THE FOREIGN POLICY
OF MODERN JAPAN

Sponsored by
THE SOCIAL SCIENCE RESEARCH COUNCIL

This volume is one of a series on Japanese society published by the University of California Press under a special arrangement with the Social Science Research Council. Each volume is based upon a conference attended by Japanese and foreign scholars; the purpose of each conference was to increase scholarly knowledge of Japanese society by enabling Japanese and foreign scholars to collaborate and to criticize each other's work. The conferences were sponsored by the Joint Committee on Japanese Studies of the American Council of Learned Societies and the Social Science Research Council, with funds provided by the Ford Foundation.

THE FOREIGN POLICY OF MODERN JAPAN

Edited by

Robert A. Scalapino

Foreword by

Edwin O. Reischauer

UNIVERSITY OF CALIFORNIA PRESS

Berkeley · Los Angeles · London

University of California Press
Berkeley and Los Angeles, California
University of California Press, Ltd.
London, England
Copyright © 1977 by
The Regents of the University of California
ISBN 0-520-03196-2
Library of Congress Catalog Card Number: 75-15219
Printed in the United States of America

Contents

Contributors

HANS H. BAERWALD is Professor of Political Science at UCLA. He is the author of *Japan's Parliament: An Introduction* (1974), and *The Purge of Japanese Leaders Under the Occupation* (1959), as well as numerous articles about Japanese politics.

MICHAEL K. BLAKER is presently a research associate at the East Asian Institute, Columbia University, and until recently he directed the Japan policy studies program sponsored by the United Nations Association. His scholarly studies include a monograph on Japan's pre-World War II negotiating behavior and articles on Japanese diplomacy, its foreign policy decision-making processes, and American-Japanese security relations.

GERALD L. CURTIS is Associate Professor of Political Science and Director of the East Asian Institute, Columbia University. He is the author of *Election Campaigning, Japanese Style* (1971) and editor of *Japanese-American Relations in the Seventies* (1970).

HARUHIRO FUKUI is Associate Professor of Political Science at the University of California, Santa Barbara. While a research associate with the Brookings Institution he participated in a research project on the politics of American-Japanese relations. He is also the author of *The Japanese Liberal-Democrats and Policy Making* (1970) and several articles on Japanese politics and foreign policy decision-making.

DONALD C. HELLMANN is Professor of Political Science and Asian Studies at the University of Washington and is currently serving as Director for Asia of the Commission on Critical Choices for Americans. His publications include *Japanese Domestic Politics and Foreign Policy* (1969) and *Japan and East Asia* (1972).

CHALMERS JOHNSON is Professor of Political Science at the University of California, Berkeley. He is the author of *An Instance of Treason, Ozaki Hotsumi and the Sorge Spy Ring* (1964), *Conspiracy at Matsukawa* (1972), and numerous other works on the politics of eastern Asia.

MASATAKA KOSAKA is currently Professor of International Politics in the Faculty of Law at Kyoto University. His publications include many books and articles in Japanese and *Options for Japan's Foreign Policy*, Adelphi Papers no. 97 (1973).

MAKATO MOMOI is Professor of the National Defense College, Tokyo, and an official of the National Defense Agency. He has been a prominent commentator and writes on Japanese defense issues.

SADAKO OGATA is Associate Professor of Political Science at the International Christian University (Tokyo) and currently serving as Minister and member of the Japanese Delegation to the United Nations General Assembly. She is the author of *Defiance in Manchuria: The Making of Japanese Foreign Policy, 1931–1932* (1964), and many articles in both Japanese and English on Japanese foreign policy, American-Japanese relations, and Chinese-Japanese relations.

EDWIN O. REISCHAUER is University Professor at Harvard University and a former U.S. Ambassador to Japan. He is the author of a number of studies on Japan, East Asia, and American-Far Eastern relations, including *Wanted: An Asian Policy* (1955) and *Beyond Vietnam: The United States and Asia* (1967).

SEIZABURO SATO is Associate Professor of Japanese Politics at the University of Tokyo. His recent publications include *Japanese Attitudes toward the World* (1974) and *Political Thought in the Meiji Restoration* (1975).

GARY R. SAXONHOUSE is Associate Professor of Economics and Co-Director of the Research Seminar on Japanese Economic Organization at the University of Michigan. He has written numerous articles on Japanese economic history, American-Japanese economic relations, and econometric theory, which have appeared in such journals as the *American Economic Review*, the *Quarterly Journal of Economics*, and the *Journal of Political Economy*.

ROBERT A. SCALAPINO is Professor of Political Science at the University of California, Berkeley, and editor of *Asian Survey*. He is the author of numerous works on Japan, China, Korea, and U.S. Asian policies, the most recent of which are *Japanese-American Relations in a Changing Era* (1972), *Asia and the Major Powers* (1972), and *Asia and the Road Ahead* (1975).

AKIO WATANABE is Associate Professor of International Relations at the University of Tokyo (Komaba). He is the author of *The Okinawa Problem: A Chapter in Japan-U.S. Relations* (1970) and various articles on Japanese foreign policy making.

Preface

Despite the close relations between the United States and Japan during the past thirty years and the growing number of person-to-person contacts via economic interaction, student exchanges, and various conferences, true communication between our two peoples is still at a relatively rudimentary stage. The reasons are many. Even in situations where language barriers are reduced—and in most settings, these remain formidable—the challenge of conveying to those of another culture the nuances and subtleties that derive from one's own societal experiences and thought processes is a prodigious one.

In a small way, our conference on Japanese foreign policy represented progress in this respect. For five days, January 14–18, 1974, seventeen scholars—almost equally divided between Japanese and American—met in the mid-Pacific, on Kauai, Hawaii, focusing their attention on selected aspects of Japan's foreign policy. An effort was made to encompass both the major issues or aspects of policy and the central institutions involved in the policy-making process. Some participants employed the case-study approach; others wrote as generalists. A variety of methods were used, as will become apparent.

In addition to the individuals whose papers are included in this volume, James William Morley, Edwin O. Reischauer, Royama Michio, and Robert E. Ward participated, serving as discussants. The papers were subsequently revised, both to take account of the initial criticisms and to include later developments when relevant.

Our effort was to select scholars from both cultures having different specialities and coming from different generations. A certain premium was placed on younger scholars in an effort to take advantage of differences in training and perspective. As many of the participants of both nationalities bridged in some measure the linguistic-cultural gap by virtue of their training and experience, communication in this instance flowed with minimal difficulty. Exchanges were lively and to the point. On a number of subjects, there was no agreement, as some of the papers will indicate. Disagreements, however, did not conform to nationality, nor were they absolute in most cases, being rather a matter of degree.

    We are much indebted to the Joint Committee on Japanese Studies of the
American Council of Learned Societies and the Social Science Research Council for its support of the conference, as a part of a series of conferences reflecting
various disciplines which it has sponsored on Japan. David Sills was invariably
a thoughtful and perceptive representative of the Social Science Research
Council who worked with us.

    We are also deeply indebted to Edwin O. Reischauer, who consented to
write the Foreword. Special appreciation must be expressed to Susan Alitto,
who labored long and well in the highly complex task of bringing diverse
writing styles into some conformity. And to the University of California Press,
whose cooperation equals its standards, we pay grateful tribute.

ROBERT A. SCALAPINO

December 23, 1975
Berkeley, California

Foreword

EDWIN O. REISCHAUER

Modern Japanese foreign policy is a subject of bewildering complexity and also vagueness. It involves most facets of the intricate and fast-changing society of Japan and also the interaction of the Japanese with an even more diverse and unstable world which surrounds them. It is hard to come to grips with and almost impossible to pin down in fixed words within the limits of a single volume.

Attempts by one author to present a neat unitary view of the whole of Japanese foreign policy always appear to others to be limited, superficial, or somewhat biased. Multiple views from a variety of stances, though possibly confusing and even contradictory in places, are more likely to produce a better concept of the whole. It is like the exploration of the surface of the moon or some distant planet: a selection of pictures from diverse angles and different degrees of closeness is more likely to give a better concept of the lay of the land than any one shot, no matter how finely focused.

Unlike a moon-scape, however, Japanese foreign policy is undergoing constant change. One approach would be to concentrate only on the present moment, but to do so would be to lose the sense of motion. Again, as with angles of vision, a variety of approaches in time, some basically historical, others focused on specific contemporary aspects of the problem, gives a chance for a deeper understanding and some sense as to where Japan may be heading.

The present volume is an attempt to deepen our understanding of Japan's foreign policy by viewing the subject in a variety of different ways. It is the outgrowth of a conference of American and Japanese scholars held geographically midway between the two groups on the Hawaiian island of Kauai in January 1974. The essays of which it consists were in their earliest form papers presented at this conference. They were each discussed at length by the assembled group of experts, which included a few like myself who had not written papers but were there merely for the discussions. Subsequently each author revised his essay on the basis of the criticisms and suggestions of others with differing areas of specialization and angles of vision and in line with suggestions for their coordination made by the conference chairman and editor, Robert Scalapino. The result is this volume.

I found the original presentation of the papers at Kauai a most stimulating experience and have once more been rewarded by reading over the revised papers. In this Foreword I would like to prepare the reader a bit for what to look for in these essays and to say a word or two of caution about some features of the terrain which may still be missing or obscure in this particular assortment of views.

The table of contents is itself a sort of analysis of how these essays fit together. First come three essays grouped under the heading "Decision-Making and the Foreign Policy Process." In the first two, Haruhiro Fukui and Hans Baerwald explore the Japanese Foreign Ministry and the Diet as key elements in the decision-making process on foreign policy. In the third, Michael K. Blaker analyzes the style of Japanese diplomatic negotiations as revealed in a number of specific prewar examples and a few taken from the postwar period.

The second rather loose grouping of three essays has the title "Interests: Public and Private." In the first, Akio Watanabe analyzes recent Japanese public opinion on certain foreign policy issues as revealed through public opinion surveys. The other two are detailed studies of specific foreign policy issues, both having to do with the economic side of the spectrum. These are Gerald Curtis's careful study of the proposed Japanese exploitation of the Tyumen oil fields in Siberia and Sadako Ogata's analysis of the attitudes and actions taken by the Japanese business community in the normalization of relations with the People's Republic of China in 1972, presented as a case study of the role of business in the formulation of foreign policy.

These two essays lead naturally into the next section on "Economics and Foreign Policy," which is made up of three essays of broader scope. Masataka Kosaka looks outward from Japan in analyzing Japan's changing international economic policies, whereas Gary Saxonhouse looks from the changing international economic environment inward to the opportunities and problems this has created for Japan. Chalmers Johnson's essay, in contrast to these other two, is a detailed study of the organizational history of MITI, the Ministry of International Trade and Industry, and its influence on Japan's economic foreign policies.

The next section, entitled "Security Issues," shifts attention to this other main aspect of Japan's foreign policy. It consists of two essays both general in nature but approaching the problem in different ways. Makoto Momoi gives a detailed history of the Self-Defense Forces and the changing concepts of their strategic mission. Donald Hellmann discusses the reasons why Japan since the war has kept a very low profile in security matters and why he believes this may be changing.

The final section, labeled "A Summary," is appropriately reserved for two papers, one by an American, the other by a Japanese, which attempt an overview of the whole. Again the approaches are different enough to avoid undesirable duplication. Seizaburo Sato takes a broad historical view of the attitudes and perceptions the Japanese have brought to their foreign policy problems and also gives some consideration to their mechanisms for policy formulation. Scalapino, while glancing back at history, concentrates on an analysis of the position in which Japan now finds itself. He discusses the possibilities of Japan moving away from its present close association with the United States to some other bilateral relationship or, more plausibly, a position of neutralism or equidistance from all the acknowledged power centers of the world. On balance, Scalapino doubts the probability of any such move and expects only small, incremental changes rather than some dramatic reshaping of Japan's foreign policies.

Sato in his paper suggests a three-way division of the foreign policy problem. There are first the realities of the international environment and national power, then the internal attitudes toward international matters, which may limit or skew the perceptions of the problems posed, and finally the mechanisms by which the nation goes about formulating foreign policies, which again may limit or distort the decisions made. This last phase of the subject is related to the broader subject of the Japanese decision-making process in general, which of late has been a lively topic of interest among those concerned with Japanese matters.

Exactly a year before the Kauai conference, another conference in the same series was held on the Hawaiian island of Maui and led to the publication of a volume entitled *Modern Japanese Organization and Decision Making*, which was edited by Ezra Vogel, the conference chairman.* While many of the essays in this book bear on the organization and decision-making of business firms, labor unions, and work groups and on other subjects little related to foreign policy, others concern the organization of the bureaucracy and its procedures as well as the influence of big business, intellectuals, and the newspapers on policy decisions, which are all subjects of direct relevance to the formulation of foreign policy.

In the present volume a number of essays are concerned with this problem. It is a central interest in Johnson's lengthy essay on MITI as well as Fukui's and Baerwald's papers on the Foreign Ministry and the Diet. Watanabe's study of public opinion bears on it, as do also Blaker's work on tactical style in diplomatic negotiations and Ogata's study of the business community's role in

*Berkeley and Los Angeles: University of California Press, 1975.

one specific problem, while Sato too considers the subject briefly but in more general terms.

The essays in this and the earlier Vogel volume greatly expand our understanding of the decision-making process in Japan as it bears on foreign policy, though by their very nature they do more to clarify the operations of parts of the machine than the integration of these various parts into a working whole. We learn of the functioning of some of the key ministerial bureaucracies which, as everyone knows, are the original drafters of most policies and legislation and represent the institutional memory and continuity of the Japanese government. We also learn of the organs for handling foreign policy matters in the Diet and something of the attitude of the public, the influence of business, the role of intellectuals, and the power of the mass media. But there is still much to be clarified about how these popular, political, and bureaucratic elements fit together in policy formulation.

Divergent policies of the various ministries must be harmonized under the overall supervision of the cabinet, and bureaucratic planning must also be brought into line with what the Diet majority is willing to enact into legislation. In this second problem, the cabinet, of course, as the "executive committee" of the Diet and the controller of the bureaucracy, has a key role in meshing bureaucratic policies with political opinions. But the various organs of the Liberal Democratic Party, which forms the Diet majority, seem to play an even more important role. In particular, the party's Policy Affairs Research Council and its various committees serve as a diverse and flexible forum where divergent opinions within the party, clashing views of the ministries, and the opinions of various outside pressure groups can all be heard and a viable consensus achieved. This process of blending varied political and administrative views and achieving a balance in foreign policy between political and bureaucratic pressures is still an area that needs clarification.

The influence of outside pressure groups and public opinion on foreign policy also needs more exploration. Ogata's case study bears out Gerald Curtis's conclusion in his essay in the Vogel volume that the direct influence of big business on policy is now much less than had once been assumed, but the pressures of business and other outside forces nonetheless do have a role that needs more study. Certainly public opinion in general and the mass media more specifically exercise an influence on the attitudes of politicians and thus on the formulation of policy. A politician, after all, must be responsive to the views of his supporters to be elected. Although most experts agree that domestic matters loom far larger than foreign policy for most voters, still popular attitudes undoubtedly serve as a constraint on politicians in foreign policy matters, which they no doubt apply in turn to the bureaucrats.

Even when politicians do not fear for the votes that sustain them, they may be influenced in their actions by public clamor and direct political action.

Foreign policy has normally been the area in which the ruling Liberal Democratic Party felt itself most vulnerable to attack through determined obstruc-
tionism by the opposition parties in the Diet, popular demonstrations in the
streets of Tokyo (which like all the major cities leans in its sympathies toward
the opposition), and criticism by the mass media, which as metropolitan
phenomena tend to share in the leftward lean of the city populations. There can
be little doubt that both direct and indirect popular pressures on Diet politicians have been constraining influences on Japanese foreign policy, helping to account for its seeming timidity and admitted "low posture." In fact, the
role of the politician both in terms of his responsiveness to public attitudes and
pressures and in turn his restraining influence on bureaucratic policies appears
to be the key central link in the process of policy formulation that still needs
careful study and elucidation.

Whatever the mechanisms for formulating foreign policy, the chief determinants are inevitably the actual international realities and the national
perception of these. As Scalapino points out, Japan has witnessed a complete
transformation of its relationship to the outside world in the roughly dozen
decades since the coming of Perry in 1853. In fact there has been a series of
sweeping changes which cumulatively have produced an almost 100 percent
reversal of the basic conditions in which Japan finds itself.

Before 1853 Japan was as close to complete political and strategic isolation
and economic autarchy as any developed country in modern times could
possibly be. But suddenly it found its economy menaced by the cheap machine
production of the West and even its political independence threatened. By
heroic efforts it achieved military and economic security against the West and
won back legal equality by getting rid of the so-called unequal treaties. In the
process, however, the Japanese came to see their strategic interests in broader
terms than the old isolationism and, like the countries of the West, embarked
on a policy of achieving security through imperial expansion. Again Japan
proved successful, and by the time of the First World War it possessed a burgeoning empire and was clearly the paramount power of its quarter of the
globe.

Japan, however, had meanwhile started to industrialize, as a necessary part
of its policy of achieving security through "enriching the country and strengthening the military" (fukoku kyōhei). Industrialization increasingly forced Japan
out of the shelter of its old autarchy and made it dependent on foreign raw
materials as well as export markets abroad to pay for them. When imperial expansion began to run into what was in time to prove the quagmire of nascent
nationalism, the Japanese paused briefly in the 1920s to consider the possibility
of security through peace and international trade. The world depression, however, helped throw the decision against this course and back to the seizure of a

large enough empire to support the industrial economy that was emerging in Japan. This proved the wrong choice, and Japan went down to utter defeat and destruction.

After the war, under favorable international conditions, largely produced by the United States, as Saxonhouse explains in his essay, Japan staged a seemingly miraculous economic recovery. But it emerged from the war shrunken to the size it was in the days of economic independence and isolation, though with more than three times the population of that time. It found itself even more completely outclassed in military strength by the nuclear superpowers than it had been in its days of peril in the mid-nineteenth century. It had become entirely dependent for life on an advanced industrial economy, which in turn depended on the natural resources and markets of the whole world. No other major country relied as heavily as Japan on resources and markets located so far away in distant areas of the globe. In this sense, Japan had moved in twelve decades from being the world's most isolated country to being the most global.

It would be hard to imagine a greater change in the international position and national power of a country, and the Japanese were completely aware of this frightening transformation. The sense of smug security of Tokugawa times and the proud confidence in their own military powers of a half-century earlier had given way to a clear realization that Japan was pitifully vulnerable to any disruption of trade and itself possessed no defense against nuclear attack in a world that continued to be riven by deep ideological and emotional fissures.

It is not surprising that popular perceptions in Japan of the meaning of these changes has remained confused and in sharp conflict. Some persons have perhaps underreacted, clinging to outworn concepts, but even more appear to have overreacted and jumped to false conclusions. This confusion in popular Japanese attitudes is one of the reasons why Japanese foreign policy is so hard to come to grips with. Emotions run high on many aspects of foreign policy. The weight of public opinion and popular pressure is hard to gauge. Public rhetoric often seems little related to the detailed actions of government and business.

There is also a confusion in perceptions of another sort. The Japanese started their modern period convinced that they were in essence an "Eastern" country merely employing "Western" techniques, and from this some of them developed the concept of being the leaders and champions of Asia against an oppressive West. But at the same time, other Japanese saw their nation as spiritually departing from Asia to become "civilized" and modern. Neither concept proved correct, but the old ambiguity remains. There can be no doubt that the Japanese now find their most numerous contacts and the closest parallels to their contemporary society in North America and Western Europe. At the same time, they feel uncomfortably distinct as the one great industrialized land of non-Western cultural background, and geographically, of course, they remain in East Asia. Attitudes toward the outside world and perceptions of international problems remain the most confused and confusing aspects of Japanese foreign relations. This is an area that calls for much more thorough exploration. Three of the Japanese contributors, Watanabe, Kosaka, and Sato, comment cogently on this side of the problem, but more study is needed.

Given the startling shifts in the surrounding environment and in Japan's relative power and given the ambiguities of Japanese attitudes and the confusion of perceptions, it is surprising that Japan's foreign policy has remained as stable as it has since the war. One reason for this undoubtedly was the favorable environment the United States created during the first two postwar decades. Japan was able politically to stay quite safely out of sight behind the American international stance, while concentrating on its own economic recovery in an economically open world the United States had helped shape. Of equal importance was a tacit consensus among leadership elements in Japan, and probably among most of the people as well, on a policy of putting economic growth above all other goals. Japan developed a diplomatic style of reacting flexibly to others, while avoiding initiatives itself and concentrating on its own economic objectives. Judged by the results, it would be difficult to find a country that has been more successful in its postwar foreign policies.

But as the essays of Kosaka, Saxonhouse, Hellman, Sato, and Scalapino all show, conditions have changed greatly in the past few years. Japan has grown economically too large and the American economic and strategic stance has become too uncertain to permit Japan safe refuge in the lee of American policy. The vital relationship between Japan and the other indurialized nations, which also include Japan's chief sources of food and raw materials, has become extremely complex and threatened by new tensions. Japan probably needs to develop a more positive attitude in its relations with these countries, in place of its passive, reactive policies of the past, if the external economic environment is to remain healthy and favorable for Japan. More care must also be devoted to relations with the largely preindustrial countries, which are essential sources of raw materials for Japan and now form a large part of the international political environment. And there is need for a cautious though friendly and carefully balanced policy toward the two great rival Communist powers, which may become more important sources of Japanese raw materials in the future and in any case are both uncomfortably close to Japan.

Some scholars have suggested that in this period of new and more difficult foreign policy problems, the Japanese decision-making process may prove too complex and uncertain to produce decisions of adequate clarity and wisdom. In other words, Japan may become dangerously immobilized in its foreign policies. This possibility makes the decision-making process all the more important a subject of study. The process is perhaps more complex than in other countries and certainly more of it proceeds out of sight—that is, not in open parliamentary hearings and debates but in the more hidden consultations of party committees and in quiet negotiations between party factions, between ministries, between politicians and bureaucrats, and between outside pressure groups and opposition parties and those in power. My own judgment is that these procedures are as capable of coming up with the necessary decisions as are our own, possibly being somewhat more cumbersome and slower but at the same time producing decisions that are more likely to be supported by a consensus and are therefore less likely to be soon overturned. But these are matters on which no one can be certain, and much more study is needed.

A more serious problem than the decision-making process is the confusion in popular Japanese attitudes and perceptions about the world environment and Japan's place in it. This confusion is aggravated by the depth of hostility and distrust within Japanese politics, which is a direct outgrowth of the years of intellectual repression and heavy indoctrination during the 1930s and the war years. Differences of view are greatly magnified by unhappy memories as well as by new ideologies. In addition, all Japanese are deeply aware of Japan's frightening vulnerability. These psychological factors combine to give a certain volatility to what since the war has otherwise proved to be an extraordinarily stable and generally predictable democratic political process. These psychological pressures also suggest that, regardless of the complexities of the decision-making process, a new foreign policy consensus may not be easy to reach.

Despite these doubts, however, I tend to agree with Scalapino in expecting no sudden shifts in Japanese foreign policy but rather small incremental changes. In fact, I feel this process is already well under way. I do not look for the shift on defense policies that Hellman seems to expect. On the other hand, a friendly equidistance toward China and the Soviet Union already seems to have been established and is proving basically sound. There seems to be general agreement that more efforts must be made to smooth relations both with the oil-rich and the resources-poor nonindustrialized countries, though such general principles are, of course, easier to formulate than to embody in concrete policies. The first shock of the oil crisis produced dreams in Japan of an independent economic policy, but these ebbed during the next two years, leaving a renewed realization of the crucial importance of close cooperation with the other industrialized nations, which come closest to having the same interests and goals as Japan and account for more than half of Japan's trade. This has been especially true with regard to the United States, which alone provides a quarter of Japan's imports, mostly essential food and raw materials, and more than a quarter of its export market. Perhaps this is the reason why the successful imperial visit to the United States in October 1975 produced a general feeling that the visit symbolized a new stage in Japanese-American relations of true equality and deepened mutual understanding.

The judgments I have expressed here, of course, may not be accepted by everyone. Admittedly they are based on only an incomplete understanding of present realities, which by their own uncertainty make the future all the more obscure. The thirteen contributors to this volume would probably come up with as many variant interpretations of the present situation and future prospects. But one thing is sure. If the reader will look with these thirteen authors from their various angles of vision at the different aspects of the foreign policy terrain they describe, he will certainly be in a much better position to make his own judgments on these matters.

I

Decision-Making and the
Foreign-Policy Process

Policy-Making in the Japanese Foreign Ministry

HARUHIRO FUKUI

There are two broad and interrelated reasons for the study presented here. The first is my feeling, apparently shared by most students of public policy and policy-making, that professional bureaucrats play an important, though not necessarily dominant, role in the formulation as well as implementation of crucial policy decisions, both domestic and foreign. The second is my unhappiness, which may also be widely shared, about the paucity of serious studies of the professional administrative bureaucracy in Japan, especially the foreign-policy bureaucracy.

Although it is apparent that the bureaucracy plays an important role in the operation of modern government in general, the centrality or dominance of that role, especially in the making of foreign-policy decisions, is not as evident.[1] Specifically, there are some important disagreements and inconsistencies in the current literature relating to the role of the foreign-policy bureaucracy in Japan. At one pole, some argue that the bureaucrats' role is central, dominant, and growing.[2] At the other, a few have found the role of bureaucrats to be marginal in specific policy-making cases.[3] Between these two poles, probably the majority of specialists in both Japan and the United States acknowledge the importance—but not necessarily the centrality—of the bureaucrats' role in "typical"

1. See my discussion on the role of the bureaucracy in "Bureaucratic Power in Japan," in Peter Drysdale and Hironobu Kitaoji, eds., *Japan and Australia: Two Societies and Their Interaction* (forthcoming).

2. For example, see Ikeda Masaaki, "Rippō katei no mondai ten," in Ashibe Nobuyoshi, ed., *Gendai no rippo* (Tokyo: Iwanami Shoten, 1967), pp. 272–283; Misawa Shigeo, "Seisaku Kettei katei no gaikan," in Nihon Seiji Gakkai, ed., *Gendai Nihon no seitō to kanryō* (Tokyo: Iwanami Shoten, 1967), pp. 14–18.

3. For example, see Donald C. Hellmann, *Japanese Domestic Politics and Foreign Policy: The Peace Agreement with the Soviet Union* (Berkeley and Los Angeles: University of California Press, 1969), pp. 24, 25, 135, 142.

3

policy-making situations.[4] These differences reflect the complexity and variability of actual policy-making situations and the roles of various actors, including bureaucrats, in those situations.

At the level of generalities one may point to the variability and contradictory
pressures of certain parametric or environmental factors.[5] The bureaucrats' expertise and control over vital information no doubt work for the importance of
their role in policy-making situations. The bureaucrats' position is further
strengthened by the relative impotence of both the cabinet, which is officially
charged (by the constitution) with the management of foreign as well as
domestic affairs, and the ruling LDP, which numerically dominates the Diet,
the highest and sole law-making organ of the state. It is well known that neither
the cabinet nor the LDP functions on its own as an active and effective policy-
maker, mainly because of the lack of manpower and skills necessary for effective policy-making operations, but also because of the divisive effects of
intraparty factionalism. Both depend on professional bureaucrats for the information, administrative expertise, and manpower that go into the making of
policies.

On the other hand, there are factors working against bureaucratic control of
policy-making processes, especially in the foreign policy area. The administrative bureaucracy as a whole is constitutionally subordinate to the Diet. In
theory, and to a large extent in practice, bureaucrats are subordinate to politicians, both individually and collectively. Among the bureaucrats compartmen-
talized into ministries and agencies, those in the Foreign Ministry are relatively
weaker, if not the weakest, in terms of political power and "clout." In recent
years, their shares of annual government expenditures and the authorized
number of government employees have been the second smallest among the
twelve ministries of the central government. Their influence on a foreign minister's decisions and actions is usually limited and on those of a prime minister
even more so. The political leaders not only use sources of information and
policy advice other than Foreign Ministry bureaucrats, but often decide and act
against the latter's explicit recommendations.[6] The direct influence that the
Foreign Ministry bureaucrats are able to bring to bear on the Diet or the LDP
is generally far more limited than what their counterparts in the other ministries, notably Finance and MITI, seem to be able to wield. Last but not least,
they have been engaged in periodic and often bitter interministry jurisdictional
and policy disputes and rivalries (especially with MITI bureaucrats), which
have further weakened their position in the overall political arena.

4. For example, see Akio Watanabe, *The Okinawa Problem: A Chapter in Japan-U.S. Relations*
(Melbourne: Melbourne University Press, 1970), chap. 6; and my "Foreign Policy Making
in Japan: Case Studies for Empirical Theory" (paper delivered at the Annual Meeting of the
Association for Asian Studies, April 1–3, 1974, Boston).
5. For a detailed discussion, see my "Bureaucratic Power in Japan."
6. Ibid.

One can argue either way about the relative importance of the Foreign Ministry bureaucrats in the making of Japanese foreign policies, depending on what combination of the preceding factors one chooses to emphasize. Other important reasons for the disagreements and inconsistencies in the current literature are the differences in the type of policy issues involved. It is reasonable to expect the role of the ministry bureaucrats to vary from central to marginal, depending on the type of issues at stake. If the issue is routine and noncontroversial, involving essentially a continuation or marginal, incremental change of the status quo, the decisions (or nondecisions) may well be made "bureaucratically"—mainly by the bureaucrats, with little intervention from politicians or interest groups. If the issue is politically sensitive and highly controversial, the decisions may be made "politically"—more or less directly by political leaders, with the bureaucrats playing a subordinate or marginal role. We may assume that politicians, who depend directly on the support of the electorate for their status and power, are more sensitive and vulnerable than the bureaucrats to the pressure of public opinion and mass media. As the role of politicians increases in a controversial situation, so does the influence of the general public and media, except in a severe external crisis when the decision-making initiative shifts to a handful of political leaders without an accompanying increase in the participation or influence of public opinion in the decision process. In any event, the role of bureaucrats in any given policy-making situation relates, as a rule, to the political sensitivity and controversiality of the issue involved.

In actuality, of course, many other factors come into play. The personalities and other idiosyncratic attributes of the participating politicians and bureaucrats may have an important bearing both on the decision process and the decisions themselves. The general political conditions—such as the state of party politics, the level of popular discontent, or the proximity of a Diet election—may determine the degree to which an issue becomes controversial. And the presence of other concurrent issues and how they relate to the particular issue in question can have a significant impact on the way it is dealt with by politicians, bureaucrats, and others.[7] All these important factors tend to make actual policy-making processes more complex and variable; they must be carefully examined in each specific case. It is small wonder, then, that we should find inconsistencies and contradictions in the arguments and conclusions of the scholars.

Despite, or because of, such complexity and variations, the role and behavior of the foreign-policy bureaucracy should be studied systematically and in detail. The fact that the bureaucrats appear to play a dominant role in routine policy-making situations and do not seem to play a comparable role in con-

7. See Thomas L. Brewer, "Issue and Context Variations in Foreign Policy," *Journal of Conflict Resolution*, March 1973, pp. 89–111.

troversial situations calls for investigation and explanation. Unfortunately, specialists both in Japan and elsewhere have given little attention to the environment and behavior patterns of the Japanese foreign-policy bureaucracy. There are only three Japanese-language sources on the subject, each of which has its own particular limitations, and not a single work of any scholarly significance or interest in any other language.[8] As a result, both specialists and the general public are largely ignorant about the operations of a ministry which may have important bearings on their lives, professionally or otherwise.

The primary purpose of this article is, then, to begin to fill this unfortunate gap in the current scholarship on Japanese foreign policy and foreign policy-making. Its focus is deliberately narrow. I shall concentrate on identifying the dominant patterns of the policy-relevant decision-making process in the Japanese Foreign Ministry and on drawing a collective profile of the bureaucrats who participate in the process.[9] As this is a study limited to a consideration of the Foreign Ministry bureaucracy and its policy-making behavior, I shall not seek to weigh the relative role of the Foreign Ministry bureaucracy in the overall foreign policy-making process of the Japanese government.[10]

For information used in this study I have depended substantially on four documentary sources published by the Japanese government, and on personal interviews with forty-one Foreign Ministry officials and several knowledgeable journalists.[11] The sample of officials included all ranks above the seventh man

8. Gaimushō Hyakunen Shi Hensan Iinkai, ed., *Gaimushō no hyakunen*, 2 vols. (Tokyo: Hara Shobō, 1969), a semiofficial history of the Foreign Ministry which contains much useful and factual information, but an almost straight descriptive study with little attention to analytical or theoretical concerns. Kawamura Kinji, ed., *Gaimushō* (Tokyo: Hōbunsha, 1956), the only secondary work dealing directly with the Foregin Ministry bureaucracy. It remains informative and interesting today, despite its date of publication and journalistic style. Banno Masataka, *Gendai gaikō no bunseki* (Tokyo: Tokyo Daigaku Shuppankai, 1971), a more recent and scholarly work, but the topics it covers are more traditional than contemporary and more European than Japanese.

9. "Policy" may mean different things to different people. Allison and Halperin equated it with "authoritative aspirations, internal to a government, about outcomes." See Graham T. Allison and Morton H. Halperin, "Bureaucratic Politics: A Paradigm and Some Policy Implications," in Richard H. Ullman and Raymond Tanter, eds., *Theory and Policy in International Relations* (Princeton, N.J.: Princeton University Press, 1972), p. 46. Destler defines "policy" as "not what we aspire to accomplish but what the government actually does." M.I. Destler, *Presidents, Bureaucrats, and Foreign Policy* (Princeton, N.J.: Princeton University Press, 1972), p. 4; see also the alternative meanings he cites on p. 18. My definition of "policy" as used in this essay is close to but somewhat narrower than Halperin's. It may be formulated as "authoritative, purposive, and *subject-specific* aspirations of those who represent or act on behalf of a government."

10. For a more detailed discussion on these subjects, see my "Bureaucratic Power in Japan" and "Foreign Policy Making in Japan."

11. The government documentary sources are *Gaimushō shokuin ryakureki: Shōwa 45-nen* (Tokyo: Ministry of Foreign Affairs, n.d.); *Shōwa 45-nen 10-gatsu hensan Gaimushō shokuin rekinin hyō* (Tokyo: Ministry of Foreign Affairs, n.d.); Ōkurashō Insatsukyoku, *Shokuin roku* (Tokyo: Ministry of Finance Printing Office, 1971, 1973), vol. 1; and *Gaimushō no hyakumen*, *vol. 2*.

The interviews were conducted during two trips which I made to Japan—September 1971 to July 1972 and February-March 1973—in conjunction primarily with three case studies I

Table 1
Breakdown of Foreign Ministry Officials Interviewed

Rank	Number	Office affiliation	Number
Permanent vice-minister	1	Minister's Secretariat	5
Deputy vice-minister	2	Asian Affairs Bureau	8
Bureau director	3	American Affairs Bureau	5
Counselor (in bureaus)	3	European and Oceanic Affairs Bureau	2
Division head	12	Middle Eastern and African Affairs Bureau	1
Deputy division head	6	Economic Affairs Bureau	3
Assistant deputy division head	8	Economic Cooperation Bureau	1
Ambassador	1	Treaties Bureau	4
Counselor (at embassy)	3	United Nations Bureau	3
First secretary	1	Public Information and Cultural Affairs Bureau	3
Second secretary	1	Washington embassy	6
TOTAL	41		41

in the line of command at the Tokyo headquarters (the *jiseki jimukan* or assistant deputy division head) and the fourth man at an embassy overseas (in this case, the second secretary in Washington, D.C.). A breakdown of these forty-one officials by rank and office of current affiliation is given in Table 1. These interviews do not in any way represent a scientifically chosen probability sample, and the information drawn from them cannot be handled as though it came from such a sample. I am not attempting to do, for example, what Bernard Mennis did with his sample of American foreign-policy officials.[12] My analysis will be essentially qualitative rather than quantitative. My "random" (nonstatistical) sample also includes officials at ranks above those included in the Mennis sample.

Although it is not my intention to attempt a full-fledged comparative analysis, I have drawn on several studies of the United States' foreign-policy bureaucracy in order to keep speculations in a comparative perspective. I will

had undertaken jointly with Brookings Institution scholars. See the forthcoming Brookings studies in U.S.-Japanese relations by Priscilla Clapp, M.I. Destler, Hideo Satō, and myself. Among the journalists I interviewed, not including those interviewed exclusively for the Brookings studies, are Kikuchi Ikuzō (*Asahi*); Tominomori Eiji (*Asahi*); Ishizuka Toshijirō (*Mainichi*); Miyoshi Osamu (*Mainichi*); and Watanabe Tsuneo (*Yomiuri*).

12. See Bernard Mennis, *American Foreign Policy Officials* (Columbus: Ohio State University Press, 1971), chap. 2.

make a few passing references to these studies to suggest further investigations into what appear to be interesting similarities or contrasts.

THE PROCESS PATTERN

The complexity of the policy-making process in the Foreign Ministry is confusing not only to outsiders, but apparently even to those inside the bureaucracy.[13] There are different ways in which decisions are made or, perhaps more appropriately, *evolve*. One important distinction is between bureaucratic and political decisions. The first would deal with routine, noncontroversial situations involving technical or administrative decisions of no political significance. Discussions and consultations are largely contained within the bureaucracy, but also involve, as a rule, all officials with jurisdictional interest in and responsibility for the particular policy subjects. Information and ideas flow both horizontally and vertically among the officials but in an orderly manner through well-defined channels close to the image conveyed by the conventional model of *ringisei*.[14]

13. Interviews: an official in the First American Affairs Division, American Affairs Bureau, Oct. 19, 1971; and an official in the China Division, Asian Affairs Bureau, May 1, 1972. One division head categorically denied that there were any set patterns of decision-making in the ministry.

14. Tsuji Kiyoaki explained the *ringisei* as follows: "It is used to refer to a system whereby administrative plans and decisions are made through the circulation of a document called *ringisho*. This is drafted in the first instance by an official of low rank. It is then circulated among other officials in the ministry or agency concerned who are required to affix their seals if they agree with the policy proposed. By complex and circuitous paths the document gradually works its way up to higher and higher administrators, and finally reaches the minister or top executive official. When he approves the *ringisho*, the decision is made." Kiyoaki Tsuji, "Decision-Making in the Japanese Government: A Study of Ringisei," in Robert E. Ward, ed., *Political Development in Modern Japan* (Princeton, N.J.: Princeton University Press, 1970), pp. 457–458. See also Bernard S. Silberman, "Ringisei: Traditional Values or Organizational Imperatives in the Japanese Upper Civil Service, 1868–1945," *Journal of Asian Studies*, Feb. 1973, pp. 251–264.

Burton Sapin gives the following description of the American parallel to *ringisei*: "Operating under well-established rules, the communications people send the *action copy* of an incoming telegram or dispatch . . . to the appropriate bureau and information copies to other departmental units and outside agencies that have an interest in the matter. . . .

"The effort is to make clear where responsibility lies. It is then incumbent upon the responsible bureau and officials to see that the matter is checked out and appropriate documents 'cleared' with other interested offices and officials. This means getting either positive approval or at least an initialled willingness to let the item go through to the next highest level or to the level at which formal action can be taken. (As in many other bureaucracies, the man who finally signs the document and sends it out over his signature is usually not the one who has drafted it.)

"Such a system would seem to leave considerable room for 'end-running' officials and units with differing views, for pushing papers through without 'clearing' with all the interested parties. As a matter of fact, this is not a major problem. . . . an official or a unit that has been bypassed once on some matter in which it has an interest will raise such an uproar and make life so difficult for those who have tried to 'end-run' them that it is not likely to happen a second time." Burton M. Sapin, *The Making of United States Foreign Policy* (Washington, D.C.: The Brookings Institution, 1966), pp. 116–117.

In situations involving more politically sensitive or controversial issues, politicians and others, such as interest-group leaders and people from the mass media, extensively intervene and take the decision-making initiative. Information and opinions may still flow horizontally among officials of equal ranks in the different compartments of the bureaucracy as well as vertically among those of different ranks within each compartment. The flow is, however, neither smooth nor orderly, but is often short-circuited and confused. The whole process tends to move in a fashion far from the image conveyed by the *ringisei* model.

An important tendency that relates to the distinction between routine and controversial situations is that the number of participants within the ministry tends to be in inverse proportion to that of participants outside the ministry. In routine cases, relatively more ministry bureaucrats and relatively fewer outsiders participate, whereas in controversial cases the opposite tends to be true. In either case, however, the number of participating officials is not very large. Even in routine situations, the lower limit of participation seldom extends beyond the assistant deputy division head level. More typically, it stops at the deputy division head (*shuseki jimukan*) rank. At the upper end, the spread cannot extend beyond the permanent vice-minister, who is the highest career official in the ministry. Thus, most decisions are made at or close to the summit of the ministry's personnel structure.[15]

The lateral range of participation is determined by the number and kind of bureaus and divisions with jurisdictional interest in, and responsibility for, the type of issue involved. The bureaus are divided into geographic and functional groupings, although a policy issue is typically both geographic and functional in character.[16] This does not mean, however, that geographic and functional bureaus normally get involved in the same issues, for jurisdictional responsibilities are divided rather neatly between the two categories. Bilateral issues are assigned to the geographic bureaus, whereas multilateral problems go to the functional bureaus. Thus, the responsibility of the United Nations Bureau is fairly easy to define. The Treaties Bureau, on the other hand, tends to get in-

15. Interview, Kikuchi Ikuzō (reporter, Political Affairs Department, *Asahi shimbum*), April 19, 1972.

16. In 1970 there were four geographic bureaus: Asian Affairs; American Affairs; European and Oceanic Affairs; and Middle Eastern and African Affairs. The functional bureaus were Economic Affairs; Economic Cooperation; Treaties; United Nations; and Public Information and Cultural Affairs. In addition, there were three departments: Research and Analysis; Consular and Emigration Affairs in the Minister's Secretariat; and Cultural Affairs in the Public Information and Cultural Affairs Bureau. For a simple chart of the Japanese government ministries and agencies, see Administrative Management Agency, Japanese Government, *Table of Organization of the Government of Japan*, Dec. 1971. The most recent reorganization of the Foreign Ministry occurred in 1969 and resulted in the integration of political and economic functions in all geographic bureaus, except American Affairs. For a brief discussion of the reorganization and its effects, see *Gaimushō no hyakunen*, 2:772–773. For comparison, see the bureaus in the U.S. State Department as described in Sapin, *Making of Foreign Policy*, pp. 119–120.

volved in all kinds of issues dealt with by the Foreign Ministry, regardless of
whether they are bilateral or multilateral, foreign policy or domestic and political in nature. With the exception of the Treaties Bureau, however, simultane-
ous and competitive involvement of a geographic and a functional bureau in
the same issue is rare, if not impossible.

Over a routine, noncontroversial matter, intraministry consultations take
place across division and, frequently, bureau lines among officials of appropriate ranks. These officials participate in the process in a matter-of-fact
and ritualistic fashion with no special sense of commitment or group solidarity.
When the issue involved is highly sensitive and controversial, a much more
compact and well-defined group is formed on an ad hoc but predictable basis.
It consists usually of the permanent vice-minister, a bureau director or two
(including the Treaties Bureau director), one or two counselors (again one
from the Treaties Bureau), and a few division heads and deputy division
heads. Occasionally one of the deputy vice-ministers participates as a principal
member of the team, while an assistant deputy division head or two may serve
as auxiliary members.

The Foreign Ministry team charged with policy formulation relating to the
reversion of Okinawa in the middle of 1969, for example, consisted of the vice-
minister, the directors of the American Affairs and the Treaties bureaus, one
counselor each from those two bureaus, and the heads of the First North
American Division and the Treaties Division.[17] A deputy vice-minister played a
rather insignificant role as a coordinating officer. Similarly, policy formulation
preparatory to Prime Minister Tanaka's trip to China in the fall of 1972 was
assigned to a group made up of the vice-minister, the directors of the Asian
Affairs and the Treaties bureaus, and the heads of the Chinese Affairs and the
Treaties division.[18] In both cases there were several others who were consulted
but the burden of decision-making lay clearly with the small groups described.

Within the operational decision-making unit of the highly sensitive type, the
vice-minister is doubtless the commanding officer. He is not only senior to all
other members both in age and rank, but also the vital link between the ministry team and the foreign minister, the prime minister, and other extramural
participants. As a former holder of the office stressed, a vice-minister is usually
well acquainted with the views and feelings of the political leaders, particularly
the prime minister and foreign minister.[19] And it is, of course, the political
leaders who hold the power of approval over the ministry officials' decisions
(recommendations) and ultimately determine the foreign policy of Japan. In
practice, however, the vice-minister is not always an active leader of the team,
and often not even an active participant in its work. This is partly because a

17. This is discussed in the forthcoming case studies cited in footnote 11.
18. See my "Foreign Policy Making in Japan."
19. Interview: Shimoda Takezō (justice, Supreme Court; former vice-minister of foreign affairs),
July 18, 1972.

vice-minister is responsible for the entire range of the ministry's official activities, which leaves him little time to devote to any particular problem, policy-
related or otherwise. It also depends on the personality and personal interests of
the individual who happens to occupy the position. For example, Shimoda,
who was interested in political matters, played an active, indeed dominant, role
in the shaping of the ministry's policy on the Okinawa problem while he was
vice-minister. His successor, Mori, did not actively involve himself in the issue,
presumably because he was more of an economist and had a certain amount of
distaste for a predominantly political issue.[20]

The same applies to the bureau directors. They are in a position to play a
central role in the work of the decision-making group and often do. As often,
however, they find themselves almost as busy as the vice-minister with the multiple demands made by various segments of their bureaus. That same condition
tends also to prevent them from acquiring a great deal of specialized knowledge
about particular issues. Preoccupied with administrative and personnel matters
and frequent trips to the Diet during its annual sessions, a bureau director is
often unable to devote much time and attention to a single policy issue even if
personally he would want to do so. A counselor, who is officially the bureau
director's aide, can and does fill in this gap to some extent. His position,
however, is often referred to as the "mezzanine" (between the bureau director
upstairs and the division heads downstairs) and is somewhat ambiguous both
in terms of responsibilities and functions. This ambiguity tends to inhibit
whatever initiative he might theoretically take. Real action, even in a controversial or crisis situation, thus tends to take place close to the bottom of the
decision-making group structure—the level of the division head.[21]

Division heads have in fact always been the linchpin of the decision-making
machinery in the Foreign Ministry in crisis as well as routine situations. For example, in the summer of 1938, German foreign minister Ribbentrop sent the
Tokyo government a secret message suggesting a tripartite military alliance
among Germany, Italy, and Japan. The Ministry of the Army was promptly
appraised of its arrival and contents, but in the Foreign Ministry, only the
head of the First Eurasian Affairs Division and his immediate subordinates
were informed of it sooner than three weeks after its arrival.[22] The abortive
Hull-Nomura negotiations preceding Pearl Harbor in 1941 involved, as far as
the Foreign Ministry was concerned, only four officials in the American Affairs
Bureau—the bureau director and counselor, and the head and deputy head of
the First American Affairs Division.[23]

20. Interview; Kikuchi Ikuzō.
21. Major responsibilities for preparation of Prime Minister Tanaka's trip to the People's
Republic of China in 1972 were carried by China Division head, Hashimoto, and Treaties
Division head, Kuriyama. Interviews: officials in the Asian Affairs and Treaties bureaus, March 5
and 6, 1973.
22. *Gaimushō no hyakunen* 2:407.
23. Ibid., pp. 465, 602.

In the postwar period, the decisions relating to the Soviet-Japanese negotiations in 1955–1956 were made within the Foreign Ministry largely
between the counselor for European Affairs and the head of the Sixth European and American Affairs Division (in charge of East European affairs).[24] Referring to the more contemporary situation, one head of an important and
busy division declared that a division head and his deputy were a mini-foreign
minister and a mini-vice-minister respectively.[25] Another division head defined
the division as the hub of activity in the ministry.[26]

One comes away from a series of interviews with ministry officials with an
image of a typical division head that is similar to Elder's profile of a country
desk officer in the U.S. State Department.

A country desk officer . . . may be low man on the totem pole so far as seniority in
policy-making is concerned, yet he wields significant power in the formulation of
American foreign policy. With a considerable degree of truth, it may be said of
him that he is both wheelhorse and sparkplug of the decision-making process.

. . . The desk man's influence at all levels in the decision-making process stems
from his detailed knowledge of an area and his role as a drafting officer. Unless he
is really out of step, it is easier for his bosses to concur or make minor revisions
than to disagree and upset his apple cart. The "tyranny of the written word"
works in his favor. On day-to-day routine matters, the desk officer is the cock of
the walk.

. . . College-trained and usually in his late thirties or early forties, the Foreign Service type desk officer is personable and intelligent, possessing some verbal skill,
considerable initiative, and a sense of responsibility.[27]

In terms of the ranking structure, Japanese division heads are the equivalent of
American office directors rather than country desk officers.[28] They are, as a
rule, not in their thirties but in their early or mid-forties. Moreover, country
desk officers are found only in the geographic bureaus of the State Department,
but in Japan both functional and geographic bureaus have division heads.

Regardless of the original source of the initiating action, pressure, or inspiration, few problems requiring an official intraministry decision of some significance bypass the division head with jurisdictional interest in the issue involved.
Acting as the "wheelhorse and sparkplug" of an ad hoc decision-making group,
the division head draws on the manpower and intellectual resources available

24. Kawamura, *Gaimushō*, pp. 41–42.
25. Interview, an official in the American Affairs Bureau, Oct. 19, 1971.
26. Interview, an official in the Minister's Secretariat, April 7, 1972.
27. Robert E. Elder, *The Policy Machine* (Syracuse, N.Y.: Syracuse University Press, 1960),
pp. 19–27.
28. See Sapin, *Making of U.S. Foreign Policy*, p. 120.

in his division. There are, however, severe limitations on such resources. The vertical range of participation in the policy-relevant decision process does not extend below the assistant-deputy head level, even in routine cases. In fact, below this level there are not many officials who are "qualified" to participate in the business of intradivision deliberations on policy issues.[29] With some minor variations, each division has only three "qualified" men—the head, deputy head, and assistant-deputy head, the last of whom usually heads an intradivision coordinating desk (*sōmu-han*). Each of the remaining country or functional desks is headed by an official who is, in the ministry's bureaucratic jargon, a "noncareerist."[30] The desk-level staff discharges essentially sub-decisional clerical duties.

When the first round of intradivision work is done, whether or not it results in a definite recommendation, the division head may go directly to the bureau director or, if any divisions in or outside the bureau are also involved, to his counterpart in those divisions. In the latter case, the principle of the *ringisei* applies, but probably to a lesser extent than it apparently does in some other ministries of the Japanese government or in the U.S. Department of State. With or without intervening lateral consultations at the division head level, the recommendation, usually put down on paper, goes up the ladder for approval to the bureau director, the vice-minister, and eventually, the foreign minister. Frequently, there are disagreements among the officials—especially if the issue involved is controversial—and the initial recommendation is returned for revisions. More face-to-face consultations take place, counselors and even a deputy vice-minister get involved, and the revised and re-revised recommendation "travels up and down the floors" of the ministry. The "tyranny of written word" may work in favor of the division head. At least one official was emphatic that, compared with other ministries such as Finance, the Foreign Ministry tends to give its division heads considerable discretion in decision-making.[31] The rule of seniority, however, is rigidly observed; a division head cannot and does not go directly to the vice-minister or minister against the will of the bureau director and counselor.[32] A division head is thus a powerful man, but the true test of his effectiveness is his ability to work with and not against his bureau director.

The participation of the deputy vice-ministers and counselors in the intramural decision-making process is irregular and variable. The role of the parlia-

29. For a fuller discussion on this point, see the next section of this article.

30. Note that the term in the American usage refers to a higher-ranking political appointee. A more precise meaning of the term as used in the Japanese Foreign Ministry will be given in the next section.

31. Interview, a secretary to the foreign minister, June 29, 1972.

32. Needless to say, this does not preclude a division head or a counselor from briefing the vice-minister or even the minister, usually with the knowledge and approval of the bureau director.

mentary vice-minister is generally insignificant.[33] Although he is normally a
member of the Senior Officials' Conference (Kanbu-kai), he is never an active
member, and the conference group is not even a very effective decision-making
group. Nor does he intervene in the intraministry decision process. His function is primarily to help facilitate communications between the ministry and
the Diet.[34] Kawamura concluded seventeen years ago that a parliamentary
vice-minister was a "living tape recorder used to answer questions in the
Diet."[35] Usually with no background or even interest in foreign policy, and
regarding the job essentially as a liability in his political life, he memorizes relevant (and irrelevant) facts and figures prepared by ministry officials with
which to respond to the questions asked by Diet members in committee
meetings and plenary sessions.

An ambassador and the counselors at an overseas post do not directly participate in the decision-making process at the headquarters. Their function is
primarily information-gathering. There is, however, a fine distinction between
gathering and processing information, on the one hand, and policy formulation, on the other. Decisions must be based on relevant information. He who
collects, selects, and manipulates information inevitably has substantial power to influence, often determine, the decisions based on such information.
Moreover, the official functions of the foreign-service officers stationed overseas,
from ambassadors down to second secretaries or below, include advising the
ministry headquarters and the foreign minister on questions of policy relating
to the area under their jurisdiction. That an ambassador is invariably a senior
careerist official with a rank nominally higher than that of the vice-minister
makes the impact of his advice significant and sometimes critical.[36] When a
decision is taken under the pressure of specific actions by a foreign government
and is therefore directly linked to formal or informal negotiations with that
government, an ambassador often acts as the chief negotiating officer.[37] In such
a situation, the ambassador can and does play a leading role in the decision-
making process despite his physical remoteness from the headquarters. His immediate subordinates—the counselors and first secretaries—also get deeply
involved in the process.

Although the decision-making group and process are characteristically in-

33. There was, however, the case of a parliamentary vice-minister representing peanut
growers' interests in his election district successfully pleading with the prime minister
against liberalizing import of foreign peanuts. The source for this interesting information did
not want to be quoted.

34. Interview, Ōnishi Masao (parliamentary vice-minister of foreign affairs), Feb. 3, 1972.

35. Kawamura, Gaimushō, p. 155.

36. An ambassador is appointed by the prime minister with the emperor's attestation.

37. The forthcoming monographs by Brookings scholars cited in footnote 11 discuss the roles of
Ambassador Shimoda in the negotiations for the reversion of Okinawa and of his successor,
Ushiba, in the textile negotiations.

sulated from the body of ministry personnel outside the vertical and lateral ranges of involvement indicated, machinery for broader participation and coordination is not totally lacking. At the division level, the coordinating desk operates to keep the work of several geographically or functionally specialized desks effectively linked to one another. At the bureau level, division heads usually meet twice a week at the Division Head Conference (Kachō Kaigi) to debate issues of common interest and concern.[38] Officials above the bureau director rank participate in the Senior Officials' Conference, which meets two or three times a week.[39] Finally, there are the annual conferences for heads of overseas diplomatic and consular establishments.

None of these conferences, however, serves as decision-making machinery. They are designed merely to provide opportunities for officials to exchange information and ideas without taking positions or even making recommendations on policy matters. Kawamura and his collaborators commented that the Senior Officials' Conference was an occasion for bureau directors to read superficial reports on the activities of their bureaus; Banno attaches a slightly more positive quasi-decision-making function to it.[40] A principal member of the conference dismissed it as a device either to absolve a particular official of his responsibility for a wrong or controversial decision by implicating others or to appease a minority group of dissidents by giving them an opportunity to air their grievances, though with no significant consequences.[41]

That the Foreign Ministry is not really equipped with decision-making machinery operating on a ministrywide basis is an important part of its tradition. In prewar days, a line of officials affiliated with one or two particular bureaus and divisions also made decisions, which the vice-minister and minister then ratified and presented to the prime minister as the will of the ministry.[42]

Another tradition among senior ministry officials is a belief in what could be called policy-making by improvisation and a distrust of comprehensive long-

38. Interview, an official in the Second Southeast Asian Affairs Division, Asian Affairs Bureau, June 5, 1972; Kawamura, *Gaimushō*, pp. 85-86.

39. In the summer of 1972 the Senior Officials Conference had three meetings a week, one of which was attended by the foreign minister. The regular members were the vice-minister, two deputy vice-ministers, bureau and department directors, director of the Minister's Secretariat, chief protocol officer, and director of the Foreign Service Institute.

40. See Kawamura, *Gaimushō*, pp. 41, 86; Banno, *Gendai gaikō no bunseki*, p. 190.

41. Interview, an official in the American Affairs Bureau, Oct. 14, 1971. Sapin discusses the State Department's equivalent of the *kanbukai:* "At his staff meetings, held up to recently three times a week at 9:15 A.M., the Secretary meets with all his high-ranking officials (usually of Assistant Secretary rank and higher), giving them an opportunity to bring matters before their colleagues and the Secretary. What can be accomplished, however, is severely limited by the size of the group and the relatively short time available (usually less than forty-five minutes) for the global review of problems that take place." Sapin, *Making of U.S. Foreign Policy*, p. 115.

42. *Gaimushō no hyakunen*, 2:182.

term planning.[43] Prewar attempts to build strong policy-planning and co-ordinating machinery in the ministry included the appointment, in 1936, of an Organization Reform Committee. The committee proposed the concentration of planning functions in a Political Affairs Bureau, but the proposal was defeated. The opposition held the "pragmatist" view that policy-planning could not be divorced from day-to-day routine operations and, therefore, was best undertaken by each of the conventional geographic bureaus.[44] The primary function of the Research Department in the prewar period was to collect intelligence relating to the Soviet Union.

Since World War II, the ministry has included policy research and planning as a part of its serious business only during the period of the Allied Occupation, when Japan was temporarily deprived of its independent diplomatic authority and policy research and planning was necessarily divorced from practice. There is a Research and Analysis Department in the minister's secretariat, which in theory engages in comprehensive and coordinated policy investigation and planning.[45] In practice, it is not even as effective as the now defunct Policy Planning Council of the U.S. State Department.[46] The regular bureaus view the Research Department's activities with suspicion, and potential disputes over jurisdiction severely circumscribe that department's role.

The absence of effective ministrywide machinery for decision-making and policy coordination enhances the autonomous discretionary power of each bureau. As if out of an instinct to avoid being ruled by the law of jungle, which could result from such a situation, the bureaus have learned to live by rules for peaceful coexistence which emphasize noninterference in each other's internal affairs and mutual respect for the territorial integrity of all. This spirit also nourishes and strengthens the ad hoc decision-making groups formed along bureau-division lines. The Foreign Ministry is thus characterized by subsystem dominance in which the individual bureaus and divisions are the basic units of decision-making and action and the individual bureau directors and division heads enjoy a large measure of freedom—within the limits defined by the rule of seniority—to map out their course of action on any specific policy issue at hand.

The lines of jurisdictional interests and responsibility are clearly drawn between the bureaus. The American Affairs Bureau attends to matters relating to policy toward the nations in North, Central, and South America and does not meddle in issues arising between Japan and China, which are handled by

43. Interview, an official in the Minister's Secretariat. More will be said later about this subject.
44. *Gaimushō no hyakunen*, 2:69-76.
45. See "Shoshō jimu yōran: Gaimushō," in *Shokuin roku* 1:137.
46. For comparison, see Destler's analysis of the problem of policy planning and coordination in the U.S. foreign policy bureaucracy in Destler, *Presidents, Bureaucrats, and Foreign Policy*, chap. 8. See also earlier discussions of the State Department Policy Planning Council in Elder, *The Policy Machine*, p. 72, and Sapin, *Making of U.S. Foreign Policy*, pp. 112-113.

the Asian Affairs Bureau. The Economic Affairs Bureau has jurisdictional interests in problems of international monetary and trade policy, but the Middle Eastern and African Affairs Bureau has the primary responsibility for negotiating with an Arab country on oil imports. Each geographic bureau tends to develop a special geographic "identity" or bias. For example, the American Affairs Bureau tends to have a sympathetic view of American government actions, and division heads tend to identify with the particular governments and countries with which they deal. First North American Affairs Division Head Chiba Kazuo had warm feelings for State Department and American embassy officials, just as China Division Head Hashimoto Hiroshi pleaded with passion for a "forward-looking policy" toward the People's Republic of China.[47] Only the periodic and frequent rotation of personnel from one bureau to another seems to keep this kind of geographic bias from seriously interfering with interbureau and interdivision relations.

The only notable exception to the rule of jurisdictional separation, as noted earlier, is the role of the Treaties Bureau. Acting as the general legal counsel and adviser for the entire ministry, this bureau tends to intervene in wide-ranging policy and administrative issues. Its functions are considerably broader than those of the legal adviser's staff in the U.S. Department of State.[48] In a way, the bureau combines the functions of the State Department's legal adviser and Congressional Relations Bureau. Acting as the central reservoir of knowledge and wisdom on all legal aspects of the nation's foreign relations, the Treaties Bureau officials, especially the bureau director and the head of its Treaties Division, assist and advise not only their colleagues and superiors in the ministry itself but, even more importantly, the foreign minister and the prime minister. During the Diet sessions, the Treaty Bureau officials make themselves constantly and continuously available to the cabinet leaders. In fact, without the bureau officials' help, the cabinet leaders would be unable to answer most of the sharp questions asked by opposition members on details of the government's transactions with foreign governments. The director of the bureau provides an authoritative interpretation of the most controversial or obscure provision in an international treaty or agreement; he and his staff supply the copious references to precedents and theory to support the prime minister's and foreign minister's positions on sensitive foreign policy issues before the Diet and the nation.[49] The office of the Treaties Division has a corner

---

47. Interviews, officials in the divisions concerned. See the interesting accounts of the prewar China Bureau officials' opposition to the policy of aggression against China pursued by the military and promilitary members of the cabinets in *Gaimusho no hyakunen*, 2:279-230, 293, 315-318, 327-328, 332-337.

48. On the role and function of the Legal Adviser's Office, see Richard B. Bilder, "The Office of the Legal Adviser: The State Department Lawyer and Foreign Affairs," *American Journal of International Law*, July 1962, pp. 633–684.

49. Interview, an official in the Treaties Division, Nov. 25, 1971.

of a bookshelf for several thick files of "Hypothetical Questions Asked and Answers To Be Given," on which political leaders rely for correct and proper answers to all kinds of questions that are likely to come up in Diet foreign policy debates.

In the years immediately following the end of the postwar Occupation, when major foreign policy efforts concerned settlement of various war-related claims and accounts with foreign governments and laying legal foundations for new relationships, the role of the Treaties Bureau was particularly important. Even in the more recent years when political and economic issues tend to over-shadow purely legal problems, it remains the keystone of the ministry's domestic political as well as foreign relations.[50] The intimate involvement with the Diet no doubt influences the outlook of the bureau's officials, who are general-ly more sensitive to the pressures and exigencies of domestic politics than offi-cials in the other, particularly geographic, bureaus. By intervening in the work of virtually all segments of ministry personnel involved in policy-related decision-making, the Treaties Bureau exerts substantial unifying influence, no doubt contributing to the "legalistic" mentality so often attributed to the ministry and its officials.[51] As with the other bureaus, however, only the direc-tor, one of the three division heads and his deputy, and perhaps the counselor participate directly in the intraministry and extramural counseling services relating to any specific policy issue.

With the Treaties Bureau complement added, the size of the ad hoc decision-making body still remains extremely small (seldom more than ten officials), especially in situations involving controversial issues. In such a situa-tion, the personal attributes of a few particular officials become an especially important factor in the determination of the decision process and its outcomes. As one official pointed out, the central question then becomes which persons happen to occupy the strategic posts at the critical points in the process.[52]

THE ACTORS

In 1970 there were about 2,600 "officials" employed by the Foreign Ministry.[53] Of this number, 310 held the top-ranking posts above deputy division head and its equivalents either at the Tokyo headquarters or in overseas diplomatic and consular missions. The basic biographical data on these officials are presented in Table 2. The average bureau director was fifty-three years old. He was born

50. Interviews, a secretary to the prime minister, Feb. 24, 1973; an official in the American Affairs Bureau, Oct. 19, 1971.

51. See relevant comments in Kawamura, *Gaimushō*, pp. 24–25.

52. Interview, an official in the Treaties Bureau, Nov. 25, 1971.

53. Jinjiin Ninyōkyoku, *Shōwa 45-nendo ni okeru ippanshoku no kokka kōmuin no ninyō jōkyō chōsa hōkoku* (1970), p. 29, table 2 (1).

Table 2

Biographical Data on Average High-Ranking Foreign-Service Officials

	No.	Age	Year of entry into F.S.	Years between entry and high office	Age at high appointment	HFSE certificate (%)	Judicial or administrative certificate	Tokyo University Law Faculty graduate (%)
Headquarters								
Reserve ambassador	5	59	1935	15.6	40	100	0	80
Vice-Minister	1	59	1935	15.0	39	100	0	100
Deputy vice-minister	2	58	1938	12.0	38	100	0	100
Director, minister's secretariat	1	47	1940	12.0	39	100	0	100
Counselor, minister's secretariat	4	56	1940	17.2	42	50	0	25
Bureau director	9	53	1941	15.5	39	100	0	77.7
Deputy bureau director	1	51	1942	18.0	41	0	100	100
Department director	3	56	1940	15.6	41	100	0	100
Counselor	18	52	1942	18.6	43	38.8	61.2	66.6
Division head	49	43	1950	17.4	41	87.7	6.1	71.4
Research officer	13	50	1943	23.0	46	46.1	0	38.4
Secretarial officer	4	41	1955	15.0	38	100	0	50.0
Others*	5	53	1940	18.4	42	80.0	20.0	60.0
Overseas								
Ambassador	90	57	1938	14.9	39	93.3	3.3	78.8
Minister	19	53	1941	18.0	41	47.3	52.7	84.2
Consul-general	39	55	1940	21.7	46	33.3	41.0	46.1
Counselor	47	51	1943	20.8	45	27.6	51.0	53.1
TOTAL (Mean)	310	52	1942	17.9	42	66.1	22.3	66.4

SOURCES: *Gaimushō shokuin ryakureki: Shōwa 45-nen*, 1970; Ōkurashō Insatsukyoku, *Shokuin roku* (Tokyo: Ministry of Finance, 1971, 1973), vol. 1.

*3 protocol officers, 1 librarian, 1 government representative to Expo '70.

in 1917, during the First World War; entered the ministry's service in 1941, the year of Pearl Harbor; and has since served nearly thirty years. The counselors were only one year younger than the modal bureau director. The division heads were exactly ten years younger, having been born in 1927 during the early days of the prewar militarist upsurge, and having entered the service in 1950, about a year before the San Francisco Peace Treaty. Except for ministers, counselors, and research officers, the overwhelming majority had successfully passed the Higher Foreign Service Examination (HFSE) before their entry into the service. Except the secretariat counselors and research officers, an overwhelming majority of the others who had not taken the HFSE had passed one of the two prewar civil service examinations of roughly equal level and prestige (the Higher Administrative Service Examination or the Judicial Service Examination). In fact, 272 of the 310 officials counted, or 87.6 percent, had passed one of these examinations; 205, or 66.1 percent, had passed the HFSE.

In the entire 2,600-man work force of the ministry, those who held HFSE certificates numbered 585, or 22.5 percent. Holders of Middle Foreign Service or Language Trainee certificates numbered 428, or 16.4 percent, and 287, or 11.0 percent, had Lower Foreign Service Examination certificates.[54] The remainder either held prewar Administrative or Judicial Service certificates or none at all. There was a sharp line of distinction regarding both the highest rank that could be attained and the pace of promotions between those who did and those who did not hold an HFSE or a prewar Administrative or Judicial Service certificate. The middle and lower examination certificate holders and the language trainees were, as a rule, not eligible for appointment above the deputy division head level. Even among those who had been appointed to the higher ranks before 1970, there were substantial differences among the three categories of officials (those with HFSE certificates, those with Administrative or Judicial Service certificates, and those without any of these certificates—the noncareerists) in the length of time spent between the date of entry into the service and the date of first appointment to a high ranking post. Table 3 shows the degree of those differences.

Not surprisingly, 206, or 66.4 percent, of the 310 high officials in the ministry were also graduates of Tokyo University Law Faculty. Of the 205 with HFSE certificates just about 80 percent (165) were Tokyo University Law Faculty graduates. Naturally correlation between graduation from the Tokyo University Law Faculty and the speed of promotions after entry into the ministry's service was also high. It was, however, not as high as the correlation between the type of entrance examination certificate and the pace of promotions as

54. During the 1945–1970 period, an average of 17.6 HFSE certificate holders were appointed each year. The 1961–1970 average was somewhat higher at 22.3. Middle Foreign Service and Language Trainee examination recruits were fewer in number: an annual average of 16 during 1947–1969 and 13.7 between 1959 and 1969. See *Shōwa 45-nen 10-gatsu hensan Gaimushō shokuin rekinin hyō,* pp. 316–322, 328–331.

Table 3
Differential Pace of Promotions in the Foreign Service

Number of years between entry and appointment to high office	HFSE certificate holders	Administrative & judicial examination certificate holders*	Noncareerists	Total
14 years or less	69 (33.7%)	4 (5.8%)	4 (11.1%)	77 (24.8%)
15–19 years	114 (55.6%)	36 (52.2%)	2 (5.6%)	152 (49.0%)
20 years or more	22 (10.7%)	29 (42.0%)	30 (83.3%)	81 (26.2%)
Total	205 (100%)	69 (100%)	36 (100%)	310 (100%)

$$x^2 = 113.819/p < .001 \qquad\qquad \text{Gamma} = .734$$

SOURCES: *Gaimushō shokuin ryakureki: Shōwa 45-nen;* Ōkurashō Insatsukyoku, *Shokuin roku,* vol. 1.
*The slow pace of promotions among prewar Administrative and Judicial Service Examination certificate holders is due largely to the fact that many of them obtained the certificates in mid-career. None of the 4 in "14 years or less," 10 of the 36 in "15–19 years," and 13 of the 29 in "20 years or more" categories passed either examination in mid-career, after several years in the service. Virtually all of the HFSE certificate holders, in contrast, passed the examination on graduation from college before entering the service.

suggested in Table 3. The relevant chi square and gamma values were respectively 57.102 ($p < 0.001$) and 0.125.[55] Therefore, the type of entrance examination certificate was relatively more important than graduation from Tokyo University Law Faculty, although the two were closely interrelated.

The true dimension of the elite versus nonelite or, to use the bureaucrat's jargon, careerist versus noncareerist, distinction becomes more visible and dramatic when one looks at the next level of officials: the deputy division head at the headquarters, and the first secretary (embassies) and consul (consulates) overseas. Holders of HFSE certificates are relatively few at this level. Of the fifty-one deputy division heads identified at the headquarters in 1970 only five were in the elite certificate-holding group. Corresponding figures for first secretaries and consuls were respectively 48 out of 120 and 6 out of 54.[56] Their mean dates of birth and entry into the service are given in Table 4. The average

55. For a more general discussion of the importance of academic background in the promotion system of the Japanese government bureaucracy, see Akira Kubota, *Higher Civil Servants in Postwar Japan* (Princeton, N.J.: Princeton University Press, 1969), chaps. 4, 5; Shimbori Michiya, *Gakubatsu* (Tokyo: Fukumura Shuppan, 1969), chap. 3.
56. Excluded from these figures were 101 first secretaries and 21 consuls who were permanent affiliates of other ministries or agencies as well as 4 first secretaries whose agency affiliation could not be determined.

Table 4
Career Comparison of Middle-Level Foreign Service Officials

	Deputy division head		First secretary		Consul	
	Careerist	Noncareerist	Careerist	Noncareerist	Careerist	Noncareerist
Mean date of birth	1934	1915	1931	1917	1927	1917
Mean date of entry	1956	1940	1955	1946	1954	1940

SOURCES: *Gaimushō shokuin ryakureki: Shōwa 45-nen;* Ōkurashō Insatsukyoku, *Shokuin roku,* vol. 1.

careerist deputy division head was eighteen years younger than the average noncareerist colleague. The age differences in the two categories of first secretaries and consuls were respectively fourteen and ten years. The careerists had reached one of these ranks within about fifteen years after their entry into the service; the noncareerists had spent twenty-four to thirty years. These are rough estimations, but the differences are unmistakable. A fifty-five-year-old noncareerist deputy division head works side by side with a thirty-six-year-old careerist at the same rank and about the same salary. The few exceptional cases of noncareerists reaching the division head or consul-general rank notwithstanding, there is a very high barrier between one class of officials and the other.[57]

Among the careerists, promotions are based largely on seniority. Unless one makes some serious mistakes, one is normally assured of periodic reviews and promotions. Most eventually attain the rank of counselor or bureau director at headquarters, or minister, consul-general, and even ambassador overseas. Promotions are, however, by no means automatic. Final decisions regarding specific cases are made by the vice-minister in consultation with the director of the minister's secretariat and the head of the Personnel Division in the secretariat.[58] In addition to the principle of seniority, which is always respected, the decisions are based on evaluation reports submitted semiannually on January 1 and July 1 by each official's immediate superior, and kept in the personnel files for use in the periodic review process. This system makes merit an important factor in personnel decisions.

There are important differences in the way the system actually operates in the Japanese Foreign Ministry and in the U.S. State Department.[59] First,

57. See also Kawamura, *Gaimushō,* p. 117.

58. Interview, an official in the Personnel Division, Minister's Secretariat, Jan. 28, 1972. Promotions of bureau directors and above are, however, subject to approval from the foreign minister, the prime minister, and occasionally other LDP leaders.

59. For comparison, see the description of the annual "efficiency reports" in the State Department and their effects on the behavior of American foreign service officers in Smith Simpson, *Anatomy of the State Department* (Boston: Houghton, Mifflin, 1967), pp. 20, 38.

Japan has no equivalent to the "selection out" or "up-or-out" dismissal system of the State Department, and voluntary resignations are few.[60] Second, there are virtually no lateral transfers of personnel into the Foreign Ministry from other ministries, public agencies, or outside the government bureaucracy. The substantial number of officials who are sent by various other ministries to overseas diplomatic and consular establishments are not permanent transfers; they return to their home ministries on termination of their overseas appointment. Thus, except for the annual accretion by recruitment of twenty or so fresh college graduates, the size and composition of the ministry's careerist population change little over time. Third, there is no factionalism based on school ties, presumably because so many come from a single school anyway, and none, so far, based on ideological or policy differences.[61] All these factors combine to make the careerist life fairly comfortable and pleasant, apart, of course, from the pressure of work itself; they generate in the holder of an HFSE certificate a strong sense of identification with and loyalty to the ministry. Virtually all the officials I interviewed reacted very negatively to my queries about "possible" disputes and conflicts among them. A division head known to have long held a minority view on an issue important to him emphatically denied that his colleagues and superiors had erred and should therefore repent.[62]

Another interesting and important attribute of the Foreign Ministry careerists is the generalist orientation and emphasis in their training and professional outlook. The tendency in Japan is just as conspicuous and consistent as in the U.S. foreign service where, it has been said, an ambitious officer learns early that "specialization in finance, science, and especially labor, is the kiss of death."[63] Periodic and frequent rotation assures that every careerist will become a generalist superficially familiar with many functional and geographic areas but a specialist in none. Table 5 shows the average number of areas the various high-ranking officials had worked in by 1970. Even the relatively young division heads had served in at least two and a half of the six functional areas and three of the ten geographic areas.[64] Although more officials have served in some areas (such as economic and information or Western Europe and North America) than in others (such as consular affairs-emigration and international organization or Eastern Europe and Central and South America),[65] emphasis has been placed consistently on making everybody in the elite corps a good all-

60. Interview, an official in the Minister's Secretariat, Jan. 28, 1972. On the "selection out" rule, see Sapin, *Making of U.S. Foreign Policy*, p. 332.

61. In the 1930s there were running battles in the ministry between the pro-German, promilitary "Axis" faction and its opponents loosely referred to as the "Anglo-American" faction. See *Gaimushō no hyakunen*, 2:142, 145, 172, 181-183, 422.

62. Interview, an official in the China Division, May 1, 1972.

63. David H. Davis, *How the Bureaucracy Makes Foreign Policy* (Lexington, Mass: Lexington Books, 1972), p. 19.

64. For comparison, see Simpson, *Anatomy of the State Department*, p. 33, and Sapin, *Making U.S. Foreign Policy*, p. 128.

65. This is discussed more fully in my "Bureaucratic Power in Japan."

Table 5
Average Number of Areas
in which High-Ranking Foreign Service Officials Have Served*

	N	Functional areas at headquarters**	Geographic areas at headquarters***	Geographic areas of overseas missions
Bureau director	9	2.6	2.2	3.3
Counselor (headquarters)	18	3.0	2.0	3.1
Division head	49	2.5	1.4	2.9
Ambassador	90	2.8	1.5	4.2
Counselor (overseas)	47	2.7	1.3	3.2
TOTAL	213			

SOURCE: *Gaimushō shokuin ryakureki: Shōwa 45-nen*

*The average period of service in one area is estimated to be three years.
**Secretariat, consular affairs-emigration, economic affairs, treaties and agreements, international organization, and information-research.
***Northeast Asia, Southeast Asia, Southwest Asia, North America, Central and South America, Near and Middle East, Africa, and international organizations.

around generalist. Specialization has definitely not been a factor in the operation of the rotation or promotion system.

The Middle Foreign Service Examination group is not one of specialists either. Both the Higher and Middle examinations test general knowledge, and the Foreign Service Institute gives in-service training with a generalist emphasis to both groups.[66] The only specialists in the ministry are the language trainees, most of whom specialize in languages other than English, especially "exotic" languages such as Norwegian, Polish, Bengali, or Swahili.[67] This is a very small

66. As given in 1971, the HFSE covered, in its first part, constitutional law, international law, economics, diplomatic history, either administrative or civil law, either finance or economic policy, one foreign language (English, French, German, Spanish, Russian, or Chinese), and general intelligence. The second part consisted of oral tests in constitutional law, international law, economics, conversational ability in one foreign language, and hearing and writing ability in the foreign language; a comprehensive written test in unspecified subjects relevant to the duties of a foreign service officer; a group discussion and interview; and a physical examination. The Middle Foreign Service Examination included, in its first part, general intelligence, composition (in Japanese), jurisprudence, international law, economics, one foreign language (English, French, German, Russian, Spanish, Portuguese, Italian, Dutch, Arabic, Persian, Urdu, Hindi, Burmese, Thai, Vietnamese, Indonesian, Chinese, or Korean). The second part had oral tests in jurisprudence, economics, conversational and writing ability in one foreign language, an interview, and a physical examination.

For a description of the Foreign Service Institute Training programs, see Gaimushō Kenshūjo (Foreign Service Institute), ed., *Gaimushō Kenshūjo jūnen shi* (1956), Part 2.

67. Further discussion is contained in my "Bureaucratic Power in Japan."

group and part of the noncareerist personnel precluded from advancement to the high-ranking positions. Thus, in the entire work force of the ministry, specialization is minimal and limited to several hundred language experts.

So far I have presented an essentially biographical profile of the Foreign Ministry careerist corps. To draw a psychological and ideological profile is considerably more difficult. I will limit myself to discussion of a few salient aspects and tendencies that seem relevant and important to understanding the decision process in the ministry.

A careerist's professional life is a generally pleasant and satisfactory one, free from peer group competition or in-group factional strife. A sense of quasi-familial cordiality and solidarity prevails among his colleagues both at the headquarters and especially at an overseas post, where personal ties among the generally small staff tend to be even more intimate than in Tokyo. This groupism combines with the effects of seniority rule and the practice of semi-annual performance evaluation reports to generate a powerful pressure for conformism and agreeableness. Observations on the "high degree of the yes-man spirit" among American foreign-service officers and the fact that they tend to be "compromisers rather than contesters, avoiders of argument rather than dynamic leaders," also apply to Japan.[68] Above all, Japanese foreign-service officers try to avoid rocking the boat and express only views they believe will be agreeable to their superiors.[69] One official went so far as to assert that minority and dissident views are systematically weeded out in the decision system so completely committed to groupism and conformism.[70] Although such statements tend to exaggerate the degree of internal unity and minimize the conflicts of ideology and opinion that do exist among the ministry officials, conformism has been an important, probably dominant, tendency in the Japanese Foreign Ministry.

The careerists' political views and attitudes are characterized by ambivalence and a sense of dilemma. For example, the role of public opinion in the formulation of the nation's foreign policy is readily recognized. The official of the Public Information and Cultural Affairs Bureau insisted that his colleagues in the ministry should pay much greater attention to the trends of public opinion, instead of being absorbed in guessing what is on the minds of their superiors.[71] In the same breath, however, he condemned the general public as emotional, myopic, and irresponsible. One official in the American Affairs Bureau echoed this view but mentioned the materialist concerns of the public as the more disturbing problem.[72] According to him, the public became emotionally interested in a foreign-policy issue only if it involved material gains or

68. See Simpson, *Anatomy of the State Department*, pp. 8, 35.
69. Kawamura, *Gaimushō*, pp. 25, 100.
70. Interview, an official in the Public Information and Cultural Affairs Bureau, Nov. 12, 1971.
71. Ibid.
72. Interview, Oct. 14, 1971.

losses to the people themselves; in the absence of such issues, the people were generally indifferent.

There is a similar ambivalence in comments on politicians, whether as members of the Diet or of the parties. I encountered on the one hand, especially among officials of relatively junior ranks, an eloquent and well-formulated view that it is the politicians' job to decide the basic domestic and foreign policies of the government, and officials in the ministries ought to limit their efforts to implementing those decisions. An official in the Treaties Bureau, who held and supported such a view, argued that the policies of the ministry were not made by ministry officials, but by government leaders, and properly so. Another official in the Asian Affairs Bureau said that Japan's policy toward the People's Republic of China was for the cabinet, not the Foreign Ministry, to decide.[73] A division head in the Economic Affairs Bureau was more philosophical and elaborate.[74] He explained that in most other ministries and agencies, officials presented recommendations to their ministers without any alternative options. The Foreign Ministry did not and must not do so, because that would violate the principle of democratic control of foreign policy. Decisions must be left to the Diet and elected representatives of the people.

On the other hand, many officials argued just as eloquently that politicians could not be entrusted with the important business of foreign policy-making because of their ignorance, parochialism, and general lack of competence. Thus an official, who asked not to be quoted, explained that a politician was somebody whose entry into the bureaucracy had been thwarted by his inferior academic achievement and, therefore, he was a jealous and helpless man. A bureau director referred to ranking cabinet ministers' ignorance about foreign countries and their affairs and emphatically concluded that a professional foreign-service official was incomparably better equipped to guide the nation in its foreign relations.[75] A much younger second secretary at the Japanese embassy in Washington fully agreed with the view that a foreign service official was far more intelligent and knowledgeable about problems of foreign policy than a politician.[76] Some referred also to prevalent corruption among politicians and compared this with the bureaucrat's "incorruptibility and integrity"; others mentioned the "subservience" and generally unprincipled attitude of the ruling LDP toward the opposition parties as a main reason for their unhappiness with politicians.[77] The belligerency with which some officials discussed politicians and party politics seems to reflect a latent fear and distrust of

73. Interview, June 5, 1972.
74. Interview, Jan. 31, 1972.
75. Interview, Nov. 12, 1971.
76. Interview, a second secretary, Japanese Embassy in Washington, D.C., May 24, 1973.
77. Interview, a deputy vice-minister, Oct. 25, 1971.

them. After all, bureaucrats at the upper ranks are vulnerable to interventions from political leaders which can determine promotions and even their entire professional career.

The officials' views on the substance of Japan's foreign relations seemed more straightforward. They assured me time and again of their commitment to the basic law of postwar Japanese foreign policy—continued military alliance and economic cooperation with the United States—as "absolutely necessary" for Japan's survival and well being.[78] They also accorded high priority to relationships with the "democratic" nations of Western Europe. On the other hand, the USSR and the People's Republic of China have been potential adversaries, if not actual enemies, in the postwar (Cold War) mental framework of Japan's foreign relations. This view has persisted, at least with regard to the USSR. According to one top-ranking official, the People's Republic of China still lacked the power and ability to formulate and implement a global strategy, but the USSR possessed such power and ability and was actually intent on dominating the world.[79] For the other nations of Asia, the traditional Foreign Ministry attitude has been one of indifference mixed with contempt.[80] For nations of the Middle East and Africa and, indeed, even those in the Indian subcontinent, there is that characteristic foreign service officer argot, "West of Burma." Asia east of Burma is not desirable, but tolerable; the nations beyond are a diplomat's limbo. One does everything to avoid being transferred to that part of the world.[81]

Although these traditional notions and prejudices still persisted among the officials I interviewed in 1971–1973, there was some evidence that they were no longer as widely and unquestioningly shared as they had been ten or fifteen years earlier. Even Hōgen Shinsaku emphasized the need for increased mutuality and equality in U.S.-Japanese relations. A division head mentioned the rapidly decreasing credibility of the U.S. "nuclear umbrella" and noted that there was a growing feeling among his colleagues that Japan could well do without it.[82] An *Asahi shimbun* reporter, Kikuchi Ikuzō, referred to the increasingly defiant mood among younger foreign-service officers. On the other side of the coin, the attitude toward the People's Republic of China and perhaps also the USSR was changing in 1971, especially after the mid-summer "Nixon shocks."[83] Kikuchi also noted an important change in the climate of

78. Interviews, officials in the Minister's Secretariat and the Economic Affairs and Public Information and the Cultural Affairs bureaus.

79. Interview, with a deputy vice-minister who was known for his exceptionally articulate view of the USSR and communism partly because of his personal experiences with Soviet officials. He served in the Japanese embassy in Moscow in 1944–1946 and again in 1959–1961. At the headquarters, too, he served in divisions dealing directly with the USSR.

80. See relevant comments in Kawamura, *Gaimushō*, pp. 108–110.

81. I owe many of my thoughts on this subject to Kikuchi Ikuzō.

82. Interview, an official in the Economic Affairs Bureau, Jan. 31, 1972.

83. See my "Foreign Policy Making in Japan."

opinion regarding Asia, although the change did not extend to the "West of Burma" regions. According to his observations, Korea had become "popular" and so had Southeast Asian countries such as Thailand, Indonesia, and Malaysia, especially among the younger foreign-service officers. This seems to point up a change in the foreign-policy perspectives of Foreign Ministry careerists. It is probably very uneven in its range and intensity among the different age cohorts, but of sufficiently large dimensions to influence the decision process in the ministry in the years to come. These changing perspectives, the ambivalence in domestic political outlook, and some of the other important sources of strain on intraministry operations which I have identified in this section can cause future problems and liabilities for the Foreign Ministry decision-making system and its major actors.

PROBLEMS AND PROSPECTS

The most obvious and probably the most fundamental source of tension lies in the existing personnel system which discriminates against noncareerists as a matter of principle. Despite the partial validity of the argument that those who had passed the HFSE were generally better educated and more knowledgeable about subjects relevant to foreign service than those who had not, the illogicality and inequity of the system are obvious. One's lifetime career is determined with virtual finality by one's performance on the entrance examinations. On admission to the service, one is assigned to either the elite or the nonelite class; no matter how hard one works and how much one improves in abilities relevant to the service, one cannot move from one class to the other. There is no second chance to prove one's worth through a comprehensive, across-the-board examination at mid-career. Theoretically, a noncareerist may take or retake the HFSE. In practice, the high premium placed on fresh college graduates puts the mid-career man at such a disadvantage that few consider this a real option. Many, including careerists in the ministry, recognize the irrationality of the system. One interviewee pointed out that because of the discontent generated by the system, the ministry was losing a significant number of capable Middle Examination Certificate holders to private firms.[84] He hoped that some reform would soon be undertaken to eliminate the most flagrantly discriminatory aspects. Although what specifically had to be done was never clear, most with whom I talked supported the idea of reform in these areas.

Apart from the inherent inequity of the system, the systematic exclusion of noncareerists from the high ranks has caused a severe shortage of manpower at the strategic levels of decision-making. The problem has been chronic—it was just as serious in the 1930s as now[85]—but it has appeared to be getting pro-

84. Interview, a secretary to the Foreign Minister, June 29, 1972.
85. *Gaimushō no hyakunen*, 2:79-80.

gressively worse in the early 1970s. Given a workload which has been growing at a staggering rate, it is a near miracle that the small careerist corps,
spread out so thinly over the bureaus, divisions, and overseas missions (three to
four men per division), has managed to steer the nation clear of so many
hidden reefs and sandbars in the turbulent sea of postwar international politics.
Add the near total absence of specialists, and the feat appears even more surprising. The success or, more accurately, the avoidance of failures, has owed
much to fortuitous circumstances and the skill of the officials in maximizing the
output of their decision-making efforts by concentrating their limited resources
in a few select areas. The techniques are "single-issue-ism" and "policy-making
by improvisation."

The first of these techniques has never been explicitly formulated, but the
basic idea is familiar to both the officials themselves and observers outside the
bureaucracy. As one official explained, it refers to the way all available manpower in a given ad hoc decision-making unit is devoted to a single major issue
to the exclusion of all others.[86] The focal issue may be the normalization of
diplomatic relations with the USSR, the revision of the U.S.-Japan Mutual
Security Treaty, the reversion of Okinawa, or rapprochement with the People's
Republic of China, but the basic rule is one major issue at a time. The Cabinet,
the LDP, and other ministries suffer from a shortage of skilled manpower as
much or more than the Foreign Ministry, so the technique has actually been
applied by the entire Japanese government. Some attribute the development of
this technique (or tendency) to cultural factors, but it seems more logical to
relate it to the obvious shortage of manpower.[87]

When the vice-minister, one of the two deputy vice-ministers, the director of
a busy bureau, such as American Affairs, and a couple of division heads are
preoccupied with one important issue, it is no doubt difficult for the ministry to
deal simultaneously with another major issue or issues falling in the jurisdictional territory of that same bureau. For example, the ministry did not and
could not begin immediately to work seriously on the task of normalizing
relations with the People's Republic of China in the wake of President Nixon's
announced rapprochement in the summer of 1971. The top officials in the
ministry and Treaties Bureau were still occupied with the Diet debate on the
U.S.-Japanese agreement for the reversion of Okinawa.[88] Even if the attitude of
the People's Republic of China toward the Sato cabinet had been more flexible

86. Interview, Febr. 24, 1973. It is interesting to note that similar single-issue-ism has been
observed in the media coverage of foreign news in the United States. See Bernard C. Cohen,
"Mass Communication and Foreign Policy," in James N. Rosenau, ed., *Domestic Sources of Foreign
Policy* (Glencoe: Free Press, 1967), pp. 195-212.
87. Kiuchi Akitane, for example, attributed it to the "insular mentality" and inexperience
of Japanese officials and politicians.
88. Interviews, some officials in the China Division, March 6, 1973.

at the time, it would have been impossible for the Japanese government and Foreign Ministry to get ready for immediate formal negotiations on the complex politicolegal issues; the matter had to wait for half a year until early 1972.

What I call policy-making by improvisation is also familiar to the officials. It is closely related to single-issue-ism and frequently referred to as *anken-shugi*, or a case-by-case approach. As explained by one official, it is based on the belief that a policy is not and cannot be "made" prior to action, but must "evolve out of a series of actions taken in response to the pressure of events or circumstances."[89] In its purest form it stands on the proposition that a policy is either a sequence of actions or a logical thread that *retrospectively* ties such actions together. Again it seems obvious that this approach is born largely out of necessity caused by the shortage of manpower and talent available for systematic long-term policy-planning. In a way, the more complex the issues of international politics and foreign policy become, the more tempting this type of earthy pragmatism may be. It is, however, essentially a form of adventurism which depends primarily on intuition and snap decisions without reference to a larger perspective.

Alternatives to single-issue-ism and policy-making by improvisation would be the development of a capability to deal with several important policy issues simultaneously and on the basis of systematic advance planning. As immediate and sufficiently drastic expansion of the total ministry work force is unlikely, considering the well-known positions of both the Finance Ministry and the National Personnel Authority, a multi-issue potential would require a substantial change in the internal allocation and utilization of existing manpower resources. The steps necessary to achieve such a change are bound to hurt important segments of the present personnel and to provoke intense opposition.

First and foremost, the discrimination against noncareerists built into the present personnel system would have to be substantially reduced, if not completely eliminated. Second, selective specialization in certain functional and geographic areas might be encouraged and rewarded.[90] Making language trainees eligible for appointment to the higher ranks would be helpful, but more fundamentally, specialization in a wide range of functional areas, such as science and resource economics, would be necessary. Both measures would touch the most sensitive aspects of the personnel system—namely the entrance examinations and promotions—and would not be easy to effectuate. Third, a procedure for encouraging greater competition and diversity and discouraging complacency would be desirable. The "up-or-out" rule as practiced in the U.S. State Department is harsh and apparently subject to abuse. It can inhibit and even kill initiative rather than encourage it. The absence of a procedure to cope with chronic nonperformers—the current situation in the Japanese Foreign

89. Interview, an official in the Research Department, April 7, 1972.
90. For comparison, see Elder, *The Policy Machine*, pp. 182–183.

Ministry—is equally questionable, but certainly many, perhaps the majority of the officials would object to the introduction of the American procedure. Fourth, creation of machinery for central policy-planning, coordination, and control might be desirable. This would not be easy either, given the absence of a centralized planning tradition in the ministry and the lack of goodwill exhibited by the regular bureaus toward even the relatively small fifteen-man staff in the current Planning Division of the Secretariat.[91]

Although such reforms are not likely to be undertaken in the immediate future, it seems almost certain that without some changes along the lines suggested, the ministry is bound to face a crisis of formidable proportions before long, to the detriment of its own interests and, more importantly, the larger foreign-policy interests of the Japanese people. There are indications that this danger is increasingly recognized and becoming an important subject of internal debate among concerned officials. Whether reform measures are taken will depend on the outcome of this debate as well as on the pressures from the changing domestic and international environment.

Closely related to the discontent about the present personnel system and decision-making procedures, and stimulating the internal debates on the question of organizational reform, are the divisions and conflicts arising from generational differences among officials. These generational conflicts are mostly latent as yet, but many admit the importance of these differences in decision-making. One division head contrasted the "forward-looking" attitude of the younger officials to the "passive and negative" posture of the older generation.[92] Another talked about the gap of consciousness between the "war-timers" and "postwar-timers."[93] A newspaper reporter observed the conflict between "yes-man" bureau directors and independent-minded division heads.[94] The main divisions thus seem to be between officials who entered the foreign service before or during the Second World War and those who entered after the war.

One important factor involved is the differential psychological impact of the wartime experience. The role of traumatic personal experience and its memory in the shaping of a nation's foreign policy has been discussed in varied contexts. Deutsch and Edinger wrote, for example,

In all countries, the making of foreign policy is influenced by the legacy of the past. Not only among the small groups of influential persons but also among the broad masses of the voters, memories of the past help to shape the images of what foreign policy is and what it could be—what tasks any present or future foreign policy could accomplish, what persons and institutions should accomplish them, and by what methods. People turn to memories for answers to their basic questions:

91. Interview, an official in the Research Department, April 7, 1972.
92. Interview, an official in the American Affairs Bureau, Oct. 19, 1972.
93. Interview, an official in the Economic Affairs Bureau, Jan. 31, 1972.
94. Interview, Kikuchi Ikuzō.

"What are we?" "What do others expect of us?" and "What should we expect of ourselves?" In all countries, memories thus fashion expectations. Everywhere they influence the interplay between foreign policy and the continuing process of national self-perception and self-definition.[95]

As Table 2 suggested, the vice-minister and deputy vice-ministers of 1970 entered the foreign service a few years before 1941, the year of Pearl Harbor; the modal counselor, whether at the headquarters or at an overseas post, entered during the war; but the modal division head did not enter until five years after the war. It is also relevant that a large percentage of the high-ranking officials had actually served in the military services during the war. These percentages for selected categories of officials are given in Table 6. Altogether, 99, or 31.9 percent, of the 310 high-ranking officials had served in the armed services. In fact, all the ranks above counselor level have heavy, though varying, concentrations of people who served with wartime military forces.

Not only those who joined the armed services, but probably all who lived their young adult life in the war years carry the psychological mark of that traumatic experience. In some ways, those who stayed in the foreign service during the war may carry deeper psychological scars. The overwhelming majority of those who went into the armed services were drafted and were no more

Table 6
Percentages of Foreign Service Officials
with Military Service Experience

	Number	Percent
Bureau director	9	44.4
Counselor (headquarters)	18	66.6
Division head	49	10.2
Ambassador	90	31.1
Minister	19	68.4
Consul-general	39	48.7
Counselor (embassy)	47	25.5

SOURCES: *Gaimushō shokuin ryakureki: Shōwa 45-nen;* Ōkurashō Insatsukyoku, *Shokuin roku,* vol. 1.

95. Karl W. Deutsch and Lewis J. Edinger, *Germany Rejoins the Powers* (Stanford: Stanford University Press, 1959), p. 11. See also Kenneth E. Boulding, "National Images and International Systems," *Journal of Conflict Resolution,* June 1959, reprinted in Harold K. Jacobson and William Zimmerman, eds., *The Shaping of Foreign Policy* (New York: Atherton Press, 1969), pp. 164–165.

enthusiastic about the war than those who stayed in the foreign service. On the other hand, those who were spared induction, often because of the importance of their civilian duties, were involved or implicated in the promilitarist versus antimilitarist controversies in the bureaucracy. It is impossible for this author to adequately measure the impact of the experience on their contemporary political and foreign-policy views, but it is probably substantial. A division head, himself a member of the postwar generation, and who asked to remain anonymous, described an aspect of that impact as follows:

Virtually all bureau directors and counselors were "committed" to the war in one way or another. Now, on the one hand, they want to justify their actions in those days, and, on the other, they have doubts about their judgments on current events and problems. They tend to be overly cautious about deciding their courses of action regarding a foreign-policy issue.

Another official, of the deputy division head rank and who also did not want to be identified, complained that war-timers were "inscrutable" and resentful. According to this official, they were a terribly unhappy lot whose misery could not be assuaged either by higher salaries or better posts.

Such subtle psychological factors are hard for an outsider to detect, much less analyze. One common characteristic of their biographic background is, however, objectively identifiable and quite conspicuous. Many of the war-timers spent the early part of their professional career in what was, strictly speaking, not foreign but domestic services. During and immediately following the war, Japan did not have regular diplomatic relations with the rest of the world. Its diplomatic transactions were very limited between 1941 and 1951. As a result, a large number of Foreign Ministry officials had no work to do in their own ministry and therefore went to the special wartime and postwar government agencies, notably the Postwar Liaison Office, the Economic Stabilization Agency, or the Ministry of International Trade and Industry. The percentages of Foreign Ministry officials who temporarily worked in those other agencies are given in Table 7. Kawamura argued that these officials learned their "servility" toward Americans in those Postwar Liaison Office days and retained it into the mid-fifties.[96] The same deferential attitude toward the United States seems to continue to characterize many, if not all, of this generation of officials.

A no less important and much more readily ascertainable consequence of having been born and having reached adulthood before or during the war was the lack of in-service professional training and direct exposure to foreign relations in a normal diplomatic setting during the first and perhaps crucial years of their career. They are now criticized by their younger colleagues for their clumsiness in foreign languages, particularly English, and in their personal relationships with their counterparts in foreign governments. This

96. Kawamura, *Gaimushō*, pp. 29–30.

Table 7
Percentages of Officials Who Have Served in Other Agencies
in the Postwar Period

	N	Postwar liaison offices	Prime minister's offices agencies	MITI
Bureau director	9	55.5	88.8	22.2
Counselor				
(headquarters)	18	72.2	66.6	50.0
Division head	49	8.1	24.4	28.5
Ambassador	90	64.4	64.4	40.0
Minister	19	73.6	78.9	31.5
Consul-general	39	69.2	61.5	48.7
Counselor (embassy)	47	53.1	59.5	29.7

SOURCES: *Gaimushō shokuin ryakureki: Shōwa 45-nen;* Ōkurashō Insatsukyoku, *Shokuin roku,* vol. 1.

characterization does not apply to prewar-timers, who entered the foreign ser-vice in the thirties and had some proper professional training before the war. In fact, some of them have been regarded as complete diplomats with prodigious linguistic prowess and impeccable social manners.[97] Yet, the fact that many war-timers have less than the complete confidence of the postwar-timers was very evident from statements I heard from members of the younger generation.

If reform is going to be undertaken before long, it will no doubt be due to growing pressure from the ranks of these younger officials. It is unthinkable, at the time these words are written at any rate, that the older generation—those above the division head rank—will undertake on their own initiative the kinds of reforms I have suggested. But there are prewar precedents for possible ac-tions by today's Young Turks. It was, after all, the seventy-odd members of the Ryōyūkai (Society of Friends and Associates), all junior officials below the rank of division head, who memorialized Foreign Minister Arita in 1936 for a reform of the ministry's moribund personnel system and organizational structure so that it might cope more effectively with the growing influence of the military.[98] Each generation of junior officials has had grievances against the old-timers of their days and has often registered those grievances in one form or another.[99] In the early 1970s there was again frequent articulation of disaffection and frustra-tion among members of the up-and-coming generation reaching or just about to reach the bottom level of ministry decision-makers. A sense of crisis was

97. Ibid., pp. 188–201.
98. *Gaimushō no hyakunen,* 2:59–60. For other examples, see also pp. 128, 296.
99. For pertinent comments, see Kawamura, *Gaimushō,* pp. 185–187.

again spreading, no doubt triggered by the events of 1971. This may well prove an ephemeral "mood." Against the background of the obvious inadequacies and liabilities of the existing system, it seems more likely to lead to some reforms, perhaps piecemeal and gradual rather than sweeping and drastic.

Among the increasingly restless young officials of the Foreign Ministry, I noted some indications of an impatient, defiant, and cocky posture of self-assertion, with heavy nationalistic overtones. Such indications were certainly not unique to the Foreign Ministry bureaucrats in Japan of the early 1970s. One would detect a similar posture and rhetoric among young politicians, such as those Liberal Democrats associated with the Seirankai (Summer Storm Society). More generally, there was an unmistakable upsurge of nationalist rhetoric in the post-Nixon-shock Japan. What is significant, however, is that the young Foreign Ministry officials were apparently joining, if not leading, the bandwagon in an increasingly articulate and self-conscious way. This too may be another passing mood. Or it may be a sign of a healthy self-confidence finally regained by a rising generation of Japanese twenty-five years after the war and defeat. My feeling is that it is more than a mood and that it will affect the general orientation of Japanese foreign policy—including the controversial issues of national security and rearmament—in important ways in the years to come. The Young Turks in the Foreign Ministry of the 1920s and 1930s fought, at least temporarily, the rising tide of militarism and adventurism in foreign policy. Today's Young Turks may be beginning to fight against postwar pacifism and "economic diplomacy" in the name of an independent foreign policy. This may not be such a terrible, much less surprising, thing after all. What would be unfortunate, and probably disastrous in its consequences, would be for the bureaucrats to join the nationalist bandwagon, not by conscious and carefully considered choice, but by drift and out of exasperation. The kinds of reforms suggested here might not prevent this from happening, but the continuation of single-issue-ism and improvisation in decision-making would surely encourage adventurist tendencies in one form or another.

Much remains to be studied concerning the Japanese foreign-policy bureaucracy before we can gain an adequate understanding of how important and not-so-important foreign policies are made, or evolve, and why. Our current knowledge and understanding is particularly inadequate with regard to decision processes in routine, noncrisis situations, which no doubt account for the majority of real-world cases. Virtually no case studies have been undertaken to systematically describe and analyze such processes. My effort here has deliberately been narrow in scope and tentative in its conclusions. Hopefully, however, it represents at least a small step in the direction of linking the organizational structure of the Foreign Ministry with the decision-making process.

The Diet and Foreign Policy

HANS H. BAERWALD

Untrammeled executive authority over foreign affairs is the rule in most political systems. Japan is no exception, despite the horrendous consequences suffered by its people because of the extensive military influence over foreign policy from the late 1920s to the disastrous summer of 1945.

The Japanese military were not just an instrument of authoritarian control over the execution of foreign policy. They were an active, and at times predominant, shaper of the decision-making process. The memory of that fact has had a significant effect on the conduct of postwar Japanese foreign affairs. It has meant that until quite recently Japanese foreign policy has been so low-profile—or, as the Japanese themselves would say, so "low-posture"—that it has barely been visible. Foreign Ministry "Blue Papers" notwithstanding, many Japanese are convinced that their country does not have any foreign policy as such—a criticism that is by no means unique to the Japanese.

Although the posture of the Japanese Diet in foreign affairs is increasing, its actual role is still minimal. To explore some of the reasons why the parliament remains a relatively impotent participant in foreign policy-making, we must first consider the institutional arrangement of the Japanese government. Constitutionally, Japan has a parliamentary political system. This means, among other things, that as long as the prime minister and his cabinet have a working majority in both chambers of the national legislature, the Diet is nothing more than a ratifier of decisions that have been made by the prime minister and his colleagues—providing, of course, those decisions are reasonably acceptable to his party and the electorate. In this respect, there is nothing to distinguish the manner in which the Japanese Diet is tied to the cabinet's decisions from the operations of other parliamentary systems.

A second factor in the Diet's weak role in foreign policy-making is the character of Japan's political party system. For some twenty years the LDP has—year in, year out—controlled a substantial working majority in both chambers of the Japanese Diet. Prior thereto, in the postwar period, Japanese foreign policy was largely formulated in Washington, D.C., or by the American proconsuls charged with overseeing the Occupation in Tokyo. "By the end of December 1945, the Japanese Government had no relations with the outside world except through the Supreme Commander [of the Allied Powers], and arrangements were being made for the repatriation of Japanese representatives in foreign countries."[1] Furthermore, it was only with utmost caution that the Japanese government began to emerge from America's protective guidance after the peace treaty was officially ratified in the spring of 1952. For all intents and purposes therefore, to the extent that the members of the Diet have participated in the formulation of Japanese foreign policy, it has been the representatives of the LDP who have had a controlling voice.

Two complicating factors are provided by the inner structure of the LDP—a coalition of factions (a description equally valid for the leading opposition, the JSP) and the fact that LDP foreign-policy views are fundamentally at variance with those espoused by all other political parties—the JSP, the Kōmeitō, the JCP, and to a lesser extent the DSP. The disparity in *Weltanschauung* has complicated the search for consensus among the diverse party representatives in the Diet, a factor that is of more than passing significance given the high priority accorded to consensual decision-making in Japanese society.

Indeed, the apparent divergence between the foreign-policy goals of the LDP and those of its critics has resulted in frequent failures to achieve any broadly based consensus. In any case, managers of Japan's foreign policy have often been forced to devote their primary efforts to delicate negotiations among the factions inside the LDP in order to achieve the agreement necessary for realization of their goals. Once agreement within the LDP has been attained, the opposition parties can be safely ignored because of the overpowering majority that has been enjoyed by the LDP in the Diet since 1955. In turn, this has meant that debate over foreign policy generally takes place within the policy-making councils of the LDP or between the LDP and the officials of the Japanese government directly concerned with foreign policy—primarily officials in the ministries of Foreign Affairs and International Trade and Industry.

Simultaneously, there occur debates among the factions in the JSP or between it (as a party) and other opposition parties. These internal debates may occasionally surface inside the Diet; but generally they have been resolved before each case is presented in the Diet, and there is little open attempt to seek accommodation. Thus it is also from the perspective of Japanese political reali-

1. "Control of Japanese External Affairs," *Political Reorientation of Japan, Report of the Government Section, S.C.A.P.* (Washington, D.C.: Government Printing Office, 1949), p. 7.

ties that the Diet can be perceived as a rubber stamp for the will of the governing LDP.

THE INSTITUTIONAL SETTING

The Diet's role in foreign policy rests on the following provisions of the 1947 Japanese constitution. First, the Diet is "the highest organ of state power . . . and . . . the sole law-making organ of the state." Second, it is accorded the function of approving treaties, which requires a simple majority vote by both chambers, but the Representatives' decision is final regardless of the action or inaction of the Councillors, providing that thirty days of a Diet session remain. Third, it is the forum to which the prime minister and relevant members of his cabinet submit reports on international affairs.[2] Thus the Diet is a sounding board for the cabinet to disseminate important developments in Japanese foreign policy; it approves treaties concluded between Japan and foreign governments; and it must pass any new domestic legislation that international obligations might require.

It has become customary for the prime minister and his foreign minister to present their formal messages to the Diet as one of the first orders of business once a new session has been convened. These pronouncements generally provide an overview of past achievements and set forth major goals for the coming year. In turn, leaders of the opposition parties are accorded an opportunity to present their respective positions and to raise pertinent questions—officially termed interpellations—to the prime minister and his colleagues.

Interpellations have something of the quality of debates in that alternative views are articulated. However, issues are seldom directly joined by the participants in this process. Although interpellations are initially conducted in the plenary sessions of each chamber, the Committee on the Budget in each chamber provides an additional forum for airing issues. These committees do not restrict their jurisdiction to deliberations on the budget, but have become the stage for an analogue to the famous "question periods" in the British House of Commons. By providing these forums for the ventilation of pressing international developments together with steps being contemplated by the Japanese government in the field of foreign affairs, the Diet does contribute to the open discussion of state matters. For purposes of the dissemination of information (and, regrettably, obfuscation), these interpellations play an important role. There is little agreement, however, on what impact they have on the process of formulating foreign policy.

Each chamber of the Diet also has separate committees on foreign affairs. They, too, provide forums for the public discussion of international treaties and

2. *Constitution of Japan*, chap. 4, art. 41; chap. 4, arts. 60, 61; and chap. 5, art. 72.

related matters. Similar functions are performed by the committees on the cabinet that have jurisdiction over matters of national security, a subject that remains under the control of the prime minister's office despite the existence of a defense agency.

In December 1973, House of Representatives Foreign Affairs Committee Chairman Kimura Toshio permitted me to observe a three-hour public meeting of his committee.[3] Oil, the energy crisis, and Japan's Middle East policy were the major topics concerning which the committee members grilled Foreign Minister Ōhira Masayoshi and his several subordinates (experts whose testimony was required). Considerable time was devoted to exploring how many qualified Arab specialists were in the Foreign Ministry, what rank they had achieved, and whether service in a Middle Eastern country had constituted a plus factor in a foreign service officer's career. In general, Foreign Minister Ōhira and his subordinates painted a rather gloomy picture in their responses. Nonetheless, they made promises to the committee that corrective measures designed to upgrade the number, quality, and status of Middle East specialists were being actively undertaken. All parties had representatives on the committee, and each was accorded a predetermined period of time for questions. Liberal Democrats, who represented the government party, were seemingly as stern as opposition party representatives in their questions.

Chairman Kimura later told me that the affairs of the committee are governed by a board of directors (*riji kai*) consisting of five LDP members, two Socialists, and one Communist. They meet privately prior to an open committee session. The Kōmeitō and DSP currently only have "observers" on the board of directors; they attend sessions of the *riji kai*, but do not vote. In the past, the Foreign Affairs Committee had also held executive sessions for the entire committee. This practice, however, was discontinued after the December 1972 House of Representatives election, during which the Communists increased their strength in the Diet and began urging that the executive sessions be discontinued, because, they alleged, such sessions had allowed private "deals" to be made between the majority LDP and the minority opposition parties.

These plenary and committee discussions may become the focal point for greater participation by members of the Diet in the formulation of Japanese foreign policy. Chairman Kimura, for example, disagreed with my contention that, due to the nature of their internal organization, these sessions have not yet acquired a substantial level of importance. He countered with the assertion that his being chairman of the Foreign Affairs Committee and having the opportunity to question cabinet ministers and other government officials about matters of great concern to Japanese voters—he specifically cited the oil and

3. I would like to express my gratitude to Chairman Kimura for his courtesy and for granting me an hour-long private interview in his private office on the same day (Dec. 18, 1973).

soybean crises because they affected the daily lives of millions of citizens—would substantially improve his chances for reelection.

This plus factor for a committee chairman, and for committee members whose visibility in the press is increased in proportion to the questions they can ask, unfortunately does not prove that committee sessions influence government policy in the realm of foreign affairs. The ability of the majority party to control the legislative process is too great. Plenary sessions are, of course, presided over by the Speaker in the House of Representatives and the President in the House of Councillors. Committee activities are directed by chairmen. All of these individuals are selected, more often than not, in conjunction with a reorganization of the cabinet.

Personnel decisions of this sort have become ever more deeply intertwined with the balancing of factional forces in the LDP. Therefore, those who are selected for these leadership roles in the Diet generally tend to be loyal partisans of the majority party and, more important, staunch supporters of the specific coalition of faction leaders who constitute the LDP's "mainstream" during their tenure. Consequently, they can be expected to control matters under their jurisdiction in accordance with the wishes of their party's leadership. Obviously, it is a system that is not designed to encourage the exercise of independent initiative.

Kōno Kenzō's election as president of the House of Councillors in the summer of 1971 is often cited as presaging a trend toward greater independence on the part of a presiding officer of that House vis-à-vis the prime minister and his cabinet. Undoubtedly, his victory was a revolt against then Prime Minister Satō Eisaku and his chosen instrument in the second chamber, outgoing President Shigemune Yūzō. I believe that the disobedience was temporary, however. When Tanaka Kakuei succeeded Satō as prime minister and LDP president in July 1972, his factional coalition consisted of his own grouping and those led by Miki Takeo, Ōhira Masayoshi and, belatedly, Nakasone Yasuhirō. Nakasone had become the leader of the largest group remaining from the faction led by the late Kōno Ichirō, who had been House of Councillors' president Kōno Kenzō's older brother. The elder Kōno had been Satō's major opponent at the time that the latter succeeded Prime Minister Ikeda Hayato in the fall of 1964. Hence, it was natural for Kōno Kenzō to lend himself to a revolt against Satō's leadership when the opportunity to do so arose in the form of a contest for the presidency of the House of Councillors.

An entirely different situation came into being with Tanaka's accession to the prime ministership. Kōno Kenzō probably cannot be described as an ardent Nakasone follower. The latter is too young in comparison to Kōno's senior standing. Nonetheless, factional ties do exist between Kōno and Nakasone. As long the latter remained in the mainstream coalition supporting then Prime Minister Tanaka, it could be anticipated that Kōno's deviationist tendencies vis-à-vis his party leader would not be substantial.[4] It is the intraparty factional relationship within the LDP, therefore, which for the time being controls the dynamics of influence between the LDP president and cabinet prime minister on the one hand and the presiding officers of the two Houses of the Diet on the other.

Presiding officers of the two chambers are assisted by Committees on House Management (Giin Un'ei Iinkai), each of which is presided over by a member of the majority party, and each of which has a board of directors whose distribution of party representation reflects the ratio of seats held by all of the parties in that chamber. This means that the majority party effectively controls all of the levers of power in the Diet's legislative machinery.[5]

The *gichō* (chairman of the House, that is, speaker or president) and the *iinchō* (committee chairmen) have virtually dictatorial powers over the conduct of affairs under their jurisdiction. They control the agenda, even to the point of changing it—literally at the last minute.[6] Technically, they are supposed to make such changes only after consultation (without debate) with their colleagues; but this procedural formality is occasionally overlooked if the press of events is sufficiently heavy.

In effect, these provisions have transferred all of the levers of the Diet's legislative machinery into the hands of the majority party. Once the majority party—in its inner councils—has made its decision, the Diet becomes the playing field for the LDP's game plan. If the majority party wishes to extend deliberations on a particular item in the arena of foreign affairs—for example, the Nuclear Non-Proliferation Treaty—it can utilize the Diet's machinery to prolong the process of approval virtually indefinitely. If the majority party decides that the time has come to rush the Diet's approval of a treaty—for example, the revised Mutual Security Treaty with the United States in the spring of 1960—then it can utilize its control over all loci of power in the Diet's legislative machinery to have the necessary action taken with lightninglike speed.

All participants, whether members of the majority or minority parties, recognize this reality. Hence, they are aware that their participation is rarely

4. For further details, see my *Japan's Parliament: An Introduction* (New York: Cambridge University Press, 1974), pp. 76–78.

5. There are a few special committees in the House of Representatives and a small number of standing and special committees in the House of Councillors that are chaired by members of the opposition parties. These committees, however, generally do not have jurisdiction over sensitive subjects and, in any case, the LDP can exercise its control by means of its majority on the committees' board of directors.

6. *The Diet Law*, chap. 6, art. 55: "The President of each House shall fix the order of the Day and notify it to the House in advance": chap. 5, art. 48: "The Chairman of each Committee shall arrange its business and maintain order in the Committee." *Rules of the House of Representatives*, chap. 8, sec. 2, art. 112: "When the Speaker deems it necessary, or upon a Member's motion, he may alter the order in the agenda, or add new items to it after consulting the House without debate." A similar provision is found in the *Rules of the House of Councillors*, chap. 8, sec. 2, art. 88.

anything more than a charade. Of course, their deliberations may have some impact on public opinion, which in turn may have some impact on the next election. All of this presupposes that the Japanese public is heavily influenced in its electoral behavior by questions of international relations. This presupposition is, at the very least, open to considerable doubt. In this connection, it is worth noting that the JSP has not obtained great political benefits by emphasizing foreign policy goals in its action program.

Members of the Diet have responded to these institutional restraints and opportunities in a "creative" fashion whenever crisis situations have arisen. It must be remembered that the major crises of parliamentarianism in Japan have revolved around questions of foreign policy—for example, the Mutual Security Treaty with the United States or the treaty reestablishing diplomatic relations with the Republic of (South) Korea. On both occasions it was clear from the outset of the Diet session that the governing LDP's support for the treaty at issue ensured its eventual approval. It was equally clear that the opposition parties, especially the JSP, which was still influential in 1960 and 1965—in comparison to its relative decline in the 1970s—was opposed to the treaties and was determined to do all within its power to block the approval process, or at least delay approval for as long as possible.[7]

Both of these episodes have been described at length elsewhere.[8] However, without a brief recapitulation of how the Diet ratified these treaties, it would be difficult to comprehend the extent of the acrimony over aspects of Diet procedure that has become so consequential for the Japanese. In both instances, accepted norms of parliamentary procedure were twisted and strained almost to the breaking point. It could be argued that neither case is "typical"; on the other hand, both tested the survival capacity of the system and therefore vividly illuminate the Diet's capacity to respond to situations of stress. It is for the latter reason that they have been selected for illustrative purposes here.

The crisis over the ratification of the revised U.S.-Japan Treaty of Mutual Cooperation and Security of 1960 involved several factors.[9] First was the content, which provided that the United States and Japan would continue to be bound to each other in an alliance that would strengthen the military security interests of both partners; this relationship was desired by the governing Liberal Democrats, but vociferously opposed by the Socialists. Second, Japan's then Prime Minister Kishi Nobusuke had become an unusually controversial

7. The position of the DSP was ambiguous. It was one of opposition, but not so much to the treaties themselves as to some of the parliamentary tactics that were being brought into play by the LDP and the JSP.

8. See Robert A. Scalapino and Masumi Junnosuke, *Parties and Politics in Contemporary Japan* (Berkeley and Los Angeles: University of California Press, 1962); George R. Packard, *Protest in Tokyo* (Princeton: Princeton University Press, 1966); Hans H. Baerwald, "Nikkan Kokkai," in Lucian W. Pye, ed., *Cases in Comparative Politics, Asia* (Boston: Little, Brown, 1970), and *Japan's Parliament*.

9. For the full text of the treaty, see Packard, *Protest in Tokyo*, pp. 364–367.

political leader by virtue of his background and his style of governance; his critics emphasized his role as a minister in Prime Minister Tōjō's wartime cabinet and his autocratically bureaucratic approach toward his party colleagues as well as his parliamentary opposition. Third, the JSP, aided and abetted by the major trade union federation, Sōhyō, and the highly militant national student organization, Zengakuren, had pledged themselves to an all-out campaign in an effort to delay or possibly block the ratification process. Fourth, the timing of Diet procedure was partially dictated by external events, of which the most significant was the planned visit of U.S. President Dwight Eisenhower—a projected event that was ultimately canceled.

Each of these elements contributed to the climactic confrontation that transpired during the night of May 19–20, 1960. By then it was no longer the treaty itself that provided the focus for all of the parliamentary maneuvers. Instead, it was time. President Eisenhower was scheduled to arrive on June 19. Prime Minister Kishi wanted to present him with a gift (*omiyage*), namely, the ratified treaty. Under the rules of procedure, if the House of Representatives voted for ratification with one calendar month still remaining in a given Diet session, any action by the House of Councillors would be superfluous.[10]

Initially at issue for that memorable evening session was whether the Liberal Democrats could achieve a vote to extend the length of that day's Diet session. That proved to be difficult: the Socialists had blockaded the corridors leading from the Speaker's room to the plenary chamber, preventing the presiding officer from convening the session so that a vote could be taken. Regular police forces—who are to be sharply distinguished from regular Diet guards—had to be called by the Speaker to remove the opposition members and their assistants from the passageways so that he could reach his raised seat and open the plenary session.

His objective attained, the Speaker adjusted the agenda on his own authority instead of following prescribed Diet procedure. Although technically the Speaker has the authority to fix the "order of the day" (the agenda), it is normally the Committee on House Management—on which the opposition parties have representatives in proportion to their percentage of seats in the House—that formulates the program for a given plenary session. On the evening of May 19, according to Speaker Kiyose Ichirō, normalcy was prevented by the Socialists' obstructionist tactics.[11] The Socialists, on the other hand, viewed the Speaker's behavior as dictatorial and constituting another in a series of maneuvers designed by Prime Minister Kishi to negate their efforts to have the proceedings conform to the Diet Law and the Rules of the House of Representatives.[12] In quick succession, those members of the House of Representatives who were in

10. *Constitution of Japan*, art. 61.
11. Interview with Mr. Kiyose in his Diet chambers, May 31, 1963.
12. Packard, *Protest in Tokyo*, pp. 237–239, 240–241, 275–276.

attendance at the evening session (only LDP members, and they with some notable exceptions) voted to extend the Diet session, took a brief recess, reconvened, and voted their approval of the treaty.

Many of the same tactics marked the Diet's approval of the treaty reestablishing diplomatic relations between Japan and the Republic of Korea in 1965. In this instance, the LDP leadership, with the reluctant concurrence of the opposition parties, established special committees in both chambers to conduct hearings on the basic treaty, an agreement on fishing rights, and domestic legislation governing the status of Koreans resident in Japan. (An alternative strategy would have been to allow relevant standing committees to handle the separate elements of the package: the Foreign Affairs Committee to consider the treaty; the Agriculture, Forestry, and Fisheries Committee to consider the fishing agreement; the Judiciary Committee to ponder the domestic legislation). As the Socialists were opposed to the treaty, they embarked on delay tactics that included being dilatory in finding members to serve on the special committees. In contrast, members of standing committees are selected at the beginning of each Diet session.

Deliberations in the special committees became bogged down in the lengthy questions that opposition members posed to cabinet ministers and their assistants. All concerned understood that the purpose of the questions was to prolong proceedings rather than to enlighten fellow parliamentarians or the public at large. Consequently, government spokesmen responded as briefly and evasively as possible, in turn raising the ire of their interlocutors. After the hearings had dragged on for ten days, House of Representatives Special Committee Chairman Andō Kaku recognized a fellow LDP member, Fujieda Sensuke, in the midst of a lengthy question from one of the Socialists. In the ensuing din—in Japan, too, interrupting a member who has the floor is considered bad form—no one, including the committee scribes, could clearly hear what Mr. Fujieda was saying. Nevertheless, when it was made public, the committee record contained a full report of Fujieda's motion: he moved to cut off debate, to have the committee vote its approval of the legislative package, and to empower the chairman to report the committee's decision to the plenary session.

It required three days of intensive backstage maneuvering to get to the point at which the plenary session could be convened. One of the concessions that the oppositionists wrung out of the Liberal Democrats during the process was that motions of no confidence could be introduced and discussed at the plenary session. Such motions normally take precedence. As the hours and days of the plenary session dragged on, mired in the bog of motion after motion of no confidence against certain cabinet ministers and other responsible officers, LDP representatives became ever more frustrated over the lack of progress toward Diet approval of the treaty.

Once again, the majority party took matters into its own hands. In the midst of a third consecutive all-night session, Speaker Funada Naka resorted to the simple device of changing the agenda. In less than a minute, the assembled representatives voted to cut off discussion and to approve the treaty package. Understandably, the LDP's leadership had planned the details of this midnight performance with great care, including plans for three groups of relatively young and husky LDP representatives who—at a given signal—rushed from their desks to provide protective cordons around all points of access to the Speaker's raised dais against the anticipated onslaught of disgruntled Socialists. The latter, in turn, afterward accused their secretary-general, Yamamoto Kōichi, of not having alerted them to the possibility of a surprise move on the part of the LDP at that particular session. Some Socialists even went as far as to allege that Yamamoto had been party to a private agreement with his LDP counterpart in permitting the unilateral action by Speaker Funada.[13]

Whatever the facts, what ultimately counted was that the governing LDP obtained the necessary Diet approval for both treaties. The substantive policy questions had already been determined in intraparty deliberations prior to the beginning of the Diet session, so each side's tactics during the session revolved around manipulation of time rather than the substance of the treaties at issue. Hence, it is understandable that the minority parties should embark on a series of delaying devices. For them, the principal issue was whether the approval of the treaties could be delayed even if they could not be blocked. To counter the minority parties' tactics, especially in the face of a threatened upset to its timetable, the majority party was willing to utilize its control over all phases of Diet procedure—some of which had been originally designed to allow the minority a voice in controlling the Diet's internal machinery. The issue for the majority was to obtain Diet approval and, if possible, to do so within the time specified without alienating the minority from at least minimal support for parliamentary norms. The most prominent weapon was the forced vote (*kyōkō saiketsu*), which, in effect, allows the majority to run the affairs of the Diet single-handedly.

These tactical devices have been used only in extreme circumstances thus far. All participants recognize, at least in their private comments, that an excessive utilization of such tactics would seriously strain the willingness of all concerned to abide by the rules of parliamentary procedure in other instances when the legislative proposals are less controversial. Nonetheless, the use of near-violent delaying tactics by the minority and the near-violent "forced vote"

13. I picked up these allegations during the course of extensive interviews with members of the Diet, their assistants, and Japanese newspapermen during the autumn of 1965. Positive confirmation of the allegations proved to be impossible to obtain. However, it is believed significant that Yamamoto was subsequently replaced as party secretary-general and, possibly even more important, that he also changed his factional affiliation from then JSP Chairman Sasaki Kōzo to that of Sasaki's long-time rival, Eda Saburō.

tactics of the majority do color all aspects of Diet procedure. Those who are on the majority side recognize that if the discussion does not go favorably, the forced vote tactic is always available. Those on the minority side recognize that their words alone, no matter how eloquent—or irresponsible—will have little influence on the workings of the legislative process. It is no wonder therefore that tactics based on the manipulation of time rather than on a discussion of the issues take precedence in the calculations of the antagonists in the parliamentary struggle.

On occasion, the memory of these tactics and the possibility that they would again be used influence the decision of the government (that is, the cabinet) on whether to submit a particular treaty to the Diet for deliberation. For example, the memories of the 1960 "struggle over the security pact" (*ampo tōsō*) influenced the decision not to resubmit the treaty to the Diet in 1970 for a specified extension (five or ten years). In that instance, there was an alternative of extending the treaty on a year-to-year basis, which did not require Diet approval. To be sure, the decision either avoided or blunted confrontations in the Diet and demonstrations outside the Diet compound. It also diminished the Diet's constitutional mandate to be the locus of treaty approval.

One can, of course, argue that impasses of this kind are the consequence of some fault in the organization of the Diet or its internal procedures. One can also argue that the relationship between the majority and minority has not yet been fully resolved within the overall context of Japanese society. It is my position that the fundamental problem is not related to either of these hypotheses, but that it rests on the fact that the foreign-policy goals of the LDP and the various opposition forces are irreconcilably divergent.

CONSTRAINTS ON THE DIET

Three major factors have impeded the capacity of the Diet to play an important role in the formulation of Japanese foreign policy. The first is the imbalance of representation between the majority party and its varied opposition parties. The second is the divergence of goals as enunciated by the LDP and its opponents. The third is the style of intraparty decision-making which creates blockages that preclude accommodation among the parties.

Since 1955, when the JSP temporarily reunited its two wings and the conservatives responded by splicing the Liberal and Democratic Parties into the LDP, the latter has had a substantial majority in both chambers of the Diet. Beginning with the House of Representatives election of 1958, the first after the LDP had been organized, that party has won roughly 60 percent of the House seats at each succeeding election, despite the fact that the popular vote for LDP candidates has steadily declined from a high of 57.8 percent in 1958 to a low of 46.6

percent in 1972. LDP campaign managers have been enormously astute in maximizing the translation of popular votes into party seats. Only with the December 1976 election did the LDP slip to a precarious position, depending upon independent conservatives for a bare majority in the lower house.

The opposition parties have fared considerably less well over the same period. In the 1958 election, the JSP won 33 percent of the seats in the House of Representatives with over 35 percent of the popular vote. After its split into the JSP and DSP in 1959–1960, the JSP never controlled more than 30 percent of the seats, and the DSP never in excess of 8 percent prior to 1976. With the emergence of the Kōmeitō as a force to be taken seriously in the Diet, and the renewed vitality of the JCP manifested by the results of the 1969 and 1972 elections, opposition to the majority party became splintered, in turn complicating the process of challenging LDP hegemony.

The parties have obtained basically similar results to date in elections for the House of Councillors. The July 7, 1974 "Tanabata" contest for roughly one-half of the seats in the Diet's Second Chamber came close to ending the LDP's hegemony. However, the conservatives emerged victorious, albeit with a paper-thin majority—only three seats in excess of the bare minimum of 127 councillors.

All of this has meant that the LDP has not had to share its policy-making powers with the opposition parties, or pay much heed to their foreign-policy positions. From a practical standpoint, the difficult problem has been to ensure that all factions within the LDP continue to support the foreign policies deemed important by the party's leadership. Most of the latter process, unfortunately, has been and is hidden from view, inasmuch as it takes place behind the closed doors of the LDP's Policy Research Council (Seichōkai), or in meetings between representatives of the Foreign Affairs Section (Gaimu Bukai) of the Seichōkai and officials of the Foreign Ministry, MITI, or leaders of major LDP support groups, such as the Federation of Economic Organizations (Keidanren).

In the field of foreign affairs, it is the Foreign Affairs Section of the LDP's Policy Research Council that appears to play a controlling role in determining what the party will formally sponsor in the Diet. This can include advocating that a treaty be placed on the Diet's legislative calendar or that the LDP publicize its position on a controversial foreign policy issue. A veteran LDP member, Ōhashi Takeo, stated it clearly: "On daily business, it is the Bukai that is nearly always supreme. Afterwards, the only remaining problem in the Diet is dealing with the opposition parties. Within the government party, arrangements are made in the Bukai."[14]

14. Ōhashi Takeo-shi danwa sokki-roku (Tokyo: Naisei-shi Kenkyū-kai, 1972), p. 169. I am deeply indebted to Professor Watanabe Akio, a Kauai conference colleague, for his sending me a copy of this revealing booklet.

My own interviews with members of the Diet generally confirm Mr. Ōhashi's views. However, one caveat requires brief elaboration. In instances when there are substantial disagreements inside the LDP—in the recent past, issues in this category would include the disposition of the Kim Tae-jung affair, the Civil Aviation Treaty with the People's Republic of China, and the Nuclear Non-Proliferation Treaty—LDP factions reportedly use the private meetings of the Foreign Affairs Section to argue their positions. In this instance I am using "factions" in their dual meaning: groups inside the LDP that are identified with particular party leaders as well as party groupings that cut across the personal factions and are identified with general policy orientations, such as the Asia Study Group, the Afro-Asian Study Group, and the Blue Storm Society (Seirankai).[15]

The foregoing is not intended to paint a complete picture of all the individuals and groups that participate in the policy-formulation and decision-making processes in foreign policy-making. To do so would take one very far afield, assuming that it were within the realm of the possible. Rather, it is intended to indicate that the Diet is excluded from the preliminary stages, at which the basic decisions are made. Furthermore, representatives of opposition parties and organizations affiliated with them (such as the major trade union federations) are thereby blocked from having an effective voice.

Disputes over foreign policy also take place within the councils of the JSP, during which attempts to make adjustments on differences among that party's factions tend to preoccupy its leaders. Sometimes these disputes surface at JSP conventions. More often, however, the airing and tentative resolution of alternative proposals takes place behind closed doors at party headquarters. Furthermore, attempts to achieve a common foreign-policy stance among the JSP, the Kōmeitō, the JCP, and the DSP also generally take place outside the halls of the Diet and are, thus, difficult to observe.

This style of policy-making effectively undermines whatever role the Diet may play as a stage for observing and assessing the behavior of the public's representatives, whose constitutional responsibilities include the approval of treaties with foreign governments and the discussion of specific policy proposals in the realm of foreign affairs. That which does transpire on the public stage provided by the Diet committee meetings or plenary sessions has been carefully and meticulously programmed beforehand.

Thus, if the script demands confrontation among the antagonists, then the opposition will use tactics of delay and obstruction, and the LDP will counter with a "forced vote." In this way the participants can keep faith with their particular supporters among the attentive public. In the end, the majority always wins, of course; but the opposition parties will have proved their sincerity by us-

15. Mr. Ōhashi also refers to these, but in an earlier context, the period of normalizing diplomatic relations with the Soviet Union in 1956. Ibid., p. 125.

ing every legal—and occasionally extralegal—tactical device to thwart the majority's awesome superiority. These confrontations can give the appearance of straining the bonds that hold parliamentary procedure together, but they also provide a catharsis by means of which irreconcilable positions—while upheld to the bitter end—result in public acquiescence of that which the majority wills. These confrontations, too, have gradually become more and more carefully prearranged.[16]

If, on the other hand, the script calls for accommodation among the majority and at least some minority parties, this too is carefully arranged in preparliamentary negotiations. Such accommodations rarely involve matters of substance (such as the specific provisions of a treaty), but rather involve the timing of the submission of a treaty to the Diet for its approval or the enunciation of a slight alteration in a given aspect of foreign policy. Especially if matters of principle are involved, this process requires the utmost in discretion in its execution; insofar as possible, the participants must be accorded the appearance of not having compromised their commitment. By its very nature, therefore, it cannot take place under that harsh glare of publicity to which sessions of the Diet are subjected.

Both of these factors—the imbalance of representation between the LDP and its opponents and the adjustment of views within the ranks of the respective antagonists—would have modest consequences were it not for the rhetoric of mutual distrust and suspicion between them. It is close to impossible to find some common ground between the claim by one side that the U.S.-Japan Security Treaty should be the linchpin of Japanese foreign policy and the other side's desire for that treaty's abrogation. It is equally difficult to reconcile the stance that Japan should have formal diplomatic relations only with South Korea and the position that such ties should be established with both North and South Korea.

Such highly visible disagreements may disappear as the external setting of internal relationships changes from superpower conflict to uneasy détente. Nonetheless, memories of earlier disagreements linger, partly because mutual trust is lacking. An observer gains the impression that some members of the LDP simply cannot take seriously the possibility that they could ever trust —not to mention accommodate themselves to—the views of some Socialists, and even more, the Communists. Some of the latter also are more comfortable with the simplicity of blanket opposition to all views of their Liberal Democratic colleagues.

This built-in hostility, which has so effectively prevented any discussion of foreign policy issues among the parties and incapacitated the Diet as an open

16. At any rate, that is my interpretation of certain episodes that I have witnessed. For readily understandable reasons, prior agreements concerning the length and style of confrontations that antagonists might have made with each other cannot be publicly admitted.

forum, may also be in the process of dissolving. One reason is the changed atmosphere in international relations. Another is the precarious position of the LDP in the Diet.

At present, the LDP controls both chambers by very narrow margins, with its fate uncertain in the 1977 House of Councillors election. It is entirely possible that House of Councillors' president Kōno Kenzō, who designates himself as "without party affiliation" (mushozoku), would vote with the LDP on matters of organizing the House if it came to a crunch. Nonetheless, whatever partisan proclivities he might wish to entertain are constrained even now by the large number (121 out of 252) of oppositionists who naturally wish to exercise their influence as fully and effectively as possible.

As a consequence, the LDP may shortly be forced to pick up some support from current opposition party members. Doing so could either take the form of a formal coalition (less likely), or receiving their concurrence on specific bills (more likely). From an ideological perspective—in terms of known policy preferences—the Democratic Socialists are most available for aiding the LDP in providing a few, much-needed extra votes on items of urgent priority. Yet the DSP's stance is complicated by its need to maintain some semblance of an independent posture vis-à-vis the LDP. Another possibility is that the LDP's leadership will woo either the Kōmeitō or the moderates in the JSP's Eda faction. Both have the advantage, for the LDP, of being numerically larger than the DSP. Both also are considerably sterner, by comparison to the DSP, in their criticism of LDP policies and programs—especially on such crucial issues as the Mutual Security Treaty and educational reform measures.

The foregoing, of course, is still in the realm of speculation. The impact of the 1977 House of Councillors' election remains as an item for future observation. That which can be asserted with some certainty is, first, the LDP will be forced to be far more circumspect in its relations with the opposition parties; second, the opposition parties are still deeply split and remain in a complex relationship with each other; third, the JSP, Kōmeitō, and DSP will be faced with the difficult choice of either limited cooperation with the LDP, or continuing to play a more telling obstructive role. In any case, the Diet's role as a forum for policy-making might be enhanced. It could mean that the LDP could not continue simply to ignore the opposition parties *inside the halls of the Diet*. It might also mean that some of the oppositionists would demand an end to forced-vote tactics as the price for limited cooperation.

These prospects, however, are not the only ones that might be considered. Another equally plausible one is that the LDP's coalition partner (for example, the DSP) is so beguiled and bedazzled by one or two of its members sitting in the cabinet that it does not raise any serious objection to the use of steam-roller tactics vis-à-vis the remaining opposition parties. In effect, the only change would be a slight alteration in the cast of principal actors without any basic change in the effectiveness of the minority parties; they would remain barred from *effective* participation, as has been the case since 1955.

Speculation on these and other alternatives does serve to underline what I consider to be the basic problem of Diet members in formulating and approving foreign policy. Effective power is in the hands of the majority, as in all parliamentary systems. If that majority does not wish the minority's representatives to participate in a meaningful fashion, it certainly can prevent them from doing so. Furthermore, given the factionalized character of the LDP, that party's support for specific policies is normally the product of extensive intraparty negotiations. A compromise with the formal opposition would require most—if not all—factions of the LDP to shift their positions. Achieving agreement within the LDP is normally extremely difficult given the delicate balance between the mainstream and antimainstream coalitions that is the inevitable by-product of factionalism. Once achieved, renegotiating the agreement to make it acceptable to the opposition is well nigh impossible, especially as there are always elements within the LDP that cannot accept any idea put forth by oppositionists, especially members of either the JSP or the JCP.

CONCLUSION

The Diet has not played a central role in Japan's foreign affairs in the postwar period, primarily because of the wide gulf in attitudes and goals between the majority LDP and the minority parties. As a consequence, policy formulation and effective decision-making power remain in the hands of the LDP's leadership, government bureaucrats in relevant ministries and agencies, and leaders of important LDP support groups. That which transpires in the Diet is in accordance with drafts of dramatic productions written elsewhere. Possibly I am placing too much emphasis on the amount of control forces external to the Diet impose on what the Diet ultimately decides. As Professor Fukui and several other participants in the Kauai conference pointed out, researchers apparently have a tendency to depreciate the importance of what they study—partially out of concern that they might glorify their own research, partially out of fear of being overly identified with their subject. Nonetheless, in my own case, I am relying far more on the observations of members of the Diet (obtained in countless interviews) than on my own perceptions. A remaining possibility is that members of the Diet, or any other institution, are incorrect in their analysis of their own role or function. If so, we are at a methodological impasse.

For me, the generalization that individual members of the Diet are almost overwhelmingly powerless remains as a fact of life. The "party line" is laid down by LDP, JSP, JCP, Kōmeitō, or DSP headquarters. Prior to its determination, there may well be considerable jockeying for position among factions—especially in the LDP and JSP, or among support groups that influence the respective party positions. Subsequent thereto, however, deviation from agreed-on doctrine is extremely rare and, when it does occur, risky. One example may be worth citing. At the time of the approval of the Partial Nuclear Test-Ban Treaty in 1963, one JCP member, Shiga Yoshio, voted for the treaty in defiance of his party's position. He was expelled from the party for his deviation. This example is not intended to prove that all parties are monolithic. Each of them, with the exception of the JCP and possibly the Kōmeitō, are riven by serious intramural disputes. My point is that these disputes are resolved at the preparliamentary stage of the legislative process. This means that they remain largely hidden from public view, except insofar as they are partially filtered through the pages of the newspapers or through the spoken news of the radio and television networks.

Thus far the system has worked in the sense that decisions made in the halls of the Diet have been accorded acceptance by the Japanese public. Everyone in the Diet, be he a member of the majority LDP or of a minority party, dutifully acts out his predetermined role (party discipline is virtually unquestioned as far as formal voting is concerned), and that which has been decided—public demonstrations to the contrary notwithstanding—receives support until another crisis arises.

In a society that has been as deeply divided—at least at the level of rhetoric—on foreign policy as Japan over the last quarter-century, the achievement of public acceptance of government policy in foreign affairs is not to be deprecated. From this perspective, the Diet has played a consequential role as the stage upon which the society's inner fissures over foreign policy can be transmuted into symbolic conflicts among designated combatants.

Nonetheless, this process, which reduces the Diet to a safety valve and little else, does raise some anxieties regarding the future of parliamentarism in Japan. Possibly the fundamental question is how long the participants in the Diet, whether they belong to the LDP or to the opposition parties, are willing to allow themselves to act out periodic scenes of near violence. In the case of the LDP there is always the danger that some group will advocate crushing the opposition forces altogether. In the case of the opposition parties there is the equal danger that frustration over being noninfluential will lead to the advocacy of revolutionary tactics. Fortunately, neither of these alternatives is currently a probability. Yet as long as such radical reactions are in the realm of the possible, alternatives to the Diet's relative impotence need to be considered.

The objective of making the Diet into the forum for public airing of foreign policy issues might be achieved if the parties and their representatives would allow themselves to be less rigid in adhering to the "party line" as currently decreed in preparliamentary intra- and interparty negotiations. Such relaxation still tends to be perceived as a luxury, because the foreign policy differences of the major antagonists (the LDP on one side, the JSP and JCP on the other) are believed to be irreconcilable, so that no amount of discussion can resolve them. In the meantime, therefore, the only alternative is to conduct negotiations relating to the timing and degree of confrontation—and this in private—rather than over issues of substance in public. Hence, the task of building bridges of mutual confidence is a crucial requirement. Should that requirement be met, the Diet could become a forum for real debate instead of the stage for combat.

It is entirely possible that these changes can and will be made. Japan is no longer involved in rehabilitating itself from a frightfully destructive war and in becoming a major force in international affairs. Both of these goals have been realized. Second, the external environment is no longer bipolar, so that the Diet itself need no longer be riven by vestiges of attitudes formed during the height of the Cold War. However, these transformations in attitude and style of behavior could not be expected to take place overnight.

There is, of course, no guarantee that Japanese foreign policy would be "better," as measured by some ideal yardstick, even if the Diet should play a larger role in its formulation. Nonetheless, it is my conviction that popularly elected representative bodies mirror, far more accurately than largely anonymous and nonresponsible (to the public) bureaucracies, the aspirations and disparate interests of the citizenry. It is for this reason that the Diet should play a larger and more meaningful role in the formulation of Japanese foreign policy.

Probe, Push, and Panic:

The Japanese Tactical Style in International Negotiations

MICHAEL K. BLAKER

*"Even if there is no hope, I would like
to persist to the very end."*

War Minister Tōjō Hideki
during the 1941 U.S.-Japanese negotiations

Successful performance in international negotiations, or "winning," results from an effective application of bargaining power. Bargaining power can be defined as the capacity to generate intended negotiating outcomes. Bargaining power and, by extension, "success" depend on a government's ability to shape the negotiating environment through selected strategies and tactics to suit its prearranged objectives. A negotiating strategy is an overall bargaining design, a general plan for advancing discussions through successive stages toward some desired conclusion. It is implemented by more specific tactics, framed (at least ideally) in a comprehensive set of instructions containing the moves to follow under shifting bargaining conditions, a list of contingency or fallback plans, and some estimate of the negotiating range.

The negotiating strategies and tactics of many nations, particularly those of Western Europe, appear to be rather similar. Their general attitudes toward negotiations, domestic decision-making processes, and observable bargaining behavior do not permit the analyst to identify anything resembling coherent, identifiable, national negotiating "styles." Communist and totalitarian states

55

also seem to form a separate grouping, as they share broadly analogous patterns of negotiating behavior.[1]

But all nations do not negotiate alike. And a national bargaining style—the composite of those behavioral patterns appearing repeatedly in the negotiating experience of a particular nation—is in many cases distinguishable. Such recurrent patterns do seem to appear in the negotiatory conduct of Japan's diplomatic representatives before the Pacific War. Moreover, these prewar bargaining habits were not broken by the Japanese surrender, the demise of the emperor system, or the creation of a constitutionally based system of parliamentary democracy. Japan, in short, has displayed a distinctive and enduring negotiating style under widely varying domestic and international conditions.[2]

A few caveats should be mentioned concerning the use of negotiating strategies and tactics as an organizing concept. To begin with, the volitional character of these moves must be emphasized. There is a distinction between planned and unplanned behavior, between tactics purposefully chosen to influence the opposition and those adopted more or less inadvertently, in-

1. The existing literature on the subject of international negotiations has stressed Soviet-American bargaining encounters, particularly the postwar disarmament conferences, and Chinese Communist negotiating conduct. In-depth analysis of other states is lacking even though the inclusion of other major actors in the international system is clearly a needed next step in the evolution of a general theory of negotiation.

As examples of work in this field, one may refer to Raymond Dennett and Joseph E. Johnson, eds., *Negotiating with the Russians* (Boston: World Peace Foundation, 1951); Arthur Lall, *How Communist China Negotiates* (New York: Columbia University Press, 1968); Nathan Leites, *Styles of Negotiation: East and West on Arms Control 1958–1961* (Santa Monica, Calif.: Rand Corporation document no. D8994ARPA, 1961); John W. Spanier and Joseph L. Nogee, *The Politics of Disarmament* (New York: Praeger, 1962); Kenneth T. Young, *Negotiating with the Chinese Communists* (New York: McGraw-Hill, 1968).

2. This paper is based primarily on research conducted for a doctoral dissertation at Columbia University dealing with Japan's international negotiatory behavior before the Pacific War. When I first considered adding material on the postwar Japanese bargaining experience, I thought that the differences between postwar and prewar behavior would justify dividing the paper into two sections. After evaluation of the differences of the 1955–1956 Soviet-Japanese negotiations for normalization of diplomatic relations and the recent U.S.-Japanese textile negotiations, the differences did not seem sufficient to support such a division. I have therefore incorporated comments on these two postwar cases into the material on prewar Japanese bargaining conduct.

The prewar cases from which illustrations are drawn for this article are the Sino-Japanese negotiations for the Shimonoseki Treaty, 1895; the bargaining for the first Anglo-Japanese Alliance, 1901–1902; the Russo-Japanese negotiations for the Portsmouth Treaty, 1905; the Sino-Japanese negotiations for the Twenty-One Demands, 1915; the Russo-Japanese Alliance negotiations, 1916; the negotiations leading to the Lansing-Ishii Agreement, 1917; the Nishihara loans bargaining (Sino-Japanese), 1918; the Versailles Conference, 1918–1919; the Dairen Conference (Soviet-Japanese), 1921; the Washington Conference, 1921–1922; the Changchun Conference (Soviet-Japanese), 1922; the Peking Conference (Soviet-Japanese), 1924–1925; the London Naval Conference, 1930; the Chinese Eastern Railway negotiations (Soviet-Japanese), 1932–1935; the Anti-Comintern Pact negotiations and subsequent bargaining to strengthen that agreement (Japan, Germany, Italy), 1936–1939; the Tripartite Pact negotiations (Japan, Germany, Italy), 1940; the Soviet-Japanese Neutrality Pact bargaining, 1941; and the U.S.-Japanese negotiations before Pearl Harbor, 1941.

dependently of their anticipated effects on the opposing side. There are certain
negotiating moves that are observable to the outside analyst, but they may be
so ingrained in a nation's style of diplomatic interaction that they are pursued
unconsciously. In Japanese negotiating practice, for example, an individual
diplomat, in the pre-1945 era, frequently explained his inability to concede with
the claim that, although he personally favored compromise, the army or the
navy or Japanese public opinion would absolutely forbid it. Even if the assertion had been the true reason for his intransigence, the diplomat himself was
probably unaware that he was using "tactics," that he was deliberately bringing in this argument as a maneuver to buttress the Japanese position. In fact,
these statements seem to the analyst to be most often little more than self-
serving apologetics to curry favor with the other side. No matter what the intention, however, this kind of argument probably seems deliberate to opposing
diplomats who lack the knowledge necessary to distinguish it from consciously
calculated tactical actions.[3]

It would be inappropriate to treat nondeliberate actions in the same manner
as purposefully selected tactics. Pervasive, nondeliberate patterns of behavior
do partially mold a nation's negotiatory style and contribute substantially to
victory or defeat. However, they fall somewhat outside the rubric of tactics, at
least as that term is construed in this study. Tactics comprise only the deliberate devices, ploys, or moves that a government adopts as part of an overall
strategic plan to manipulate the bargaining environment to conform to its own
ends. They are intentional actions designed to induce desired reactions from
one's opponents. Of course, the line between deliberate and nondeliberate action is not easy to draw.

Attempts to relate bargaining ends and means within the total negotiating
context must be analyzed on this explicit, intentional level. If an outcome favors
one side, an observer should not assume that the favorable terms necessarily
stemmed from an adroit tactical combination; nor should he presume that a
side was necessarily aware of the consequences of its own behavior. Such
assumptions exclude other possibly causal linkages and can impair an accurate
evaluation of bargaining performance. For example, Komura Jutarō is often
somewhat unjustifiably lauded for his diplomatic prowess in dealing with the
Russians at the Portsmouth Conference in 1905. One author has gone as far as
to say that Komura, by his own efforts at the negotiations, rescued half the
island of Sakhalin for Japan.[4] In reality, Komura's personal success was highly

3. Bryant Wedge and Cyril Muromcew, "Psychological Factors in Soviet Disarmament
Negotiations," *Journal of Conflict Resolution*, vol. 9, no. 1 (March 1965), pp. 18–36; also F.G.
Bailey, *Strategems and Spoils* (New York: Shocken, 1969), p. *xiii*.

4. As Thomas Schelling points out, "an observer can seldom distinguish with confidence
the consciously logical, the intuitive, or the inadvertent, use of a visible tactic." See Schelling,
"An Essay on Bargaining," *American Economic Review* vol. 46, no. 3 (June 1956), p. 286.
"Visibility" appears to be Schelling's standard of tactical credibility. See Ibid., pp. 287, 296.
See also Fred Charles Iklé, *How Nations Negotiate* (New York: Harper and Row, 1964), for
several brief comments on conscious versus unconscious moves.

fortuitous, arising not from his own bargaining skills, which on close study appear mediocre in this negotiating encounter, but from Japan's military occupation of half the island, plus the quite accidental last-minute arrival in Tokyo, via informal channels, of information to the effect that Russia was willing to relinquish Southern Sakhalin. It is notable that the Tokyo government secured this data *after* having decided to abandon its Sakhalin claim entirely![5]

A second general point to remember is that decision-makers face severe uncertainties and limitations in selecting strategies and tactics. In choosing bargaining tactics, as in any other sphere of decision-making action, governments often have a mind-boggling gift for unleashing forces leading to entirely unintended effects. Naturally, policy-makers try to select from a number of choices the alternative best calculated in their view to achieve the goal they have in mind. But they are constrained by many factors such as limited knowledge, domestic political pressures, or personal prejudices. When viewed in retrospect, moreover, the seeming lack of any sequential or logical coherence in a given tactical combination may stem in part from the fact that tactics are often chosen at the last possible moment or developed ad hoc, under the fluid pressures of actual bargaining. Also, an apparent absence of overt manipulative tactics may itself be a tactic.

Third, one should not exaggerate the purely gaming aspect of bargaining—the extent to which government leaders, empty of conviction, may pretend to set some arbitrary minimum position and then coldly adopt manipulative devices to force it through. It may be true, of course, that how the other side perceives a move is more relevant than the original intentions behind it; still, blatantly Machiavellian tactics or obviously frivolous ploys run the constant risk of alienating the other side. According to negotiating mores, "tactics," "ploys," or "gambits" have pejorative connotations. Thus, governments deny earnestly they are using tactics at all—such denial being, of course, itself a tactic!

The point is this: although bargaining positions often seem to rest on ambiguous (and one might think therefore adjustable or flexible) standards such as national defense, justice, or special interests, one must not dismiss this as meaningless rhetoric to the extent that a solid, if partially hidden, core of vital policy interests is overlooked. The stakes in most bargaining situations are exceedingly high to all parties, and tactics reflect this grave concern.

Fourth, this study deals with maneuvers targeted on the opposing side, with tactics having one central goal—to win the other side over to one's point of view. Tactical decisions unfold within a domestic political context and may therefore serve these purposes in place of, or parallel to, wholly bargaining objectives. There is, after all, a distinction between deliberate stalling for some hoped-for advantage and inevitable delay because of governmental impasse;

5. Kamimura Shin'ichi, *Gaikō gojūnen* (Tokyo: Jiji Tsūshinsha, 1960), p. 32.

between intentional ambiguity and unavoidable vagueness stemming from indecision; and between the intentional leaking of opposing demands and public
disclosure of confidential information either inadvertently or otherwise by dissidents at home. This paper excludes or deemphasizes these and other tactics
aimed principally at a domestic audience, although their occasional impact on
bargaining strategies is recognized. However, communication tactics—conscious distortion, intentional vagueness, deliberate withholding of information
—are included when directed at the negotiating adversary. Likewise, tactics
aimed at third parties are considered when designed to improve the terms of
agreement.

A final caveat is that no nation is free to choose any tactical assortment to
implement its bargaining goals. Attitudinal constellations deriving from firmly
imbedded cultural patterns inhibit bargaining choices either by proscribing
certain moves or by predisposing a side to favor others. Further, decision-
making/communication processes affect the range and type of tactical options.
These two general factors determine the pattern of a nation's bargaining
strategies and tactics. Stated somewhat differently, a nation's negotiating
strategies and tactics are, on the broadest level, the combination, culmination,
or expression—the observable end result—of leadership attitudes toward international affairs, and national domestic decision-making and communication
processes.

Besides these two general variables, moreover, there are four other factors or
subvariables that affect the tactical mixture in any given case: the character of
the decision-making group and the personalities of its members; the subject
matter under negotiation; the relative power position of the sides; and the
bargaining stage (how far negotiations have progressed toward a settlement).
In addition to attempts to restrict voluntarily one's own bargaining freedom of
action as a commitment tactic, these and possibly other factors combine to
eliminate potentially available moves, leading to strikingly consistent leitmotifs
in the negotiating practice of a specific nation.

STAGE ONE: PRELIMINARY PROBING TACTICS—
MAKING A SITUATION NEGOTIABLE

Japan's leaders and diplomats undertake both formal and informal prebargaining efforts with remarkable drive and determination. Some of their early moves
are intended partly to persuade, to sell a position to the other side. But they are
mostly information-gathering exercises designed to assess chances of agreement
by securing the opponent's view of Japan's position. In every case, Japan expends tremendous amounts of diplomatic energy sounding out the other side
(sempō no ikō o tsukitomeru) and exchanging views with them (iken no kōkan).

This lengthy and cautious Japanese prelude to formal negotiations regularly takes place informally and in private, mirroring a characteristic desire for strict secrecy at each stage. The sounding-out process normally coincides with official decision-making conversations within the government and arrival of early intelligence and diplomatic reports from abroad. This information on anticipated opposing and third-party positions constitutes one important basis for establishing initial Japanese positions. A typical example was Foreign Minister Uchida Yasuya's instructions to negotiator Makino prior to the Versailles negotiations in 1918: "Before presenting our already established demands to the Allied Powers, we should first exchange views with them, altering our demands somewhat by deleting or abbreviating sections, while we continue to work on those policies as yet not completely decided upon."[6] There is a comparatively greater concentration of energies on obtaining a unified Japanese position in prenegotiation deliberations in Tokyo than on learning the opponent's position or establishing an effective dialogue with the adversary before negotiations begin.

Japan's prebargaining tactical style is defensive. With some minor variations depending on the adversary, the principal goals are to tie the hands of the other side in advance; to block the formation of anti-Japanese public sentiment abroad; to deter or eliminate entirely any third-party interference in bilateral negotiations (especially with weaker states); to narrow the scope or range of subjects to be discussed; and to gain explicit or tacit opposing concurrence by removing from the agenda items thought to be inimical to Japan's interests. Unlike the Soviets, who are notorious for the great number and frequent irrelevance of their demands, Japanese bargainers carry along a very short shopping list, consisting mostly of staple items. More than anything else, this Japanese defensiveness betrays an intense fear of submission, or the appearance of submission, to foreign diplomatic or military pressure. Constant anxiety over possible disapproval or active pressure by more powerful states explains much of Japan's emphasis on cautious, defensive moves during the preliminary bargaining stage. In every negotiating context the Japanese seek to avoid open confrontations, to reduce risks, and to insulate themselves from potential criticism or attack.

During the preliminary period, the Japanese try to secure commitments from the bargaining opponent which will restrict the range of topics to be discussed and exclude items that are of peripheral significance or subjects that might place the Japanese on the defensive. If the sounding-out process is designed to ascertain the nature of the adversary's stance, these moves are intended to make sure he will hold to it once bargaining begins. For Japan,

6. Foreign Minister Uchida to Makino Shinken, Dec. 9, 1918, in Gaimushō, *Nihon gaikō bunsho* (1918) (Tokyo: Nihon Kokusai Rengō Kyōkai, 1936–) vol. 3, p. 649.

efforts to secure opposing commitments through understandings (*ryōkai*), consultations (*uchiawase*), and preconditions (*senketsu jōken*) are central to its prebargaining approach. In negotiating the first Anglo-Japanese Alliance, for
example, Japan firmly rejected a British bid to include India within the proposed alliance framework.[7] Japan's chief concern in negotiations with Germany
and Italy during the late 1930s was whether to include, as targets of the alliance, states other than the Soviet Union, as Berlin staunchly advocated.[8]

Those in charge of Japanese policy for the Versailles negotiations wanted to
concentrate their resources on just a few issues, to exclude from the discussions
countries not directly involved, and to keep certain subjects, which Japan considered *faits accomplis* (*kisei jijitsu*), off the agenda entirely. Japan's bargaining
strategy was simple—focus on its "exclusive interests" (cession of Germany's
North Pacific and Shantung holdings) and play everything else by ear. The
idea was to ignore those issues with which Japan was not directly concerned, to
"evaluate the progress of the situation" as it developed, and cooperate "as
much as possible" with the Allies on matters of shared concern.[9] Japanese
diplomats were to secure privately, separately, and in advance, definite assurances from the major powers that Japan's claims to former German interests in the Pacific and China were legitimate. Explicit tactical instructions,
however, were not given.

Similarly, before the Washington Conference, Japan attempted to obtain
from Britain and the United States explicit, formal commitments to exclude
Far Eastern problems from the talks. And for the 1930 London Naval
Conference, the Japanese delegation was instructed to achieve 70 percent of
parity vis-à-vis the United States and Britain in auxiliary craft and cruisers and
the submarine tonnage level reached by the end of 1931. To anchor this position, particularly the demand for 70 percent of parity in heavy cruisers,
Japanese leaders conducted an extensive propaganda campaign in Japan and
sought to get advance guarantees of British and American support. Wakatsuki
Reijirō, the chief Japanese negotiator, even stopped over in Washington with
his entourage on the way to London in what was a doubly futile effort to work
out an "arrangement" with American leaders and to rally U.S. public opinion
behind the Japanese position.

A concern with third-party responses is the principal motivation of such preliminary moves as attempts to mobilize public opinion abroad or to align with
another country to increase Japan's bargaining leverage. It also helps explain

7. Ian Hill Nish, *The Anglo-Japanese Alliance* (London: Athlone Press, 1966), pp. 208,
211–212.
8. Nihon Kokusai Seiji Gakkai, eds., *Taiheiyō sensō e no michi* (Tokyo: Asahi Shimbunsha,
1962), vol. 5, pp. 26–30 (hereafter cited as *TSM*).
9. Yoshimura Michio, "Nichi-Ro kōwa jōyaku no ichisokumen," *Kokusai seiji* 3 (1960):
124.

Japanese tactics in bilateral dealings with weaker countries. At Shimonoseki and in the Twenty-One Demands negotiations, for example, Japan's strategy was to move swiftly and secretly, create a *fait accompli,* and then convince the powers to acquiesce in the agreement. Throughout the Twenty-One Demands negotiations, Tokyo kept one ear constantly attuned to reactions abroad and formulated its plans on the basis of expected foreign responses. Thus, the main reason Foreign Minister Katō Kōmei rejected negotiator Hioki Eki's plan for high-pressure tactics was his belief that such methods would stir up foreign criticism and invite interference or even intervention by the Powers. Instead, he ordered Hioki first to exhaust all "diplomatic means."[10] In many prewar bilateral negotiating situations, the goal was to establish a *fait accompli* that could later be traded off for some advantage. Japan's military occupation of Sakhalin before the Portsmouth Conference, its quick seizure of German holdings in late 1914 prior to the Twenty-One Demands, and its occupation of North Sakhalin prior to negotiations with the Soviet Union in the early 1920s are but a few examples. Once a *fait accompli* was created, it could be compromised later, but only for some sort of compensation (*daishō*).

In zealous pursuit of its own bargaining interests during this early phase, Japan is occasionally guilty of placing excessive faith in the tacit promises and commitments of the opposition or third parties. Examples are Japan's indignation during discussions with Russia in 1916 when, from Tokyo's point of view, Russia seemed to renege on assurances given by Kozakov in preliminary conversations in the Japanese capital;[11] its overdependence on the well-known Katō-Grey correspondence in 1914 to the effect that Britain would diplomatically underwrite Japan's China policies;[12] and, at Versailles, its premature belief that Colonel House's personal support for the Japanese racial-equality demand spelled automatic success at the conference.[13] Also, in 1905, Japan placed too much trust in Theodore Roosevelt's personal ability to bring the Russians around to accepting the Japanese position before the Portsmouth Conference.

On occasion, Japan's over-optimism stems from wishful thinking rather than from commitment. In 1895, for example, Itō and the other genrō knew before the Shimonoseki Conference that the powers would react sternly against any exorbitant Japanese demands, but they forged ahead anyway with, as it turned

10. Katō to Hioki, Feb. 18, 1915, in *Nihon gaikō bunsho* (1915), vol. 3, pp. 171–172; Katō to Hioki, Mar. 8, 1915, in ibid., p. 210.

11. Reference is to the chief of the Far Eastern Department of the Russian Foreign Ministry, Grigorii Kozakov, who visited Japan with Grand Duke Georgii Mikhailovich in January 1916. Gaimushō, *Nichi-Ro kōshō shi* (Tokyo: Gaimushō, 1955), vol. 2, p. 344; also Ishii to Inoue, May 4, 1916, in *Nihon gaikō bunsho* (1916), vol. 1, pp. 143–144.

12. See, for example, A. Whitney Griswold, *The Far Eastern Policy of the United States* (New Haven: Yale University Press, 1964), p. 182.

13. See Unno Yoshio, "Pari kōwa kaigi to Gaimushō," *Rekishi kyōiku,* vol. 15, no. 1 (1967), p. 49; also Kobayashi Tatsuo, ed., *Suiusō nikki* (Tokyo: Hara Shobō, 1966), p. 692.

out, disastrous results.[14] At Versailles, Tokyo leaders believed they had assurances that China would not contest the validity of an improved Japanese position on the continent and were "surprised" when they met opposition.[15] In the Twenty-One Demands negotiations, it is hard to understand Japan's "surprise" at China's flat rejection of the most severe set of conditions (Group Five) and Peking's disclosure of the demands to other countries and the press.[16] In the 1955–1956 Soviet-Japanese normalization talks, Japan began negotiations with unwarranted optimism because they overestimated the strength of their bargaining position.[17] Japanese newspaper sources indicate that the Japanese thought the Soviets might offer generous concessions in exchange for a resumption of diplomatic relations, an optimism which is especially curious in view of the strong Japanese fear and distrust of the Soviet Union. Concessions were expected on the repatriation of Japanese prisoners-of-war (the sine qua non of a peace treaty), on the Northern Islands, and on Japan's bid for entry into the United Nations. Japan also hoped for a comprehensive fishing agreement, an exchange of trade representatives, and a Soviet renunciation of reparation obligations. On the controversial northern-territory issue, the *Sangyō keizai shimbun* claimed that the Soviet Union would have to return not only the Habomais and Shikotan but also the Kuriles and South Sakhalin.[18]

All basic Japanese bargaining instructions contain a solid core of totally unalterable demands on which the other side cannot expect any generosity from Japan. The game plan relating to questions clearly within Japan's minimum position is inflexible and incorporates few if any fallback provisions, for success is assumed. The negotiator is therefore allowed scant personal freedom in carrying out tactical plans on these issues. He is expected to hold doggedly to the position prescribed by Tokyo and, if he encounters determined resistance, to communicate with his government immediately and await further instructions.[19]

On less essential items, there are some anticipated Japanese compromises.

14. Hilary Conroy, *The Japanese Seizure of Korea 1868–1910* (Philadelphia: University of Pennsylvania Press, 1960) pp. 286–287. Yamagata was concerned that exorbitant Japanese demands would displease the Powers and wanted to work out some arrangement with Russia, although he stopped short of suggesting a softening of the demands. See Roger F. Hackett, *Yamagata Aritomo in the Rise of Modern Japan, 1838–1922* (Cambridge, Mass: Harvard University Press, 1971), pp. 165–166.

15. Their assumption was based on the October 1917 Sino-Japanese agreement on Shantung and Tsou's informal visit to Japan prior to the conference.

16. Gaimushō Hyakunen Shi Hensan Iinkai, ed., *Gaimushō no hyakunen* (Tokyo: Hara Shobō, 1969), vol. 1, p. 612.

17. I.I. Morris, "Japan and the Moscow Negotiations with the Soviet Union," *The World Today* 11 (August 1955):358; also Savitri Vishwanathan, *Normalization of Japanese-Soviet Relations 1945–1970* (Tallahassee: Diplomatic Press, 1973), p. 88.

18. *Sangyō keizai shimbun*, May 26, 1955.

19. The original instructions for the Portsmouth Conference, for instance, ordered: "If the conference does not go as planned, then wait for instructions." *Nihon gaikō bunsho* (1905), vol. 5, p. 239.

Concessions are not ruled out. Japanese leaders were willing before the London
Conference, for instance, to sacrifice relatively minor items in order to win their
main objectives. Depending on the conference "situation," negotiators were
authorized to compromise on auxiliary craft (destroyers and light cruisers) or
even to drop this category entirely and focus on heavy cruisers, and to accept a
weaker three-power, as opposed to a five-power, agreement.[20]

Regarding the disposition of these less crucial items—conditions falling
within the "bargaining range"—the absolute size of authorized Japanese concessions is small. Moreover, when setting forth the outer boundaries of compromise, decision-makers seek refuge in ambiguity. The word most frequently
used in basic instructions to indicate the range of discretionary latitude is a flac-
cid "somewhat" (*tashō*). For example, the Japanese cabinet decision approving
London Naval Conference instructions declared in part that, "as long as it does
not compromise our naval capability, it is acceptable to make some sacrifices
on light cruisers and destroyers."[21] Other such terms commonly appearing in
instructions are "to a certain extent" (*aru teido made;* Washington Conference),
"to some extent" (*jakkan no teido made*) or "as much as possible" (*dekirukagiri;*
both in 1916 Russo-Japanese Alliance negotiations), or "as far as conditions
permit" (*jijō no yurusu kagiri;* Portsmouth Conference and Versailles, among
others). For the 1955–1956 Soviet-Japanese negotiations, Matsumoto Shun'ichi
was permitted some "flexibility" (*danryokusei*) on the handling of the Japanese
demands for the Kuriles and South Sakhalin and was instructed to "push for"
the return of the islands of Etorofu and Kunashiri.[22] But the precise extent of
his personal discretionary latitude on the territorial question was uncertain at
the outset. Even later, revised instructions remained ambiguous—he was to
seek "as far as possible" to obtain Etorofu and Kunashiri.[23]

Leaders in Tokyo are also imprecise when discussing the timing of concessions. They prefer to watch and wait, to retain maximum flexibility as long
as the basic substance of their position is not jeopardized. Here again the
phrase "as far as conditions permit" is often inserted into negotiating instructions to describe when negotiators should pursue particular items, submit

20. "Instructions for the London Naval Conference," in Gaimushō, *Nihon gaikō nempyō
narabini shuyō bunsho* (Tokyo: Hara Shobō, 1965) (hereafter cited as *NGN*), vol. 2, pp. 139–
142, reflecting a cabinet decision of Nov. 26, 1929. Or consider Matsuoka's instructions for
the Neutrality Pact on North Sakhalin rights: "We have no objection to some compromise
[on this issue]." Horinouchi Kensuke, Andō Yoshirō, and Narita Katsushirō, "Nichi-Doku-I
dōmei; Nisso chūritsu jōyaku," in Kajima Heiwa Kenkyūjo, ed., *Nihon gaikō shi* (Tokyo:
Kajima Kenkyūjo Shuppankai, 1971), vol. 21, p. 278.

21. "Instructions for the London Naval Conference," *NGN*, vol. 2, p. 142.

22. Matsumoto Shun'ichi, *Mosukuwa ni kakeru niji: Nisso kokko kaifuku hiroku* (Tokyo: Asahi
Shimbunsha, 1966), p. 31. Also Donald C. Hellmann, *Japanese Domestic Politics and Foreign
Policy: The Peace Agreement with the Soviet Union* (Berkeley: University of California Press,
1969), pp. 59–64.

23. Matsumoto, *Mosukuwa ni kakeru niji*, p. 49. These revised instructions were dated Aug.
27, 1955.

proposals, offer trades, or withdraw demands. Thus, Washington Conference instructions contained an entire subdivision headed "matters to be demanded depending on the conference situation" (*kaigi no jōsei ni yori shuchō subeki jikō*).[24] In practically every case, initial instructions are studded with the words "at an appropriate opportunity" (*tekitō na kikai ni*) or "at an appropriate time" (*tekitō na jiki ni*) to indicate the timing of concessions. The exact method, timing, and amount of compromise over the limited number and size of items in Japan's "bargaining range," then, is usually left up to the diplomat, depending on conference conditions. This sample from Washington Conference instructions captures the spirit well: "Show a compromising attitude to some extent depending on the situation at the conference" (*kaigi no jōsei ikanni yoritewa aru teido made kōjō no seishin o shimesu*).[25]

Anticipated Japanese concessions are few, but from the way initial instructions stipulate how even these meager offerings might be presented, one would think Japan was surrendering its Three Sacred Treasures. According to starting instructions, negotiators are to retreat only when all else fails. Thus Katō instructed Hioki in late 1914: "Make every effort to push through on the basis of Plan *A*, but if unavoidable [*yamu o ezaru ni*], use Plan *B*."[26] Japan's Washington Conference delegates were advised, "If it is unavoidable [*yamu o enai baai niwa*], we have no objection to excluding some territory."[27] And during the London Naval Conference the Japanese government first cabled its representatives, "If circumstances make it inevitable [*jijō yamu o ezaru baainiwa*], it is acceptable for you to conclude a three-power rather than a five-power pact."[28]

Beginning Japanese instructions also seem to assume that the opposition must make the first concession, after which Japan will respond with concessions of its own. Perhaps Japanese leaders feel more comfortable compromising once the opposing side has demonstrated its "good faith" (*kō'i; zen'i*), "sincerity" (*sei'i; seijitsu; seishinsei'i*), or "spirit of compromise" (*jōhoteki seishin*)

24. "Instructions for the Washington Conference," in *Shidehara Kijūrō* (Tokyo: Shidehara Heiwa Zaidan, 1955), pp. 208–215. The "Instructions for the London Naval Conference" provided, "If you are unable to reach an agreement on capital ships, it is acceptable just on auxiliary vessels. This question will depend on the situation, the order of discussion, and the method of negotiation." Katō's initial instructions concerning the Twenty-One Demands stated, "Bring up the question of returning Kaiochow Bay at an appropriate time" (*tekitō no jiki ni*). See Katō to Hioki, Dec. 3, 1914, in *Nihon gaikō bunsho* (1914), vol. 1, p. 567. There are differing views on the limits of authorized Japanese compromise in these negotiations. Kawamura Kinji claims that Matsumoto was instructed to press for the Kuriles and South Sakhalin, to try especially hard for the Habomais and Shikotan, but if these efforts should fail, to sign a peace treaty without settling the territorial issue. Kawamura Kinji, ed., *Gaimushō* (Tokyo: Hōbunsha, 1956), pp. 65–66.

25. "Instructions for the Washington Conference," *Shidehara Kijūrō*, p. 214.

26. "Instructions for the Sino-Japanese Negotiations," Katō to Hioki, Dec. 3, 1914, in *Nihon gaikō bunsho* (1914), vol 1, pp. 561–590.

27. "Instructions for the Washington Conference," *Shidehara Kijūrō*, pp. 208–215.

28. "Instructions for the London Naval Conference," *NGN*, vol. 2, p. 140.

by conceding first. Also, a prior opposing concession provides an important face-saving justification for a Japanese countercession.

Positionally, the main purpose of Japanese prebargaining tactics is to refrain from an early commitment to concede, reserving maximum "freedom of action" (*jiyū kōdō*) until negotiations actually begin. Although Japanese leaders and diplomats seek firm preliminary commitments from negotiating opponents, they stubbornly balk at reciprocating with advance promises of their own. In multilateral negotiating settings, this Japanese wish for positional maneuverability is translated into attempts to occupy a detached, middle-of-the-road position. For instance, Japan's Washington Conference plenipotentiaries were advised to adopt an "impartial attitude";[29] for the London Naval Conference the delegation was similarly instructed not to favor any side but to assume a "fair and impartial attitude." Japan's London representatives were told that if problems arose between the Anglo-American Powers and France and Italy, or just between France and Italy, they were to stay in the middle, act as intermediary, and provide "good offices" if needed.[30]

In terms of its bargaining position, Japan begins negotiations with several points clearly in its favor. This was especially true in the prewar period when Japan was usually the offensive side, that is, the party seeking to alter the status quo in its favor by the presentation of clearly revisionist demands. It was, to put it badly, fighting over someone else's marbles. A Japanese concession meant allowing the other side to keep more of what it already had. Therefore, Japan's claims that its concessions were "generous," "bearing the unbearable," or were being offered in a "magnanimous and just spirit" (*kōsei kanyō taru taido*) rang particularly hollow. And yet, despite Japan's seemingly powerful offensive potential in the prewar era, in practice its prebargaining plans were mostly thematic variations on basically defensive strategies. In terms of style at least, this defensive pattern has continued to be a characteristic pattern of Japanese negotiating practice in the postwar period as well.

Why are the Japanese so consistently defensive in their negotiating approach? Of course, their emphasis on preliminary checking moves (securing prior understandings, arrangements, and commitments through a sounding-out process with the opposition) itself has defensive overtones. Beyond that, Japanese enthusiasm for this early-phase activity is a blend of several cultural ingredients: a preference for behind-the-scenes maneuvering; a penchant for meticulous planning; and a conspicuous distaste for premature commitment. Moreover, given their fondness for domestic decision-making meetings that

29. "Instructions for the Washington Conference"; also *Gaimushō no hyakunen*, vol. 1, p. 800. Japan was reluctant to accept the U.S. agenda as it would restrict its freedom of action. At the London Naval Conference Japan chose to formulate its own proposals rather than just to respond to the initial American draft.

30. "Instructions for the London Naval Conference," *NGN*, vol. 2, p. 140; also Unno Yoshio, "Rondon kaigun gunshuku kaigi" *Kokusai seiji* 3 (1959):39.

have been artfully rigged ahead of time, the stress Japanese negotiators place on preliminary moves is not surprising. Knowing they will be tied closely to this initial negotiating program once the government (and, in the prewar period, the emperor) has sanctioned it, and that their political lives in some sense rest on its successful execution, politically accountable government leaders are understandably hesitant and cautious.

The dread of interference from more powerful countries also leads Japan to use defensive tactics. Both Japan's bargaining goals and the moves designed to obtain them are conditioned by this deep-seated fear. It is a defensive calculation—arising from an acute Japanese sensitivity to hostile foreign public and government opinion or to direct power confrontations—that is primarily responsible for smoothing over the jagged edges of proposed Japanese demands, yet this also brings opening positions close to real minimums. Such fears are also a chief reason why Japanese leaders delay decisions until the last minute in the hope that an irreversible decision might not have to be made at all. These fears also help to explain why initial instructions on unresolved questions are often vague and brief (although such ambiguity results, too, from genuine policy ambivalence). To be sure, taking the initiative in bargaining implies a clarity of objectives that Japan in most cases has lacked.

To preempt foreign criticism and to avoid being forced on the defensive, Japan occasionally makes what might be called anticipatory concessions, the net effect of which is to soften opening lines even more. The decision to jettison from its list of Portsmouth Conference conditions the demand that Russia dismantle all military fortifications in Vladivostok was no doubt aimed at pleasing the American president, who opposed the item.[31] Again, before the Washington Conference, Japan elected in advance to drop several terms to avoid inviting foreign mistrust.[32]

A desire to ward off foreign criticism has led to still other preliminary tactics—for example, operating through an intermediary (such as Manchukuo during negotiations for the sale of the Chinese Eastern Railway, 1933–1935), appointing "observers" who would both represent Japan's interests and assess prospects for possible government level talks (such as at the 1921 Dairen Conference), and, more broadly, relying heavily on private and informal channels of diplomatic interaction. One sample of this last pattern will suffice. Prime Minister Konoe, during 1941, could not openly admit how desperate Japan's situation had become in large part because the military had staked its reputation on a series of preceding decisions. For reasons of prestige or, if one will,

31. Gaimushō, *Komura gaikō shi* (Tokyo: Kuretani Shoten, 1953), vol. 2, p. 62.
32. *TSM*, vol. 1, p. 38. Before the Changchun Conference, Japan decided to withdraw voluntarily from the Maritime province to avoid the embarrassment of having to withdraw in response to pressure if it continued the occupation. George Alexander Lensen, *Japanese Recognition of the USSR: Soviet-Japanese Relations 1921–1930* (Tallahassee: Diplomatic Press, 1970), pp. 49–50.

"face," he therefore favored initiating talks with the United States through private channels, shifting to official levels (involving a minimal number of persons) only when there was some prospect of success. Finally, if these moves brought promising results, Konoe, who was personally close to the military, was to arrange a settlement himself.[33]

Despite strenuous and energetic preparations, the Japanese also tend to commence negotiations with several handicaps. For one thing, their initial positions are tactically barren. The preliminary goal is disarmingly simple—to push through preset plans as speedily and completely as possible. But from a tactical standpoint, the absence of clearly defined policies on some questions, the sparseness of officially authorized concessions, and the near total lack of artificially inflated or sham demands simply pave the way for later trouble. If pressed forcefully on some issue, Japanese diplomats are told merely to "explain our position fully," or to "make every effort" to convince the other side, or to "cable for further instructions." How they are to proceed if initial policies fail, or how far they should retreat, are not spelled out at this stage. The only tactic, if that is the proper term, is to provide for at least some fallback positions. This is clearly a defensive approach, and even here Japanese diplomats have precious little to work with, scant wherewithal for offers and exchanges. Therefore, the Japanese negotiator's position is delicate. The sheer rigidity of original positions goes far to guarantee that conflicts will arise between the negotiator and the home government over their respective spheres of bargaining competence and the policies appropriate for meeting shifting conference conditions. Without settled policies on each question, and substantial, clear-cut fallback areas, the negotiator is highly vulnerable to charges of being uncompromising and disinterested in reaching agreement.

Japanese diplomats are appalled at the thought of leaping into a totally open, free-wheeling bargaining situation. They prefer pragmatic, low-risk methods. They want, if at all possible, to stack the bargaining deck in advance, to guarantee success by creating situations of strength as translated into various preliminary agreements, arrangements, and *faits accomplis*. These maneuvers predictably consume considerable time; final decisions are often postponed until the last minute. In at least two prewar cases (Versailles and the Tripartite Pact negotiations), Japanese bargaining policies were still unsettled when negotiations formally got underway. It also appears that Japan started negotiations with the Soviet Union in 1955 without having established its minimal position on the crucial Northern Islands question.[34] Most recently, before the second round of textile talks, begun in late 1970 in Washington, the Satō government decided to press forward with negotiations without the prior ap-

33. Imai Seiichi, "Naikaku to tennō, jūshin," in Hosoyā Chihiro et al., eds., *Nichi-Bei kankei shi* (Tokyo Daigaku Shuppankai, 1971), vol. 1, p. 31.

34. *Nippon Times*, Oct. 1–2, 1955 (after July 1, 1956, called *Japan Times*).

proval of domestic textile manufacturers. The initial Japanese proposal that supposedly incorporated both the views of the industry and the government was publicly dubbed a mere "position paper" by the minister of MITI.[35] In these typical cases, the Japanese government made a tactical error by leaving too much undecided, thereby placing additional pressure on a sadly inadequate Japanese decision-making organization to react quickly and flexibly to reach important decisions while negotiations were in progress.

During the prebargaining stage, then, Japanese government leaders and negotiators hope to trap the opponent or third parties in a web of advance agreements, arrangements, and understandings that function like preconditions. Japan's preliminary strategy is cautiously pragmatic and basically negative: avoid conflict with stronger powers, detour around potentially vexing items, and, at the same time, make sure that an ultimate agreement is possible.

STAGE TWO: THE BARGAINING PHASE

The middle bargaining phase begins after initial positions have been developed and articulated by all sides. During this stage the emphasis turns to soft-spot probing, exchanges, inducements, and cautious testing; the intrinsic rhythm of concrete bargaining interaction emerges. The premium is now placed on improvisation, speed, and ingenuity. But for Japan, unfortunately, any modification of original bargaining plans is excruciatingly difficult. Bound by rigid instructions and directed by relatively uncompromising leaders in snail-paced policy-making groups in Tokyo, Japan's negotiators are at a clear disadvantage during this fluid and uncertain middle period.

Manipulating the means of commitment

Unity. Unity is always a key concern in bargaining. The adversary must be denied an opportunity to split one's ranks, to exploit real or potential divisions to its own advantage. One of the most critical tasks facing governments in international bargaining, therefore, is to demonstrate conclusively that leaders and negotiators stand together, backed unswervingly by the people.

Throughout the pre-World War II period, the press, members of the Diet, and many individuals and factional groups in the government itself were less flexible in bargaining policy than those responsible for making and executing policy. In at least two prewar cases—Shimonoseki and the Twenty-One Demands—organized public opinion may have forced the Japanese government to adopt a more assertive negotiating posture than officials originally con-

35. *Japan Times,* Nov. 10, 1970.

templated.[36] Similarly, in the postwar period, major newspaper opinion, the opposition parties, and intellectuals, with few exceptions, have attacked any Japanese concessions and have urged the government to be firm and unyielding in diplomatic negotiations.

An uncompromising public in particular provides Japanese leaders and diplomats with a powerful commitment device to buttress their arguments against compromise. And they have not failed to take full advantage of the weapon. At the Washington Conference, for instance, Katō Tomosaburō declared that Japanese "public opinion" viewed acceptance of the Hughes plan as "total capitulation";[37] at another point he warned that "public opinion" would never allow the Four-Power Treaty to apply to Japan proper and would never accept anything less than a 10:7 naval ratio.[38] Negotiator Ishii Kikujirō told Secretary of State Lansing in 1917 that, if the United States did not agree to recognize Japan's "special interests" in China, the "Japanese people" would attack the government and the opposition in the Diet would blame the Gaimushō.[39] In February 1956 when Soviet leaders demanded that Japan abandon its claim to the Southern Kurile islands (Etorofu and Kunashiri), bargainer Matsumoto Shun'ichi intimated that a "troublesome" situation would arise if the Soviet Union should ignore intense Japanese public feelings that the two islands rightfully belonged to Japan.[40] Though it is hard to assess whether the Japanese public actually holds such convictions (in which case negotiators simply are describing an existing state of affairs) and the degree to which the government at any given time is responsive to this opinion, it is clear that Japan's negotiators, when in need of a supportive argument, will nearly always add a pinch of "public opinion" to harden the tactical mix.

In addition to an uncompromising electorate, the existence of relatively hardline elements either in the government or in a position to exert pressure on the government (such as the opposition parties) also gives negotiators a convenient reason not to comply with opposing demands for concessions. During the 1930 London Naval Conference, for instance, Foreign Minister Shidehara told Ambassador Castle in Tokyo that he was "personally willing to accept the

36. Mutsu Munemitsu, *Kenkenroku* (Tokyo: Iwanami Shoten, 1958), pp. 193–194; Marius Jansen, *The Japanese and Sun Yat-sen* (Cambridge, Mass.: Harvard University Press, 1954), pp. 183–186; Hackett, *Yamagata Aritomo*, p. 164. For the analogous Portsmouth instance, see Shumpei Okamoto, *The Japanese Oligarchy and the Russo-Japanese War* (New York: Columbia University Press, 1970). As Hackett observes: "In both instances [1894–1895 and 1904–1905] the demands of popular opinion far exceeded the position taken by the government." See his *Yamagata Aritomo*, p. 230.

37. Actually there was some public disagreement over the issue. *Gaimushō no hyakunen*, vol. 1, p. 833.

38. Sadao Asada, "Japan and the United States, 1915–1925" (Ph.D. thesis, Yale University, New Haven, 1963), pp. 233–234.

39. Robert Lansing, *The War Memoirs of Robert Lansing* (Westport, Conn.: Greenwood Press, 1970), p. 294; Shigemitsu Osamu, "Ishii-Ranshingu kyōtei," *Kokusai seiji* 6 (1958):72.

40. Matsumoto, *Mosukuwa ni kakeru niji*, p. 84.

American position but was afraid of the navy."[41] Late in the 1955–1956 Soviet-Japanese normalization talks, negotiator Kōno Ichirō told Khrushchev that although he and others were willing to shelve the territorial question, a group of LDP members had forced passage of a party resolution calling for immediate return of the Habomais and Shikotan. He asked Khrushchev to "understand" this political situation.[42]

Resolve (ketsui). One of the more common Japanese arguments to show commitment is to declare, in effect, "we mean business." Thus, at an Imperial Conference late in 1941, Foreign Minister Tōgō Shigenori observed, "if [the United States] reflects upon the fact that Japan is resolved, I think it must give some thought to our demands."[43] Or, "The United States seems from the outset to have believed that its economic pressure would force Japan to surrender but, if it recognizes that Japan is resolved . . ."[44] At the Washington Conference, Tokyo ordered Katō to explain to Hughes "that we are resolved to make the fortifications issue indivisible from a naval limitations agreement."[45]

Bargaining norms. Words alone cannot convert a determined government or the negotiators representing it.[46] Nevertheless, despite the yawning gap often existing between the public utterances of officials and the innermost reasons for bargaining action, diplomats behave as if their arguments make some difference and, if nothing else, their public and private statements add yet another dimension to their negotiating style.

Japan uses the conventional idiom of negotiation when making proposals. This involves two steps. First, when a Japanese resistance point crumbles and a shift in position becomes necessary, the rationale for the change is elaborately described. Typically, these statements justify a new move as an attempt to push negotiations toward a settlement, to promote good will between parties, or to show Japan's willingness to make "great sacrifices."[47]

41. Castle to Cotton (Acting Secretary of State), Mar. 7, 1930, in U.S. Department of State, *Foreign Relations of the United States: Far Eastern Series* (Washington, D.C.: Government Printing Office, 1930), vol. 1, pp. 49–50.
42. Matsumoto, *Mosukuwa ni kakeru niji*, p. 144.
43. Sanbō Honbu, ed., *Sugiyama memo* (Tokyo: Hara Shobō, 1967), vol. 1, p. 410, trans. in Nobutaka Ike, trans. and ed., *Japan's Decision for War: Records of the 1941 Policy Conferences* (Stanford: Stanford University Press, 1967), p. 232.
44. *Sugiyama memo*, vol. 1, p. 415, trans. in Ike, *Japan's Decision for War*, p. 238.
45. "Instructions on the Arms Limitation Question," Jan. 14, 1922, *NGN*, vol. 2, p. 2.
46. Iklé, *How Nations Negotiate*, pp. 154–155, 200.
47. For example, "Out of consideration for the overall work of the conference, Japan will not press this issue but . . ." (Versailles); see Makino Shinken, *Kaikoroku* (Tokyo: Bungei Shunjū Shinsha, 1949), vol. 3, p. 184; and "Japan, in view of the overall situation, is taking a broad perspective on these questions out of its desire to conclude the negotiations swiftly"; see Gaimushō, ed., *Nisso kōshō shi* (Tokyo: Gannandō Shoten, 1969) pp. 303–304. See also Komura to Katsura, Aug. 23, 1905, in *Nihon gaikō bunsho* (1905), vol. 5, p. 486.

The second step is to establish a fresh commitment at the next resistance level. By declarations of fealty to the new position, Japan seeks to counter pressures toward further compromise inherent in such bargaining norms as reciprocating concessions or revising one's "minimum." Japan therefore portrays its draft proposals as magnanimous (*kanyō, kandai*), as just and fair (*kōsei datō*), or as its absolute minimum (*zettaiteki saishōgen*). Examples from the Twenty-One Demands negotiations illustrate Japan's consistent use of this technique:

This proposal, containing exceedingly generous demands aimed at achieving peace, represents our true minimum, with no room whatsoever for compromise [first offer].

These are our last concessions [second offer].

These are absolutely our final concessions—our lowest minimum [a later offer].

There is no room at all for compromise on this draft [still a later revised draft].

This is our final revised draft [another draft, two weeks later].[48]

In building these successive commitment points, there is the danger of going too far, to the point of actually convincing the opposition that a nonfinal position is final—a point aptly illustrated in the following comment by prewar foreign minister Tōgō:

I used in my instructions [to Nomura in 1941] language which in other circumstances might have been unduly strong. Parenthetically, the State Department seems to have felt that my language showed that we had no genuine desire to reach a settlement; such phraseology in my instructions as "this is our final proposal," or "so and so is absolutely necessary," was played up by the prosecution in the IMTFE [International Military Tribunal for the Far East] as if it had made a great discovery—that Japan was delivering an "ultimatum." This, of course, is absurd—even in ordinary commercial transactions a "final offer" is not inevitably the last proposal, and *a fortiori* the same is true in diplomacy. I had myself the experience, while serving abroad and conducting negotiations, of receiving from Tokyo an instruction saying that I should bear in mind that the current proposal was the final one—then to have it followed by another, and another, in the same language.[49]

In the postwar period, Japan has faced even greater difficulty in building credible fallback positions, partially because officials have been willing to express publicly their personal views on negotiations. For instance, during the Ushiba-Flanigan segment of the lengthy U.S.-Japanese textile negotiations

48. See these telegrams selected from the diplomatic correspondence: Katō to the Chinese Minister, Feb. 3; Katō to Hioki, Feb. 16; Hioki to Katō, Mar. 25; Hioki to Katō, Apr. 7; Hioki to Katō, Apr. 26; in *Nihon gaikō bunsho* (1915), vol. 3.

49. Shigenori Tōgō, *The Cause of Japan*, trans. Fumihiko Tōgō and Ben Bruce Blakeney (New York: Simon and Schuster, 1956), p. 149.

several years ago, the Japanese side submitted what it labeled its "final" position on November 14, 1970, at only the second meeting. Negotiator Ushiba announced this to be Japan's "minimum" but then undermined the assertion by
stating, "If the United States concedes, we will too." MITI chief, Miyazawa,
also raised the possibility of Japanese concessions: "the Japanese proposal is intended to see how far the U.S. side will compromise." Miyazawa, a hard-liner
in these negotiations, also declared publicly that a textile settlement was impossible unless Japan capitulated! On November 21, Foreign Minister Aichi
confessed that the November 14 proposal had not been Japan's final draft after
all, and another Japanese "final draft" (*saishuan*) was formulated and presented
on November 28. Only five days later, Miyazawa "could not say" whether
Japan might concede further.[50]

During the 1955–1956 Soviet-Japanese negotiations, Japanese bargainers
repeatedly returned to Tokyo for "consultations" and, on their arrival, a hue
and cry was raised in the Japanese press for the government to agree on a firm
bargaining position.[51] At no point, however, did the government develop a
supraparty negotiating policy, nor, for that matter, did any one faction support
the same policy throughout the negotiations. Foreign Minister Shigemitsu
publicly aired views different from and on occasion opposite to those of his own
prime minister! During the middle phase of these negotiations, Prime Minister
Hatoyama admitted that it would be "exceedingly hard" for Japan to persuade
the Russians to surrender Kunashiri and Etorofu.[52] Some months later, with
his government's policy clearly providing that Japan would sign a treaty only
when the two islands were returned, Hatoyama stated that the islands had "no
value except in time of war."[53] LDP leaders hurriedly conferred and issued a
statement correcting Hatoyama's "slip of the tongue." What the prime minister had meant to say, the statement claimed, was that the "territorial problem
is not fixed."[54] It was errors such as this which later prompted *Time* magazine
to level this charge against the ailing Japanese leader: "We are not worried
about Hatoyama's body, we're worried about his mind!"[55]

Slogans and set phrases. Another means of expressing bargaining commitment is
through slogans and set phrases. Like Wilson's "Fourteen Points" or FDR's
"Four Freedoms," they can usefully join together otherwise disparate items,
placing them all on the same level. They can then be presented as a neatly
wrapped package, take it or leave it. Slogans can serve important domestic

50. *Japan Times*, Nov. 12, 21, 1970; *Asahi shimbun*, Nov. 15, Dec. 4, 1970.
51. "Consultations" refer to the territorial issue between the negotiator and Prime Minister Hatoyama. See, for instance, *Nippon Times*, Oct. 1, 1955.
52. *Asahi shimbun*, Nov. 13, 1955.
53. *Mainichi shimbun*, June 6, 1956.
54. *Asahi shimbun*, June 7, 1956.
55. *Time*, Sept. 24, 1956, p. 30.

goals as well by welding together possibly dissident factions, stimulating patri-
otic fervor, or spurring on the people to great sacrifices. If made relevant to the
bargaining context, they can suggest resolve, determination, and unity. By
sheer repetition, moreover, they can acquire a certain credibility, or at least so it
is hoped by those employing them.

Japan is adept at sloganeering—that is, at articulating its bargaining commitments in set phrases or principles. In the prewar period Japan was most
often the offensive negotiating side, the party obligated to show the logical connection between items on its list of demands. At Versailles, for example,
Japan's position was founded on the so-called *sandai gensoku* (three great
principles). Apart from establishing a convenient basis for commitment, the
device performed a significant linkage by elevating one "principle" (racial
equality), which was outside Japan's actual minimum, to the same level as
Japan's key territorial demands (cession of Shantung and the German islands
in the North Pacific).[56]

A similar pattern is discernible at the 1930 London Naval Conference, where
Japan's negotiating stance was founded on the "three great policies" of which
the most critical was a demand for 70 percent of parity in heavy cruisers. The
other two conditions were far less crucial to Japan and original instructions
even provided for some compromise on these points. Still, the "policies" and
the fixed percentage ratios they reflected were political doctrine in Japan, and
certain Japanese naval leaders had staked their reputations on winning all
three demands. Small wonder that they would have nothing to do with
Stimson's attempt to persuade Japan to settle for an amorphous "naval
superiority."

Manipulating the tools of persuasion

Along with attempts to prove their position immovable are Japanese moves
to induce the opponent to accept that position. These persuasive devices
—whether verbal arguments, positional maneuvers, or coercive tactics—are
aimed at pressuring the other side to alter its basic stance.

The calculated quid pro quo. Behind Japan's handling of positional shifts and
issue linkages is a consistent wish to create and sustain the appearance of an
even, symmetrical exchange. Traditional Western bargaining norms, such as

56. The racial equality question was added late and never acquired the urgency of Japan's
other demands. Break-off, for instance, was not a seriously debated alternative if the racial
equality claim were to fail. See the record of the Gaikō Chōsa Kai meeting, Apr. 21, 1919, in
Suiusō nikki, p. 468; Uchida to Msui, Apr. 21, 1919, in *Nihon gaikō bunsho* (1919), vol. 3, p. 242;
and Uchida to Matsui, Apr. 23, 1919, in ibid., p. 249.

reciprocal concessions, revision of starting positions, and give-and-take, are vividly reflected in Japan's tactical use of exchanges and mutual concessions as inducements.

On the rhetorical level, Japanese appeals to bargaining norms are frequent—especially to "the spirit of mutual compromise" (*gojō no seishin*) or its shorter rough equivalent "good faith" or "sincerity." For instance, to attract Russian concessions at Portsmouth, Komura vowed, "If Russia shows a willingness to concede one step, then we will too."[57] Or as Wakatsuki told Stimson at the 1930 London Naval Conference, "If you can appreciate my own good faith, then you must respond with good faith."[58]

On this verbal level Japan tries to show that it has compromised more, is more reasonable, and is more interested in resolving the problems under discussion than the other side. In addition to good faith or sincerity, other Japanese bargaining norms, such as patience, fairness, or great effort, appear regularly in the records as persuasive devices, as in these examples from the Twenty-One Demands negotiations in 1915:

We cannot accept your proposal since it lacks *good faith*.

If you demonstrate *a sincere attitude*, we shall discuss Group 5. . . . I have strict instructions to urge your side to show *sincerity*.

If you have *good faith* you should meet with us three times a week. [italics added.][59]

Beneath such rhetoric is a rock-hard Japanese disdain for making unilateral concessions (*ippōteki jōho*), for giving up something for nothing. Their original proposals and subsequent offers are tied explicitly to concrete and substantial compromises from the other side. For example, certain Tokyo leaders were incensed in November 1941 when the United States failed to respond to Japan's so-called *"A"* proposal with an answering draft.[60] Whenever negotiator Yoshizawa made a concession at the Peking Conference in 1924–1925, he would add expectantly, "now it's your turn."[61] During U.S.-Japanese bargaining over tex-

57. *Komura gaikō shi*, vol. 2, p. 89; Kuroki Yukichi, *Komura Jutarō* (Tokyo: Kōdansha, 1968), p. 611.

58. Wakatsuki to the Japanese Government, Mar. 15, 1930, *NGN*, vol. 2, p. 145; and answering instructions, in ibid. p. 149.

59. In order of citation, these are Hioki to Katō, Feb. 9; Hioki to Katō, Feb. 10; Katō to Hioki, Feb. 14 (see also record of Feb. 18, Katō meeting with Chinese minister in Tokyo distilled in Katō to Hioki, Feb. 18); and Hioki to Katō, Mar. 6, *Nihon gaikō bunsho* (1915), vol. 3.

60. Nishi Haruhiko, *Kaisō no Nihon gaikō* (Tokyo: Iwanami Shoten, 1965), p. 121; Liaison Conference, Nov. 13, 1941, *Sugiyama memo*, vol. 1, pp. 415–416, trans. in Ike, *Japan's Decision for War*, pp. 244–247.

61. Gaimushō, Archives, Meiji-Taishō 251 106 28, *Nichi-Ro kokkō kaifuku kōshō ikken, Pekin kaigi jumbi uchiawasekai gijiroku*, meeting of Oct. 27, 1924, pp. 711–714. During these negotiations, each time Yoshizawa presented a Japanese draft proposal he asked the Soviet negotiator to give in out of a "spirit of mutual compromise." This, according to Yoshizawa, was the "fair" procedure. Ibid., meeting 46, Dec. 27, 1924, pp. 836–858; and meeting 47, Dec. 29, 1924, pp. 867, 882.

tiles in 1970, Prime Minister Satō declared that since Japan had conceded several times, it was Washington's "turn." Continued U.S. intransigence, he thought, would show that it lacked the "spirit of mutual compromise" essential to a solution of the problem.[62]

Thus, there is a regularized cadence of Japanese offers within the general maneuvering for positional advantage that occurs in negotiations. By being the side to submit the original draft (*gen'an*), or by merely presenting a compromise draft (*dakyōan*), a new draft (*shinteian*), or a revised draft (*shūseian*), Japan tries to gain a tempo, to transfer the responsibility for concessions to the other side, and looking ahead perhaps to the final bargaining phase, shift the blame for any break-off onto the opponent.

Though they expect significant opposing concessions, Japanese negotiators, principally because of the sparseness of officially authorized compromises, can never offer much in return. Even as they admit in the abstract the need for concession, compromise, and flexibility, their actual offers are usually nominal, occasionally fictitious, and sometimes downright phoney.

Highly inflated initial demands. One common method of minimizing real concessions and taking advantage of situational pressures to reciprocate concessions is to incorporate sham conditions into a basic negotiating platform, elevate them to the level of other "genuine" demands, and try to barter them off for some gain. In the Portsmouth, the Twenty-One Demands, and the 1921 Dairen Conference negotiations, Japan presented highly inflated initial demands.

Japan opened the Portsmouth meeting with two sham demands—that Russia surrender ships interned in Chinese ports during the war and limit its naval forces in the Far East—thrown in simply as bargaining tools. Negotiator Komura was empowered to withdraw the two demands if necessary. Before letting them go, however, he tried to trade them for Japan's major demands —Sakhalin and an indemnity. Komura made his phony offer in language identical to that which the Japanese typically use when presenting genuine concessions. He stated that, moved by a "sincere desire" (*seijitsu naru kibō*) to reach agreement, the Japanese would withdraw the demands for naval force limitation and surrender of interned ships if the Russians were willing to consider "in a spirit of conciliation" (*chōwa no seishin o motte*) the questions of the cession of Sakhalin and the reimbursement of war expenses.[63] Komura's ploy, totally transparent to the Russians, accomplished nothing.

It is difficult to consider Japan's harsh Group Five conditions during the Twenty-One Demands negotiations as truly sham proposals. Initial govern-

62. According to Fukuda Hajime, chairman of the LDP special textile policy committee, *Asahi shimbun*, Dec. 12, 1970.

63. *Nihon gaikō bunsho* (1905), vol. 5, pp. 482–483.

ment instructions did label these items as "completely separate" but at the same time referred to all five groups as "demands" (*yokyū*).[64] It was only after China leaked the demands to the Powers, who then started to pressure Japan, that Tokyo introduced a distinction between its Group Five "wishes" (*kibō*) and its other "demands." Even in the face of intense foreign pressure, Japan had backed off only slightly from these items by the time it issued its final ultimatum.[65]

The few times Japan has tried highly inflated demands it has failed to gain anything, mainly because they are obviously specious, outside the range of serious consideration. Subsequent Japanese withdrawal of such proposals has not served to enhance the credibility of fallback positions or to induce opposing concessions.

Postponement (*atomawashi*). Another hallowed bargaining precept is that chances of reaching agreement on major issues are improved if the sides first come to terms over less significant problems. This is the "domino" effect—each bargain that is struck, however unimposing in and of itself, bolsters mutual trust, enlarges expectations, and raises prospects of securing an overall agreement. As a tactical matter it may be profitable for a negotiator to concede on relatively insubstantial problems at the beginning and then to use these previous concessions later as proof of his "good faith," to shift the initiative for compromise to the opponent, and to extract counterconcessions on more critical items.

Postponement is a common Japanese tactic, particularly on key issues involving measurable rights and interests. By comparison, the Japanese have been much more willing to concur "in principle" to vague abstractions like the "Open Door," the right of "equal opportunity," or Chinese "territorial integrity." But they never concede quickly on issues of pivotal concern.

During the Twenty-One Demands talks, negotiator Hioki postponed debate on certain Japanese conditions each time he encountered stiff Chinese resistance.[66] In these negotiations, postponement was prompted by the desire not to

64. "Instructions for the Sino-Japanese Negotiations."
65. The Chinese side had leaked the demands by Feb. 15, 1915. Even though Katō told the Chinese minister to Tokyo on Feb. 18 that Japan would be unaffected by European and American opinion concerning the demands, Japan was plainly compelled by the Chinese action to admit the contents of the previously secret Group Five to the Powers and, later, to offer concessions because of foreign protests and anticipated pressure.
Only the demand for joint police forces was actually dropped from Group Five before the May ultimatum. Before China leaked the demands Japan had been talking of conceding somewhat on this group (see Hioki to Katō, Feb. 12), but mostly the Japanese tried to trade off items in it for gains on conditions they perceived as more vital in groups Two and Three (see Katō to Hioki, Apr. 12, 1915). Both in *Nihon gaikō bunsho* (1915), vol. 3.
66. Katō to Hioki, Feb. 26; Katō to Hioki, Mar. 8; Katō to Hioki, Mar. 24 (cable 269); Hioki to Katō, Mar. 27; Katō to Hioki, Mar. 28; and Hioki to Katō, Apr. 17; in *Nihon gaikō bunsho* (1915), Vol. 3, pp. 191, 210, 265–267, 268–269, and 331–332.

antagonize the Powers by an immediate use of force, not to terminate the negotiations, and to delay a settlement on Group Five that might run counter to
the original Japanese position. But the scheme was a tactical disaster. It permitted the Chinese to separate the demands and to trade one off against
another. More crucially, by pushing too hard and too long for plainly unacceptable demands, Japan gave the Chinese time to mobilize their surprisingly
potent resources in the form of support from foreign allies. By the end, Japan
was on the defensive and China could confidently reject concessions on some
key issues. Similarly, once it had become evident during the 1940–1941 Neutrality Pact negotiations that Japan could not persuade the Soviets to surrender North Sakhalin and, in fact, might even have to liquidate its coal and oil
holdings there, the Tokyo government repeatedly sought to defer these matters
until later.[67] Finally, Japan's pre-Pearl Harbor efforts to reach a modus vivendi
with the United States worked in the same framework—settling immediate
problems (Japanese withdrawal from Indochina, rescinding the U.S. order
freezing Japanese assets) and postponing resolution of thornier questions such
as China and the Tripartite Pact.

Impasse within the government over major changes in the Japanese position
is a factor leading to postponement, as illustrated by the recent textile negotiations. A 1970 Japanese plan for a U.S.-Japanese experts' conference was
postponed because of MITI and Gaimushō disagreement. Also in these negotiations, MITI resistance to concessions and the Satō government's inability to
obtain textile manufacturers' support led to postponement tactics in the form of
a general proposal for voluntary restrictions on textile exports with details
deferred until later.[68]

It is only against the backdrop of Japanese domestic politics that one can understand why a Japanese negotiator will try to postpone an item until later
when compromise seems inevitable. Most Japanese negotiators defer controversial items to the end simply because they are not authorized to concede. As
initial Japanese bargaining decisions are reached only after herculean preliminary work, subsequent changes involving substantial concessions also require
monumental effort. Delaying resolution of particular issues is perhaps not so
much a Japanese tactic, therefore, as the nearly inescapable concomitant of rigid bargaining procedures, highly dedicated negotiators, and a deep-rooted fear
of anything that smacks of capitulation to the other side.

67. Tatekawa had argued that a treaty should be concluded before taking up North Sakhalin concessions and other problems. Matsuoka, obviously on the defensive, attempted to
defer definite resolution of the concessions: "At the earliest opportunity we shall try to settle
issues relating to the North Sakhalin concessions in the spirit of mutual compromise." *TSM*,
Vol. 5, p. 293.

68. *Asahi shimbun* and *Japan Times*, Dec. 8–9, 1970.

Contingent offers: "You go first." Another persistant Japanese persuasive device is the contingent offer. Japanese tend to make their own concessions explicitly dependent on and therefore subsequent to opposing concessions. In bargaining, such Japanese contingent offers function as preconditions—being the logical extension into formal negotiations of their prebargaining technique of securing opposing commitments and promises. Moreover, Japanese middle-stage offers, promises, and other responses are often quite ambiguous, as are the prebargaining efforts to escape commitment.

During the 1916 negotiations with Russia, negotiator Motono was specifically instructed neither to divulge the details of Japan's offer of arms and ammunition nor to show a willingness to discuss a treaty of alliance until after Russia had agreed to cede the entire Harbin-Changchun section of the Chinese Eastern Railway.[69] At the Dairen Conference five years later, Japan demanded that the Far Eastern Republic (*inter alia*) destroy all military fortifications in Vladivostok, pledge never to maintain naval forces in the Pacific, and lease North Sakhalin to Japan for eighty years as compensation for the Nikolaevsk incident, after which Japan would withdraw its forces occupying North Sakhalin. Throughout these negotiations, Japanese bargainer Matsushima Hajime refused to commit himself to an evacuation date more specific than "as soon as possible," and even when he mentioned one toward the end of the negotiations, his offer had so many qualifications that Soviet acceptance was out of the question.[70]

During the 1941 U.S.-Japanese discussions, Tokyo's September 6 proposal in effect asked Washington to perform a series of actions (stop interfering with Japan's management of the China incident, resume commercial relations, close the Burma Road, cease all aid to Chiang Kai-shek, and contribute to economic cooperation between Japan, Thailand, and the Netherlands East Indies) and to refrain from several others (increasing its forces in the Far East, acquiring military rights in Thailand, the Netherlands East Indies, China, or the Far Eastern part of the Soviet Union). Only after the United States had conceded to all these demands was Japan to offer its own concessions (no advance beyond Indochina, withdrawal from French Indochina after the establishment of a "just" peace, a guarantee of Philippine neutrality, and an "independent" Japanese interpretation of obligations under the Tripartite

69. Ishii to Motono, Feb. 15, 1916; Ishii to Motono, Feb. 17, 1916; Motono to Ishii, Feb. 19, 1916; in *Nihon gaikō bunsho* (1916), vol. 1, pp. 120–124. Motono was to keep the exact quantity of arms and ammunition vague at first, stating merely that Japan would provide "as much as we can," or "to a certain extent" (*jakkan no teido made*). See *Nichi-Ro kōshō shi*, vol. 2, pp. 323–326.

70. *TSM*, vol. 1, pp. 211–214; Lensen, *Japanese Recognition of the USSR*, pp. 26–30.

Pact to assist Germany and Italy in the event the United States joined the European conflict).[71]

In dealing with weaker adversaries Japan has combined the contingent offer with the package deal. In this way Kawakami Toshihiko in conversations with

Figure 1
Positional Adjustment Sequence during the
Chinese Eastern Railroad Negotiations, 1933–1935

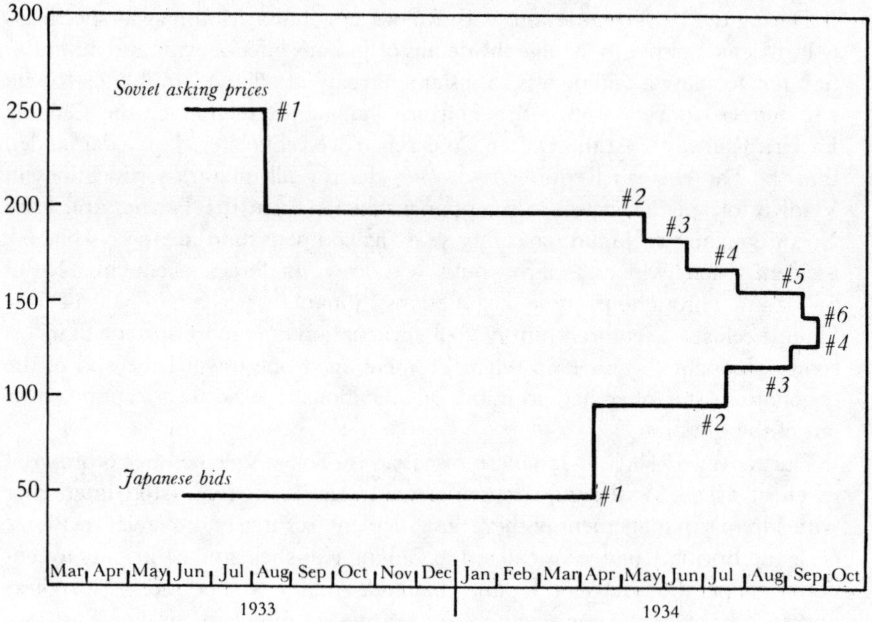

*Price in millions
of rubles*

*Movement from original position
(in millions of rubles)*

Move:	#1	#2	#3	#4	#5	#6
Soviet Union:	–50	–10	–20	–10	–15	–5
Japan:	–50	–20	–10	–10		

71. Imperial Conference, Sept. 6, 1941, records in *Sugiyama memo*, vol. 1, pp. 313–314, 321–323, trans. in Ike, *Japan's Decision for War*, pp. 135–136, 152–163. The preliminary draft which eventually culminated in the September 6 decision had included these jokers: *"dekirukagiri sumiyaka ni"* (as quickly as possible), concerning Japan's withdrawal from China; *"jishuteki ni okonau"* (to be determined independently), regarding Japan's obligations under the Tripartite Pact if the United States entered the European War; and *"kōsei naru kiso"* (fair basis), to describe the standard by which U.S. economic activity in China was to be judged. Matsumoto Shingo, "Nichi-Bei kōshō to Chūgoku mondai," *Kokusai seiji* 2 (1967):85.

Soviet negotiator Adolph Joffe in 1923 offered to set a definite date for evacuating North Sakhalin only if Joffe first agreed to accept all Japan's demands, and to grant certain specific rights in North Sakhalin for a given period of time.[72] During the Twenty-One Demands negotiations, Japan's strategy was first to secure Peking's acceptance, in principle, of all its conditions, after which Japan would present its exchange items (*kōkan jōken*) or inducements (*yūin jōken*) including the return of Kiaochow to China. To add insult to injury, Japan even attached extra strings to the package in the form of conditions to the Kiaochow offer.[73]

Gradual retreats from starting positions. Once the need to compromise has been accepted during bargaining, the question is how. For Japan, the answer invariably is slowly and grudgingly. This Japanese predeliction for step-by-step retreat from initial positions is perhaps most evident in negotiations dealing with subject matter capable of precise measurement. Figure 1 shows the gradual increase in Japan's bids, in decreasing amounts for each bid, for the Chinese Eastern Railroad during negotiations with the Soviet Union between 1933 and 1935.[74] Figure 2 illustrates Japan's positional shifts during the London Naval Conference, showing its firm stand on heavy cruisers and its readiness to adjust tonnages in other ship categories. Also clear in this figure is how closely the final outcome compared with Japan's original position.[75] Another example is the way Tokyo backed off on the northern territorial issue during the 1955–1956 negotiations with the Soviet Union:

1. Demand the Habomais, Shikotan, the Kuriles, and Sakhalin.
2. Demand Habomais, Shikotan, South Kuriles (Etorofu and Kunashiri); refer the disposition of the North Kuriles and South Sakhalin to an international conference.
3. Demand Habomais, Shikotan; drop demand for international conference if Soviets will cede South Kuriles.
4. Demand Habomais, Shikotan (immediate return); Soviets to negotiate on South Kuriles as part of later peace treaty; disposition of North Kuriles and South Sakhalin subject to provisions of San Francisco Treaty.
5. Demand Habomais, Shikotan (immediate return); South Kuriles return when U.S. returns Okinawa to Japan, Japan will renounce claims to North Kuriles and South Sakhalin.

72. This was very similar to the approach employed right up to the start of official negotiations in Peking in 1924. Kobayashi Yukio, "Nisso kokkō juritsu no ichi dammen," *Rekishi kyōiku*, vol. 9, no. 2 (1961), p. 28; also *Nisso kōshō shi*, pp. 62–63.
73. "Instructions for the Sino-Japanese Negotiations."
74. Derived from material in *Nisso kōshō shi*, pp. 297–304.
75. Derived from *TSM*, Vol. 1, pp. 65–68.

Figure 2
Japan's Positional Adjustment Sequence during the
London Naval Conference, 1930

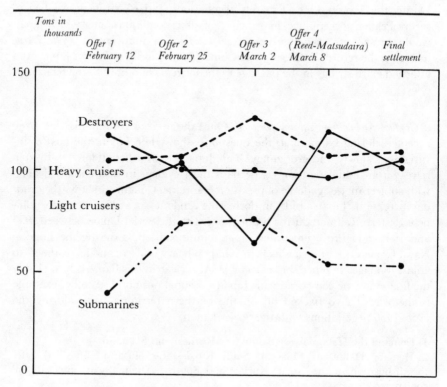

6. Demand Habomais, Shikotan (immediate return); Soviets to negotiate on South Kuriles as part of later peace treaty.
7. Sign normalization agreement, deferring territorial issue.[76]

STAGE THREE: THE TACTICS OF LAST RESORT

In international negotiations, according to Iklé, each party has a constant three-fold option—to compromise, to terminate, or to continue bargaining.[77] Of course, these alternatives exist throughout negotiations, but at some more or

76. It should be noted that this list sets forth positions as they developed during these ne-gotiations; Tokyo had not established these fallback positions in advance. Derived from Mat-sumoto, *Mosukuwa ni kakeru niji;* Hellmann, *Japanese Domestic Politics and Foreign Policy;* and *Japan Times*, May 1955–November 1956 (prior to July 1, 1956, *Nippon Times*).
    77. Iklé, *How Nations Negotiate*, pp. 61–62.

less identifiable point a choice must be made. By this stage, the nature and firmness of opposing minimums have been tested, a number of bargains struck, fallback positions exhausted, and the negotiator has dispatched his views of the chances of wringing further concessions from the other side. Moreover, contextual pressures inherent in bargaining (time, reciprocating concessions, domestic factors, third party influences) have served to constrict remaining options even more. With evaporation of the desire to go on bargaining, at least in the manner of stage two, negotiations advance to the final phase.

Final-stage Japanese decisions

Self-commitment moves are at the heart of Japanese tactical style and a principal source of their bargaining strength. Its leaders and diplomats are adept at fastening themselves securely to a position through a variety of commitment devices and then stubbornly refusing to let go. In fact, they are far more skillful at commitment than at persuasive techniques. Such Japanese tactics as watchful waiting, avoiding early commitment, deferring major concessions until the opponent has compromised, submitting plainly unacceptable demands again and again, mobilizing domestic public opinion behind their most extreme conditions, all have the effect of contributing to rigidity and forcing Japan on the defensive as negotiations approach their dénouement. When thwarted in obtaining bargaining goals, there seems to be no alternative except to persist. The result, virtually without exception, is that the Japanese find that they have painted themselves into a corner by decisions they have made or failed to make during the preliminary and middle stages. Final decisions —whether to sever negotiations, to compromise, or to resort to arms—are complicated by earlier Japanese commitments. These decisions can be taken only after the most wrenching reappraisal of previous bargaining policy. The Japanese talent for self-commitment, ironically, makes uncoupling from earlier positions agonizingly difficult.

Implicit in final Japanese bargaining decisions is a two-step justification process: a thorough cleansing of preceding decisions until they are free of any policy blemishes, followed by an often frenetic search for ways of shifting any fault for losses incurred, or to be incurred, away from the leaders/negotiators themselves. These devices do not, of course, enable policy-makers to escape final choices and decisions. They structure the framework within which a final, and politically safer, decision can be reached, with very little room for adjustment.

Conscience-clearing devices. Before Japanese government leaders can transfer blame for failure elsewhere, they first seek to reaffirm the absolute purity of their original policy.[78] It is equally important in this conscience-clearing process to prove that earlier devisions were reached only after the most "careful deliberations" and that "due caution" had been exercised.[79] A third cluster of Japanese bargaining norms—'patience," "calmness," and "bearing the unbearable"—are evident in this policy justification process. Like "great efforts" or "due caution," these also imply unyielding dedication, but they further suggest such Japanese bargaining ideals as stoic impassivity, imperturbability, and coolness under fire. And perhaps more than the previous two categories, this group of norms imparts an aura of arrogance.[80] Finally, it is maintained that Japan has been "reasonable," "fair," "moderate," "magnanimous," and "compromising" throughout negotiations, both in its general attitude and its presentation of concrete concessions. In short, it is typically asserted that the Japanese government has done everything possible by "compromising what is compromisable," and has made "great sacrifices" to show its "good faith."[81]

Another Japanese pattern in structuring final bargaining moves is to dispel any doubts about their choice. Phrases such as "unavoidable" (*yamu o ezu*), "nothing else but to" (*hoka wa nashi*), or "no room but to" (*yochi wa nashi*), suggesting despair, fatalistic resignation, and even desperation, are scattered throughout closing Japanese bargaining statements. Whatever the substance of the final decision itself—concession, threat, ultimatum, breakoff—it is invariably framed as "bearing the unbearable." This is the product of a kind of

78. At least in part, this means detailing how punctiliously various Japanese bargaining norms have been followed. It is common, for instance, for the Japanese government and those representing it to rationalize final moves with the assertion that "great efforts" have been made, albeit in an ultimately futile cause. Thus, "our plenipotentiaries met repeatedly with the British and American delegates but, *despite our having exerted every effort* to obtain our demands, there was no convergence of opinion." See "Final Instructions to the Japanese Delegation to the London Naval Conference," Apr. 1, 1930, *NGN*, Vol. 2, pp. 149–150.

79. For example, "On the heavy cruiser issue, our delegates followed their instructions and we employed *great caution* [*shinchō*]. After *careful consideration* [*seisa*], we have decided . . ." See ibid., p. 155.

80. To wit, "For over half a year *we have endured what is difficult to endure*. Our endurance up to now stems from our desire for peace. But *there is a limit to our patience.*" Or, "The Japanese government has tried to bring negotiations to a successful conclusion and has *borne the unbearable* to avoid complications in the situation." See "Final Ultimatum," Twenty-One Demands negotiations, May 7, 1915, *NGN*, vol. 2, pp. 402–404.

81. Thus, "in our conduct of negotiations we have had the most sincere and fair attitude" (*shinsei to kōsei naru taido*). See Tōgō statement before the Nov. 5, 1941, Imperial Conference, *Sugiyama memo*, Vol. 1, p. 420, trans. in Ike, *Japan's Decision for War*, p. 213. To see how these various norms were combined in final stage communications, one might consider the following cursory content analysis of the Nov. 4, 1941 instructions from the Japanese government to Ambassador Nomura Kichisaburō in Washington, which contained three criticisms of the opposition (for being "uncompromising," for doubting Japan's "intentions," and for having ignored previous Japanese compromises); ten self-congratulatory statements (two references each to Japanese "sincerity," "careful deliberations," "patience," "peaceful intentions," and "past compromises"); four comments that reflected on the gravity of the situation itself; five exhortations for Nomura to exert "great efforts"; and two appeals to Nomura to adhere to his instructions. Tōgō Shigenori, *Jidai no ichimen* (Tokyo: Kaizōsha, 1952), pp. 217–219.

situational determinism whereby ending moves are described so as to cast Japan as the helpless victim of circumstance (the commonest of many Japanese phrases expressing this idea is *"kyūchi ni ochiita"* or "we have fallen into a difficult spot"), buffeted about by forces beyond its control. "No matter how long we wait," negotiator Wakatsuki warned Tokyo at the waning stage of the 1930 London Naval Conference, "they will never concede."[82]

Another characteristic feature of final Japanese decisions is that they are generally structured as being between two polar alternatives (typically *"nisha takuitsu"* or "two things, pick one"). As Wakatsuki posed final options for Tokyo in 1930, "we must give in or leave."[83] In negotiations with the United States in 1941 the Japanese perceived their choices as indescribable hardship (*gashinshōtan*) or war, and although both options were denigrated, the less favored one (in this case *gashinshōtan*) was pictured as particularly unappetizing.[84] Similarly, at the closing stage of the protracted U.S.-Japanese textile negotiations, the Japanese side perceived only two alternatives: "to make wholesale concessions or to terminate negotiations" (*zenmenjōho suru ka, chūdan suru ka*).[85]

The effort of Japanese policy-makers to preclude or erase any personal blame for failed policies is partially served by the Japanese habit of limiting final choices. Reduction of the number of choices limits the possible decisions and, by implication, the chances for failure or an embarrassing situation where someone must bear responsibility for miscarried policies. "We have no choice" is, in effect, the perfect ex post facto rationalization permitting individual or collective redemption from the stigma of bargaining failure.

Shifting the blame. Having officially declared themselves free of any mistakes or mismanagement, the architects of Japanese negotiating policy then seek to pin the blame on someone or something else. Beneath attempts to transfer the blame is the belief that Japanese policies are intrinsically correct. Therefore, any conflict arising during bargaining must be the unfortunate (and by implication avoidable) consequence of some kind of misunderstanding, diplomatic bungling, or mistaken translation. Although bargaining policies themselves can never admittedly be wrong, the agents who have administered policy or their methods can be, at least in the sense that they failed to work as anticipated.

The negotiator and his techniques are often singled out for criticism when initial plans have gone astray. He is most frequently charged with timidity,

82. Wakatsuki to the Japanese government, Mar. 15, 1930, *NGN*, Vol. 2, p. 146.
83. Ibid.
84. See Liaison Conference, Oct. 31, 1941, *Sugiyama memo*, vol. 1, p. 362, trans. in Ike, *Japan's Decision for War*, p. 198.
85. *Asahi shimbun*, Dec. 14, 1970.

with having failed to push hard enough to win (thus violating the Japanese negotiating norm of great efforts). He is on occasion accused of violating his instructions, miscommunication, linguistic incompetence, or even disloyalty. Another frequent target is the negotiating methods that have been employed. To offer just one example, in the following citation a former Japanese diplomat attacks slipshod prebargaining work for the breakdown of the first round of Soviet-Japanese negotiations for sale of the Chinese Eastern Railway in 1933:

There had been no informal exchange of views before negotiations; nor had there been any special consultations concerning how the conference would be handled. . . . For both sides to submit proposals reflecting just their own one-sided points of view was totally inappropriate . . . and . . . rather like amateur *sumō* wrestlers who lunge forward without first toeing the mark.[86]

Final-stage tactics

Last-ditch moves to save the situation. The numbing uniformity of Japan's tactical style is most openly exposed during the culminating phase. Although leaders and diplomats have already flung themselves repeatedly against opposing positions in search of agreement without major compromise, they feel compelled to try once more, to turn to what might be termed tactics of last resort.

Unbending Japanese faith in the rightness of their bargaining plans leads to inflexible decisions throughout negotiations, inhibits compromise, and blocks understanding of other viewpoints. It thus produces much hand-wringing by officials, an atmosphere of crisis, and sharply defined final choices.

Japanese self-righteous resolve also implies averting open confrontations, deferring concessions, and retreating gradually from original positions. This attitude fosters the belief that if only the right method could be discovered, difficult final adjusting decisions might not have to be made at all. By this reasoning, any issue can be settled with the proper means. Japan's reliance on devices to adjust the trappings rather than the substance of positions, then, finds expression in the conviction that if the right negotiator can be found, if Japan's "true intentions" (*shin'i*) can be communicated clearly to the other side, if there can be a "man-to-man discussion" (*hito to hito to no hanashiai*), or a "frank exchange of views" (*fukuzō naki iken no kōkan*), or if someone can come up with a dramatic gesture or the right formula, it is possible to "achieve a breakthrough" (*nankyoku o dakai; kyokumen o dakai*) and "save the situation" (*jikyoku o shūshū*).

Japan's final stage techniques—the closest Japan ever comes to a genuine combination of moves—are conceived more as communication devices than as tactics. These actions are based on the proposition that the opponent has failed to grasp the inner substance of what Japan is trying to achieve. According to

86. Morishima Moritō, *Imbō, ansatsu, guntō* (Tokyo: Iwanami Shoten, 1950), p. 107.

this reasoning, once such a misunderstanding is swept away, the opposing side, at last able to understand the actual situation, will quickly and spontaneously accede to Japanese terms and sign an accord without delay.

The direct personal appeal. Prominent in final stage Japanese bargaining behavior is an emphasis on direct personal contact with opposing negotiators or leaders, a method previously most evident at the prebargaining phase. A common move is the last minute personal appeal to opposing negotiators—the ultimate great effort—which, if abortive, can help the Japanese pin the blame for failure on the other side.

In 1939 an inability to transmit messages clearly to Germany and Italy lay behind Foreign Minister Arita's suggestion that Prime Minister Hiranuma cable Hitler and Mussolini personally to explain Japan's policy and to ascertain the final German and Italian positions on a proposed tripartite connection. Others in Tokyo wanted Hiranuma to go to Berlin in person. Arita wanted the prime minister to bypass "untrustworthy agents" (Ōshima Hiroshi in Berlin and Shiratori Toshio in Rome) in order to inform German and Italian leaders of Japan's point of view directly and frankly. This was the genesis of the later "Hiranuma message."[87]

This tactic also stems from the need to overcome impasse within the Japanese government, to have someone shoulder the responsibility for adverse bargaining fortunes. During final-hour government deliberations in 1915 over whether to present an ultimatum to the Chinese, the genrō Yamagata, disturbed by Western complaints about Japan's policies and tactics in the negotiations, blamed Foreign Minister Katō for the deadlock. He put the question bluntly to Katō: "If you admit this responsibility, is it not your duty to proceed to China as special ambassador and attempt a final settlement?"[88]

When the Japanese-Soviet Neutrality Pact negotiations stalled in late 1940, principally because the Japanese army, navy, and Foreign Ministry would not agree on the scale of commitment to the Axis that Japan should undertake under the proposed accord, Foreign Minister Matsuoka decided to take personal command of the negotiations, travel to Moscow himself, and "at a stroke" (*ikkyo ni*) conclude an agreement. But he left Tokyo the following March with no intention of altering earlier Japanese offers already proved to be insufficient for a settlement. In the face of judgments by both former negotiators (Tatekawa Yoshitsugu and Tōgō Shigenori) that Moscow would spurn his proposed nonagression pact and would make Japan liquidate its existing concessionary holdings in North Sakhalin, Matsuoka put his faith in German promises of help in pressuring the Russians to accept his proposals. He even

87. *TSM*, Vol. 5, pp. 120, 426–427; Arita Hachirō, *Bakahachi to hitowa iu: ichi gaikōkan no kaisō* (Tokyo: Kōwadō, 1959), p. 99.
88. Cited in Hackett, *Yamagata Aritomo*, p. 288.

thought he could convince Russian leaders to let Japan purchase North Sakhalin outright.[89] But Ribbentrop's mediation with the Soviets proved useless; in fact, he exaggerated Japan's desire for an agreement and as a result stiffened Soviet resolve to make Japan relinquish its North Sakhalin holdings. Matsuoka's other ploys (such as scheduling his Berlin visit ahead of the Moscow negotiations for a psychological impact on the Soviets) were equally impotent. Indeed, his pilgrimage to Berlin and Moscow was by any measure a failure, as Japan eventually settled for about what had been anticipated by more pragmatic minds all along.

Perhaps the best known of the prewar examples are Japan's crisis resolution tactics during the 1941 negotiations with the United States.[90] Here again Japanese leaders hoped to reach a settlement merely by adjusting their negotiating methods, as illustrated by Tokyo's initiatives in August to arrange a Konoe-Roosevelt summit meeting. Japanese leaders claimed that their efforts to organize the meeting proved their good faith and that the conference would enable the two countries to break the deadlock at a stroke.[91] And the "Konoe message" proposing the meeting seemed to deny the grave differences that divided Washington and Tokyo at that time, blaming a "lack of understanding" (*ishi no sotsū*) and "mutual suspicion and misapprehensions" for deteriorating relations and declaring that to eliminate such causes of discord,

I [Konoe] wish to meet Your Excellency *personally* for a *frank exchange of views....* I consider it ... of urgent necessity that [we] should meet first to discuss *from a broad standpoint* all important problems ... and explore the possibility of *saving the situation* [Italics added].[92]

The summit conference plan miscarried because several top American leaders, especially Secretary Hull, wanted explicit Japanese commitments and concessions in advance. Kurusu Saburō's heralded mission to Washington three months later was likewise little more than a gesture, as he carried no new concessions with him. His rescue operation was inspired by the hope that something could be done, as Kurusu put it, "to tide over the present abnormal situation." Despite his personal eagerness for a quick settlement, such a prospect was bleak at that late date.[93]

Prime Minister Hatoyama's journey to Moscow in October 1956 to restart the stalled normalization talks with the Soviet Union is a postwar example of

89. *TS* vol. 5, pp. 286–287; Horinouchi, *Nihon gaikō shi*, Vol. 21, pp. 278–284.

90. Other examples are Gotō Shimpei's mission to Moscow during the late 1920s when fishing negotiations had foundered, and similar attempts in earlier years by Inoue Kaoru, Itō Hirobumi, and Ōkubo Toshimichi.

91. *Sugiyama memo*, Vol. 1, pp. 92, 420, 558.

92. Note dated Aug. 26, 1941, *NGN*, vol. 2, p. 543.

93. Dec. 1, 1941 memorandum in Department of State, *Peace and War: United States Foreign Policy, 1931–1941* (Washington, D.C.: Government Printing Office, 1943), p. 822; also pp. 794–795, 806.

similarly motivated Japanese bargaining behavior. Although two previous negotiators (Matsumoto Shun'ichi and Shigemitsu Mamoru) were convinced that the Russians would not surrender on the key territorial issue, Hatoyama felt a personal effort would "wring maximum concessions from the Soviets."[94]

During the final stage the Japanese negotiator or his representative will informally sound out opposing leaders to test if their positions are firm and if further concessions might be forthcoming. These initiatives are motivated by a desire to open up the heart, to speak frankly, and to have a free and open (*jiyū taikan*) exchange of views. At the 1924–1925 Peking Conference, for example, after Soviet negotiator Lev Karakhan offered what he called "final" concessions and threatened breakoff if Japan refused to comply, Yoshizawa then tried the personal touch. He called on Karakhan alone to see if another Soviet draft proposal might be forthcoming. As one might imagine, Karakhan yielded nothing beyond his previous "final" offer.[95]

When the London Naval Conference talks reached a crisis, Wakatsuki requested an informal meeting with MacDonald to convey his intense personal commitment to obtain an agreement. Reminding MacDonald of his orders to leave the conference if Japan's demands were not met, Wakatsuki confided darkly that the slightest Japanese compromise would imperil his political reputation and his life. But he scoffed at these risks "if some way could be found to make the conference succeed." In his memoirs Wakasuki seems much impressed with the impact this declaration of resolve had on MacDonald. Wakatsuki recorded that MacDonald was "moved" by the admission, "shook my hand and quietly left the room." The next day Wakatsuki met Stimson privately to settle remaining differences on the cruiser ratio problem. In his later account of the meeting, the Japanese head negotiator is struck by the fact that Stimson simply penciled in tonnage figures on a piece of paper ("If he had been Japanese, he would have used an abacus"), and that they were personally able to hammer out a tentative settlement on the spot.[96]

At multilateral conferences or in bilateral settings in which Japan is on the defensive, Japanese diplomats usually initiate such personal crisis-resolution meetings. To cite a postwar example, when talks with the Soviets had broken down in early 1956, it was the Japanese negotiator who sought a private meeting with Soviet bargainer Malik "in view of the gravity of the situation." Matsumoto felt that the territorial question might be settled if only both sides

94. *Asahi shimbun*, Aug. 19, 1956. More details appear in Hatoyama's memoirs: "When Shigemitsu's negotiations ended, I felt that, as the person most responsible for the negotiations, I would have to go to Moscow and handle the final bargaining myself." See Hatoyama Ichirō, *Hatoyama Ichirō kaikoroku* (Tokyo: Bungei Shunjū Shinsha, 1957), p. 195.

95. *Pekin kaigi gijiroku*, meeting 43, Oct. 30, 1924, supp. p. 747; Leonid Nikolaevich Kutakov, *Nisso gaikō kankei shi*, trans. from the Russian by the Soviet Diplomatic Research Council (Tokyo: Tōe Shoin, 1965), vol. 1, p. 84.

96. Wakatsuki Reijirō, *Kofūan kaikoroku* (Tokyo: Yomiuri Shimbunsha, 1950), pp. 352–353.

could have a full and frank (*jūbun kaku'i naki*) exchange of views. Malik refused.[97]

A variation on this theme appeared when the U.S.-Japanese textile talks were on the verge of collapse late in 1970. Fukuda Hajime, chairman of the LDP special textile committee, was chosen to head a small delegation to Washington to achieve a breakthrough in the negotiations (*kōshō o dakai suru tame*). To accomplish this goal, the mission was to communicate that non-agreement on textiles might bring down the Satō government, that Japan had exerted "every effort" toward a settlement by making sizable concessions, and that many Japanese textile firms were going bankrupt. Besides conveying these messages to the Americans, however, Fukuda and the others had an unstated objective: to assess the mood in the United States and, on returning to Japan, to help work out a compromise with domestic textile manufacturers. As it turned out, they played a pivotal role in this process.[98]

The compliant Japanese negotiator and arbitrary action (dokudan senkō). Understanding Japan's final stage bargaining style requires an appreciation of the precarious position of the Japanese negotiator. He is subjected to intense pressures. Trapped in a web of overlapping and often conflicting loyalties and obligations—to his own domestic bureaucratic group, his own policy preferences, his individual political ambitions, and the overall success of the negotiations—he is weighted down with duties and responsibilities, buoyed up by high hopes. Despite his inflated expectations, however, he is usually relegated to a subordinate role and given limited discretionary authority. As the extent of his authorized power nearly always embraces larger issues of policy responsibility within the government, he is frequently cautioned "not to go too far." When he is given more substantial authority, its precise extent is often ambiguous. If he wants to exercise his own discretion beyond the lines drawn in his instructions, he is ever aware that any such move must be approved by Tokyo—an unlikely prospect, especially if he asks in advance. The pluralistic and particularistic features of the Japanese political system mean that he must bargain with Tokyo as much as with the opponent. At prewar international meetings (such as the Versailles Conference, the Washington Conference, or the London Naval Conference) he was asked to command mistrustful, recalcitrant, and occasionally openly rebellious dissidents who often elevated their own interests above those of the government or negotiating leaders. Finally, he is repeatedly placed in an awkward position because the Japanese political system does not tend to allow clear decisions to be made quickly. Therefore, he is caught squarely in the crossfire, stranded in a situation requiring flexibility while controlled by leaders of a political system in which the methods of operation seemingly defy any hope of flexibility.

97. Matsumoto, *Mosukuwa ni kakeru niji*, p. 83.
98. *Asahi shimbun*, Dec. 14, 1970 and Oct. 8, 1971; *Japan Times*, Dec. 15, 1970.

In view of these pressures, it is scarcely surprising that the Japanese negotiator is rarely in full accord with government policy. Often his policy preferences collide frontally with those of his superiors in Tokyo, and he tends to be more amenable to compromise than they.[99] Compared to the leaders in Japan, nearly every negotiator studied here was more willing to believe opposing bargainers when they claimed "this is our final offer."

A typical example is negotiator Ushiba during the U.S.-Japanese textile negotiations in 1970. According to press accounts, Ushiba was unhappy that Tokyo urged him to break the impasse in the negotiations without providing him with the means to do so in the form of revised instructions. Able only to repeat previous Japanese positions, he finally saw "no alternative" but to accept the American proposals.[100]

Further, the Japanese negotiator has tended to act according to his relatively pliant views, to take matters into his own hands when put on the spot in bargaining. He has frequently taken unsanctioned positions despite the chance that such independent moves might not be underwritten later in Tokyo. Briefly, he has tended to resort to what in Japanese is called "arbitrary action."

Typically, arbitrary action includes, first, moves taken in violation of explicitly prescribed orders: offering unsanctioned commitments, twisting the meaning of instructions, ignoring government orders, failing to transmit messages to or from the opposition, or refusing to carry out instructions. Second, there are less blatant infractions, independent actions taken by the negotiator without explicit bargaining orders: initiating discussions or sounding out the opponent in such a manner as to promote personal preferences over those of the government, failing to report information quickly, and, when faced with ambiguous instructions, neglecting to clarify them but instead adapting them to suit his own purposes. A third, much more subtle, and in its long-term consequences perhaps more pernicious, variation of arbitrary action is the Japanese diplomat's habit of interposing himself between his own government and the bargaining adversary. Here too he contravenes traditionally accepted Western standards of negotiating conduct. After all, it is one thing to apologize for government indecision, delay, or inaction; it is altogether another matter to hint that one personally opposes government policy.

Nearly every diplomat whose performance was reviewed for this study had used one or more of these variations of arbitrary action. In fact, the practice has

99. The roster of these comparatively flexible prewar negotiators is long: Hayashi Tadasu, Motono Ichirō, Ishii Kikujirō, Makino Shinken, Katō Tomosaburō, Yoshizawa Kenkichi, Wakatsuki Reijirō, Ōshima Hiroshi, Shiratori Toshio, Tatekawa Yoshitsugu, Tōgō Shigenori, Matsuoka Yōsuke, Nomura Kichisaburō, Kurusu Saburō. It includes bargainers of all persuasions—hard and soft line, civilian and military, continental expansionist and liberal internationalist. In the two postwar cases Japanese bargainers were also more conciliatory than the government. Only Komura (Portsmouth Conference) and Hioki Eki (Twenty-One Demands), among all negotiators studied, were exceptions to this rule.

100. *Japan Times*, Nov. 2 and 23, Dec. 15, 1970.

been so common in Japanese negotiating behavior as to seem the norm rather than the exception.

It is during the crisis phase of bargaining that the Japanese negotiator most often exceeds, ignores, or distorts his instructions, usually by making unauthorized commitments or concessions. In November 1941, for instance, Kurusu and Nomura presented Japan's "*B*" fallback plan prematurely and without approval, feeling that further negotiations on the basis on Japan's previous, less-compromising "*A*" draft would be pointless.[101] In August 1956 during the closing stage of Soviet-Japanese normalization talks in Moscow, negotiator Shigemitsu thought he should wind up the negotiations even if that meant making unsanctioned concessions. On his own initiative he informed the Russians of his personal willingness to accept their proposal to return to Japan only the Habomais and Shikotan. He told Tokyo that efforts to gain more territory would be fruitless and risky. "Postponing the [territorial] issue will merely hurt our prestige, put us in a disadvantageous position, and might even threaten prospects for obtaining the Habomais and Shikotan. I am convinced we can safely compromise at this time."[102] And the next day he added: "An agreement acceptable to the Japanese people is impossible to achieve. Viewing the situation objectively, we must give in."[103] Shigemitsu was overruled.

Arbitrary action has been the Japanese bargainer's response to tensions largely caused by inadequate policy-making processes, the political system's incapacity to reach quick, unambiguous decisions. Time and again the decision-making apparatus bogs down over trivia and detail or becomes immobilized by bitter political rivalries. The resulting impasse creates a policy vacuum which the negotiator is repeatedly tempted, and in the end feels forced, to fill.

Threats and warnings. Threats and warnings, the heavy artillery of bargaining, can be analyzed on two levels. First, there are pressuring moves, operative mostly within the negotiating context, whose projected penalties include escalating demands, delaying, refusing to agree, recalling a negotiator, or breakoff. Their main risk is simply nonagreement.

That Japanese leaders and negotiators consider nonagreement seriously in every case is convincing testimony to their tenacity. In some prewar situations, such as the Twenty-One Demands, Shimonoseki, and the 1924–1925 Soviet-Japanese negotiations, the Japanese used threats of breakoff at every stage though most often during the crisis period. A Japanese threat of breakoff is usually linked to a final offer, such as Matsuoka's declaration, one day before

101. For these and other independent Japanese diplomatic actions taken during the 1941 U.S.-Japanese negotiations, see *TSM*, vol. 7, pp. 173–187; Hosoya Chihiro, "Gaimushō to chū-Bei taishikan," in Hoyosa et al., *Nichi-Bei kankei shi*, vol. 1, pp. 209–226; and Kurusu Saburō, *Hōmatsu no sanjūgonen* (Tokyo: Bunka Shoin, 1948), p. 98.

102. Matsumoto, *Mosukuwa ni kakeru niji*, p. 111.

103. Ibid., p. 112.

agreement was reached on the Neutrality Pact in 1941, that he had made his "last concession" and would leave Moscow if it were rejected.[104] When presenting final stage proposals at Shimonoseki in 1895, Itō warned the Chinese "these are absolutely our final concessions. No discussion on them will be tolerated. Just answer yes or no."[105] A decade later at Portsmouth, Komura, unhappy with the Russian response to his "final" offer, made undisguised plans to return to Japan and even had his hotel bill totaled up, just two days before both sides came to terms.[106]

Other threats occur outside the conference room and depend mostly on tacit communication for their effectiveness in bargaining. Examples of such extraconference techniques are seizing the adversary's fishing vessels, creating some sort of incident, harrassing opposing nationals, or refusing to allow the opposition to send messages in code (as actually happened in preliminary armistice negotiations at Shimonoseki in 1895 and in talks preparatory to the Peking Conference).

Direct pressure tactics are unusual in Japanese negotiating practice. Only five of the bargaining interactions examined here (Shimonoseki, Portsmouth, Twenty-One Demands, Chinese Eastern Railway, and the 1941 U.S.-Japanese talks) were conducted against a backdrop of possible violent action. And in only one instance (Twenty-One Demands) were extraconference pressuring devices used while negotiations were in progress. In this case negotiator Hioki badgered the Chinese side ceaselessly for leaking information, delaying, and failing to show a "compromising spirit." His efforts unavailing, Hioki finally complained, "threats are about as productive as the east wind blowing in a horse's ear."[107] Such frustration led to sterner measures, the dispatch of troops to Manchuria and Shantung, and eventually to the ultimatum which forced Peking to capitulate.

Japanese bargaining threats are expressed ambiguously. As Mutsu Munemitsu pointedly advised Li Hung-chang at Shimonoseki, "It would be unfortunate [*ikan*] if you don't agree with us and the talks are broken off."[108] Japan's 1915 ultimatum alluded ominously to the "necessary steps" Japan would take if China failed to submit a "satisfactory reply" by (this part was bitingly explicit) May 9 at 6 P.M.[109] Such circumlocutory threats do have an advantage of unpredictability, but they are also susceptible to misinterpretation (as was the case with a well-known 1941 Japanese message that Washington intercept-

104. *TSM*, Vol. 5, p. 293.

105. Mutsu, *Kenkenroku*, p. 240; also *Nihon gaikō bunsho* (1895), vol. 1, pp. 357–358 (April 11, 1895), pp. 361–362 (April 13, 1895), and pp. 414, 417–419.

106. *Komura gaikō shi*, vol. 2, p. 105; Okamoto, *The Japanese Oligarchy and the Russo-Japanese War*, p. 150.

107. Hioki to Katō, Mar. 27, 1915, *Nihon gaikō bunsho* (1915), vol. 3, pp. 264–267.

108. Mutsu, *Kenkenroku*, p. 404.

109. *NGN*, vol. 1, p. 403.

ed and perhaps wrongly translated as "things are automatically going to happen").

Final face-saving devices. When Japanese negotiators have been repeatedly rebuffed in attempts to push through their demands, they face a new situation by the final bargaining stage—not just another resistance point but a stark challenge to the central Japanese goal of victory without undue complications. This challenge is most serious if the other side has already made substantial concessions, for bargaining norms require the reciprocation of compromises. In these circumstances another technique surfaces: the last-ditch attempt to salvage something when earlier plans have gone awry and Japan decides to compromise.

At least five techniques are used to remove some of the sting from these closing compromises. First, the concession is discounted as the "inevitable product of extenuating circumstances" that have "forced" Japan, totally against its will, to accept the opponent's "illegitimate" demands.

Second are attempts to explain away the compromise as meaningless. At the London Naval Conference, Japan's acceptance of slightly less than its advocated ration of 70 percent of parity was dismissed as only a "temporary" inferiority. The final Japanese statement explaining the concession further provided that Japan was free to watch and wait because resolution of the issue was deferred until a conference in 1935.[110] The argument in effect was that the agreement did not impose constraints on Japan but permitted strengthening of its naval forces as the economy recovered from the depression.

A third method is to link the Japanese retreat to some opposing compromise, no matter how inconsequential. It cannot be openly admitted—for reasons of "face"—that pressure, threats, or overambitious Japanese policies have forced a concession. Thus, citing the London case once more, Tokyo's final decision to accept the American "compromise draft" was painstakingly explained in terms of earlier British and American concessions.[111]

A fourth technique, likewise a form of denial or avoidance, is to defer resolution of a problem until later, a final-stage extension of postponement. Matsuoka, for instance, was able to obscure his concession to Soviet leaders on the North Sakhalin issue in April 1941 by deferring a definitive settlement for "a few months."[112] Attempting to insert general statements explaining their position into conference records (such as at Versailles) is yet another variation of this common Japanese device.

A final face-sustaining method is to paper over unresolved conflicts, hiding potentially unpopular bargains in secret "understandings" or protocols, and

110. *NGN*, Vol. 2, pp. 154–155.
111. *NGN*, Vol. 2, pp. 154–155.
112. *TSM*, Vol. 5, pp. 293.

taking refuge in calculated ambiguity—in order to gain an agreement. Camouflaging unsettled issues allows each side to interpret the agreement later as it wishes. Paradoxically, through the fiction of an "agreement," the sides, in holding to their positions and resisting a settlement, can in effect bring it about. For example, in the Lansing-Ishii "Agreement" the shapeless standard of "geographical propinquity" was used to anchor equally blurred Japanese "special interests" in China. It is well known that both sides held vastly divergent conceptions of the degree of Japan's interest.[113] But had an explicit articulation and resolution of these dissimilar views been attempted, agreement would have been impossible.

Such face-saving techniques serve a vital domestic political function. By reducing the apparent size of concessions, they help to soften the potential reverberations of compromise, to placate the opposition at home, and to preempt postbargaining opposition attacks. By providing the government with a method of retrieving something, however small, they partially deter accusations that leaders have sold out to the opponent. Their chief target is domestic, although they are secondarily aimed at public and government opinion abroad.

Shifting the blame onto the opponent. When termination of negotiations rather than compromise is the chosen Japanese alternative, another face-saving tactic is commonly used: transfer the blame onto the other side. There is nothing surprising in this. In any decision to suspend a bargaining relationship—either temporarily by postponement or delay or permanently because of hopeless deadlock or resort to armed force—there is always considerable maneuvering by all sides to throw the onus onto the opponent.

Strictly, no single party is exclusively at fault. And yet, for several reasons, Japan repeatedly appears culpable when negotiations are about to be suspended or terminated. Further, Japanese officials seem to accept this burden passively, even willingly. Note, for example, this entry from the Saionji-Harada memoirs when the London Naval Conference had reached a showdown: "Saionji wanted a settlement because even if it should be France or Italy that brought about a rupture of the talks, it would be Japan's shilly-shallying . . . that would make it possible, and Japan will have to bear responsibility for such a rupture."[114] It seemed to Tokyo that they faced a Hobson's choice at that stage of the conference—reject the U.S. "compromise draft" and take the

113. Although recognizing its "flexibility," Tokyo was reluctant to accept the "amorphous" phrase "special interests." Motono to Satō, Oct. 6, 1917, in *Nihon gaikō bunsho* (1917), Vol. 3, p. 788.

114. Harada Kumao, ed. *Saionji-Kō to seikyoku* (Tokyo: Iwanami Shoten, 1956), vol. 1, p. 28, entry for March 25, 1930. With minor changes, as trans. by Thomas Mayer-Oakes in *Fragile Victory, Prince Saionji and the 1930 London Treaty Issue from the Memoirs of Baron Harada Kumao* (Detroit: Wayne State University Press, 1968), p. 98.

blame for a breakdown, or give in and be forced to modify long-standing national defense policies.[115] It was largely the desire to avoid responsibility for breakdown (plus the threat of an Anglo-American front against Japan) that led ultimately to the compromise engineered by the Hamaguchi cabinet.[116]

At the Washington Conference, Katō feared that continued Japanese persistence would merely create a similar dilemma in which Japan would either have to accept the U.S. proposals and be accused of capitulation in Japan, or reject them and cause the conference to collapse. If the conference failed, he felt, Japan would be responsible.[117] In the recent U.S.-Japanese textile negotiations there were scattered official and public Japanese accusations of American intransigence and disinterest in settling the issue. But most Japanese reacted to these stalled negotiations by blaming themselves. Compromises by Japan, it was claimed, were the only way to unlock the dispute and gain an agreement.[118]

Why do the Japanese so intimately identify their own concessions (or other action) as the sine qua non for an agreement? It takes two to negotiate, and the cause of failure rests as much with the side taking, for asking too much, as with the side being taken from, for not conceding enough. The following generalizations may help explain this tendency: Japan's leaders and diplomats so deeply internalize their commitment to agreement that they cannot imagine the other side blocking a settlement; by this stage they are generally on the tactical defensive for not conceding earlier; they are highly image-conscious and sensitive to potential foreign criticism; they recognize that the opponent has made compromises that Japan should reciprocate; and they realize that their own cumbersome decision-making processes have exacerbated difficulties during negotiations.

Whatever the reason, their heavy concern with responsibility for the breakdown (and implied policy failure) leads to a sometimes frantic campaign to cast the blame onto the other side. Bargaining norms, of course, preclude

115. James B. Crowley, *Japan's Quest for Autonomy: National Security and Foreign Policy, 1930–1938* (Princeton: Princeton University Press, 1966), p. 56. Officially there were four alternatives: (1) rejection of the U.S. proposal: (2) presentation of a new, revised draft; (3) acceptance of the U.S. proposal without alternation; and (4) acceptance of the proposal with "appropriate" reservations. The final option was chosen. *NGN*, vol. 2, pp. 150–154. See also Wakatsuki to Shidehara, Mar. 14, 1930, cited in *Gaimushō no hyakunen*, vol. 1, p. 925.

116. Admiral Takarabe was also anxious that Japan not be blamed for the breakoff, even though he differed from Wakatsuki in judging that there was room for further negotiation. He wished to extend the conference and try to force the opposition to accept the blame for any failure. *TSM*, Vol. 1, p. 72.

117. Asada, "Japan and the United States," pp. 232, 235; Thomas H. Buckley, *The United States and the Washington Conference, 1921–1922* (Knoxville: University of Tennessee Press, 1970), p. 86.

118. Gaimushō officials were especially given to such statements. *Japan Times*, Nov. 12, 17, 1970. Satō (in *Asahi shimbun*, Nov. 27, 1970) rejected rumors that he had reached a "secret agreement" with Nixon at their summit meeting a month before. Satō claimed the two leaders had merely agreed to "handle the issue in a spirit of mutual compromise" (*gokei-gojō seishin de yaru*).

any Japanese admission that the adversary has compromised (which implies reciprocation) or has any but the most malevolent of motives, tactics, and policies. Japan's references to opposing intransigence, unresponsiveness, bad faith, and the like are couched in the accepted idiom of bargaining. Thus, "the American government, adhering steadfastly to its original assertions, has failed to display in the slightest degree a spirit of conciliation. The negotiations made no progress" (U.S.-Japanese negotiations, 1941).[119] Or,

The Chinese May 1 reply completely failed to meet our expectations or to show good faith. . . . Moreover, the Chinese have scarcely responded at all to our concession to return Kaiochow, made at painful cost and in good faith. Their reply is empty rhetoric and totally lacks good faith and sincerity. [Twenty-One Demands negotiations].[120]

To give another example, in 1895 at Shimonoseki both Mutsu and Itō wanted to transfer responsibility for a rupture of the negotiations onto the Chinese.[121] And at the Portsmouth Conference ten years later, by making minor concessions early in the negotiations, the Russians effectively built up pressure on Japan to concede, a pitfall the Japanese did not avoid very skillfully.[122] The Japanese side sought to elude blame and worked out an arrangement with Roosevelt whereby he would make a final personal appeal to the czar. If the move proved unsuccessful, the blame for breakoff would fall upon Russia.[123] Komura wanted to break off the negotiations and issue a public statement listing Japanese concessions and blaming Russia for termination. But Komura's superiors in Tokyo elected to submit, because they feared being blamed for failure of the negotiations and were more aware than Komura of how the war situation had turned against Japan.[124]

Final-stage combinations. When termination of bargaining is the selected Japanese option, a pattern of ending moves surfaces. This typical closing sequence has four parts: (1) set a deadline or time limit for agreement on Japanese terms; (2) urge negotiators to exert "great efforts" to reach a settlement by "diplomatic means" before the deadline; (3) refuse, as before, to make Japan's own offers explicit; and (4) terminate negotiations with the claim that "we have no choice," blaming the other side for breakdown.

Toward the end of the Dairen Conference Japan decided to terminate the negotiations unless the Far Eastern Republic (obviously backed by the Soviet

119. U.S. Dept. of State, *Peace and War*, p. 833.

120. "Final Ultimatum," May 7, 1915, *NGN*, vol. 1, pp. 402–404.

121. Mutsu, *Kenkenroku*, p. 6.

122. *New York Times*, Aug. 16, 1905.

123. Eugene P. Trani, *The Treaty of Portsmouth: An Adventure in American Diplomacy* (Lexington, Ky.: University of Kentucky Press, 1969), p. 139.

124. *Komura gaikō shi*, vol. 2, p. 105; Komura to Katsura, Aug. 17, 1905, and "Substance of Cabinet Meeting concerning Japanese-Russian Informal Conference at Portsmouth," supp. 1 to telegram from Katsura to Komura, Aug. 28, 1905, *Nihon gaikō bunsho* (1905), Vol. 5, pp. 284 and 301.

Union) submitted to a ten-day ultimatum. At the same time the Japanese government ordered its representatives to make "final efforts" to induce the Far Eastern Republic to give in. The Far Eastern Republic, however, rejected the ultimatum, mainly because Japan failed to include a specific date for withdrawal from Russian territory.[125] Although Japan had already decided to withdraw, the insistence of the Far Eastern Republic on a definite date somehow made the Japanese doubt their motives. The result was a Japanese breakoff, and an accusatory statement:

> Whereas Japan has . . . throughout the negotiations maintained a sincere and conciliatory attitude, the Chita delegate entirely ignored the spirit in which we offered concessions and brought up one demand after another, thereby trying to gain time. Not only did he refuse to entertain Japanese proposals, but declared that he would drop the negotiations and return to Chita immediately.

> The only conclusion from this attitude of the Chita Government being that they lacked the sincerity with which to try to bring the negotiations to fruition, the Japanese Government has instructed their delegate to quit Dairen.[126]

Similarly, at the Changchun Conference, negotiator Matsudaira was ordered to leave if Tokyo's demands were not accepted by a fixed date (end of September 1922). If the Soviets failed to concede, he was to announce publicly that the Russians were wholly at fault for termination. Despite several later Russian concessions of minor importance, Japan continued to balk at giving a precise date for withdrawal from North Sakhalin, claiming that Tokyo would make that decision "independently." Ending the talks on September 25, Matsudaira issued a public statement blaming the Soviets for the breakoff.[127]

This terminating sequence parallels that used by the Japanese in the 1941 negotiations with the United States. Tokyo leaders set a deadline of which Washington (through "magic") was aware, exhorted negotiators Nomura and Kurusu to do everything in their power to gain an agreement, inserted jokers (concerning a withdrawal date from Indochina and China) in each offer, asked the American side to trust Japan and its true intentions, terminated the talks according to a previously set deadline, and blamed the United States for the collapse of the negotiations.

SUMMARY

From Perry to the present, the Japanese style of international negotiation has been dominated by a philosophy of risk minimization and confrontation

125. *Nisso kōshō shi*, pp. 47–51; Lensen, *Japanese Recognition of the USSR*, p. 41.
126. Lensen, *Japanese Recognition of the USSR*, pp. 42–43.
127. *Nisso kōshō shi*, pp. 69, 70–71; Lensen, *Japanese Recognition of the USSR*, p. 76.

avoidance. Japanese policy-makers seem to prefer doing nothing when it is safe to do nothing and act only when the pressure of events forces them to act. They have consistently focused on the risks and dangers of an aggressive bargaining style rather than on the opportunities such initiatives might present. Such a passive mentality makes those in charge of bargaining in Tokyo underestimate their bargaining power and appear hesitant and indecisive.

It has also helped strike purely manipulative tactics from the list of possible Japanese negotiating tactics. In the pragmatic Japanese negotiating approach there is little room for highly exaggerated demands, threats, and extraconference pressuring devices that seem dangerous and likely to fail. Instead, the ideal Japanese negotiating scenario involves little if any real negotiation but prearranged bargains hammered out behind-the-scenes, safely sheltered from public scrutiny. Ironically, even though the Japanese have adopted policies specifically designed to skirt premature commitments and to keep options open, they often find those options sealed off by the final negotiating stage.

Domestic Japanese political habits and practices greatly bear on Japanese negotiating behavior. Its fragmented, inner-directed government processes, in which participants tend to put their own interests above all others, have an onerous impact on negotiating performance, and especially on timing, flexibility, and speed. In short, the political structure itself imposes limits on Japanese negotiating conduct. The combative pluralism of the system was perhaps most starkly revealed in the army-navy-Foreign Ministry rivalries of the 1930s. But competition and compromise was built into the system even then; no single group wielded uncontested political authority. Since the war the relative strength of the military has fallen drastically whereas that of the Diet, the media, and opposition parties has grown. But particularistic competition continues to be the basic feature of Japanese politics. In place of army-navy disagreements, there are intra-LDP factional rivalries or Gaimushō-MITI disputes. Although the substance of issues and the arena of conflict have changed somewhat in the postwar period, similar factors continue to be involved in the equation. The divisiveness of the political system continues to have the effect of impeding the smooth execution of Japanese bargaining policy.

Before negotiating policy is determined, certain knotty political issues must be unraveled—who will be responsible for a decision, who will mediate among rival factions, who will make the personal sacrifices needed to cement a decision. The problem is more political (that is, forging a sustainable domestic coalition) than tactical (weighing alternatives and gauging opposing positions and moves). Leaders and negotiators focus their bargaining resources on what they regard as manageable and realizable objectives. This intensive Japanese prebargaining work has the incidental but significant effect of shearing extravagant or extraneous demands from Japan's conditions before negotiations begin. But starting negotiations with comparatively modest demands, preshrunk through lengthy domestic debate, leaves Japan perilously close to its real minimum. A Japanese negotiator must begin work with few arrows in his quiver—perhaps several nominal concessions and a specious demand or two. By necessity, he tends to gamble everything on a single, unyielding formula. If that formula fails, however, he has few fallback plans in reserve.

The portrait which emerges from this study is that of a nation exceedingly committed to winning in bargaining. The analysis, moreover, has identified many of the tactical expressions of this commitment. Japanese bargaining style is molded by a conviction that their goals are just, proper, and fair. "Just" policies, it is felt, should win simply because they are "just," if only their intrinsic "justness" can be communicated to the other side, if they are resolute, if they push hard enough, and if the other side appreciates their "sincerity." This attitude leads the Japanese to reject elaborate strategies and tactics but to rely instead on sheer persistence to win. The vaunted diffidence of the Japanese is scarcely visible when they are pressing their own case. They show commitment by threats of breakoff, assertions that they have the solid backing of Japanese public opinion, and reminders of their own sincerity (*sei'i*), resolve (*ketsui*), patience (*nintai*), and compromising spirit (*dakyoteki no seishin*). They stick to the issues agreed on for discussion, avoiding histrionics, useless rhetoric, or whimsical shifts in position. Sham demands are unusual but, when presented, are pursued perfunctorily and dropped quickly, in hopes of winning an exchange or some tactical advantage. New conditions are extremely rare once negotiations begin. Thus, the Japanese are relentless and tenacious rather than ruthless or pugnacious (except, possibly, when dealing with far weaker opponents such as China or Korea in the prewar era).

This pattern of Japanese bargaining tenacity is most evident in their almost frantic final stage search for ways to salvage initial goals without major concessions. They spurn the middle path and cling to original positions to the bitter and often hopeless end, even at the risk of breakdown. The most typical Japanese crisis stage technique, in fact, is to push once again, holding fast to earlier positions, even to badly eroded or untenable ones, while seeking to conjure up some winning method. Final stage Japanese tactics include direct appeals to opposing negotiators and ordering their bargainers to open the heart (*kyoshintankai*), reveal Japan's true intentions, and make a "last effort" (*saigo no doryoku*) to uncover the method that at a stroke can save the situation. It is as if determination alone is the key to negotiating success, that victory is attainable by adjusting the superficial means of negotiation rather than by compromising on substantive issues.

Japanese compromise behavior also reflects a narrowly defined conception of self-interest. They neither seek to locate islands of common ground between the sides nor do they easily grasp the adversary's point of view. Rhetoric aside, Japanese negotiators in practice stick doggedly to original positions. Concessions tend to be (1) made late, at the late-middle or final stage, after being postponed as long as possible; (2) broken down into small pieces and parceled out slowly and grudgingly; (3) contingent on opposing compromise; and (4) embellished with face-saving rationalizations to soften the blow when it lands. And having made a concession of consequence, Japanese bargainers hold even more tenaciously than before to what remains of their original demands.

The Japanese game plan for bargaining victory seems to proceed via a definable sequence: first, to probe carefully opposing thinking in order to gauge what is obtainable and to set manageable goals; second, to harness all available bargaining resources to force through these apparently realizable conditions; and finally, to continue to press for these demands even when their fortunes have soured and at the risk of terminating negotiations. It is the simplest sort of strategy—know what you want and push until you get it.

It is an open question whether the Japanese bargaining behavior outlined here is distinguishable from that of other countries. Until the negotiating style of various countries has been subjected to critical, in-depth study, it is impossible to delineate with any precision the unusual, the distinctive, or the unique features of Japanese negotiatory style. And even if it were discovered that many (or most) countries resort to the tactics used by the Japanese, such a finding would not necessarily vitiate the importance of this characteristic Japanese approach. Rather, the pivotal issue is why, given the vast range of potential bargaining moves, Japanese leaders and negotiators have tended to use the same ones and to exclude others with such remarkable consistency. Taken individually, therefore, any one of the bargaining tactics described here may not be uniquely Japanese, but the manner in which Japanese bargaining moves are combined, emphasized, and repeated provides a recognizable and probably unique dimension to their international negotiating behavior.

II

Interests:
Public and Private

Japanese Public Opinion and Foreign Affairs: 1964–1973

AKIO WATANABE

The relationship between public opinion and public policy is exceedingly complex.[1] The two have a reciprocal influence on each other, with various intervening institutions such as political parties, pressure groups, and the mass media also exerting their impact on the relationship. Moreover, public opinion affects policy in ways that cannot be clearly measured or predicted. Accordingly, it is difficult to treat public opinion as a social phenomenon, fixed and observable with some measure of precision. It is even more difficult to isolate this factor from others in order to focus on its role in foreign policy formulation.

Cognisant of these methodological problems, I shall rely chiefly on data from opinion polls to describe the main characteristics—the distribution pattern and the change over time—of Japanese opinions and attitudes that relate to international problems. Attempts to uncover specific public opinion trends and make predictions on their future direction would require taking into account, in addition to the simple distribution patterns, the structural distribution according to occupation, class, age, and political party affiliation. Unfortunately, with a few exceptions, limitations of space and data availability preclude such an undertaking.

1. For the conceptual themes used in this paper, I drew on various earlier works, especially these: V.O. Key, Jr., *Public Opinion and American Democracy* (New York: Knopf, 1961); H.L. Childs, *Public Opinion* (Princeton, N.J.: Van Nostrand, 1965); and Karl W. Deutsch and Lewis J. Edinger, *Germany Rejoins the Powers* (Stanford: Stanford University Press, 1959).

I have taken V.O. Key's definition of public opinion, namely, "those opinions held by private persons which governments find it prudent to heed."[2] As policy relevance is a precondition of public opinion in this definition, one must know what opinions about what issues are thought by decision-makers to be worth considering. It is conceivable that public opinion analysts might concentrate on opinions having little relation to the actions of decision-makers, or overlook issues to which the latter attach great importance. Nevertheless, the existence of numerous public opinion surveys on a certain matter is some proof that society generally considers that problem important, hence policy-makers cannot completely ignore it.[3] Moreover, in Japan various government organizations, including the Foreign Ministry, as well as the large newspapers are important public-opinion poll-takers.[4] Thus the collective opinions of Japanese voters, as manifested in these opinion polls, exert some influence on the thoughts and actions of policy-makers.

I shall limit the period under consideration essentially to the recent decade, 1964–1973. This is a convenient time period with several advantages. It includes the seven years of the Satō administration plus the short periods preceding and following Satō's tenure, and thus has a unity of its own. It also encompasses a wide range of international changes and events that have had important implications for Japanese foreign policy: for example, the carrying out of a series of nuclear experiments in China; the prolongation of the Vietnam War and the consequent weariness of the U.S.; and the surfacing of political consequences stemming from Japan's postwar economic advances.

Moreover, this period may be distinguished from the preceding "postwar" period in the sense that it has been a time during which significant—albeit gradual—changes occurred in Japan's attitudes toward the outside world. These changes have taken place against the background of important shifts in the international situation, such as the changing relationships among China,

2. Key, *Public Opinion*, p. 14.

3. For example, writing on the subject of the Satō administration's China policy, Kimura Toshio, then deputy chief cabinet secretary, made reference to the results of opinion polls conducted by several newspapers. He cited them in support of the argument that relations with the Nationalist government on Taiwan should not be sacrificed for friendship with Peking. See his article, "Satō naikaku no taichū shisei," *Azia kotarii*, Vol. 3, no. 2 (April 1971), pp. 18–20. Also see Satō Eisaku's interview with Endō Shūsaku in *Shūkan Asahi*, April 26, 1974, pp. 140–141, in which the former premier frankly confessed that, while in office, he read and cared about the popularity surveys conducted by newspapers.

4. Out of 555 opinion surveys reported to the public relations division of the prime minister's office for the period from April 1970 to March 31, 1971, 47 were conducted by national government agencies, 92 by prefectural bodies, 210 by municipal institutions, 75 by newspaper publishers, and so on. Nationwide surveys amounted to 75, of which those conducted by national government agencies and newspaper publishers numbered 29 and 27 respectively. See Naikaku Sōridaijin Kambō Kōhōshitsu, comp., *Yoron chōsa nenkan* (Tokyo: Ōkurashō Insatsukyoku, 1971), pp. 8–9; hereafter cited as *Nenkan*, followed by the year of publication.

the U.S., and the Soviet Union, and the increased fluidity thereby caused in Asian international politics. Thus, although Japan has continued to deal with the problems inherited from the earlier period, it has also had to face several new problems. The context within which public opinion has been shaped thus includes changes in Japan's basic foreign policy orientation under the new conditions, including a trend toward international multipolarity and Japan's growing awareness of its own strength.

MAJOR TRENDS IN JAPANESE OPINIONS ON FOREIGN POLICY

Evaluation of This Era.

To understand the Japanese people's expectations and aspirations vis-à-vis their country's foreign policy, it is first necessary to discover how they evaluate their experiences during the nearly thirty years since the war and relate them to the entire course of modern Japanese history. The results of public opinion surveys taken over the last several years show that the majority of Japanese give an affirmative evaluation to the postwar period.

In July 1970, 48 percent of a cross-section of Japanese people (over sixteen years of age) responded that they had "gained something" from the changes in Japanese society over the past twenty-five years. The number of positive responses far outstripped either those who answered that they had "lost something" (24 percent), or those who gave no answer or fell into the "other" category (28 percent).[5] The results of this survey correspond closely with those of a survey taken two years earlier, in which nearly one out of two persons agreed that "life is better in the postwar period than it was in the prewar days," 28 percent answered that "it was easier to live in the prewar days," and 23 percent answered "other" or gave no answer.[6] When asked more specifically to differentiate materially and spiritually between the pre- and postwar periods, sixty-three Japanese in every hundred found the postwar period materially better, 16 percent found it worse, and another 16 percent gave no answer. Spiritually, 39 percent found the postwar period better, 36 percent found it worse, and 18 percent saw "no change."[7] These results indicate that, although most Japanese believe that the radical changes in their society during the postwar years have generally improved life, some also regret the social disorders and loss of traditional mores that have accompanied the changes.

5. A nationwide opinion poll conducted by the Mainichi Shimbunsha in July 1970, cited from *Nenkan* 1971, pp. 560–561. Subsequent references to polls will give, in order, the name of the pollster, the date of the survey, and the source.
6. Asahi Shimbunsha, Aug. 1968, *Asahi shimbun,* Sept. 20, 1968.
7. Mainichi Shimbunsha, July 1970, *Nenkan* 1971, pp. 560–561.

From a broader historical view, the Japanese tend to feel that the postwar
period is, like the Meiji period, a good era. For example, in a public opinion
survey on the occasion of the one-hundredth anniversary of the Meiji Restoration, over half the respondents gave a favorable evaluation to both the Meiji
period and the postwar period; only 6 and 18 percent respectively replied that
either the Meiji or postwar period was not good. (Those who could not answer
either positively or negatively account for 19 percent for the Meiji period and 22
percent for the postwar period. The remainder gave "don't know" answers.)
The period from the beginning of the Shōwa through the defeat (1926–1945)
contrasts with these two periods. Those who viewed it in a negative way (58
percent) far outnumbered those who viewed it positively (13 percent) and
those who could answer neither way (15 percent). For the Taishō period
(1912–1925), opinion was divided as follows: 24 percent remembered it
favorably, 18 percent remembered it unfavorably, and 29 percent declined to
answer.[8]

The results of a newspaper survey, also in 1968, indicate a similar pattern
with respect to the Japanese people's historical memory. The question was, "If
you were to compare the Meiji, Taishō, and Shōwa periods, what would be
your impression of each?" Respondents were given four pairs of contrasting
adjectives and asked to select the one in each pair that was closest to their image of each period. As shown in Table 1, most respondents thought that the

Table 1
Japanese Images of the Modern Periods in Their Society
(by percentage of responses)

	Meiji	Taishō	Shōwa (early)	Shōwa (late, postwar)
Progressive	32	8	7	43
Conservative	16	20	16	7
Vigorous	31	8	16	23
Stagnant	5	28	11	3
Stable	16	25	13	21
Disorderly	27	16	38	20
Bright	11	9	9	32
Dark	9	18	36	10
Other/no answer	17	21	14	7
TOTAL	164	153	160	166

SOURCE: Asahi Shimbunsha, Aug. 1968, *Asahi shimbun*, Sept. 20, 1968.

8. Sōrifu, March 1968, *Nenkan* 1968, pp. 206–207.

postwar period was progressive and vigorous, a "bright" period, but their views were about evenly divided on whether it was stable or disorderly. Evaluations of the Meiji period were somewhat similar. In contrast, early Shōwa was remembered as a dark, disorderly period. Although Taishō was certainly a stable period, its evaluation as a stagnant, conservative, dark period suggests that the so-called Taishō liberalism did not make a deep impression on the minds of ordinary Japanese.[9]

Thus, people feel that Japan's course since the Meiji Restoration, even if beset with frustration and failure along the way, has as a whole been successful.[10] Two successes in particular—rapid modernization following the Meiji Restoration and brilliant recovery after the war—are firmly implanted in the people's memory. The vision of a past "golden age," along with a general expectation that the future will be better than the present, is often connected with various dissatisfactions concerning existing conditions.[11] In present-day Japan, however, the memory of the glorious past, the anticipation of a good future, and the fundamentally positive attitude toward the present (or toward the postwar period that has brought about the present) appear to mutually reinforce one another.

This generally positive Japanese attitude toward the present and future naturally derives from a sense of sufficiency and consciousness of improvement in each individual's private life. Those who are more or less satisfied with their present pattern of living have repeatedly fallen in the range of 53–58 percent in surveys conducted over the past seven or eight years. If those who are completely satisfied are added, the figure reaches 58–65 percent. About one-third of the people are somewhat dissatisfied with their own lives, but only 5 percent are extremely dissatisfied. Those who feel that their own standard of living has improved over the previous year always exceed one-quarter, while approximately one-third are optimistic about the prospects for the future.[12] Of course, responses to a question about the degree of satisfaction with one's personal life broadly reflect the respondent's feelings about income, position, work, family, housing, leisure, and health, and do not necessarily correspond to his feelings of

9. Asahi Shimbunsha, Aug. 1968, *Asahi shimbun*, Sept. 20, 1968.

10. In June 1966, six out of ten voters in the Tokyo area answered that they were proud of their country's history, another 7 percent said there was nothing in particular to be proud of, and 20 percent replied "it has little more than common merit." Tōkei Sūri Kenkyūjo, July 1966, *Nenkan* 1967, p. 110.

11. In response to the question, "what will Japan be like in the twenty-first century?" 55 percent responded that Japan would be considerably better off, 17 percent answered that there would be no great change, and only 9 percent forecast that things would be worse. The remainder gave either other answers or no answer. See Asahi Shimbunsha, Aug. 1968, *Asahi shimbun*, Sept. 20, 1968.

12. A series of opinion surveys conducted by the prime minister's office, entitled "The Living Conditions of the Japanese People," summarized in *Gekkan yoron chōsa* (cited hereafter as *Yoron chōsa*), Oct. 1971, pp. 8, 14, and Sept. 1972, p. 8.

satisfaction toward political and social problems.[13] Nevertheless, when asked "do you feel that postwar Japan as a whole has been advancing in a favorable direction?" sixty-seven out of one hundred Japanese took a positive attitude whereas less than one out of eight answered negatively.[14]

Even the growing awareness since the late 1960s of new problems accompanying the country's "excessive" industrialization—such as pollution, environmental destruction, and economic friction with foreign countries—has not shattered the general approval of the postwar era. Although nearly two out of three persons in a March 1971 nationwide survey mentioned increased public pollution (kōgai) as an unfavorable concomitant of economic growth, 27 percent still thought that the economic growth had, on the whole, brought good things to the country; only 14 percent thought the impact had been bad. (Another 29 percent of the respondents answered ambivalently, and 18 percent were not prepared to give an answer.) When asked whether the preceding answers also referred to their personal lives, more than six out of ten respondents answered in some degree affirmatively; only 8 percent answered negatively.[15] Moreover, people who thought that their society was moving in the right (desirable) direction increased from 43 percent in October1971 to 49 percent in August-September 1972; those who did not decreased from 21 percent to 15 percent.[16] Despite the urging from some quarters that the Japanese must rethink the basic premises upon which they have built their prosperous postwar economy, it seems unlikely that citizens at large will be led to discard their acquired ways of thinking. It is still too early to pass judgment on the impact of the recent "oil crisis," but it may well prove to be shallow and transient.

13. For example, a Mainichi Shimbunsha poll in November 1969, interviewed two thousand persons over sixteen years of age on the "degree of satisfaction" they felt regarding both their private lives and political matters. Their responses, by percentage, follow:

	Completely satisfied	Rather satisfied	Rather dissatisfied	Completely dissatisfied
Private life	20	51	21	7
Political matters	5	35	38	19

See Nenkan 1970, pp. 523–524. See also Nihon Chiiki Kaihatsu Senta, ed., Nihonjin no kachikan (Tokyo: Shiseidō, 1970), pp. 169–171; and Kokumin Senkōdo Chōsai Iinkai, ed., Nihonjin no manzokudo (Tokyo: Shiseidō, 1972). The last is a survey of popular attitudes toward living conditions, based on a multivariate analysis taking into account nine variables including income, job, and housing.
14. Naikaku Sōridaijin Kambō Kōhōshitsu, Oct. 1968, Nenkan 1969, p. 107.
15. Sōrifu, March 1971, Yoron chōsa, Nov. 1971, p. 9.
16. Sōrifu, Aug.-Sept. 1973, Yoron chōsa, April 1974, p. 25.

The Legacy of the War

Conceivably, the positive image of the postwar period is the reverse side of the dark memory of the Pacific War and the defeat. Two out of three Japanese cited the Pacific War when asked what event they considered the most important for Japan in the past one hundred years (up to three answers were allowed). The atomic bomb or military defeat were also mentioned by 22 percent of the people. When these figures are contrasted with 14 percent for the Meiji reforms, 13 percent combined for the Sino-Japanese, the Russo-Japanese, and the First World wars, and 12 percent for the Great Kantō earthquake, it becomes clear that the experience of World War II remains the most deeply ingrained memory among the Japanese.[17] This is not difficult to understand considering that about 40 percent of all adult Japanese have experienced war as soldiers or have suffered damage from air raids, and that those who have themselves been injured in battle or by war damage (3 percent) combined with those who have lost a close relative in the war (17 percent) reach 20 percent.[18] Of course, the damage and loss of life during World War II was not as great in Japan as in Germany, Russia, and China, but the dramatic experiences of Hiroshima and Nagasaki have doubtless given a unique coloring to the adverse memories of the war in Japanese minds.[19]

One distinguishing characteristic of the attitude of Japanese toward the war is their exceedingly weak consciousness of having actively supported their war leaders or the wartime principles. In Germany, even in 1948 when the memory of defeat was still fresh and strong, 41 percent of the adults said expressly that they had once supported the Nazis (43 percent of the German people actually voted for the Nazis in 1933), and many still believed that the principles of National Socialism were sound.[20] There is no comparable data for Japan, but the very fact that this kind of question did not occur to Japanese pollsters is suggestive. In other words, Japanese rarely remember the war in terms of ideas or causes to which they themselves were devoted; it is almost as if they remember it mainly as a misfortune that befell them.[21] This characteristic of the Japanese public's memory of the war may raise doubts as to whether, and to what extent, postwar Japanese pacifism is founded on moral conviction. From a pragmatic view, however, the failure the Japanese associate with their war ex-

17. Asahi Shimbunsha, Aug. 1968, *Asahi shimbun,* Sept. 20, 1968.
18. Yomiuri Shimbunsha, June 1969, *Nenkan* 1970, p. 491.
19. Sankei Shimbunsha, Aug. 1972, *Yoron chōsa,* Oct. 1972, p. 78. In this survey twelve hundred persons, between ages fifteen and sixty-five and living in the Tokyo and Osaka areas, were interviewed over the telephone. Seventy-six percent stated it was necessary to remind young people of the tragedy of Hiroshima and Nagasaki.
20. Deutsch and Edinger, *Germany Rejoins,* p. 15.
21. See Sabata Toyoyuki, *Sensō to ningen no fūdo* (Tokyo: Shinchōsa, 1967).

periences contrasts with their postwar experiences of success, and undoubtedly
works to support the postwar "spirit."

This new "success," of course, was not guaranteed from the beginning.[22] On
the contrary, the desire to wipe away the feeling of humiliation and loss of confidence brought on by unpreceded defeat supplied the psychological energy
for the postwar Japanese recovery. Until recently, efforts to get back what
Japan lost in the war—independence, prosperity, honor, international position,
and national self-confidence—have consistently formed the main theme of
Japanese foreign policy. With each solution to a troublesome diplomatic
issue—for example, recovery of independence with the conclusion of the peace
treaty, admission to the U.N., conclusion and implementation of reparation
agreements with Asian nations, restoration of Russo-Japanese and Sino-
Japanese relations, and final admission to the club of advanced industrial
nations with the abolition of the application of article 35 of GATT and Japanese acceptance of article 8 of the IMF—successive cabinet leaders have
announced "the end of the postwar period." Premier Satō made the most recent such statement on the occasion of the return of Okinawa.[23]

In the process of these postwar recovery efforts the Japanese were naturally
encouraged by the memory of the Meiji era. Although actual postwar conditions, both internally and internationally, resembled many experiences of the
1920s, the postwar Japanese did not identify as much with the democracy and
cooperative international diplomacy of the Taishō era as with the Meiji era.
Comparison with the Meiji period seemed more appropriate because of the
similarities with respect to rapid social change and the fervent pursuit of an improved international position.

The end of the war also brought a sense of relief and liberation to many
Japanese. With time, this memory of liberation has become stronger than the
feelings of humiliation associated with the defeat. In 1972, 44 percent of the
Japanese welcomed the anniversary of the end of the war (August 15) with
feelings of rejoicing connected with the return of peace; only one-fourth of the
people remembered the sorrow of the defeat.[24] Thus, one of the psychological
motivations for Japanese postwar efforts—wiping away the feelings of humiliation—has greatly weakened even if it has not yet completely disappeared. Yet,
if opinions are sought regarding the unsolved territorial problem with Russia
and the U.S. military bases remaining inside Japan (including Okinawa), only

22. In the mid-1950s, one foreign observer painted a gloomy picture on the prospects for
Japan's recovery, not only in politicomilitary terms, but also economically. See James T.
Watkins IV, "Background of Japanese Foreign Policy," in Philip B. Buck and Martin
Travis, Jr., eds., *Control of Foreign Relations in Modern Nations* (New York: Norton, 1957),
p. 756.

23. See Akio Watanabe, "Japanese Postwar Foreign Policy Thinking: An Analysis of Government Speeches in the Diet," in Seizaburo Sato and Roger Dingman, eds., *Japan's Perceptions of the World* (forthcoming).

24. Sankei Shimbunsha, Aug. 1972, *Yoron chōsa*, Oct. 1972, p. 78.

one-third of the people agree with Premier Satō that "the postwar period ended with the return of Okinawa"; about half feel that "the postwar period has not yet ended."[25] Attempts, however, to keep war memories alive—such as the recent movement to edit and publish the record of the so-far untold story of the Tokyo air raids—are more likely to cause Japanese to recall the sacrifices of the war than to rekindle any malice toward old enemies.

Japan's Image of Itself as a Middle Power

A survey conducted in July 1970 asked the following question: "It is often said that before the war Japan was a first-class nation, but after the war it fell to a fourth-class position. What class do you feel Japan belongs in today?" The largest number, 31 percent, ranked Japan as a second-class nation; 22 percent said third-class, 18 percent said first-class, and 7 percent said fourth-class.[26] Roughly similar results were obtained from a slightly different question: "Do you feel Japan today is viewed as being important by the rest of the world?" The breakdown of responses to the four choices—from "extremely important" to "not important at all"—was 19 percent, 49 percent, 14 percent and 1 percent.[27]

A commonly accepted view among Japanese and foreigners alike is that Japan, after having suddenly fallen to a fourth-class position as a result of the defeat, has finally recovered to a position as a second-ranking nation. Japan, which throughout the greater part of its history has had no real equals, has grown accustomed to regarding its neighbors as either inferior or superior in terms of civilization, power, and wealth. When Japan was under the influence of the great Chinese civilization, the country was in a subordinate position, but secretly ranked itself above its small neighbor, Korea. Contact with the West liberated Japan from the idea of immutable hierarchy among nations and taught Japanese to apply an index of power—which, unlike morality, was capable of rapid elevation—to relations among nations. Although the Japanese worked their way up to a position among the great powers—all of which were Western, Christian peoples—and although they thought they had gained the sought-after status as an equal, Japan was still the only non-European major power and was ceaselessly tormented by feelings of isolation and segregation.

25. Ibid.
26. Mainichi Shimbunsha, July 1970, *Nenkan* 1971, pp. 560–561.
27. NHK (Japanese Broadcasting Company), Feb. 1966 (a national sample of 5,400 persons between the ages of fifteen and sixty-nine), *Nenkan* 1966, p. 323. In a poll jointly taken by the four local newspapers (Hokkidō Shimbunsha, Chūbu Nippon Shimbunsha, Nishi Nippon Shimbunsha, and Tokyo Shimbunsha) in November 1967, sixteen persons in every hundred ranked Japan as among the most important in the world community, 64 percent as second-rate, 17 percent as third-rate, and 1 percent as fourth-rate. See *Nenkan* 1968, p. 498.

At times, these feelings moved the country to search for its ultimate values again in the Asian civilization from which it had undertaken a process of separation.

Postwar Japanese have come to place greatest emphasis on economic development as the measure of Japan's international relations. "Economic diplomacy," a rather vague term with a variety of meanings in actual application, is a frequently used term by Japanese leaders and very influential in shaping public attitudes. For example, in a public opinion survey of May 1970, respondents were asked to select from a given list the one or two most important things Japan should do to become a big power. Thirty-seven percent chose "expand economic strength," 33 percent said "elevate the people's standard of living," and 23 percent replied "consolidate social welfare and social capital investment." The fewest, only 4 percent, chose "develop great military power." (Fifteen percent said "promote international cooperation and increase aid to the developing countries.") The same survey also asked, "in what field do you think Japan is doing most to contribute to world peace?" Responses included 21 percent for technical assistance, 17 percent for economic assistance, and 14 percent for cooperation with the U.S. Seventeen percent did not think Japan was contributing in any field, 30 percent gave "don't know" answers, and only 1 percent answered military power.[28]

On another occasion, respondents were asked to rate the effectiveness of the following five methods for ensuring Japan's future security: (a) strengthen military power; (b) promote economic cooperation with all countries; (c) become more active in diplomatic negotiations; (d) improve the people's livelihood; and (e) promote cultural exchange with other peoples.[29] Significantly, the economic, cultural, and diplomatic methods were each supported by 75 percent, whereas the military route was thought ineffective by almost half (see Table 2). Moreover, a breakdown by party affiliation does not reveal any great differences in an evaluation of the nonmilitary methods. Supporters of the JSP, JCP, and the Kōmeitō believe somewhat less in the effectiveness of economic cooperation than supporters of the LDP and DSP, but when those with reservations are included, the difference is small—about 75 percent of JSP, JCP, and Kōmeitō supporters as opposed to 80 percent of LDP supporters. In attitudes on the effectiveness of military power, however, the differences among the supporters of the various political parties are clear: six out of ten LDP supporters believe in its effectiveness (12 percent of these without reservation); but six out of ten JSP and Kōmeitō supporters and about three-quarters of JCP supporters are skeptical of the effectiveness of military power. These differences reflect the different party positions on policy issues such as the strengthening of the Self-Defense Forces and the continuation of the Japanese-American Securi-

28. Yomiuri Shimbunsha, May 1970, *Nenkan* 1971, p. 537.
29. Mainichi Shimbunsha, April 1972, *Yoron chōsa*, July 1972, p. 72.

Table 2

Japanese Opinions on How to Insure Their Country's Security
(by percentage of responses)

	Very effective	Somewhat effective	Not too effective	Not at all effective	Others/ no answer
a. Military power	6	34	32	14	14
b. Economic cooperation	32	43	9	2	14
c. Diplomatic negotiations	33	42	9	1	15
d. Peoples' livelihood	31	39	13	2	15
e. International exchange	37	38	9	2	14

SOURCE: Mainichi Shimbunsha, April 1972, *Gekkan yoron chōsa* (cited hereafter as *Yoron chōsa*), July 1972, p. 72.

ty Treaty. As a whole, however, belief in the effectiveness of military power is rather low even among LDP supporters.

The idea that economic power is the basis of national strength and the factor on which international relations ultimately depends, is not a new position for Japanese citizens nor peculiar to Japan. Indeed the stress on economic development has spread throughout the world today. Postwar Japanese, however, given their recent history, have had special reasons for promoting economic development and de-emphasizing military power. The catastrophic costs of war and the extraordinary success of the developmental program naturally contribute to a great faith in economic power. Today, the vast majority of Japanese know that Japan stands third behind the United States and the USSR in GNP, and nearly three out of four believe that their country belongs to the advanced nations.[30]

Postwar Japan has also had few incentives for competing internationally on a military level. Of course, certain considerations during the period just after the return of sovereignty—for example, the urgent need to increase production to a level that could support the people's livelihood and the importance of not provoking the suspicions of neighboring peoples toward a formerly expansionist nation—made large-scale rearmament clearly impossible. Subsequent changes in both internal and external conditions have not basically shifted the balance against extensive military power. As a small, densely populated, resource-poor

30. Ibid; and Hokkaidō Shimbunsha, Chūbu Nippon Shimbunsha, Nishi Nippon Shimbunsha, and Tokyo Shimbunsha, Nov. 1967, *Nenkan* 1968, p. 497.

nation, Japan must depend heavily on the international environment for its survival and development. As this critical fact determines its position in the world and limits its options, Japan is extremely sensitive to the impact of events outside its borders. At an earlier point, in the 1930s, this caused Japan to embark on an overseas adventure when it was forced into a corner. Today, however, a similar vulnerability has caused Japanese leaders to urge the maintenance of "a peaceful, prosperous international society" and the practice of "international cooperation" as of "vital importance" for Japan.[31] In postwar Japan, it has been establishment policy to consider the political and economic costs of a strong dependence on military power too great in terms of probable achievements, given current political, military, and technological factors.

Such a position is made easier because the Japanese have had little feeling of being exposed to a direct, concrete threat from an external enemy during the postwar period. For example, when asked "at present, from what country is an attack [on Japan] possible?" about one-fourth to one-fifth of the Japanese public usually answers that for any country (or situation) to cause an attack is unthinkable. As about one-third of the people give "don't know" answers, less than 50 percent of the respondents can conceive of any country being hostile to Japan.[32] Table 3 illustrates a similar breakdown of Japanese opinion on the likelihood of an attack from outside in the near future.

Table 3

Japanese Opinions on the Likelihood of an Attack*

(by percentage of responses)

	Likely	May or may not	Not likely	Absolutely unthinkable	Others/ no answer
June 1968	3	43	40	5	9
October 1969	5	35	47	7	6
April 1972	4	43	39	8	6

SOURCES: Mainichi Shimbunsha, June 1968, *Mainichi shimbun*, July 1, 1968; Mainichi Shimbunsha, Oct. 1969, in Naikaku Sōridaijin Kambō Kōhōshitsu, comp., *Yoron chōsa nenkan* (hereafter cited as *Nenkan*) (Tokyo: Ōkurasho Insatsukyoku, 1970), p. 545; and Mainichi Shimbunsha, April 1972, *Yoron chōsa*, July 1972, p. 70.

*The question was, "Do you feel that in the near future there is a danger that Japan—including Okinawa—will be attacked by another country or be involved directly in a war?"

31. Gaimushō, *Waga gaikō no kinkyō* 16 (Tokyo: Ōkurashō Insatsukyoku, 1972), p. 81.

32. Tōkei Sūri Kenkyūjo, *Tokyo teiki chōsa no kekka*, Research Report General Series 28 (Tokyo: Tōkei Sūri Kenkyūjo, 1971), p. 76. I am grateful to Shigeki Nishihira of the institute for the use of this source.

Chart 1

Japanese Perceptions on the Levels of International Tension

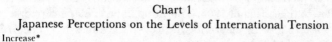

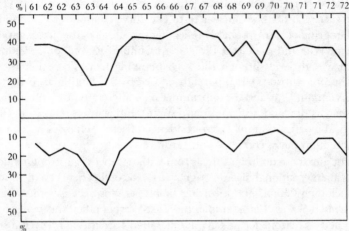

*The percentage of those who said that the danger of Japan's becoming involved in a war had increased.
**The percentage of those who said that the danger of Japan's becoming involved in a war had decreased.

SOURCE: Tōkei Sūri Kenkyūjo, *Tokyo teiki chōsa no kikka* (Tokyo, 1971), p. 76.

Although the Japanese do not have a strong feeling of being exposed to an imminent threat from without, they do feel a generalized indirect threat from the international tensions connected with the global and regional activities of the American, Russian, and Chinese "superpowers." A survey, conducted twice a year since the mid-1950s, has asked voters within the twenty-three wards of Tokyo, "looking at recent world activities, do you think the danger of Japan's becoming embroiled in a war has decreased or increased?"[33] The results of this survey, which are graphically illustrated in Chart 1, indicate a substantial reduction in the degree of international tension perceived by the Japanese in the period from the autumn of 1963 to the spring of 1964. Perhaps this low point reflected such international developments as the establishment of the Washington-Moscow hotline (June 1963), the Partial Nuclear Test Ban Treaty (August 1963), and Japan's acceptance of article 8 of

33. Ibid., p. 78.

the IMF and admission to OECD. According to the chart, however, the Japanese returned to the stern realities of international politics with a sudden increase in their perception of international tension in the period from the autumn of 1964 to the spring of 1965. This jump in people's perception of tension came just as Japan was celebrating the Tokyo Olympics, but concurrently came the news from Moscow about Khrushchev's dismissal and from Peking about the success of its first nuclear test. The curve continues to rise until its peak in the spring of 1967, probably reflecting the effects of the prolongation of the Vietnam War and the Great Proletarian Cultural Revolution in China. It remains at a high level through the 1968 bombing halt. Thereafter the undulations become substantial, apparently caused by the continuous uncertainties of the Vietnam War and the appearance of a different type of international conflict (such as the Sino-Soviet border dispute). If this interpretation of Chart 1 is correct, the perceptions of Tokyo residents reflect the changes in the international situation fairly correctly and sensitively.

When the Japanese do feel a threat from without, there is a strong tendency to see it as an international dispute originating in a conflict between the nuclear powers (including China) and involving Japan perhaps because of its alliance with the United States. For example, the East-West conflict and nuclear war are often cited as reasons for anxiety about Japan's security, and even a small percentage have mentioned the U.S. as a country that could possibly threaten Japan (6 percent in December 1968, 7 percent in June 1969, and 3 percent in September 1969). The largest number consistently point to a threat from the Soviet Union. Although the perceived threat from China has been second after that from the USSR, it declined conspicuously in the late 1960s.[34]

In short, postwar Japan feels confident and satisfied at having been able to achieve and maintain a strong economic position among the world's advanced countries. With its pragmatic view of international relations, the nation has been able to avoid preoccupation with cultural or ideological conflict, whether in the form of Western versus Oriental civilization (which tormented the prewar Japanese) or in the form of communism versus liberal democracy, the issue so prevalent in the postwar world. As no urgent problems existed which required the exercise of military power for their solution, a military force sufficient to allow full-fledged participation in global power politics has seemed prohibitively expensive. Thus, backed by its abundant economic strength, contemporary Japan has endeavored to increase its international position and voice in the world moderately, while retaining its self-image as a middle power and avoiding any great psychological strain. Present-day Japan, in sum, is not

34. See Sōrifu, Nov. 1965, *Nenkan* 1966, p. 149; Asahi Shimbunsha, Dec. 1968, *Asahi shimbun*, Jan. 5, 1969; Yomiuri Shimbunsha, June 1969, *Nenkan* 1970, p. 492; and Asahi Shimbunsha, September 1969, *Nenkan* 1970, p. 498. See also my article, "Okinawa henkan; hembo suru Nichi-Bei domei," *Chūō kōron,* Aug. 1971, pp. 108–109.

striving to become a superpower or to take a leading role in international politics.

A Resurgence of Nationalism?

In light of the factors enumerated here, how should one evaluate the revival of Japanese nationalism in recent years? If one takes nationalism to mean an over-all positive attitude toward things Japanese and being Japanese, it is not difficult to discover a strengthening of this attitude. For example, during the Occupation (1951), a sample of Japanese were asked, "compared with civilized nations such as England and the United States, do you think Japan is inferior?" (The phrasing of the question itself was typical of Japanese psychology in those days!) Nearly one-half (47 percent) of the respondents asserted that the Japanese were inferior whereas only 23 percent said that they were not.[35] Similar surveys in subsequent years, however, indicate the extent to which the Japanese have regained their self-confidence: those who answered that Japanese were superior to Westerners increased from 20 percent in 1953, to 33 percent in 1963, and to 47 percent in 1968; those who thought Japanese were inferior fell from 28 percent in 1953, to 14 percent in 1963, and to 11 percent in 1968.[36] Aside from whatever notions exist on the superiority or inferiority of Japanese, these survey results reflect a natural pride in being Japanese and the widespread feeling that the Japanese way of life is the most compatible. In October 1971, 65 percent of adult Japanese felt without reservation that they were glad they had been born Japanese, and another 21 percent agreed with reservations. Only 3 percent, either with or without reservations, were not glad to have been born Japanese.[37]

Among the youth (seventeen to twenty-two years old), however, the positive attitude toward being Japanese is weaker than the average and the trend in recent years has been downward. Moreover, the feelings of Japanese youth for their country are weaker than those of West German, English, and French young people of the same age.[38] Some argue that the reservations toward their country among Japanese youth reveal that the inferiority complex toward foreigners is still deeply rooted. Others say that Japanese youth, having been exposed to different values and increased international contacts, have either fallen into confusion or been able to take a more objective look at their own country.

35. Yomiuri Shimbunsha, Aug. 1951, *Yomiuri shimbun*, Aug. 31, 1951.
36. Tōkei Sūri Kenkyūjo Kokuminsei Chōsa Iinkai, *Dai-2 Nihonjin no kokuminsei* (Tokyo: Shiseidō, 1970), p. 160.
37. Sōrifu, Oct. 1971, in *Yoron chōsa*, Nov. 1972, p. 22.
38. The following survey results show how Japanese youth compare with West European

Two strong tendencies, however, emerge from recent surveys: the higher the education, the greater the number of answers with reservations; and the older the respondents, the greater their awareness of being Japanese in connection with such objects as the national flag, the national anthem, and the emperor. Moreover, as age declined among respondents, there was a tendency for them to think of themselves as Japanese when they had personal contact with foreigners and when they were exposed to foreign literature and films.[39] Thus, it seems that the greater reservation about being Japanese among the younger generation indicates that they are looking objectively at their own country as just one nation in the midst of great international diversity.

The feelings of national belonging were probably stimulated to a degree by the heightened moods during the 1964 Olympics and Expo 1970. Today such traditional symbols of the state as the flag and the anthem are emotionally a part of the majority of Japanese. For example, Table 4 shows the results of a survey just after the Olympics in December 1964 on feelings about the flag (*hinomaru*) and the anthem (*kimigayo*). Interestingly, whereas older people con-

Table 4

Japanese Responses to the State Symbols
(by percentage)

	Favorable*	Not Favorable	Indifferent	Others/no answer
The flag	69	2	4	23
The national anthem	71	8	2	19

SOURCE: Sōrifu, Dec. 1964, *Nenkan*, 1965, p. 102.
*The total of the various expressions of "good feelings."

youth in the percentage of their responses to a question on whether they have pride in their mother country:

		Affirmative	Negative	Noncommittal
West German	(1966)	72	13	15
British	(1966)	84	10	6
French	(1966)	90	4	6
Japanese	(1966)	64	13	23
Japanese	(1967)	70	6	25
Japanese	(1970)	53	16	31

For the data for Japan, see Sōrifu, Nov. 1967, *Nenkan* 1968, p. 171; on the other countries, Nihon Risāchi Sentā, "Wakamono no ishiki," *Yoron chōsa*, April 1972, p. 56.
39. Mainichi Shimbunsha, Dec. 1971, *Yoron chōsa*, May 1972, p. 77.

nect their consciousness of being Japanese with such state symbols, younger
people tend to relate to traditional cultural characteristics such as old-fashioned
Japanese houses, scenery, and kabuki.[40] A November 1970 survey, for example, asked young people, "of what does Japan have to be proud?" The largest
number, 38 percent, selected its traditions and its distinctive culture, followed
by those who opted for the beauty of the country (34 percent), the diligence of
the people (29 percent), the war-renouncing constitution (25 percent), and the
guarantee of its people's freedom (20 percent).[41] Although these responses are
somewhat stereotyped, they seem to reflect a recent trend in public opinion—that rapid economic growth together with accompanying social changes
and environmental destruction have aroused concern about things other than
material benefits.

These signs of the recovery of national confidence and pride do not, however,
suggest revival of a fanatical nationalism having an important political meaning. Rather, the attitude is characterized by a moderate easy-going posture
among postwar Japanese, who feel relieved of the earlier self-imposed burden of
world leadership, and who now have had their deeply rooted inferiority complex mitigated by the postwar rise of cultural relativism and a pragmatic value
system. For better or worse, postwar Japanese are not so easily moved to pur-
ism and perfectionism as they were in prewar days. For example, those who
found beauty or nobleness in Mishima Yukio's suicide (November 1970) did
not exceed 10 percent; the vast majority of people thought the act was barbaric,
foolish, or useless.[42]

In general when there is a large gap between the aspirations and the capabilities of a people regarding the international role of their country, that
nation's policies can easily disturb the status quo. In present-day Japan, however, the aspirations and the reality of Japan's international role are harmonized to a greater extent than ever before. The results of many public
opinion surveys show that the people do not attach much importance to Japan's playing a leading role in international politics. In a 1970 survey, over one-
third of the respondents cited the growth of economic power and the elevation
of the people's standard of living as conditions for international greatness; one-
sixth cited an increase in international cooperation and aid to the developing
countries; and only 4 percent stressed the strengthening of the military.[43] When
asked in December 1971 to choose the one most desirable route for Japan to
follow henceforth, 53 percent of the adult Japanese respondents answered that

40. Ibid.
41. Sōrifu, Nov. 1970, *Nenkan* 1971, p. 159. In this poll, young persons between the ages of
fifteen and twenty-three were interviewed and allowed to give multiple answers.
42. Yoron Kagaku Kyōkai, Dec. 1970, and Sankei Shimbunsha, Nov. 1970, both in *Yoron
chōsa*, Feb. 1971, pp. 80–82.
43. Yomiuri Shimbunsha, May 1970, *Nenkan* 1971, p. 537. Respondents were allowed to
give multiple answers.

Japan should become a welfare state, greatly outnumbering the 20 percent that said Japan should seek to aid the developing countries and to achieve peaceful coexistence. Characteristically, only 3 percent each thought that Japan should become a militarily strong power or a leader in international politics. Moreover, only 9 percent advocated "economic superpower status."[44]

Whether viewed as excessively cautious due to the past experience of failure, lethargic due to the long withdrawal from power politics after the war, or purely selfish and indifferent about the fate of other peoples, the vast majority of Japanese do not urge their country into larger efforts and concerns with foreign relations. Rather, they unmistakably direct the country to take up its own internal problems first. This introverted tendency, not the oft-mentioned resurgence of expansionistic nationalism, may well pose substantial problems for Japan's foreign policy elites in the years to come.

OPINION-POLICY RELATIONSHIP ON CERTAIN SELECTED TOPICS

In the context of these general public attitudes relating to foreign affairs, I shall examine the relation between public opinion and government policy on a select number of major foreign policy issues arising in the decade 1964–1974: (1) the establishment of diplomatic relations with the Republic of Korea; (2) the China problem; (3) relations with the Soviet Union; (4) U.S.-Japanese relations, especially with regard to the Mutual Security Treaty; and (5) Japan's defense policy, including nuclear armament.

Korea

With the establishment of diplomatic relations with the Republic of Korea in 1965, the Japanese government finally resolved a problem that had existed since the restoration of Japan's independence in 1952. The problem had been exacerbated by strong Korean government attitudes and the deep-seated antipathy of the Korean people toward the Japanese, stemming from the bitter memory of Japan's colonial administration of their country. Some Japanese also objected to establishing formal relations with South Korea, ostensibly on the grounds that such an action would aggravate the international Cold War in

44. Asahi Shimbunsha, Dec. 1971, *Yoron chōsa*, May 1972, p. 83. The options in this questionnaire were (*a*) Japan should aim at a great power status by continuing to follow a policy of high economic growth; (*b*) Japan should aim at becoming a welfare state rather than a great power; (*c*) Japan should aim at becoming a great power, militarily strong enough to defend itself on its own ability; (*d*) Japan should aim at becoming a leading power in the arena of international politics; (*e*) Japan should seek peaceful coexistence among nations through giving aid to the underdeveloped countries; and (*f*) other answers.

East Asia by recognizing only one of the contending regimes on the Korean peninsula. Despite an outcry from the opposition parties and some antigovernment groups, however, the Ikeda administration carried negotiations with the Republic of Korea nearly to completion before Ikeda was forced to resign due to ill health. His successor, Eisaku Satō, completed the task with the signing of the Basic Treaty between Japan and the Republic of Korea on June 22, 1965.

From the signing of the Japan-Korea treaty to the exchange of ratification documents the following December, popular Japanese support for the treaty gradually declined while opposition to it grew. During this period, monthly surveys in the Tokyo area asked the question, "what do you think of improving Japan-Korea relations by restoring formal diplomatic ties?" As shown in Table 5, the percentage of respondents either firmly or moderately in favor of the treaty declined from 64 to 54 percent and those opposed grew from 8 to 13 percent. There was also an increase in the number of persons unable to make up their minds on the issue.[45] Although the changes were not dramatic, they were significant because they took place during the period in which the treaty was much discussed in the Diet and the newspapers.

No doubt the opposition parties' loud protests against the government's action, and the playing up of this in the Japanese mass media, affected public opinion on the treaty. In October 1965, 56 percent of the Japanese public replied that they had read about the Japan-Korea treaty in newspapers and magazines or heard about it on radio and television, whereas less than 7 percent answered that they had attended public meetings held by various political parties on the subject.[46] Moreover, those who opposed Diet ratification of the treaty far outnumbered those who held adverse opinions on the treaty itself. In other words, it was not the purport of the treaty but the way it was handled in the Diet that caused the public alienation.[47]

Table 5

Japanese Opinions on the Treaty with the Republic of Korea
(by percentage of responses)

	Absolutely necessary	A good thing	Not necessary	Absolutely objectionable	Don't know/ no answer
October 1965	11	53	5	3	28
November 1965	9	49	8	3	31
December 1965	8	46	9	4	34

SOURCE: Jiji Tsūshinsha, Oct.–Dec. 1965, *Nenkan*, 1966, p. 288.

45. Jiji Tsūshinsha, Oct.–Dec. 1965, *Nenkan* 1966, p. 288.
46. Jiji Tsūshinsha, Oct. 1965, *Nenkan* 1966, p. 290.
47. Jiji Tsūshinsha, Nov. 1965, *Nenkan* 1966, p. 291.

The effect of these political events on the popular Japanese image of Korea is revealed in a series of nationwide monthly opinion surveys conducted by the Jiji Press (Jiji Tsūshinsha). Respondents were asked to select from a prepared list of the nine or ten countries—the U.S., USSR, U.K., France, West Germany, Switzerland, the People's Republic of China, India, the Republic of Korea, and North Korea (which was added after July 1970)—the three countries they liked best and the three they liked least.[48] The results of these surveys are summarized in Charts 2 and 3. Although the Republic of Korea has consistently remained among the countries most disliked by the Japanese, a close examination of the survey results reveals some meaningful shifts in attitudes. Mutual distrust and ill feeling, which had taken deep root during the Syngman Rhee administration, lingered even after the relatively pro-Japanese government under Pak Chung-hi came to power in Korea and the Ikeda administration resumed the long-shelved negotiations with South Korea. After 1963, however, the feelings in Japan toward South Korea improved and paved the way for the Satō cabinet to proceed with the final negotiations.

A temporary decline in negative feeling toward Korea after ratification of the treaty in October 1965 was followed by a period of intensified tension, probably because of the bitter criticism of the government's action in implementing the terms of the treaty, particularly reparations and other monetary settlements. This period lasted for a few years until the late 1960s, when the situation finally returned to a more normal pattern (see Charts 2 and 4). This fluctuation in Japanese feelings toward Korea suggests that, although popular attitudes toward individual countries are usually fairly stable and resistant to change, political events of the day can have an enormous effect on them. The variations in Japanese opinions on China and the United States also support this hypothesis.

China

In reviewing Japanese attitudes toward China over the past decade or so, one is immediately struck by their volatility. Throughout the greater part of the 1960s, the People's Republic of China, together with the Soviet Union, remained a major object of Japanese fear and animosity. Between 1966 and 1968 the Japanese disliked China even more than Russia, but by the early 1970s Japanese feelings toward China began to show a sudden warming. The pace of change was especially great, even abnormal, before and after Premier Tanaka's

48. The monthly surveys conducted by the Jiji Press throughout the country are reproduced in the consecutive volumes of *Nenkan*, 1960 to the present. The results for recent months are available in *Yoron chōsa*.

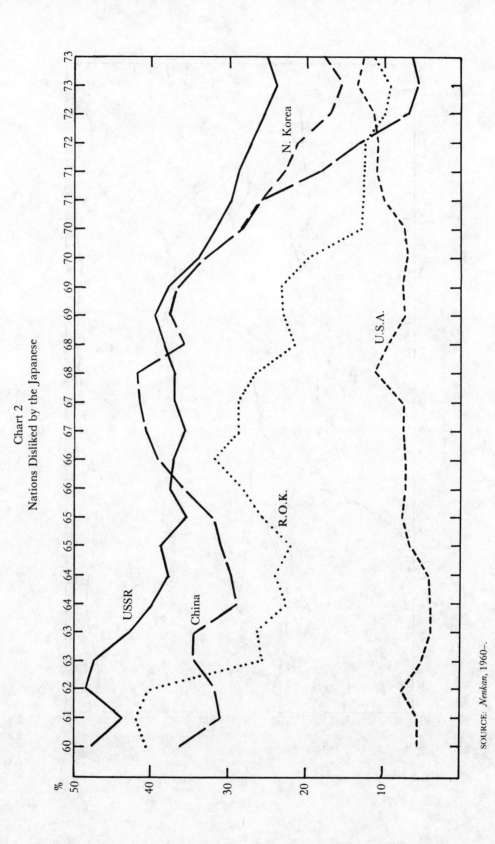

Chart 2
Nations Disliked by the Japanese

USSR

China

N. Korea

R.O.K.

U.S.A.

%
50
40
30
20
10

60 61 62 63 64 65 66 67 68 69 70 71 72 73

SOURCE: *Nenkan,* 1960–.

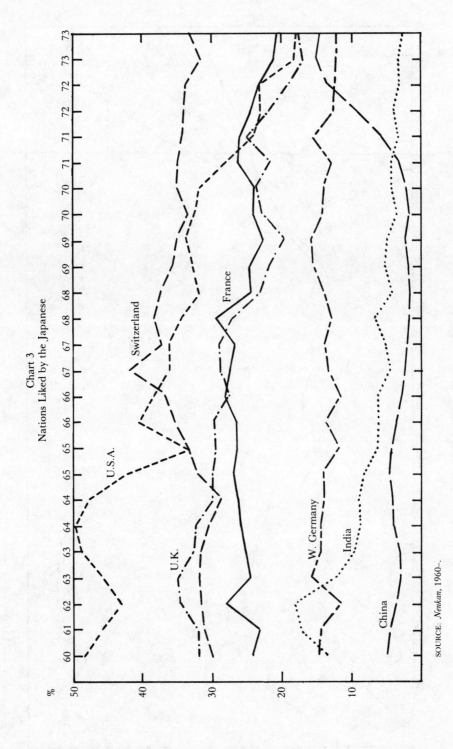

Chart 3
Nations Liked by the Japanese

SOURCE: *Nenkan*, 1960–.

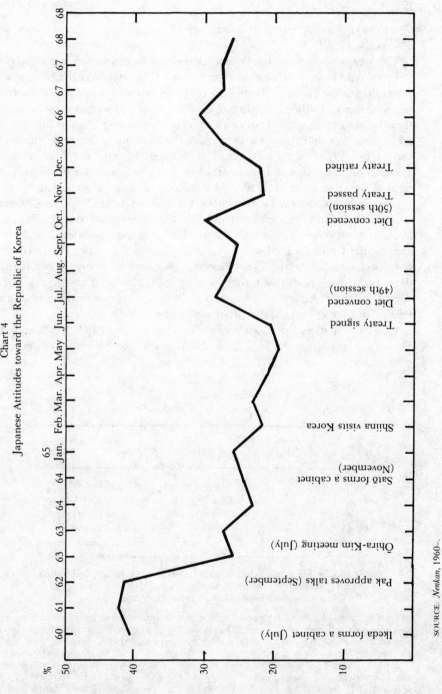

Chart 4
Japanese Attitudes toward the Republic of Korea

SOURCE: *Nenkan*, 1960–.

visit to Peking in September 1972 (the period of the so-called China boom; see Charts 2 and 3).[49]

The idea of recognizing the Peking regime had always found support among more than 30 percent of Japanese voters. Even at the height of the Chinese excesses during the Cultural Revolution, only one in ten Japanese firmly objected to recognition. At the same time, a similarly small proportion—usually less than 10 percent—had no reservations about abandoning Taiwan in order to make friends with Peking. Consequently, the majority of Japanese either favored a two-China formula if it could be arranged, or could not make up their minds about the status of Taiwan. Table 6 shows two typical distribution patterns of Japanese opinion on the China issue in the pre-Nixon period.

Contrary to common belief, neither the "China boom" nor the "Nixon shock" (Nixon's announcement in mid-July 1971 of his planned visit to Peking) had any great effect, at least in an immediate sense, on Japanese opinion regarding the China issue. Table 7 specifically shows the results from two surveys conducted before and after Nixon's announcement. In further comparing these 1971 survey results with those in the 1960s, there is, if anything, a slight decline in the "don't know" group and a small increase in opinion favorable to Peking, but the changes are far from significant.

Other international developments concerning China in 1971–1972, such as Peking's admission to the U.N., also had little effect on Japanese popular opi-

Table 6

Japanese Opinions on China

(by percentage of responses)

	February 1964		June 1967	
Formal ties with Peking		U.N. seat*	U.N. seat	for
		pro 11	8	Peking
Pro	38	con 16	31	Two Chinas
		don't know 11	--	Undecided
Con	7		8	Taipei
Don't know	55		53	Don't know

SOURCES: Jiji Tsūshinsha, Feb. 1964, *Nenkan*, 1964, p. 220; and Kyōdō Press (Tsushinsha), June 1967, *Nenkan*, 1968, p. 419.

*Only of those who favored formal ties with Peking.

49. The extent of the "China boom" at that time may be inferred from the fact that, in a poll taken immediately after Premier Tanaka's visit to Peking, 98 percent of those interviewed knew about that event. A total of 69 percent said that they had read or heard about the Sino-Japanese joint communiqué issued at the conclusion of the premier's visit. See Jiji Tsūshinsha, Oct. 1972, *Yoron chōsa*, Dec. 1972, p. 82. This can be compared with 96 percent of the American public that had heard about the atomic bomb only a few days after it was dropped in Hiroshima. See John M. Fenton, *In Your Opinion . . .* (Boston: Little, Brown, 1960), p. 36.

Table 7

Effects of U.S.-China Rapprochement
on Japanese Attitudes toward China
(by percentage of responses)

	U.N. seat for Peking	U.N. seat for Taipei	U.N. seats for both	Don't know
January 1971	11	7	34	48
Late July 1971	13	6	31	49

SOURCE: Nihon Risāchi Sentā, Jan. and July 1971, *Yoron chōsa*,
Nov. 1971, p. 75.

nion with regard to China. These events may have influenced the gradual shift
in Japanese opinion favorable to an early establishment of formal ties with
Peking (Table 8 summarizes the results of various surveys taken in the early
1970s), but their impact should not be exaggerated. The relatively large proportion of Japanese which had always supported recognition of the People's
Republic of China actually began to increase as soon as the Chinese Cultural
Revolution wound down. By mid-1968, 42 percent of the people interviewed
replied that Japan should restore relations with Peking as soon as possible, and
another 37 percent favored friendly relations short of formal ties. The status
quo approach—the "trade but no political relations" formula—and the con-

Table 8

Japanese Opinions on Establishing Formal Relations
with the People's Republic of China
(by percentage of responses)

	Yes, immediately	Yes, as soon as possible	No need to make haste	Not necessary at all	Don't know/ no answer	TOTAL
Mar. 1970*	16	47	23	4	10	100
Apr. 1971	11	44	13	1	31	100
(Jul. 1971 Nixon reveals his plan to visit China)						
(Oct. 1971 China is admitted to U.N.)						
Nov. 1971	14	44	13	1	28	100
(Jul. 1972 Tanaka forms a new cabinet)						
Aug. 1972	17	45	13	1	24	100
Sept. 1972	19	45	13	2	22	101

*The 1970 survey is included for reference, although it is difficult to compare it directly
with the others because its questions were phrased rather differently.
SOURCES: The March 1970 results from Mainichi Shimbunsha; the others from Jiji
Tsūshinsha, *Yoron chōsa*, June 1971, p. 67; Jan. 1972; Oct. 1972, p. 75; and Nov. 1972, p. 74.

tinuance of formal relations with the Nationalist government in Taiwan were chosen by 5 percent and 2 percent of respondents respectively (the remaining 14 percent gave no answers).[50]

The really significant shift in Japanese opinion regarding China occurred only after Premier Tanaka actually visited Peking and successfully concluded an agreement with China. In polls taken shortly after the premier's visit, about one out of three Japanese adults strongly approved his action, calling it "a very good thing." Another 50 percent answered that "it was all right," and less than 3 percent disapproved (the remaining 11.5 percent were uncommitted).[51]

The major international developments in 1971–1972, however, probably did affect the sharp increase in Japanese popular support for breaking relations with Taiwan so that an early rapprochement with Peking would be possible. As there was not a large change in the amount of sympathy for Taiwan, probably many who had previously been noncommittal swung over to support the establishment of ties with Peking (see Table 9). No doubt the impact of Sino-American rapprochement and China's admission to the United Nations put the troublesome issue of Taiwan's international status in a substantially different context, easing Japanese psychological inhibitions about making a decision against Taiwan.

The Japanese, however, still suffered certain qualms of conscience in making this embarrassing choice between Peking and Taipei. In October 1972, shortly after the government made the decision to sever diplomatic relations with

Table 9

Japanese Opinions on Severing Relations
with the Nationalist Government on Taiwan
(by percentage of responses)

| | Among those in favor of relations with Peking | | | | | Those opposed to immediate relations with Peking, thus in favor of retaining relations with Taiwan (columns 3 and 4 Table 8) |
| | (column 1 and 2, Table 8) | | | | | |
	Yes, without hesitation	Yes, if necessary	No (two Chinas)	Other/ don't know	Sub-total	
Apr. 1971	2	7	34	12	55	14
Nov. 1971	5	15	28	11	59	14
Aug. 1972	4	18	28	12	62	14
Sept. 1972	5	15	30	14	64	15

SOURCES: Jiji Tsūshinsha, *Yoron chōsa*, June 1971, p. 67; Jan. 1972; Oct. 1972, p. 75; and Nov. 1972, p. 82.

50. Mainichi Shimbunsha, June 1968, *Mainichi shimbun*, June 21, 1968.
51. Jiji Tsūshinsha, Oct. 1972, *Yoron chōsa*, Dec. 1972, p. 82.

Taiwan, only 6 percent of the Japanese approved of the action without reservation and 15 percent expressly disapproved. As many as 51 percent of the people answered rather timidly that it was "the only possible thing to do," and the remaining 21 percent gave "don't know" answers. Such a reserved attitude was quite in contrast with the positive and almost naive approval of the government's action in establishing relations with Peking. Thus, the Taiwan problem was an important factor in the formulation of Japanese opinions on the China issue. The barrier, however, was not insurmountable; there existed a permissive consensus among the Japanese in relation to the China problem.[52]

Russia

Undramatic but steady progress in Soviet-Japanese relations in the decade 1964–1973 includes the Soviet-Japanese Aviation Agreement, which made possible the opening of air routes between Tokyo and Moscow in January 1966 and between Niigata and Khabarovsk in March 1971; the Consular Agreement (July 1966); regular ministerial consultations (the first in July 1967, when Japanese Foreign Minister Miki visited Moscow, and the second in January 1972, when Soviet Foreign Minister Gromyko visited Japan); and a gradual increase in trade under the long-term trade agreements between Japan and the Soviet Union (the volume of trade doubled from U.S. $514 million in 1966 to $1,098 million in 1972). These developments, however, attracted little public attention. A survey conducted in Hokkaidō in 1966 indicates that less than 40 percent of the people knew of the agreements on trade, aviation, and consular exchange, but nearly three out of four people were aware of such problems with the Soviet Union as the obtaining of permission to visit graves on former Japanese islands, the negotiations for a fishery agreement, and the protest against the capture and internment of Japanese fishing boats and their crews.[53]

Among the various problems in Russo-Japanese relations, the territorial issue has naturally attracted the greatest attention from the Japanese. From both legal and historical perspectives, the Japanese government has claimed the islands of Habomai and Shikotan because they are an integral part of Hokkaidō (which never came under foreign control), and Etorofu and Kunashiri because they belong to what the Japanese call the Southern Kuriles, sovereignty over which—according to the Japanese position taken during the normalization talks with the Soviet Union in 1956—Japan did not renounce in the San Francisco Peace Treaty. A solution to this territorial question, the Japanese government argues, should precede conclusion of a peace treaty. The Russians, however, contend that the territorial question has already been

52. As for the concept "permissive consensus," see Key, *Public Opinion*, pp. 32–33.
53. Governor's Office of Hokkaidō, May 1966, *Nenkan* 1967, p. 242.

solved and, therefore, does not stand in the way of a peace treaty. Despite considerable argument between the two governments since the early 1960s, there is no indication that they will resolve this issue in the near future.

In the past, certain promotional groups, such as the Association for the Promotion of the Return of the Northern Territories and the Federation of the Former Inhabitants of Chishima and Habomai, as well as some governmental or semigovernmental agencies, such as the Prefectual Office of Hokkaidō and the Council for Affairs concerning the Northern Territories (an institution created in October 1969 under the supervision of the prime minister's office) have tried to stir up public opinion over the territorial issue. Their efforts notwithstanding, a poll conducted in May 1966 indicated that even the public in Hokkaidō showed less interest in the problem of the Russian-occupied islands than in the question of Okinawa.[54] The opinion surveys summarized in Table 10, however, seem to demonstrate that the campaign to build up an informed opinion on the Northern Islands has had some effect.

Despite anti-Russian agitation by ultranationalistic groups and increased public awareness, however, it seems unlikely that Japanese public opinion will become sufficiently aroused over the Northern Islands question to embarrass the government. In May 1966, only 17 percent of the public insisted on the immediate and unconditional return of the Soviet-occupied islands. Another 15 percent held the view that Japan should make Russian return of the islands a condition in the withdrawal of U.S. forces from Japan. The majority (40 percent), however, replied that Japan should not foolishly jeopardize peaceful relations with the Soviet Union—which were necessary for the smooth handling of such pragmatic matters as fishing and trade agreements—by doggedly adhering to its claim to the islands.[55]

In fact, the more familiar the territorial issue has become, the less hotheaded the public has become. In 1966, 74 percent of Hokkaidō voters gave affirmative answers to a question as to whether the Japanese government should proceed more vigorously with its negotiations with the Soviet Union on the territorial issues; the figure declined to 72 percent in 1969 and 66 percent in 1970.[56] By the early 1970s, Japanese opinion on the problem divided as follows: approximately one-third of the public felt that Japan should aim at getting all four islands back; about one-quarter would be content with only the two tiny islands adjacent to Hokkaidō; and the remainder (about 40 percent) was undecided.[57] Moreover, if the Russians were to provide some kind of assurance on their willingness to negotiate over the Southern Kuriles problem, the govern-

54. In Hokkaidō, 34 percent of the voters showed a greater interest in Okinawa than in the Northern Islands, 29 percent said they were more interested in the Northern Islands, 8 percent were equally interested in both, 9 percent in neither, and 20 percent gave "don't know" answers. Ibid., p. 240.

55. Ibid., p. 242.

56. Ibid., *Nenkan* 1967, pp. 240–242; 1970, pp. 220–222; and 1971, pp. 309–311.

57. Jiji Tsūshinsha, Feb. 1972, *Yoron chōsa*, April 1972, p. 87.

Table 10
Awareness in Hokkaidō of the Territorial Problems
with the Soviet Union
(by percentage of responses)

		May 1966	June 1969	Aug. 1970	
	very much		52	19	63
	fairly			44	
Those who showed an interest in the issues	not very much	n.a.	31	25	31
	not at all			6	
	don't know		17		6
Those who had talked about the matter with their friends or family		23	33		39
Those who were aware	a. that the four islands were under Russian occupation	84	87		92
	b. that the San Francisco Treaty and the Soviet-Japanese Joint Declaration contained provisions relevant to the problem	26	36		39
	c. that the Japanese government had been asking Russia to return the islands	76	88		89
	d. that some groups had been engaged in the campaign for the return of the islands	60	74		84

SOURCE: Governor's Office of Hokkaido, *Nenkan*, 1967, pp. 240–242; ibid., 1970, pp. 220–222; and ibid., 1971, pp. 309–311.

ment would probably not have much trouble in building up a consensus for a compromise solution.[58] Although the pending problem over the Northern Islands has been and will continue to be an important reason for Japanese ill-feeling toward the Russians, there seems little possibility that anti-Russian agitation will score any great success in the subdued ideological tension marking the recent international scene.

58. In January 1971, for instance, those insisting on the prompt return by the Soviet Union of all the four islands (35 percent) were outnumbered by those approving the idea that Habomai and Shikotan should be recovered first (57 percent). Sankei Shimbunsha, Jan. 1972, *Yoron chōsa*, March 1972, p. 90.

Chart 5
Degree of Japanese Public Interest in Various Issues

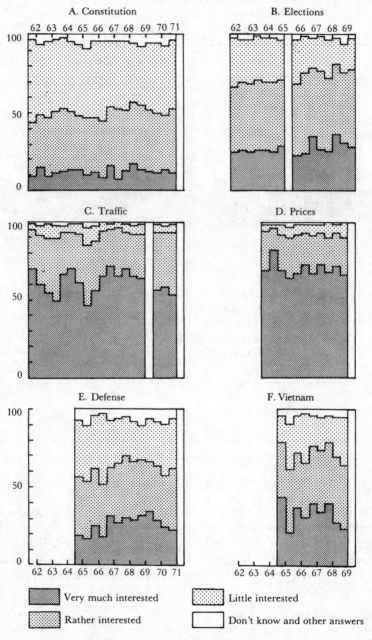

A. Constitution	B. Elections
C. Traffic	D. Prices
E. Defense	F. Vietnam

Very much interested   Little interested

Rather interested   Don't know and other answers

SOURCE: Tōkei Sūri Kenkyūjo, *Tokyo teiki chōsa no kekka*, pp. 46-49.

The United States

Since the end of the war, the Japanese public has had a generally favorable impression of the United States, but several events over the past few years have tarnished this image of America. The sharp fall in American popularity in 1965, as illustrated in Chart 3, was probably caused by the beginning of heightened U.S. intervention in the Vietnam War which commenced in the spring of that year. No doubt the critical reports in leading Japanese newspapers on the American actions in Vietnam impressed the Japanese public; in August 1965, 94 percent of the people surveyed said that they knew about the war in Vietnam; 87 percent had heard of the Vietcong, and 79 percent knew of the American bombing of North Vietnam.[59] It is difficult, however, for the mass media to keep the man in the street constantly interested in such a topic as the Vietnam War. Unlike such subjects as constitutional issues, elections, prices of commodities, and traffic troubles, which attract a fairly stable level of public interest, popular concern over the Vietnam War issue fluctuated over time (see Charts 5 *A–F*). In May 1965, 28 percent of those interviewed in Tokyo cited the Vietnam War as one of the current topics to which they paid particular attention when reading the newspaper. Only six months later, barely one out of twenty citizens in Tokyo referred to the news on Vietnam as an item that evoked their special interest.[60] The basic image that the mass media conveys on a particular event, however, seems to remain rather stable in the public mind. In a series of public opinion studies conducted from 1965 to 1969, 30 to 40 percent of the citizens of Tokyo usually blamed the United States for the war in Vietnam; those who blamed the Vietcong, North Vietnam, Communist China, or the Soviet Union never reached that figure, even when added together.[61]

The United States regained some popularity after the initial excitement over the Vietnam War died down, but it slipped again during 1967–1968. The gradual deterioration of the American image in Japan during these years was related to the Japanese fear, groundless or not, of becoming involved in the United States military actions in Southeast Asia. Although, as the Japanese government explained, the visits to Japanese ports by U.S. nuclear-powered submarines and aircraft carriers fell within the terms of the U.S.-Japan Security Treaty, the frequency of these port calls, as well as the greatly intensified U.S. use of Okinawan bases, seemed to increase the danger in the eyes of the Japanese public.

The situation was further complicated by the fact that the reversion of Okinawa was becoming a hot issue in Japanese politics. Both the American deci-

59. Asahi Shimbunsha, Aug. 1965, *Nenkan* 1966, pp. 296–297.
60. Tōkei Sūri Kenkyūjo, spring and autumn 1965, *Nenkan* 1966, pp. 151–152.
61. See Tōkei Sūri Kenkyūjo, *Tokyo teiki chōsa no kekka*, pp. 46–49.

sion to return the Ogasawara islands in 1968 and the agreement between the United States and Japan the following year for the return of the administration of Okinawa to Japan within a few years obviously had some effect in preventing the further aggravation of Japanese feelings against the Americans. By some irony of fate, however, the actual reversion of Okinawa, a gesture of American friendship with Japan, was finalized at a time when American-Japanese friendship reached its lowest ebb since the end of the Pacific War. By then new issues had emerged, such as the economic friction over textiles and currency as well as diplomatic confusion over China. The wild fluctuations in the popularity indices (especially those concerning America and China) shown in Charts 2 and 3 indicate the degree to which these events had an injurious effect on U.S.-Japanese relations.

Despite the unhappy experiences of recent years, however, the majority of Japanese still have great expectations for the future of Japanese-American friendship. In a recent poll, for example, nearly two-thirds of the respondents replied that in spite of Sino-Japanese rapprochement, they did not think it necessary for Japan to abandon its traditional policy of friendship with the United States.[62] At the same time, public opinion in Japan, as in any country, is inconsistent in many ways. Although 37 percent of the public surveyed in a 1971 poll named the United States as one of the three countries on which they believed Japan could rely, another 37 percent answered negatively to a question in the same survey as to whether the Americans kept faith with foreign peoples (31 percent answered affirmatively). Moreover, nearly half responded that Japan was understood by the Americans better than by any other people, but 45 percent of the same sample supported the statement that the United States, as a great power, was inclined to disregard the interests of small and weaker nations.[63]

What bearing do such psychological fluctuations have on the Japanese view of the Security Treaty with the United States? The soundings of opinion on this subject are difficult to compare because they were conducted by different pollsters who framed their questions in divergent ways. If one sorts them out by type, however, broadly similar patterns can be observed. There is, moreover, one series of surveys conducted twice a year since 1960 in Tokyo by the Institute of Statistical Mathematics (Tōkei Sūri Kenkyūjo) according to which unfavorable opinion on the Security Treaty was strongest (nearly one out of two citizens) at the time of its signing but gradually declined, with the result that nine years later the balance had turned almost completely in favor of the treaty. These studies are reproduced in a summarized form in Table 11. After 1970, the situation began to be reversed but not to such an extent that the balance was decisively upset.[64]

62. Sankei Shimbunsha, Oct. 1972, *Yoron chōsa*, Dec. 1972, p. 85.
63. Mainichi Shimbunsha, Oct. 1971, *Yoron chōsa*, Dec. 1971, pp. 78–79.
64. Tōkei Sūri Kenkyūjo, *Tokyo teiki chōsa no kekka*, p. 72.

Table 11
Japanese Attitudes toward the Mutual
Security Treaty with the U.S.
(by percentage of responses)

	Pro	Con	Other	Don't know
1960 spring	20	46	6	29
1960 autumn	33	37	2	28
1962 spring	28	29	5	38
1967 spring	39	26	11	24
1969 autumn	40	22	8	30
1970 spring	36	28	7	29
1971 spring	35	31	5	29

SOURCE: Tōkei Sūri Kenkyūjo, *Tokyo teiki chōsa no kekka*, p. 72.

Other polls (represented in Tables 12 *A–E*) confirm the main outlines of the trends in Japanese opinion on the Security Treaty presented in Table 11. Despite the apparent confusion and inconsistencies among these polls, they do reveal (1) that the balance is, on the whole, in favor of the treaty, although firm supporters number only about one in ten persons; (2) that although a sizable number of individuals are still opposed to the treaty, a considerable proportion appear to be only mildly opposed, as evident in the large percentage of persons who take a noncommittal position whenever such an option is available; and (3) that uncommitted persons have increased in recent years.

Certainly no one can predict how the balance will swing in the future. That will depend, one may conjecture, on future international developments as well as on how effectively the various political forces in Japan are able to influence the public's sentiments. Table 13 affords some clues on Japanese attitudes toward the Security Treaty by party affiliation. Apart from the Communists, who were definitely opposed to the treaty, each group contains a large proportion (about 40 percent) of uncommitted persons.[65] Their attitude will inevitably affect the balance.

Recent international developments, including the Sino-American rapprochement, have reduced the need for Japan to choose between the American alliance and Chinese friendship, which in turn has helped to undermine the opposition to the American treaty. On the other hand, these developments have given rise to the argument that, in view of the seemingly reduced international tension in Asia, Japan need rely less than in the past on the United States. Japan's response to the retrenchment of American military presence abroad has also been ambiguous. Although their fear of becoming unintentionally in-

65. *Mainichi shimbun*, July 1, 1968.

Table 12
Results from Various Surveys
on Japanese Opinion regarding the Mutual Security Treaty with the U.S.
(by percentage of responses)

A. Do you think the U.S.-Japan Security Treaty is useful for the maintenance of peace and the security of Japan?

	Yes, very useful	Yes, think so	No, don't think so	No, even harmful	Other	Don't know
Dec. 1967	11	43	12	5	0	29
Dec. 1969	15	47	15	5	0	19

SOURCE: *Nenkan*, 1968, p. 430; and 1970, p. 546.

B. Do you think the U.S.-Japan Security Treaty is useful for the purpose of maintaining Japan's security?

	Very useful	May be useful	Not very useful	Even harmful	Undecided	Other	Don't know
Mar. 1968	12	33	21	--	11	1	22
Apr. 1968	12	43	17	--	10	1	17
June 1969	12	35	4	2	26	--	20

SOURCE: Yomiuri Shimbunsha, March and April 1968 (surveys to investigate the effect of President Johnson's announcement of the termination of air raids on North Vietnam on Japanese public opinion), *Yomiuri shimbun* , Apr. (22, 1968. Other results from *Nenkan*, 1970, p. 493 (the 1969 poll was worded somewhat differently).

C. Is the U.S.-Japan Security Treaty in the interests of Japan?

	Yes, it is	No, it isn't	Undecided	No answer
Jan. 1969	33	29	--	40
Sept. 1969	37	34	--	24
June 1970	37	14	24	22
June 1971	34	20	26	20

SOURCE: *Asahi shimbun*, Jan. 5, 1969; *Nenkan*, 1970, p. 499, and 1971, p. 552; and *Yoron chōsa*, Aug. 1971, p. 72.

Table 12 (*continued*)

D. Japan has a security treaty with the U.S. for the defense of the country. Are you for or against this treaty?

	For	Against	Undecided	Other/ no answer
Mar. 1960	22	36	15*	27
June 1968	30	20	43	7

SOURCE: *Nenkan*, 1959, p. 135; and *Mainichi shimbun*, July 1, 1968.
*Not interested.

E. Do you think the U.S. Japan Security Treaty is useful for the maintenance of the security of Japan?

	Yes, it is useful	No, it isn't useful	No, it is even harmful	Other/ no answer
Apr. 1969	52	23	14	11
Oct. 1969	58	20	12	10
Apr. 1972	48	25	14	13

SOURCE: *Nanken*, 1970, pp. 476, 513; and *Yoron chōsa*, July 1972, p. 69.

volved in international conflicts through the treaty commitment with the United States is now greatly reduced, Japanese can no longer be sure about the U.S. intention to remain in Asia. U.S. credibility has become a growing question. Thus, it seems unlikely that a popular consensus can be formed in Japan on the U.S.-Japanese alliance in the near future.

National Defense

Although the problem of national defense is not yet the object of serious discussion in Japan, it has drawn fairly constant interest from a substantial proportion (approximately 60 percent) of the voters in the Tokyo area (see Chart 5 *A–F*). In 1968–1969, political parties and newspapers, in anticipation of a decision on the renewal of the U.S.-Japanese Security Treaty in 1970, vigorously took up the national defense issue, thereby possibly producing a rise in popular concern on the question at that time.[66] Some business leaders have also begun to articulate more openly their views on matters such as the creation of "inde-

66. Tōkei Sūri Kenkyūjo, *Tokyo teiki chōsa no kekka*, pp. 46–49.

Table 13
Breakdown by Party Affiliation
of Japanese Opinion regarding the Mutual Security Treaty with the U.S.
(by percentage of responses)

	Favorable	Unfavorable	Noncommittal	Other/no answer
Total	30	20	43	7
By party support				
Liberal Democratic	48	6	41	5
Dem. Socialist	33	27	39	1
Kōmei	19	34	40	7
Socialist	16	39	41	4
Communist	7	72	17	4

SOURCE: *Mainichi shimbun*, July 1, 1968.

pendent defense capabilities," the need for a sufficiently developed weapons industry to "nationalize" the equipment for the Self-Defense Forces, and the maintenance of sea-lane security for bringing in the resources vital to the Japanese economy.

In June 1968, two out of three Japanese voters were somewhat familiar with the three so-called nonnuclear principles—that Japan will not acquire, produce, or bring in nuclear weapons—and in October 1969, a little over 60 percent of the public were aware that a decision on the Mutual Security Treaty would be made the following year.[67] More important than popular awareness on the defense problem, however, is how meaningfully and intelligently the policy options are presented to the public. Here, the situation is not satisfactory, although it has improved over some years ago when the defense issue was almost taboo among Japanese intellectuals. With these basic facts in mind, I shall attempt to analyze the major trends of popular opinion regarding two specific questions: the nature of the Self-Defense Forces, and the desirability of Japan's nuclear armament.

In September 1969, three persons in four approved in principle the maintenance of Self-Defense Forces and only one out of ten disapproved. In another poll taken at the same time, a little more than 40 percent supported the statement that Japan should keep both the Mutual Security Treaty with the United States and the Self-Defense Forces, 13 percent voted for the abrogation of the treaty, and another 10 percent rejected both the treaty and the Self-Defense Forces.[68] On the strength of these figures, the Defense Agency claimed rather boastfully in its first White Paper (published in 1970) that the "people now

67. Mainichi Shimbunsha, June 1968, *Mainichi shimbun*, July 1, 1968; and Hokkaido Shimbunsha, Chubū Nippon Shimbunsha, Nishi Nippon Shimbunsha, and Tokyo Shimbunsha, Nov. 1969, *Nenkan* 1970, p. 518.
68. Naikaku Sōridaijin Kambō Kōhōshitsu, Sept. 1969, *Nenkan* 1970, pp. 105, 109.

Table 14
Japanese Attitudes toward the Self-Defense
Forces
(by percentage of responses)

	For	Against	Undecided	Don't know
Dec. 1953	51	31	--	18
July 1954	60	23	--	17
Feb. 1971	46	33	8	13

SOURCE: Yomiuri shimbunsha, Dec. 1953 and July 1954, *Yomiuri shimbun*, Jan. 6, 1954, and July 11, 1954; Naikaki Sōridaijin Kambō Kōhōshitsu, Feb. 1971, *Nenkan*, 1971, p. 203. The question in the 1971 survey was whether Japan should have armament for purely self-defense purposes or should have none at all.

have a well-developed understanding of the security policies adopted by their government" and that the "majority of the public is appreciative of the raison d'être of the Self-Defense Forces."[69]

A long-range view, however, does not support the optimism of this White Paper. A comparison of the quoted data—which incidentally were all from polls conducted by government agencies—with the results of similar polls in earlier periods reveals not an increase but a decline in support for the Self-Defense Forces (82 percent in 1965, 77 percent in 1967, and 75 percent in 1969), as well as steadily growing disapproval of them (5 percent in 1965, 6 percent in 1967, and 10 percent in 1969). Although the balance was definitely on the affirmative side, the figures do not support a conclusion that the debates on national defense were helpful in building up enlightened support for the government's defense policy. In fact, although those who feel that Japan should not maintain any armament under any circumstances do not constitute a very large proportion (18 percent), about 30 to 40 percent of the Japanese voters are not well disposed toward the Self-Defense Forces for financial, constitutional, or other reasons.[70] Table 14 illustrates the relatively insignificant changes in Japanese opinion on the Self-Defense Forces over the twenty-some years since their creation in July 1954.

Questions regarding the nature and size of a country's defense forces, however, have little meaning without a consideration of the basic aims of the country's defense policy and its relevance to current international circumstances. Japanese public opinion has not yet crystallized on the place of the Self-Defense Forces in the nation's military set-up as a whole, especially in view of the uncer-

69. Bōeichō, *Nihon no bōei: bōei hakusho* (Tokyo: Ōkurashō Insatsukyoku, 1970), p. 63.
70. Sōrifu, Nov. 1965 and Sept. 1969, *Nenkan* 1966, p. 146, and 1970, p. 108.

tainties about the future of the American alliance. Indicative of the fluidity of the situation is the divergent way in which questions on the subject are phrased in various opinion polls.

Although the variation in survey formats makes it difficult to present the relevant data in a meaningful way, several points and trends regarding popular Japanese views on the nation's defense policy do emerge from the polling results compiled in Table 15. First, there is a fairly regular pattern in the division of opinion, with the exception of that in the most recent poll. Second, popular responses can change substantially depending on the phrasing of the questions. In the latest poll, the support for option *A* obviously declined be-

Table 15
Japanese Opinions on Defense Policy
(by percentage of responses)

	Options*	A	B	C	D	E	Other/ no answer
Pollster/Date							
Mainichi	Oct. '69	22	21	24	9	8	16
Kyodo	Dec. '69	20	14	24	12	9	22
Kyodo	Apr. '70	24	10	22	11	8	25
Mainichi	Apr. '72						
Total		12*	20**	21	11	17***	19
By party affiliation							
LDP		26	22	22	5	9	16
DSP		6	27	28	11	21	7
Kōmeitō		4	17	28	11	20	20
JCP		4	9	15	41	22	9
JSP		5	18	17	16	26	18
No party		5	20	22	13	20	20

SOURCES: *Nenkan*, 1970, pp. 514, 546; ibid., 1971, p. 520; and *Yoron chōsa*, July 1972, p. 69.

*Options: The wording is that used in the Mainichi poll in October 1969 and is similar throughout, unless otherwise noted. Options *A, B, C, D,* and *E* correspond roughly to the party policies of the LDP, DSP, Komeito, JCP, and JSP, respectively.

A: To maintain the present Security Treaty and strengthen own defense capabilities in accordance with the growth of national power (* plus rely on America's nuclear umbrella).

B: To modify the Security Treaty to permit the U.S. to use base facilities on Japanese soil in emergency only, and to establish an independent defense set-up (**plus secure a nonaggression treaty between East and West).

C: To liquidate the Security Treaty by stages while aiming at the maintenance of complete neutrality.

D: To abrogate the Security Treaty and seek neutrality and national security on Japan's own ability.

E: To abrogate the Security Treaty and realize an unarmed neutrality (***plus conclude a nonaggression treaty among Japan, the U.S., China, and the USSR).

cause of the addition of "American nuclear umbrella"; options B and E were favorably affected by the additional mention of idealistic proposals for "non-aggression" arrangements. Third, there is a wide diversity of opinion within any single party group. Even among Communist supporters, who generally share the same opinions, nearly six out of ten showed an inclination toward ideas more in line with the policies of the other parties (especially those of the Kōmeitō and the Socialists) than with the policy of the JCP (represented by option D). Within the other groups, little more than one-quarter of each party's supporters favored their own party policy. (The respondents were not told which position was in line with which party's policy).

Perhaps the most obvious indication from Table 15 is that there is no clearly discernible, fixed trend with respect to Japanese opinion on national defense. Therefore, its future depends on policy leadership from the political parties and other opinion leaders. Many Japanese, however, remain skeptical on pragmatic as well as idealistic grounds about the usefulness of armed force in resolving any international problems Japan may face. This fundamental attitude is certain to influence Japan's decisions on future defense policy.

Japanese caution on the use of armed force is also relevant to the controversial question of Japan's acquisition of nuclear weapons. The Chinese nuclear program and arguments about the credibility of America's nuclear umbrella have greatly transformed the intellectual atmosphere in which the Japanese deal with this once-dangerous topic. Nevertheless, there are no clear-cut indications that the Japanese public is any more favorable to the country's nuclear armament. Opinion studies on this subject over the past several years indicate that 15 percent of the public at most favors Japanese acquisition of nuclear forces, whereas from 60 to 80 percent categorically reject the idea. However, one-quarter to one-third of the Japanese people think that, whether they desire it or not, Japan is likely to arm itself with nuclear weapons in the future, as long as the present conservative leaders remain in power.[71]

In another interesting study of the opinions of Japanese leaders in various walks of life, 78 percent did not think it wise for Japan to "go nuclear." Only one out of a hundred favored a nuclear policy, and 20 percent answered that the decision should be left to future generations.[72] As a nuclear policy has not yet become a serious choice among either political or intellectual leaders of the country, no one can be sure that the Japanese will not change their views about nuclear armament. Nevertheless, recent trends in public opinion do not manifest any signs of a revolutionary departure from the traditional nonnuclear policy.

71. See, for example, Mainichi Shimbunsha, June 1968, *Mainichi shimbun*, July 1, 1968; and Yomiuri Shimbunsha, June 1969, *Nenkan* 1970, p. 492.

72. A poll conducted in the summer of 1972 by Yomiuri Shimbunsha of the views of 296 persons selected from academic, journalistic, business, bureaucratic, and defense circles on the subject of Japan's defense and foreign policies. See Yomiuri Shimbunsha, *Nihon no gaikō anzenhoshō*, Tokyo Kaigi Hōkokusho, 3 (Tokyo: Kaigi Jimukyoku, 1973), p. 76.

CONCLUSION

Some social psychologists argue persuasively that public opinion data frequently suffer from distortions simply because they are based on "a kind of invalid
self-report in which opinion expression is deflected from private indifference
toward endorsement of perceived consensus."[73] Respondents in surveys—particularly in a society such as Japan where conformity with others' views is
highly valued—tend to echo as their own those opinions they have already
heard expressed and defended, especially in the mass media. This fact raises
the important question of the distinction between "real" and "perceived" public opinion for all who observe or are involved in the policy-formulation process. Hence, Kishi Nobusuke, Japan's premier at the time of the controversial
revision of the U.S.-Japanese Security Treaty, could assert that he would count
on the "inaudible voices" (*koenaki koe*) of the silent majority rather than on those
articulated through the opposition parties and media.

There is some evidence that since treaty revision crisis of 1960, Japanese
leaders have become more cautious (or even timid) about offending the *vox
populi*. Japanese politicians have become, for better or worse, public-opinion-
minded. To the extent that pollsters' reports are becoming a major source of
the policy-makers' knowledge about public opinion, it may be reasonably assumed that the people's voice, as reflected in the polls, is affecting the decision-
makers' perception of important policy issues and their assessment of feasible
responses to those issues.[74] For example, public opposition to the establishment
of diplomatic relations with the Republic of Korea (or government apprehension over possible domestic confusion comparable to that surrounding the preceding cabinet's forceful handling of the Security Treaty issue) apparently
caused the Ikeda administration to delay its actions.[75] The prolonged handling
of the matter certainly helped detract from the force of the critical arguments.
Similarly, the Satō cabinet decided, on the basis of public opinion and in spite
of arguments from important members of the LDP, not to propose an extension
of the Security Treaty by an explicit arrangement with the United States in
June 1970 when the treaty became eligible for further negotiations.[76]

Although public opinion acted as a constraint on policy innovation in both
cases, it did not prevent the government from taking the action it deemed

73. Milton J. Rosenberg, "Images in Relations to the Policy Process: American Public
Opinion on Cold-War Issues," in Herbert C. Kelman, ed., *International Behavior* (New York:
Holt, Rinehart and Winston, 1965), p. 286.
74. See footnote 3 and Misawa Shigeo, "Seisaku ketteikatei no gaikan," in Nihon Seiji
Gakkai, ed., *Gendai Nihon no seitō to kanryō* (Tokyo: Iwanami Shoten, 1967), p. 21.
75. For a similar view, see Kōsaka Masataka, "Yoshida Shigeru igo," in his *Saisho Yoshida
Shigeru* (Tokyo: Chūō Kōronsha, 1968), p. 139.
76. A fairly detailed account on the intraparty decision-making process about this issue is
given in Asahi Shimbunsha, *Jimintō: hoshu kenryoku no kōzō* (Tokyo: Asahi Shimbunsha,
1970), pp. 77–111.

necessary. Public opinion merely delayed governmental policy on the Korean issue. On the Security Treaty issue, government and party leaders themselves were not convinced of the merits of substantive changes. Possibly future governments will feel more constrained by domestic opinion, especially in their attempts to accommodate the country's policies to the requirements of international life such as the increased demands from developing areas for economic and technical aid.

More typical of the impact of Japanese public opinion on foreign policy in the past, however, has been its role as a *stimulus* for a more self-assertive "autonomous diplomacy." The Japanese people, while accepting the sheer necessity and even the wisdom of the American alliance, have also felt that the alliance has limited their country's independence. Therefore they have tended to define and review Japanese diplomacy according to whether it has reduced or increased the nation's dependence on the United States. Both the reestablishment of diplomatic relations with the Soviet Union in 1956 and the revision of the American Security Treaty in 1960 were assessed in such terms, although the government never really succeeded in persuading the people that the treaty revision was to enable Japan to stand on an equal footing with the United States.

In these terms, both the reversion of Okinawa and the establishment of diplomatic relations with the People's Republic of China illustrate the impact of public opinion on policy innovation. The growing public demand for more acceptable solutions to the Okinawa issue, however, was more of an embarrassment than an encouragement to the Japanese government.[77] And although the Japanese people welcomed the establishment of diplomatic relations with the People's Republic of China, the merit of that move was substantially reduced by the fact that Washington, not Tokyo, had initiated the rapprochement with Peking.

Future historians may well write that the establishment of Sino-Japanese diplomatic relations brought to an end the era in which relations with the United States completely dominated Japanese thinking about international affairs. It is too early to predict what will eventually emerge from a reconsideration of the basic assumptions underlying Japanese foreign policy, but irrespective of the outcome, Japanese public opinion will have an important bearing on both the shape of a new consensus and the process by which it is made.

77. See Akio Watanabe, *The Okinawa Problem: A Chapter in Japan-U.S. Relations* (Melbourne, Australia: Melbourne University Press, 1970), especially chap. 11. A more detailed analysis on the various aspects of the political process leading up to the Satō-Nixon communiqué on Okinawa of November 1969 is provided in Nihon Kokusai Seiji Gakkai, ed., *Okinawa henkan kōsho no seiji katei* (Tokyo: Yūhikaku, 1975).

The Tyumen Oil Development Project and Japanese Foreign Policy Decision-Making

GERALD L. CURTIS

Japanese businessmen, acting through an organization called the Japan-Soviet Economic Committee (Nisso Keizai Iinkai) have been discussing for several years with Soviet authorities the possibility of Japanese participation in the development of the oil resources of the Tyumen region of Siberia.[1] But as of mid-1975, Japanese businessmen and Soviet authorities involved in these discussions had been unable to arrive at a mutually acceptable agreement. The project appeared to have been shelved for the foreseeable future, although it remained on the agenda of the Japan-Soviet Economic Committee.

In dealing with the evolution of Japanese policy concerning Tyumen we are dealing in effect with what is a Japanese nondecision. Although it is difficult to assign precise weights to the several factors involved in Japanese policy in the absence of a final and clear decision, it is possible to identify the variables involved and to formulate hypotheses about their relative importance. In doing so we can also indicate the developments that would need to occur if the present Japanese nondecision on Tyumen were to be turned into a decision to participate in this large and extremely expensive project.

I am particularly concerned with analyzing the policy of the Japanese government concerning Tyumen, a policy that consists of three major elements: (1) a refusal to become a direct party to the negotiations and an insistence that

1. The official English name of the committee is the Japan-Soviet Business Cooperation Committee, but I will refer to it simply as the Japan-Soviet Economic Committee.

an agreement be concluded between Japanese business leaders and Soviet authorities before the Japanese government enters negotiations in any formal manner; (2) a determination by the political leadership to keep separate the issue of participation in the Tyumen project from the northern islands' reversion question, despite strong pressures for a different policy from within the bureaucracy; and (3) a refusal to permit Japanese business participation in the Tyumen project without the participation of United States companies in some form. My purpose in this article is to analyze the reasons for this policy, the process by which it was formulated, and the implications of such a policy for the conduct of Japanese foreign relations.

JAPAN'S ENERGY PROBLEM

Japanese energy problems did not begin with the Yom Kippur War. Before the war broke out in October 1973, and before Japan was subjected to the Arab oil boycott, business and government leaders were concerned about, and seeking ways to reduce, Japanese dependence on the Middle East and the "majors" for its oil supply.[2]

To anyone familiar with the basic facts of Japan's situation in regard to energy resources, the reasons for intense Japanese interest in the abundant natural resources of Siberia are self-evident. Japan, like all industrial countries, has tremendous needs for energy and presently satisfies them primarily by oil.[3] It is the world's second largest consumer of petroleum and the world's largest importer of crude oil. It is dependent on outside sources for 99.7 percent of its oil, 80 percent of which comes from the Middle East.[4] In 1969 Japan accounted for 8.4 percent of the world's demand for oil, and by 1980, as Japanese energy requirements grow faster than the average world rate, this figure is expected to jump to 14 or 15 percent. The entire increase, of course, will have to be satisfied by imports (see Table 1).

One important characteristic of the Japanese oil industry is the extent to which it is controlled by foreign, primarily American, capital. Despite Japan's dominant position in the international oil market, independent Japanese com-

2. The research for this section of the paper was conducted in the summer of 1973 before the outbreak of war in the Middle East. I have left it largely unchanged because more recent data were not easily available, but, more importantly, because the discussion reflects the fact that present Japanese energy policy has roots that go back before the October War in the Middle East and the subsequent oil boycott.

3. Petroleum accounted for 74.9 percent of Japan's primary energy supply in fiscal 1972. That percentage is expected to decline only fractionally by 1980. The United States depends on petroleum for about 46 percent of its energy.

4. Mainly from three Middle Eastern countries: Iran, Saudi Arabia, and Kuwait.

Table 1

Petroleum Requirements of the World and Japan

	Requirements (in million tons)			Average yearly percentage change	
	1960	1969	1980	1960–1969	1969–1980
World	881	1739	3714	7.4	7.9
Japan	25	146	560	19.6	13.0
	(2.8)*	(8.4)	(15.1)		

SOURCE: Adapted from Japan Economic Research Center, *Japan's Economy in 1980 in the Global Context—The Nation's Role in a Polycentric World* (Tokyo, March 1970), p. 85.
*Figures in parenthesis are Japan's share of world demand.

panies account for less than 10 percent of the total supply of Japan's crude oil.[5] Japan lives, as a popular phrase in Japanese energy circles has it, under a "major's umbrella" (*meijā no kasa*). Six of the major oil consortiums account for some 60 percent of Japanese crude oil imports, and other independent American companies for an additional 12 percent. Five of these majors account for 43 percent of Japan's oil refining and 47 percent of distribution. If one adds independent foreign companies to these figures, foreign capital controls over 50 percent of the refining and distribution of oil for Japan.[6] A Foreign Ministry report characterized this situation as one in which most of the oil reaching the Japanese consumer is "strings-attached oil" (*himotsuki genyu*) (see Table 2).[7]

The central role played by American firms in the Japanese oil market is the consequence of policies undertaken in the early postwar period, when Japan had neither the capital nor the technology to develop its own overseas sources. As long as these companies were able to meet the rapidly increasing demands for oil in Japan, little attention was given to developing the Japanese oil industry. This situation has changed dramatically in recent years as the awareness of possible oil shortages has increased, as oil-producing countries acting through OPEC have begun to negotiate effectively with the majors for

5. Japan's share of the international oil market is 16.7 percent. The United States is second at 13.4 percent. West Germany, France, Italy, and England together account for 51 percent, and, of these countries, the largest is England at about 13 percent. Masuda Satohiro, "Sekiyu sangyō no genjō to mondaiten," in Tsūshō Sangyōshō Oaijin Kanbō Chōsaka Hen, *Nihon no energugii mondai* (Tokyo, 1972), p. 77.

6. Gaimushō, Keizaikyoku Hen, *Nanajūnen ni okeru shigen gaikō* (Tokyo: Keizai Kyoku, 1972) pp. 83–84. See also Sakisaka Masao, *Kokusai sekiyu jōsei to enerugii mondai* (Tokyo, 1972); Tsūshō Sangyōshō, *Nihon no enerugii mondai.*

7. Gaimushō, *Shigen gaikō,* p. 84. The dominant role of foreign oil companies in the Japanese market is reflective of a more universal phenomenon. The world's eight major oil companies account for 64 percent (in 1969) of the total petroleum supply in the market world economy. They account for 55.5 percent of the world's oil production, 47.8 percent of its refining, and 49.9 percent of its distribution.

Table 2
Japanese Dependence on the Majors (1972)
(thousand kiloliters)

		Quantity	Percentage
Majors	Caltex	31,442	16.1
	Esso	20,115	10.3
	Mobil	17,772	9.1
	Gulf	14,842	7.6
	Shell	23,826	12.2
	British Petroleum	2,344	1.2
	CFP (France)	4,296	2.2
	TOTAL	114,637	58.7
Other	Getty	8,202	4.2
foreign	UNOCO	9,569	4.9
companies	Other U.S. corporations	5,078	2.6
	Soviet Union Oil Export Corp.	1,953	1.0
	TOTAL	24,802	12.7
Japan	Arabian Oil	18,553	9.5
	North Sumatra Oil	586	0.3
	Others	36,716	18.8*
	GRAND TOTAL	195,294	100.0

SOURCE: Adapted from Gaimushō, Keizaikyoku Hen, *Nanajūnedai ni okeru shigen gaikō,* (Tokyo, 1972), p. 113.
*Handling is done by trading companies; the basic suppliers are for the most part the majors.

higher prices, and as the general state of Japanese-American relations have deteriorated.

Japan now finds itself in a particularly serious situation. It does not participate in the negotiations between OPEC and major oil consortiums, but must pay the price they agree on; it is dependent on one of the most politically unstable regions of the world for most of its oil supply and, as recent developments have shown, it can be rather successfully subjected to economic blackmail by the Arab states; it has an oil industry that controls less than half of the refining and distribution operations in Japan and has had little significant involvement with oil exploration and development.

Over the past few years Japan has been moving toward the adoption of new policies for securing oil resources. Its so-called resources diplomacy (*shigen gaikō*) has been characterized by a leitmotif that stresses autonomy while at the same time emphasizing interdependence. The ways in which these two objectives interact in the Japanese search for stable oil supplies are of direct relevance for an understanding of Japanese policy on the Tyumen issue.

The Japanese desire to move toward a more "autonomous" position in the world oil market was reflected in clear terms in the MITI interim report on energy: "In order to achieve the objective of securing a stable and reasonably priced supply, it is necessary for Japan to maintain its freedom of action, to be independent in spite of influences from other countries in the full range of activities of petroleum enterprises from the development of crude oil imports to refining and distribution."[8] For the past several years the Japanese have also expressed a desire to get out from under the "majors' umbrella." As the MITI report noted, "The consuming countries have had to bear the final burden of the OPEC problem [i.e., the increased cost of petroleum] without having had an opportunity to express their position. It made them recognize the importance of participating actively in the international petroleum market."[9]

Recently there has been a marked increase in the number of Japanese firms entering into oil development projects and in the number of new companies formed for the purpose of seeking oil development concessions. In a one-month period between January and February 1973, for example, there were announcements that the thirty-six companies of the Fuyo group would set up the Fuyo Petroleum Development Corporation, that the Sumitomo Group would set up the Sumitomo Petroleum Corporation, and that the group led by the Daiichi Kangyō Bank would establish a World Energy Development Corporation.[10] The government has moved to strengthen the publicly owned Japan Petroleum Development Corporation to encourage it to seek oil concessions and, through the offer of tax and other incentives, it is attempting to encourage both the consolidation and vertical integration of Japanese oil industry firms. The objective, as the MITI interim report defined it, was to bring 30 percent of Japan's oil from "autonomous" Japanese sources by 1980.[11]

8. Ministry of International Trade and Industry, "Interim Report by the Petroleum Sub-Committee for the Advisory Committee for Energy" (mimeo), p. 16. The Japanese text of the report is included in Tsūshō Sangyōshō, *Nihon no enerugii mondai*, pp. 313–335.

9. Ibid. The Japan Economic Research Center made the same point in a report which observed: "In case confusion results from an aggravation of confrontation between these consortiums and the monopolistic organizations of supplier countries, Japan will be hit hardest." Japan Economic Research Center, *Japan's Economy in 1980 in the Global Context: The Nation's Role in a Poly-Centric World* (Tokyo, March 1970), pp. 54–55.

10. Information from the [Japan] Institute of Energy Economics, "Energy in Japan," *Quarterly Report* 20 (March 1973).

11. Tsūshō Sangyōshō, *Nihon no enerugii mondai*. By April 1975, much of the intense Japanese business interest in overseas oil development had cooled in the face of what the *Asahi shimbun* characterized as "nationalism in oil, dry holes, and mounting losses." As the newspaper pointed out, many business enterprises had lost interest in such projects because of the difficulty of securing adequate capital in a time of domestic recession and because Japanese business is "assuming the risk of exploration and development and the host country stands to take the profits, if any." See *Asahi Evening News*, March 31, 1975. It seems unlikely that the MITI objective of bringing 30 percent of Japan's oil from "autonomous" Japanese sources by 1980 will be realized.

During the 1972 fiscal year, ending March 31, 1973, there was a tremendous increase in the growth in Japanese overseas petroleum investment. There was a 100 percent increase in Japanese equity holdings abroad, with U.S.$780 million of the $1,781 million of securities acquired representing a 22.5 percent interest in Abu Dhabi Marine Areas (ADMA), a firm holding concession rights for a thirty-year period to two rich oil fields in Abu Dhabi.[12] Of U.S.$243 million investment in "overseas branches," $218 million went to Kuwait, apparently to upgrade the facilities of the Japanese-owned Arabian Oil Company. The Middle Eastern share of Japanese investment jumped from 8 percent at the end of Japanese FY 1971 to 20 percent as of March 31, 1973. The increase in Japanese Middle Eastern investment is indicated graphically in Figure 1.

Japanese dependence on Middle Eastern sources of oil has made it wary of moves that might push it to the forefront in any effort by consumer nations to challenge OPEC. The statement of MITI Minister Nakasone during a visit to Iran in the spring of 1973 that Japan would not join any consumer's group aimed at confronting OPEC was the most clear expression of a view apparently widely shared in the Japanese bureaucracy—well before the Middle East erupted in new crisis.[13]

The events of the last half of 1973 intensified the Japanese search for autonomy. But autonomy is a complicated concept. It means for Japan both the diversification of oil resources in order to reduce dependence on the Middle East and the development of a supply structure that would put Japan less at the mercy of the majors than it has been in the past. But Japanese policy toward the major oil consortiums is also complex. Japan has been attempting both to get out from under the majors' umbrella and to buy into several of the majors' development projects in order to benefit from their technological skill and gain a voice

12. The other partners in ADMA were the Abu Dhabi government with 25 percent, Compagnie des Françaises Petroles with 25 percent, and British Petroleum with 27.5 percent. The Japanese investor, the Japan Oil Development Co., projected that during the thirty-year period of the concession it would bring 350 million tons (about 2,285 million barrels) of oil to Japan and return a profit of U.S. $876 million by the time the concession ran out. By 1975 the picture was remarkably different. The Abu Dhabi government had increased its share in ADMA to 60 percent and cut the daily flow by more than 40 percent of its capacity of 570,000 barrels. The possibility of a 100 percent takeover of ADMA by the Abu Dhabi government made the foreign partners reluctant to invest new funds in further exploration and development. As a result, the Japan Oil Development Co. showed a loss in 1974 of ¥8,590 million and a total deficit of ¥12,773 million. See *Asahi Evening News*, March 31, 1975.

13. The Foreign Ministry, for instance, in an energy report, repeatedly cautioned against a policy of alienating OPEC: "Looking at the next ten to fifteen years, if the world's main oil-consuming nations including our country become inevitably more and more dependent on the oil produced by OPEC countries, then it is essential that our country's oil and resource diplomacy take appropriate new directions toward developing countries and particularly toward OPEC and, in conformity with this, develop a bold new concept and achieve policies in accordance with it." Gaimushō, *Shigen gaikō*, p. 193. The report suggested that Japan "reflect on our economic great-powerism, total identification with the United States, and our making slight of resource-rich developing countries." Ibid., p. 47.

Figure 1
Trends in Japanese Overseas Private Investment
(in millions of U.S. dollars and percentage of total)

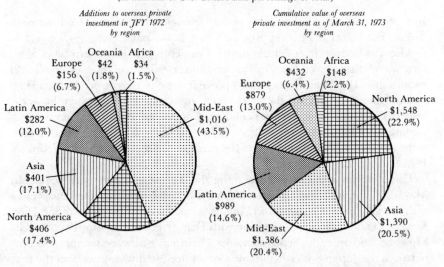

*Additions to overseas private
investment in JFY 1972
by region*

*Cumulative value of overseas
private investment as of March 31, 1973
by region*

Total increase: U.S. $2,338 million   Total cumulative value: U.S. $6,773 million

SOURCE: U.S. Department of State, Office of Media Services, *Special Report on Japan's Overseas Investment—Growth and Change* (Washington, D.C.: Government Printing Office, 1973).

in their global energy policies. An autonomous energy policy in Japanese terms is not necessarily an independent energy policy. Prime Minister Tanaka, for example, enthusiastically pronounced a theme of cooperation and interdependence when he traveled through Western Europe in the fall of 1973: to the British he proposed that the Japanese participate in the development of North Sea oil resources; to the French, that they undertake a joint venture in developing natural resources in Africa; and to several European countries, that they develop a complex "swapping" agreement whereby Japanese would invest in resource development projects in one area and be able to obtain resources from another.

This dual Japanese concern for autonomy and interdependence runs throughout the government's deliberations on the Tyumen oil development project. The Tyumen project has been attractive to Japan because of its relevance to the search for diversified sources of supply. But the central reason for

Japanese refusal to participate in the project is that, under present circumstances, it would have to participate alone.

THE TYUMEN OIL PROJECT

In 1966, at the inaugural meeting of the Japan-Soviet Economic Committee in Tokyo, the Soviet delegation proposed that Japan participate in a project to develop the petroleum resources in the Tyumen region of western Siberia, an area about the size of France with enormous estimated reserves of oil and natural gas. The Japanese expressed polite interest in the project, but made no serious moves to pursue the discussions until April 1971, when Japanese leadership of the Japan-Soviet Economic Committee indicated interest in resuming substantive talks on Tyumen. They asked the Soviets to present a concrete proposal at the fifth session of the joint committee scheduled for February 1972.[14]

Thus, serious discussions concerning the Tyumen project were begun. In May 1971, the Japanese ambassador to the Soviet Union discussed the project with Soviet Premier Kosygin; in August a leading LDP member of the Diet, Kosaka Zentarō, discussed the issue with Deputy Prime Minister Beybakov in Moscow; and in early September, the chairman of the petroleum subcommittee of the Japan-Soviet Economic Committee met in Moscow with the first deputy minister of trade to further pursue the Tyumen question. When the Soviet minister of trade visited Tokyo in the same month, he discussed a possible Tyumen project with then Prime Minister Satō and with the Finance and MITI ministers, Fukuda Takeo and Tanaka Kakuei.[15] These preliminary discussions leading up to the fifth joint meeting were capped by the visit of Soviet Foreign Minister Gromyko to Japan in January 1972. During his much-publicized visit, Japan and the Soviet Union agreed to open discussions on a peace treaty in order to put Japanese-Soviet relations on a more "stable basis," and they also agreed to accelerate discussions concerning Japanese participation in Siberian development.

The Japanese-Soviet Economic Committee is of central importance in organizing Japanese business participation in Siberian development projects. Formed in 1965, the Japanese committee has gradually expanded in size and

14. For an account of the discussion at the first four joint economic committee meetings, see David Hitchcock, Jr., "Joint Development of Siberia: Decision-Making in Japanese Foreign Relations," *Asian Survey*, March 1971; information on the original joint proposal can be found in John T. Stephan, "Soviet-Japanese Cooperation for the Development of Siberia," paper prepared for the Third International Cultural Conference, Fukuoka UNESCO Association, Fukuoka, Japan, Aug. 22–24, 1972.

15. This chronology is based on information contained in the report of the Fifth Joint Japan-Soviet, Soviet-Japan Business Cooperation Committees. Nisso, Sonichi Keizai Iinkai, *Dai gokai gōdō kaigi hōkokusho* (Tokyo, Feb. 1972).

complexity. It is made up of some one hundred members of Keidanren (Federation of Economic Organizations) and the Japan Chamber of Commerce and Industry chosen by the leaders of these two organizations, Uemura Kōgorō and Nagano Shigeo, who served as the committee's co-chairmen.[16] Although officially an independent organization, the committee has in practice become a part of the Keidanren structure.

The committee has a large number of subcommittees and sub-subcommittees, each dealing with a specific aspect of Siberian development. The subcommittee responsible for the Tyumen project negotiations is the petroleum committee (sekiyu iinkai). It is headed by Imazato Hiroki, chairman of the board of the Nihon Seikō Company and the Overseas Petroleum Development Company and, as Chart 1 indicates, it is made up of the heads of leading financial and industrial institutions.

Since 1968 the Japanese-Soviet Economic Committee has negotiated three important Siberian development agreements. The first was for the development of timber resources in the Soviet Far East, for which the Japanese provided U.S.$160 million in credits. A second agreement, signed in 1970, involved a Japanese commitment of U.S.$80 million for the construction of a port at Wrangel Bay. A third agreement in 1972 involved Japanese credits in U.S.$40 million for the purchase of machinery and other equipment in return for which Japan would be able to import 8 million cubic meters of wood chips and 5 million cubic meters of wood pulp at international prices over a ten-year period.[17] At the fifth joint economic committee meeting in Tokyo in February 1972, the Soviet Union presented five proposals for Japanese participation in Soviet resource development projects, all of which involved loans and credits from Japan far greater than in any of the previous agreements. Two project proposals, involving oil in Tyumen and natural gas in Yakutsk, required bank loans running into several billions of dollars.

When representatives of the Soviet Union had first brought up a Tyumen proposal in 1966, they asked for Japanese assistance in building a 7,800-kilometer pipeline from Tyumen to Nakhodka. By the time of the fifth joint economic committee meeting in 1972, the Russians had already completed a 3,400-kilometer portion from Tyumen to Irkutsk. At the meeting, the Soviets proposed that Japan provide a bank loan of over one billion dollars to enable the Soviet Union to purchase large pipes and other equipment and materials necessary for constructing 4,400 kilometers of pipeline from Irkutsk to Nakhodka, for constructing large storage facilities and a shipping terminal, and for increasing the capacity of the existing pipeline between Tyumen and Irkutsk. In return, the Soviet Union offered to supply crude oil to Japan at the

16. That is until 1974, when Mr. Uemura was succeeded by Dōkō Toshio as president of Keidanren.
17. Information primarily from "Saikin no Nisso kankei," Sōrifu chōsa geppō, March 1973; and Asahi shimbun, Dec. 7, 1972.

Chart 1
Petroleum Committee Members

Chairman: Chairman, Overseas Petroleum Development Co.
Members: Pres., Petroleum Federation
           Pres., Petroleum Mining Federation
           Vice-Pres., Japan Export-Import Bank
           Pres., Petroleum Development Public Corp.
           Pres., Electric Works Federation
           Pres., National Federation of Banks
           Pres., Tokyo Electric Power Co.
           Pres., Kansai Electric Power Co.
           Pres., Shinnihon Steel Co.
           Pres., Nihon Kokan
           Pres., Sumitomo Metal Co.
           Pres., Idemitsu Petroleum Co.
           Pres., Maruzen Petroleum Co.
           Pres., Japan Mining Co.
           Pres., Taikyo Petroleum Co.
           Pres., Kyodo Petroleum Co.
           Pres., Alaska Petroleum Development Co.
           Chairman, Fuji Bank
           Pres., Tokyo Bank
           Pres., Japan Industrial Bank
           Pres., Soviet Trade Organization
Advisers: Chief of Europe and Asia Bureau, Foreign Ministry
           Chief of International Finance Bureau, Finance Ministry
           Chief of Trade Bureau, Ministry of International Trade & Industry
           Chief, Bureau of Mines and Coal, MITI
           Chief of Trade Promotion Bureau, MITI

SOURCE: Nisso, Sonichi Keizai Iinkai, *Dai gokai gōdō kaigi hōkokusho* (Tokyo, Feb. 1972).

rate of 25 to 40 million tons annually over a twenty-year period.[18] Since the February 1972 meeting, however, the Soviet Union has changed the terms of its offer several times.

In June 1972, a technical mission led by Imazato Hiroki visited Tyumen.[19] As a result of its observations, the mission concluded "that seen from the technical viewpoint, the Tyumen project is worth pursuing."[20] In October of

18. See Nisso, Sonichi Keizai Iinkai, *Gōdō kaigi,* especially pp. 37–54.

19. The following brief chronology of developments on the Tyumen negotiations will help facilitate later discussion. It is largely based on information reported in the *Asahi shimbun* and *Nihon keizai shimbun* for the period February 1972 to April 1974.

20. The Team of Experts [report on its trip to the Soviet Union], *Japan-Soviet Economic Committee, Petroleum Subcommittee Report* (Tokyo, 1972, in English), p. 4.

that year, Foreign Minister Ōhira visited Moscow, and in January 1973, he
and Prime Minister Tanaka both made a special point of clearly separating the
Tyumen issue from the question of the return to the northern islands. In
March, Prime Minister Tanaka, in a letter to Secretary Brezhnev, called for
negotiations for a peace treaty and stressed the importance of achieving an
agreement on the Tyumen project for the long-term economic relations between the two countries. On May 10, Imazato announced that he would lead
a joint business-government delegation to Moscow in June to negotiate a basic
agreement with the Soviet Union on the Tyumen project.

From the middle of May, however, there was a sudden turn away from what
looked like rapid progress toward an agreement. On May 25, the Soviet Union
asked that the Imazato visit and the sixth meeting of the joint economic committee, which was scheduled for July, both be postponed. Imazato went to
Moscow in August and, on his return, announced that the Soviet and Japanese
top leadership of the joint economic committee would meet at the end of September in Tokyo and that the sixth meeting of the whole committee would be
held early in 1974. At the end of September, the head of the Japanese Export-
Import Bank went to Washington and Moscow where he apparently had
preliminary discussions concerning the size and interest rate for a partially
government-financed Japanese bank loan for the Tyumen project. Developments took another serious turn in September, when the Soviet Union suddenly
announced a modification of its original proposal: instead of an annual supply
to Japan of from 25 to 40 million tons of crude oil, it would supply 25 million
tons at the maximum; and because of inflation and changing exchange rates,
Japanese participation would cost considerably more than one billion dollars.

In October 1973 Prime Minister Tanaka visited Western Europe and the
Soviet Union. In Germany he suggested that the West Germans participate in
the Tyumen project, an invitation that came to the surprise and vexation of the
Japanese businessmen involved in the project negotiations. In Moscow he
issued a joint communiqué with Brezhnev reaffirming Japanese interest in
Siberian development and promising government support for the Tyumen
project once an agreement had been worked out between the Soviet authorities
and the Japanese business leaders involved. On his return to Tokyo he indicated his willingness to have the government cover 80 percent of the financing
of the bank loan—in contrast to a previous position that the government would
assume no more than 70 percent of the financing—and that the government
would probably agree to keep the interest rate under 6 percent as the Soviets
had demanded.

To further complicate this picture, rumors spread in late October that the
Russians were planning to build a large refinery at Nakhodka, and that the
Idemitsu Petroleum Company had been working outside of the Japan-Soviet
Economic Committee structure to negotiate an agreement for purchasing oil

from this facility. It also became clear that American interest in participating in the project, which had been dwindling throughout the summer, had reached a new low.

Then, in March 1974, the Soviet Union introduced a major new factor into the negotiations. It indicated that it had revised its earlier plans to transport oil from Tyumen to Nakhodka entirely through a pipeline and now planned to ship the oil part of the way over a second trans-Siberian railroad. If the Japanese wanted to participate in the Tyumen project, they would have to contribute to the building of the rail line. The price for the right to buy Tyumen oil had gone up from an original figure of U.S.$1 billion to an estimate of U.S. $3.3 billion.[21] Besides the increased dollar costs, the Soviet linking of Tyumen oil development to a second Siberian railroad project intensified the already considerable Japanese concern over the political and military implications of the Tyumen development scheme. Although some Japanese business leaders professed to see the railroad as simply another way to transport oil across Siberia, the Japanese government saw serious strategic implications in the proposal.[22] Its mounting concern over the increasing financial cost of the Tyumen project, the difficulty of securing adequate guarantees of supply, the military implications of a trans-Siberian pipeline and second trans-Siberian railroad, and the impact of the project on Japan's relations with the People's Republic of China had led, by the spring of 1974, to a virtual standstill in the Tyumen project negotiations.

THE TYUMEN PROJECT AND JAPANESE
BUSINESS-GOVERNMENT RELATIONS

The Japanese government has endeavored to insulate the Tyumen project as much as possible from the political and security concerns the project itself engenders. The proposed pipeline would run near the Sino-Soviet border and would significantly increase Soviet military capabilities in the Far East. China has opposed Japanese participation in the project for this reason. The pipeline construction across Siberia to Nakhodka also raises problems for Japanese defense planning because it would increase Soviet conventional military capabilities in the region closest to Japan. This concern is intensified by the prospect of a second trans-Siberian railroad. Finally the Tyumen project is intertwined with Japanese-Soviet discussions of a possible peace treaty. One of the ostensible reasons for a treaty is the need to put Japanese-Soviet relations on a more stable basis, thereby making possible long-term credit arrangements and a more extensive economic relationship. An agreement on Tyumen, simply because of the sheer size of the Japanese investment involved and the govern-

21. *Nihon keizai shimbun*, April 3, 1974.
22. See, for instance, the comments of Uemura and Nagano in *Nihon keizai shimbun*, April 3 and 4, 1974, and in *Tōyō keizai*, April 20, 1974, pp. 18–26.

ment financing required, would have the effect of reordering Japanese government policy on investment and trade with the Soviet Union.

The Japanese government response to these issues was not to attempt to resolve the largest ones first, but to encourage Japanese business leaders in the Japan-Soviet Economic Committee to work out a basic agreement with Soviet officials on the Tyumen project within guidelines established by the government and in close consultation with the relevant government agencies. This refusal by the Japanese government to become a party to the Tyumen project negotiations has greatly chagrined the Soviet Union.

Japanese business leaders involved in the negotiations, importantly, have also opposed this government policy. They have argued that the government should work out a government-to-government agreement on the basic principles to govern cooperation in the project and that, on this basis, the Japan-Soviet Economic Committee would then work out the details of a general agreement.[23] In December 1971, Imazato presented a written brief to government leaders, saying that the project was beyond the capacity of business to handle alone. He argued that "full government support" was necessary for the smooth progress of the negotiations and asked that the government authorize MITI Minister Tanaka to head a delegation of government, business, and LDP representatives to Moscow in the spring of 1972 to negotiate with the Soviet government.[24]

The Japanese government did appoint representatives from MITI and from the Finance and Foreign ministries as official advisers to the petroleum subcommittee of the Japan-Soviet Economic Committee, but it did not establish a proposed committee of representatives from MITI, the Finance and Foreign ministries, and the Economic Planning Agency (a committee intended to serve as a formal liaison with the businessmen's group). Neither was the Tanaka trip realized, although government officials joined as "observers" a delegation that visited Tyumen in the spring of 1972 under the leadership of Imazato. The basic position of the Japanese government that it would not become directly involved in the negotiations was reflected in the Brezhnev-Tanaka joint communiqué issued at the conclusion of Prime Minister Tanaka's visit to Moscow in October 1973.[25]

23. See the discussion at the fifth Joint Economic Committee meeting, Nisso, Sonichi Keizai Iinkai, *Gōdō kaigi*.

24. *Asahi shimbun*, Dec. 30, 1971. After the Soviet Union indicated its desire that Japan help build a second trans-Siberian railroad, Imazato again called for direct government participation in the negotiations; he argued that the issue had become a "political matter." *Nihon keizai shimbun*, July 4, 1974.

25. Until the Brezhnev-Tanaka talks the Soviet Union had insisted that Japanese government participation in the project was an "absolute condition," arguing that the Japanese government should make its position clear on allowing the use of Export-Import Bank financing for a bank loan and that it should become a direct party to the negotiations. See, for example, the statement to this effect by Soviet ambassador to Japan Troyanovsky in a speech in Tokyo on Jan. 26, 1973, quoted in *Asahi shimbun*, Jan. 27, 1973.

The Japanese government's decision to stay behind the scenes has lent a particular character to business-government relations in the Tyumen decision-making process and to Soviet-Japanese negotiations on the issue. Japanese business leaders, in their discussions with Soviet authorities, often have spoken for both business and government. As one government publication remarked, in discussing a planned trip by Imazato to Moscow, "Chairman [of the petroleum committee] Imazato is to go to the Soviet Union in April 1973 to negotiate with the Soviets on the issues raised by the Japanese government."[26]

Close business-government consultation has been maintained throughout the negotiations, partly to ensure that, in their negotiations with Soviet authorities, Japanese business leaders do not commit themselves to agreements that the government is unprepared to support. But tug and pull between businessmen eager to bring about a successful resolution of the negotiations and a government exceedingly wary of being drawn into a project with the military and political implications of the Tyumen proposal continue to characterize government-business relations on the issue.

During 1972, in the period immediately following the Soviet proposal at the fifth joint economic committee meeting, considerable resistance to the Tyumen project surfaced in several government ministries. The Finance Ministry argued that the interest on a loan should be at a rate of at least 6.5 percent. The Export-Import Bank, which would have to arrange government financing for the loan, expressed reluctance to commit itself to a project involving the enormous sums required for the Tyumen proposal. MITI was hesitant about the project because of concerns over some of the technical issues involved in the development scheme and because it favored a deferred payments arrangement (that would give Japan some control over Soviet purchases) rather than the bank loan on which the Soviets insisted. The Defense Agency raised questions about the military implications of the project and about the impact on relations with China. Finally, elements in the Foreign Ministry resisted a government declaration of support for the Tyumen project because of a desire to link Japanese participation in the project to demands for a return of the northern islands.

By the middle of 1973, however, it appeared that many of the economic issues had been resolved. Although the government continued to insist that it would not be a party to the negotiations until a general agreement was signed, it did use a variety of forums to make clear that it would support a bank loan to the Soviet Union in the amount of approximately one billion U.S. dollars, that the Export-Import Bank would cover 70 to 80 percent of the financing, and that the interest rate would be low.

Issues raised by the Japanese side concerning technical problems related to the exploitation and transportation of Tyumen's oil also were largely resolved.

26. "Saikin no nisso kankai." As it turned out, the trip was not realized.

The report of the delegation of Japanese engineers and government officials headed by Mr. Imazato, which visited Tyumen in June 1972, concluded that Tyumen did have the reserves and the Russians the necessary technology to develop and deliver a stable supply of crude oil to Japan. The group observed that it was necessary to "clarify the characteristics of the Tyumen crude oil, especially its sulfur content," but that in terms of quality, "it is worth conducting sales negotiations for the oil."[27]

Whenever Japanese-Soviet negotiations on Tyumen have seemed to be moving toward agreement, the Soviet Union has made significant changes in its proposal, largely in the direction of increasing the cost to Japan for participating in the project. There are several possible reasons for such Soviet behavior: it has calculated that Japan has become so desperate for new and diversified sources of energy that it will pay a much higher price for Tyumen oil than was earlier anticipated; as the Tyumen negotiations have developed, conflicting views within the Soviet decision-making hierarchy have emerged forcing ad hoc adjustments in the Soviet proposal to satisfy various domestic constituencies concerned with the project; or in the aftermath of successful OPEC efforts to raise the price of oil, the Soviet Union has become increasingly concerned with its own long-term energy needs and with the problem of maintaining a sufficient supply of oil to Eastern Europe.

Domestic demand for oil in the Soviet Union is increasing rapidly; one estimate suggests that Russia's demand for oil will increase by 8 percent a year between 1972 and 1980, whereas output will increase by only 6 percent.[28] Furthermore, Eastern European needs for oil also are expected to increase rapidly in the coming years, and there is a question whether the Soviet Union can provide for this demand and sell a great deal of oil to other countries at the same time. The problem is complicated by the fact that even if oil reserves in Siberia are proved to be as great as the Soviet government estimates, demand is likely to increase faster than the Soviet ability to get the oil out of the ground, even with outside technological and financial assistance.

Soviet statements in the winter and spring of 1974 suggest that Tyumen may have been relegated to a much lesser order of priority than other Siberian development projects in Soviet negotiations with Japan. Soviet government representatives stressed, for example, that the proposal for the building of a second trans-Siberian railway was relevant only to the Tyumen proposal; that a failure to bring about Japanese and Soviet agreement on this issue should not prevent them from moving forward on other projects such as the development of natural gas in Yakutsk or oil in Sakhalin.[29]

27. *Petroleum Subcommittee Report*, p. 12. The report of the team of experts confirmed that the sulfur content of Tyumen oil ranged from 0.8 to 1.5 percent. The question was not one of the Soviet ability to deliver low sulfur oil, but one of how high a price the Japanese would have to pay for "clean" oil.

28. *The London Economist*, Feb. 23, 1974, p. 47.   29. *Nihon keizai shimbun*, April 2, 1974.

TYUMEN AND THE NORTHERN ISLANDS

With the return of Okinawa, increasing attention has come to be focused in
Japan on the issue of the northern islands. Japanese demands for the return of
the four islands of Shikotan, Habomai, Etorofu, and Kunishiro, occupied by
the Soviet Union since the end of the Second World War, have grown in intensity in the past few years. The return of the islands is supported by the mass
media and all political parties, although they differ over how the return would
be best obtained.

Japanese government emphasis on the return of the northern islands after
the Okinawa reversion has been evident in a variety of government actions and
pronouncements. In the spring of 1969, the government announced that the
four northern islands would appear as Japanese territory on all maps.[30] For
those who thought that the postwar era ended with the return of Okinawa,
Prime Minister Tanaka reminded them in a Diet speech in June 1973 that "it
can be said that the postwar era does not end until the northern islands are
returned to Japan."[31]

Throughout 1972 the Japanese government, and the Japanese media,
grasped for any indication that the Soviet Union might be softening its position
on the northern islands issue. Gromyko's visit to Tokyo in January 1972 and
the agreement reached then to commence peace treaty negotiations were widely interpreted in Japan as a Soviet willingness to compromise on the territorial
question because, for Japan, a major reason for a peace treaty is the settlement
of this issue. In July a report by the Kyodo correspondent in Moscow quoted
unidentified Soviet sources as saying there was a possibility that the Soviet
Union would "lend" the islands to Japan as a way to solve the problem; the
report received wide coverage and a prompt denial by the Soviet government.[32]
In August an interparty Diet delegation returned from a trip to Moscow with
the report that the Soviets seemed willing to discuss the territorial issue during
peace treaty negotiations, but that it should not be at the top of the agenda.[33]
Despite these Japanese reports of possible flexibility in the Soviet position, the
Soviet press and Soviet leaders in their public statements continued to maintain
that the issue was already resolved and that the Japanese would have to accept

30. See Hitchcock, "Joint Development of Siberia," p. 288.
31. Quoted in *Japan Times*, June 30, 1973.
32. *Asahi shimbun*, July 15 and 22, 1972.
33. *Asahi shimbun*, Aug. 19, 1972. This visit by an interparty delegation was a result of the
Gromyko visit to Tokyo. At that time the Japanese government complained of the Soviet
pattern of dealing only with the opposition parties. Since then a Japanese-Soviet Parliamentary Exchange Program has been established, led in Japan by LDP member Ishida Hakuei
and including members from all the political parties, including the JCP. Ishida led a delegation of representatives from all of Japan's political parties to Moscow in the early fall of 1973.

that fact.[34] In September 1973, the Diet adopted a resolution, co-sponsored by all political parties, calling on the government to demand the return of the northern islands.[35]

When Foreign Minister Ōhira visited Moscow in October 1972 for the first round of peace treaty discussions, the *Asahi shimbun* took the opportunity to remind the Soviets that "the demands for the return [of the northern islands] is not at all, as the Soviets say, something 'publicized by a few politicians' but is the fervent desire of the entire nation."[36] Later, in the following March, *Asahi shimbun* returned to the same theme, warning that improving economic relations alone could not provide a base for friendly Soviet-Japanese relations:

The voice of the Japanese people is one in demanding the return of Kunashiro and Etorofu. Until the Soviet Union demonstrates understanding of that, the Japanese people will continue to have doubts about the professions of peace on the part of the great power, the Soviet Union. The dialogue between the leaders of Japan and the Soviet Union cannot evade this problem.[37]

With Soviet and Japanese interest in the joint development of Siberian resources, and with increasing Soviet interest in a peace treaty with Japan, the question of the possible linkage between the northern islands and Japanese participation in Siberia has emerged as an important issue of strategy in Japanese diplomacy. Some voices within the bureaucracy and the ruling party have supported such a linkage strategy, whereas other elements in the bureaucracy and in the business community have been opposed to the idea of tying together economic participation in Siberian development with the political question of the northern islands.

The press has not argued explicitly that Japan should refuse to cooperate in large Siberian development projects unless the Soviet Union returns the Northern Islands. But elements in the Foreign Ministry and in the LDP did make such arguments, at least through the latter half of 1972. The argument for linking the two issues is based on the assumption that if Japan accepts the Soviet proposal in Tyumen, it, in effect, would make the reversion of the northern islands virtually unobtainable. Agreement to pursue large-scale investment in Siberia, financed with enormous bank loans rather than with credits for specific purchases, would undercut Japan's bargaining position in negotiations on the territorial issue. If Japan indicates that the present structure of Japanese-Soviet relations imposes no significant constraints on Japanese-Soviet economic cooperation, there would be little incentive for the Soviets to try

34. Soviet statements on the northern islands through 1972 are summarized in "Saikin no Nisso kankei."
35. See *Japan Times*, Sept. 21, 1973.
36. *Asahi shimbun*, Oct. 22, 1972.
37. *Asahi shimbun*, March 11, 1973.

to resolve the territorial question. Such a view found particularly strong support among Foreign Ministry bureaucrats involved in Soviet affairs.[38]

The available evidence indicates, however, that the business community as well as the Finance Ministry and MITI have generally opposed any attempt to involve Tyumen and other Siberian projects in a strategy for obtaining Soviet concessions on the northern islands. Their opposition seems to have been motivated by a belief that linking the two could result in the successful resolution of neither; that diversification of energy resources was of more immediate crucial importance to Japan than the reversion of the islands; and that agreement to cooperate in Siberian development could possibly help create an atmosphere within which discussion of the settlement of the territorial question could be more fruitfully conducted.[39]

When Foreign Minister Ōhira returned from Moscow in October 1972, where he unsuccessfully had sought a meeting with Brezhnev, he remarked that because of Soviet obstinance on the northern islands, the government would have to study further its position on a peace treaty and on the Tyumen question.[40] The question was resolved in January 1973 by a decision of the top political leadership—specifically Prime Minister Tanaka and Foreign Minister Ōhira—to separate the Tyumen and northern islands issues. When the result became clear, it infuriated the group in the Foreign Ministry and the LDP that had been insisting on a quid pro quo between Tyumen and the northern islands. In a speech on January 16, Ōhira stated that when the Japanese business and Soviet authorities reach a more advanced stage in their talks [on the Tyumen project], we will cooperate. I do not want to consider tying in political questions such as the return of the Northern Islands. Economic issues should be taken care of as economic issues."[41] On the following day, Ōhira met with the Soviet ambassador to Japan and repeated the government position. Because of the great differences in Soviet and Japanese opinion on the northern islands issue, there would be a need for much further negotiation. The Tyumen question should be separated from those negotiations. He emphasized that, when the Soviet authorities and the Japanese business leaders came to a basic agreement on Tyumen, the government would support it in a positive manner.[42]

38. Interministry differences on the strategies to be adopted vis-à-vis the Soviet Union are discussed in several interpretive newspaper articles. See especially *Nihon keizai shimbun*, March 1 and Oct. 11, 1973; *Asahi shimbun*, March 7, Aug. 23 (editorial), and Oct. 11, 1973; *Nihon keizai sangyō shimbun*, Oct. 8, 1973; *Yomiuri shimbun*, July 9, 1973.

39. The *Nihon keizai shimbun*, for instance, in an article on the Tyumen project, suggested that one of the important reasons for the government's decision to separate the two issues was that holding back on Tyumen "could push the Soviet Union too far and have adverse consequences for Asian stability." *Nihon keizai shimbun*, March 1, 1973. Also, the *Asahi shimbun* suggested that Tanaka would attempt to move the Siberian discussions forward to create a "good mood" for the peace treaty negotiations. *Asahi shimbun*, Oct. 15, 1973, p. 2.

40. *Asahi shimbun*, Oct. 25, 1972.

41. *Asahi shimbun*, Jan. 18, 1973.

42. *Asahi shimbun*, Jan. 18, 1973.

The government had not indicated prior to January 1973 that its support for the Tyumen project would require a successful resolution of the northern islands question, but only in January did it make clear that it wanted to separate the two issues. In his letter to Brezhnev in March 1973, asking for a summit meeting to discuss a peace treaty, Tanaka made no direct references to the territorial question, but did stress the importance of reaching agreement on the Tyumen project.[43] In his discussions in Moscow with Brezhnev in October 1973, Tanaka stressed Japanese demands for the reversion of the northern islands. But in the joint communiqué issued at the end of the visit, the two issues again were clearly separated. Tanaka expressed his government's willingness to support Japanese participation in Siberian development projects, and both sides indicated that they would pursue discussions early in the following year on a peace treaty and on "issues remaining from the wartime period," that is, the northern islands issue. After he returned to Japan, Tanaka met with business leaders in the Japan-Soviet Economic Committee and again stressed that the two issues were separate and that the business leadership should pursue the Tyumen negotiations.[44]

There were two major reasons for the Tanaka administration's decision to separate the Tyumen and northern island questions. One was a pragmatic judgment that a linkage strategy would probably not achieve its objective—that the Soviet Union would rather do without Japanese investment in Tyumen than compromise on the territorial question. The argument made by many business leaders—that Japan needed Tyumen as much as Tyumen needed Japan and that the Soviets knew this—was a compelling one. Soviet threats to turn elsewhere for financial support seem to have convinced the government that any attempt to tie the two issues together could result in the development of Tyumen without Japanese participation.

The second reason relates to the general Japanese government strategy for dealing with the political and security ramifications of the Tyumen project. By linking the two issues, Japan itself would be politicizing a matter it has been intent on depoliticizing as much as possible.[45] Chinese support for Japan's territorial demands, expressed most pointedly in Chou En-lai's speech before the

43. *Asahi shimbun*, March 7, 1973; *Japan Times*, March 8, 1973. The omission of any mention of the territorial issue was noted by the Hungarian newspaper *Magyarorzsag*: "Tanaka's letter made no mention of Japan's territorial demands on the Soviet Union—a new type of flexibility of the Japanese, showing a readiness to separate the sets of questions awaiting solution." Quoted in the *Japan Times*, March 25, 1973.

44. Tanaka's visit to Moscow and the substance of the joint communiqué are discussed in the daily newspapers. See especially *Nihon keizai sangyō shimbun*, Oct. 8, 1973, p. 1; *Asahi shimbun*, Oct. 11, 1973, p. 4; *Nihon keizai shimbun*, Oct. 11, 1973, p. 3. For the reaction of business leaders to Tanaka's visit and Tanaka's meeting with business leaders, see *Nihon keizai shimbun*, Oct. 13, 1973, pp. 1 and 2; Oct. 17, 1973 (evening), p. 1; Oct. 18, 1973, p. 3; *Asahi shimbun*, Oct. 17, 1973 (evening), p. 2.

45. Or, as the *Yomiuri shimbun* put it, it would contradict its efforts to paint the Tyumen project as a "simple business deal" (July 9, 1973).

Tenth Party Congress, only contributed to a Japanese fear that Tyumen might draw it directly into the Sino-Soviet dispute.

By stressing Japanese demands for a reversion of the islands in his discussions with Brezhnev, Tanaka was responding to strong domestic pressures for a hard-line approach to the territorial question. But by continuing to separate the two questions, he was indicating his commitment to a strategy that had emerged earlier in the year. If one element in that strategy was to keep the government out of direct negotiations on the project, a second was to keep Tyumen out of the Japanese-Soviet negotiations on the northern islands and a peace treaty.

In December 1974, Tanaka was succeeded as prime minister by Miki Takeo. In January 1975, Miki sent his foreign minister, Miyazawa Kiichi, to Moscow for the first high-level governmental talks concerning a Japanese-Soviet peace treaty since Tanaka's trip in October 1973. In contrast to the emphasis placed on the Tyumen project and other Siberian development schemes in the Tanaka-Brezhnev talks, the discussions between Miyazawa and Soviet Foreign Minister Gromyko apparently were concerned almost exclusively with the northern islands issue. In Japanese newspaper accounts of the meetings, including one *Sankei* article that claimed to reveal the "inside story" of the talks, no mention was made of discussion on Tyumen or other Siberian development projects.[46] The joint announcement issued by Miyazawa and Gromyko at the end of their talks reconfirmed the governments' desire to conclude a peace treaty, but indicated no progress on resolving the northern islands question and made no mention of cooperation in the development of Siberia.

On February 13, 1975, Brezhnev sent a letter to Miki suggesting that the two governments conclude a treaty of friendship and cooperation and continue negotiations on a formal peace treaty.[47] Such a friendship treaty supposedly would provide a framework for more extensive economic intercourse and would enable the Japanese government, which was negotiating a friendship treaty with Peking, to demonstrate that it was not tilting toward China and away from Moscow. This new Soviet proposal drew a negative response from the Miki government. In a letter to Brezhnev in late April, Miki apparently avoided responding directly to the new Soviet proposal and reaffirmed his government's interest in concluding a peace treaty as quickly as possible.[48]

The first six months of the Miki administration saw a virtual shelving of the Tyumen issue and a deadlock in negotiations on the northern islands and peace treaty questions. One of the Tanaka government's reasons for separating the questions of the return of the northern islands and possible participation in

46. *Sankei shimbun,* Feb. 3, 1975. See also *Asahi shimbun,* Jan. 19, 1975; *Nikkei shimbun,* Jan. 18, 1975.

47. *Mainichi shimbun,* Feb. 14, 1975.

48. The letter was not made public, but a summary of its contents is reported in *Mainichi shimbun,* April 26, 1975.

the Tyumen development—its concern to keep the Tyumen issue from drawing Japan into the vortex of the Sino-Soviet dispute—has become more pressing under the Miki cabinet. Chinese insistence that a Sino-Japanese treaty of friendship include a clause pledging both governments to resist "hegemony" in Asia is viewed in Moscow as being aimed specifically at Russia and has resulted in a vigorous Soviet effort to convince Japan not to agree to the inclusion of such a clause. As far as the Tyumen project is concerned, these developments have only reinforced the Japanese government's determination not to allow Japanese business participation in the Tyumen project without some kind of American involvement.

THE AMERICAN CONNECTION

Japanese government determination to effect an American connection in the Tyumen development scheme results from a number of concerns. For one, the cost involved in the Tyumen development project is staggering. As originally proposed by the Soviet Union, the Tyumen project was to be a bilateral venture, setting it apart from proposals concerning Yakutsk natural gas or Sakhalin oil development, both of which were conceived as involving both American and Japanese capital. But from early in the Tyumen discussions, the Japanese endeavored to involve Americans in the project. Imazato, for instance, talked on numerous occasions of the United States "standing behind the Japanese" in the negotiations with the Soviet Union and of the business community and the government's determination to bring American companies into the project.[49] As the price of participation has grown, Japanese business leaders have become increasingly concerned to get American companies to take over part of the financial burden.

Responses of American companies to Japanese invitations to join the Tyumen project have not been enthusiastic. There is a widely shared skepticism whether the return on the investment required for participation in Tyumen

49. On one occasion Imazato remarked to Soviet representatives that "the Gulf Oil Company wishes to participate in the Tyumen oil project. Of course, in principle, it will be only Japan and the Soviet Union that will sit at the conference table. Gulf will sit back of the Japan side." *Petroleum Subcommittee Report*, p. 156. On another occasion when Imazato was in Moscow, he reportedly said: "We would like to carry out the development [of Siberian resources] among the three countries. The owner of the resources is the Soviet Union. . . . If Japan can get the permission of the Soviet Union, it can participate in U.S.-Soviet cooperation, and if the Soviet Union permits, the United States can cooperate with the Japan side in cooperation between Japan and the Soviet Union. . . . In the Tyumen oil project, it is the Soviet Union and Japan that will sit at the negotiating table, and U.S. companies will probably cooperate with the Japanese side. If U.S. firms invest 10 to 15 percent of the capital, it will make it easier for the Japanese side, and the government would welcome it." Quoted in Takamatsu Yasuo, "Bei-Chū-So 'sekiyu takyokuka gaikō' no danmen," *Zaikai*, Aug. 5, 1972, p. 156.

would be large enough to make the project worthwhile, particularly after the Soviet Union reduced the maximum amount of oil it would provide annually while tripling the price of participation. American oil company executives, more than their Japanese counterparts, apparently are also skeptical about the extent of the Tyumen reserves and the ability of the Russians to get the oil out of the frozen steppes of Siberia and to their customers in the amounts promised.

American investment in Tyumen is complicated by the failure of the United States and the Soviet Union to conclude a trade agreement and by the present lack of American government support for large-scale American investment in the Soviet Union. Japanese businessmen have clung to the hope that, if necessary, American companies could participate through the use of Eurodollars, but as long as the American and Soviet governments find it impossible to arrive at a trade agreement that is acceptable to both the Soviet Union and the American Congress, and in the absence of strong American government encouragement of Japanese-American joint investment in Tyumen, American participation in the project appears increasingly unlikely.

Cost considerations are of relatively secondary importance, however, in accounting for the Japanese government's desire for American participation in the Tyumen project. Siberia will eventually be developed, with or without Japanese participation. In 1975, for example, the Soviet Union was scheduled to spend a record U.S.$3.7 billion on capital outlays for its oil-producing industry. Of this, more than $2.3 billion was to be invested in construction and installation, with the largest volume of work scheduled for the Tyumen region.[50] The question that preoccupies Japanese policy planners is how Japan can participate in and benefit from this development and, at the same time, protect itself from the strengthened Soviet military capabilities in the Far East that will result from the region's development and secure credible guarantees of long-term supply. The policy of relying on its alliance with the United States to offset Soviet military power in the Far East continues to be central to Japanese defense planning; the desire for American participation in the Tyumen project is an effort to reinforce the American commitment in Northeast Asia. The objective of Japanese policy is to create a situation in which the Soviet Union could not easily take actions inimical to the security interests of Japan without at the same time directly threatening American interests. For Japan, traditionally suspicious of Russian intentions and commitments and particularly concerned about the stability of its oil supply, American involvement in Tyumen could provide some increased measure of confidence that the Soviet Union would live up to its side of the agreement to supply oil for the full twenty-year contract period. As far as Tyumen and other Siberian oil and gas development projects are concerned, the evolving Japanese policy appears to be one of attempting to construct a broad range of joint projects, creating a complex of

50. *Oil and Gas Journal*, March 3, 1975, p. 44.

intertwining relationships among the U.S., Japan, and the Soviet Union, which would reinforce their mutual dependence and reduce the chances that Japan could be isolated and pressured into taking actions against its interests.

Perhaps most important in accounting for the Japanese government's insistence on American participation in the project is its concern about the impact of this project on Japan's relations with China. Chinese leaders have expressed apprehension about the project for obvious reasons. As mentioned earlier, the proposed Tyumen-Nakhodka pipeline would run close to the Sino-Soviet border enhancing Soviet military capabilities there. The Soviet decision to build a second Siberian railroad only heightened Chinese anxieties, particularly when accompanied by statements such as that made by Soviet Oil Minister Shashin that "you can only send oil through a pipeline, but by rail you can ship anything you want," presumably including soldiers and military hardware.[51]

On a number of occasions the Chinese have indicated concern over possible Japanese participation in the project, but they have signaled that they would be less opposed to a Tyumen project that involved the United States than one that involved Japan alone. This view was stressed, for example, during discussions between Chinese leaders and a group of Japanese businessmen in Peking in September 1973. As reported by the group's leader, former Keidanren president Uemura Kōgorō, "the Chinese would not say yes or no about the [Tyumen] project because they do not want to interfere in [Japan's] internal affairs." Mr. Uemura went on to say that the Chinese, although still unhappy, believe that the joint Japanese-American financing now envisaged for Siberian development would be "better" than solitary Japanese investment.[52] In a January 1975 meeting with senior LDP member Hori Shigeru, Chou En-lai again urged the Japanese to take a cautious attitude vis-à-vis Siberian investment and to seek joint Japanese-American participation in those development projects it did want to undertake.[53]

The Chinese have also increased their own offers of oil to Japan. In 1973, Japan imported one million tons of oil from China. Imports the following year increased almost fivefold to 4.9 million tons. Estimates for 1975 were that Japan would import about 8 million tons of Chinese oil. The Chinese, in fact, were willing to sell more oil than the Japanese could buy and criticized Japan for not fulfilling its contracts for oil imports in 1974.[54] In January 1975, the Japanese government sent its first official "oil mission" to Peking to begin discussions of possible government-level agreements for long-term supply. In February and March, Japanese companies signed contracts for the importation of 7.8 million tons of oil from China in 1975 at a price 70 cents lower per barrel

51. *Oil and Gas Journal*, June 10, 1974, p. 43.
52. Quoted in *Christian Science Monitor*, Sept. 14, 1973, p. 2.
53. *Asahi shimbun*, Jan. 21, 1975.
54. *Tokyo shimbun*, Jan. 24, 1975.

than that of the previous year.[55] Chinese imports from Japan in 1974 were up by 90.9 percent over the previous year. The 34 percent increase in its exports to Japan was entirely in crude oil. Other exports declined by 5.3 percent, and the resulting trade imbalance in favor of Japan was a record high of U.S. $683,220,000, an increase of more than ten times the previous year's Japanese balance of $67,320,000.[56] Oil exports to Japan, accordingly, are likely to play an increasingly important role in enabling China to pay for Japanese imports. Although the Chinese decision to make more oil available to Japan at competitive prices cannot be attributed primarily to its concern to forestall a major Japanese investment in the Tyumen project, the consequence of Chinese policy in 1974 further undercut Japanese enthusiasm for the Tyumen development proposal.

Japanese concern with Chinese attitudes regarding the Tyumen project have alternately grown and waned and grown again in intensity over the past several years. Particularly in the early stages of Soviet-Japanese negotiations on the Tyumen project there was a rather broadly shared feeling in Japanese government and business circles that Japan would be better off in the Tyumen project than out, regardless of the Chinese attitude. It was assumed that the Soviet Union would proceed with the pipeline construction with or without Japanese assistance and possibly with other foreign capital. In October 1973, after the Soviet Union announced that it was cutting the maximum amount of oil to be supplied to Japan from the Tyumen fields, the Japanese press paid considerable attention to a rumor that West Germany had made an attractive offer to the Soviet Union to buy Tyumen oil and that the Soviets were trying to reduce the promised supply to Japan in order to supply Germany.[57] Some Japanese even worried about a possible American move to go into the Tyumen project and leave Japan out, a fear of a kind of Siberian *atamagoshi gaiko* (over the head [of Japan] diplomacy) such as had been exercised by the United States in preparing for President Nixon's visit to Peking. Some government officials also expressed concern that a decision to stay out of Tyumen, seemingly based largely on Chinese objections, could seriously and adversely affect Japan's relations with the Soviet Union, convincing the Soviet Union that Japan was hopelessly subservient to Chinese demands and possibly leading to Japanese exclusion from other Siberian projects.

Increasingly, however, Japanese government officials appear reluctant to go forward with the Tyumen project over strong Chinese objections, particularly as the terms of the project proposal itself have become less and less attractive. Consequently, to the extent that the Tyumen project is still alive, it hinges more than ever on American participation. In the complex relationships among China, the Soviet Union, Japan, and the United States, American business par-

55. *Nihon keizai shimbun*, Feb. 19, 1975; *Mainichi shimbun*, March 10, 1975.
56. *Mainichi shimbun*, Feb. 22, 1975.
57. *Nihon keizai shimbun*, Oct. 10, 1973.

ticipation in, and American government support for, the Tyumen project could assuage Chinese fears that the Soviets might utilize the new oil supply system for military actions against China; Japanese participation alone would serve only to heighten Chinese anxieties. The Chinese could at least hope that U.S. involvement would be a deterrent to Soviet military action in the area, a deterrent strength that Japan does not possess.

In general one gets the impression that Japan would be willing to suffer Chinese "unhappiness" in order to get Siberian oil, but that it is determined to avoid being caught alone in the cross-pressures created by Soviet-Chinese relations. The way for Japan to avoid being so caught is to introduce American interests into the project.

CONCLUSIONS

Japanese participation in the Tyumen project is conceivable in the event that one of three developments occurs. One is that the Japanese government, in its desire to obtain new sources of energy and to be actively involved in the development of Siberia, rejects political and military implications of the Tyumen project and plunges into it without American participation. Although such a move cannot be entirely ruled out, it seems highly improbable that the present government would commit itself to a project in the Soviet Union of such enormous dimensions without some kind of American participation. Even in the event that an opposition coalition should come to power in Japan, the chances for a positive unilateral decision on Tyumen would be minimal because almost any opposition coalition imaginable would be even more concerned with Chinese reactions than the LDP government.

A second possibility would be a decision by the Soviet Union to greatly reduce the price of Japanese participation. It is difficult to judge the extent to which changing Soviet policy on Japanese participation in Tyumen has simply represented bargaining tactics. Having once raised the cost of Japanese participation to such a high level, a sudden offer by the Soviet Union to retreat, for example, to its original proposal might make the project look so attractive for Japan that political and military concerns would be overwhelmed by a new wave of enthusiasm for participation in Tyumen development. But to suggest this possibility is probably to give the Soviet Union more credit for bargaining skill than it deserves. Although the Soviet Union may eventually attempt to compromise with Japan on the conditions for participation, the concessions offered are not likely to be dramatic enough to create the kind of psychological reaction that this scenario requires.

The most likely development one can envisage that would bring about an agreement on Tyumen between Japan and the Soviet Union is one in which Japan proves successful in obtaining the participation of American capital in the project. Only American involvement can moderate Japanese government anxieties about increased Soviet military capabilities in the Far East, the prospects of a stable supply, and the impact of the project on Japan's relations with China, and thereby make a Japanese investment worth the risk.

But there are several factors that inhibit such a development. American companies are extremely skeptical of the economic merits of the Tyumen project, and the American government has been reluctant to encourage them to cooperate with Japan. For American foreign policy, the Tyumen project is but part of the larger issue of U.S. policy concerning Siberian development and U.S.-Soviet economic intercourse. Unless and until this issue is resolved in favor of expanded trade and investment with the Soviet Union, it is unrealistic to expect any U.S. government encouragement of American participation in the Tyumen project.

Despite the somewhat misleading rhetoric in Japan of an "autonomous foreign policy" (*jishu gaikō*), the Tyumen issue highlights the fact that Japan has been seeking anything but a "go it alone" policy in pursuit of its national interests in the new environment created by the demise of the bipolar structure of international relations. The desire for American participation in Tyumen is not the consequence of Japanese inability to break loose from a postwar policy of dependence on the United States, but the result of a pragmatic consideration of Japanese national interests in a new international setting. Conceivably, Japanese involvement in Tyumen without United States participation would have been more easily realized if the bipolar structure of the international system had continued. Within that earlier postwar international context the Japanese government could feel confident that United States national interest would dictate a policy of coming to Japan's aid if its security or economic viability were threatened. That kind of confidence in the American alliance no longer exists, and Japan today is seeking a more highly structured pattern of interdependent relations with other states than it has had in the past. In the context of international relations in East Asia, the end of the U.S.-Japanese relationship of the cold war era has made the strengthening of Japanese-American ties all the more essential from the Japanese perspective.

The breakdown of bipolarity does not necessarily increase Japanese foreign policy options. On the contrary, the emergence of a so-called multipolar international system and the American policy of détente have in many important respects acted as a further constraint on Japanese diplomacy. The Japanese response to the uncertainties created by the present structure of international politics has been an effort to avoid alienating anyone. The emphasis has been on minimizing risks rather than maximizing advantages. Japanese government decision-making on Tyumen has been slow and cautious, not because of organizational or cultural imperatives, but because of a conscious attempt to achieve goals while minimizing risks. In the case of Tyumen, such a policy requires American involvement in the project. American détente policy has made untenable important basic assumptions of postwar Japanese foreign policy (that the world system is bipolar and that the coincidence of Japanese and U.S. national interests is sufficient to guarantee Japanese security in the broadest sense); it has not as yet contributed to building a structure of interdependence—its ultimate goal but Japan's present preoccupation.

The Business Community
and Japanese Foreign Policy:

Normalization of Relations with
the People's Republic of China

SADAKO OGATA

It is widely believed that the business community plays a major part in the decision-making process of public policy in contemporary Japan.[1] Particularly since the fall of 1973, when inflation became the most important political issue, public opinion has turned sharply against business, and labor and citizens' groups have focused their attack on Keidanren (the Federation of Economic Organizations) and the economic ministries. Among students of Japanese politics, however, the trend seems to be away from emphasizing the power of big business or the intimacy of government-business relations. In fact, the business community represents differing interests, which lead to a diversified impact on the decision-making system. A realistic appreciation of the business-community role in the decision-making process requires greater attention to the range of business influence in specific situations.

Any discussion of the business community raises the problem of identifying the group in question. Structurally, the business community might be considered to be comprised of three layers of business groups: *zaikai* (the leaders of major economic organizations); *gyōkai* (the industrial interests); and *kigyō*

1. I wish to thank the following for the time and assistance they provided me in carrying out the present research: in Keidanren (Federation of Economic Organizations), Uemura Kōgorō (president), Horikoshi Teizō (vice-president), Kotō Rikuzō (senior managing director), and Satō Masatake (counsellor); in Keizai Dōyūkai (Japan Committee of Economic Development), Hasegawa Kaneshige (vice-president, and president of Sumitomo Kagaku) and Yamashita Seiichi (managing director); in Nisshō (Japan Chamber of Commerce and Industry), Nagano Shigeo (president and chairman of the board of Shin Nihon Seitetsu); in the Memorandum Trade Office, Okazaki Kaheita; and journalists Suzuki Yukio (*Nihon keizai shimbun*), Hirata Masami (*Kyōdō tsūshin*), Hakojima Shinichi (*Asahi shimbun*).

(the individual corporations). Each layer functions as an adjuster of the different and competing interests in the layer below. Much debate over the power of business in Japan has concentrated on zaikai influence and given insufficient attention to the role of gyōkai in the internal workings of the business community.

The term *zaikai* literally means the financial or economic world, but in the present-day mass-media context, it has come to refer to a group of major industrial and financial leaders who devote considerable time to the activities of one or more of the primary economic organizations: the Federation of Economic Organizations; the Japan Committee for Economic Development (Keizai Dōyūkai); the Japan Chamber of Commerce and Industry (Nippon Shōkō Kaigaisho or Nisshō); and the Federation of Business Managers (Nikkeiren). Zaikai are generally regarded as a power elite who represent the interests of the business community as a whole rather than of individual businessmen.

In contrast to zaikai, gyōkai represent specific industrial interests, which range from finance and commerce to manufacturing, and from large to small entities. Among the most powerful and best established gyōkai are steel, electricity, and banking. The major function of gyōkai leaders is to adjust the competitive interests among individual corporations within their own gyōkai sphere. Furthermore, the close ties between industry and the administrative bureaucracy are formed at the gyōkai level. Through so-called administrative guidance, the economic ministries influence gyōkai, while gyōkai attempt to ensure that the ministries will take their interests fully into account. Gyōkai also serve as the primary unit for political contributions. They contribute publicly to the LDP fund-raising organization called Kokumin Kyōkai as well as privately to individual politicians who are sympathetic to their particular interests or who are contenders for party leadership.

Whether the general interests promoted by zaikai prevail over the particular interests of gyōkai and individual corporations depends on the issue in question. On the issue of trade and capital liberalization, which developed mainly in relation to the United States, zaikai took the initiative in advocating liberalization, whereas the adjustment of particular business interests lagged far behind. On Japan's normalization of relations with the People's Republic of China, particular business interests took the lead and entered the China market, whereas zaikai hesitated because of the uncertain national and international political situation surrounding China. These two examples reflect the politically conservative nature of the top layer of the business community, whose zaikai leaders could make great strides in a situation involving relations with friendly free enterprise countries such as the United States, but would take extreme caution vis-à-vis socialist states, especially those with no diplomatic relations with Japan.

An important point in a discussion of the business community deals with the relationship between business and politics. In the existing medium constituency system, neither zaikai nor gyōkai nor individual corporations are effective vote-getters—in sharp contrast to area-based groups such as farmers, fishermen, or some textile manufacturers. Under normal circumstances, the business community contributes to conservative political parties without making specific demands; its primary concern is to ensure the continued maintenance of the free-enterprise system, which it identifies with conservative-party rule. As long as this system prevails, the business community can influence the formulation of specific economic policies through its close contacts with the administrative bureaucracy. Adjustment of interests relating to such matters as the annual national budget, taxation, trade, and tariff is made through consultations among the zaikai and gyōkai leaders, the ministries in charge, and the Policy Affairs Research Council of the LDP.

In a crisis situation, when the stability of the conservative party is threatened and when public opinion turns critically against the government, the business community assumes a pressure-group character and makes political demands on the government and party leadership. In 1953–1954, when bitter power feuds in the two conservative parties allowed the socialist parties to achieve substantial gains in the general election, zaikai leaders pressed for the merger of the conservative parties. The founding of the LDP in November 1955 was in response to the public desire for political stability, a desire shared by the business community. Another crisis situation developed over the U.S.-Japan Security Treaty in 1960, when business leaders were alarmed by the potential power of the organized masses and again came to the rescue of the LDP. The business community has also inspired and promoted the choice of Ikeda as prime minister, Ikeda's "doubling national income" policy and low political posture, and the establishment of the Kokumin Kyōkai as the LDP fund-raising machine.

To understand the range of business influence in a given situation, this article examines the role of the business community in the process of Japan's normalization of relations with the People's Republic of China. The Satō government's prolonged indecision on this issue caused the business community to take the lead in calling for early normalization of relations with Peking. Thus, it cleared the way for the Tanaka government to recognize China in the fall of 1972. The China case has certain unique features. First, it was a highly charged national issue. Second, when the business community, which had been involved in the China market through individual gyōkai and corporations, was forced by the People's Republic to take a political stand in order to maintain business ties with China, it began to move quickly, in line with the rapid changes in the international political scene. The decisions of the business community at all three levels reflect the thought and behavior pattern of this group collectively. They also indicate the range of variables that influence business as a major constituent part of the Japanese decision-making system.

ECONOMIC RELATIONS
BETWEEN JAPAN AND CHINA,
1949–1970

After the founding of the People's Republic in 1949, Japan maintained close economic relations with China in spite of the absence of diplomatic relations. In principle, China insisted that no separation should be allowed between politics and economics, but, in practice, trade continued at an expanding rate, especially after 1965, until it reached a total of U.S. $822 million in 1970. By then, Japan had become the primary trading partner of China, accounting for 20 percent of China's total trade.

In the course of the 1949–1970 period, trade relations between Japan and China went through several distinct phases, which derived from changes in international and domestic political conditions.[2] In terms of international politics, the period can be divided into two phases. The first phase started shortly after the founding of the People's Republic and was governed by the laws of the Cold War. It lasted until 1960, when intensified Sino-Soviet conflict forced China to turn more toward trade with Japan, despite the serious political problems separating the two countries.

Within Japan, the China issue caused divisions among the public, between the ruling party and the opposition parties, and within the LDP itself. The government maintained the policy of respecting her formal diplomatic ties with the Nationalist government while allowing trade with China through non-governmental channels. Differences existed among succeeding cabinets as to the importance of their commitment to the Nationalists. During the Kishi government (February 1957 to July 1960) and the Satō government (November 1964 to July 1972), Japan veered closer to the Nationalists, and its relations with the People's Republic were greatly strained. During the Kishi years, trade relations with the People's Republic were broken off; in the Satō era, they kept expanding in spite of the political attacks leveled at Satō. Economic factors obviously accounted for this difference, but the intensified Sino-Soviet conflict was also a determinant.

2. For an excellent analysis of Japan-China relations during 1949-1967, see Haruhiro Fukui, *Party in Power: The Japanese Liberal-Democrats and Policy Making* (Berkeley and Los Angeles: University of California Press, 1970). Fukui divides the period into five phases. I have divided the period into two phases in order to emphasize the changes in international political structure.

Phase One: 1949–1960

The small-scale trade that commenced between Japan and China shortly after the founding of the People's Republic declined drastically with the Korean War, and with the enforcement of the trade embargo by the United States and the Western allies. In April 1952, the Soviet Union sponsored the International Economic Conference in Moscow in order to break through the Western embargo. China, in need of trade with non-Communist countries, took the occasion to conclude eleven trade agreements with neutralist nations (such as Finland, Pakistan, Burma, and Ceylon) which had already extended diplomatic recognition to the Peking government. With those countries that accepted the embargo policy—including Japan—China concluded nongovernmental trade agreements. From then on, China's policy was to utilize trade contacts in an effort to pressure these governments to reverse their restrictive China policy.[3]

The first of a series of nongovernmental trade agreements between the People's Republic and Japan was reached in June 1952; the second followed in 1953. Within Japan, several groups, consisting of socialists, conservative politicians, and business leaders mainly from the Kansai area, organized to promote economic and political relations with China. The China-Japan Trade Promotion League (Chū-Nichi Bōeki Sokushinkai) and the Parliamentary League to Promote Sino-Japanese Trade (Nitchū Bōeki Sokushin Giin Renmei) were among the first.

The government's attitude toward China at that time was still ambivalent. Although Prime Minister Yoshida signed a separate peace treaty with the Nationalist government in Taiwan in 1952, he seems to have favored closer relations with China especially in trade. He requested the cooperation of Murata Shōzō, former president of Osaka Shōsen and wartime Japanese ambassador to the Philippines, in helping to improve relations with China. In 1952 Murata visited Peking, and in 1954 he formed and became president of the Japan International Trade Promotion Association (Nihon Kokusai Bōeki Sokushin Kyōkai).[4] Most of the Japan International Trade Promotion Association leaders were also leaders of the National Council for the Restoration of Diplomatic Relations with China and the Soviet Union (Nitchū Nisso Kokko

3. See Miyashita Tadao, *Chū-Nichi bōeki no kenkyū* (Tokyo: Nihon Gaisei Gakkai, 1955), for a discussion of the Japan-China trade in the early Cold War period.

4. Among the board members of the association were conservative politicians, such as Takasaki Tatsunosuke and Kitamura Tokutarō, and business leaders, such as Hiratsuka Tsunejirō (president of the Japanese Fishery Association or Dai Nippon Suisankai), Suga Reinosuke (president of the Association of Electric Works or Denki Jigyō Rengōkai), and Okazaki Kaheita (formerly of the Bank of Japan and wartime director of Shanghai Kakō Shōgyō Ginkō).

Kaifuku Kokumin Kaigi). Politically, they were opposed to Yoshida and belonged either to the Progressive Party or to the Hatoyama faction of the Liberal Party.

With the signing of the peace treaty with Taiwan, Japan encountered opposing pressures from the two governments in Taipei and in Peking. The Nationalist foreign minister, Yeh Kung-chao, made known the Taiwan view that Japan's formal resumption of trade with the Mainland was a violation of the peace treaty. Peking, on the other hand, bitterly opposed both the Japanese Peace Treaty and the separate treaty with Taiwan.

Under the circumstances, the Japanese government moved gradually toward an official policy that separated politics from economics in dealings with China. During the Hatoyama and Ishibashi governments, however, various steps were taken to encourage the growth of trade with China. In 1955, the third Japan-China Nongovernment Trade Agreement and the Japan-China Fishery Agreement were concluded. In the same year, China held its first trade fair in Tokyo and Osaka, and, in the following year, the first Japanese trade fair opened in Shanghai and Peking. Trade between Japan and China expanded rapidly, reaching U.S. $150 million in 1956. The events were in line with Hatoyama's advocacy of a more independent diplomacy and the conclusion of the peace agreement with the Soviet Union in October 1956. Hatoyama did not, however, attempt to reverse the diplomatic ties established with the Nationalists.

The generally cordial relations between Japan and China worsened after Kishi Nobusuke became prime minister in February 1957. The Nationalist government in Taiwan, in the form of a letter from Chiang Kai-shek to Kishi, threatened to terminate trade talks in Taipei if the Japanese government continued to expand trade with the Mainland. Kishi was more susceptible to these pressures than his predecessors. He made a trip to Taipei in June and reportedly went as far as to encourage Chiang to realize his goal of retaking the Mainland. The Nagasaki flag incident in the wake of this trip led to the termination of trade relations between China and Japan in May 1958. In the following year Japan's exports to China dropped by one-fourteenth, and imports dropped a little over one-third. China abrogated all trade contracts, causing enormous financial losses to the Japanese companies concerned. This experience had a profound effect on the business community, making it extremely cautious in its subsequent dealings with China.

China followed up its attacks on the Kishi government with the promulgation on July 7, 1958, of the "three political principles," which were to have a binding effect on future relations with Japan. The principles stipulated that the Japanese government should (1) immediately abandon words and actions hostile to the People's Republic of China; (2) cease to participate in a "plot to create two Chinas"; and (3) refrain from obstructing the normalization of relations between the two countries.

While taking strict measures against the Kishi government, China encouraged the visits of Japanese groups who were opposed to Kishi. On a visit to Peking in March 1959, Asanuma Inejirō, secretary-general of the JSP, publicly denounced U.S. imperialism as the "common enemy of the Japanese and Chinese peoples." Alarmed by the strained Japan-China relations, former Prime Minister Ishibashi visited Peking in September, and the following month Matsumura Kenzō made his first postwar visit, accompanied by LDP Diet members Takeyama Yūtarō, Ide Ichitarō, Furui Yoshimi, and Tagawa Seiichi, all of whom became actively engaged in the China issue in succeeding years. Together they formed a pro-Peking faction within the LDP, which developed into the Asian-African Problems Research Association (Ajia-Afurika Mondai Kenkyūkai) in 1965 and stood in opposition to the pro-Taipei Asian Problems Research Association (Ajia Mondai Kenkyūkai) organized in 1964.

Phase Two: 1960–1970

The Sino-Soviet conflict came into the open in 1960 in the form of border disputes and attacks on the Soviet Union in the Chinese Communist Party organ *Red Flag.* The Soviet Union withdrew 1,390 technicians from China and abrogated over three hundred bilateral agreements and contracts. Coincidentally, the U.S.-Japan Security Treaty controversy forced the resignation of the Kishi cabinet.

The succeeding Ikeda cabinet reverted to the policy of increasing trade and communication with China at the nongovernmental level. In August 1960, Chou En-lai disclosed China's new and less stringent trade policy toward Japan to the visiting representative of the China-Japan Trade Promotion League, Suzuki Kazuo. Generally known as the "three principles of trade," it outlined three forms of trade which could develop between Japan and China in the new period: (1) trade guaranteed by an official agreement between the two governments; (2) trade supported by nongovernmental agreements and contracts between private Japanese firms and appropriate Chinese corporations; and (3) trade specially designed to suit the interests of small Japanese enterprises wholly dependent on Chinese supplies of raw materials and arranged by particular organizations, such as the Japan Council of Trade Unions (Sōhyō) and the All-China Federation of Trade Unions.

To select the private Japanese firms to enter into contracts with Chinese corporations, China solicited the assistance of the China-Japan Trade Promotion League and the Japan International Trade Promotion Association. Gradually these organizations came to exercise great power; they chose firms that accepted the principle of no separation between politics and economics and the "three political principles." The selected firms were designated as "friendly

firms" and became the main trade route between the two countries. Number-
ing about three hundred, most of the friendly firms were small, with fewer than
ten employees.

Although China could manipulate and carry out trade with the friendly
firms on its own terms, these firms did not have the financial basis or the
business capacity to undertake the large-scale transactions that China began to
want. With the intensified Sino-Soviet conflict, China needed long-term trade
programs. Thus, Chou En-lai invited Matsumura Kenzō to discuss the possibility of expanding trade with Japan, and Prime Minister Ikeda supported
and encouraged Matsumura's efforts.[5] Takasaki Tatsunosuke, who went to
China in December 1962 accompanied by Okazaki Kaheita, followed up on
Matsumura's work. By then the conservative politicians and business leaders,
including Okazaki, had left the Japan International Trade Promotion Association, which had become increasingly dominated by the Japanese Communists.
Okazaki feared that the existing trade through the friendly firms might never
develop into official trade for two reasons: it did not involve the manufacturers
sufficiently and could not result in exports of industrial plants; and it did not
involve government officials, but consisted only of antigovernment elements. He
felt that new trade programs had to be designed to realize what to him was the
most important objective, that of establishing diplomatic relations with China.[6]

While in China, Takasaki signed a memorandum with Liao Cheng-chih,
then deputy chief of the Chinese Staff Office of Foreign Affairs, on a five-year
trade program between the two countries. Commonly referred to as the *L-T*
trade, this program envisaged export and import transactions at an annual
average of U.S. $180 million. China's main export items were specified as coal,
iron ore, soy beans, maize, salt, and a few other agricultural products; its main
import items were to be steel materials, chemical fertilizers, and agricultural
machinery. The *L-T* trade had semigovernmental qualities with the maintenance of permanent missions in Tokyo and Peking.

The Japanese mission was a product of circuitous collaboration between
government and private business. MITI used its market research funds to
finance the mission in Peking; it allowed two officials to participate in the trade
delegation headed by Okazaki in 1963 and appointed minor ministry officials
to the Peking mission. Gyōkai groups participating in the *L-T* trade supplied
the rest of the mission staff. According to Okazaki, China always treated the
L-T trade officials as government representatives.[7]

Conclusion of several long-term contracts for the export of industrial plants
to China accompanied the *L-T* trade arrangement. The most important
contract was for the export of a vinylon plant, agreed on between Kurashiki

5. Tagawa Seiichi, *Nitchū kōshō hiroku* (Tokyo: Mainichi Shimbunsha, 1973), pp. 32–34.
6. Interview with Okazaki Kaheita, Aug. 29, 1973.
7. Ibid.

Rayon and the China National Technical Import Corporation; for the first time the Japanese government permitted use of the Export-Import Bank credit for the plant purchase. When Nan Han-chen, chairman of the China Council for the Promotion of International Trade, visited Japan in 1964, the then minister of MITI, Satō Eisaku, met with him and expressed willingness to permit deferred payment for industrial plants if a third country would act as guarantor. Satō was the first cabinet member to confer with an official from the People's Republic.[8]

As soon as Satō became prime minister in November 1964, however, his attitude toward China began to change. He proved more susceptible than his predecessor to the pressures of the Nationalist government in Taiwan, which was determined to prevent Japan from exporting plants to China on a deferred payment basis. Satō's *volte face* became evident when the government denied Export-Import Bank credit to Dai Nihon Bōseki and Hitachi Zōsen in January 1965. In the course of the Diet debate, the prime minister disclosed that former Prime Minister Yoshida had promised the Nationalist government in May 1964 that Export Bank credits would not be used to finance Japanese exports to China. In protest, China abrogated the contract with Dai Nihon Bōseki and an earlier freighter-building contract with Hitachi Zōsen. These developments led to another period of strain between Japan and China. Satō's visit to Taiwan in 1967 and his communiqué with President Nixon in 1969 were interpreted as acts inimical to China.

The early days of the Satō government also witnessed growing polarization over the China issue among the public, nongovernmental groups, and the political parties. The Cultural Revolution accelerated this trend as conflict between Peking and the JCP resulted in the dissolution of a number of groups such as the Japan-China Trade Promotion League and the purging of Communist Party members from friendly firms and pro-China organizations. As a result, the friendly firms' trade with China came under the sole influence of those totally committed to the promotion of Chinese interests. With the Communist Party ousted, the left-wing groups within the JSP, together with the pro-Peking elements within the LDP, emerged as the main champions of the Chinese cause.

The pro-Peking elements of the LDP played two important functions. Within the party, over eighty members organized the Asian-African Problems Research Association on January 28, 1965. The association's membership cut across factional lines, although its main supporters came from the Kōno, Matsumura, and Ōno factions. Outside the party, the pro-Peking elements of the LDP took part in the negotiation and promotion of the *L-T* trade, and the subsequent "Memorandum Trade" (which replaced the *L-T* trade) was based

8. Okazaki Kaheita and Tagawa Seiichi, "Yatto sono hi ga otozureta," *Gekkan ekonomisuto*, Oct. 1972, pp. 116–117.

on a memorandum that was renegotiated each year. Furui Yoshimi, Okazaki Kaheita, and Tagawa Seiichi spent weeks negotiating the terms of the political communiqué that formed the most important part of the trade agreement itself. The dilemma confronting the negotiators was their search for a formula that would satisfy the Chinese government's strong disapproval of Satō government policies, but would not wholly undermine their position as members of the LDP. Invariably these political communiqués emphasized that the two policies of no separation between politics and economics and the "three political principles" should be upheld as the guiding rules in Japan-China relations.[9]

In opposition to the efforts of the pro-Peking elements within the LDP, the pro-Taipei elements organized the Asian Problems Research Association in December 1964. Their purpose at that time was to prevent Prime Minister Satō, who had just taken office, from taking a pro-Peking course. The pro-Taipei group was led by Kaya Okinori and comprised the mainstream of the party including the majority of the Kishi, Satō, and Ishii factions. They were ideologically anti-Communist and believed that national security required that Taiwan and South Korea be protected from takeover by Communist regimes. They never actually opposed trade with the People's Republic, but insisted that Japan should not promote trade at the expense of its relations with Taiwan and the United States. In other words, Japan's relations with China should never go beyond the existing practice of separating politics and economics. Working closely with the pro-Taipei LDP members and binding them with the pro-Taipei elements among business leaders, ex-bureaucrats, and publicists was the Japan-Republic of China Cooperation Committee (Nikka Kyōryoku Iinkai). This committee was formed in 1956 following the visit to Taiwan of a China-Japan friendship mission led by Ishii Mitsujirō.[10] The Japan-Republic of China Cooperation Committee received official patronage, and among its activities were biannual meetings in Tokyo and Taipei. Increasingly it served as the channel through which the Nationalists attempted to prevent the political and business communities from turning toward the People's Republic of China.

Although economic relations between Japan and the People's Republic were frequently obstructed by political changes, they showed rapid growth, especially after 1965. By 1970 Japan had become China's primary trading partner. The Japanese business community tried to circumscribe political restrictions and to make the most out of the practice of separating politics and economics. The top zaikai leaders followed official policy and did not openly approach the China

9. For detailed account of the *L-T* and *M-T* trade negotiations, see Tagawa, *Nitchū kōshō hiroku.*

10. Kishi Nobusuke headed the committee; the standing directors were Sawada Renzō (former Japanese ambassador to the United Nations), Horikoshi Teizō (vice-president of Keidanren), and Yatsugi Kazuo (standing director of the National Policy Research Association or Kokusaku Kenkyūkai).

market. In fact many of them actively participated in the Japan-Republic of China Cooperation Committee. Individual gyōkai and corporations, however, while retaining their business ties with Taiwan, attempted to promote business with the People's Republic by setting up dummy friendly firms and participating in the *L-T* trade.

Chou En-lai's "Four Conditions" and the reaction of the business community

In April 1970, China enunciated new criteria for trade contracts with Japanese firms. Under what became known as Chou En-lai's "four conditions," firms that assisted Taiwan or South Korea through trade or investment, or assisted the war in Indochina, were to be excluded from the China market.

These strictures were aimed at alleviating two frustrations that China had endured in its dealings with Japan. First, China's attempt to use trade contracts for political purposes had not produced the desired results. Neither the friendly firms nor the Memorandum Trade firms could promote Chinese demands to the point of reducing economic and political relations with Taiwan, or of realizing diplomatic relations with China. Thus Japan became the primary trade partner of Taiwan as well as of China. Second, China had become increasingly concerned over Japan's defense build-up and economic predominance in Asia, especially after the 1969 Sato-Nixon communiqué that linked Japan's interests with the security of Taiwan and the Republic of Korea. The Chinese leaders, jointly with North Korean officials, launched a campaign attacking Japan's "imperialist designs" on Taiwan and Korea and the revival of Japanese militarism.

On April 15, 1970, the opening day of the Canton Trade Fair, which included the mass participation of Japanese firms and businessmen, Chou En-lai stated to the leaders of the Japan International Trade Promotion Association that "China could not allow Japanese enterprises that supported the reactionary policies of the Satō government and pushed into the Taiwan market." The fertilizer industry was cited as an example.[11] A few days later, on April 19, Chou En-lai repeated his position in an interview with leaders of the Memorandum Trade delegation, which included Matsumura Kenzō, Furui Yoshimi, and Fujiyama Aiichirō. At this interview, Chou elaborated his policy in the form of four conditions: (1) no trade would be allowed to those who assisted Taiwan and South Korea; (2) no trade would be allowed to those who invested in Taiwan and South Korea; (3) no trade would be allowed to those who produced weapons for the American war of aggression against Vietnam, Laos, and Cambodia; (4) no trade was intended with American companies in Japan.[12]

11. *Nihon keizai shimbun,* April 16, 1970.
12. Ibid., April 20, 1970.

On April 28, Hagiwara Teiji, managing director of the Japan International Trade Promotion Association, announced the final version of the "four conditions," which, interestingly, was considerably more rigorous in application than what Chou En-lai had originally proposed. The "no trade is *intended* with American companies in Japan" in the original became, in the final version, "no trade is *allowed* to American joint ventures or American-owned companies."[13] Officials of both the Japan International Trade Promotion Association and the Memorandum Trade indicated that dummy friendly firms had to sever relations with their parent companies, or that the parent companies themselves had to clarify their position on China.[14] Okazaki Kaheita later commented that the Japanese themselves tended to be expansive in their interpretation of the "four conditions," a tendency he ascribed to a peculiar Japanese characteristic of wanting to win support of, if not to please, their partners. He also indicated that many small friendly firms tended to display their loyalty for fear of being ousted from the China market.[15]

Chou En-lai's "four conditions" caused considerable confusion in Japanese business circles, most of which had some business ties with China as well as with Taiwan and South Korea. Two groups in particular had to make a quick decision—those who were heavily dependent on the China market, and those who were dummy firms of the large trading companies. The problem was especially acute for Sumitomo Kagaku, for the Chinese trade authorities had branded that firm, together with Mitsubishi Jūkōgyō, Teikoku Jinken, and Asahi Dow Chemical, as typical violators of the "four conditions." The charges against the Sumitomo Kagaku Company were that it had "assisted South Korea and Taiwan," and more specifically that its chairman of the board, Doi Masaji, was an active participant of the Japan-Republic of China Cooperation Committee.

Sumitomo Kagaku did not hesitate in accepting Chou's "four conditions." The company had to take the gyōkai interest into consideration (chemical fertilizer and steel were the two major industrial interests that had become heavily involved in the China market), in addition to the fact that China imported over half of Sumitomo Kagaku's yearly chemical fertilizer production. According to Hasegawa Kaneshige, president of Sumitomo Kagaku, however, it was not only the importance of the existing China market, but also the long-range limitations of the Taiwan market that prompted his acceptance of the "four conditions." He felt that China promised a brighter prospect, for the best business in Taiwan was already under American control, leaving little room for Japanese interests.[16] After conferring with presidents of companies belonging to

13. *Asahi shimbun,* April 29, 1970.
14. Ibid., April 28, 1970, and May 11, 1970.
15. Interview with Okazaki Kaheita.
16. Interview with Hasegawa Kaneshige, Oct. 4, 1973.

the Ammonium Sulphate Industry Association (Ryūan Kōgyōkai), Sumitomo Kagaku announced that Chairman of the Board Doi would no longer attend the Japan-Republic of China Cooperation Committee and, through Okazaki Kaheita in the Memorandum Trade Office in Peking, notified China of its acceptance of Chou's "four conditions." China recognized Sumitomo Kagaku's request, and repeated that any other company that withdrew from the Japan-Republic of China Cooperation Committee and accepted the "four conditions" could take part in the China trade.[17]

Sumitomo Kinzoku Company was the first Japanese steel firm to announce its acceptance of the "four conditions." Chinese trade authorities had requested the five major steel companies—Shin Nihon Seitetsu, Nihon Kōkan, Sumitomo Kinzoku, Kawasaki Seitetsu, and Kōbe Seikō—to accept Chou's "four conditions" before entering into business negotiations at the Canton Trade Fair. Hyuga Hosai, president of Sumitomo Kinzoku took the lead and notified China that the company "had not conducted any act in the past that might be in violation of the 'four conditions' and planned to abide by them in the future."[18] In fact, Sumitomo Kinzoku had been careful to avoid large-scale business involvement in Taiwan. President Hyuga is said never to have set foot on Taiwan in order to keep a clean record.[19] Within a few days, Kawasaki Seitetsu, Nihon Kōkan, and Kōbe Seikō also notified China of their acceptance of the "four conditions."

Special circumstances surrounding Shin Nihon Seitetsu, the largest steel firm in Japan, put policy implications on its position which could not be solved in simple business terms. Shin Nihon Seitetsu had invested heavily in Taiwan and South Korea. Moreover, its chairman of the board, Nagano Shigeo, was also president of the Japan Chamber of Commerce and Industry, a top zaikai leader, a close supporter of Prime Minister Satō, and an important member of the Japan-Republic of China Cooperation Committee. After considerable debate over the economic and political impact which the company's acceptance of the "four conditions" might have, Shin Nihon Seitetsu notified Chinese trade authorities that it "understood" the "four conditions" in their literal meaning, without specifying whether it would attend the coming July meeting of the Japan-Republic of China Cooperation Committee to be held in Tokyo.[20] To China's further demand for the firm to clarify its position vis-à-vis the July meeting, Shin Nihon Seitetsu replied that it could not withdraw because it was the policy of the company to promote trade with all countries and its participation in the committee was purely for economic reasons.[21] China did not approve Shin Nihon Seitetsu's interpretation of the "four conditions," and their traders at the Canton Trade Fair had to leave without obtaining any contracts.

17. *Asahi shimbun*, June 5, 1970.   18. *Nihon keizai shimbun*, May 9, 1970.
19. Ibid., June 6, 1970.   20. *Asahi shimbun*, May 15, 1970.
21. Ibid., May 23, 1970.

Thereafter, Shin Nihon Seitetsu became the pivotal point on which both the Japan-Republic of China Cooperation Committee and such pro-Peking groups as the Japan International Trade Promotion Association, applied great pressure to win it over to their respective side.

The widespread existence of dummy firms placed the trading companies in a particularly difficult situation with regard to the "four conditions." With the exception of Nichimen Jitsugyō, which China had designated as a friendly firm and which kept its dummy firm in Taiwan, the large trading companies had been trading with China through their dummy firms. Mitsubishi Shōji traded through Meiwa Sangyō, the largest friendly firm; Mitsui Bussan had Keimei Kōeki and Daiichi Tsūshō; Sumitomo Shōji had Taika Bōeki; Itochū had Shin Nihon Tsūshō; and Marubeni Iida had Wakō Kōeki. As Kimura Ichizō, managing director of the Kansai Japan International Trade Promotion Association, emphasized, the Chinese position was not merely a request that the dummy companies terminate their relations with the parent companies, but a demand that the parent companies themselves abide by the "four conditions."[22] Of the nine major trading firms, Mitsubishi Shōji, Mitsui Bussan, Itochū, and Marubeni Iida were members of the Japan-Republic of China Cooperation Committee. As they did not express any intention of withdrawing their dummies, they were cut off from the China market. Sumitomo Shōji, Kanematsu Gōshō, Nisshō Iwai, and Ataka Sangyō—trading companies based in the Kansai area—expressed their intention of supporting the "four conditions." Their share in the Taiwan and South Korea market had been considerably less, and they were not members in the Japan-Republic of China Cooperation Committee.

Wakō Kōeki, the dummy firm of Marubeni Iida, exemplifies the case of complete submission to Chou's "four conditions." Forced to decide between remaining in China trade or with the parent company, it chose to cut its Marubeni Iida contact in terms of capital, personnel, and even office building. On June 29, Wakō Kōeki openly presented a letter of protest to Marubeni Iida, in which it denounced the latter's determination to attend the fifteenth general meeting of the Japan-Republic of China Cooperation Committee.[23] Wakō Kōeki's display of eagerness won it a place in the China market. President Kokubu Katsunori, in a press interview announcing its return to "friendly trade," stated that he would endeavor to change the position of the four major trading firms and would oppose Japanese militarism. He further expressed his political belief that it was "necessary to fight for the resignation of the Satō government in order to improve Japan-China relations."[24]

Indeed, the fifteenth general meeting of the Japan-Republic of China Cooperation Committee that was held July 6–8 became the rallying point between

22. *Nihon keizai shimbun,* May 12, 1970.
23. Nitchū Bōeki Sokushin Giin Renmei, *Shiryō geppō* 36 (July 1970).
24. *Asahi shimbun,* July 25, 1970.

the pro-Peking and pro-Taipei forces. The Japan International Trade Promotion Association issued a statement on June 18, denouncing the Japan-Republic of China Cooperation Committee and particularly branding Mitsubishi, Mitsui, Itochū, and Marubeni Iida for serving as the "economic nucleus of revived Japanese militarism."[25] A similar statement was made on June 30 in the name of 134 friendly firms.[26] On July 3, seven organizations connected with Japan-China "friendly trade" held a national meeting to denounce the Japan-Republic of China Cooperation Committee, and declared that any business organization that attended the fifteenth general assembly would be regarded as in violation of the basic rule of Japan-China trade and would be cut off from the China market.[27]

The Japan-Republic of China Cooperation Committee regarded the fifteenth general assembly as the battle ground on which to defend its existence as well as to prevent the business community from rushing into the China market.[28] Yatsugi Kazuo, managing director of the conservative National Policy Research Association wrote an "open letter to Chou En-lai" in *Shin kokusaku* (the organ paper of the association), in which he strongly protested Chou's intervention in Japanese domestic matters.[29] Apparently much persuasion went into ensuring a record high attendance at the meeting: thirty-six business firms sent representatives, including Nagano Shigeo of Shin Nihon Seitetsu. In the course of the general assembly, Yatsugi directed his main efforts toward preventing the Nationalist delegates from producing their version of the "four conditions"—such as a statement in the final communiqué announcing that Taiwan would exclude business firms that had any dealings with the People's Republic. Yatsugi felt that such a request would clearly divide the Japanese business community into pro-Peking and pro-Taipei groups, a division that would be detrimental to Japanese business.[30]

In effect, however, the Nationalist government did exclude some firms that accepted the "four conditions." The Japanese business community as a whole tried not to take sides, adopting a wait-and-see policy toward international political developments. None of the economic organizations issued any formal statement. However, Uemura Kōgorō, president of Keidanren and permanent committee member of the Japan-Republic of Korea Cooperation Committee, stated that his position was to "disregard the 'four conditions,'" and warned the business community not to become upset over this matter.[31] Prime Minister Satō, as well as pro-Nationalist LDP leader Ishii Mitsujirō, seemed to share Uemura's views. They particularly felt that Chou's "four conditions" should not intrude into Japanese relations with the Republic of Korea.[32]

25. Nitchū Bōeki Sokushin Giin Renmei, *Shiryō geppō* 36 (July 1970).   26. Ibid.
27. *Nihon keizai shimbun*, July 4, 1970.
28. Yatsugi Kazuo, "Waga sengo ki," *Tōyō keizai*, April 14, 1973.
29. *Shin kokusaku*, June 25, 1970.   30. Ibid., July 25, 1970.
31. "Shū yongensoku ni urotaeruna," *Zaikai*, June 15, 1970.
32. *Nihon keizai shimbun*, May 29, 1970.

In analyzing the reaction of business corporations that accepted the "four conditions," two features stand out. First, all of them already had stakes in the China market. Fertilizer and steel together accounted for over 70 percent of Japan's exports to China, with machinery coming next at 12.4 percent, and textiles at 4.5 percent.[33] It is little wonder that the chemical and steel industries, with the exception of Shin Nihon Seitetsu, were the first to accept the "four conditions." Such textile companies as Tōyō Rayon, Kurashiki Rayon, Yunichika, and Asahi Kasei followed suit. In the machine industry, Komatsu Seisakujo was the first to accept the "four conditions." Its former president, Kawai Ryōsei, had been a pioneer in the China market, and his son and successor, Ryōichi, had promoted China trade and even served on the Memorandum Trade delegation in 1969 and 1971. Kubota Tekkōsho, Hitachi Seiki, and Tōshiba Kikai also accepted the four conditions.

The second feature is that these industries were based largely in the Kansai area, with the Sumitomo group taking the lead: Sumitomo Kagaku was the first to rescind its membership in the Japan-Republic of China Cooperation Committee, and Sumitomo Kinzoku took the initiative in accepting the "four conditions." Sumitomo Shōji was the first of the largest trading companies to become committed to the China market. The Sumitomo attitude can be accounted for largely in historical terms. Since prewar times, the Chinese continent had been its main area of activity. Moreover, it is said that when Saionji Kōichi decided to move to Peking in 1958, Ogura Masatsune, former general manager of the Sumitomo zaibatsu, gathered together the leaders of the Sumitomo group to confer with Saionji concerning the group's future strategy toward China.[34]

Other Kansai-based industries shared Sumitomo's concern for China. A strong nostalgia for the China market still lingered among prewar business leaders in the area. They frequently attributed the decline of Kansai business to the loss of the China market and hoped that revival of the China trade would allow them to recover the lost ground.[35] Another consideration is that, in general, the Kansai business community possessed a stronger sense of independence from governmental influence than did Tokyo business. The Kansai business leaders believe that business should not be hampered by political differences, and they have taken a stronger initiative in promoting East-West trade than have the Tokyo leaders. For example, Matsubara Yosaburō, president of Hitachi Zōsen, concluded ship-building contracts with China in 1963; Ōhara Sōichirō, president of Kurashiki Rayon Company, negotiated the first vinylon plant export to China; and Hyūga Hosai of Sumitomo Kinzoku made a breakthrough advance to China in 1965. The positive Kansai attitude toward the China market is borne out by an opinion poll of ninety-four business

33. Ibid., May 3, 1970.   34. Ibid., June 6, 1970.
35. Interview with Hasegawa Kaneshige.

leaders who responded to the Kyōdō News Agency questionnaire in the summer of 1971. To the question on whether Japan should recognize China before the United States did, only 1.9 percent of the Tokyo business leaders answered "yes," in contrast to 26.2 percent from Osaka and Nagoya. On the question of whether Japan should start negotiating for the resumption of diplomatic relations with China immediately under the Satō government, 46.2 percent of the Tokyo leaders answered in the affirmative, compared with the 61.9 percent from Osaka and Nagoya. On the future of the China market, 69 percent of Kansai and Nagoya leaders expected it to grow to a total volume of U.S. \$1.5 to 2 billion in five years; 57.9 percent of the Tokyo leaders held similar expectations.[36]

THE CHANGING INTERNATIONAL ENVIRONMENT AND THE SHIFT IN THE BUSINESS COMMUNITY

Although a segment of the Japanese business community already having strong business interests in China agreed to Chou En-lai's "four conditions," it was the rapid new developments on the international scene that caused an increasing number of corporations and some zaikai leaders to gravitate toward China. Emerging from the isolationist era of the Cultural Revolution, China embarked on a new foreign policy of vying for leadership and recognition on the global stage. In the final analysis, it was in response to Chinese invitations that Canada recognized the People's Republic on October 13, 1970, that the majority supported the Albanian Resolution at the Twenty-Fifth United Nations General Assembly on October 20, 1970, and that the United States reversed its policy of containment toward China in the spring of 1971. These international developments reached their climax with President Nixon's announcement on July 15, 1971, that he would visit Peking. At the same time, Chinese authorities energetically sought support for their position among the Japanese business community and general public outside the pro-Peking groups by unfolding their so-called ping-pong and invitational diplomacy.

As China's international prestige rose, Chinese efforts to win friends met with remarkable success in Japan. On December 9, 1970, 379 Diet members from all the major parties joined forces to organize the suprapartisan Dietman's League for the Restoration of Ties with China (Nitchū Kokkō Kaifuku Sokushin Giin Renmei). Fujiyama Aiichirō served as president of the League, which set out to mobilize all pro-Peking forces, including business, to exert pressure on the government.[37] Toward the end of March 1971, the Dietman's

36. *Shin ehime,* Sept. 1, 1971.
37. Some newspaper reports suggest that close contact, including financial support, existed between Ni-Chū Giren (the Federation of Representatives from Japan and China) and the business community, especially Keizai Dōyūkai. The writer was unable to find any evidence of this from any of the newspaper correspondents or businessmen interviewed.

League and the JSP jointly sponsored a People's Congress for Restoration of Diplomatic Ties between Japan and China (Nitchū Kokkō Seijōka Kokumin Kyōgikai), and also attempted to cooperate with Kōmeitō-sponsored organizations.

Changes also took place in the business community. Corporations that previously had had no large business in China now began to move in directions they hoped would win future access to the China market for them. Toyota Motors, which had been exporting trucks to China through its affiliate, Hino Jidōsha, led the way. The Japan International Trade Promotion Association had been trying to persuade Toyota for some time to accept the "four conditions."[38] And neither domestic nor foreign business prospects were bright for the automobile industry in the 1970s. The company then started such careful preparations for entering the China market as training its personnel in the Chinese language, collecting materials on the China market, and contacting the Memorandum Trade Office.[39] Vice-President Katō of Toyota Jidōsha Hambai stated in a New Year interview with the press that China, in terms of international politics and business, was the crucial issue of the 1970s and that he was ready to put his full force into export there.[40]

When China launched its "ping-pong" diplomacy, therefore, Toyota proved extremely receptive. On April 9, 1971, while leading the Chinese team at the World Meet in Nagoya, Wang Hsiao-yun, the managing director of the Chinese People's External Friendship Association and one-time chief representative of the Liao Cheng-chih Trade Office, visited the Toyota factory and conferred with the management. Shortly thereafter, Toyota announced that it had presented to the Japan International Trade Promotion Association its request to participate in the spring 1971 Canton Trade Fair, and that it had attached to the request a document stating that it would not make any direct investments in Taiwan and South Korea, although it would continue its commercial contracts based largely on technical assistance and services.[41] On April 24, Vice-President Katō stated that he planned to communicate formally his intention to visit China.[42] Nissan, Honda, and other automobile manufacturers followed Toyota's lead.

By 1971, subtle changes were taking place in the Chinese enforcement of the "four conditions." Toyota's experience was definitely different from the experiences of the previous year, when the conditions were applied more indiscriminately. When Tōyō Bearing accepted the "four conditions" on May 15, 1971, China allowed it to retain its joint venture in Taiwan—providing it did not increase its Taiwan investment—on the grounds that the venture

38. *Nihon keizai shimbun,* Dec. 4, 1971.

39. "Sekai senryaku de gekitotsu suru Toyota, Nissan no kōdō," *Zaikai,* Dec. 15, 1971, pp. 98–100.

40. *Nihon keizai shimbun,* Jan. 1, 1971.

41. *Asahi shimbun,* April 23, 1971.   42. *Nihon keizai shimbun,* April 25, 1971.

amounted to less than 100 million yen.[43] By showing a growing flexibility in the application of its "four conditions," China sought to accelerate the rush of the Japanese business community into the China market.[44]

During his one-month stay in Japan, Wang Hsiao-yun proved very energetic in promoting contacts with business leaders. He conferred with the presidents of the Sumitomo group companies and invited them to visit China. The highlight of his trip, however, was his meeting with the Keizai Dōyūkai leaders on April 24. This was the first occasion on which zaikai leaders established formal contact with a high-ranking Chinese official. Among the four economic organizations, Keizai Dōyūkai had taken the greatest interest in China since the mid-1950s. It had kept close contact with Okazaki Kaheita and had even planned to send a mission to China in 1964 under the leadership of Shōji Takeo. With a membership composed of individuals rather than gyōkai or corporations, Keizai Dōyūkai was generally freer to air new opinions. It considered its special role to be the task of looking and planning ahead of the times.[45] In its 1971 New Year message, Keizai Dōyūkai announced that one of its major objectives in the coming year would be "to endeavor to find ways to cause China to participate in international society, from the viewpoint of bringing about peaceful coexistence."[46] Keizai Dōyūkai's positive attitude to the China issue was shown by the appointment to the vice-presidency of Kawai Ryōichi, president of Komatsu Seisakujo. Kawai was widely regarded as the businessman best acquainted with China, and Komatsu Seisakujo was the first machine manufacturing concern to accept the "four conditions." President Kikawada Kazutaka consulted closely with Kawai in deciding on Dōyūkai's policy toward China.[47]

The April 24 meeting was arranged through Kimura, who was to play an increasingly important role as liaison between Chinese authorities and Japanese business leaders.[48] This meeting did not produce any agreements or concrete results, as the Chinese side repeated their adherence to the no-separation principle, the "three political principles," and the "five peace principles." Keizai Dōyūkai considered the "five peace principles" to be in line with its position, but took no stand on the other principles. After the meeting, however, Kikawada held a press interview in which he stated that "the improvement of China-Japan relations was a national problem."[49] Yamashita observed that one had

43. *Asahi shimbun*, May 16, 1971.   44. Interview with Kotō Rikuzō on Sept. 22, 1973.
45. Interview with Hasegawa Kaneshige.   46. *Asahi shimbun*, Jan. 19, 1971.
47. Interview with Yamashita Seiichi on Oct. 11, 1973.
48. The Keizai Dōyūkai leaders who attended the April 24 meeting were Kikawada Kazutaka, president of Tokyo Denryoku; Nakayama Sōhei, former president of the Industrial Bank of Japan; Iwasa Yoshizane, chairman of the Board of Fuji Bank; Imasato Hiroki, president of Nihon Seikō; Kawai Ryōichi, president of Komatsu Seisakujo; Suzuki Haruo, president of Shōwa Denkō; Yamashita Seiichi, managing director of Keizai Dōyūkai; and Kimura Ichizō, managing director of Kansai Japan International Trade Promotion Association.
49. *Asahi shimbun*, April 25, 1971.

to support the judgment that "the world situation surrounding China would change drastically in the first part of the 1970s."[50]

Meanwhile, Shin Nihon Seitetsu remained unchanged in its position toward the People's Republic. Also on April 24, Chairman of the Board Nagano Shigeo stated to the press that "the company position has always been to deal with anybody that is a good partner from a business standpoint" and that he was not thinking of "announcing withdrawal from the Japan-Republic of China Cooperation Committee or of making any promises in advance."[51] Apparently, however, Nagano was left in an extremely difficult position. The company was shut out of China at a time when the domestic market was stagnant and voluntary restrictions had to be placed on steel exports to Europe and to the United States. According to *Asahi* correspondent Hakojima Shinichi, who was covering the business leaders, Nagano carefully avoided making any further commitments to Taiwan such as visits or receipt of special honors, and brooded over the question of whether or not to attend the Japan-Republic of China Cooperation Committee meeting scheduled for the following July. He did not want to be left behind other business leaders, but at the same time he could not move easily because of his close association with Prime Minister Satō.[52]

President Nixon's announced visit to China, ironically, saved those business leaders who had remained undecided, particularly Nagano. On July 16, 1971, the day after Nixon's announcement, President Inayama of Shin Nihon Seitetsu declared that the company would not be represented at either the Japan-Republic of China or the Japan-Republic of Korea Cooperation committee meetings. Nagano was quoted as saying, "the game is almost over!" Within six weeks the company reversed its stand and recognized the "four conditions." At the same time, in anticipation of greatly reduced attendance, Yatsugi Kazuo and Horikoshi Teizō decided to cancel the invitations to business representatives to attend the Japan-Republic of China Cooperation Committee meeting.[53]

In August 1971, a second high-ranking Chinese mission was dispatched to Japan on the occasion of the funeral services for Matsumura Kenzō. It was headed by Wang Kuo-chuan, vice-president of the China-Japan Friendship Association. During his one-week stay, he made contact with various political and business leaders. Again, a most important meeting was held with Keizai Dōyūkai leaders. Kikawada was said to have been reluctant to meet with Wang because of the publicity given to every move he took on China, but Imasato Hiroki insisted on holding a meeting and tried especially hard to include Nagano, who was not a Keizai Dōyūkai member. The result was Wang's

50. Ibid., April 30, 1971.

51. Ibid., April 25, 1971.

52. Interview with Hakojima Shinichi on Oct. 6, 1973; also Kimura Ichizō, "Nitchū keizai kōryū o tegakete nijūnen," *Zaikai*, Sept. 15, 1972.

53. *Asahi shimbun*, July 23, 1971.

meeting with Kikawada, Imasato, Iwasa, Nakayama, and Nagano, assisted by Hagiwara Teiji, the managing director of the Japan International Trade Promotion Association. Aside from an agreement that an exchange of leadership visits was highly desirable for the improvement of Japan-China relations, nothing much was settled. It was the fact that the meeting took place that had great impact. Now Nagano was definitely established among those who held a positive stand toward China. Now that he and Kikawada—top zaikai figures heading two of the four major economic organizations, leaders of the two most powerful gyōkai, as well as heads of Japan's largest corporations—called for closer relations with the People's Republic, the mainstream of the business community gravitated rapidly toward Peking. Prime Minister Satō was said to have been infuriated by the behavior of Nagano and the other business leaders.[54]

With the announcement of Nixon's visit to Peking, eventual Japanese recognition of the People's Republic also became a foregone conclusion. The differences were over the timing and manner of recognition; and here Satō found himself left behind, while the business community started to move ahead. Within the LDP, Miki Takeo was the first main faction leader in the cabinet to respond to the Nixon announcement. On July 19, 1971, Miki, who had always spoken in support of "peaceful coexistence" with the People's Republic but had not clarified his position toward the Nationalists, admitted that relations with the Nationalist government might have to be sacrificed for the more important cause of normalizing relations with the People's Republic. Miki also conferred with Wang Kuo-chuan and turned increasingly toward Peking, eventually taking a trip there in April 1972.

China, in the meantime, took full advantage of the favorable tide in Japan, and began its campaign of "invitational diplomacy." In the course of 1971, a record number of 5,718 Japanese were invited to China. In the past, Chinese authorities had invited members of leftist friendship associations, opposition-party leaders, and pro-Peking members of the LDP, but now they began to opt for influential Japanese businessmen irrespective of their political positions and past records. Two missions of businessmen, one consisting of Kansai leaders, the other of Tokyo leaders, visited China in the fall of 1971.

The Japan International Trade Promotion Association, particularly its managing director, Kimura Ichizō, was largely responsible for the selection and staging of the missions to China. Since the spring of 1971, the Kansai branch of the association had been trying unsuccessfully to persuade Kansai business leaders to organize a mission, but the leaders had hesitated over taking an action so opposed to government policy.[55] The announcement of Nixon's trip banished all doubts, and an all-Kansai business leader mission was quickly

54. Interview with Hakojima Shinichi.
55. "Ukabi agatta posto Ashiwara taisei," *Zaikai*, Sept. 15, 1971, p. 88.

formed to leave for China on September 15.[56] The mission consisted of the presidents of the Japan Chamber of Commerce and Industry, Kansai Keieisha Kyōkai, Kansai Keizai Dōyūkai, Ōsaka Kōgyōkai, and two vice-presidents of Kankeiren; it was headed by Saeki Isamu. That Saeki led a China mission just when Japan seemed about to establish closer ties with the People's Republic is considered to have further strengthened his leading position in the Kansai business community.[57] Before leaving on its trip, the Kansai China mission stated that it was accepting the "five peace principles" and the "three political principles," and was committed to the normalization of relations between Japan and China.[58]

The setting up of a Tokyo business leaders' mission followed a more complicated course. China's invitation came in the form of a letter, personally delivered by Kimura Ichizō, from Kuo Mo-jo, honorary president of the Japan-China Friendship Association, to Kikawada Kazutaka.[59] Kikawada first planned to make a personal visit, but other leaders of the Keizai Dōyūkai urged him to take the occasion to send a Dōyūkai mission. The Japan International Trade Promotion Association as well as Imasato Hiroki were eager to have Nagano Shigeo participate so the mission might include a substantial number of major business figures.[60] Keizai Dōyūkai leaders expected the dispatch of their mission to have a strong effect on political and economic circles.[61]

On October 14, the Tokyo businessmen's China mission was organized with Shōji Takeo, former president of Keizai Dōyūkai and former president of the Japan Monopoly Corporation, as its leader. It was an all Keizai Dōyūkai mission with the addition of Nagano Shigeo.[62] Initially, no consensus seemed to exist among the mission's participants with regard to the Chinese proposals, particularly the "three political principles."[63] With the acceptance of the People's Republic of China into the United Nations on October 25, 1971, however, Shōji stated that he was now able to visit China on the basis of the "three political principles," and the other members were also ready to commit

56. "Hōchū taiken kara teigen suru," *Kikan chūō kōron*, winter 1971, pp. 228–230.

57. "Kansai zaikai hōchū misshon dōkōki," *Zaikai*, Nov. 1, 1971, pp. 118–121.

58. *Asahi shimbun*, Sept. 16, 1971.

59. Kikawada wrote a letter thanking Kuo Mo-jo for sending flowers to Matsunaga Yasuzaemon preceding his death. Matsunaga had been a pioneer in power development and a business leader since prewar times.

60. Statement of Hakojima Shinichi. Hakojima recounted that the consensus of the *Asahi shimbun* reporters who accompanied Editor-in-Chief Gotō Motoo and the Tokyo businessmen's mission to China was that the main target of the Chinese authorities was Nagano Shigeo. The Chinese authorities must have formed their judgment on the basis of comments made by Japanese visitors, especially the Japan International Trade Promotion Association.

61. Statement of Yamashita Seiichi.

62. The members consisted of Kikawada Kazutaka, Imasato Hiroki, Iwasa Yoshizane, Kawai Ryōichi, Minato Moriatsu, Nakajima Masaki, and Nagano Shigeo.

63. *Asahi shimbun*, Oct. 15, 1971.

themselves to these principles. When the mission returned from its nine-day trip on November 22, it issued a statement stressing "the need to strive for the realization of the resumption of diplomatic relations between Japan and China."[64]

CHINA'S REPRESENTATION IN THE UNITED NATIONS AND THE REACTION OF THE BUSINESS COMMUNITY

With the question of the People's Republic's representation in the United Nations settled, the entire business community shifted its position and started calling for early normalization of relations with China. President Uemura of Keidanren, who had been holding back in the bid for China, stated for the first time at the Keidanren Council meeting on December 16, 1971, that "once China has been admitted to the United Nations, we must expect an early resumption of normal relations with China."[65] Prior to the U.N. vote, although Uemura had expressed his readiness to abide by the outcome, he had supported Prime Minister Satō's decision to sponsor the resolution requiring a two-thirds majority to expel Taiwan. In fact, throughout most of 1971, Keidanren had not taken a stand on the China issue, because it felt that no resolution could win the support of all its members.[66]

The last business leaders to adjust themselves to the changing international situation were the executives of the trading companies and their respective related companies. Company groups such as Sumitomo, Mitsui, and Mitsubishi are the successors to former zaibatsu. Usually they have two centers of gravity: the banks, which are the primary source of capital for related companies; and the trading companies, which negotiate contracts for the manufacturers in the group. Generally, these groups of companies show the greatest strength and cohesion when they engage in a project involving the development of a new area. The Sumitomo group had advanced to the China mainland with Sumitomo Shōji acting as its principal contact point. Now that international acceptance of the People's Republic seemed imminent, Mitsui Bussan and Mitsubishi Shōji had to make serious preparations for their own shifts of position. The particular problem for the trading companies was one of timing: they could move neither too quickly nor too slowly lest their related companies and customers be unable to establish their desired contacts.[67]

Already in the fall of 1971, Mitsui Bussan and Mitsubishi Shōji had started preparing for the coming change. Although they still supported the Japan-Republic of China Cooperation Committee, they began to send less-senior board members to the meetings or attend only subcommittee meetings on

---

64. "Hōchu o oete," statement, Keizai Dōyūkai.   65. *Keidanren geppō*, Jan. 1972, p. 5.
66. Interview with Kotō Rikuzō.   67. Interview with Hakojima Shinichi.

trade. After the United Nations vote on China, the presidents of Mitsui Bussan and Mitsubishi Shōji both issued statements welcoming China into the United Nations and expressing their desire to return to the China market. They continued to remain in the Taiwan and South Korea markets, however, and also continued to support the China policy of the Satō government until June 1972, when President Wakasugi of Mitsui Bussan and President Fujino of Mitsubishi Shōji finally accepted the "four conditions." Wakasugi explained that he could no longer wait for the government's recognition of China; recognition seemed to be taking much longer than he had expected.[68]

President Fujino coupled the announcement supporting the "four conditions" with a surprise statement that the Mitsubishi group was planning to send a mission to Peking. He further disclosed that the group had begun to prepare for the mission immediately after China's admission to the United Nations.[69] According to Kimura Ichizō, managing director of the Kansai Japan International Trade Promotion Association, he first met Tajitsu Wataru, chairman of the board of Mitsubishi Bank through President Hyūga of Sumitomo Kinzoku, who had asked him to help realize Tajitsu's wish to visit China. Kimura repeatedly consulted with Tajitsu and in June finally obtained China's approval.[70] It had been generally assumed that China disapproved of the Mitsubishi group, especially because Mitsubishi Jūkōgyō had been singled out as "inimical" by the Chinese authorities. Indeed, the Mitsubishi Jūkōgyō leadership was known for its "hawkish" attitude. After Chairman of the Board Kōno Fumihiko led the Mitsubishi mission to Taiwan in 1965, various companies of the Mitsubishi group started to invest heavily in Taiwan. Moreover, President Makita Yōichiro, as recently as September of the previous year, spoke mockingly of those who tried to get on the bandwagon to China.

China's invitation to the Mitsubishi group came in July 1972, and three leading figures of the group—Chairman Tajitsu of Mitsubishi Bank, President Fujino of Mitsubishi Shōji, and President Koga, who had succeeded Makita at Mitsubishi Jūkōgyō—left for China on August 14. They did not present any documents in support of the "four conditions" prior to their departure, but merely prepared materials to show their existing business interests in Taiwan and South Korea. At the same time the Mitsubishi mission was in the People's Republic, Chairman Kōno Fumihiko of Mitsubishi Jūkōgyō visited Taiwan, formally on business, but actually to win the approval of the Nationalists on the course that Mitsubishi was taking. It was unusual for two missions to be dispatched simultaneously to Peking and Taipei. It was even more unusual that they were both received.

68. *Asahi shimbun,* June 14, 1972.
69. Ibid., June 8, 1972.
70. Kimura, "Nitchū keizai kōryū o tegakete nijūnen," p. 111.

The Mitsubishi mission to China was notable on two counts: the royal welcome accorded the mission by the Chinese authorities; and the complete change in attitude shown by the Mitsubishi group. The media were full of stories of Mitsubishi's "sumptuous *volte face*." Apparently, China thought it advantageous to make use of Mitsubishi's outstanding industrial power.[71] Mitsubishi Jūkōgyō's arms production power alone might have been the real cause of China's interest.[72] On Mitsubishi's part, there was definitely a feeling that the time was ripe for change. Mitsubishi, which had always operated in close alliance with the government, now judged that the resumption of diplomatic relations was imminent and took steps to prepare for the large-scale economic exchange that was expected to follow. Tajitsu's position was that Mitsubishi could mobilize its wide-ranging industrial power to undertake various big projects needed for China's economic development.[73] The Mitsubishi mission to China was followed by a Tokyo businessmen's mission led by President Inayama of Shin Nihon Seitetsu. The latter's objective was also to study the nature of economic relations between Japan and China after full diplomatic relations were established. The Furukawa, Fuyō, Sanwa, and Mitsui groups similarly sent missions.

By the time Mitsui and Mitsubishi groups took steps to enter the China market, the internal political scene had begun to show quick changes. Prime Minister Satō's withdrawal from the LDP presidency became increasingly certain at the beginning of 1972, and prospective successors started taking positions on the China issue. Miki Takeo, who was the first of the main faction leaders to take a pro-Peking stand, traveled to China himself in April and clearly called for the abrogation of the treaty between Japan and the Republic of China. Ōhira Masayoshi, in December 1971, also took the position that the existing peace treaty with the Republic of China was not valid for the purpose of terminating war between China and Japan. The two leading contenders for the LDP presidency, Fukuda Takeo and Tanaka Kakuei, the ministers of Foreign Affairs and MITI in the Satō cabinet, did not come out in clear support of normalization with China. Apparently Tanaka was determined to undertake diplomatic recognition of the People's Republic once he was elected premier, but he refrained from expressing open support of such a move lest it cost him votes at the coming election.[74] Nevertheless, as MITI minister, Tanaka had one advantage over Fukuda—MITI had always taken a more positive policy toward China than the Ministry of Foreign Affairs as a result of the belief that Japan had a strong stake in economic intercourse with China. Thus, Tanaka could

71. Comment of Matsumura Masanao, son of Matsumura Kenzō and president of Mitsubishi Sōko, quoted in "Mitsubishi grūpu no Chūgoku e no henshin," *Gekkan ekonomisuto*, Oct. 1972, p. 132.
72. Statement, Hakojima Shinichi.
73. "Mitsubishi grūpu no Chūgoku e no henshin," p. 131.
74. See Tagawa, *Nitchū kōshō hiroku*, pp. 336–344.

state on January 18, 1972, that MITI was prepared to permit the use of Export-Import Bank loans to China as soon as contracts were concluded and applications were presented, and to open a new section within the ministry to deal with China.[75] One reason for Tanaka's success in the LDP election on July 5 was that he, together with Ōhira, Miki, and Nakasone, could advocate "changing the tide" of the Satō government in a direction that had already been taken by the business community and was supported by the general political mood of the country.

After Prime Minister Tanaka visited Peking and established full diplomatic relations with the People's Republic of China, the business community formed two new organizations to deal with China and Taiwan. On November 21, 1972, the Japan-China Economic Association (Nitchū Keizai Kyōkai) was set up to serve as the organ of the business community in its contacts with China.[76] At its inception, some expected the association to become the main economic pipeline by absorbing the Memorandum Trade, which was to be terminated by the end of 1973, and the friendly firms' trade under the Japan International Trade Promotion Association. The latter attempted to strengthen its position by appointing Fujiyama Aiichirō as president in June 1973, but its fate will depend largely on how much China will allow it to handle future trade.

The Exchange Association (Kōryū Kyōkai)—so named because of the difficulty in agreeing on a term for the Republic of China authorities—was formed on December 1, 1972. Its functions are not limited to economic relations, but also include semigovernmental activities on behalf of Japanese nationals and interests in Taiwan. Its funds are based on contributions from the business community, but the operation of the offices in Taiwan is financed by the government. The association uses the building of the former Japanese embassy in Taipei and the former Japanese consulate in Kaohsiung. Horikoshi Teizō, vicepresident of Keidanren and long-time supporter of the Japan-Republic of China Cooperation Committee, became president of the association, with former Japanese ambassador to Taipei Itagaki Osamu as chairman of the council. In fact, the association undertakes functions similar to those of the Memorandum Trade Office. The terms of its activities are designated in an agreement concluded between the Exchange Association and its counterpart in Taiwan.[77]

75. *Nihon keizai shimbun,* Jan. 19, 1972.

76. Inayama Yoshihiro became president, and Kawai Ryōichi became chairman of the council, which was composed of sixty-five big business leaders. President Uemura of Keidanren, President Ashiwara Yoshishige of Kankeiren, President Kikawada of Keizai Dōyūkai, President Nagano of the Japan Chamber of Commerce and Industry, President Saeki of the Osaka Chamber of Commerce and Industry, and Okazaki Kaheita served as advisers. For details concerning the Japan-China Economic Association, see Inayama Yoshihiro, "Nitchū keisai kyōkai no hossoku ni atatte," *Keidanren geppō,* Jan. 1973, pp. 52–54.

77. For details concerning the Exchange Association, see Horikoshi Teizō, "Kōryū kyōkai no hossoku ni atatte," *Keidanren geppō,* Jan. 1973, pp. 55–59.

With the organization of the Exchange Association, the Japanese business community completed its adjustment to changed political circumstances. Now the principle of "no separation between politics and economics" became valid for relations with the People's Republic of China, and the separation principle was applied to Taiwan, where trade still continued at an expanding rate.

CONCLUSION

The process leading to Japan's normalization of relations with the People's Republic of China represented a crisis situation for the business community in which it was forced to take political decisions in order to pursue its business objectives. Throughout the period, the major determinant was the changing international political situation, to which the Japanese government seemed incapable of reacting promptly. The apparent delay was caused largely by commitments to past U.S. policies of containing the People's Republic of China and supporting the Nationalist government on Taiwan both diplomatically and economically.

Under such circumstances, the kind and degree of relationship with the government functioned as a crucial factor in determining the position of various business groups. The greater the distance from government, the easier it was for corporations and business leaders to shift their position in favor of the People's Republic. During the friendly firms' trade period, small and medium-sized companies largely monopolized the China market. Once Chou En-lai presented the "four conditions," corporations that were already heavily dependent on the China market took the lead in accepting these terms. The early conversion of the Sumitomo group can be explained to a certain extent by the fact that it was based in Kansai, an area that has traditionally depended largely on the China market and shown relative independence from government patronage. The late conversion of Shin Nihon Seitetsu proved the weight of government influence, for Shin Nihon Seitetsu alone among major steel corporations chose to remain outside the China market for over a year, at a time when the steel industry was in need of new markets.

The shift of zaikai leaders toward China came well after a sizable portion of individual corporations and gyōkai had expressed acceptance of Chou's "four conditions." Among zaikai leaders, Keizai Dōyūkai, whose self-assigned role was to serve as the conceptual-planning organ of the business community, was the first to confer with visiting Chinese missions and to send a mission to China. Nagano's extensive hesitation was due not only to Shin Nihon Seitetsu's long-standing government patronage, but also to his close contact with top government leaders, especially Prime Minister Satō. President Uemura of Keidanren was the last of the zaikai leaders to turn to China. His identification with the government was total. To the writer, Uemura defined his role as "semiofficial," for he often found himself regarded as the representative of the entire business community. As such, he believed that he could not visit China before the establishment of diplomatic relations, but he felt that he was obliged to go once diplomatic ties were formed.[78]

The decisions of individual corporations and business leaders vis-à-vis China were the outcome of a weighty balancing process between pursuit of business interests and adherence to government policy. What pushed the balance in favor of pursuing business interests were changes in the international scene. The present case study indicates that one of the outstanding features of the business community was its susceptibility to change. The business community kept its feelers out for any sign of change in the international environment surrounding China, and was deeply affected by events such as Canada's recognition of China, the results of the U.N. vote on Chinese representation, and various U.S. maneuvers toward China. President Nixon's announcement that he would visit China was of critical importance and the single most significant cause of the change in the Japanese business community. Having acted for so long on the basis that Japan follows every step taken by the United States, the business community was confident that by moving with President Nixon it was heading in the direction that the Japanese government was bound to follow. Finally, the People's Republic's entry into the United Nations was interpreted as international recognition of China's legitimacy and caused even those adamantly opposed at an earlier point to accept China's new status.

The decision-making process of the business community suggests that, in a situation involving a friendly state such as the United States, it is unlikely that top zaikai leaders would head a movement opposing official policy. At the same time, they would not take any action against individual corporations or gyōkai that breach official policy in pursuing specific business interests. Corporations or gyōkai were left to make their own choice on the China issue until the top leaders took the cue from the international scene and cast their lot with the new tide.

What then was the impact of the business community on the total decision-making process leading to the normalization of relations with China? Unlike the process under usual conditions, the business community could not act in close contact with the administrative bureaucracy. As the top leadership started to gravitate toward China, however, the business community as a whole began to assume a pressure-group character. This initially took the form of either supporting Peking's terms for normalization or pointing to the need to act in line with changing international circumstances. Second, the business community proved itself highly responsive to Chinese overtures and took definite steps, such as conferring with visiting Chinese officials or sending mis-

78. Statement Uemura made to me on Oct. 21, 1973.

sions to China. Its opinions and actions became increasingly attuned to the pro-Peking elements of the LDP, which by then had joined with the opposition parties and various pro-China groups in an all-out bid for the normalization of relations with China. The business community thus became involved in the nationwide process geared to changing the internal political environment.

It is more difficult to ascertain the specific nature of interaction between the business community and the political parties. Pro-Peking groups, such as the Japan International Trade Promotion Association, did succeed in manipulating influential business leaders and friendly firms as well as the media.[79] In a sense, the business community was a pawn of the diplomatic offensive of the People's Republic, although business leaders themselves had definite interests that they believed they could pursue by taking a pro-Peking position. The actual influence of the business community on the LDP cannot be estimated without undertaking a detailed study of intraparty politics involving China. However, it may be said that the pro-Peking shift, especially of the top zaikai leaders, influenced the contenders to the premiership to turn more decisively in favor of accepting Peking's terms for normalization of relations with Japan. In other words, the conversion of the business leaders helped accelerate the pro-Chinese trend within the mainstream of the LDP and drove the Satō and Fukuda factions out of power.

The process leading to normalization of relations with China suggests that decision-making was a result of a complicated and multiple interaction among, as well as within, the government, the parties, and the various nongovernmental groups. No one played a dominant part in the decision-making process, least of all the government leaders. External stimuli had decisive impact. Within these limits, however, the role of the business community should not be minimized, for it was the business community after all that cultivated, maintained, and promoted actual ties with the People's Republic throughout the postwar era. Furthermore, businessmen accelerated the change of the political climate not only among the general public but also among the major factions of the LDP. Thus, they helped realize the formation of a new cabinet that was committed to a new line of policy toward China.

79. Hirokoshi Teizo told me on July 19, 1973, that he believed the pro-Peking avalanche was a result of conspiracy.

III

*Economics and
Foreign Policy*

The International Economic
Policy of Japan

MASATAKA KOSAKA

I

Many observers of Japan have been impressed by the contrast between Japan's worldwide economic activity and the nationalistic orientation of its economic policy. Certainly the global character of Japan's trade in the mid-1970s is indisputable. Only twenty years ago Japan's trade, which was then mainly with the United States and other Asian countries, represented only 1.5 percent of total world trade. But Japanese economic activities expanded throughout the 1960s to every corner of the world and, in the 1970s, accounts for more than 6 percent of total world trade. The decline of Southeast Asia's share in Japan's trade is revealing. In 1955 Japan sold more than 20 percent of its exports to Southeast Asian countries; in the 1970s it amounts to little more than 10 percent, less than Japan's current trade with Western European countries. Table 1 shows the regional breakdown of Japan's exports over the past seventy years.

A global approach to economic matters, which tries to avoid dependence on any one place, is emerging in Japan. The country has achieved some good results with its policy of diversification, especially in expanding its sources for raw materials. With the exception of oil, Japan does not rely on any specific country or area for particular materials.[1] Japan has also had some success with its attempts to diversify its markets, although the geographical distribution of its trade is still somewhat lopsided. Trade with its largest partner, the United States, amounted to 30 percent of the total in 1970, but the percentage of the total for the top five trade partners shows a better balance. Among the advanced industrial countries, only Britain has an equally dispersed pattern (see Table 2). If the sample is enlarged to include the top ten trade partners, the

1. *Strategic Survey 1971* (London: International Institute for Strategic Studies, 1971), pp. 59–60.

207

Table 1

Region	1901	1911	1926	1935	1950	1960	1970	1974
Less Developed	46.2	49.5	55.4	72.5	60.9	51.1	40.8	47.1
Asia	46.1	49.3	52.9	63.7	46.3	37.0	31.2	32.7
(China) [a]	32.4 [a]	26.0 [b]	21.6	17.6	2.4	0.1	2.9	3.6
Colonies	3.4	14.5	15.3	23.8				
East and South Asia						32.2	25.4	22.9
West Asia (Middle East)						3.4	2.8	6.2
Africa	0.1	0.1	1.8	5.6	8.9	7.3	5.7	8.9
Latin America	0.0	0.1	0.7	2.9	5.7	7.5	6.1	9.1
Others						0.7	0.8	–
Developed	53.5	50.4	44.6	27.3	39.0	44.0	52.6	45.8
North America	29.0	28.1	36.8	16.5	22.5	27.6	33.6	25.9
(U.S.A.)	27.7	27.3	35.7	16.3	21.7	24.7	30.7	23.0
Europe	22.9	20.1	5.2	7.9	12.0	11.5	14.8	15.1
Oceana	1.7	2.3	2.6	2.9	3.6	4.9	5.4	4.8
Communist Bloc						1.8	5.4	7.1

SOURCE: Calculated from *Main Statistics of Japan since Meiji* for 1901–1960 and from *Japan Export Monthly* (December 1970) for 1970.

[a] Prewar export to Manchuria is included in the figures for China.
[b] Includes export to Hongkong.

Table 2

The Share of the Five Top Trade Partners in the Total Trade of Major Countries, 1969

Exports	1st	2nd	3rd	4th	5th	Total of the Five
Japan	U.S. 31.0	Korea 4.8	Hong Kong 3.8	Formosa 3.8	Liberia 3.0	46.4
U.S.	Canada 24.1	Japan 9.2	U.K. 6.1	W. Germany 5.6	Mexico 3.8	48.4
W. Germany	France 13.3	Holland 10.2	U.S. 9.4	Benelux 8.2	Italy 8.2	49.3
U.K.	U.S. 12.4	W. Germany 5.7	Ireland 4.5	Australia 4.5	France 4.3	31.4
France	W. Germany 20.4	Benelux 10.7	Italy 10.3	Holland 5.9	U.S. 5.4	52.7

Imports	1st	2nd	3rd	4th	5th	Total of the Five
Japan	U.S. 27.2	Australia 8.3	Iran 5.4	Canada 4.5	Philippines 3.1	48.5
U.S.	Canada 28.8	Japan 13.6	W. Germany 7.2	U.K. 5.9	Italy 3.3	58.8
W. Germany	France 13.0	Holland 11.6	U.S. 10.5	Italy 9.7	Benelux 9.3	54.1
U.K.	U.S. 13.5	Canada 6.1	W. Germany 5.6	Holland 4.9	Sweden 4.0	34.1
France	W. Germany 22.2	Benelux 11.4	Italy 10.1	U.S. 8.4	Holland 6.3	58.4

SOURCES: *Japan Export Monthly* (Dec. 1970); and United Nations, *Statistical Yearbook, 1970.*

pattern becomes clearer: although Japan's trade with the United States constitutes an indispensable base, it has successfully diversified the rest of its trade. Even by 1974, Japan's trade with the United States had declined to 23 percent of the total; by 1980, the global character of Japan's economic activities should become still clearer.[2]

Japan's attempts to spread its economic interests more widely reflects its geographic position. As an island country, it has easy access to every nation with ports. Moreover, modern transportation technology has nullified the distance factor, and big tankers and bulk carriers have brought a sharp reduction in freight charges. Freight charges per ton in 1960 were $5.50 for iron ore and $5.82 for crude oil; by 1969, they had dropped to $3.65 and $2.93 respectively. Modern technology has also increased average transportation mileage which, in effect, has reduced the distance between Japan and other countries and helped the global expansion of Japan's economic activities.[3]

The second characteristic of Japan's economy, the nationalistic orientation of its economic policy, is also indisputable, although it has sometimes been exaggerated and the recent modifications have been underestimated. The basic principle of Japan's trade policy has been, at least until recently, to enhance exports and limit imports, and to achieve this end it has adopted an intricate system of trade regulation. After Japan joined GATT in 1955, it built up a tariff system characterized by (1) low rates for primary products and high rates for finished goods—tariff escalation; (2) low rates for capital goods and high rates for consumer goods; (3) low rates for products not currently produced in Japan or likely to be produced in future and high rates for those that were or could be produced in Japan; (4) protection for infant industries; (5) protection for industries that employed many workers even if they were declining or stagnating; (6) low rates for daily necessities and high rates for luxury goods; (7) low rates for special goods such as materials used for education, cultural purposes, or medical care.[4]

With the growing liberalization of the trade systems of the world in the 1960s, Japan experienced increased pressure to liberalize its own trade, but it did not respond quickly. For example, tariff escalation—the pillar of Japan's import policy—was still evident in 1970. The result was a poor horizontal division of labor with the other countries. Although the percentage of Japan's imports in finished goods expanded from 7.7 percent in 1967 to 25.5 percent in 1970, it was still much smaller than that for other industrial countries, where the average was 50 percent.[5] Moreover, the concentration of Japan's exports within relatively few industries—another result of the policy to stimulate exports—increased the imbalance. According to a GATT report,

2. *Nichi-Bei keizai no chōki tenbō: 1980* (Tokyo: Nihon Keizai Kenkyu Center, 1973), p. 249.
3. *Shigen mondai no tenbō* (Tokyo: MITI, 1971), pp. 94–102.
4. *Nichi-Bei keizai*, pp. 295–296.   5. Ibid., pp. 301–307.

Japan's total exports of manufactures amount, in values, to less than 60 percent of the corresponding exports of the Federal Republic of Germany. Yet among Japan's principal product groups there are nine in which Japan supplies more than a third of combined OECD exports of the same products, and these nine groups include one-quarter of Japan's total exports of manufactures. In contrast, there are only four product groups in which the Federal Republic of Germany is a similarly preponderant OECD supplier, and these four groups comprise only 6 percent of the Federal Republic of Germany's manufactured exports.[6]

After 1968, when Japan's balance of trade began to record a substantial surplus, the demands for liberalization of its trade policies became stronger, and in the beginning of the 1970s Japan finally took substantial measures to correct the situation. Unfortunately Japan's attitude during this period was not a positive one; rather it represented a passive adaptation to the outside pressure. Such an attitude created distrust among other countries and retarded desirable changes in Japan's economic structure. For example, Japan's schedule of tariff escalation conformed to the world average only after modification of the tariff system in November 1972. The effects of the change naturally were not to be seen immediately.

II

What are the roots of Japan's nationalistic economic policy? One must begin the query by examining Japanese history, for the economic policy of Japan today is a product of its history. First, Japan had to start life in the international community as a weak and undeveloped country. Japan had closed its doors to the world for more than two hundred years before the Western powers forced them open again. It was a natural psychological reaction for the Japanese to regard these Western powers as a threat. There were practical reasons as well. Japan experienced serious disturbances in its economy—for example, in its monetary system—when it was forced to discard isolationist policies and enter the international order. Moreover, the Western powers were industrialized whereas Japan was still agrarian. Many manufactured goods streamed into Japan, which could export only raw materials and foods in exchange. In the first year of the Meiji era (1867), raw materials comprised 71 percent of Japan's exports, whereas finished goods accounted for only 7 percent. Even in the twenty-sixth year of Meiji (1893), after major efforts had been made to produce and export finished goods, such products still amounted to only 26 percent of the total, in contrast to 51 percent for raw materials and 20 percent for foods.[7]

Moreover, as most studies on Japanese trade have indicated, Japan did not

6. *Japan's Economic Expansion and Foreign Trade: 1955–1970* (Geneva: GATT, 1971).
7. Tsurumi Sakichio, *Nihon bōeki shi kō* (Tokyo: Ganshodo, 1939), pp. 305–306.

have the capability to manage the trade business due to its inexperience and the lack of appropriate organizations.[8] Dependence on foreign trading companies put Japanese manufacturers in a disadvantageous position, and with the loss of its tariff autonomy Japan could not mitigate the impact of Western industrial power. Therefore, the aim of Japan's early international economic policy was to secure the country's continued existence by recovering tariff autonomy, creating trading companies and a merchant marine, and stimulating the growth of industry and the export of finished industrial goods. As the task was urgent and Japan was underdeveloped, the state took primary responsibility. As one author argued,

England opened trade relations of its own free will. But Japan was forced by the Americans to do so. English people are clever and good at industry, while the Japanese are not.

England is very well developed and so are the people. But Japan is underdeveloped, and so are the people. Many are still lazy and their abilities have not been developed. When England liberalized her trade, she was the most advanced country, but Japan, at the time of liberalization, was inferior to every other country.[9]

Such a beginning gave a defensive cast to Japan's international economic policy.

By the beginning of the twentieth century, Japan had become a semi-industrialized country, but the more favorable position did not bring about a more positive and internationalist approach because too many difficult tasks still remained. There were, however, some important new developments in the 1910s and 1920s.[10] Japan had secured the minimum conditions for its existence with its victory in the Russo-Japanese War. The country also became aware of new frontiers for commercial expansion. Thus, when internationalism and pacifism emerged as the dominant ideas in the world after the First World War, Japan adopted its "New Diplomacy." This new public policy, also known as the "Shidehara Diplomacy," regarded economic intercourse as the central concern of international relations.

The Japanese experience with its New Diplomacy, however, was not a happy one. Although the gospel of internationalism was attractive as an idea, the facts of international relations were harsh and lent support to those in Japan who advocated a defensive and nationalistic policy. First, the productivity of Japanese industry was still low because the country was not yet highly industrialized. It was therefore difficult to find markets for Japan's finished

8. Ibid., pp. 283–297. Also Asakura Kōkichi, *Nihon bōeki kōzō ron* (Tokyo: Hoppon Shoten, 1955), p. 40.

9. Ibid., pp. 35–36.

10. Iriye Akira, "Heiwa teki hatten shugi to Nihon," *Chūō Kōron*, Oct. 1969.

industrial goods, and became possible only with the strong support of the government. These conditions influenced the policy of even Shidehara, the champion of the New Diplomacy, and led to Japan's tough position on the tariff problem involving China. One reason for the failure of the Peking Tariff Conference, which began in October 1925, was Japanese opposition to the introduction of a surtax prior to the establishment of a formal system.[11] The Japanese government opposed the tax out of fear that the Japanese textile industry might lose the competition with the Chinese textile industry in the field of low quality textile goods. Moreover, Japan could not compete with the other industrialized countries in the high quality goods market. Such difficulties were typical of those encountered by a semideveloped country.

Second, Japan had a tremendous need to export because it had to import raw materials for its industry. Thus, the balance of payments problem appeared during the initial stages of industrialization and became chronic. The difficulties increased after the First World War when the system of free trade collapsed and the trends toward protectionism appeared. Even in the 1920s, world trade did not grow rapidly, but the situation deteriorated as many countries adopted outright protectionism after the Great Depression of 1929. Such developments put Japan in an agonizing situation, for it could not retaliate against those countries that provided its raw materials. In 1951, the Japanese Foreign Ministry published the following assessment of the situation in the 1930s:

Japan astonished the world by increasing her exports in 1933 in the midst of the depression . . . and the future looked bright for the Japanese. . . . But Japan could increase exports only to those countries [or areas] that treated the Japanese goods on more or less equal and free terms, such as England . . . the Near and Middle East . . . Latin America, Thailand, and Manchuria. . . . Exports to countries that had adopted a protectionist policy, such as the Soviet Union, the United States, Australia . . . did not increase.[12]

After 1935, even the former free trade countries began to adopt protectionist measures, and Japanese exports could no longer grow. Japan reacted by treating those countries with a freer system favorably and those with protectionist systems less favorably. "But Japan could not limit the imports from such countries as the United States, Germany, Australia, New Zealand, Canada, Sweden and Denmark, irrespective of their trade policy, because the imports from these countries consisted of raw cotton, wool, timber, pulp, oil, iron, copper, nickel,

11. Iriye Akira, *After Imperialism* (Cambridge, Mass.: Harvard University Press, 1965), pp. 76–78.
12. Ministry of Foreign Affairs, *Tsūshō jyōyaku to tsūshō seisaku no hensen* (Tokyo, 1951), pp. 711–716.

and machine goods, all of which were essential to Japanese industry." Japan's
economic policy could not pursue the lofty goal of internationalism but had to
try to secure the necessary goods with a nationalistic policy.

Third, the virtual ban on Japanese emigration influenced the Japanese attitude toward international society, even though it was not directly related to
trade policy. In the early 1920s many Japanese sought a solution for Japan's
overpopulation in emigration. One author wrote in 1922, "If the League of
Nations was really created with the aim of permanent peace for all human beings, and if the coexistence of people is the ideal on which world peace is to be
built, the world should sympathetically help us to solve our many unhappy
problems resulting from overpopulation."[13]

One can argue, of course, that these expectations were unrealistic and that
Japan later succeeded in solving its problem without emigration. Nevertheless,
the Japanese at the time looked to the example of other countries that had used
emigration to solve their overpopulation problems, especially during the nineteenth century. With Japanese expectations so high, it was a serious blow when
the Japanese proposal for a "Declaration of the Equality of Races" was not
adopted by the Versailles Peace Conference and when in 1924 the United
States adopted its immigration act legally banning Japanese immigrants. The
Japanese considered this rank discrimination; the rejection of Japanese immigrants turned internationalism into a hollow ideal.[14] Moreover, it strengthened the suspicion that Japan, a nonwhite country, was treated less favorably
for racial reasons. Such suspicions had been gaining currency in Japan ever
since Japan had become one of the powers and begun to experience resistance
to its growth.[15]

Thus, Japan discarded its brief experiment with internationalism to follow
the course of ultranationalism. Ultranationalism was discredited by the Second World War, but the views and experiences of the 1920s and 1930s have remained in Japanese consciousness: as Japan has no natural resources, its first
priority must be their acquisition; extraordinary efforts to increase exports are
necessary in order to pay for raw materials; Japan is in a weak position because
it is less industrialized than the Western countries; and Japan is in a disadvantageous position politically because it is the only nonwhite industrial country.
These feelings make up the underpinnings for Japan's defensive and nationalistic international economic policy.

13. Iriye, "Heiwa teki hatten shugi to Nihon."
14. After the passage of the immigration act, the slogan "independent foreign policy"
(jishu gaikō) began to be advocated as an alternative to the policy of cooperation with the
West.
15. For example, the "yellow peril" theory gave serious concern to many Japanese after
the Russo-Japanese War. See Takakura Tetsuichi, ed., Tanaka Giichi denki (Tokyo), vol. 1,
p. 459.

III

As the contemporary situation is very different from that of the past, one might expect that the old memories and attitudes have been weakened and largely replaced with a new perspective. The remarkable success of Japan in the past twenty years, however, has not only made Japan powerful, but also vulnerable, and some of its weaknesses are now more visible. It is true that Japan currently finds it less difficult to export its industrial goods; in some sectors (steel and shipbuilding, for example) the Japanese dominate the scene. Thus, the traditional objective of Japanese economic policy—promotion of exports—is no longer a difficult task. But even before the recent oil crisis, there was growing apprehension among Japanese policy-makers concerning the future of the nation. As Japanese economic activities have rapidly expanded in scope and increased in volume, they have encountered higher barriers abroad. The Japanese consider many of the barriers counter to the principles of free trade, and sometimes they attribute them to the fact that Japan is the only non-Western industrial nation in the world. To this must be added the increasingly difficult task of obtaining the raw materials necessary for their industry at reasonable prices—not merely oil, but other products as well. Thus, the Japanese have discovered that the old problems—the unique nature of Japan and the lack of raw materials—still persist, although in different form.

Recent events clearly indicate that these concerns are not without reason. The uniqueness of Japan and the lack of raw materials create real problems, ones difficult to solve. Moreover, the resistance that the Japanese have increasingly encountered abroad is a natural consequence of the increased strength of their economy and their slowness in making adjustments to the new situation. Some criticism of Japan's protectionist policy and its delay in import liberalization is justified, but the adjustments needed have never been simple.

First, it is not enough to rely wholly on principles of free trade, for they can work only with intricate compromises. It would be naive to suppose that under the rules of fair competition, a country may expand its exports indefinitely. To do so can bring serious disorders to the economies of other countries, pushing them to adopt protectionist regulations that violate the basic principles of free trade. To avoid such dire consequences, a country must take care not to adversely affect the stability and growth of other economies. It must accept the fact that free trade needs some control and that it is generally the countries with surplus exports which must regulate themselves. But such self-control is a delicate task. Usually the weaker side seeks more control, while the stronger promotes the principles of free trade. As every country has strong sectors as well as weak ones, any trade negotiations involve a complex give-and-take process, and even then developments can lead to serious conflicts.

Thus self-regulation of certain exports became a thorny issue between the United States and Japan. The textile issue, for example, is a delicate matter due to the structure of that industry. But when outside considerations further complicated the textile negotiations in the early 1970s, the result was a relatively serious confrontation. Both governments were rather clumsy in their handling of the problem, but other factors exacerbated the problem. First, the impression that concessions were being required of Japan as the price for the reversion of Okinawa had unfortunate psychological effects on the Japanese. Second, the American demands for Japanese self-regulation were not based on solid economic arguments, but were motivated by domestic political considerations, a factor that did not receive enough attention from the Japanese government.[16] Also, the Japanese did not realize that short-term concessions could result in long-term gains. Perhaps they had not yet come to a full understanding of the new situation created by their strong economy and the concessions this would sometimes necessitate.[17]

Second, it is not always easy to determine what constitutes protectionism. Many Japanese feel that they are unjustly accused of protectionism, especially with regard to their so-called non-tariff barriers. Much of the criticism of Japanese economic policy touches on these non-tariff barriers, the most notorious of which is the "administrative guidance" that MITI provides to Japanese industries. Some criticism is certainly well-founded, but often the picture is overdrawn.[18] Although it is true that many foreigners have difficulty operating in the Japanese market, some too easily attribute their troubles to non-tariff barriers because these represent a vague concept that can be used in many ways. Non-tariff barriers, however, are not something that the government can create or demolish at will. They consist mainly of the differences in business conventions and customs as well as the differences in the social structures

16. Gary Saxonhouse, "A Review of Recent U.S.-Japanese Economic Relations," *Asian Survey*, Sept. 1972.

17. The Japanese textile manufacturers evinced an awkward defensiveness. Just as the negotiations approached their conclusion, the press reported that Vice-President Miyazaki of the Textile Industry Federation had belatedly indicated a willingness to comply with the American demands for a period of two years. This was a signal of weakness, whereas in these particular negotions Japan was in a position of strength. If Japan was going to concede that much, moreover, it would have been more effective to have done so a few months earlier. The attitude of the Japanese textile manufacturers, however, becomes understandable in view of the intransigent attitude of the American textile manufacturers. Therefore, the textile negotiations may not have been the best case to prove my point. Nevertheless, the lack of a sense of enlightened interest on the part of the Japanese with respect to the general issue was undeniable and added many difficulties. Moreover, few individuals argued for a concessional position by Japan, even outside the textile industry. For a typical Japanese view of the negotiations, see Kubota Akira, "Nichi-Bei sen'i jyūrokunen sensō," *Chūō kōron, Keiei mondai*, winter 1971.

18. A typical argument is found in Håkan Hedberg, *Nihon no chōsen*, the Japanese translation of the original *Das japanska utmaningen* (Stockholm: Bonniers, 1969). Although the author puts his argument in a generally friendly tone, he is rightly severe on this point.

within which businessmen operate in different societies.[19] Therefore, those who do not have sufficient knowledge of the business and social conventions of a given country are adversely affected. Non-tariff barriers exist in every nation in one form or another, but the Japanese language and conventions are so different from those of other industrial nations that it is difficult to assimilate them quickly. Theoretically, Japanese should suffer from similar difficulties when operating abroad. But the Japanese have had to operate in Western countries for a long time, so they have managed to learn Western conventions. The rest of the world, however, has long neglected the Japanese market. Still, the much-criticized hard-sell methods of Japanese merchants can be attributed to their insufficient understanding of the conventions of others. On the whole, the uniqueness of Japan's society and culture seems to be the root of the trouble.

The uniqueness of Japan has created problems at two different levels. On one level, it leads to misperceptions and hasty judgments. For example, attempts from abroad to explain the favorable competitive position of the Japanese economy in terms of its cheap labor suffer from a hidden sense of superiority and do not come to grips with the realities. Arguments that make value judgments on the basis of the different cultural and social structure of Japan suffer from cultural egocentricity. These prejudices are natural, but misleading.

An unfortunate effect of these misunderstandings is that, by providing easy but false explanations for problems, they create confusion and lead to overlooking a serious issue on a second level—can the system of free trade work in a heterogeneous system? Most people seem to suffer from the illusion that the system of free trade works smoothly unless some "bad guys" interfere—an illusion that takes different forms depending on whether the perspective is Japanese or Western. Westerners start with their perception of the disruptive impact of Japanese economic expansion, attribute it to the different cultural and social system of Japan, and, blinded by cultural egocentricity, make unwarranted value judgments. The Japanese tend to absolve Japan of blame for any surplus in the balance of trade, no matter how large, as long as the country has observed the formal conventions of free trade.

Both are wrong. The system of free trade is a fragile one and feasible only under certain premises, one of which is that there must be certain homogeneity among the countries in the system. The problem of non-tariff barriers, for example, should not be insurmountable in a homogeneous system, but it can represent a very difficult problem under highly diverse international conditions. Like the balance of power system, the free trade system may not be able to operate smoothly if conditions are too heterogeneous. This is one basic question

19. G.C. Allen, "Japan's Place in Trade Strategy," in Hugh Corbet, ed., *Trade Strategy and the Asian-Pacific Region* (London: George Allen and Unwin, 1970).

that Japan and the other industrial nations must face today. Japan creates problems precisely because it injects too much heterogeneity into the system.

As noted, the lack of raw materials is a primary cause for concern among Japanese today. After World War II, two conditions operated to reduce the problem of raw material supply for Japan. First, the postwar world economic system guaranteed free trade and free access to raw materials fairly well. Therefore the Japanese could survive by processing imported raw materials and exporting the product to gain money with which to import more raw materials. Second, the volume of raw materials that Japan needed was small and could be obtained by one means or another. Toward the end of the 1960s, however, these conditions changed and the Japanese began to experience difficulties.

Due to its rapid growth since the 1950s, the volume of raw materials that Japan must now import to maintain its industrial activities has become colossal. As shown in Table 3, 90 percent of Japan's raw materials now comes from abroad, including all its aluminium and nickel and 99.7 percent of its oil. Japan is least dependent on others for lead and zinc, but half of these needs are still supplied from abroad. Japan's dependence on outside sources for raw materials has existed for a long time, and the difficulties have not proved insurmountable. But toward the end of the 1960s, Japan's share in the total world consumption of raw materials rose to nearly 10 percent. In the non-Communist world, Japan is second only to the United States in the amount of raw materials

Table 3
Japan's Dependence on Foreign Sources for Raw Materials,
1970

Item	Demand	Home Production	Dependence on others (%)
Copper (thousand tons)	880	215	75.6
Lead (thousand tons)	216	98	54.6
Zinc (thousand tons)	681	310	54.6
Aluminum (thousand tons)	885	0	100
Nickel (thousand tons)	91	0	100
Iron ore (million tons)	111.0	13.2	87.9
Coal (million tons)	59.2	12.8	78.5
Crude oil (million kl)	204.1	0.7	99.7
Natural gas (million m³)	3,662	2,387	34.8
Uranium (thousand st)	0.7	--	100.0
TOTAL 10 billion yen	323	31	90.0

SOURCE: MITI, *White Papers on Natural Resources* (Tokyo: MITI, 1971), p. 9.

it consumes. As the United States has considerable natural resources of its own, Japan has become the largest importer of raw materials. Its share in the world trade of raw materials is now roughly 12 percent, as is shown in Table 4, and under present conditions it is destined to grow.

In the meantime, the international situation with regard to raw materials has changed. By the end of the 1960s, total world consumption had become enormous, and the supply of several mineral resources began to fall short of demand. Moreover, some supplying countries have become dissatisfied with the terms of trade or the fact that they have remained the suppliers of raw materials but have not succeeded in their own industrialization. Thus they have become more demanding in their terms of trade and have begun to ask for new types of economic relations with the industrial nations so that they themselves can become industrialized.[20] These factors have made it more difficult for Japan to obtain the raw materials required.

It is wrong to think that Japan is severely handicapped by its lack of raw materials. In today's world of global interdependence, such actions as embargos will take place only under exceptional circumstances, and, given proper efforts in technological development, the shortage of raw materials in an absolute sense is unlikely for the forseeable future. Japan should continue to be able to obtain raw materials through regular commercial transactions. In fact, no country today can operate its industries without importing a considerable amount of raw materials from abroad.

Table 4
Major Raw Material Trade Shares
(in percentage)

	Japan	U.S.	U.K.	Soviet bloc	Others
1965	9.1	12.2	10.1	9.6	59.0
1966	11.8	14.1	10.8	10.5	52.8
1967	11.9	11.3	9.1	8.7	59.0
1968	12.9	12.2	9.3	8.2	57.4
1969	11.8	11.4	8.2	7.6	61.0
Growth per year	14.5	4.5	1.1	0.6	

SOURCES: United Nations, *Monthly Bulletin of Statistics*, March 1970; MITI, *White Paper on Natural Resources* (Tokyo: MITI, 1971).

20. Their new attitude was dramatically shown by the OPEC actions in 1969, 1971, and subsequently, but such an attitude was increasingly revealed even during the 1960s, as demonstrated by the two resolutions in the United Nations concerning rights over natural resources (1961 and 1966).

Nevertheless, the lack of raw materials presents two special problems for Japan. First, reliance only on commercial transactions will not be sufficient to guarantee the necessary supply of raw materials in the future, given Japan's economic projections. Therefore, a 1971 MITI White Paper proposed diversification in the acquisition of raw materials by adding two new methods for obtaining them: (1) to advance funds to countries that produce raw materials in exchange for guarantees of supply; and (2) to invest in the exploration for raw materials at Japan's own risk.[21] The White Paper particularly emphasized the second approach because (1) it would contribute directly to an increase in world production of raw materials; (2) it would guarantee supply through the development of special ties with the countries that own the raw materials; and (3) it would improve the terms of trade.[22] Such efforts will certainly improve the situation if they succeed, but this type of policy demands substantial political capabilities, because the close and special ties produced through investment tend to create complicated political problems. Unless direct investment is accompanied by wise political action, the situation can easily deteriorate.

Second, importation of large amounts of raw materials can create a formidable balance of payments problem. Japan must export an enormous flow of manufactured goods to pay for the vast supply of raw materials from abroad. As most supplier countries do not have large home markets, Japan has contrived to have a surplus in trade elsewhere—with the United States, Southeast Asian countries, and Europe. But Japan may find it difficult to maintain such a trade surplus now that the amount necessary to pay the bill has become so great. Japan's trade surplus with countries other than those that supply raw materials can become greater than they can tolerate, as past events have so graphically illustrated. The difficulties have recently increased, with the sharp rise in the prices of raw materials—a trend that promises to continue. The development of the supplier countries, which are in most cases the less-developed ones, will help alleviate the problem but will not eliminate it. Importing a large amount of raw materials and financing it by trade surpluses elsewhere is not an uncommon policy, but to seek to practice it on such a large scale as is necessary for Japan creates a difficult problem both for it and for the world.

In exerting a greater effort than others to promote exports, therefore, Japan must pay special attention to the composition of its trade, and in this respect it will continue to be different from most other industrialized nations. In sum, Japan is unique, not only socially and culturally, but also economically. Although it is not easy for Japan to maintain and enhance its livelihood under such circumstances, it is also not easy for other nations to accommodate to such a nation in the world system. Naturally, therefore, Japan has become an object of criticism and various countermeasures as it has risen from a negligible posi-

21. *Shigen mondai no tenbō*, pp. 196–204.
22. Ibid., p. 199.

tion in the world economy to one of the largest traders. Naturally also, such reactions have caused deep anxiety in Japan and revived the traditional fear that the country may be isolated from the world. Many Japanese are obsessed with the vulnerability and weakness of their country; the result is their continued defensive and nationalistic approach to the international affairs.

IV

A defensive and nationalistic approach to international affairs, however, cannot solve Japan's problems. It is inappropriate for a global trading nation, and therefore counterproductive. The system of free trade is essential for Japan's prosperity, to a much larger degree than it is for other countries. Undoubtedly every nation, including the United States, would suffer if the system of free trade were to collapse. The United States, however, could survive if barter should become the order of the day; it would be utterly impossible for Japan. Japan's balance of trade can be maintained only multilaterally; the large volume of raw materials Japan must import cannot be paid for by exports to supplier countries alone, because their markets are usually small. Therefore, if many countries were to insist on bilateral balance, Japan would suffer greatly. Without a successful effort to maintain a trade balance on a global scale—in other words, the system of free trade—Japan cannot live.

These conditions require a positive internationalist policy within which Japan makes a greater effort to communicate its nature and especially its uniqueness to the rest of the world. A few individuals have realized the obvious need for cultural exchange,[23] but the main thrust of Japan's policy has continued to be defensive and nationalistic. As rationality does not lie in this direction, what are the factors that make the Japanese choose this approach over a positive internationalist one? Perhaps the basic reason lies in the essentially closed and conservative nature of the Japanese system. The Japanese manner of decision-making and Japanese attitudes toward norms both reveal these aspects of the system.

A substantial number of studies on the Japanese decision-making system are now available. Most observers agree on the following points: it is basically group or consensus decision-making, and consists of many lengthy sessions in which each participant begins to express himself in a very vague and noncommital way and gradually reaches his conclusions in more concrete fashion, in accordance with what appears to be the consensus. A fatherlike figure usually presides and serves as a middleman who lends his authority to the process by announcing the decision. Undoubtedly such a system has several advantages: it

---

23. The establishment in 1972 of the Japan Foundation was the product of the realization, but the past performance of Japan in this field makes one skeptical of its future.

promotes a sense of participation as it enlists the opinions of almost all the constituent members; it prevents the appearance of "drop-out" or "maverick" tendencies; and it facilitates the execution of the decision because many have participated in the process and thus understand the decision and feel committed to it. Thus, such scholars as James Abegglen and Herman Kahn consider this decision-making method a source of the dynamism of Japanese society because it enables the mobilization of the total energies of the society.[24]

But consensus decision-making also has several disadvantages. First, it takes time, not only because so many meetings are necessary to give everyone a chance to state his opinions, but also because it is difficult to overrule the opposition. The Japanese are not happy with majority decisions and a decision made by consensus must satisfy the desires of nearly everyone, or at least it must not neglect anyone in too obvious a manner. Therefore, a convinced or stubborn minority can delay a decision and possibly block it altogether.

Second, decision-making by consensus tends to become a system of mutual irresponsibility which results in confusion, because the responsibility and the competence of leaders and led are not clearly defined. Therefore, when faced with an unpleasant decision, everyone tends to be evasive. Such defects were apparent in the decision-making of the Japanese government during the Second World War.[25] Also, the need to maintain a façade of consensus makes it hard to arrive at clear-cut decisions in difficult cases. The solution often is an extremely vague formula, which becomes the cause of a greater confusion afterward. Whether the potential virtues or the defects of the Japanese decision-making system manifest themselves more strongly depends on the circumstances. The Japanese are not always slow to act even within their time-consuming process. Clearly, the Japanese system is weak under the conditions of stress and crisis, but if the nature of the crisis is simple, the Japanese can usually react; if it is complicated, on the other hand, confusion and irresponsibility are likely to ensue.

Two unfortunate corollaries to the Japanese system of consensus decision-making are an inability to act with foresight and the closed nature of the system. Consensus is obtained without great difficulty when the nature of the task is clear. Often, for instance, the Japanese have been good at adapting to strong, decisive pressures from outside. But when the situation is blurred, they are in trouble. As planning ahead, by definition, means to act within an uncertain situation, it is difficult to obtain consensus on measures aimed at dealing with long-term issues and problems. Such decisions, to be sure, are difficult for any country, but even more so for the Japanese. Yet long-range planning is

24. Herman Kahn, *The Emerging Japanese Superstate* (Englewood Cliffs, N.J.: Prentice-Hall, 1970), chap. 2.

25. Zbigniew Brzezinski, *The Fragile Blossom* (New York: Harper and Row, 1972), p. 50.

precisely what is required of Japan now, especially in the economic sphere. Even if the Japanese, taking action belatedly, manage to reorganize aspects of the Japanese economy, the unfortunate impact of the delay on other countries cannot be undone. If the theater of action were limited to Japan, quick and concerted action after long and cautious deliberation would still work. But the theater of action for the Japanese is now much wider.

Another unfortunate aspect of the Japanese decision-making system is its insensitivity to demands from outside when these conflict with demands from within. Thus, even minor domestic interests cannot easily be sacrificed for the sake of necessary adjustments to the outside world, because the first priority is to obtain consensus within the country. The Japanese attitude on the protection of its agricultural sector represents a typical case. Japan's protectionist policy toward agriculture has not been criticized only by foreign countries, but has also caused notoriously high food prices in Japan and hurt such groups as blue- and white-collar workers and artisans. Only the farmers benefit directly. If food imports were liberalized, the majority of Japanese could obtain food more cheaply. Yet the movement in Japan for the liberalization of food imports has been much delayed. The majority interest is clearly with the critical foreigners and the Japanese nonagricultural sectors; but although these groups are not powerless, they are also not decisive. Unless and until the farmers themselves are persuaded to accept a different policy and a consensus is created, change with respect to agricultural trade policies will be slow.[26]

Another important factor is the Japanese attitude toward rank and norms. Many have pointed out that the Japanese conception of the international order is hierarchical: at any given time, there is a definable rank order between any two nations, whereby one is higher, the other lower. Such a concept also manifests itself in the Japanese attitude toward themselves and other people: they are obsequious to superiors but haughty to inferiors, and excessively preoccupied with self.[27] Although such a thesis applies more accurately to traditional Japan, it still holds true in considerable measure today. In the Meiji period, the Japanese tended to classify the countries of the world as "highly civilized," "semicivilized," or "backward."[28] In a later version the categories became "first-rate power," "second-rate power," and "third-rate power," and now they are "super-power," "middle power," and "small power." Although such classifications can be found everywhere, the Japanese seem to be more intensely conscious of them. As Herbert Passin writes,

26. The Japanese have also shown a tendency to be greatly concerned with their image in the world, and therefore susceptible to criticism from abroad. By its very nature, however, such a pattern of change is not easy to discern and document.

27. This has been pointed out by many. For example, Edwin O. Reischauer, *The United States and Japan* (Cambridge, Mass: Harvard University Press, 1958), p. 109; and W.G. Beasley, *The Modern History of Japan* (New York: Praeger, 1965), p. 310.

28. The term was coined by Fukuzawa Yukichi.

It is probably fair to say that in general, international ranking is more important to individuals in Japan than in most other countries. Japanese have a strong tendency to rank themselves on the basis of the ranking group with which they are primarily identified (in this case the nation). A member of a low-ranking group, however high his personal rank, will always tend to be related below the member of higher-ranking groups. . . . Because the individual's self-ranking and his ranking by his "significant others" are so dependent upon the ranking of his group in a world of competitive, striving groups, the concern for Japan's position in the world tends to penetrate farther down into the population than would be the case in most other countries.[29]

These attitudes arise from both structural features of Japanese society and historical experience. Ranking is very important in the human contact of the Japanese. "Effective communication depends upon careful attention to the subtly calibrated cues of relative standing. All three of Japan's major encounters with the outside world have had a similar structure: backward Japan feels obliged to absorb a foreign civilization and, through absorbing it, catch up with it."[30]

Whatever its roots, the hierarchical concept of international society is still the basic framework within which Japanese classify their nation as a latecomer. Their strong desire to improve Japan's position is clearly an important source of the Japanese dynamism. But such a concept has made it difficult for the Japanese to establish healthy horizontal relations with equals. Also, under such a rubric, taking initiatives in shaping and maintaining international order cannot become a basic task for the Japanese. Their task is to catch up with their superiors.

Such a tendency is strengthened by Japanese attitudes toward norms. In their eyes, norms are something that are either given from above or called forth by the situation. They are not created by men through multilateral action. Therefore, Japanese will observe norms when they are given in a clear form. Otherwise they tend to behave as they wish. This passive view toward norms can be understood as a reflection of the Japanese view of society. Japan is a natural nation-state; the idea that a state is created by common will and contract has not existed in Japan. Japan has existed and will exist, regardless of the will and actions of its people. Hence, norms are considered to be created by nature, not men. Given the tradition of authoritarian rule in Japan, moreover, to the extent that a norm is created by men, it is by superiors and not by the common efforts of all citizens.

29. Herbert Passin, "Socio-Cultural Factors in the Japanese Perception of International Order," *Annual Review 1952: Japan Institute of International Affairs*, p. 53. See also Nakane Chie, *Tate shakai no ningen kankei* (Tokyo: Kodansha, 1967).
30. Passin, "Socio-Cultural Factors."

A recent study found that the Japanese entertain a rigorous attitude toward law.[31] A heavy majority favored the death penalty for certain crimes, for example, and a surprisingly large number of respondents regarded adultery as a punishable offense.[32] But at the same time, those polled calmly condoned minor breaches of law for a very characteristic reason: the respondents, including those who had broken a given law themselves, answered that such a breach was not bad because other people also did not observe the law concerned.[33] The view of contract was also interesting. Although a substantial majority of respondents considered it necessary to have a clear, written contract, they also thought that the contract could be interpreted liberally, with significant changes of content if the situation changed.[34] Clearly the Japanese ethic is basically a situational one.[35] In a word, it is what nature creates, and not what men make.

The Japanese look on norms in international society in a similar vein. As Kyōgoku Junichi wrote,

There does not exist in Japan a real feeling that Japan and the Japanese, with their individuality, are related with other nations, also with their individualities, and that the Japanese contribute to the civilization of others, and others to the civilization of Japan. . . . The world has been a "given" surrounding Japan, which makes a real impact on Japan, but which cannot be modified by the efforts of the Japanese. The world is nothing but the "framework" or the setting which can change only mysteriously.[36]

The logical conclusion from such a view of the world is that the task for the Japanese is to adapt wisely to the international situation to secure its national interests, and not to try to change or create the mysterious framework.

V

Thus we have arrived at a curious and strikingly paradoxical fact. The conservatism and closedness of the Japanese decision-making system and the passive attitude toward norms are decisive factors in Japan's defensive and nationalistic economic policy. Such a policy is now counterproductive, but it is the other side of the very factors that have contributed to the success of Japan's industrializa-

31. Nihon Bunka Kaigi, *Nihonjin no hō ishiki* (Tokyo: Shiseidō, 1973).

32. Should adultery be punished? Yes 52% No 22% Should the death penalty be abolished? Yes 15% No 84%

33. For example, the rationing law, which existed during and after the Second World War, and traffic regulations.

34. Those who favored a liberal interpretation amounted to 64.3 percent, in contrast to 31.6 percent for those who insisted on a rigorous interpretation.

35. Classic studies of the Japanese ethic, which are still valuable, are to be found in the works of Watsuji Tetsurō. *Fūdo* is a representative one.

36. Kyogoku Junichi, *Gendai-minshusei to seijigaku* (Tokyo: Iwanami-Shoten, 1969), p. 170.

tion and economic expansion. The Japanese have been good at absorbing and assimilating foreign civilizations.[37] Their system has succeeded in generating enormous energy among the people, and on the whole they have wisely adapted to the changes in the world situation.

The closedness and even the conservatism have contributed to Japan's success. Because Japan is a closed system with some windows open—some call it a semipermeable system[38]—the disruptive effects of international intercourse have been relatively few. The Japanese have been able to pick and choose and then respond to external impacts with nationally cohesive efforts. This style developed because Japan, long in a distant corner of the world, both has had to and has been able to learn from a distance.[39] Though the actual distance has decreased since the middle of the nineteenth century, the system has persisted and, on the whole, continued to benefit Japan.

It has been only recently, when intercourse with the outside world has grown to such a degree, that Japan's style has begun to produce problems. The vigorous activities of the Japanese on a global scale and a defensive and nationalistic economic policy grow from the same roots, namely, the basic "institutions" of Japanese society. In a word, the basic contradictions marking Japanese economic policies are inherent in its society.

There can be no easy solution to the contradictions, but one need not be pessimistic or desperate even if this analysis is accepted. Few countries have the ability to play a world role, and it is hard for citizens or their leaders to identify their nation's vital interests in such a vague and abstract setting as "the global system." Also, it is difficult for anyone to find both rational and effective ways to contribute to the world with its perplexing diversities and innumerable problems. Only when a country outgrows its original inhibitions and defects of ability and perspective, can it become a global actor, assuming its integral capacities for that role.

Can Japan become a constructive global actor, especially in the economic realm? Or will Japan fail to break through its old defensive, nationalist proclivities in spite of its pressing needs? If the former is the case, Japan can contribute to the world by the very virtue of the fact that it *is* a unique country. If the latter occurs, Japan's economic growth will stop rather abruptly at a certain point, and the consequent frustration may well cause a crisis not only in Japan but also in a number of other countries in the world.

37. It is well known that foreign civilization was "Japanized" as soon as it was taken in by the Japanese. Confucianism, Buddhism, Chinese characters and paintings, all were adapted by the Japanese. Tsuji Zennosuke regards this assimilation as one of the main characteristics of the Japanese civilization. See his *Kaigai kotsū shi wa* (Tokyo: Naigai Shoseki, 1930), chap. 1.

38. Umezao Tadao coined the term in his *Henkaku to jyoho* (Tokyo: Chūō Kōronsha, 1971), p. 286.

39. Passin, "Socio-Cultural Factors." I have expanded on this idea in my *Kaiyō kokka Nihon no kōsō* (Tokyo: Chūō Kōronsha, 1965).

MITI and Japanese International Economic Policy

CHALMERS JOHNSON

Bureaucracies are not normally objects of popular affection, even when they appear to promote popularly supported goals, and Japan's Ministry of International Trade and Industry (MITI) is no exception in that respect.[1] Given that MITI has presided over—if not actually brought about (its precise contribution is one of the most controversial subjects of modern political economy)—the fastest growing industrial economy that ever existed and has administered the growth of Japanese foreign trade at a rate some three times greater than the growth rate of all international trade during the postwar generation, it is perhaps not surprising that some of Japan's overseas competitors have criticized MITI. In addition to the familiar epithets of "ubiquitous MITI" and "notorious MITI," some foreigners have dubbed it "the ministry of one-way trade" and "the corporate headquarters of Japan, Inc."

At the same time, observers sensitive to what Japan has achieved acknowledge that "MITI is a body which has no exact equivalent in other nations, neither in its wide scope nor in its formidable reputation" and that "MITI [has come] to wield more power and have more say-so in how companies conduct their business than any other similar ministry in a non-Communist country."[2]

1. In Japanese, MITI is known officially as the Tsūshō Sangyō Shō, which is commonly shortened to Tsūsanshō.
2. P.B. Stone, *Japan Surges Ahead, the Story of an Economic Miracle* (New York: Praeger, 1969), pp. 48–49; and Kimpei Shiba and Kenzo Nozue, *What Makes Japan Tick* (Tokyo: Asahi Evening News Co., 1971), p. 174. Also note the comment of Kazushi Ohkawa and Henry Rosovsky, "Japan must be the only capitalist country in the world in which the government decides how many firms there should be in a given industry, and then sets about to arrange the desired number." MITI is the government agency that performs these tasks. See Ohkawa and Rosovsky, *Japanese Economic Growth* (Stanford: Stanford University Press, 1973), p. 223. On the idea of "Japan, Inc." and the role of the government in it, see James C. Abegglen, "The Economic Growth of Japan," *Scientific American*, vol. 222, no. 3 (March 1970), pp. 31–37.

Even the former head of the U.S. Council of Economic Advisers, Herbert Stein, told the 1973 convention of the American Economic Association that the United States may "need an economic planning agency like the Japanese or French," and "pointed to the . . . Japanese Ministry of International Trade and Industry for a model for the United States."[3]

In contrast to these more or less grudging testimonials to MITI's achievements as a bureaucracy, citizens of Japan have often been scathing in their comments about the ministry. Some Japanese have called it "pro-big business," a "department store of government," the "Toranomon [section of Tokyo] Ginza," the "Toranomon office of Yawata Steel," and an "intermediate station en route to the *zaikai.*" Other Japanese wits have labelled it "the son of Economic Animal," "the bureau for hiding industrial pollution problems," "the office in charge of raising prices," "industry's education mama" (*sangyō no kyōiku mama,* a reference to the Japanese mother who devotes all of her energies to shepherding her son through the Japanese educational maze), and, more recently, after Japanese industry had matured and begun to rebel against MITI, a "disappointed education mama" (*shitsui no kyōiku mama*).[4] Nevertheless, most Japanese have been enthusiastic supporters of economic growth, regarding the transformation of Japan from the shattered hulk of 1945 to the status of the world's third most productive economy with pride and not a little awe; many besides old trade and industry bureaucrats are prepared to defend MITI's policies as wise and proper in overall conception, if not necessarily in every detail or some of their unforeseen consequences.

Like most popular catch phrases, each characterization contains a bit of the truth, and each could be and has been argued in serious descriptive and

3. *New York Times,* Dec. 30, 1973, p. 1.
4. Compare the following: Tsūsanshō Kisha Kurabu, *Tsūsanshō* (Tokyo: Hōbunsha, 1958), p. 265; Kusayanagi Daizō, "Sahashi Shigeru, amakudaranu kōkyū kanryō," *Bungei shunjū,* May 1969, p. 173; *Business Week,* Aug. 6, 1960, pp. 100–104; Tsūsanshō Kishadan, "Tsūsanshō no kao," *Chūō kōron,* Oct. 1963, pp. 74, 76; Suzuki Yukio, *Keizai kanryō, shin sangyō kokka no purodyūsā* (Tokyo: Nihon Keizai Shimbunsha, 1969), pp. 46–47, 54, 77–78; Yamamoto Masao, ed., *Keizai kanryō no jittai* (Tokyo: Mainichi Shimbunsha, 1972), p. 52; and Akaboshi Jun (pseud.), *Shōsetsu tsūsanshō* (Tokyo: Daiyamondo Sha, 1971), p. 214. The pseudonym of the author of the last work means literally "Profitable Red Stars"; according to rumor, the publisher had to add the word *"shōsetsu"* (fiction) to the title in order to avoid governmental efforts to prevent publication. There is nothing fictional about the book, including the use of proper names. For an exchange of views on the pros and cons of MITI's image, see the roundtable discussion by Ōjimi Yoshihisa, then vice-minister of MITI; Dokō Toshio, then president of Tōshiba and vice-president of Keidanren; Suzuki Haruo, then vice-president of Shōwa Denkō and a leader of Keizai Dōyūkai; and Horikoshi Teizō, then vice-president of Keidanren, in Sangyō Seisaku Kenkyūjo, ed., *Tsūsanshō 20-nen gaishi* (Tokyo: Sangyō Seisaku Kenkyūjo, 1970), pp. 26–39. Also note the comment of Ohkawa and Rosovsky, "The popularity of this ministry [MITI] is not great, even among certain industrialists, but in view of Japan's performance as a technology importer it would be hard to argue that private initiative has been stifled by excessive government interference." *Japanese Economic Growth,* p. 222.

analytical writing. But this recitation of diverse views does show that MITI is an extremely complex institution, with shifting and intricate relationships with big business, other ministries, and within itself as a large bureaucratic organization—an institution that most outsiders and some insiders continue to oversimplify grossly. Nothing requires greater stress than the time-frame in attempts to generalize about MITI's relationship to the economy, or about Japanese government-business relationships in general. For example, to say that one of MITI's main tools of policy implementation is its informal "administrative guidance" of particular industries—an easily demonstrable proposition—ignores the fact that administrative guidance was less pronounced in the 1950s than in the 1960s because in the 1950s MITI possessed more direct means of control; it was less pronounced in the 1970s than in the 1960s, because by the 1970s some of MITI's other policies had brought about stable oligopoly in certain key industries, thereby lessening the need for administrative guidance. MITI is far too complex, and the Japanese economy far too dynamic, to be apprehended by any cliché.

The subject of MITI and Japanese trade and industry is also too big for a single essay. Thus the orientation of this paper is toward only one aspect of MITI's activities—international economic policy. Even so, the subject must be both narrowed and expanded. It is impossible to talk about MITI's policies in the international economic arena without first identifying and characterizing MITI itself. At the same time, as Japan is changing, so the Japanese bureaucracy is changing, and MITI is changing. This attempt to intercept each of these moving targets is necessarily restricted to the twenty-five years after the founding of MITI in 1949.

THE ECONOMIC BUREAUCRACY

All parties, foreign and domestic, engaged in almost any form of economic transaction in Japan testify to MITI's pervasive and potent influence. But if one asks what is the basis of this power, there is a good deal of confusion and no simple answer. Of the five ministries and one agency that make up what the Japanese public calls the "economic bureaucracy" (MITI, the ministries of Finance, Agriculture and Forestry, Transportation, and Construction, and the Economic Planning Agency), MITI is the smallest ministry and controls the smallest ministerial budget. In terms of political influence, MITI is notoriously weak (compared with Finance and Agriculture) in the number of retired officials it sends to the Diet; although six of the twelve postwar Japanese prime ministers through Prime Minister Tanaka have been former civil servants, only one (Prime Minister Kishi) was a former trade and industry civil servant. In 1973, MITI administered some 121 laws that regulated the operation of the

Japanese economy (140 laws in 1967),[5] but knowledgeable observers argue that these laws are vague. In addition, "the outsider cannot evaluate the degree of government control merely by reading the laws. Informal verbal requests from ministry officials in Tokyo can be fully as effective as direct controls would be in Western Europe or the United States."[6] Perhaps true, but why should Japanese entrepreneurs listen to the informal verbal requests of bureaucrats and accept such requests as if they had the force of law?

Serious questions exist about the nature of the government-business relationship in Japan; unfortunately many English-language attempts to answer them have merely compounded the difficulties. Some foreign commentators see the Japanese government, and particularly MITI, as virtually dominating the economy, fostering its growth through protectionism, subsidies, tax breaks, and direct orders to individual enterprises, euphemistically called "administrative guidance." This explanation is often self-serving; it is commonly invoked by foreign interests seeking anti-Japanese protective legislation in their own countries or as an excuse for their own comparatively poor performance. As an explanation of the Japanese government-business relationship, and of MITI's role in that relationship, it is inadequate; it is unable to explain why the Japanese economy, allegedly dominated by an official bureaucratic apparatus, outperforms every other bureaucratically directed economy in the world, and it ignores the widely held (and not unsubstantiated) view in Western countries that official bureaucracy is synonymous with low efficiency.

An alternative explanation, advanced by some scholars and by the U.S. Department of Commerce, is that Japan enjoys a unique, culturally derived capacity for social cooperation and organization.[7] In this view, the Japanese government-business relationship is one of "rolling consensus," and the result is "Japan, Inc." Although closer to the truth than the first view, this position fails to record the intense competitiveness that exists in the private sector and among the bureaucracies. It also ignores the widespread and often heated criticism that the Japanese press and public have directed at the bureaucracies, particularly MITI. When a former administrative vice-minister of MITI asks his fellow officials to ponder the significance of the popular slogan *mukashi gunjin, ima kanryō* (it used to be the militarists, now it's the bureaucrats), his

5. For a list of all laws administered by MITI in 1973 and the bureaus that have jurisdiction over them, see *Tsūsan handobukku 1974* (Tokyo: Shōkō Kaikan, 1973), pp. 363–367. For the figure as of March 1967, see Maeda Yasuyuki, "Seisaku kainyū no henshitsu to tsūsan kanryō," *Keizai hyōron*, Feb. 1968, p. 35.

6. Leon Hollerman, *Japan's Dependency on the World Economy* (Princeton, N.J.: Princeton University Press, 1967), p. 158.

7. Eugene J. Kaplan, director, Far East Division, Bureau of International Commerce, U.S. Department of Commerce, *Japan: The Government-Business Relationship* (Washington, D.C.: Government Printing Office, 1972), p. 24.

warning cannot be dismissed as mere public griping or as a manifestation of Japan's well-known exposé journalism.[8]

The idea that Japanese economic decision-making occurs through a process of consensus formation is widespread in the West, but this view raises at least as many questions as it answers. Does "consensus" mean that there is little or no conflict in Japanese government-business relations? If so, how, precisely, do MITI and business leaders agree on such delicate matters as a particular firm's investment priorities? What happens when everyone cannot be gotten on board? Is it possible to engineer consent, and, if so, who does it and how is it done? What is the difference between consensus in Japan and jawboning, lobbying, logrolling, pork barreling, influence peddling, and other ordinary, dubious, or corrupt practices used in Western governments and legislatures for producing agreement without confrontation?

Rather than discarding the concept of consensus, which does point in the direction of Japanese reality, I must insist on two qualifications to its use: (1) there is a serious danger of oversimplification, particularly of confusing a Japanese ideal with actual practice; and (2) however consensus may be reached at a given time or on a given issue, it is a process that changes its meaning, content, and typical procedures over time. Several cases suggest that norms of consensus have developed primarily as a way of overcoming the ever-present danger of absolute deadlock among Japan's highly competitive groups.

Jurisdictional disputes appear to be the very life-blood of the Japanese bureaucracy. MITI itself identifies five basic policies that were the ministry's special areas of responsibility during its first twenty years of existence (1949–1969)—industrial rationalization, trade promotion, enlargement of productive capacity, nurturing of medium and smaller enterprises, and development of industrial technology—but in none of these areas did it have exclusive jurisdiction.[9] When former administrative vice-minister of MITI, Ōjimi Yoshihisa, told a visiting Industry Committee of the Organization for Economic Cooperation and Development that "there are . . . two subject areas in which MITI has fully inclusive competence covering all industries; one of these is the field of international trade, and the other, that of small and medium-sized business," he was simply wrong on the first and disingenuous about the second (as small and medium-sized business has consistently attracted only half-hearted attention from MITI).[10] The Temporary Administrative Study Committee (Rinji Gyōsei Chōsa Kai), appointed by the government to investi-

8. Sahashi Shigeru, "Kanryō shokun ni chokugen suru," *Bungei shunjū*, July 1971, p. 109.

9. Tsūshō Sangyō Shō, *Tsūshō sangyō shō nijū nen shi* (Tokyo: Tsūshō Sangyō Shō, 1969), p. 5.

10. Organization for Economic Cooperation and Development, ed., *The Industrial Policy of Japan* (Paris: OECD, 1972), p. 45.

gate the bureaucracy and recommend measures for its simplification, reported in 1964 on fifty-three instances of joint jurisdiction between two or more ministries over the control of international trade alone; only MITI was a party in all cases.[11] As late as 1971, the press was still commenting that the various recommendations of this and two or three successor committees had not been implemented, so one may consider this a continuing situation.[12]

In the broad area of international economic policy, with the exception of international monetary policy, which is handled exclusively by the Finance Ministry (although with a great deal of comment from MITI and the Economic Planning Agency), there is no policy area where one ministry is in total control. Moreover, Japan lacks a single coordinating agency—such as the Office of Management and Budget in the United States seeks to be—to reconcile differences of viewpoint among the ministries. Each ministry jealously guards its own *nawabari* (sphere of influence), and all members of a particular ministry develop a marked *nawabari ishiki* (territorial consciousness). Former MITI Vice-Minister Sahashi has lamented that bureaucrats tend to put the interests of their organization before those of the nation, and all students of the Japanese bureaucracy have noted its extraordinary "sectionalism."[13]

Coordination among ministries does, of course, go on, usually beginning at the subsection level and, on very exceptional matters when the bureaucracies are unable to reach a consensus among themselves, going up to the cabinet. These bureaucratic agreements are more likely to be forged on the basis of compromise and trade-offs than on the basis of argumentation and purely rational considerations. There are innumerable examples of intrabureaucratic disputes. MITI and the Ministry of Transportation argue publicly over whether oil should be moved by truck or pipeline and about who controls it in either form; MITI and the Ministry of Construction argue about who has jurisdiction over the technology for prefabricated housing; MITI and the Ministry of Posts and Telecommunications argue about who will be responsible for developing new computer software; and MITI and the Ministry of Finance, the two most powerful and prestigious ministries in the government, argue about almost everything, commonly *not* reaching a consensus.[14]

MITI and the Ministry of Foreign Affairs must cooperate with each other in the administration of international economic relations, but there have been historic conflicts between the two. One example will suffice to illustrate how

11. Rinji Gyōsei Chōsa Kai, *Kyōkan kyōgō jimu no kaikaku ni kan suru iken* (Tokyo: Committee print, Sept. 1964), vol. 4, app. 10, pp. 112–123. The final report of this committee is available as *Gyōsei no kaikaku* (Tokyo: Jiji Tsūshin, 1967), 541 pp.

12. *Japan Times,* editorial, Dec. 13, 1971, p. 14.

13. Sahashi, *Bungei shunjū,* July 1971, p. 108.

14. A good example of bureaucratic deadlock can be seen in the divergent positions taken by MITI and the Ministry of Finance for the Japanese-American trade conference at Hakone, July 1972. See Yamamoto, ed., *Keizai kanryō no jittai,* p. 49.

some of these conflicts are resolved. In the late 1950s, MITI and the Ministry of Foreign Affairs jointly sponsored the establishment of a research institute for the study of Asian and Third World affairs, the Ajia Keizai Kenkyūjo (literally, the Asian Economic Research Institute, but known officially in English as the Institute of Developing Economies). A few years later MITI sought to change the institute's status from that of a private foundation to a governmental special corporation within MITI's jurisdiction. The Ministry of Foreign Affairs objected to this as an infringement on its *nawabari*. The issue ultimately came to embroil Prime Minister Kishi, Foreign Minister Fujiyama, and MITI Minister Ikeda. Kishi personally asked the MITI vice-minister, Ueno Kōshichi, to back down on his ministry's proposal, for Fujiyama was a close associate of the prime minister's and had intervened with him. Ueno held fast, however, relying at least in part on the fact that Kishi was MITI's most illustrious alumnus in the political world. Kishi finally agreed to give the institute to MITI, but only on the condition that Ueno would have to think of some compensation for the Foreign Ministry. Ueno therefore traded jurisdiction over the (overseas) Agricultural Development Center (Nōgyō Kaihatsu no Shidō Sentā) to the Foreign Ministry in return for MITI's sole control over the Institute of Developing Economies. Fortunately for the institute itself, which is one of the most highly regarded in the world, MITI's influence rests very lightly on its internal research activities.[15]

Interministerial competition and rivalry is an aspect of all known governments, but it is particularly pronounced in Japan for reasons that can only be alluded to here. These include the traditions of the bureaucracy dating from the Meiji period, the characteristic of lifetime employment within a single ministry, the fact that the bureaucracy's position in the Japanese social system was if anything enhanced rather than weakened by the Allied Occupation, and the circumstance that the ruling political party draws about a quarter of its Diet members from among retired career officials. Former MITI Vice-Minister Sahashi believes that the bureaucracy is the only major institution in Japan that has gone relatively unchanged in terms of its most basic characteristics (such as clannishness, elitism, factionalism) since the Itō cabinet of 1885, while the rest of society has changed around it.[16] As for competitiveness in Japan,

Competition . . . must be pursued under cover to some extent. . . . Problems associated with competition carried out at the individual level can be lessened if

15. This story was recounted by former Vice-Minister Ueno himself in a collection of memoirs of all of the surviving MITI vice-ministers. See Seisaku Jihō Sha, ed., *Kaikoroku sengo tsūsan seisaku shi* (Tokyo: Seisaku Jihō Sha, 1973), pp. 76–77.

16. *Bungei shunjū*, July 1971, p. 109. Yamamoto Masao of the *Mainichi shimbun* wrote in 1972 that Japanese bureaucrats are by nature "undemocratic, inflexible, and anti-people." *Keizai kanryō no jittai,* p. 15. This is mentioned solely to illustrate that such opinions of the bureaucracy are not exclusive with Sahashi.

the competition is between or among groups. Those who identify with the group to which they belong can put out extra effort to enhance the group's competitive position without incurring social opprobrium. On the contrary, this effort will bring an individual social praise. Lively competition can exist among families, schools, universities, religious sects, and government agencies.[17]

MITI's competitiveness stems from these general cultural traits of its society and from factors in its own peculiar history. Government administration of trade and industry can be traced back to the first year of the Meiji Restoration. The first direct ministerial ancestor of today's MITI was the Ministry of Agriculture and Commerce, created in 1881. During and after the First World War, powerful pressures from agricultural interests for greater governmental attention led to the division of the Ministry of Agriculture and Commerce in 1925 into the Ministry of Agriculture and Forestry and the Ministry of Commerce and Industry, the latter being MITI's immediate predecessor. All the post-World War II administrative vice-ministers of MITI entered the ministry during the 1930s and 1940s when it was the Ministry of Commerce and Industry, and although the postwar change of name reflected an important change of focus, there was direct continuity in personnel, functions, and outlook.

In 1943, the Ministry of Commerce and Industry was turned into the Ministry of Munitions. Prime Minister Tōjō served concurrently as the first minister of munitions, and Kishi Nobusuke was his administrative vice-minister. On August 26, 1945, just prior to the arrival of the American Occupation forces, the Ministry of Munitions was changed back into the Ministry of Commerce and Industry. On May 25, 1949, as part of the U.S. Occupation's efforts to get the Japanese economy back on its feet, the Ministry of Commerce and Industry was overhauled and its name changed to the Ministry of International Trade and Industry. MITI itself underwent another major reorganization in 1952 after the American Occupation forces had left, and it remained virtually unchanged until July 1973, when it was again thoroughly reorganized.

In a certain sense, MITI is a classic example of a bureaucracy that has pursued suicidally successful policies. Old MITI officials regard the ministry's "golden age" as approximately 1935 to 1955, when it ran an almost totally controlled economy of one form or another (war mobilization, war production, and postwar rationing). In fact, Hirai Tomisaburō, who entered the Ministry of Commerce and Industry in 1931 and rose to be vice-minister of MITI between 1953 and 1955 (in 1974 he was president of New Japan Steel), once worried about what would happen when liberalization came to the Japanese economy, because there was not an official left in MITI who had had any experience with an open, uncontrolled economy, all had joined the ministry after he had).[18]

17. Nobutaka Ike, *Japan, the New Superstate* (Stanford: Stanford University Alumni Association, 1973), p. 46.
18. Hirai's memoirs, in *Kaikoroku sengo tsūsan seisaku shi*, p. 43.

MITI spokesmen like to argue that MITI gave up its absolute control powers in 1952 with the abrogation of the Temporary Demand and Supply Adjustment Law (Law no. 32, promulgated September 30, 1946), even though most observers would put the date in 1964, when the liberalization of international trade and payments took place. In any case, MITI officials note longingly that the Ministry of Finance still has *control* of the banks, Agriculture and Forestry still regulates farming, and all other ministries still have clearly defined powers and bailiwicks.[19] MITI alone has lost its old controlling raison d'être, and it has succeeded so brilliantly in promoting trade and industrial growth that its basic constituency, big business, is not sure how much more administrative care it still needs from MITI. The ministry is a little like a poverty agency that has actually succeeded in eliminating poverty. Needless to say, as would all bureaucracies in a similar position, MITI set out to find new functions and, by the 1970s, had clearly succeeded in doing so. Throughout the 1950s and 1960s, however, it was anxious to keep the functions that it still possessed and to expand them at the expense of other ministries, sometimes confusing its own bureaucratic needs with the interests of its clients, Japan's traders and industrialists.

In 1948–1949, the trade and industry bureaucracy had twenty-four thousand employees. After independence and with the decline of controls, it lost ten thousand. Since then the MITI personnel count has slowly climbed higher, but has remained the smallest among the economic ministries.[20] The relative sizes of the various economic bureaucracies in terms of their official allocation of personnel, as of December 1971, are indicated in Table 1.

One characteristic way that MITI has compensated for its relatively low numbers and has enlarged its overall influence is through sending temporary transferees to other ministries and agencies, an activity in which all ministries engage, particularly the broadly gauged agencies with major policy responsibilities. MITI and the Ministry of Finance have competed vigorously over the years to see which could spread its influence the farthest. MITI began its life in 1949 seriously in the red in terms of its transferee balance with the Ministry of Foreign Affairs, but by the 1960s it had turned this situation around and enjoyed a black-ink account vis-a-vis all ministries except Agriculture and Forestry. Agriculture and Forestry accepted no MITI men but sent its own officials to MITI to fill the posts of chief in the Chemical Fertilizer Department, chief of one of the chemical fertilizer sections in the Light Industries Bureau, and chief of the Agricultural and Marine Products Section in the International Trade Bureau. Such transferees retain their lifetime career commitment to the agency they first joined, whether they return to it or not. In Kubota's analysis of a large sample of Japanese higher officials, some 70.8 per-

19. *Tsūshō sangyō shō nijū nen shi*, p. 5.
20. Tsūshanshō Kisha Kurabu, *Tsūsanshō*, p. 259.

Table 1
Personnel Sizes of the Japanese Economic Bureaucracies*
(December 1971)

	Subtotal	Total
Ministry of Agriculture and Forestry		
Home Office	96,470	
Food Agency	25,960	
Forestry Agency	40,158	
Fishery Agency	1,895	
		164,483
Ministry of Finance		
Home Office	76,510	
National Tax Administration Agency	51,334	
		127,844
Ministry of Transportation		
Home Office	32,824	
Maritime Safety Agency	10,996	
Maritime Accidents Inquiry Agency	41	
Meteorological Agency	6,150	
		50,011
Ministry of Construction		32,592
Ministry of International Trade and Industry		
Home Office	14,068	
Patent Agency	1,924	
Small and Medium Enterprises Agency	170	
		16,162
Economic Planning Agency		552

SOURCE: Japanese Government, Prime Minister's Office, Administrative Management Agency, *Table of Organization of the Government of Japan* (Tokyo: Ōkurashō insatsu kyoku, 1972).
*The agencies listed as subentries are under the parent ministry's jurisdiction and control but possess an independent secretariat.

cent of all bureaucrats started and ended their careers within their native bureaucracies, while some 82.5 percent of MITI bureaucrats and 90.1 percent of Ministry of Finance bureaucrats did so.[21]

Tables 2 and 3 report on the status of transferees to and from the Ministry of Foreign Affairs. MITI has by far the largest number of officials among non-Foreign-Office bureaucrats serving in overseas posts, but in exchanges between the home offices of the ministries, as late as 1964 Foreign Affairs sent more officials to MITI than it received in return. MITI maintains the largest exchange of officials with the Foreign Ministry of any ministry dealing with it, although the trend has been toward reduced exchanges since the high levels of the early fifties.

MITI sends its biggest number of transferees to the Science and Technology Agency, and it also has a large contingent in the Environmental Protection Agency. A MITI man by tradition holds down the job of director of the Equipment Bureau in the Defense Agency, and there are MITI officials located strategically in the cabinet secretariat, the cabinet legislation bureau, the General Affairs Bureau of the National Defense Council, the Pollution Control Committee, and the Fair Trade Commission.[22]

By far the most famous case of an export-of-officials war for the control of another agency and of resistance by that agency against the acceptance of the imported bureaucrats was that between MITI and the Finance Ministry for control of the Economic Planning Agency (EPA). As the descendant of the Occupation-period Economic Stabilization Board—which the established ministries resisted as long as they could and moved in to control when the Occupation authorities made resistance impossible—the EPA today does not have operational functions. But it is strategically placed to influence policy, and it played the central role in the government's commitment to the Income Doubling Plan of 1960. By tradition and a great deal of maneuvering, a MITI man has held the EPA's administrative vice-ministership (the post that controls relations with the cabinet and the Diet), the directorship of the agency's Coordination Bureau, and several other positions. In 1973, there were thirty-one MITI transferees working in the EPA, including the highest career official in the agency. Some writers have characterized the EPA as a "branch store of MITI" (*Tsūsanshō no demise*). On the other hand, the Ministry of Finance traditionally has held the critical position of chief of the secretariat, where matters concerning personnel are decided, and it also has controlled the EPA budget.

Four of the first five vice-ministers of the EPA went on from that post to become the vice-minister of MITI itself (see Chart 1), a practice which greatly irked the career officials of the EPA. This monopolization by MITI bureaucrats of the EPA's top post was a major source of frustration to the EPA economists, who were trying to upgrade their service and to get out from under the

21. Akira Kubota, *Higher Civil Servants in Postwar Japan* (Princeton, N.J.: Princeton University Press, 1969), p. 103, table 31, and p. 107, table 33.
22. *Tsūsan handobukku 1974*, p. 335.

Table 2

Officials from Agencies Other than the Foreign Ministry
in Overseas Legations

Mission	MITI 64	MITI 73	MOF	MAF	MOL	MOT	MOP	MOE	MOJ	MOC	DA	PA	JNR	STA	EPA	MOW	1964 Totals
United States	2	2	3	1	1	1			1		5			2	1		17
Canada	1	1	1	1		2											4
Mexico	1	1															1
Brazil	1	1	1	1		1											4
Argentina	1	1	1														2
Chile	1	1															1
U.K.	2	2	3	1	1	1					1			1			10
France	2	1	2					1			1	1		1			8
Austria		1							1								2
Belgium	3	3	2	1													6
Italy	1	1	1	1								1					4
Holland	1	1															1
Germany	1	2	1	1	1						1			1			5
USSR	1	1	1	1	1						2			1			6
Switzerland	2	2	2	1	1	1	1										8
OECD (Paris)	2	3	2	1		1						1			1		7
Yugoslavia																1	1
Lebanon			1														1
Turkey											1						1

Country						
U.A.R.	1					1
Iran	1		1			2
South Africa	1					1
Nigeria	1					1
Kenya	1					1
Thailand	1	1		1	1	5
Pakistan	1	1				2
Taiwan	2					2
Malaysia	1					1
Burma	1	1				2
Cambodia		1				1
Philippines	2	1	1			4
Indonesia	1	1	1		1	5
India	2	1	1	1	1	6
Australia	1	1				2
Spain	1			1		
Poland	1					
Singapore	1					1
Vietnam	1					
Korea	1					
Saudi Arabia	1					
Egypt	1					
Tanzania	1					

(Consulates)																	
New York	2	2	5									1					8
San Francisco	1	1															1
Toronto	1	1															1
Vancouver		1															
Hamburg	1		1														1
Sydney	1	1	1														2
Hong Kong	1	1															3
TOTAL	45	55	31	16	4	8	1	1	1	3	14	6	1	7	2	1	141

SOURCES: Data for all agencies are for 1964 as reported by Rinji Gyōsei Chōsa Kai, *Kyōkan kyōgō jimu no kaikaku ni kan suru iken* (Tokyo: Committee print, Sept. 1964), vol 4, app., pp. 128–129. The supplementary comparative column on MITI for 1973 is from Tsūsan Handobukku Henshū Iinkai, ed., *Tsūsan handobukku 1974* (Tokyo: Shōkō Kaikan, 1973), pp. 346–350.

Abbreviations of ministries and agencies

MITI	Ministry of International Trade and Industry	MOC	Ministry of Construction
MOF	Ministry of Finance	DA	Defense Agency
MAF	Ministry of Agriculture and Forestry	PA	National Police Agency
MOL	Ministry of Labor	JNR	Japanese National Railways
MOT	Ministry of Transportation	STA	Science and Technology Agency
MOP	Ministry of Posts and Telecommunications	EPA	Economic Planning Agency
MOE	Ministry of Education	MOW	Ministry of Welfare
MOJ	Ministry of Justice		

Table 3

Interministerial Loan of Officials

between the Foreign ministry and the Other Economic Ministries and Organizations

The upper figure is the number of officials from other agencies sent to the Foreign Ministry. The lower figure is the number of Foreign Ministry officials sent to other agencies.

Year	EPA	FTC	MOF	MAF	MITI	MOT	JETRO	Keidanren	AKK	OECF	BOJ	NKG	KG	EIB	OTCA
1950	–	–	–	–	–										
	21	5	5	2	60										
1951	–	–	–	–	–										
	14	4	10	2	62										
1952	–	–	–	–	6		–								
	13	2	5	1	56		2								
1953	–	–	–	–	6		–				1				
	4	2	4	1	31		2								
1954	–	–	–		4		–				1				
	3	2	1		26		2								
1955	–	–	–		5	–	–				1				
	2	2	1		24	2	2								
1956	–	–	4	–	12	–	–				2				
	2	2	1	1	24	2	1								
1957	–	–	4	–	11	–	–	–			2				
	1	2	1	1	23	2	2	1							
1958		–	4	–	9	–	–				2				
		1	1	2	19	2	2								
1959	–	–	4	–	9	–	–				3				
	1	1	1	3	15	2	2								
1960	1	–	4	–	10	–	–	–			4				
	1	1	1	4	15	2	2	1							
1961	1	–	4	–	9	–	–	–			4				
	–	1	2	4	16	2	2	1							

Year	EPA	FTC	MOF	MAF	MITI	MOT	JETRO	Keidanren	AKK	OECF	BOJ	NKG	KG	EIB	OTCA
1962	1	–	4	5	6	2	–	–	4	–	–	–	–	–	4
	1	1	2	–	13	–	1	3	–	1	–	–	–	–	–
1963	1	1	5	4	6	3	–	1	4	–	1	–	2	1	4
	1	–	–	5	10	–	1	2	–	1	–	1	–	–	–
1964	1	1	4	5	10	3	–	1	4	–	1	–	3	1	4
	1	–	–	–	10	–	1	2	–	1	–	1	–	–	–

SOURCE: Rinji Gyōsei Chōsa Kai, *Kyōkan kyōgō jimu no kaikaku ni kan suru iken* (Tokyo: Committee print, Sept. 1964), vol. 4, app., p. 172.

Abbreviations of ministries, agencies, and organizations

EPA Economic Planning Agency (and its predecessors)
FTC Fair Trade Commission
MOF Ministry of Finance
MAF Ministry of Agriculture and Forestry
MITI Ministry of International Trade and Industry
MOT Ministry of Transportation
JETRO Japan External Trade Organization (Nihon Bōeki Shinkōkai)
Keidanren Keizai Dantai Rengōkai (Federation of Economic Organizations)
AKK Ajia Keizai Kenkyūjo (official translation: Institute of Developing Economies)
OECF Overseas Economic Cooperation Fund (Kaigai Keizai Kyōryoku Kikin)
BOJ Bank of Japan
NKG Nihon Kōgyō Ginkō (Industrial Bank of Japan, Ltd.)
KG Nihon Kangyō Ginkō (Nippon Kangyo Bank, Ltd.)
EIB Export-Import Bank (Nihon Yushutsunyū Ginkō)
OTCA Overseas Technical Cooperation Agency (Kaigai GijutsuKyōryoku Jigyōdan)

Chart 1
*MITI's Control of the Vice-Ministership of the
Economic Planning Agency,
1952–1973*

Career* Branch	VM**	Vice-minister	Dates at EPA
1. MITI	VM	Hirai Tomisaburō	8/1/52–11/17/53
2. MITI		Nagamura Teiichi	11/17/53–7/2/54
3. MITI	VM	Ishihara Takeo	7/2/54–11/25/55
4. MITI	VM	Ueno Kōshichi	11/25/55–6/15/57
5. MITI	VM	Tokunaga Hizatsugu	6/15/57–5/13/60
6. MITI		Koide Eiichi	5/13/60–7/10/62
7. MITI		Ōbori Hiromu	7/10/62–10/25/63
8. MITI		Matsumura Keiichi	10/25/63–6/10/65
9. MITI		Nakano Shōichi	6/10/65–7/18/67
10. MITI		Kawade Chihaya	7/18/67–9/20/68
11. MITI		Takashima Setsuo	9/20/68–12/5/69
12. EPA		Shikano Yoshio	12/5/69–July 1972
13. EPA		Yano Tomoo	July 1972–7/1/73
14. MITI		Nitta Kōichi	7/1/73–1974

NOTE: The Economic Council Agency (Keizai Shingi Chō) was established on August 1, 1952. On July 20, 1955, its name was changed to Economic Planning Agency (Keizai Kikaku Chō). From August 1, 1952 until July 31, 1957, the highest nonpolitical, career post in the agency was entitled "deputy director" (*jichō*). After 1957 the post was renamed "administrative vice-minister" (*jimu-jikan*).

*MITI means Ministry of International Trade and Industry career official; EPA means Economic Planning Agency career official.

**VM means that the particular official went on from the vice-ministership of the Economic Planning Agency to become the vice-minister of the Ministry of International Trade and Industry.

control of the two senior economic ministries. During 1963–1964, EPA officials tried to work with the secretariat and the Ministry of Finance to place the distinguished economist Ōkita Saburō, one of their own members, in the vice-ministership but they failed. An EPA man did not make it to the top until 1969, when MITI was definitely slipping in its position of power throughout the government, and Finance was expanding its sphere of influence. The EPA people did, however, succeed in 1960 in stopping MITI from using their vice-ministership as a preparatory post for the MITI vice-ministership; after 1960 the EPA vice-ministership became instead a final post before retirement for high MITI officials. In fact, the dispatch of an official to the top EPA post from MITI after 1960 became a tactic in internal MITI factional struggles, because the person who became the EPA vice-minister could not come back to MITI and was thus out of the running for the biggest prize of them all, the MITI vice-ministership itself.

It is not surprising that the shift in status of the EPA vice-ministership from stepping-stone to terminal position came in 1960, when the Income Doubling Plan was launched. Several leading Japanese students of official policy-making have alleged that the competition between MITI and Finance over the EPA and the aspirations of the EPA officials for independence all interacted with the plan itself and influenced both its nature and the decision to proceed with it.[23] This bureaucratic infighting has neither strengthened the EPA nor improved the indicative planning powers of the Japanese government. Although it would be erroneous to stress these bureaucratic rivalries to the point of overlooking the very real successes of the Japanese economic bureaucracy as a whole, or of ignoring the extent to which rivalries are mitigated by personal and university-class ties and mediated by political leaders, it is at the same time necessary to insist that such rivalries do exist, are potent, and should be expected in a bureaucratic structure as large and as entrenched as that of Japan.

We can now indicate where the various bureaucracies normally stand with regard to international economic policy. The Ministry of Foreign Affairs, through its Economic and Economic Cooperation bureaus, generally takes a liberal position on trade matters but is hampered by having no natural constituency within Japan (being composed of a small bureaucracy whose members usually retire later than other officials into positions of minor influence) and by having the reputation for being "internationalist" (which in recent decades has translated into a reputation for being accommodating toward the United States). The Ministry of Finance is the most prestigious and allegedly the most powerful economic bureaucracy, and its International Finance Bureau clearly holds a commanding position with regard to international monetary affairs. Its reputation is one of liberalism on trade matters, but it is regarded as conservative when it comes to dispensing foreign aid. It is also said to suffer from poor internal coordination among its individually powerful bureaus, resulting in its exercising more of a veto power or negative influence on policy than taking a positive leadership role. The Ministry of Agriculture and Forestry is openly protectionist on matters concerning imports that might adversely affect its constituents, the farmers, and it is politically influential because the LDP's power base is in the countryside. It is also one of the few economic ministries that has some of its retired officials in the opposition parties.

23. The basic source is Itō Daiichi, "Keizai kanryō no kōdō yōshiki, 'shotoku baizō keikaku' o chūshin to shite," in Nihon Seiji Gakkai, ed., *Gendai Nihon no seitō to kanryō* (Tokyo: Iwanami Shoten, 1967), pp. 78–104. Also see by the same author, "The Bureaucracy: Its Attitudes and Behavior," *The Developing Economies*, vol. 4, no. 4 (Dec. 1968), pp. 446–467. In addition, see Tsūshanshō Kisha Kurabu, *Tsūsansho*, pp. 259–261; Tsūshanshō Kishadan, *Chūō koron*, Oct. 1963, pp. 84–85; Suzuki, *Keizai kanryō*, pp. 113–119; and Yamamoto, ed., *Keizai kanryō no jittai*, pp. 162–164.

MITI has been traditionally protectionist in the areas of trade and capital liberalization, but for the stated reason of promoting Japan's international competitiveness rather than as a matter of principle. It is liberal on agricultural trade, which is not within its jurisdiction. It long stood for increased trade with mainland China and the Soviet Union, clashing often with the Foreign Ministry on these issues. It is the ministry most commonly chosen second after the Ministry of Finance by university students who have been accepted for government service, and it has a reputation for extensive internal democracy, which contrasts with other rather dour ministries, such as Foreign Affairs and Finance.[24] Although heavily criticized in the late 1960s for putting gross national product ahead of net national welfare, MITI is prepared to defend its record and possesses some of the most outspoken and candid representatives in the ranks of Japanese officialdom.

Policy of all kinds in Japan has been made almost exclusively by the bureaucracy, particularly during the period before the two conservative parties merged (1955), but persisting well into the 1970s. The bureaucracy also has tended to resent attempts by politicians to interfere with the bureaucratic policy-making process, although there are notable exceptions and differences among ministries.[25] During the late 1960s and early 1970s, particularly under the Tanaka government, political influence over the bureaucracy increased in response to public criticism of unpopular official policies or the consequences of earlier policies, such as pollution. The older pattern is still, however, the norm: policy originates with a ministry, is coordinated by the bureaucrats themselves, ratified at the ministerial and cabinet levels, given the stamp of approval by the LDP, and, if necessary, enacted into law by the Diet. Some observers believe that the enormous power of the bureaucracy combined with the strong representation of ex-bureaucrats within the Diet adds up to a virtual collapse of the executive and legislative branches of government into a single branch, dominated by the executive; although this tendency is present, the actual situation is too dynamic to be characterized by so sweeping a generalization.[26]

24. The university students' comment is "Ōkurashō de nakereba Tsūsanshō" (If the Finance Ministry doesn't come through, then MITI). On MITI's internal democracy, see the observations of former Vice-Minister Yamamoto Shigenobu, in *Kaikoroku sengo tsūsan seisaku shi*, pp. 162–163.

25. As an example within MITI, when Ōhira Masayoshi became MITI minister in November 1968, new parliamentary vice-ministers (Diet members, one from each house) were also named. One of them sought to find out what went on inside the ministry, but the bureaucrats went to great lengths to shut him out, even changing the names of official ministerial conferences to so-called private informal liaison gatherings. The MITI bureaucrats were very displeased to have one of their parliamentary vice-ministers attempting to do anything more than was customary for a man in his position—maintaining contact with the Diet. See Akaboshi, *Shōsetsu tsūsanshō*, pp. 169–172.

26. For arguments that the executive and legislative branches have virtually merged, see, for example, Misawa Shigeo, "Seiji kettei no gaikan," in *Gendai Nihon no seitō to kanryō*, pp. 5–33; and Sahashi Shigeru, *Bungei shunjū*, July 1971, p. 112.

MITI's POWERS

One area of marked parochialism in Western, primarily American, studies of Japanese society is concerned with the role and rule of law in general and of administrative law in particular. This is, of course, not true of the work of Western specialists on Japanese law, but they are extremely few in number. Meanwhile, the general historical, sociological, and anthropological traditions of Western Japanology combine to suggest that law plays only a minor part in the regulation of Japanese society, that the Japanese have a low "legal consciousness," and that in order to understand how Japan works, one must direct attention to the covert, indirect, informal norms of daily or of political and economic life. This is far too big a subject to deal with here other than to signal its importance, but it often seems as though Americans believe that Japanese—or other peoples—are not legal-minded simply because they are not legalistic, or litigious, in precisely the way Americans are. This attitude derives not only from a widespread American scholarly disbelief in the explanatory value of studying Japanese law but also from a general American ignorance of the continental European legal tradition, from which Japanese law draws much of its inspiration and to which it continues to look for new examples and precedents.[27]

Although it is undoubtedly true that Japanese do not sue each other as frequently as Americans do, and that there is an entirely different "culture" surrounding the law and legislation in Japan from that in the United States, it is equally true that the powers of MITI rest fundamentally on a series of laws, that changes in these laws provoke the most intense political involvement, that virtually the entire higher bureaucracy in Japan received an education in the law, and that the legality of, for example, administrative guidance by the bureaucracy has been and remains a major point of dispute in active Japanese politics.

The essence of MITI's power derives from its legally sanctioned "license and approval authority" (*kyoninkaken*), something that it has exercised in varying degrees and over changing activities since the Meiji period.[28] All analysts of

27. See Chalmers Johnson, *Conspiracy at Matsukawa* (Berkeley and Los Angeles: University of California Press, 1972). The best single volume on Japanese law in English is a collection of articles by Japanese scholars. See Arthur T. von Mehren, ed., *Law in Japan* (Cambridge, Mass.: Harvard University Press, 1963).

28. The term *kyoninkaken* (permission and approval authority) is a general concept covering *menkyo* (licenses), *tokkyo* (patents), *kyoka* (permits), *ninka* (approvals), and *shōnin* (endorsements). In a more general sense, it extends to the government's legal authority to require or carry out *tōroku* (registration), *kensa* (inspection), *kentei* (certification), and *todokede* (notification). Each must be distinguished and studied in terms of its practical application. The Petroleum Industry Law of 1962, for example, includes requirements for permission (*kyoka*) to engage in petroleum refining, approval (*ninka*) for capital investment, advice (*kankoku*) on production, and numerous reports (*todokede*) to be submitted to MITI concerning a firm's operations. The last has been put to an unusual use. If MITI does not approve of

MITI agree that the ministry's increased reliance on administrative guidance during the 1960s was a direct result of the loss of significant portions of its license and approval authority due to economic liberalization. Some MITI officials and some industrialists prefer the procedures of administrative guidance to the procedures of legally explicit ministerial licensing and approval, but this does not necessarily mean that they lack legal consciousness, only that they recognize the advantages to them of being free of legal constraints in certain respects. At the same time, there are numerous critics who are prepared to see administrative guidance continue but who demand that it be brought under the rule of law and be formally authorized in legislation.

MITI's basic enabling legislation is its establishment law of 1949, rewritten in 1952 and modified frequently since then.[29] MITI historians regard it as a historic piece of legislation in that for the first time it provided a basis in a Diet-enacted law for the ministry's work, whereas prior to 1949 the ministry's existence and most of its orders rested only on Imperial ordinances. Article 3(2) of the establishment law authorizes MITI "to regulate and inspect the production and circulation of mining and manufacturing products," while article 4(13) authorizes MITI "to formulate plans concerning fundamental policies for production, distribution, consumption, and foreign trading of commodities (including electric power) under its jurisdiction." Article 4 further says that "the exercise of this authority must be in accordance with law," which is where the controversy over administrative guidance begins.

Beyond this basic law, MITI has been charged with the implementation of other major laws, which give to the government licensing and approval authority—that is, control—over numerous productive and commercial activities. These laws form the real bedrock on which MITI's powers rest. As examples from the past, one might mention the Important Industries Control Law of March 1931 or the National General Mobilization Law of April 1938, and the lush growth of ordinances derived from them. Without question the two most important pieces of legislation in MITI's postwar arsenal have been the Foreign Exchange and Foreign Trade Control Law (Law number 228 of December 1, 1949) and the Foreign Investment Law (Law number 163 of May 10, 1950).[30] These laws gave MITI approval powers over how virtually all

what a firm is doing, even though its power is limited to receiving reports in the affected area, it will cause the firm to alter its behavior through the simple expedient of refusing to accept unfavorable reports. On the licensing and approval authority and MITI's licensing powers, see Ringi Gyōsei Chōsa Kai, *Kyoninkara no kaikaku ni kan suru iken* (Tokyo: Committee print, Sept. 1964), vol. 6, p. 3, and app., pp. 84–103. On the Petroleum Industry Law of 1962, see "Gyōsei shidō no jittai o arau," *Tōyō keizai* 3796 (April 6, 1974):29–31.

29. Texts of these laws (law no. 102 of May 24, 1949, and law no. 275 of July 31, 1952) may be found in Tsūsanshō Daijin Kanbō Chōsa-ka, *Tsūshō sangyō shō shijū nen shi* (Tokyo: Tsūsan Shiryō Chōsa Kai, 1965), pp. 481–509 and 584–607.

30. Partial English translations of these laws may be found in Robert S. Ozaki, *The Control of Imports and Foreign Capital in Japan* (New York: Praeger, 1972), pp. 143–186.

short-term and long-term capital funds were to be spent in Japan, even though they were not, as Maeda has shown, as powerful or all encompassing as some of the legislation MITI had administered earlier.[31]

Although these laws were drafted in cooperation with Allied Occupation authorities and enjoyed their explicit approval as a means of solving Japan's then-chronic balance of payments difficulties, MITI officials put these laws to a use that the Americans scarcely imagined (the Americans thought that they were temporary and would soon be rescinded).[32] An official MITI history records,

In December [1949] MITI's main tool was enacted—the Foreign Exchange and Foreign Trade Control Law. Its direct objective was to control inadequate foreign exchange in order to import food and other daily necessities, machinery required for rationalization, and the raw materials needed for export goods; its more important uses were for industrial rationalization, industrial protection, and the promotion of exports. . . . In May 1950 the Foreign Investment Law was promulgated. It differed from the Foreign Exchange and Foreign Trade Control Law in that the latter provided rules for ordinary exchanges, whereas the new law was to provide control over the introduction of technology and foreign capital. . . . Through the policy use [seisaku-teki unyō] of the Foreign Investment Law and the Control Law, technology, funds, and materials were funneled to enterprises.[33]

In 1964, when Japan liberalized its international trade under pressure from its foreign trading partners, these laws were greatly restricted in their applicability and fell into disuse (although they were not abrogated). By shifting from article 14 to article 8 status in the International Monetary Fund, Japan had to end its controls on foreign exchange in current international transactions and its restrictions on the convertibility of yen held by nonresidents. Similar changes occurred in 1967 with the beginning of the liberalization of capital transfers to and from Japan. It was precisely these liberalizing developments that led to the controversy within the government and society over whether the fragmented nature and high debt-to-equity ratios of Japan's key industrial enterprises produced the so-called excessive competition phenomenon and left Japan's industries highly vulnerable to foreign take-overs. It also produced the bureaucratic crisis over what MITI's future role should be after it lost its direct control powers over foreign trade—what Suzuki calls "MITI's neurosis."[34] The ministry responded to these shifts in Japan's basic orientation toward the rest of the world, first, by drafting a new fundamental law for itself and introducing it

31. Maeda Yasuyuki, *Keizai hyōron,* Feb. 1968, pp. 35–37, contains a useful survey of the laws and ordinances administered by MITI.
32. See Supreme Commander for the Allied Powers, *History of the Nonmilitary Activities of the Occupation of Japan,* vol. 50: *Foreign Trade,* declassified Feb. 27, 1970. Copy in U.S. National Archives, Washington, D.C., and microfilm copy in the possession of the author.
33. *Tsūshō sangyō shō nijū nen shi,* pp. 5, 7.
34. Suzuki, *Keizai kanryō,* p. 45.

into the Diet, where it aroused a storm of protest and ultimately died, and second, by turning to administrative guidance of the economy through numerous informal, ad hoc channels.

The controversy surrounding the famous Draft Law of Special Measures for the Promotion of Designated Industries (Tokutei sangyō shinkō rinji sochi hōan, known simply as the Tokushinhō) of 1962 and 1963 illustrates the centrality of the role of law in Japanese administration, the importance of European examples and precedents in Japanese practice, and the bureaucratic infighting between MITI and the Ministry of Finance. Behind this bill and MITI's later actions was the ministry's belief that Japan's industries were not prepared in 1964 to compete on an equal basis in the international commercial arena. Although the reasoning of MITI on this subject is persuasive to the writer, the discussion here has nothing to do with these broader issues of economic analysis and judgment; the present treatment is directed exclusively to MITI as a bureaucratic actor within the Japanese political system.

In 1961, after the Japanese government had already committed itself to liberalization, Sahashi Shigeru, who had worked in MITI since 1937, became director of MITI's powerful Enterprises Bureau. One of his first actions was to call the first secretary in the Japanese embassy in Paris, Morozumi Yoshihiko, back to Tokyo. (Both Sahashi and Morozumi later served as vice-ministers of MITI: Sahashi from October 1964 to April 1966; Morozumi from June 1971 to July 1973.) While in Paris, Morozumi had studied French indicative planning, and he had witnessed the so-called invasion of Europe by United States capital. He and Sahashi both believed that Japan needed new strategies for its economy in the coming liberalized age—strategies that would forestall an American capital invasion of Japan similar to what had occurred in Europe and that would allow the government to continue strengthening Japanese business to meet the competition. Sahashi learned from Morozumi of a scheme that French planners called the *économie concertée;* he adopted it for a plan that MITI would describe variously as the "mixed economy" (*kongō keizai*), the "cooperative economic structure" (*kyōchō keizai taisei*), "public-private cooperation" (*kanmin kyōchō*), a shift from "control" (*tōsei*) to "inducement" (*yūdō*). In the 1970s the Japanese press called it the "growing together of the public and private sectors" (*kanmin yuchaku*).[35]

On the French concept, an authority on French economic administration, Stephen S. Cohen, writes,

35. See, *inter alia,* Tsūsanshō Kishadan, *Chūō kōron,* Oct. 1963, pp. 74–75; *Kaikoroku sengo tsūsan seisaku shi,* memoirs of Matsuo Kinzō (vice-minister July 1961–July 1963), Imai Zen'ei (vice-minister July 1963–October 1964), and Sahashi Shigeru; Akaboshi, *Shōsetsu tsūsanshō,* pp. 23–33; *Tsūshō sangyō shō nijū nen shi,* pp. 11–12; M.Y. Yoshino, *Japan's Managerial System* (Cambridge, Mass.: MIT Press, 1968), pp. 185–188; Seisaku Jihō Sha, *Tsūsanshō, sono hito to soshiki* (Tokyo: Seisaku Jihō Sha, 1968), pp. 11, 33, 35–37; and *Tōyō keizai,* April 6, 1974, p. 28.

The *économie concertée* is a partnership of big business, the state, and, in theory though not in practice, the trade unions. The managers of big business and the managers of the state run the modern core of the nation's economy—mostly the oligopoly sectors. Positive cooperation—not conflict, as in a market ideology—is its motor. The state is not a silent partner; it is an initiating, active partner. It intervenes in every aspect of economic affairs, encouraging, teaching, sometimes, even threatening. Its purpose is to promote economic modernization: greater efficiency, greater productivity, greater expansion. The partnership works for the general interest; and it works outside the traditional political arena. Parliament and the constellation of institutions that surrounds Parliament are not necessary for the smooth functioning of the system. . . . The *économie concertée* is the new higher civil servants' favorite model of economic and social organization. It is fundamentally an attitude of cooperation between the stewards of the state and the managers of big business.[36]

France was not the only source of inspiration to the Japanese planners. They were also interested in Italy; in fact, MITI had already drawn on Italian precedents for the law establishing the Japan Synthetic Rubber Company, Ltd., of 1957 and the Aircraft Industry Promotion Law of 1958, which set up the Japan Aircraft Manufacturing Corporation. The latter firm designed, built, and sold (to Piedmont Airlines in the United States, among others) the YS-11 transport airplane. Both the synthetic rubber and aircraft firms were so-called national policy companies, established in areas where private capital was simply too weak to finance them and where strong governmental financial aid and protection were required. MITI officially acknowledges that these companies share an "affinity in conception" with the Italian IRI system, which Votaw describes as follows:

Most of the Italian government's extensive participation in the economic sector of society is carried on through two large public companies: ENI [Ente Nazionale Idrocarburi, in the petroleum field] and Istituto per la Ricostruzione Industriale (IRI). The latter dates back to the Mussolini days, is approximately twice the size of ENI, and has well over one hundred subsidiary and affiliated companies engaged in everything from shipping and aircraft to steel, automobiles (Alfa Romeo), and banking. Unlike ENI, however, IRI is less of a "business firm" and more of a "government bureau" engaged in supervising business firms.[37]

Based on Morozumi's information, his own worries about the effects of liberalization, and the continental European precedents, Sahashi set out to draft the Tokushinhō. He also, together with his superiors in MITI, established a joint civilian-official deliberation council (*shingikai*) to make a searching an-

36. *Modern Capitalist Planning: The French Model* (Cambridge, Mass.: Harvard University Press, 1969), pp. 51–52.
37. Dow Votaw, *The Six-Legged Dog, Mattei and ENI* (Berkeley and Los Angeles: University of California Press, 1964), p. 72.

alysis of the competitive strength of the Japanese economy.[38] This new body, set up in April 1961, was entitled the Industrial Structure Investigation Council (Sangyō Kōzō Chōsa Kai) and headed by the late Ojima Arakazu, then chairman of the board of Yawata Iron and Steel and a former vice-minister of the Ministry of Commerce and Industry. The council's five-volume report, which remains one of the most comprehensive investigations of any economy in the world, influenced Sahashi's draft law and caused him to modify parts of it.[39]

Sahashi's Tokushinhō, which he and MITI liked to describe as a "breakwater against the tides of liberalization," was a complex bill. It called for government assistance in the reorganization of industries with weak international competitive ability; the encouragement of mergers in order to produce concentrations on a par with the rest of the world; the giving to MITI of powers of tax relief, financing, and the ability to make exceptions to the Anti-Monopoly Law; and government-private cooperation through a series of councils composed of representatives from MITI, industry, and finance, set up to reach mutually acceptable decisions on structural changes and investments in each industry.

Forces in the Diet combined to defeat the "charge of the Sahashi regiment," as the press at the time called it. The Fair Trade Commission rose to the defense of the Occupation-created Anti-Monopoly Law; in fact, so bitter was its opposition that a few years later, when the commission wanted to establish a discussion group (kondankai) on the Anti-Monopoly Law, and MITI chose Sahashi as its delegate, the commission said that it would give up the idea rather than accept him.[40] The opposition political parties ripped into the idea of

38. On the nature and importance of shingikai in Japanese public administration, see Yung Ho Park, "The Governmental Advisory Commission System in Japan," Journal of Comparative Administration, vol. 3, no. 4 (Feb. 1972), pp. 435–467; and by the same author in Japanese, "Shingikai-ron," Jichi kenkyū, vol. 48, nos. 5–6 (May and June 1972), pp. 20–38 and 81–96.

39. See Sangyō Kōzō Chōsa Kai, Nihon no sangyō kōzō, 5 vols. (Tokyo: Tsūshō Sangyō Kenkyū Sha, 1964). The council of 1961 was created in addition to, and did not duplicate, the old Industrial Rationalization Council (Sangyō Gōrika Shingikai), set up in December 1949, which had performed yeoman service throughout the 1950s. It had been MITI's primary forum for the exchange of views between the ministry and industrial leaders and the place where industrialists could examine and modify the innumerable MITI plans for specific structural innovations in the Japanese economy. Following the failure of the Tokushinhō in the Diet, the Industrial Structure Investigation Council and the Industrial Rationalization Council merged in January 1967 to become the Industrial Structure Council (Sangyō Kōzō Shingikai). This body, headed during the early 1970s by the then president of Keidanren, Uemura Kōgorō, is MITI's most prestigious channel for communicating its ideas to the business community (of some thirty-six shingikai operated by MITI) and its main means for indirectly implementing the principles of the failed Tokushinhō. See Obayashi Kenji, "'Nihon kabushiki kaisha' no shukuzu, sankōshin no kanmin kyōchō-buri," Nikkei bijinesu, July 26, 1971, pp. 68–70.

40. Kusayanagi Daizō, Bungei shunjū, May 1969, pp. 162–163; Kaikoroku sengo tsūsan seisaku shi, pp. 146–147.

"public-private cooperation," scaring everybody with the spectre of a revival of bureaucratic control. Elements of the business community did not believe that the proposed measures were necessary and adopted a "liberal" stance (Ishizaka Taizō of Keidanren is commonly identified as the leader of these groups).

Most important, the Ministry of Finance was opposed because it saw MITI infringing on its own territory—finance—and it mobilized most of the banking world against the MITI bill. MITI has long been critical of the "overloan" characteristic of Japanese industrial financing (the extent to which firms are financed largely by bank loans rather than by the sale of equity shares), a point on which most foreign analysts would concur with MITI, but the Ministry of Finance and the Bank of Japan, which are the underwriters of the overloans, came to the defense of their clients, the banks. The person usually identified as the leader of this contingent of anti-Tokushinhō forces was Usami Makoto, then president of the Mitsubishi Bank. Sahashi himself blamed the Ministry of Finance above all others for the defeat of his bill: "The Ministry of Finance bureaucrats know nothing about industry. They don't know the living economy at all. The only thing they can do is to find fault with the policies which others think of through enormous efforts and to cut the budget. They lack all creative vision about how to advance Japan or how to see the economy develop dynamically."[41] Whatever the merits of Sahashi's views, the Tokushinhō itself languished in the Forty-Third, Forty-Fourth and Forty-Sixth Diets and never came to a vote.

However, as all analysts agree, the recession of 1965 and the first capital liberalization of 1967 led to the principles of the Tokushinhō being implemented anyway—through a series of industry-specific laws that either already existed or were newly enacted, through administrative guidance, or through the Industrial Structure Council being given responsibility for reviewing and approving individual enterprise investment decisions. It seems clear that although many business leaders suspected the motives of MITI in advancing the Tokushinhō—they really did fear the restoration of heavy bureaucratic controls over the economy—many of them agreed with MITI's diagnosis of what was needed for the Japanese economy in the "new age."

MITI's reliance on specific laws for individual industries rather than on one or two overarching laws carries with it consequences that alarm some Japanese analysts more than the broadly based statutes. Legislation such as the postwar Petroleum Industry Law, Electric Utility Industry Law, Gas Utility Industry Law, Cotton Textile Industry Law, Machine Industry Promotion Law, and Electronics Industry Promotion Law bears a close family resemblance to the 1937–1938 laws (such as the Synthetic Petroleum Enterprise Law, the Iron and Steel Enterprise Law, the Machine Tool Manufacturing Enterprise Law, and

41. Quoted in Suzuki, *Keizai kanryō*, p. 130.

the Aircraft Manufacturing Enterprise Law) that formed part of the basis for the controlled economy during the Pacific War.

Moreover, such legislation tended to reinforce the vertical structure that existed within MITI prior to 1973, for each industry law was assigned to the exclusive jurisdiction of a single MITI bureau. MITI's so-called primary bureaus (*genkyoku*) were notorious for becoming spokesmen for their client industries. Serious questions have been raised about the degree of expertise a bureau director and his staff could have on a given industry, particularly when the director holds the job for no more than two or three years, resulting in his becoming the captive of the industry's trade association for his data-base and other necessary information. The trade associations of each industry can be quite powerful, and a prudent MITI bureaucrat will not normally challenge them if he wishes to leave the position of director of a *genkyoku* with his reputation as an administrator intact.

Another objection is that some industry laws turn out to be only "convenience laws" (*kamben hō*)—not regulatory legislation but covers for administrative guidance and for an extremely close, occasionally corrupt, relationship between officials and businessmen. No law is necessarily typical, but one may take the Petroleum Industry Law of 1962 as an example. It vests authority in MITI to authorize the refining and sale of petroleum products, to approve the installation or expansion of refining facilities, to pass on annual production plans, to establish a range of standard selling prices, and to demand and receive reports. What actually goes on appears to be a refiners' cartel that would be illegal if it were not protected by the presence of MITI officials at meetings of competing firms—or at least so the prosecutors of the Tokyo High Procuracy charged in May 1974, when they indicted officials of the Petroleum Association of Japan and twelve petroleum companies on charges of criminal price-rigging.[42] Laws such as the Petroleum Industry Law, as well as informal administrative guidance in general, are hard to police and can easily turn into what some economic analysts call a "fairy's cloak" (*kakure-mino*), a magic cape that makes invisible what would be illegal if it were visible.[43]

Administrative guidance is distinct from the legally sanctioned license and approval authority of a ministry in that it does not rest on a specific law, only on the general establishment act creating a ministry. Bureaucrats can "recommend" (*kankoku*), "request" (*yōsei*), "advise" (*jogon*), or "mediate" (*chūkai*) on any matter within their jurisdiction as specified in the establishment law of their ministry or agency.[44] The cabinet legislation bureau defines administrative guidance (*gyōsei shidō*) as a device designed to "enable an administrative agency to induce the party or parties concerned to take or not to take a certain

42. *Nihon keizai shimbun*, May 29, 1974; *Asahi shimbun*, May 29, 30, 1974.

43. *Tōyō keizai*, April 6, 1974, p. 33. On the Petroleum Industry Law of 1962, also see Peter R. Odell, *Oil and World Power* (Harmondsworth: Penguin, 1970), pp. 124–126.

44. Maeda, *Keizai hyōron*, Feb. 1968, p. 38.

action in such a way that a given objective of the agency may be achieved with the cooperation of the party or parties thus approached."[45] The bureau adds that there are three restrictions on its use: (1) it has no legal binding power; (2) it must be confined to the "duties and functions" of the administrative agency concerned; and (3) if it involves behavior that comes within the purview of the Anti-Monopoly Law, the administrative guidance must be in accordance with one of the laws which specifically allow for exceptions to the Anti-Monopoly Law.[46]

We cannot review here all of the interesting ramifications of administrative guidance by MITI. A few points must be made, however. First, the most common example of administrative guidance is a MITI *kankoku sōtan*—a recommendation for curtailed operations—in industries where exemptions from the Anti-Monopoly Law have been authorized by law. These recommendations actually direct each company in an industry to reduce production by a specified amount and for a given period to correct depressed conditions due to "excessive competition"; they constitute a "voluntary" agreement to restrict exports or production.

Second, MITI prefers administrative guidance to formal legal procedures because it is faster, less disruptive, and more flexible. Industrialists prefer administrative guidance because they trust MITI and because they do not have to open their books to inspection by the Fair Trade Commission, as they would have to do if they sought to establish a legally permitted, formal "depression cartel" under the terms of the various amendments to the Anti-Monopoly Law.

Third, although various foreign governments, notably the United States, have often been critical of administrative guidance, they are in fact one of the prime causes of its existence. In order to maintain their reputations as pure free traders, foreign governments do not wish to enact their own restrictions against Japanese imports that may be disrupting one of their domestic industries. Therefore, they pressure Japan into "voluntarily restricting" its exports of a given product to the foreign market. Once such an agreement is reached, someone in Japan has to decide on the exact production and export allocations that will be assigned to each manufacturer under the terms of the voluntary export-restriction agreement. MITI does this chore—and it does so through administrative guidance. The United States, for example, has no specific import restrictions against Japanese goods, but it has some forty-nine agreements

45. *Japan Times*, June 3, 1974.
46. Laws authorizing exemptions to the Anti-Monopoly Law include the Export-Import Transactions Law of 1952, the Medium and Smaller Enterprises Stabilization Law of 1952, the Coal Industry Rationalization Law of 1955, the Textile Industries Facilities Regulation Law of 1956, and the amendment of Sept. 1, 1953, to the Anti-Monopoly Law itself. See Kanazawa Yoshio, "The Regulation of Corporate Enterprise: The Law of Unfair Competition and the Control of Monopoly Power," in von Mehren, ed., *Law in Japan*, p. 496.

with Japan under which Japan voluntarily restricts its exports to the United States, the largest number of such restrictions among all of the advanced capitalist nations.[47] As Eleanor Hadley laconically remarks, "Import quotas imply export cartels."[48]

Fourth, perhaps the most interesting form of administrative guidance is "mediation." In MITI, this involves high-level brokerage carried out by the vice-minister or a bureau director in order to solve a basic problem when it arises in the industrial world, such as the merger of the Yawata and Fuji steel companies, the salvaging of Maruzen Petroleum from financial ruin, or the amalgamation of the Prince Automobile Company with Nissan Motors. Such mediation, or the use of the good offices of the government to bring the parties together, is delicate, invariably oral (as is all administrative guidance, for that matter), and usually completely secret from the public until after it has been accomplished. In the Nissan-Prince merger, for example, the public is still unclear about precisely what role the bureaucracy played and about who led whom in the maneuvering, the bureaucracy or the representatives of the firms.[49]

Finally, administrative guidance is sometimes taken as evidence of the weakness of the "rule of law" in Japan, but this is not necessarily the case. Administrative guidance became salient during a period of very rapid and fundamental change in the Japanese economy; its rise correlates with the decline of parts of the licensing and approval authority of the government. However, Japanese understand the use of administrative guidance to be unusual and temporary, and a great deal of attention has been directed by Japanese scholars and jurists to its precise legal meaning and to ways in which it can either be codified into law or prohibited by law.[50] If Americans are to say that Japanese are careless about the law, Japanese could as easily reply that Americans are so legalistic as to be careless of the economy. In any case, former Vice-Minister Sahashi's opinion on the purposes of administrative guidance comes close to representing the views that prevailed throughout MITI during the period under study:

47. Amaya Naohiro, "Immediate Economic Problems between Japan and the United States and Their Long-Range Prospects" (Tokyo: MITI Information Office, March 6, 1973), p. 25.

48. *Antitrust in Japan* (Princeton, N.J.: Princeton University Press, 1970), p. 388. See also Gene Gregory, "Now It's 'Orderly' Sales," *Far Eastern Economic Review*, July 22, 1972, pp. 38–39. Gregory notes that "the imposition of voluntary restraints entails the formation of an export cartel for the product or industry to be regulated."

49. Maeda, *Keizai hyōron*, Feb. 1968, p. 38. On the Maruzen Petroleum case, see Sahashi Shigeru, *Ishoku kanryō* (Tokyo: Daiyamondo Sha, 1967), pp. 240–245.

50. See "Gyōsei shidō no kihon mondai" [special collection of articles], *Jurisuto* 342 (March 15, 1966):21–63; and "Tokushū: dokkinhō to gyōsei shidō," *Jurisuto* 566 (July 15, 1974):14–51.

It is dangerous to determine a priori that "free competition is a good thing and cooperation is a bad thing." There is desirable competition and useless competition within the general category of free competition. A clear difference exists between the economy of [Adam] Smith's time, when equipment was small-scale and it was relatively easy to drop out of competition, and the contemporary economy with billions of yen invested in capital equipment and where natural selection through free competition causes great confusion. The result of competition in the latter case is only social misery.[51]

As should be apparent, MITI is a powerful ministry even though it expends only a small budget. MITI in fact controls such a small share of the annual budget—around 1 percent—that MITI officials like to joke that their entire budget is smaller than the subsidies paid out by a single section of the Ministry of Agriculture and Forestry or the negotiated supplementary budget of the Ministry of Welfare. Table 4 offers a comparison between MITI's budget share and those of the other economic ministries.

MITI's small share of the budget (tenth out of thirteen ministries) is actually a source of bureaucratic strength; it is also a highly misleading measure of its true fiscal powers. Because MITI does not administer large subsidies, it is free of the enormous power exercised by the Ministry of Finance's budget bureau over all the other ministries.[52] If MITI had a large budget, given the fact that it wields rather slight political clout, it would definitely be subservient to the Ministry of Finance, which it is not.

The misleading aspect of MITI's low budget is that MITI also possesses the power to approve or disapprove loans made to industries by various governmental financial organs, including the Japan Development Bank (es-

Table 4

Shares of the Total Budget of the Economic Ministries
(in percentage)

	1955	1960	1965	1969
Ministry of Finance	12.17	8.49	4.20	9.62
Ministry of Agriculture and Forestry	9.45	9.38	10.66	10.54
MITI	0.70	1.01	1.50	1.36
Ministry of Transportation	2.67	2.61	2.60	2.40
Ministry of Construction	10.81	11.56	13.16	11.25

SOURCE: John Creighton Campbell, "How Powerful Is the Ministry of Finance?" (New York: University Seminar on Modern East Asia: Japan, Columbia University, Dec. 1971), p. 8.

51. *Kaikoroku sengo tsūsan seisaku shi*, p. 145.
52. Itō Daiichi, in *Gendai Nihon no seitō to kanryō*, p. 99.

tablished 1951), the Export-Import Bank (1950), the Medium and Smaller Enterprises Credit Fund (Chūshō Kigyō Kin'yū Kōko, 1953), the Electrical Resources Development Company, the Petroleum Resources Development Company, the Central Bank of Industrial Cooperatives (Shōkō Chūkin, 1936), the Productivity Headquarters (Seisansei Honbu), and several other government bodies that use post office savings, welfare annuity funds, and direct government appropriations to make loans to private firms for purchases of capital equipment.[53] The bulk of such loans has gone to the coal, electric power, steel, shipbuilding, chemical, and synthetic textile industries. In addition, MITI uses its own small budget to make what Japanese call "indicative investments"—that is, by its actions, MITI signals to the entire financial community those areas of the economy that the government wishes to support and those that it wishes to inhibit (which is usually enough to cause most bankers to grant or to refuse to make loans in the designated fields).

Firms that receive a Development Bank loan have thereby also received MITI's seal of approval (*osumitsuki*), and as businessmen say, "If the Kaigin [Development Bank] has invested money, my city bank will lend me more."[54] It is true that as the relative importance of Development Bank financing has declined over time (because of the tremendous expansion of city-bank financing), MITI's power has declined relative to that of the Ministry of Finance. Nevertheless, MITI's influence over investment decisions added to its influence over foreign trade amounts to an actual power over sums in excess of the entire national budget.[55] Needless to say, MITI uses this financial leverage to make its administrative guidance more effective—in effect, it adds the "bait" of Development Bank or other financing to its perhaps otherwise unpleasant orders. Under these circumstances, administrative guidance does not appear oppressive; it is more like what the Japanese call "a gentle pinch under the *kotatsu*" (a *kotatsu* is a foot-warmer with a quilt over it around which the whole family passes a winter evening).

Other, vaguer aspects of MITI's power position revolve around its general "influence." Except for Kishi Nobusuke and Shiina Etsusaburō, both former vice-ministers of the Ministry of Commerce and Industry and MITI's two leading political representatives, MITI men do not usually go into politics after retiring from the ministry. Those who do—Hashiguchi Takashi, Fukui Isamu, Ogasa Kōshō, Shiseki Ihei, Kawakami Tameji, Akama Bunzō, Koike Shinzō—are not normally from the MITI mainstream but rather from posts that are favorable for building political support (such as the director of one of MITI's regional bureaus or an official of the Medium and Smaller Enterprises

53. For a survey of government financial institutions, see K. Bieda, *The Structure and Operation of the Japanese Economy* (Sydney: Wiley, 1970), pp. 83–90.

54. Tsūsanshō Kisha Kurabu, *Tsūsanshō*, p. 24.

55. Maeda, *Keizai hyōron*, Feb. 1968, p. 36.

Agency). One study of Diet members in April 1966 listed the following numbers of former government officials in the House of Representatives: Ministry of Finance, 14; Agriculture, 9; MITI, 6; Transportation, 5; Welfare, 3; Foreign Affairs, 3; Labor, 2; Postal, Construction, Autonomy, and EPA, 1 each; the former Home Ministry, 21; and the former Communications Ministry, 4, for a total of 81, about 15 percent of the total membership. In the House of Councillors, the picture was similar: Agriculture, 8; Finance, 6; old Home, 6; Transportation, 5; Welfare, 5; Construction, 4; Foreign Affairs, 3; Education, 3; old Communications, 3; MITI, 2; Postal, Labor, and Defense, 1 each, for a total of 49 (18 from the national constituency and 31 from the local constituencies), about 20 percent of the total membership.[56]

It is not entirely clear what MITI's political weakness signifies. Some analysts have concluded that it means the Diet is not very important.[57] Others think that MITI is at a great disadvantage compared with the Finance and Agriculture ministries in terms of political backing. During the 1960s, when political figures with ministerial bailiwicks, such as Ikeda in Finance, Kōno in Agriculture, and Satō Eisaku in Transportation, were at the forefront of political life, there was a good deal of political maneuvering among them to gain control of or to prevent someone else from gaining control of MITI. Whatever the final judgment on the usefulness to a ministry of having a leading political supporter, MITI is today one of the three ministerial posts (along with Finance and Foreign Affairs) of which any politician aspiring to the prime ministership must have held at least one and preferably all three.

MITI's real influence is located, of course, in industry. MITI bureaucrats *amakudari* (descend from heaven) on retirement to the top echelons of every major enterprise in Japan, most importantly to the steel, electric power, trading, automotive, petroleum, and electronic computer industries, which are of special importance to the ministry.[58] Retired officials are in fact sent to such positions by the ministry as part of an official policy to help ensure the effectiveness of administrative guidance. In many industries, when a MITI official goes to negotiate with the representatives of the companies, he will be talking with men who have themselves already spent some twenty or more years in MITI, a circumstance that makes it easier for both sides to reach an agreement. Such reemployment of ex-bureaucrats in strategic posts is part of a practice the Japanese call *nemawashi*—laying the groundwork—which the Japanese recognize to be part of an "old boy" network but which many foreigners confuse as a manifestation of the famous Japanese "consensus."[59]

56. Shibuzawa Kijurō, *Kōkyū kōmuin no yukue* (Tokyo: Asahi Shimbun Chōsa Kenkyū Shitsu, 1966), pp. 9–10.

57. Itō Daiichi, in *Gendai Nihon no seitō to kanryō*, p. 100.

58. See Chalmers Johnson, "The Reemployment of Retired Government Bureaucrats in Japanese Big Business," *Asian Survey*, vol. 14, no. 11 (Nov. 1974), pp. 953–965.

59. For studies of the MITI "old boy" networks, see Seisaku Jihō Sha, *Tsūsanshō*, p. 45, and Akaboshi, *Shōsetsu tsūsanshō*, pp. 1–7.

MITI does not like to be compared with the U.S. Department of Commerce, which it regards as merely a representative of the business world within the American government; MITI prefers to think of itself as having a voice of its own, at least equal to that of the private sector.[60] As a matter of fact, this area is the most delicate for the ministry in terms of its total power position. Many cases indicate that whenever the ministry has taken a position totally opposite from that of industry, it is in deep trouble. Although all MITI leaders insist that the ministry serves the interests of the Japanese people and not just big business, it would seem that MITI, like all bureaucracies, has some difficulty in identifying the interests of the people, as distinct from those of its most immediate clients.

Former MITI Vice-Minister Ueno tells a revealing story, one that sheds some light on the general reputation of MITI. When Ueno was appointed vice-minister of the Economic Planning Agency in 1955, the director of the agency was Takasaki Tatsunosuke, who later became famous as the man who negotiated the informal trade agreements with the People's Republic of China during the 1960s. Ueno was chagrined one day to find that the director seemed to be confusing public administration with private business. The Yawata Iron and Steel Company was planning to establish a subsidiary to manufacture tin cans. Takasaki, who was the founder of the Tōyō Can Company, ordered Ueno to "stop Yawata's plans. Yawata should specialize in making raw materials and not intervene in the manufacturing side of things." Ueno replied, "I understand what you want, but the EPA has no authority to stop Yawata." To which Takasaki replied, "Of course you can. Or is it that as a MITI bureaucrat you can't resist Yawata? It is inexcusable that MITI has become Yawata's subordinate." "It is not true, sir," said Ueno. "Are you a Yawata spy, as you don't agree with me?" shot back Takasaki. Ultimately Ueno had to ask Fujii Heigo, a Yawata director, to explain to Takasaki that the problem was not within the jurisdiction of the EPA. The Yawata works were, of course, originally founded by the government and administered by MITI's predecessors until the 1930s. Takasaki therefore assumed, as many Japanese do, that MITI officials look on the interests of Yawata Steel as their own. This impression is true of many other famous firms that have received special nurturing from MITI.[61]

MITI is a powerful economic planning and regulating ministry, but it is not, as I have sought to show here, all-powerful. It exists and works within a framework of numerous competing powers and interests, all of which must be acknowledged and reconciled if effective and widely supported policies are to result. Its primary powers rest on Diet-enacted statutory authority, rather than on the funds it expends, the political power it commands, or the influence it wields. It prefers to exercise this statutory authority indirectly, through persua-

60. Suzuki, *Keizai kanryō*, p. 123.
61. *Kaikoroku sengo tsūsan seisaku shi*, pp. 71–72.

sion, advice, and inducement, but it can on occasion act authoritatively, as for example it did in the mid-1960s when it cut off supplies of coking coal to Sumitomo Metals after Sumitomo had rejected its administrative guidance. Its overall effectiveness must be rated highly, given the unprecedented success of the Japanese economy. Whatever it may have done right, in terms of its own goals, it has not done much wrong, which distinguishes it from many bureaucracies around the world. Equally to the point, it has done its work with a small staff and a small budget, a staff about half the size of the equivalent ministry in Germany and about a quarter of that in Great Britain.[62] Bureaucratic capability of this magnitude is unusual, regardless of any judgments that may be made about the propriety or desirability of bureaucracy in general.

THE INTERNATIONAL TRADE BUREAU

Japan's dependence on international trade for its very existence is so well known as to hardly need mentioning here. In a sense, the ministry in Japan charged with trade administration occupies a position somewhat analogous to a ministry of defense in other nations. Japan is resource-deficient, overpopulated, and highly industrialized; it must export in order to earn the foreign exchange necessary to pay for its vital imports of fuel and raw materials. This need to export—rather than to borrow or to permit foreign direct investment—in order to meet national goals and to provide the funds for external payments is as old as the Meiji government itself.[63] Governmental preoccupation with balance of payments problems runs through Japan's modern history like a litany, one that MITI expresses in terms of the allegedly most basic cycle of the Japanese economy: the country buys more abroad than it sells, the government dampens down business activity, domestic demand subsides, exports expand, tight money controls are lessened, domestic demand expands, imports increase and exports decrease, international payments worsen, business activity is again tightened, and so on and so on.[64]

This theme of the need to trade appears in the most unlikely places. "Pappy" Boyington, the American air ace of World War II, was shot down January 3, 1944, in the southwest Pacific. He was later interrogated on the island of Truk by the Japanese general in command of the southwest Pacific theatre, at which time the following exchange occurred:

62. Stone, *Japan Surges Ahead*, pp. 52–53.
63. See Arthur E. Tiedemann, "Japan's Economic Foreign Policies, 1868–1893," in James W. Morley, ed., *Japan's Foreign Policy, 1868–1941, A Research Guide* (New York: Columbia University Press, 1974), pp. 118–152.
64. *Tsūshō sangyō shō nijū nen shi*, p. 5. Ohkawa and Rosovsky suggest that this cycle had been overcome by the end of the 1960s because Japan had been able to accumulate large foreign exchange reserves (*Japanese Economic Growth*, p. 184), but the oil crisis of 1973 may have set it in motion again.

Then he wanted to know what I thought of the Japanese people. Well, I was diplomatic enough to say that I personally didn't have much against them, but then I
went on at great length saying what I thought of their militaristic government, and
what I thought of the atrocities I knew were committed in the Philippine Islands
and in China.

The interpreter told me that the commanding general was about ready to leave
but would like to tell me a fable and would I mind.

I answered: "Why, no, certainly not."

So the commanding general told this fable, and as nearly as I can recall—for I was
shot in the head and everything else, and was punchy, shot, and exhausted—the
fable went like this:

"Once upon a time there was a little old lady and she traded with five merchants.
She always paid her bills and got along fine. Finally the five merchants got together and they jacked up their prices so high the little old lady couldn't afford to
live any longer. That's the end of the story."

So, after having said this, the general bowed to me and went out of the room. I
couldn't help ponder that there just had to be two sides to everything, and I just
couldn't help admiring this distinguished old gent a little bit.[65]

Given Japan's history as a trading nation, one would expect that the International Trade Bureau (ITB) of MITI would occupy the vital center of the
ministry, but surprisingly enough this is not true. Of course, MITI believes in
trade and in vigorous trade promotion, but for the first twenty years of its existence MITI was internally divided between an "international trade" faction
and an "industrial" faction, with the latter usually ascendant. Commenting on
this well-known but rarely reported aspect of Japan's trade ministry, some
Japanese wits have said that MITI should properly be called MIIT, with
industry first, or referred to as the "Ministry of International Trade vs.
Industry."[66]

It is important at the outset to stress that this struggle between the two factions was not zero-sum; it was always a matter of priorities, orientations, and
policies, with the traders' faction being more "international" and "liberal" and
the industrialists' faction being more "domestic" and "nationalistic," but with
both sides always being represented. Moreover, it always involved the personalities of politicians, old loyalties to the Ministry of Commerce and Industry
(MCI), ministerial territorial disputes, and the legacies of the war and Occupation as much as it did substantive issues. With the end of Sahashi's vice-
ministership in 1966, the dispute largely came to an end, and the ministry was
more or less internationalized by new, younger leaders. By the early 1970s, it
was apparent to all in MITI that the old issues of the dispute were no longer

65. "Pappy" Boyington, *Baa, Baa Black Sheep* (New York: Putnam's, 1958), p. 247.
66. Tsūsanshō Kisha Kurabu, *Tsūsanshō*, p. 66; and Tsūsanshō Kishadan, *Chūō kōron*, Oct.
1963, p. 82.

relevant to the real problems of Japan or of the ministry. But they are relevant in one sense: the basic reform of MITI in 1973 is unintelligible without an understanding of what transpired earlier.

When the MCI was set up in 1925, it contained a small trade section (Bōeki Ka) within its Commercial Affairs Bureau (Shōmu Kyoku), but the MCI certainly did not monopolize trade administration. Bureaus in the ministries of Foreign Affairs and Finance had equal or greater responsibility for trade-related matters. In 1930, as part of the government's efforts to promote exports and to defend against the rapid contraction of overseas markets in the wake of the world economic crisis, the MCI's trade section was elevated to bureau. status.

Beginning in 1936 the army sought to create an independent trade ministry, which would be composed of the Foreign Ministry's Trade Bureau (Tsūshō Kyoku), the MCI's Trade Bureau, and the Ministry of Finance's Customs Bureau (Kanzei Kyoku) and Foreign Exchange Bureau (Kawase Kyoku). Its purpose was to concentrate all the government's energies on export expansion to earn sufficient exchange for the importation of materials needed for war and to inhibit the spending of foreign exchange on civilian goods. The plan failed because of strong opposition from the Foreign and Finance ministries, but in 1937, as a scaled-down version of the original plan, the MCI's Trade Bureau became an "external bureau" (*gaikyoku*)—that is, a semi-independent organ with its own secretariat—under strong military influence.[67] During the period of the Pacific War, MCI and the other established ministries lost virtually all jurisdiction over trade, as it was placed in the new Greater East Asia Ministry, a development that irked the Ministry of Foreign Affairs more than MCI.

Meanwhile, the MCI was transforming itself into a control-oriented, heavy-industry-centered, war production administrator. Its war efforts were not very successful—due in part to competition from the military and foot-dragging by the zaibatsu—but in the process of trying to meet wartime industrial needs, the MCI totally changed its structure and character. The MCI began its existence organized into a few broad "horizontal bureaus," organs designed to implement governmental policies and laws across the spectrum of industries. Beginning in 1939, however, it scrapped this structure in favor of so-called vertical bureaus classified by material or industry—what the Japanese call variously the *genkyoku tatewari soshiki* (vertical organization classified by primary bureaus), the *busshibetsu genkyoku-sei* (primary bureau system classified by materials), the *sangyōbetsu genkyoku-sei* (primary bureau system classified by industries), or, in

---

67. See the interview with Ueno Kōshichi, one of the MCI proponents of a trade ministry, in *Tsūsanshō 20-nen gaishi*, p. 234; Tsūshō Sangyō Daijin Kanbō Chōsa Tōkei Bu Chōsa Ka, *Tsūshō sangyō gyōsei kikō enkaku shōshi* (Tokyo, 1951), pp. 84–85; and Robert M. Spaulding, Jr., "The Bureaucracy as a Political Force, 1920–1945," in James W. Morley, ed., *Dilemmas of Growth in Prewar Japan* (Princeton, N.J.: Princeton University Press, 1971), pp. 72–73.

general, the *busshibetsu-genkyoku hōshiki* (the primary bureaus-materials classification formula).[68] Over time this change of structure led to the development of six powerful bureaus with strong links to their respective client industries— the Heavy Industries Bureau, the Chemical Industries Bureau, the Textiles Bureau, the Mining Bureau, the Coal Bureau, and the Public Utilities Bureau. This structure grew out of wartime demands, but with an occasional change of name it remained MITI's basic configuration until the reform of July 1973.

Even more typical of the war's influence on MITI's postwar form than the *busshibetsu* system is the Enterprises Bureau (Kigyō Kyoku), created on June 16, 1942. This bureau was given responsibility for transforming individual companies to bring them into the war production drive, as well as for coordinating the work of the various primary bureaus. After the war, it put its special interest in planning and industrial reorganization to work rationalizing Japan's industrial structure and attempting to enlarge its productive capacity. It also took the lead in introducing new, capital-intensive industries into the Japanese economy. Undoubtedly, the Enterprises Bureau and its subordinate primary bureaus best typify the approach and achievements of MITI as an economic planning and development agency.

There are many other aspects to the history of the primary bureaus and the Enterprises Bureau that must be put aside here. Suffice it to say that the changes in the MCI that brought about this structure are associated most closely with the names of Kishi Nobusuke, Shiina Etsusaburō, and their younger followers in this period of the MCI's development, Yamamoto Takayuki, Tokunaga Hizatsugu, and Ishihara Takeo, each of whom became a vice-minister of MITI after 1949. Some of these men are to be counted among the so-called new (or reform) bureaucrats of the late 1930s—a vague and shifting group of officials who favored a totalitarian state structure in Japan—and all were influenced by the new bureaucrats' vision of a controlled economy.[69] Referring to the leaders of MITI during the 1950s, the MITI Journalists Club contends that the real "birthplace of their spirit" (*kokoro no kokyō*) was the era in which the new bureaucrats took the stage and the *busshibetsu* was introduced into the MCI.[70]

The Allied Occupation had little effect on the MCI structure or orientation. Recreated from the Ministry of Munitions the day before the first Occupation soldier arrived in Japan, the MCI retained the *busshibetsu-genkyoku* formula, but

68. See Misonō Hitoshi, "Keizai kanryō no kinō to kongo no hōkō," *Keizai hyōron*, Feb. 1968, p. 15; Maeda, *Keizai hyōron*, p. 31; former Vice-Minister Ōjimi Yoshihisa, in *Kaikoroku sengo tsūsan seisaku shi*, p. 208; Akaboshi, *Shōsetsu tsusansho*, p. 13; and *Tsūshō sangyō gyōsei kikō enkaku shōshi*, p. 92.

69. See Robert M. Spaulding, Jr., "Japan's New Bureaucrats, 1932–1945," in George M. Wilson, ed., *Crisis Politics in Prewar Japan* (Tokyo: Sophia University Press, 1970), pp. 51–70.

70. Tsūsanshō Kisha Kirabu, *Tsūsanshō*, p. 246.

it had virtually no interest in trade and, indeed, had been out of the trade administration business for almost a decade. Even if the postwar MCI had
wanted to assume responsibility for the revival of trade, the Supreme Commander for the Allied Powers (SCAP) exercised total control in this area
through a postwar agency only tenuously connected to the MCI as an external
bureau—the Board of Trade (its own and SCAP's official translation of Bōeki
Chō).

SCAP prohibited all private trade for the first two years of the Occupation,
and even after the restrictions were eased in 1947, trade was carried on under
strict SCAP-approved, Japanese government controls. The Board of Trade,
which administered these controls, was in effect a state trading organ of the
Japanese government and one that transacted all of its business with or
through the Occupation authorities. It was heavily staffed with officials from
the Ministry of Foreign Affairs, a knowledge of English being necessary to work
in any agency directly involved with the Allied Occupation and many diplomats being available, for all foreign embassies were closed for the duration of
the Occupation. There was also a small contingent of MCI men in the Board of
Trade, most of whom later returned to MITI to work in the ITB.

In 1949, the United States changed its policies toward the occupation of
Japan and decided to do everything in its power to get the Japanese economy
back on its feet, the Americans' intent being to preserve Japan as an Allied bas-
tion in the Cold War (or at least to prevent a Communist revolution from oc-
curring there) and to end the subsidization of the Japanese people's daily living
requirements out of the American treasury.[71] Among the many policies of
SCAP's new course, one was Occupation encouragement and support of a new
ministry being proposed by the Japanese—MITI—which was conceived as a
marriage between the MCI and the Board of Trade.

Official MITI historians applaud the fact that MITI, which was created
on May 25, 1949, for the first time put the administration of both production
and trade squarely into the hands of one ministry. Overall, the idea worked
brilliantly, as the results twenty years later testified. But the parties to this
arranged marriage squabbled with each other for about their first fifteen years
together, probably because each knew a good deal more about the other than
SCAP did of either. Prime Minister Yoshida made no secret of his dislike for
the MCI bureaucracy, which he associated with the war and the controlled
economy and, of course, as one of the Gaimushō's most illustrious alumni, he
favored Foreign Office men. SCAP also seemed to prefer diplomats over trade
and industry bureaucrats, perhaps because it could converse with the former.
As a result of Yoshida's influence, the new MITI had a strong Foreign Office
coloration. At its center were two new bureaus, the International Trade Bureau
(Tsūshō Kyoku) and the Trade Promotion Bureau (Tsūshō Shinkō Kyoku),

71. See Johnson, *Conspiracy at Matsukawa*, chaps. 1 and 2.

and in the background was the Enterprises Bureau, coordinating the work of five primary bureaus. Somewhat mysteriously, the Enterprises Bureau and each of the primary bureaus had the phrase "international trade" (*tsūshō*) prefixed to their titles. It seems that this nomenclature was supposed to convey to the Allies how seriously Japan was now taking trade expansion and the American demands that it become self-supporting. Thus, from 1949 until the end of the Occupation, MITI was composed of such odd-sounding units as the Trade Enterprises Bureau (Tsūshō Kigyō Kyoku), the Trade Textiles Bureau (Tsūshō Sen'i Kyoku), the Trade Iron and Steel Bureau (Tsūshō Tekkō Kyoku), and so forth down through every bureau in the ministry. In 1952, after the Occupation, MITI was reorganized. The two bureaus concerned with international trade were combined into one—the ITB—and all the others lost their *tsūshō* prefixes. This new arrangement lasted until 1965, when the ITB was again divided into two bureaus.

The matter of names and prefixes seems trivial, but as late as 1969 old MCI bureaucrats were still worrying about the issue.[72] What rankled was that the term "Tsūshō Kyoku" for International Trade Bureau is actually the name of the prewar trade bureau of the Foreign Ministry; the MCI had always called its unit the Bōeki Kyoku. The Foreign Ministry term is perhaps a little more elegant and vague, even though it does imply the union of trade and production, which was the basic idea behind MITI, whereas *bōeki* has the ring of a down-to-earth merchant about it. The real issue, however, is of course ministerial pride and territoriality. In 1965, when the ITB was again divided into an International Trade Bureau and a Trade Promotion Bureau, MITI began to reintroduce its own and preferred word for "trade." The ITB retained the name Tsūshō Kyoku, but the new Trade Promotion Bureau was entitled the Bōeki Shinkō Kyoku. Further progress along these lines was made in 1973. The old ITB became the International Trade Policy Bureau, the official English translation for Tsūshō Seisaku Kyoku, but what is called in official English the International Trade Administration Bureau is in Japanese the Bōeki Kyoku. Old MITI men still prefer *bōeki* to the Foreign Ministry's *tsūshō*, even though the Foreign Ministry has not used the term for a generation.[73]

Exacerbating these disputes over nomenclature was the fact that from 1949 until 1956 Foreign Ministry men held the key positions in the ITB as well as in several other MITI bureaus. The first four directors of the ITB were famous Foreign Office diplomats—Takeuchi Ryūji, Ōda Takio, Ushiba Nobuhiko, and Itagaki Osamu—all of whom later served as ambassadors and had close contacts with the United States (Ushiba was a well-known ambassador to Washington in the early 1970s). Ōda explains this unusual arrangement:

72. *Tsūsanshō 20-nen gaishi*, pp. 40, 48.

73. See Tsūsanshō, *Tsūshō sangyō shō kikō oyobi kanshoku mei ra no eibun ni yoru hyōji hōhō ni tsuite* (Tokyo: Tsusanshō, July 25, 1973).

At the time [1949] we were still under Occupation, and it was well understood
that ex-diplomats had the best mentality for close contacts with the Occupation
army. It was thought that Gaimushō people would be better than MITI people for
this. This was the main reason why the ITB chief was from the Gaimushō. When
it came to heated discussions, a chief from the Foreign Ministry could probably be
more stubborn.[74]

This may have been true for the last years of the Occupation, when Takeuchi
and Ōda served, but it does not explain why the arrangement lasted until 1956.
Nor does it explain why Hirai Tomisaburō, the first director of the Trade
Promotion Bureau (always a MITI bailiwick) and a later vice-minister,
thought that by far the worst problem in trade administration was working
with Foreign Office personnel.[75] Ministerial *nawabari* was involved, as well as
some basic differences in outlook between the Foreign Ministry and MITI.

MITI has always fought Japan's economic battles on two fronts—those of
kane (money) and *mono* (things). The ITB is the planning and operational unit
in charge of the *kane* front; its responsibility is—as old ITB directors put it—to
keep Japan a "black-ink country" (*kurojikoku*). In a sense the ITB directors are
MITI's financial men, in addition to being in charge of guaranteeing imports
and promoting exports. Until 1964, the ITB controlled the foreign exchange
budget authorized by the Foreign Exchange and Foreign Trade Control Law;
its officials made all the allocations of available foreign currencies to importers
in accordance with overall MITI policies for the support of firms that manufactured for export and of new industries that contributed to a capital-intensive
structure of the Japanese economy. This gave the ITB enormous power. During the 1949–1964 period the third floor of the MITI office building, which
housed the ITB, became known as the "Toranomon Ginza" because of the
crowds of businessmen who gathered there every day seeking import funds and
export permits. The danger of corruption was always sufficiently obvious that
in the early fifties the ministry put signs on all the doors saying "Presents
Politely Refused" (*zōtōhin okotowari*), although many Japanese believe that this
did not pose too great a barrier to deliveries—at least to lower-level officials.[76]

The great achievements of the ITB in its early period were the passage of the
Export Insurance and Credit Law of 1950; the Export-Import Transactions
Law of 1952 (which permitted cartels among exporters); the negotiation of the
Japan-United States Treaty of Trade, Commerce, and Navigation of October
1953; the enactment of the Export Inspection Law of 1957; and the creation
of JETRO's predecessor in 1954, with JETRO itself (Japan External Trade
Organization) being set up by law in 1958. All this work obviously required a

74. Interview with Ōda Takio, in *Tsūsanshō 20-nen gaishi*, p. 265.

75. Interview with Hirai Tomisaburō, in *Kaikoroku sengo tsūsan seisaku shi*, p. 39.

76. Tsūsanshō Kisha Kirabu, *Tsūsanshō*, pp. 10–11; and Akimi Jirō, *Tsūsan kanryō* (Tokyo:
San'ichi Shobō, 1956), pp. 9–10.

knowledge of foreign trade, but it also required men who had worked abroad, who spoke foreign languages, and who were knowledgeable about the "culture" of international commerce—such as GATT, the IMF, the OECD, and the trends toward trade liberalization and convertibility that began to accelerate during the late 1950s. Until MITI could develop its own cadres in these areas, Foreign Ministry officials took over the responsibilities. In addition to heading the ITB itself, Foreign Ministry officials served as section chiefs of Market Sections One, Two, and Three, and the Export Section within the ITB, the Textiles Export Section in the Textiles Bureau, and some thirteen other positions.

The first MITI "native-born" (haenuki) director of the ITB was Matsuo Taiichirō, who received the post on September 16, 1956. Matsuo had long been interested in trade. During the war he worked in the Greater East Asia Ministry and during the Occupation in the Economic Stabilization Board. In 1949, he became the ITB's first deputy director; and from 1954 to 1956, he served in the embassy in Washington. After retiring from MITI in 1960, he joined the big trading firm of Marubeni-Iida, where for many years he headed its New York branch, becoming vice-president of the company in 1966. His overseas service in the Washington embassy is typical of the new crop of MITI trade officials who took over from their Foreign Office predecessors.

The ordinary MITI official before the mid-1960s was not internationally oriented; Sahashi, for example, once described himself as a "domestic-use bureaucrat" and acknowledged his weakness in foreign languages.[77] The MITI men in ITB, by contrast, were the ministry's first internationalists. Even so, they had some trouble getting themselves established in the ministry. In a 1969 roundtable discussion between three well-known former ITB directors (Matsuo Taiichirō, Komuro Tsuneo, and Yamamoto Shigenobu, all MITI career officers) and the then-current ITB director (Miyazawa Tetsuzō), Miyazawa confessed to his "seniors" that he was just learning his new job and that he had never worked overseas. Matsuo replied with a laugh (but also with a note of irony), "Work overseas doesn't actually have much influence, you know."[78]

The ITB, either in its Gaimushō period or in its MITI period, often found itself at odds with the Enterprises Bureau and the primary bureaus. In the early days, some Enterprises Bureau people believed that the foreign office men were in MITI to ensure that Yoshida's pro-American policies were carried out; and indeed, one of the main tasks of the ITB in those days was to enforce the American-inspired embargo of trade with Communist China, a policy disliked by the "industrial" faction.[79] In later periods, MITI's own ITB men were much more sensitive than their counterparts in the Enterprises Bureau to the

77. Sahashi, *Ishoku kanryō*, pp. 207, 212.
78. *Tsūsanshō 20-nen gaishi*, p. 47.
79. Akimi, *Tsūsan kanryō*, pp. 28–44, 175.

fact that liberalization of the economy was going to come faster than the industrial faction wanted and that it was necessary if Japan was to avoid retaliatory
trade restrictions from its commercial partners. During the early years of
MITI, the ITB was the ministry's most powerful bureau, representing the
political will of Yoshida that the old MCI men needed firm supervision by Foreign Office officials, and monopolizing the control of foreign exchange. But the
Enterprises Bureau slowly overtook and surpassed it for various reasons, including the lack of technical expertise in the ITB about many commodities and
industries it handled, the fact that the Enterprises Bureau was carrying out the
real transformation of the Japanese industrial structure, and the tendency of
members of the old Kishi-Shiina "control" faction to concentrate within the
Enterprises Bureau.

After 1952 and until 1963, all the vice-ministers of MITI represented the faction that had been bred in the *busshibetsu-genkyoku* period of the MCI and in the
Ministry of Munitions. Their highest priority was domestic investment to introduce into Japan a more capital-intensive, heavy industrial, high value-added
economic structure. They were not ignorant of or insensitive to trade, but they
were convinced that Japan had to be able to trade ships, steel, automobiles,
and computers, not just toys and textiles. As it turns out, theirs was the major
contribution to Japan's expansion of trade for, as Ohkawa and Rosovsky have
shown, Japan's growth was not so much "export-led" as it was "cost-reduc-
ing." Japan's trade successes did not arise primarily on the demand side—taking orders from a waiting world—but rather on the supply side—rapid cost
reduction of high-technology products for a large domestic as well as an international market. "Japan's rate of growth of exports," write Ohkawa and
Rosovsky, "has been high and well above world averages because the rate of
growth of its economy and especially of its industry has been high and well
above world averages, and not vice-versa."[80]

The Enterprises Bureau, which MITI historians call the "headquarters" for
the effort to bring about this total economic expansion, needed the ITB, but
not just because the ITB was selling domestic products abroad, or rebuilding
Japan's famous system of giant trading firms (Mitsui Bussan, Mitsubishi Shōji,
C. Itoh, Marubeni-Iida, and so forth), or importing the supplies needed for industry, but above all because it was gathering into one governmental account a
part of the funds that the Enterprises Bureau would be using to import extraordinary amounts of foreign technology and know-how. As Ohkawa and
Rosovsky conclude, "[A]utonomous investment based on borrowed technology
is the major driving force of Japanese economic growth."[81]

One of the easiest ways to compare the relative weights of the ITB and the
Enterprises Bureau in MITI's internal structure is to look at the numbers of

80. *Japanese Economic Growth*, p. 173.
81. Ibid., pp. 39–40. On the Enterprises Bureau, see Tsūsanshō, *Shōkō seisaku shi*, vol. 10:
Sangyō gōrika (Tokyo: Shōkō Seisaku Shi Kankō Kai, 1972), chap. 3.

directors from each bureau selected to fill the top career post in the ministry, that of vice-minister (see Chart 2). Excluding Yamashita Eimei, the administrative vice-minister during 1974, who is the only MITI official to have held both directorial posts and who clearly reflects the MITI "new look" of the 1970s, there have been two ITB directors selected as vice-ministers (none during the 1950s) compared with the Enterprises Bureau's six. One might also omit Yamamoto Sigenobu (vice-minister from April 1966 to May 1968), who is considered a suprafactional official, the one who began to lead the ministry toward its reform of 1973. This then leaves Imai Zen'ei, ITB director from February 1961 to July 1962 and vice-minister from July 1963 to October 1964. It is not accidental that his selection as vice-minister caused the greatest controversy in the ministry since Kishi was chosen minister of the MCI in the Tōjō cabinet (October 1941).

Imai Zen'ei joined the MCI in 1937. During the postwar era, he was always known as a leader of the "international faction." During the Occupation he served in the Economic Stabilization Board and, after MITI was formed, as head of Imports Section One in the ITB. Following the peace treaty and the establishment of normal relations with the United States, he went to Washington as first secretary in the new Japanese embassy. After completing his term overseas he returned to the home office, where he held various important posts, including that of director of the Textiles Bureau, one of the primary bureaus, from August 1958 to February 1961.

One of the more famous incidents associated with Imai's name occurred while he was director of the Textiles Bureau. Imai had been committed to the liberalization of the Japanese economy since the early 1950s, but liberalization did not actually begin until 1961, under the leadership of Prime Minister Ikeda. In a meeting between Ikeda and the leaders of MITI in 1961, the prime minister proposed that the controls designed to protect the domestic textile industry be liberalized, and Imai supported him, the only MITI official to do so and in the face of known opposition to liberalization from the textile industry and from the then minister of MITI, Shiina Etsusaburō. Imai recalls,

I approved of Mr. Ikeda's idea of the promotion of liberalization, but MITI itself was opposed to, or resisted, the open economy. . . . I myself felt the necessity for liberalization because of my experiences of the evils of the controlled economy. . . . Even some younger men in MITI were opposed to liberalization. They were afraid that the change of the economic structure to an open economy based on leadership by the private sector would weaken the powers of MITI.[82]

After serving as director of the ITB, Imai went on to become director general of the Patent Agency, a MITI external bureau. In 1963, he became the central figure in what has come to be known as the "Fukuda Typhoon," and he emerged from it as vice-minister of MITI. By tradition the outgoing vice-

82. *Kaikoroku sengo tsūsan seisaku shi*, pp. 128–130.

Chart 2

The International Trade Bureau and the Enterprises Bureau as Sources
of MITI Vice-Ministers*

From the Ministerial Reorganization of August 1, 1952
to the Ministerial Reorganization of July 25, 1973

	International Trade Bureau				Enterprises Bureau		
	VM**	Director	Period		Director	VM**	Period
1.		Ushiba Nobuhiko	8/1/52–7/16/54	1.	Nakano Tetsuo		8/1/52–8/18/53
2.		Itagaki Osamu	7/16/54–9/16/56	2.	Kiuchi Kakuichi		8/18/53–7/2/54
3.		Matsuo Taiichirō	9/16/56–7/5/60	3.	Tokunaga Hizatsugu	VM	7/2/54–6/15/57
4.		Komuro Tsuneo	7/5/60–2/3/61	4.	Matsuo Kinzō	VM	6/15/57–7/7/61
5.	VM	Imai Zen'ei	2/3/61–7/10/62	5.	Sahashi Shigeru	VM	7/7/61–7/23/63
6.		Matsumura Keiichi	7/10/62–10/25/63	6.	Shimada Yoshito		7/23/63–4/25/66
7.	VM	Yamamoto Shigenobu	10/25/63–6/15/65	7.	Kumagai Yoshifumi	VM	4/25/66–5/25/68
8.		Watanabe Yaeji	6/15/65–4/25/66	8.	Ōjimi Yoshihisa	VM	5/25/68–11/7/69
9.		Yamazaki Ryūzō	4/25/66–9/26/67	9.	Morozumi Yoshihiko	VM	11/7/69–6/15/71
10.		Miyazawa Tetsuzō	9/26/67–11/7/69	10.	Honda Sanae		6/15/71–6/23/72
11.		Harada Akira	11/7/69–6/15/71	11.	Yamashita Eimei***	VM	7/23/72–7/25/73
12.	VM	Yamashita Eimei***	6/15/71–6/23/72				
13.		Komatsu Yūgorō	6/23/72–7/25/73				

SOURCES: Seisaku Jihō Sha, ed., *Nihon no kanchō* (Tokyo: Seisaku Johō Sha, 1970), app. p. 41; and Tsūsan Handobukku Henshū Iinkai, ed., *Tsūsan handobukku 1974* (Tokyo: Shōkō Kaikan, 1973 p. 360.

*On July 25, 1973, the International Trade Bureau (Tsūshō Kyoku) became the International Trade Policy Bureau (Tsūshō Seisaku Kyoku). Between 1952 and 1973, the official translation of the Enterprises Bureau (Kigyō Kyoku) was "Industrial Policy Bureau," which although descriptive of some of the bureau's functions is not an accurate translation. On July 25, 1973, the Enterprises Bureau was renamed, literally, the Industrial Policy Bureau (Sangyō Seisaku Kyoku).

**VM: Director of this bureau was subsequently appointed administrative vice-minister (*jimu-jikan*) of MITI.

***Yamashita became vice-minister on July 25, 1973. He is the only vice-minister to have held the directorship of both the International Trade Bureau and the Enterprises Bureau. It is significant that the last post he held before becoming vice-minister was in the Enterprises Bureau.

minister of MITI names his successor, although by law the minister, a political appointee, has responsibility for all personnel assignments. In 1963, retiring MITI Vice-Minister Matsuo Kinzō named as his successor Sahashi Shigeru, then the director of the Enterprises Bureau and acknowledged throughout the ministry as the leader of the variously named Kishi-Shiina, "control," nationalist, industrial faction. Then the unusual occurred. On July 1, 1963, following a cabinet meeting of economic ministers, MITI Minister Fukuda Hajime (LDP Diet member from Fukui prefecture, member of the then Ōno faction—Funada faction after Ōno's death—former head of the political division of the Dōmei News Agency, and former parliamentary vice-minister of Labor) agreed to join a group of reporters for a cup of tea in the Upper House dining room of the Diet. In the course of their conversation, a journalist raised a question about personnel matters, to which Fukuda made a rare "positive response." He said, and all the newspapers reported, "Since MITI is a service agency, the fact that Sahashi has gotten a bad reputation with industry makes him unsuitable. I think that Imai would be good. I intend to give the next vice-minister's job to Imai."[83]

This remark set off an explosion in the ministry, compared by the MITI Journalists Club—with a good deal of hyperbole—to the army mutiny of February 26, 1936. The Sahashi faction was outraged. Work within the ministry stopped, and everyone debated the case. Some younger men went as far as to attack Fukuda, who was not an ex-bureaucrat, as a "small-time politician" trying to interfere in the affairs of MITI. This did not help relations between MITI and the Diet, where Sahashi's Tokushinhō was stymied by widespread opposition. Among the reasons for Fukuda's intervention are that (1) Fukuda and other politicians disliked the consolidation of control over MITI by the Enterprises Bureau faction; (2) Fukuda was responding to anti-Sahashi sentiment in the financial world over the Tokushinhō; (3) Fukuda and other members of the nonbureaucratic factions in the Diet distrusted the close relationship between Sahashi and former MITI Minister Satō Eisaku, whom they suspected of trying to use MITI to advance his own political interests; and (4) Imai was attractive to the more liberal leaders of the business community and had been described by Ikeda as an "able man." Thus, Imai became the new vice-minister in one of the rare cases of political intervention in bureaucratic affairs.

The story did not end there. By tradition, when one member of an "entering class" in the ministry becomes vice-minister, all other officials of that same class retire voluntarily so that he will have absolute seniority in the ministry. Imai and Sahashi were both of the class of 1937—but Sahashi did not resign. He instead went to the post that Imai had vacated, director general of the Patent Agency, and in 1964 succeeded Imai as vice-minister. Unquestionably, the

MITI elders—retired vice-ministers and bureau directors—arranged this departure from tradition as a way of healing any wounds that may have been opened and dampening down the passions of the whole affair.

Sahashi's successor as vice-minister was Yamamoto Shigenobu. He was also a former ITB director but he actually represented a new orientation in MITI as a whole and the end of the ITB-Enterprises Bureau factional struggle (although the directorship of the Enterprises Bureau continued to be the indispensable last career step before the vice-ministership well into the 1970s). Yamamoto is described in one MITI source as a "man of peace, beloved by all"; another calls him, in a typical Japanese metaphor of praise, "like transparent water" (tōmeisui).[84] Among other things he established a conference of bureau chiefs within the ministry that contributed to greater coordination and harmony. He was an old trade type, having served as first secretary in the Bangkok embassy in the early 1950s, but he was also committed to Japan's trade in heavy and advanced machinery, and with new customers. His planned expansion of Japan's trade with China in 1964 was halted only by the famous "Yoshida letter," the last interference in one of MITI's schemes by the ministry's old nemesis. After his vice-ministership, Yamamoto became the first MITI vice-minister to amakudari (move from government to business) to the automobile industry (in 1974 he was executive director of the Toyota Motor Company).

Yamamoto's most significant act was to internationalize MITI, giving it a direct negotiating role in Japan's economic diplomacy. As director of the ITB he formed half of the two-man Japanese delegation (the other was the chief of the Foreign Ministry's Economic Bureau) to the first meeting of the OECD's trade committee following Japan's admission to the organization. He attended all of the meetings of the Kennedy Round in Geneva, and in 1967, as vice-minister, he carried out the first capital liberalization—what the Japanese press, with its customary hyperbole, dubbed "the second coming of the black ships." Following Yamamoto's example, it has now become standard practice for MITI men to participate in or lead most Japanese delegations to international economic negotiations—for example, Hashimoto Toshikazu, director of MITI's Consumer Goods Industries Bureau, the successor to the old Textiles Bureau, headed the eight-member delegation to the Japanese-American talks of July 1974 to renew the textile agreement of 1971.[85] Yamamoto's vice-

---

84. *Kaikoroku sengo tsūsan seisaku shi,* p. 160; Seisaku Jihō Sha, *Tsūsanshō,* p. 85.

85. Yamamoto's internationalizing of the ITB resulted in its again being divided into two bureaus. Yamamoto explains that the bureau had grown to some eighteen sections with 530 employees. This size plus the fact that the ITB director increasingly had to meet numerous foreign delegations and personally attend international conferences made it impossible for him to administer the bureau properly. Therefore, in April 1965, the bureau was divided into the ITB, with 241 employees, and the Trade Promotion Bureau, with 258 employees. The new bureau handled primarily export matters and foreign aid. Relations between the two

ministership was thus transitional; it witnessed Japan's full emergence into the give-and-take of global economic activities, and it was the first in which radically new problems began to crowd out the old *tsūshō* versus *sangyō* disputes.

MITI is a major economic policy-making and -implementing arm of the Japanese government. Given its role, MITI is a highly public ministry (even though its internal processes are not), and when something goes wrong in the economy, it is usually blamed. During the late 1960s, MITI received a great deal of foreign criticism, but it made no impact on the ministry at all. Toward the end of the decade and into the 1970s, however, MITI became a target for widespread attacks by domestic critics, and this criticism scored. MITI was charged with having promoted growth at the expense of welfare, with having allowed environmental pollution to grow to dangerous levels, with having damaged Japan's foreign relations through its aggressive trade promotion policies, and with a host of other alleged policy failures. The industrial world itself, now fully mature and not necessarily needing further governmental protection, began to resist administrative guidance and to criticize MITI for excessive governmental interference in the private economy.[86]

At first MITI officials reacted philosophically to these developments, and tended to see the criticism as only a sign that their children had grown up. Still, public criticism of pollution and super-fast growth touched off a debate within the ministry over MITI's future role and the possible merits of "the private sector guiding the economy" versus "the government guiding the economy."[87] Finally, MITI officials began to rethink the basic questions of where Japan was going economically and of the kind of industrial structure that would be appropriate for the 1980s and beyond. They carried out some changes in the ministry's internal structure at once—such as the creation on July 1, 1970, of the Environmental Protection and Safety Bureau—but they did not unveil the ministry's new look in its full detail until July 25, 1973.

The 1974 edition of the semiofficial *Tsūsan handobukku* (Trade and industry handbook) describes the administrative reorganization of 1973 as "epochal." In his introduction, MITI administrative vice-minister Yamashita Eimei identifies the fundamental trade and industrial problems facing Japan and his ministry

new bureaus were always cordial; the sole purpose of this reorganization was to increase administrative efficiency. See Yamamoto, in *Kaikoroku sengo tsūsan seisaku shi*, pp. 173–174; and in *Tsūsanshō 20-nen gaishi*, pp. 45–46. For numbers of personnel assigned to the new bureaus, see *Tsūshō sangyō shō nijū nen shi*, endpaper chart.

86. Obayashi Kenji believes that many statements by businessmen protesting governmental interference are strictly for public consumption and that the business community only wishes to present a facade of competition, what he refers to as "Japanese-style free competition." *Nikkei bijinesu*, July 26, 1971, p. 69. However, during the late 1960s there were several significant cases in which major firms defied MITI's administrative guidance, the most famous being the Sumitomo Metals case and the Mitsubishi-Chrysler case.

87. See *Tsūsanshō 20-nen gaishi*, pp. 248–250; Akaboshi, *Shōsetsu tsūsanshō*, pp. 212–213; and Yamamoto, ed., *Keizai kanryō no jittai*, pp. 57–61.

as being, on the domestic side, environmental conservation, the problem of excessive concentration of population in some areas and excessive depopulation in other areas, and inflation. On the international side, the main problems are said to be "market friction" and "unstable currency values." As long-range problems, Yamashita lists (1) the stringency of labor supply, (2) the need to guarantee supplies of resources and energy, and (3) the need to cooperate with foreign countries. He cites eight basic goals or policies that are to guide MITI in the future: (1) the attempt to guarantee price stability and to protect the livelihood of consumers; (2) the need to build a nonpolluting society; (3) the overall development of medium and small enterprises; (4) the securing of stable supplies of resources and energy; (5) "the regulation of industrial activities for the sake of the citizens' welfare and the insuring of proper behavior by enterprises" (exact translation); (6) the building of a high-level industrial society based on a "knowledge-intensive industrial structure"; (7) the advancement of economic exchange between regions of Japan in a way that complies with each region's special characteristics; and (8) the attempt to serve the world economy through international cooperation.

In introducing his new structure in order to deal with these problems, the vice-minister singles out particularly the following organizational innovations: the creation of the Resources and Energy Agency as an adjunct organ of MITI, and the establishment within the home office's Industrial Policy Bureau of new divisions for industrial structure, business behavior, international business affairs, and price policy. Non-MITI commentators looking at the same new structure have been most warm in their praise for the decision to end once and for all the vertical structure of MITI. The new structure cuts horizontally across industries and attempts to end the one-to-one relationship between MITI bureaus and private industries.

The following is a bureau-by-bureau comparison of the new structure with the old:

1. The old International Trade Bureau continues, renamed the International Trade Policy Bureau.

2. The Trade Promotion Bureau of 1965 also continues, renamed the Trade Bureau (officially, in English, the International Trade Administration Bureau).

3. The old Enterprises Bureau has been reorganized as the Industrial Policy Bureau.

4. The Environmental Protection and Safety Bureau, created in 1970, has been enlarged and renamed the Industrial Location and Environmental Protection Bureau.

5. The Light Industries Bureau, the iron and steel sections of the old Heavy Industries Bureau, and the Chemical Industry Bureau have become the Basic Industries Bureau.

6. The Heavy Industries Bureau has been merged into a new organization called the Machinery and Information Industries Bureau; computers and aircraft are now on a par with automobiles and shipbuilding.

7. The Textiles Bureau incorporates various units from other bureaus and reappears as the Consumer Goods Industries Bureau.

8. The old Mining Bureau, whose history goes back to the Meiji period and which was renamed on June 15, 1968, the Minerals, Oil, and Coal-Mining Bureau, has been drastically upgraded into the Natural Resources and Energy Agency, a unit equal in the hierarchy to the Patent Agency and the Medium and Small Enterprises Agency directly under the minister and vice-minister.

9. The Industrial Technology Institute continues unchanged but with several new research tasks assigned.

Whereas MITI used to be organized as nine bureaus and two agencies, after 1973 it began to function as seven bureaus and three agencies. Whether this was a "new MITI" or only a new look was impossible to tell, particularly as the ministry, and Japan as a whole, were confronted almost immediately after the reorganization with the petroleum crisis of 1973 and major fluctuations in the international balance of payments. Further structural innovations seemed likely, however, as Japan sought to adjust to the rapidly changing conditions of the later 1970s.

CONCLUSION

One major deficiency of many foreign summaries of Japanese international economic policy is the failure to stress the extent to which that policy is changing. Therefore, rather than attempting to summarize this policy at a particular time, which can be misleading, I shall instead stress the direction, rate, and motivating forces of the process of change. Following Ike on Japanese foreign policy in general, one may conceive of Japanese economic policy as located on and moving between the poles of a continuum that ranges from a fully internationalist position (such as Hong Kong and Holland) to a highly nationalist, inward-looking position (such as China during the 1960s).[88] Given Japan's need to trade, it is surprising that Japan has for so long been so far away from the internationalist pole. One might expect that Japan would be a staunch defender of free trade, minimal tariff and nontariff barriers to trade, easy access to its own market in return for Japanese access to foreign markets, and internationalist in terms of its domestic economic culture. This has not been the case, but perhaps for more substantive reasons than is commonly supposed.

Japan's earlier protectionist stance is often explained in terms of the pe-

88. Nobutaka Ike, *Japan, the New Superstate*, pp. 101–103.

culiarities of Japanese society and culture—racial homogeneity, language, a continuing ethos of *sakoku* (closed country) and other historical influences, special Japanese forms of business dealing, labor-management relations, and financing—almost none of which is persuasive to Japan's trading partners given Japan's actual economic performance in the postwar world. Nor does MITI adopt such a stance. Instead, it hopes that the rest of the world will understand Japan's postwar economic achievements as a particular form of economic development. As the ministry puts it, "Japan's unparalleled high rate of growth did not come about as a result of favorable conditions. There was absolutely nothing inevitable about this achievement."[89]

In postwar Japan, the government consciously led a massive, popular, difficult campaign to develop a capital-intensive, technology-intensive industrial structure in the face of the theory of comparative costs, which would have recommended labor-intensive types of industries for a country with a large population, few resources, and little accumulated capital. Whether this structure would have resulted anyway without governmental leadership is controversial; many Japanese businessmen say so (and Ohkawa and Rosovsky leave that impression through their use of the concept of "trend acceleration" in the postwar economy). MITI does not think so, pointing in particular to what it regards as generally low quality managerial talents during at least the first postwar decade.[90] The enormous funds required to bring about this capital-intensive structure came during the first period of the campaign from Japan's low wages (and, of course, from other factors such as low social investment and low defense expenditures) and later from the high rate of personal savings of the Japanese people (which were, of course, partly forced savings due to the low welfare orientation of official policies). The main advantage to the people as a whole in the capital-intensive structure is its greater growth rate of productivity over that for light industry. As long as the investment funds could be found, the following "virtuous" cycle was set in motion: wage increases could be made without an increase in costs, which led to an increase in domestic demand, which led to an expansion of production and sales, which led to an increase in wages without a rise in costs. If Japan had pursued a comparative-costs, light-industry economic policy in the postwar world—more or less like that envisaged by the Allied Occupation authorities—it is extremely unlikely that it could have raised per capita income above that prevailing in comparably organized economies (such as in several Latin American countries).

Having largely succeeded by the mid-1960s in altering Japan's industrial structure, the government began to dismantle the controls that had made the

89. Amaya Naohiro, chief, international economic affairs section, International Trade Policy Bureau, "On Japan's Trade and Industrial Policies" (Tokyo: MITI Report JR-1 (73–2), Feb. 1974), p. 1. (The quotation has been altered slightly to correct grammatical errors.)

90. Ibid., p. 4.

building of the new structure possible and to move toward a much more open economy. Some foreign governments have been critical of the pace of this movement, but there can be no doubt about its direction along the continuum. Japan today is as close to the internationalist economic pole as any other advanced economic nation, although the alleged cultural barriers to internationalism still persist. Japan might have been less criticized during the late 1960s if it had moved faster. There seems little doubt that Japan's self-perceived vulnerability and a general sense of caution in economic liberalization caused an undue delay in revaluing its previously undervalued currency, even though it must also be stressed that the United States balance of payments difficulties during the early 1970s arose primarily from consequences of American domestic and foreign policies, and not from policies of other nations. Moreover, the oil crisis of 1973 indicated at the very least that Japanese planners were not totally paranoid when they harped on Japan's vulnerabilities.

A different way of looking at the movement in Japanese foreign economic policy is to conceive of it in terms of its relative emphasis on parameters and parameter-maintenance as distinct from an emphasis on operations and operative variables. By parameters I mean the structural characteristics of international commerce during a particular period; by operative variables I mean a country's policies for maximizing its own gains within a given parametrical structure. Amaya Naohiro, one of MITI's leading theorists, former chief of the international economic affairs section in the ITB, and during 1974 the ministry's *shingikan* (officially translated as "deputy vice-minister"), has written,

The growth of the entire world trade volume exceeded that of the world's total production, increasing from $54.7 billion in 1949 to $372 billion in 1972, an expansion of 6.8 times during a quarter of a century. [This] growth is attributable to [the] GATT and IMF systems to a great extent. Especially with respect to Japan, trade has grown by 56.1 times, far exceeding the world's average, and Japan now has the third largest trade among free countries in terms of absolute volume, surpassed only by the United States and West Germany. *Without [the] GATT and IMF systems, Japan's growth would not have been possible* [italics added].[91]

As Amaya acknowledges, Japan was fortunate in launching its heavy-industrialization campaign during a period in which the international environment was especially favorable. And yet, Japan had little to do with conceiving, bringing about, or maintaining that environment, from which it profited so handsomely. Instead, it recognized the potentialities of the environment as presented, including very low prices for basic commodities until the "oil shock," and it offered to the world a virtuoso performance in how to operate to maximize the benefits obtainable from this environment. However, over time, some analysts have come to believe that Japan was being dangerously insen-

91. Ibid., pp. 14–15.

sitive to the limits of the parameters themselves—that, for example, it should not have been necessary for the United States to pressure Japan into devoting more resources to aid the underdeveloped countries, or that the Japanese might have offered greater leadership to correct or replace the dollar-centered IMF system before it collapsed in 1971, even if American guns-and-butter policies were one major cause of the problem.

Whatever Japan might have done in the past in the way of parameter maintenance, by the 1970s it was much more concerned about parameters than it had been in previous decades. Japan vastly increased the proportion of its GNP going to foreign aid over that of the early 1960s, began actively cultivating suppliers and customers in the Middle East and Southeast Asia, undertook a program of extensive overseas investment, budgeted much larger amounts for domestic research and development than in the past, and determined to bind itself into global industrial life through joint ventures, international diplomacy, and an awakening to resource and environmental conservation. Whether these new policies will be able to perpetuate the prosperity of the first postwar generation is debatable. Nonetheless, Japan in the 1970s has accepted a role in parameter-maintenance that is often more enlightened than the actual policies of many of its critics.

One measure of this change in Japanese orientations is to be found in the varying meanings given to MITI's concept of "industrial structure," a way of thinking about economic affairs that MITI says it invented around 1960 in order to cope with the confusing problems of liberalization and to help understand the meaning of such developments as the consolidation of the European Economic Community.[92] In the early years, the concept of industrial structure (*sangyō kōzō*) was used primarily to make sophisticated international comparisons. Throughout the 1960s, MITI analyzed the structural relationships in Japan among industries, within enterprises, and internationally, and it compared these results with those from studies it made of Japan's two primary reference economies, the United States and West Germany. This work was carried on within the ministry and then referred to MITI's blue-ribbon deliberation council set up in 1961, the Industrial Structure Council. By 1974, the Industrial Policy Bureau had a full-time industrial structure section working on basic analytical problems and servicing the Industrial Structure Council, which publishes innumerable MITI reports on all aspects of the economy after a ministry-council consensus on them has been reached. The most famous of these reports are long-range and future-oriented, but many also deal with practical matters of aid and trade.[93]

92. *Tsūshō sangyō shō nijū nen shi*, p. 11.
93. See, for example, Sangyō Kōzō Shingikai Kokusai Keizai Bukai, *Nihon no taigai keizai seisaku* (Tokyo: Daiyamondo Sha, 1972), 298 pp. The chairman of the council's international economy section in 1972, under whose auspices this report was prepared and released, was Mizukami Tatsuzō, former chairman of the board of Mitsui Bussan (Mitsui Trading Company).

By the mid-1970s, the old concept of industrial structure—how did Japan's structure compare with that of international competitors—was no longer meeting the ministry's needs. The industrial structure section, under Namiki Nobuyoshi, was searching for a new concept that would incorporate the goals of environmental conservation, continued prosperity, and a "higher quality of life" that the public had come to demand after cooling off toward further high-speed growth. Namiki accepted the basic goals laid down in 1971 by the Industrial Structure Council and attempted to spell out the kinds of so-called knowledge-intensive industries that would be desirable for the future: (1) research and development (such as electronic computers, synthetic chemistry, new metals, and special ceramics); (2) sophisticated assembly (such as telecommunications equipment, business machines, and industrially made housing); (3) fashion (such as high-quality clothing and furniture, and expensive sundries); and (4) knowledge-supplying (such as data-gathering and -processing services). But Namiki found it hard to carry the current concept of industrial structure further than this, and he concluded his interim report with a new definition of industrial structure—"the theory of industrial structure is a theory of applied ethics."[94]

By 1974, the best minds in MITI were saying to the public that the people would have to decide on what the future industrial structure "should be." Clearly this was a new orientation, one that asked what kind of world Japan wanted to live in, one more attuned to parameters than to the older questions of how does our industrial structure match up against those of Europe and North America. Needless to say, however, the new definition of industrial structure would never have been relevant had the old one not been so successfully defined and achieved.

94. Namiki Nobuyoshi, chief, industrial structure section, Industrial Policy Bureau, "A Vision of Japan's Industrial Structure" (Tokyo: MITI Report JR-3(74–20), May 1974), p. 15.

The World Economy and Japanese Foreign Economic Policy

GARY R. SAXONHOUSE

THE IDEALS AND OPERATION
OF THE POSTWAR ECONOMIC SYSTEM

Near the close of the Second World War and again shortly after its conclusion, the legal framework of the postwar international economic system began to take shape. In the wake of the experience and intellectual currents of the previous twenty-five years, the commitment shown at the great conferences on the postwar economic order was truly remarkable. With the exception of the Soviet Union (which soon withdrew from the system), the major participants in the conferences that shaped the GATT and Bretton Woods agreements all shared, or unfailingly gave lip service to, a central paradigm: The unrestricted flow of goods and services across national boundaries should be the ultimate aim of foreign economic policy. Like their mid-nineteenth-century counterparts, postwar elites defined the world economic order in Ricardian terms.[1] Free trade at equilibrium exchange rates would lead to maximum world welfare, and this would occur without any country being made worse off.

With a view toward obtaining such a world order, GATT intended that each member nation-state would give up some of its sovereignty to tax and regulate its external trade in order to partially insulate the international trading system

1. For a concise summary of David Ricardo's economic thinking, see William Fellner, *Modern Economic Analysis* (New York: McGraw-Hill, 1961).

from domestic pressure groups.[2] Similarly, the Bretton Woods international financial system encouraged a pooling of some international assets among member nations to insulate the international trading system from the imperatives of domestic contracyclical economic policy. With the memory of the unfortunate experiences of the interwar period still vivid, the conferees at Bretton Woods wanted to ensure that the ideals of the liberal trading system would not be perverted by (1) the ultimately self-defeating attempt of one country to export its unemployment to its partners through competitive exchange-rate depreciation; and (2) the need for a member nation, as a matter of conscious public policy, to contract domestic employment to meet obligations incurred while participating in a liberal trading system.[3]

Even in their framing, however, the great postwar international economic agreements fell short of liberal economic goals. Repeated de jure and de facto recognition of the special economic and political interests of the major signatories sapped the force of the bold general principles enunciated in each agreement. Nonetheless, the outcome of the new arrangements was a giant step away from the economic nationalism and bloc regionalism of the 1930s. Although not fully achieved, the goal of future economic diplomacy was still unfettered international economic exchange. Depoliticizing international economic relations would be the first step in the creation of a stable world order. The major actors in these conferences clearly had regained the faith of John Stuart Mill who, one hundred years earlier, had written,

Commerce first taught nations to see with good will the wealth and prosperity of one another. Before, the patriot, unless sufficiently advanced in culture to feel the world his country, wished all countries weak, poor and ill-governed, but his own; he now sees in their wealth and progress a direct source of wealth and progress to his own country. It is commerce which is rapidly rendering war obsolete, by strengthening and multiplying the personal interests which are in natural opposition to it. And it may be said without exaggeration that the great extent and rapid increase of international trade, in being the principal guarantee of the peace of the world, is the great permanent security for the uninterrupted progress of the ideas, the institutions and the character of the human race.[4]

The strength of this renewal of faith can best be seen by contrasting Mill's version to the bitter observations of a young European refugee during the Second World War:

A textbook for the modern prince should indeed contain, in addition to Machiavelli's classic chapters, extensive new sections on the most efficient use of

2. An account of the founding and operation of GATT is given in Gerald Curzon, *Multi-Lateral Commercial Diplomacy* (London: Michael Joseph, 1965).

3. The best known discussion of the Bretton Woods conference is part of R. F. Harrod's 1950 biography, *The Life of John Maynard Keynes* (London: Collier-Macmillan, 1950).

4. John Stuart Mill, *Principles of Political Economy* (New York: Longmans, Green, 1909), p. 582.

quotas, exchange controls, capital investment and other instruments of economic warfare. . . . The extensive use of international economic relations as an instrument of national power policies has been . . . one of the main characteristics of the period preceding the outbreak of the present war.[5]

The framers of the early postwar world order did not expect that the increase in international commerce, by itself, would be enough to harmonize the varied interests of the world's nation states. The Bretton Woods and GATT arrangements were considered the economic buttresses of the world federalism that emerged with the San Francisco conference and the birth of the United Nations. Hopefully, the separation of economic transactions from the political arena would make it possible for an incipient world federal structure, such as the United Nations, to cope with a manageable level of international political transactions.

Operation of the postwar system

World federalism, as an active intellectual force exerting influence at the highest levels of government, had an extremely short life. Intellectually, the proponents of world federalism could never demonstrate, in the incisive manner of David Ricardo's algebra, that their system would improve world welfare without, in consequence, making any nation worse off. Politically, world federalism, having reached its zenith with the victory of the Allies in 1945, foundered on postwar Soviet-American mistrust and confrontation and the resurgence of the traditional nation-states in Europe. In place of the universalism characteristic of the early postwar political thinking, the Cold War bred a largely American-managed and -financed security system.

The change in the international political climate had profound consequences for the international economic arrangements hammered out in the early postwar period. The conferences that worked out the postwar economic arrangements stood for universality and reciprocity. It should be recalled that the Soviet Union was a major actor in the Bretton Woods conference. Although gold *tranches* in the International Monetary Fund and subscriptions to the World Bank were based on differing economic and financial potential, the presumption was that ultimately all nations would participate on an equal footing in a nondiscriminatory, fully convertible, international commercial and financial system. With the onset of the Cold War, however, participation in international economic institutions became circumscribed, and the system that had been intended to harmonize the economic interests among all nations took on a different cast. Free trade and multilateral clearing of all financial transactions among the non-Communist nations remained the goal of policy-makers, but

5. Albert O. Hirschman, *National Power and the Structure of Foreign Trade* (Berkeley and Los Angeles: University of California Press, 1945), p. *ix*.

the system as a whole acquired decided security overtones. The IMF and the GATT became structures for shoring up the weaker economies of the anti-Communist alliance. Analogously with the military security system, the international economic system became American-managed and -financed.

Non-Communist commodity trade:
special treatment for Japan?

Changing American policies toward occupied Japan reflected the changing views on international political and economic relations. By 1949, the early Occupation goals of reforming and democratizing the Japanese economy had given way to policies aimed at its full economic recovery so that it could serve as a vital building block in the newly envisioned American-East Asian security system. To this end, American policy-makers accorded Japan special treatment in the American-sponsored postwar economic system. Like Western Europe, Japan was allowed to severely restrict the access of American products to its market while retaining relatively free access to the American market. During the 1950s, however, strenuous efforts were made to encourage Western Europe to accept commercial and financial policies consistent with a liberal international system. No comparable pressure was exerted on Japan, in part because Japan was relatively less developed.

European policy-makers, however, were reluctant to accord Japan special privileges because of its semideveloped state and strategic position in East Asia.[6] They were disinclined to allow unfettered Japanese participation in the international economic system—especially in view of continuing Japanese truculence toward entering such a system on the same basis as the United States and Europe. Thus, Japan was not allowed to enter the GATT until 1955. Even then, European and other nations (comprising one-third of world trade) invoked Article 55 to maintain special restrictions on imports from Japan. As late as 1960, when trade among the nations of Western Europe and the United States had been substantially liberalized, goods of Japanese origin remained subject to considerable discrimination. For example, of the 1,097 products designated in the Brussels Tariff Nomenclature, France discriminated against 357 Japanese products, Italy discriminated against 228 Japanese products, and West Germany discriminated against 34 products.[7]

6. Perhaps because of the enormous differences in size in the 1950s between the United States and its major allies, the differing American, West European, and Japanese policies in the 1950s were inevitable. The economic theory of alliances suggests the larger a country is the higher it will value the output of an alliance. Larger countries will end up paying a greater than proportionate share of the general cost of an alliance. This theory is presented by Mancur Olson and Richard Zeckhauser in "An Economic Theory of Alliances," in Bruce M. Russett, ed., *Economic Theories of International Politics* (Chicago: Markham, 1968).

7. Tsūsanshō, *Kenedei-raando no keiryō bunseki* (Tokyo, 1968).

Notwithstanding the weakness of many links in the multilateral commercial relationships among non-Communist nations, the period from the late 1940s through the mid-1960s did see a great liberalizing of commercial relations. American encouragement and pressure on Western Europe was relatively successful, and a series of reciprocal tariff reductions on manufactured products reached its culmination in the reductions negotiated in the Kennedy Round agreements in 1967. During these negotiations, for the first time, Japan participated as a major actor. As trade in manufacturing products was being liberalized, however, Europe and Japan exhibited considerable reluctance on liberalizing trade in agricultural products. Indeed, the establishment of the European Economic Community's Common Agricultural Policy in 1962 suggested increasingly illiberal trade in such commodities. Although the U.S. had once permitted a lack of reciprocity in particular commodities to its own disadvantage, by the end of the Kennedy Round the United States had reestablished the principle of reciprocity. Washington did, however, continue to contribute to European integration and Japanese political stability by assenting to international commercial arrangements that permitted relatively free trade in areas where the U.S. did not have comparative advantage, and relatively and increasingly restrictive trade in commodity groups in which it did have a comparative advantage.[8]

The primacy of the dollar:
advantages and disadvantages for Japan[9]

The Bretton Woods system was built with the experience of the 1930s in mind; nations should be able to participate in a liberal international trading system without having it cause cyclical unemployment. As national participation in the Bretton Woods system required that the international demand and supply for the national currency be in balance to correct cyclical imbalances, national central banks were permitted to buy and sell national currency in exchange for international reserve assets. Given the interwar experience of national attempts to export unemployment through competitive devaluation, the postwar system sought to limit exchange-rate adjustment to instances of secular disequilibrium. Financial experts in the immediate postwar period, not anticipating the vast improvements that would occur in economic life, had a basically cyclical view of the international economy, and thus tended to dismiss the importance of secular disequilibrium and the need for exchange-rate adjustment.

8. Evidence supporting this observation is presented in A. Yamada, "Yunyū jishuku to kojin no sokei bunseki," *Bōeki to kanzei,* Jan. 1970.
9. This section is developed in more detail in Gary Saxonhouse, "A Review of U.S.-Japanese Economic Relations," *Asian Survey,* Sept. 1972.

This basically cyclical view of the international economy made it impossible for the architects of the postwar financial system to foresee the central problems of the system they had constructed. From the system's inception, gold and the U.S. dollar served as the key reserve assets. Additions to the world gold stock from mining operations, however, proved to be insufficient to provide adequate liquidity for the rapidly expanding international economy. Growing industrial uses for gold exacerbated this problem. With gold unable to meet the growing world liquidity needs, increases in international reserves could only come through U.S. dollars, and these increases could only come about through deficits in the American balance of payments. So great was the confidence in the American economy that continuing deficits in the late 1940s and early 1950s were viewed from all sides as a highly desirable means of adding desperately needed liquidity to the world economy.

In usurping the intended function of the IMF and becoming the international banker of the non-Communist world economy, the United States found itself subjected to unique standards of international behavior. On the one hand, the United States was freed from formal economic constraint on its international activities: it did not have to rely on the sales of American commodities and assets abroad to pay for its purchase of foreign commodities or of the assets and equities in foreign companies, its underwriting of other nations' defense budgets, and its stationing of troops overseas. On the other hand, quite apart from the paucity of American international activities, the nature of the evolution of the Bretton Woods system made the secular overvaluation of the dollar inevitable. The special feature of the Bretton Woods system was the fixed price between the dollar and other national currencies and, as a corollary, between the dollar and gold. The continued use of both international reserve assets in clearing international accounts rested on the stability of the relationship between them.

Although stability between the dollar and gold was the foundation of the system in the 1950s and early 1960s, the same cyclical view that ignored the need for growing liquidity also ignored the need for relatively frequent exchange-rate adjustment. If anything, the spectre of competitive devaluation led to official language that positively discouraged exchange-rate adjustment. Given the political difficulties inherent in parity changes because of their uneven impact across a national economy, an international monetary system that does not encourage such changes will likely undergo fewer than are economically necessary. Deficit nations must have international cooperation or they must devalue. Only the largess of other nations enabled the deficit United Kingdom to maintain the value of the pound in the mid-1960s. Surplus Japan needed no international help to maintain an undervalued currency through August 1971.

As the exchange-rate adjustments were made with respect to reserve assets, the system worked to secularly appreciate the dollar. Thus, the economic im-

peratives of the Cold War led to American responsibility for international
financial management which, although giving fairly free financial scope to
American international activities, handicapped the development of American
export industries and encouraged more American overseas investment than
would have been the case if the foreign exchange value of the dollar had been
kept in equilibrium. Japanese and Western European industries that were in
competition with American industries benefited from this overvaluation of the
dollar. In Europe, this improved performance came at the price of increasing
susceptibility to a takeover by American interests. Japan's tight restrictions on
direct foreign investment enabled it, through the mid-1960s, to avoid substantial American equity in its industrial advance.

*The worldwide advance of American-based
international manufacturing corporations*

Although the American experience of managing international commerce and
finance was not without precedent, the character of the American-based international manufacturing corporation in the postwar period remains unique.
What was unique was not that there was large-scale migration of capital, entrepreneurship, and technology, but rather that large American corporations
increasingly sent these elements abroad as part of a centralized global market
strategy. What made this a key feature of the postwar world economy was not
so much the dollar's role as international money (though this was clearly fa-
cilitating) but (1) the growing postwar gap in technology between the United
States and other advanced countries; (2) the complexity and malleability of the
new technology, which made it difficult for a corporate developer of a new
technology to fully recapture the rents associated with its successful development in one country except by direct participation in the use of the technology
in other countries; and (3) the improvements in communication which made
the efficient execution of a centralized global corporate strategy possible. Thus,
through the 1950s and into the 1960s, American actors probably effected the
most important transfers of technology through the instrumentality of foreign
direct investment.

Japanese reaction to this worldwide transfer of American technology contrasted sharply to the policies of Western Europe. Europe at first welcomed the
advent of American corporations, but Japan, initially with American Occupation encouragement, sought to prevent their entry. Although the earliest restrictions were designed to prevent the transfer of Japanese assets to Americans at
fire-sale prices, the restrictions in the 1950s were framed largely with an eye
to the still precarious Japanese balance of payments. Through the late 1950s,
Japan controlled the flow of direct foreign investment by allowing repatriation
of earnings only from foreign investments that had been validated by the government at the time of their entry. As such validation was given sparingly, only

IBM's willingness to forego the possibility of repatriating its earnings (together with Japanese appreciation of the extraordinarily sophisticated nature of its technology base) allowed Nihon IBM to flourish and dominate Japan's substantial computer market.[10]

With Japanese assumption of advanced-country status in the IMF and full Japanese membership in the OECD, the rationale and the legal and administrative framework for restricting and guiding foreign investment in Japan changed. Japanese officials, particularly in MITI, tended to stress the danger that substantial foreign direct investment would dampen the exceptionally rapid ongoing structural transformation of the Japanese economy. They suggested that, for largely cultural reasons, foreign management operating in such key Japanese industries as automobiles and heavy electrical equipment would find it difficult to take full advantage of the special dynamic opportunities offered by the rapidly transforming Japanese economy. Indeed, because it was widely recognized in Japan that, contrary to the prevalent business ideology, foreign-based international corporations were not truly multinational in the objective function they sought to maximize, there was fear that foreign management would consciously choose not to take full advantage of the opportunities. At the same time, the great international corporations, by their very nature, largely operated in those industries whose technology dictated oligopolistic market structures. Thus, an entrenched foreign presence in a major Japanese sector, could prevent the growth of a Japanese competitor who did attempt to take advantage of such opportunities.

More fundamentally and most particularly in the mid-1960s, major figures in the Japanese government chose to justify restrictions on foreign investment on the grounds that large Japanese-based and -dominated international corporations were necessary for the future survival of Japanese national identity. In an analysis remarkably similar to that of France's Servan-Schreiber (and as wrong in its economics as it was confused in its identification of technology with culture), the proposition was widely accepted that important advances in technology were developed only in the largest corporations and that such advances, being of exceptional value, were diffused exclusively within the corporation.[11] The large corporations, as the carriers of the most progressive technology, would come into economic, political, and cultural dominance in the last third of the twentieth century, and their international flexibility and organizational competence would come to attenuate the sovereignty of other institutions. Thus, if Japan was to participate in this new world order, restrictions on foreign direct investment were in order. Opportunities for growth within the Japanese domestic market were to be reserved for nascent Japanese-based international corporations.

10. Tsūsanshō, *Gaishikei kigyō no dōkō* (Tokyo, 1972).
11. Servan-Schreiber's thesis is presented in greatest detail in J. Servan-Schreiber, *The American Challenge* (New York: Atheneum, 1969).

These Japanese regulations and restrictions meant that, if rents for the development of technology were going to be earned from the Japanese economy, they would most likely be gained through the vehicle of a licensing agreement. Thus, many American corporations, although negative to the idea of licensing and quite capable of successfully exploiting their technology in Japan, agreed to license their technology to Japanese firms. Indeed, after standardizing for size, Japan was the world's preeminent licensee in the 1950s and early 1960s.[12]

Although it is certainly true that the transfer of technology to Japan was diminished by restrictions on foreign direct investment, the extent of the diminution was limited because (1) much of the technology Japan wanted during this period was already widely available, and typically licensors did not seem to feel that they were giving up important proprietary opportunities; and (2) most technological transfer between Japan and other countries did not appear to flow through proprietary channels at all. Although various sources attribute as much as 30 to 60 percent of the postwar Japanese economic growth to technological improvement and assimilation, as late as 1970 Japanese firms were paying no more than $500 million in licensing fees and royalties.[13] It is impossible to rationalize this small figure by assuming massive mistakes by foreign licensors and/or overwhelming monopsony power by Japanese licensees acting in concert with the Japanese government. It seems more likely that most technology and technological information either reached Japan through nonproprietary channels or was produced by the Japanese themselves. Thus, Japan's special position within the American-dominated system of international flows of technology, capital, and management, which was inextricably linked with Japan's special position within the American-sponsored international commodity trading system, was achieved at relatively little economic cost.

Postwar natural resource exploitation

If the enormous overseas expansion of American-based multinational manufacturing corporations is without precedent, the use of foreign management, capital, and technology in developing natural resources for export to advanced countries is a familiar historical pattern. Indeed, this process has provided much of the motivation for the overseas expansion of European civilization over the past five hundred years. The postwar period, with its mammoth expansion of the international petroleum industry, has seen an acceleration of foreign direct investment in natural resources. Over four-fifths of this investment has

12. This calculation is worked out in Gakujijutsu Chō, *1970—Gaikoku gijustu dōnyū nenji hōkoku* (Tokyo, 1972).

13. This analysis is discussed in more detail in Gary Saxonhouse and Hugh Patrick, "Japan and the United States: Bilateral Tensions and Multilateral Issues in the Economic Relationship," in Donald C. Hellmann, ed., *Critical Choices for Americans*, vol. XII, *China and Japan: A New Balance of Power*, (Lexington, Mass.: Heath, 1976).

been concentrated in the petroleum industry, and American-based corporations have undertaken almost two-thirds of all foreign direct investment in natural resources.[14]

While American firms were conspicuous for their presence in the worldwide exploitation of natural resources, Japanese firms were conspicuous for their absence. With the notable exception of Japanese participation in the Arabian Oil Company, through the mid-1960s Japanese overseas investment in natural resources exploitation was negligible. Despite Japan's overwhelming reliance on imported raw materials and fuels, there was almost no upstream investment. Rather than invest in natural-resource exploitation or participate heavily in most long-term purchase agreements, Japanese enterprises preferred to maintain maximum flexibility. Their tactics were a return to Japan's pre-Pacific War policies of aggressive procurement at minimum price.[15] In a world where, thanks to extensive American investment, raw materials and fuels were abundant and natural resource prices were falling, such policies were highly successful, but they had important consequences for the Japanese economy and polity.

The Japanese oil industry

In the early postwar period, Japan's complete reliance on the major international oil firms for petroleum products allowed these firms to become dominant in the refining of oil and the distribution of petroleum products within Japan. Oil was the only major Japanese industry (electronic computers at this early date were still rather exotic) in which foreign capital was able to gain substantial equity participation.[16]

MITI was not happy with this development. After 1952, it used its control over the allocation of foreign exchange for the importation of crude oil to increase refinery capacity and wholesale market shares of firms in which Japanese held a majority position. In 1962, as foreign exchange allocation became a thing of the past, the Diet passed legislation that gave MITI the legal power to ration permits for both refinery capacity and marketing facilities. This substantial effort on the part of MITI bore some fruit. By the mid-1960s, the refinery capacity and marketing position of the Japanese-dominated firms in the Japanese domestic market were almost comparable to those of foreign-dominated firms.

Nevertheless, by Japanese standards, foreign equity participation in petro-

14. Nihon Keizai Kenkyū Sentā, *Sekai no naka no Nihon keizai*, vol. 2 (Tokyo, 1972).

15. Detailed attention is given Japan's pre-Pacific War raw cotton procurement policies in K. Seki, *Nihon mengyō ron* (Tokyo, 1956).

16. Nihon Sekiyu Kyōkai, "Sōgō energy seisaku," *Sekiyu gyōkai no suii* (Tokyo, 1966).

leum refinery and distribution remained unusually high, and by both foreign and Japanese standards the industries were unusually fragmented. Almost alone among advanced industrialized nations, Japan had not a single oil firm—state-owned or private—which was vertically integrated from the production of crude oil through to final marketing operations. The oil industry in Japan was and remains divided between a relatively large number of firms that refine crude oil and a different but smaller group of firms that market petroleum products. Related to the industry's market structure, and again almost unique among advanced industrial nations, over 85 percent of Japan's crude oil is supplied by the major international oil companies.

The fragmentation of the industry was the direct result of MITI policies. Apart from the political pressure exerted by MITI, many business groups, all of whom wanted a share of what was thought of as a highly profitable business, considered it desirable to keep the industry fragmented as a means of keeping oil prices low. Where it developed that the major consumers of oil in Japan were heavy industry, for once MITI found great virtue in the competitive process. Oil was thought to be too vital to the basic thrust of the Japanese development process to allow important monopolistic elements to control its refining or distribution. The possible consequences of such fragmentation for technological change, overseas exploration, or market power in the purchasing of raw materials—all important considerations in MITI's undermining of antitrust enforcement in other areas—were deemed unimportant in this instance. Crude oil was readily available, and for much of the postwar period its price had been falling!

Post-World War II:
Nineteenth-century comparisons

In assaying the American role in organizing and managing the international economic system after World War II, the obvious standard of comparison is nineteenth-century Great Britain. In Britain's partially successful advocacy of free trade, in the role of sterling as international unit of account and store of value, in the exportation of entrepreneurship and technology, and in the exploitation of natural resources, the nineteenth-century world economy and Great Britain's role therein was never far from what American economic policy-makers were seeking in the early postwar period. Although policy-makers in both Great Britain in the nineteenth century and America after the Second World War shared a common interest in depoliticizing many facets of international economic relations, it is unclear whether they also had a common hierarchy of values. After 1947, American policy-makers justified international economic reforms largely in terms of national security. The relationship of in-

ternational economic reforms and national security for British policy-makers, at least during a number of episodes in the nineteenth century, seems most
complex.

Analogies for postwar Japan's foreign economic policies are more difficult.
Superficially, Japan might be thought of as playing Germany to the United
States' Great Britain. German influence on Japanese political, military, and intellectual organization and thought was pronounced between the 1880s and the
end of the Pacific War. Senior Japanese economic bureaucrats through the
1960s were clearly more familiar with the writings of nineteenth-century German economic protectionists such as List and Schmoller than with English
classical economists. Nonetheless, the analogy is incomplete. Although Germany had free access to the British market while it was employing highly
protectionist policies, German policies were framed within the context of an
aggressive military posture. To this extent, security of overseas raw materials
and foodstuffs was an issue of considerable concern to the German General
Staff. Autarchic policies were pursued at home at the same time that colonial
expansion proceeded (often unsuccessfully) abroad. Unlike postwar Japan,
there were numerous, energetic German efforts to pursue overseas raw materials exploitation. Finally, and perhaps most important, Germany's protectionist policies were pursued in an international economic environment that was
rapidly retreating from the high point of liberalism reached in the mid-
nineteenth century. The unhappy social consequences of the drastic fall in
wheat prices, which accompanied the westward expansion of the American
railroad, led to a general reassessment of the virtues of free trade. In addition to
Germany, France and Italy among other European countries were employing
heavily protectionist policies by the late nineteenth century. By contrast, for
almost twenty years after World War II, Japan's highly restrictive foreign
economic policies differed sharply with the gradually liberalizing outlook of
much of the rest of the non-Communist developed world. Japan's position in
the postwar world may be realistically assessed as historically unique.

TRANSITION TO A NEW
INTERNATIONAL ECONOMIC SYSTEM

The American-sponsored and -managed international economic system was
highly successful in achieving the goals for which it had been constructed. The
efficacy of international economic institutions had much to do with the
widespread economic growth and improved national well-being that were
characteristic of all non-Communist developed countries in the postwar period,
and that led inevitably to the demise of those very international economic institutions. In the early postwar world, capital stock, advanced technology, in-

ternational reserve assets, and, to a somewhat lesser extent, natural resources had been concentrated in the hands of the United States, but by the mid-1960s other major nodes of economic power had arisen. Where once the giant size, vast technological superiority, and self-sufficiency of the American economy relative to the rest of the non-Communist international economic system made the cost of economic leadership small and the legitimacy of such leadership unchallengeable, the emergence of other major economic centers changed all this. American corporate and union groups began to question America's unequal trade relations with some of its major trading partners. In turn, other major participants in the Bretton Woods system began to query the primacy of the dollar in international economic relations, suggesting, in increasingly impatient terms, that economic conditions in the United States and elsewhere no longer justified the special advantages conferred on the dollar. Similarly, the worldwide diffusion of advanced technology as well as the institutions for producing it led to increased host-country reluctance to give American-based corporations free reign to operate within their boundaries in both manufacturing and natural resource development. Indeed, the persistent, rapid, postwar growth of economically advanced countries buoyed the demand for fuels, foods, and raw materials sufficiently to allow at least some host countries to extract for themselves a good share of the economic rents associated with the exploitation of natural resources.

Growing strains in commodity trade

The growing economic strength of Western Europe and Japan made it almost inevitable that important interest groups within the United States would question the basis of international commodity trade. This questioning would have arisen even if one of the two major areas of American comparative advantage—American agricultural exports—had not been heavily and, in the case of Western Europe, increasingly restricted. The rapid growth of the advanced economies in the postwar period had produced considerable structural evolution in all nations and done much to change the worldwide distribution of productive resources. Large amounts of capital, skills, and relevant experience have accumulated where relatively little existed previously. Sizable increases in per capita income have changed the nature and amount of demand for goods and services. These epochal changes have altered national and international industrial structures. In Western Europe and Japan, the character and scale of this change has been much affected by participation in an international trading system that has continuously liberalized trade in manufactures. The United States has also experienced rapid structural evolution during the postwar period. In contrast to Western Europe and Japan, the American structural evolution was largely unaffected by participation in international trade. Long-term trends have been dominated by the increasingly capital-rich (and labor-scarce) nature of the American economy and by the relatively slow growth in the demand for goods, as opposed to services, on the part of the American consumer.[17]

For much of the postwar period, the fact of the domestic American economy's insulation from the international economy (at the same time that there was extensive American participation in the international economy in absolute terms) was widely appreciated. In the late 1960s and early 1970s, however, a cyclical downturn in the American economy coincided with a large shift from surplus to deficit in the American balance of trade and the presence of large quantities of manufactured imports from the new industries of America's leading trading partners. These new developments did much to undermine that American sense of international economic paternalism, which had sprung from relative and absolute economic strength. Although evidence was almost entirely lacking, the belief became widespread in the United States that import competition was pushing structural transformation at a pace which was socially intolerable. Liberal trade policies required that resources flow in and out of national industries in accordance with comparative advantage. As long as this process proceeds slowly little social harm is done. When this process accelerates rapidly, considerable social harm becomes a possibility. As American union leaders have been fond of pointing out, the history of economic policy in the twentieth century, and perhaps more so at other times, is the history of attempts to mitigate the unfettered ravages of the market economy. Intervention and protection is common when the determinants of structural change are domestic; should social conscience be suspended when the determinants are external?[18]

In the early 1970s, protectionist sentiment came to focus on the large, rapidly growing, export-oriented Japanese economy. Japanese exports to the United States had been growing far more rapidly than those of any other major U.S. trading partner. Indeed much of the change in the overall U.S. balance of trade can be attributed to the change, during the 1960s, of the American bilateral trade balance with Japan from surplus to very substantial deficit. As the volume and structure of Japanese exports to the United States were growing and changing, however, legal and administrative barriers, both explicit and implicit, continued to hinder the export of American products to Japan. Although popular American concern about the impact of both imports from Japan and

17. Gary Saxonhouse, "U.S.-Japanese Economic Relations."
18. In addition to the works already cited, this proposition is given careful analytical and empirical examination in Gary R. Saxonhouse, "Impact of Japanese Imports on American Economic Welfare," in Allen W. Taylor, ed., *Perspectives on Japanese American Economic Relations* (Cambridge, Mass.: Ballinger, 1974). Accompanying comments by Nate Weinberg, research director of the United Auto Workers, and George Ecklund, chief economist of the United States Tariff Commission, in the same volume, are also instructive.

Japanese restrictions on American exports was rooted in misinformation and hysteria, the slowness of the Japanese in removing these restrictions probably dealt a mortal blow to the implicit principle of lack of reciprocity in American trading relations with other non-Communist advanced economies. American willingness to accept lack of full reciprocity, already shaken by political détente, became a dead letter in the wake of Japanese inaction in the late 1960s and early 1970s.

The new American attitudes regarding continued discrimination against American products, and related social and economic threats posed by foreign and particularly Japanese imports, became manifest in 1971 with (1) the diplomatically unhappy resolution of the Japan-American synthetic textile dispute; (2) the imposition of a special 10 percent tariff surcharge on all imports as part of the Nixon New Economic Policy; and (3) the introduction of and the widespread union support for the Burke-Hartke Bill, which would have frozen foreign-manufactured products' share of American markets at the levels of the late 1960s. Although improvement in the unemployment situation in the United States in 1972 and early 1973 took the edge off rhetoric and killed the Burke-Hartke legislation, 1971 was truly a watershed in American foreign economic policy. Secretary of the Treasury Connally, moving in tandem with the Nixon-Kissinger conception of American self-interest in a multipolar world, broke sharply with the major themes in American foreign economic policy until that time.

The persistence of the hitherto unusual American posture of aggressively asserting a narrowly circumscribed view of self-interest in international trade relations can be seen most clearly in (1) the unusually large number of investigations and actions undertaken in the past three years against foreign products by the U.S. Treasury Department and the U.S. Tariff Commission under the provisions of antidumping statutes; (2) the unilateral American export embargo on soybeans in June 1973; and (3) the lack of real American initiatives in the so-called Tokyo Round of negotiations on the reduction of tariff and nontariff barriers, except in regard to European and Japanese commitments on trade in agricultural commodities.

Japan in a new era of international commercial policy. Enormous American diplomatic pressure—together with a growing appreciation of the benefits Japan might derive from full participation in a liberal, multilateral commodity trading system and a fuller recognition that most restrictions on manufactured imports would have an extremely small impact on the Japanese economy given its stage of development—has prompted major changes in Japan's policy.[19] Japan has taken active steps to remove remaining legal and administrative bars

19. Empirical work on the impact of Japanese government policies on Japan's external sector was presented in Gary Saxonhouse, "Japanese Foreign Policy and Economic Growth" (mimeo), an earlier version of the present article and available on request from the author.

hampering the import of manufactured products, and positive action to encourage American imports.[20] American pressure has also had considerable influence on the direction of Japanese exports. In keeping with the general American diplomatic posture of attempting to reduce foreign pressure on its domestic markets, the U.S. has encouraged members of the European Community to reduce their remaining, and not inconsiderable, barriers to the import of Japanese manufactured products. The partial success of this policy has been one important element in the large increase in the share in total Japanese exports directed to Western Europe during 1972, 1973, and early 1974.

Although the easing of both Japanese and European restrictions, together with the possibilities for East-West trade implicit in political détente with the Soviet Union and China, may be viewed as an important step toward achieving the early postwar ideal of truly universal liberal, multilateral trade, the new American economic policy has also had a contrary impact.[21] Some have interpreted the unilateral American embargo on soybeans as a calculated effort to ward off even stricter controls, which supposedly hysterical Japanese speculation in the spring of 1973 might have brought about. Basically, however, it represents an American attempt to deal with a domestic problem at the expense of its trading partners. This action, affecting a major source of protein in the Japanese diet, became symbolic of a whole range of food-supply problems in 1973 and 1974, and no doubt helped to tip the forces surrounding international agricultural trade policy toward increasing protection.

These events of 1973 cast considerable doubt over the already precarious prospects for liberalizing international agricultural trade and, with them, the long-term international economic interests of the United States. In 1972 and early 1973, Japanese government planners and private research organizations were forecasting a continued and fast accelerating decline of the place of agriculture in Japanese industrial structure in response to government programs of rationalization and liberalization. By early 1975, long-term forecasts assumed strenuous government effort at raising Japan's self-sufficiency in food. The share of agriculture, forestry, and fisheries in gross domestic product is assumed to be almost twice as large as had been previously projected.[22] In Japan as elsewhere, the soybean embargo has enabled the ever-tenacious farmers' organizations and Norinsho (Ministry of Agriculture and Forestry) bureaucrats to re-enter the policy mainstream.

20. The detailed discussion in Tsūsanshō, *Sekai keizai no naka no Nihon* (Tokyo, 1972), is quite explicit on this last point.
21. A discussion of Japanese economic relations with Eastern Europe, the Soviet Union, and China will be presented later in this chapter.
22. For an example of an earlier forecast, see Nihon Keizai Kenkyū Sentā, *Sekai no naka no Nihon keizai*. The later forecast is given in Nihon Keizai Kenkyū Sentā, *Sekai keizai to Nihon no shōrai* (Tokyo, 1975).

The final breakdown of the Bretton Woods arrangements

American unhappiness with the way the international trading system had evolved by the early 1970s was matched by European and Japanese impatience with the increasingly onerous asymmetries in the international financial system. By the late 1960s, many foreign economies that had once viewed deficits in American balance of payments as desirable now found themselves awash with American-created liquidity and therefore saw the American deficits as highly unattractive dollar imperialism.[23] With the increasing inroads of American-based corporate control in strategic sectors of the West European economies and the increasing unpopularity of American overseas military activities, the lack of formal economic constraints on American international activities and apparent American disinterest in bringing its balance of payments into equilibrium became almost intolerable.[24]

In view of the absence of a liquidity problem, the Americans accepted the necessity of returning their balance of payments to equilibrium. Official American reaction, however, rejected the contention that the economic and political burdens of such an adjustment should essentially fall on the United States. Moreover, it vigorously defended the acquisitional activities of American-based international corporations and the interventionist posture of American national security. From the American perspective, the problem with the Bretton Woods system was that its workings made it increasingly difficult for the United States to create sufficient external demand for dollars through foreign sale of goods and services. The failure of nations with a secular surplus in their balance of payments to appreciate their currency while secularly deficit nations were forced to devalue was over time working secularly to appreciate the dollar, the system's unit of account. American policy-makers laid the blame for international financial difficulties at the doorstep of the surplus nations, in particular Japan.

The Japanese government was aware of the American government's attitude on the need for correction of the Japanese surplus. While explicitly and quite rightly rejecting full Japanese responsibility for the malaise in the international financial arrangements, the Satō government in early 1971 announced an Eight-Point Program for reducing the extent of the Japanese surplus. Rather than appreciating the yen in accordance with official American wishes, the Satō government preferred to adjust the Japanese balance of payments through

23. The foremost expression of this view is contained in Charles de Gaulle (Terence Kilmartin, trans.), *Memoirs of Hope: Renewal and Endeavor* (New York: Simon and Schuster, 1971), p. 371.

24. Note the commentary contained in Ryutaro Komiya, "Recent U.S. Foreign Economic Policy from a Japanese Point of View," in C. Fred Bergsten, ed., *Toward a New World Trade Policy: The Maidenhead Papers* (Lexington, Mass.: Lexington Books, 1975).

(1) liberalizing import quotas and tariffs and removing a variety of export subsidies, thereby also responding to another set of insistent American demands; (2) encouraging substantial direct and portfolio investment by Japanese enterprise abroad, thereby ensuring Japanese international economic involvement proportionate to the growing size of the Japanese economy; and (3) reflating the domestic economy via government expenditures in the long-neglected areas of social welfare and social infrastructure. When this program was announced in June 1971, American government and business circles greeted it with considerable skepticism. The total package did not seem to have sufficient impact to offset quickly and substantially the burgeoning Japanese surplus and the attendant speculative pressure on the dollar. By the summer of 1971, Japanese and American attitudes had reached the classic impasse of the Bretton Woods arrangements—the surplus balance of payments nation feeling no need to move quickly and the reserve asset nation feeling unable to act. The real crisis, however, was the near impossibility for patient negotiations to resolve this deadlock. The ease of speculation was yet another flaw in the old system. Because parities were changed only rarely and long after the change had become economically necessary, the direction of the parity change was obvious and, thus, speculation was riskless. Therefore serious public and private discussion of the issue at the time of the crisis was extremely difficult.

If Japan would not appreciate, the United States would not devalue, and persistent negotiation was out of the question, the old system had to fall. The same world view that had spawned an aggressive assertion of "American interests" in international commercial policy prompted a related assertion in the international financial system. As part of the August 1971 New Economic Policy, the dollar's convertibility into gold was formally ended, and Japan and other surplus nations were bludgeoned into appreciating their currencies by official ultimata. The imposition of a surcharge on foreign imports and a new investment tax credit discriminating against producers' goods of foreign origin were also undertaken—two policy steps that would be rescinded only after surplus countries had responded in a fashion deemed appropriate by the American government. The American tactics worked; by December 1971, the Smithsonian Agreements ratified the substantial reevaluation of the yen and the mark.[25]

Official American dissatisfaction with the yen parity did not end with the Smithsonian Agreements. Feeling that the yen was still undervalued, the U.S. continued to press for further Japanese reevaluation. The initial but predictably slow response of American trade flows to the worldwide changes in exchange rates strengthened American resolve. Finally in February 1973, in the midst of continued speculation against the dollar, the United States unilaterally deval-

25. For a Japanese view of the Smithsonian Agreements and the international economic environment in its aftermath, see Hisao Kanamori, *Nihon keizai no shinjigen* (Tokyo, 1972).

ued the inconvertible dollar against gold. Shortly thereafter, all major currencies began to float against the dollar. The Bretton Woods era was finally over.

The yen in a new era of international financial relations. Although the strength of the
yen finally undermined the old system, Japan and its currency are unlikely to
play a major role in the discussions surrounding the establishment of a new international monetary system. This is largely, but not entirely, the result of a
radical change in Japan's international position after February 1973. Earlier,
after Japan's first reevaluation, the Satō government had inaugurated an
unusually relaxed monetary policy in an effort to avoid the deflationary consequences of the slackening export demand. This proved to be a bad miscalculation. The Nixon administration, with an eye to the 1972 election, employed far
more expansionary policies than anyone in Europe, Japan, and possibly the
United States expected. An unanticipated boom in world exports ensued, and
in 1973, prior to the onset of the oil embargo, wholesale prices in Japan were
accelerating at a rate of more than 22 percent annually. Although the Japanese
government began to restrict aggregate demand in an effort to cope with soar-
ing inflation, effective capacity began to contract even more rapidly due to the
reduced oil shipments from the Middle East. Inevitably, prices accelerated still
faster. Thus, relative to other balance of payments surplus nations of the early
1970s, Japanese monetary policy was unduly inflationary. These monetary
problems, together with the sharp increase in oil prices (probably affecting
Japan more than any other country, with the possible exception of Italy) and
the changing Japanese regulations on overseas investment, have made the
history of the yen since 1973 quite different from that of the German mark, the
Swiss franc, the Dutch guilder, and the French franc, not to mention a number
of the Middle Eastern currencies.[26]

The relative weakness and, for a time, the instability of the yen have aborted
the hopes of some for a major international capital market in Tokyo. Similarly,
Euroyen holdings have not become a major factor. After some promising begin-
nings, there has not been a major acceleration in the volume of world trade
denominated in yen or a major increase in foreign official holdings of yen.
Although the costs and benefits of an increased role in international financial
relations remain to be assessed, the expectation in the early 1970s was that the
yen and the deutsche mark would substantially supplement the dollar.[27] In
fact, the dollar's obituary was ludicrously premature. The deutsche mark, but
not the yen, has come into increasing international use. In consequence, Japan
had not had a major role in the discussions in the Group of Twenty and
the IMF. Although the Japanese participate in these discussions, the need to

26. The influential empirical work supporting the treatment of Japanese inflation given
here is summarized in Keizai Kikakuchō, *Keizai hakusho* (Tokyo, 1974), pp. 16–17.

27. Nihon Keizai Kenkyū Sentā, *Sekai no naka no Nihon keizai*, pp. 764–768.

accommodate the second largest economy among member nations is not obligatory.

In their own way, the Japanese still believe that their material means still do not permit their diplomats to play a major role in the discussions preceding the formal or informal establishment of a successor international financial system. This has led to the absence of a real consensus in Japan on its stake in the negotiations, and the Japanese financial policy-making machinery has yet to develop a coherent position reflecting Japanese interests.[28] Of course, Japan, along with other major actors in the world economy, states that it needs and wants a legitimate international financial system that will contribute to worldwide economic efficiency and political harmony. Nonetheless, it lacks an articulate Japanese position on the degree and means of exchange-rate flexibility in the future; the responsibilities of surplus and deficit nations; the means by which new international liquidity will be created; the future role of Special Drawing Rights relating to the dollar, gold, and other key currencies in official international financial transactions; and the degree of restriction, if any, suitable for private international capital transactions.

This failure to come to a consensus relates in some measure to fundamental disagreements within Japan regarding the very nature of the Japanese economy. Japan stands almost alone in the world as a very large economy with a rather small but nonetheless vital trade sector. Many analysts believe that the Japanese economy finally has an economic autonomy of its own. The experience with the reevaluations of the early 1970s has strengthened the hand of those economists who have long argued that the external value of the Japanese national currency makes relatively little difference and that costly domestic programs whose primary benefit is the defense of the yen at any particular value are unwise.[29] Such analysis inevitably leads to support for international monetary regimes that provide considerable scope for intervening market determination of exchange rates among national currencies without the intervention of the central bank.

Another segment of opinion within Japan, particularly within the government, fears the results of arbitrary, speculative movements in the external value of the yen rather than viewing flexibility as a means of insulating the domestic economy from foreign developments. Given Japanese dependence on imported raw materials and food, such movements might set off an unhappy spiral of cost-push inflation. Rightly or wrongly, this group believes that the sharp decline of the yen in late 1973 exaggerated the ensuing inflationary spiral. Again, particularly within the Japanese Ministry of Finance, there is great con-

28. One representative statement is given in Tsūsanshō, *Tsūshō hakusho* (Tokyo, 1974), pp. 321–327.
29. See, for example, Akihiro Amano, *An Econometric Model of the Japanese Balance of Payments and Its Policy Implications*, Japan Economic Research Center Paper no. 22 (Aug. 1973).

cern over losing the balance of payments excuse for constraining government expenditures. Clearly a Ministry of Finance thoroughly lacking in liberal traditions does not favor being replaced by the market mechanism as mediator between the domestic Japanese economy and external financial requirements.

Finally, unhappiness in the Japanese government with a formal system of flexible exchange rates is not unrelated to international political considerations. In a fully articulated, flexible exchange-rate system there would inevitably be a yen bloc. Of necessity many if not all of the non-Communist nations in East Asia and particularly Southeast Asia would tie their currencies to the yen. The real problems engendered by, and the symbolism associated with, such steps are viewed by Japanese officials as further complicating the serious Japanese political difficulties in that area of the world. Even more important than Japanese relations with Southeast Asia, there is considerable concern within the Japanese government that the appearance of currency blocs, not only in East Asia but elsewhere, would be another step down the road to a regionalism that, it is feared, might have extremely undesirable consequences for Japan.

The issues surrounding the appropriate degree of exchange rate flexibility are also related to the appropriate means for the creation of international liquidity and the relative status of national currencies and gold as reserve assets. The experiences of the late 1960s and the resulting misunderstandings between Japan and the United States have made the Japanese interested in, although not completely committed to, a system that would allow the United States to influence directly the external value of the American dollar. In the future, a needed devaluation must not come only through appreciation of other currencies. If the United States, or any other country with the concurrence of its leading trading partners, feels a change in its currency value is economically justified, systemically it should be in a position to bear the political costs of such a change. A so-called active role for the United States in connection with its balance of trade and payments suggests that there was already a consensus some years ago against further use of the dollar as a means of increasing international liquidity. The freedom the United States receives to pursue balance of trade and balance of payments objectives must be the benefit the American government receives in return for surrendering the right to pursue international activities without constraint by virtue of the dollar's reserve asset status.

The extraordinary change in trade between the oil-exporting nations and the rest of the world have suddenly put pressing international financial questions in a new perspective. Will individual nations have sufficient reserve assets to pay for imported oil? Will competitive depreciation among industrial economies become a threat once more? If the oil-exporting nations will not or cannot buy sufficient imports to match their oil exports, in what form should their earnings be held? Will these earnings be used in a politically disruptive fashion? As, relatively, the most important energy-dependent economy and as a nation that continues tight control over the inflow of capital, will Japan have balance of payments objectives inconsistent with international monetary stability? The older issues of exchange-rate adjustment and liquidity have not vanished but remain in newer guises and are being framed with increasing reference to a new locus of financial power in the Middle East.[30]

Changing view of the American-based
international corporation

Although Japanese practices regarding direct foreign investment were once viewed as backwardly mercantilist, the desire for more careful regulation of the activities of international corporations has now become widespread in less-developed countries, Canada, Western Europe, and even the United States. In part, there is a new consciousness of the lack of identity of interests among the triangle of home country, host country, and international corporation. In part, this new attitude reflects an erosion of the advanced technology, economically relevant information, and managerial expertise formerly concentrated in the United States, particularly in the hands of the larger U.S. corporations.

Host-country concerns regarding international corporations—the preemption by foreign nationals of limited host-country opportunities for gaining relevant experience, the loss of sovereignty over monetary policy, the erosion of the tax base, and the intrusion of American foreign policy into activities of domestic subsidiaries of American-based corporations—have provoked specific actions to deal with these problems. Quantitative and qualitative job quotas for domestic nationals in foreign-owned manufacturing activities have become a common regulation. For some time there have been requirements in many countries that no export restriction or regional restrictions be placed on the local subsidiaries of foreign corporations. Local opportunities for worldwide growth must not be stifled by an oligopolistic strategy of market regimentation. Finally, and closely following the Japanese practice, host countries have been seeking majority or at least 50 percent ownership of local subsidiaries. Local control, it is thought, will better ensure subsidiary activities consistent with the economic and political objectives of the host government.

Although success of these policies still requires long-term evaluation, they have already had an impact, even apart from the natural resources area. The American government is increasingly concerned lest the distribution of benefits deriving from the activities of the American-dominated international corporations move sharply away from the United States. Where once it was felt that American interests and the interests of these corporations were so similar

30. A representative Japanese statement on the quantitative dimensions of the petro-dollar problem is given in Nihon Keizai Kenkyū Sentā, *Sekai keizai to Nihon no shōrai*, pp. 83–84.

that the corporations could be relied on to preserve these benefits for the American polity and economy, this is clearly no longer felt to be the case, and recently the American government has considered retaliatory steps. The most extreme proposal to surface were the investment provisions of the Burke-Hartke bill, which would have severely restricted American direct investment abroad.

Japanese international investment policy

While much of the world has been moving closer to Japanese economic nationalism in their policies toward direct foreign investment, Japanese policies have become more liberal. Partially responding to intense foreign pressure, Japan now allows, or will soon allow, the automatic approval of fully owned subsidiaries of foreign corporations in virtually all industries except agriculture, mining, oil refining, and leather manufacture. The change, however, also reflects increased Japanese self-confidence in the competitive strength of its industry, the changing nature of the technological information required from abroad, and its increasing recognition that its own policies toward direct foreign investors affect the way in which the increasing investment activity of Japanese-based corporations are treated.

This new Japanese policy toward direct foreign investment represents a remarkable change; as recently as four years ago, Japan heavily restricted even minority ownership in joint ventures. Nonetheless, Japan is still far from having a truly liberal policy on direct foreign investment. Although Japan now permits the establishment of wholly owned foreign subsidiaries, it is still difficult for a foreign-owned corporation to obtain government approval for the purchase of an existing Japanese firm. And although explicit government approval is forthcoming for newly established ventures, many implicit barriers remain. The ultimate withdrawal in 1974 of Dow Chemical from its planned venture in the lucrative soda ash industry in Japan is a well-known case in point.

The international context of the technology market in which Japanese firms must now operate, however, makes further capital liberalization necessary. The nature of the technology and information that Japan does not now produce, and probably will not produce in the future, is increasingly difficult to license. The sophistication of the few areas in which Japan remains technologically backward is such and the producers of the technology are so few that Japan's bargaining position will be too weak to force a disentangling of information and expertise from direct equity and managerial participation in production. At the very least, Japan's weakened bargaining position is increasingly requiring the sharing of Japanese technological information in return for American technological information. This in itself is an epochal change. From a comparative perspective, even more striking than Japan's large purchases of foreign technology has been Japan's meagre sales of its own technology. Standardized by Japan's per capita GNP, the royalty fees Japan has received have been well below those of any major industrial nation in Western Europe or North America.[31]

Future Japanese overseas investment

Japan's relative lack of licensing activity abroad does not seem to indicate, however, that Japan, as a self-consciously syncretic economy, has had little technology and information to sell. Excluding military research and development since the early 1960s, the proportion of gross national product devoted to research and development in Japan is almost equal to that in Western Europe and the U.S. Moreover, these Japanese research and development efforts have been characterized by their direct commercial orientation and the unusually high percentage of their financing that comes from private sources. This emphasis on applied rather than pure research suggests that the substantial Japanese research and development base has been simply exploiting, for the benefit of the Japanese economy, the advanced technological innovations developed elsewhere. Thus, given the nature of the information and processes that get licensed, Japan's relatively modest licensing fees hardly seem to result from a lack of potentially exportable technology. More likely, given the extensive license experience within Japanese industry, Japanese manufacturers have appreciated the noninsurable risks for the licensor in licensing agreements and preferred exports, direct foreign investment, or both. Given this preference, the precedent of other advanced economies, and the pollution and land acquisition problems in Japan, many Japanese government agencies and private research institutes have projected large increases in Japanese direct foreign investment in manufacturing in the next ten years.[32]

The differences in the world environment of the 1970s as opposed to that of the 1950s and early 1960s, however, raise doubts on whether Japan will achieve the more optimistic projections. Japan does not have the monopoly on technology, the managerial expertise, or the capital that America enjoyed during its great overseas expansions. Host countries now drive harder bargains, and recent evidence clearly indicates that Japan in responding. By contrast to the wholly owned American overseas subsidiaries, the majority of Japanese manufacturing ventures are joint ventures, in which Japan often has only a minority ownership. Japan's experience over the last three years has been little different from that of other advanced economies; it suggests that projecting future Japanese foreign direct investment on the basis of the past experience of other advanced nations is bound to lead to considerable overestimation.

31. Tsūsanshō, *Tsūshō hakusho*, pp. 235–236.
32. Tsūsanshō, *Sangyō kōzō no chōki bijon* (Tokyo, 1974); and Nihon Keizai Kenkyū Sentā, *Sekai keizai to Nihon no shōrai*, pp. 83–84.

CHANGING OPPORTUNITIES FOR NATURAL RESOURCE EXPLOITATION: RESOURCE NATIONALISM, SCARCITY, AND SECURITY

As in other areas, the success of the international economic system in spurring the growth of the non-Communist advanced economies has also ultimately undermined many features of the markets for renewable and nonrenewable natural resources that have done much to facilitate this growth. Through 1960, world prices for food, nonfood agricultural raw materials, and mineral raw materials fell sharply in relation to the prices for manufactured products as well as in absolute dollar terms. After 1960, the rate of price decline of primary commodities relative to the prices of manufactured products slowed and actually began to increase in absolute dollars. By 1973–1974, prices of basic commodities had increased so much and the terms of trade between primary commodities and manufactured products had swung so sharply against manufactured products that the terms of trade returned to the 1950 relationship. Twenty years of improvement in the position of manufactured products had been wiped out.

Although the unusually rapid world economic growth explains the general trend in raw material prices, relative scarcity alone does not dictate the particular outcomes observed. A more precise explanation requires discussion of market power, nationalism, and some important real and monetary miscalculations.

One of the unforeseen factors that served to increase primary commodity prices in the 1960s was Japan itself. Of the increased exports in primary commodities between 1960 and 1970, Japan received 30 percent of wheat, 55 percent of iron ore, 22 percent of crude oil, 25 percent of soybeans, and 50 percent of wood. Almost no one, including the Japanese themselves, foresaw this explosive Japanese growth. Japanese government and business groups were in a position to assess Japanese economic growth prospects and any implications for food and raw material imports and to use such information profitably to increase worldwide supply capacity. They chose not to do so. In part because of balance of payments constraints, Japan's trading companies almost irresponsibly used the information for speculative purposes, without making any effort to change Japan's long-standing policy of maximum flexibility through avoidance of long-term commitments and equity investments. Thus, the Japanese did little or nothing, while everyone else was surprised by the buoyancy of demand, and basic commodity prices rose throughout the 1960s.[33]

33. For a discussion of this and other errors in the international context of Japanese planning, see Saburo Okita and Tomoyuki Takahashi, "International Aspects of Planning in Japan," in *Economic Planning and Macro-Economic Policy*, Japan Economic Research Center Paper no. 14 (April 1971).

In addition, the worldwide and particularly the Japanese miscalculation of Nixon administration macroeconomic policy intentions in the year before the 1972 election cumulatively resulted in a tidal wave of new world liquidity in 1972 and 1973. When joined with American disinterest in the worldwide and domestic consequences of billion-dollar wheat sales to the Soviet Union, and in view of the short-run price inelasticity of supply of primary commodities, this miscalculation inevitably contributed further to the price explosion.

With demand straining supply, the unstable political economy of primary commodity markets began to assert itself. Long unhappy with their terms of trade and with the role of foreign-dominated corporations in the exploitation of what was often their major national economic asset, and fortified by increasingly easy access to the technology, capital, and managerial expertise relevant for such exploitation, primary producing nations began in the early 1970s to extract all possible rents from foreign-owned natural-resource-exploiting ventures operating within their jurisdiction. At the same time, these primary-product-producing nations joined together in a variety of attempts to gain market power with which to alter their terms of trade. The best-known effort, the Organization of Petroleum Exporting Countries, has been remarkably successful since the Teheran Conference, and particularly since the oil embargo in late 1973, in increasing the price of crude oil and altering markedly the distribution of world purchasing power. Although such resource nationalism and the associated cartels can hardly be ignored, they should not obscure the more important (with the exception of crude oil) monetary and cyclical determinants, especially in attempting to assess the role of natural resources in the evolving international economic environment and its implications for Japanese foreign economic policy.

The future terms of natural resource availability

If the world economy grows as rapidly in the next ten years as it did between 1960 and 1970, a secular decline in the price of primary commodities is unlikely. At the same time, further sharp increases will result only from a conjunction of the same forces that were responsible for the recent jump. Thus, long-term scarcity should not act to secularly increase basic commodity prices in the foreseeable future. Known reserves for virtually all minerals and fuels remain at their historical levels. Similarly, rapid expansion in the production of foodstuffs and other agricultural raw materials, until recently limited by the lack of fertilizer capacity, should, over the next few years, return agricultural prices to levels more characteristic of the 1960s. The importance of cyclical and monetary phenomena in generating the commodity boom of the early 1970s is underscored by the sharp decline in most basic commodity prices since late 1974 (with the exception of oil). As the earlier sharp cyclical upswing buoyed prices of inelastic basic commodities, so the recent downturn has worked to depress basic commodity prices sharply. With the major exception of crude oil, virtually every important commodity entering international trade has fallen in price from peak levels by at least 20 percent.[34] In most cases, the price declines are far sharper. Indeed, if the prices in futures markets are any indication, further declines may be expected.

Although natural scarcity may not be a major consideration in the evolving world economic environment, contrived scarcity—the result of organized attempts by primary producers to exert market power—remains an important issue. Can and will OPEC continue to be an effective cartel? Will the price of oil be raised still higher in the future? Will OPEC serve as a model for other producers of primary products?

The continuing existence of OPEC as an effective cartel depends most fundamentally on the continuing willingness of Saudi Arabia and, to a lesser extent, Kuwait to accept large declines in their production and thus in their oil revenues. Both are major producers with enormous oil reserves. Given their relatively small populations, modest financial needs, and already large foreign exchange holdings, they are the only two OPEC members in a position to absorb major production cutbacks and obviate the need to assign rigid production quotas among OPEC members. The large gap at present between overall production and capacity, and the number, diversity, and fiscal needs of the other OPEC members, make it doubtful the cartel could continue to operate effectively if anything like equiproportionate cutbacks among all members were to become necessary.

The willingness of the Saudis and the Kuwaitis to underwrite the present inflated price of crude oil as well as possible future increases depends on the subtle interplay among various factors: their expectations regarding future supply-and-demand relationships for crude oil; their views on the desirability of increasing the relative economic and political power of Iran, Iraq, and Algeria by allowing them to produce crude oil near capacity at high prices, while relatively weakening the United States, Western Europe, and Japan; and their political capability to withstand pressure from Iran, Iraq, and Algeria if they should desire to do so. Any projection of the outcome is hazardous, but it is clear that in this important area of natural resources the structure of the international economic system has been changed beyond recognition. The increased price of oil by itself will have only a modest effect on the rate of economic growth in advanced nations. The concentration of economic power in national government hands of the OPEC countries, however, could, through renewed embargoes, have enormously disruptive consequences and, through politically calculated use of large foreign exchange holdings, have almost as disruptive financial con-

34. United Nations, *Monthly Bulletin of Statistics*, various issues.

sequences. Such conditions are entirely unprecedented in the postwar period and the very antithesis of the early liberal vision.[35]

The emergence of this vast power in the energy market has led directly to the establishment of countervailing institutions. Where once it was expected that the mostly American-dominated international oil companies would of necessity protect the interests of the consumer countries, now it has been clearly demonstrated that there is no such identity of interests and that new institutions are necessary if the market power of the oil-producing nations is to be curbed. Internationally, the new institution is the International Energy Agency (IEA), the potential importance of which is as significant as that of the IMF in 1946. The effectiveness of such new institutions in curbing the market power of the oil-producing nations will depend on their ability to (1) develop alternative sources of energy supply at competitive prices; (2) encourage and coordinate conservation steps among the consumer nations; (3) design consumer-nation oil-purchasing procedures to exploit potential weaknesses and mistrust among cartel members; and (4) develop crude oil stockpiles sufficient to blunt the cartel's ultimate weapon of embargo. The considerable difficulties involved in arranging significant cooperative steps among purchasing nations in all four dimensions of energy policy are best illustrated by an examination of the Japanese interest in various modes of international cooperation.

Japan and international cooperation on energy policy

Japan can hardly fail to benefit from the development of alternative sources of energy, but, under any conceivable technology in the next few decades, Japan cannot have a Project Independence. Other than some exploration on the Northeast Asian continental shelf, there is little Japan can do domestically to add to known world energy reserves. Moreover, until recently, Japan participated only modestly in overseas exploration for and exploitation of crude-oil-bearing structures. Japan's large share of oil and of imports, however, has led to considerable interest within certain governmental agencies for vastly increasing Japanese participation in exploration and exploitation.[36] Such increases would occur within the context of a restructuring of purchasing, refining, and distributing oil within Japan. Whether a continued rapid increase (a large increase from a very small base has already taken place) in such overseas Japanese efforts is in the interest of the consumer nations and Japan depends on the nature of exploration opportunities and the relative opportunity cost of Japanese resources devoted to exploration efforts, particularly in comparison

35. A study that suggests that oil-price changes, by themselves, have only a modest effect on the Japanese economy may be found in Keizai Kikakuchō, *Keizai hakusho*, p. 199.

36. Mitiyuki Isurugi, *Enerugī* (Tokyo, 1973), pp. 280–381.

with those of the U.S. and European countries. Japanese activity might benefit all consumer nations by widening the pool of exploration opportunities examined, but it could also result in redundant competition and uneconomical use of resources.

Given the previous lack of significant Japanese activity in overseas exploration and production and, therefore, the cost involved in developing expertise in this area, what benefits might Japan derive? Setting aside the contention that this might be, given the risk, an especially profitable area of investment in the future, the benefits are presumably those of counteracting the scarcity of supply in the future. Not surprisingly, in the new era of rising prices and contrived scarcity, Japan has made a historic shift away from its policy of flexibility in the procurement of raw materials. Instead, it is doing everything possible to develop and maintain long-term supply relationships through exploration, managerial, and capital participation. Yet this is also the era of natural resource nationalization, which casts doubts over whether such investment would help ensure for Japan either long-term price protection or security of supply. As long as the OPEC-contrived artificial scarcity persists in its present form virtually all rents associated with the exploration and production of crude oil will be extracted for the benefit of the host government. Moreover, recent experience suggests that a host country will take advantage of a time of supply interruption, even if it does not participate in the disruptive action itself. Japan would secure some benefits only in the unlikely event that advanced industrial nations, particularly the United States, return to the ethics of gunboat diplomacy, and the more unlikely event that Japan would participate in such efforts.

Japan, the U.S., and the international conservation issue

Although the results from increased petroleum exploration might by themselves be sufficient to significantly diminish the market power now exercised by producers of crude oil, the great expense and uncertainty surrounding new exploration has caused the great consumer nations to stress energy conservation programs in international contexts. Higher prices for oil and other energy sources will, by themselves, ensure increasing conservation as well as changes in the historical relationship between economic growth and energy use. Although some conservation will rely on newly profitable but already known technologies, much future conservation will result from new energy-saving innovations. To the extent that potential producers of such innovations perceive the possibility of collecting substantial rents in the event their innovations are successful (many energy-saving innovations may not be of this character at all), substantial individual and national efforts fully comparable to the efforts at increasing supply may be expected.

The long time horizon associated with market-led conservation activity (and, for that matter market-led exploration activity) has dictated a variety of attempts to impose, by international agreement, short-run government-managed conservation goals for consumer nations. The question, however, of how to distribute the burden of such conservation is almost as troublesome as the problem of assigning production cutbacks among crude-oil producers. The IEA's initial near-term goal was a 10 percent cutback in petroleum imports by all member nations. Many Japanese policy-making elites have stressed the inequity of such a goal: 10 percent conservation of imports is 10 percent conservation of crude oil consumption for Japan, but less than 4 percent for the United States. Moreover, 75 percent of Japanese energy is derived from crude oil, compared with only 43 percent of American energy, and there is simply less room in Japan for energy conservation than in the United States and most Western European countries. The distribution of energy for so-called comfort uses (household and transportation) is 36 percent of total usage in Japan as compared with 58 percent in the United States.[37]

Defenders of the initial IEA goal, particularly the United States, have sharply criticized the Japanese complaints. They presume that because Japan has become so dependent on oil there is considerable opportunity for taking some of the easier reconversion steps back to coal. Also, it is argued, the presumption that the opportunities for conservation in the household and transportation sectors are greater, or that conservation in these areas is in some welfare sense more appropriate or easier, can be considered thinly veiled prejudice. In fact, there is evidence that the reasonable opportunities for conservation are perhaps three times as great in the industrial and electricity-generation sectors as in the "comfort" sectors. For example, there is perhaps twice as much opportunity for energy conservation through more efficient production of paper, steel, aluminum, plastics, cement, and electricity than in working toward improved fuel economy in the proverbially energy-inefficient American automobile.[38] In this connection, it is often noted that, in international perspective, Japanese industries are relatively energy intensive in their production structure.[39]

These arguments over energy conservation burdens illustrate the inevitable subjectivity that makes explicit cooperation among consumer nations difficult. Thus, the success of the IEA programs for conservation as well as for purchasing and stockpiling depend ultimately on one or two countries taking a leadership role. Clearly most elements of these programs have large externalities and therefore cannot rely on decentralized initiative. Despite projections that in the future Japan will import from the Middle East as much crude

37. The data on which this section is based are contained in Tsūsanshō, *Tsūshō hakusho*, pp. 145–216.
38. Ford Foundation Energy Policy Project, *A Time to Choose* (Cambridge, Mass.: Ballinger, 1974), pp. 45–80.
39. Keizai Kikakuchō, *Keizai hakusho*, pp. 90–91.

petroleum as Western Europe and the United States combined, it is expected that once again it will be the United States that will bear this responsibility. Among the major demand factors in the international oil market only the United States can ever hope to reduce imported oil to a strategically unimportant part of its overall energy supply. Only the political leadership of the United States has proposed a Project Independence. Given the high value the United States has traditionally placed on strategic autonomy, its other international political goals, and its relatively rich natural-resource position (which makes the political costs of high-profile leadership bearable), this is one area of international economic relations in which the United States will assume its accustomed postwar role.

In assessing the reasons for the success of OPEC, great attention has been focused on the manner in which crude oil is purchased from producers. For example, some argue that the fully integrated American-based international oil companies—which produce crude oil, refine it into a variety of petroleum products, and then distribute them—serve the interests of the producer nations at the expense of the home country. With direct access to the consumer market, the international oil companies can attempt to pass along to the consumer the monopoly prices set by the producer nations. Thus, a centralized national purchasing agency, perhaps with some auctioning arrangement, might challenge the effectiveness of the OPEC cartel. For example, a single institution controlling access to a large American market for imported crude oil could do much to stimulate competition among the oil-producing nations. There is much to commend proposals for limiting access to the American market by a strict import quota, the rights to which would be auctioned off via sealed bids. As successful bidders might resell their import licenses, there is considerable scope for hiding the true identity of the actual bidder, which should make cheating on OPEC commitments easier.[40]

Although foreign-based vertically integrated international oil companies no longer completely dominate the Japanese petroleum industry, the concerted MITI efforts to stimulate competition at the refining and distribution stage have made it difficult for Japan to use its potentially strategic position as a large market (and in the future, possibly the largest single market) for crude oil to stimulate competition at the important prerefinery stage.[41] Consequently, as MITI has encouraged the consolidation of many Japanese industries, it is in the process of reversing previous policies in order to consolidate the comparatively large number of distributors and refiners into two or three groups, which will then be explicitly tied to Japanese exploration and overseas production ventures.

40. This analysis is presented in M.A. Adelman, "Is the Oil Shortage Real? Oil Companies as OPEC Tax Collectors," *Foreign Policy*, winter 1972/73, and further elaborated in M.I.T. Energy Laboratory Policy Study Group, *Energy Self-Sufficiency* (Washington, 1974).

41. Mitiyuki Isurugi, *Enerugi*, pp. 137–183.

Some have argued that MITI has overemphasized the establishment of a vertically integrated, Japanese-controlled oil company involved in overseas exploration and production, and neglected the development of a crude-oil-purchasing institution that would control access to the Japanese petroleum market. There is also the danger that the effort to create a Japanese "oil major" is a response to securing access to oil at a reasonable price for an era that no longer exists.

Proper evaluation of Japanese government oil-industry policies and the seeming lack of full attention to purchasing institutions require a consideration of the international negotiations on a guaranteed price floor for crude oil. With the United States government contemplating the encouragement of large capital investment (potentially at an annual rate of some $100 billion) to increase the reserves of energy available for world consumption, the prime mover in organizing international energy policy to break the market power of OPEC has acquired an interest in keeping energy prices sufficiently high to make such investment economical. Regardless of whether new sources will be located in the United States or owned by American-based corporations, the benefits of such energy sources will accrue to all consumer nations, and it seems equitable that the United States should wish to recoup its investment. Indeed, unless every effort is made to ensure that the investment can be recouped, financing from private sources will not be forthcoming. To this end, under the auspices of the IEA, the United States has attempted to seek agreement with other industrialized consuming countries to prevent oil from being sold in their respective domestic markets below an agreed common price. Although agreement in principle has been reached, the common price has yet to be established, and almost certainly there will be no agreement on the methods each should use to effect the agreement.

Given the great Japanese interest in increased energy sources, it is likely Japan will agree to some target floor price. What Japan and other energy-poor industrialized nations will do in practice once this energy is available, however, remains in some doubt. If the Japanese government believes that, for national security reasons, it is wise to limit dependence on imported Arab oil even after OPEC's market power is broken, then, of course, it will use its considerable enforcement machinery to maintain the IEA agreement. Japan might decide, however, that in a world of more abundant energy, such security issues no longer apply and that continued discrimination against the energy-using industries is not in the long-run interests of the Japanese economy. Under such a regime, the absence of a single government-sponsored purchasing agency might facilitate cheating (by making it arguably more difficult for the government to enforce its agreements). Considerable involvement in and close contact with upstream production might also contribute to the same end, while paradoxically demonstrating a potential Japanese interest in recouping its own investment.

Given the possibility that energy prices might remain high, regardless of the availability of large new sources or the development of, and conversion to, energy-saving technologies, many analysts suggest what are styled as less-expensive means of coping with contrived energy scarcity. Advocates of a low-cost institutional approach to the problems created by OPEC argue for new purchasing arrangements and more readily available modes of conservation to cope with the market power problem, while increasing stockpiles as insurance against new embargoes.[42] Widespread agreement exists in Japan, Western Europe, and the United States that—notwithstanding national evaluations of the relative merits of increased exploration, more conservation, and more attention to market structure—large petroleum stockpiles are an important component of any new energy policy. Stockpiles should be large enough to allow maintenance of normal economic activity until permanent replacement for disrupted supplies can be found. The time between the onset of the disruption and when alternative sources can be brought into production will vary nonlinearly with the size of the supply disrupted. Thus, the larger the supplies from insecure sources, the geometrically larger the necessity for stockpiles. The larger the aggregate national stockpiles, however, the more expensive they are to maintain. Although there is much international controversy over the precise point at which stockpiling will become more expensive than reliance on new technology, high-cost new sources, or increased conservation, the observed behavior of most nations indicates that the point has not been reached. Japanese stockpiles, although low by international standards, have increased by almost 50 percent since late 1973, and continued increase is inevitable. Advocates of large stockpiles in Japan have been bolstered by recent government studies showing that, providing there is slow buildup, the economic costs of maintaining a hundred twenty-day stockpiles against all imports (and thus perhaps double that against supplies from insecure areas) is, in aggregate terms, negligible.[43]

For all the Japanese attention to increasing stockpiles, its interests, as with other relatively energy-poor industrialized nations, are not entirely congruent with those of the energy-rich industrialized nations. As energy-rich nations will probably keep some domestic supplies in reserve, their larger presence in the international oil market will work to the potential detriment of Japan and similarly situated nations. Similarly, in the event of an embargo, it is not clear what access to alternative sources Japan might have as it draws down its reserves. Unlike energy-rich industrialized nations, Japan does not have the

42. M.I.T. Energy Laboratory Study Group, *Energy Self-Sufficiency*, pp. 69–72.
43. Keizai Kikakuchō, *Keizai hakusho*, pp. 115–116.

policy option of delaying the use of domestic energy resources. And it is doubt-ful that Japan can easily delay the development of foreign Japan-associated secure sources.

What are the possibilities for assertion of producer market power in other commodities? For the simple reason that no other agricultural or mineral raw material in international trade, including wheat, plays a strategic role in eco-nomic life comparable to crude oil (indeed, the international trade value of all mineral and agricultural commodities together merely equal that of crude oil), it is doubtful that such attempts will be successful or, if they are successful, that the resulting cartel actions will be sufficiently important to warrant much at-tention from economic policy-makers.

Of the primary commodities that do figure importantly in international trade there are comparatively few for which there are no readily available substitutes, either for the commodity itself or the goods it is used to produce. Even within this restricted category, the distribution of many commodities without close substitutes remains relatively rectangular. Such commodities are produced in many countries in fairly substantial amounts. In the absence of large producers willing to play the Saudi or Kuwaiti roles with respect to par-ticular commodities, it seems unlikely that cartels organized under such condi-tions can long survive.

The winnowing down of likely candidates for new cartels usually leaves but a handful of primary commodities: bauxite, phosphate rock, possibly timber, copper, and tin.[44] Of these, only bauxite producers, through actions of the Jamaican government, have had any success in raising prices through the exer-cise of market power. In contrast, copper has been a clear failure. Since 1967 a copper producers' association—CIPEC, modeled on OPEC—has been in ex-istence. Despite continuing vigorous efforts and a remarkable run-up in copper prices for a brief period in 1974, CIPEC has failed in every attempt to exert power in the copper market. Indeed, the amount of copper involved in inter-national transactions is sufficiently small that individual firms or groups of firms can, if they wish, acquire substantial positions in the copper market. Thus in late 1974, Japan became a major exporter of copper as Japanese trading firms began to unload their speculative positions—an action that helped break the back of the most recent CIPEC market action.

The effects of such Japanese action serve to underline certain aspects that are often neglected in discussions of Japan's position as a raw-material-poor, large industrialized economy. Japan imports 32 percent of the world's soybeans entering international trade, 27 percent of the corn, 24 percent of the bananas, 47 percent of the copper ore, 42 percent of the iron ore, and 40 percent of the coal. Given the absence of natural scarcity in most commodities and the small number of Japanese firms accounting for nearly all Japanese raw material im-

44. Nihon Keizai Kenkyū Sentā, *Sekai keizai to Nihon no shōrai*, pp. 50–51.

ports, it is surprising that (except with reference to Southeast Asia) there is not more discussion on Japanese exertion of market power to keep raw materials prices artificially low! Past experience, such as the role of Japanese trading firms in the pre-Pacific-War raw-cotton market, suggests that such quietly directed attempts by major importers to manipulate commodity prices are as likely as attempts at manipulation from the seller's side of the market.

THE JAPANESE POSITION
IN EAST-WEST TRADE

There is probably no better evidence that the success of the postwar international economic system also served to undermine its foundations than the changing attitudes among American policy-makers toward trade between Communist and non-Communist nations. After initial enthusiasm for universalism in the early postwar period, American policy-makers came to view institutions such as the IMF and the GATT as structures for shoring up the weaker economies of the anti-Communist alliance. The success of these institutions in promoting economic recovery and growth has given existing political institutions sufficient legitimacy and has created sufficient defense potential in Western Europe to make strident anti-Communism unnecessary and, indeed, potentially dysfunctional. Already Poland, Rumania, and Hungary have become full members of GATT, and other Communist nations are now being considered for membership in the IMF as well as GATT. In the wake of contrived energy shortages in the non-Communist industrialized economies and an increasingly well-recognized technological lag in the Communist world, policy-makers in both camps see positive advantages in increasing economic interdependence. The change in American attitudes is especially significant because, unlike the views of the Soviet Union, China, and Eastern Europe, the benefits of increased economic interdependence are not regarded as primarily direct or economic. Rather, over a short time horizon, American policy-makers seem to believe that helping to promote the economic advancement of the Communist bloc can serve other American diplomatic interests. Over a longer horizon, there is the hope—based on considerations similar to those prompting the early postwar liberal universalism—that increased economic interdependence will create powerful interests that will prevent the kind of tension that resolves itself in international violence.

For all the newly found American enthusiasm for trade between Communist and non-Communist countries, the obstacles in the path of accelerating such commercial interactions make it unlikely that this facet of the international economic system will be much different in the future than it has been during the past ten years. Although the American interest in East-West trade is relatively recent, such trade has been growing rapidly for some time. In 1953 East-West trade was 1.3 percent of world trade; by 1967 it accounted for 2.8 percent, and by 1973 it had expanded to over 4 percent of total world trade.[45] Continued rapid increase in the future, however, would probably require substantial institutional changes in Communist bloc countries, which in turn would require that they make a fundamental political decision to allow the development of substantial internal forces with great economic stakes in continuing good relations between the so-called East and West. Moreover, further rapid East-West trade growth would mean trade of a scale and in commodities that would demand a willingness of both sides to rely indefinitely and in important ways on countries long thought of as dangerous adversaries.

Even after the resolution of such political matters, a host of institutional difficulties would still remain. For example, prices in the nonmarket Communist countries bear little relation to opportunity cost and are seldom changed. In international trade, however, Communist exporters would inevitably sell their products at world market prices, which would severely constrain them in the area where they might have some competitive advantage. At the same time, any attempt to lower prices in the presence of domestic competition in import markets would almost certainly bring charges of dumping. Given irrational prices and disequilibrium exchange rates, such charges would be most difficult to refute. Throughout the postwar period the fastest growing major component of international trade has been the exchange of manufactured goods among the industrialized nations. This comprises more than 40 percent of all world trade. In the absence of a full commitment to market socialism, it is doubtful that Communist countries will be anything more than residual participants in this area of international economic interaction.

The non-Communist industrialized countries' interest in diversifying their sources for mineral and agricultural raw materials, however, helps to minimize the institutional problems in this area. In particular, Japanese interest in Soviet and Chinese raw materials will ensure continuing rapid growth in imports from Communist areas provided that relative Japanese dependence on the two areas can be kept in balance, and their overall dependence low. Overall dependence will probably not operate as a constraint, because the growth starts from an exceedingly low base relative to Japan's large resource needs and the complexity of project negotiations requires long lead times for almost every transaction. The balance consideration, however, is very important; it will be difficult for Japan to prevent almost any important arrangement from becoming a source of potential tension in the highly complex diplomatic balance in Northeast Asia. Furthermore, although it is unlikely the Japanese economy will become dependent in a significant way on China or the Soviet Union, for China, at least, economic dependence is a foreseeable danger. Almost 25 percent of China's in-

45. GATT, *International Trade 1973/1974* (Geneva, 1974).

ternational trade is with Japan. Unless China grows much more rapidly than Japan grows in the future, or unless China substantially increases the share of its GNP devoted to foreign trade while Japan does the reverse, China's interest in diversifying foreign trade sources will lead to a decline rather than an increase in the importance of China as a trade partner for Japan.

THE NEW INTERNATIONAL ECONOMIC ORDER AND JAPAN'S FUTURE

The institutions of, and the attitudes regarding, the international economic system have changed remarkably in the last half-dozen years. The postwar paradigms have unraveled. Improvements in the standard of living in many areas of the world and changes in worldwide distribution of material wealth have undermined American dominance of the international economy. These changes, together with changing political values, have also altered the American foreign-policy-making elites' conception of foreign economic policy as a clearly subordinate component of American global political strategy. The latter change has meant increasing American unwillingness to give ground on foreign economic policy in return for strengthening an anti-Communist political alliance; the former changes have meant an increasing ability of other countries to withstand new American pressures. In international commercial policy, the momentum for further reductions in tariff and nontariff barriers has been lost in the face of new, if entirely appropriate, American demands for full reciprocity; at the same time, the erection of barriers to exports has created new threats to the legitimacy of what has been achieved on the import side. In international financial policy, the end of the Bretton Woods system has left Western Europe and Japan struggling to circumscribe America's role as world banker, while by way of compensation the United States attempts to ensure ample opportunity to influence the external value of the dollar. In international direct investment policy, the economic power that is growing outside the United States with the diffusion of technology and of the means to adapt and produce technology has reduced the bargaining power of American-dominated international corporations sufficiently to allow host countries to extract a growing proportion of the rents associated with the firms' activities.

These changing host-country policies, pursued in both manufacturing and natural-resource-based industries and in both advanced industrial countries and less-developed countries, have prompted an increasingly vigorous American government reaction. Cognizant of the lack of complete identity between the interests of the American-dominated international corporation and the interests of the American economy, the American government has increasingly tended to insert itself in the bargaining between such corporations and foreign governments. In the international energy market, the American government

has adopted a postwar leadership stance (with all its positive and negative connotations) in an effort to curb the new economic and political power of the
Middle East on petroleum producers.

What do these many changes augur for the evolution of the international
economic system and Japan's position within that evolving system? There is
small prospect in the foreseeable future that the world economy will return to
an American-dominated liberal system. American banks and corporations are
materially incapable of regaining the dominant role they once held, and the
American government is politically incapable of maintaining the self-restraint
necessary to accommodate the economic needs of other nations. It is also unlikely that the world economy will break down into antagonistic regional blocs.
The enormous trade in manufactured products among industrialized countries,
the universal desire for access to the American market, and the increasing trade
between Japan and Western Europe, together with the near necessity of Amer-
ican-led cooperation among industrialized nations on international energy policy, make such a development most improbable. Japan will be economically
preeminent in the western Pacific and the Common Agricultural Policy of the
European Economic Community will survive, but these conditions will be but
one facet of the industrialized economies' relations with one another and the
rest of the world. More likely, the evolving international economic system will
come to resemble twentieth-century pluralism rather than nineteenth-century
liberalism or the regionalism of the 1930s. As under nineteenth-century
liberalism, participation in the international economic system will become increasingly global. As under the regionalism of the 1930s, the increasing lack of
shared values among major participants will leave the coordination of international economic activity less in the hands of markets and private initiative
than has been the case throughout much of the postwar period. An increasingly narrower conception of national self-interest and an increasingly greater appreciation of the role of international oligopoly and international cartel will
mean greater political intervention in international economic relations and, in
consequence, an inevitable intermeshing of international economics with other
international issues.

Pursuing a relatively narrow conception of national self-interest in the context of national goals of autonomy and stability does not necessarily mean doing violence to clearly beneficial international interaction. It means that the
U.S. and other nations will act in the future as Japan has acted throughout
much of the postwar period. It also means that an increasing variety of issues
will be treated at the highest levels of government. With international economic
issues once again requiring the attention of national political leaders, and with
issue-linkage acquiring a new legitimacy, one can expect national participation
in an increasing variety of shifting international coalitions. Optimistically, one
can hope that these new bases for occasional international alliance will serve, in
pluralistic fashion, the cause of global integration and global stability.

IV

Security Issues

Japanese Security and Postwar Japanese Foreign Policy

DONALD C. HELLMANN

Security has been a pivotal issue in postwar Japanese foreign policy. During the Occupation, deep concern for the past and future role of Japan in world affairs underlay the sweeping American-sponsored constitutional and political reforms and established the conditions on which independence ultimately was granted. During the ensuing Cold War years, alliance with the United States served both as the foundation for the integration of Japan into the international economic and political order and as the focal point of Japan's internal conflict between the conservative and opposition parties. With the emergence internationally of a more pluralistic, multipolar era, the linkages between political security affairs and economic relations have posed fresh dilemmas for Japan's strategic policy at a moment when the domestic political system is under its most serious strain since 1952. Security policy has been the point at which Japanese domestic and external politics have converged most fully and dramatically, so in considering that policy, one must look beyond the modest military forces and defense plans of the government. An evaluation of the past crises and current strategic problems from a broad political and historical perspective is required.

Japan's strategic policy can be seen simply as one dimension of Japanese-American relations. Since 1945, Japan has been either a country occupied by American troops or a defense satellite under a hegemonical alliance arrangement that has ultimately treated Japanese security interests as identical with those of the United States. The explicit ties on defense matters have been reinforced both by the cultivation of extensive bilateral economic and political relations, and by the shrill anti-American campaigns of the Japanese Left which have served to narrow the focus of the foreign-policy debate to an obsessive concern over relations with the United States. With the unfolding of the so-called Nixon Doctrine, and in the face of the monetary, trade, and resource crises that have devastated the international economic system in the last few years, this one-sided defense relationship has undergone significant changes. Still, the United States continues to hold the key to Japan's security policy; when and how Japan will move to an expanded defense posture will be shaped as much by what is done in Washington as in Tokyo.

A proper analysis of Japan's current defense problems also requires identification and elaboration of the critical variables that have shaped Japanese security policy in the past. First, what are the basic principles underlying the postwar Japanese diplomatic tradition? What are the assumptions that sustain the individual policies and shape the substantive consensus within which most domestic debate has occurred? Second, what is involved in the domestic political process, and what are the limits it imposes on the adoption of certain substantive policies (such as nuclear armament) and on the flexibility with which the leaders can respond to international crises? Finally, what has been the nature of the external environment and its influence on Japanese policy since 1945? The structure of the international system—notably the peculiar features of the bipolar world and the emergence of political and economic multipolarity—are particularly important in understanding the passive and derivative role of Japan in foreign affairs in the past. The key to Japan's current security policy in the more pluralistic and indeterminate world of scarcity lies in the links between the low politics of international economic relations and the high politics of strategy.

Despite the analytical utility in distinguishing and dealing separately with each of these variables, there is an integral and dynamic relationship among them. Indeed, it is by delineating some of these linkages that security policy can be properly placed in the context of Japanese foreign policy.

SECURITY AND PRINCIPLE

A new Japanese diplomatic tradition

The occupation of Japan provided the United States with the unique opportunity to impose on a culturally alien but industrialized society the fundamental ideals of American diplomatic tradition. This was done without the tampering influence of allies. It was also executed on a people for whom defeat had discredited the legitimacy of the political order.

As stated in the document specifying the initial postsurrender policy, the fundamental objective of the Occupation was "to insure that Japan will not again become a menace to the United States or to the peace and security of the world."[1] The means to achieve this end were to demilitarize and, above all, to democratize the nation in ways "deemed likely to stress the peaceful disposition of the Japanese people." This moralistic emphasis is fully in keeping with the Wilsonian notion that defects in the internal structure of states (such as nondemocratic characteristics) are the basic cause of war—a belief that is at the heart of the liberal American approach to foreign affairs.[2] As implemented in Japan, it represented an extreme form of the "ahistorical, moralistic, and legalistic approach" employed by the United States in World War II and applied to the international problems in Europe and Asia in the immediate postwar years.[3]

The unfettered discretion granted to the sole occupying power, the messianic idealism of General Douglas MacArthur, who dominated policy-making in the first years of the Occupation,[4] and the contrite utopianism of a senior Japanese statesman (Shidehara Kijurō) led to the insertion of Article 9 into the new constitution. The renunciation of war "as a sovereign right of the nation and the threat or use of force in settling international disputes" gave legal sanctity and symbolic dignity to pacifism within the country and placed Japan in a *sui generis* category internationally. Of the many implications that Article 9 has had for the development of postwar Japanese security policy, the most basic of all—the manner in which this "no-war" clause moved Japan from the European diplomatic tradition of power politics into the peculiarly idealist American tradition—has received remarkably little attention.

In the prewar period, Japan was deeply caught up in the imperialist power politics of East Asia in a manner consistent with the continental European style of diplomacy. Politically, the distinguishing features of this approach of international affairs involved an emphasis on the compelling, impersonal forces that shaped relations between states, on the pervasive presence of conflict, and on the necessity for substantial military capabilities.[5] Diplomacy operated in re-

1. "United States Initial Postsurrender Policy for Japan," in John Maki, ed., *Conflict and Tension in the Far East* (Seattle: University of Washington Press, 1961), p. 125.

2. See Kenneth Waltz, *Man, the State and War* (New York: Columbia University Press, 1959), chap. 4; and Arnold Wolfers and Lawrence W. Martin, *The Anglo-American Tradition in Foreign Affairs* (New Haven: Yale University Press, 1956), chap. 12.

3. See, for example, Morton A. Kaplan, *The Rationale for NATO* (Washington, D.C.: American Enterprise Institute, 1972), pp. 5–10.

4. Not only did MacArthur dominate the policies of the Occupation, but he operated, until 1948, remarkably free from all outside influences, including that of his own government. George F. Kennan, *Memoirs, 1925–1950* (Boston: Little, Brown, 1967), pp. 376–385.

5. For an English synopsis of the history of Japanese diplomacy and security prior to World War II, see James B. Crowley, *Japan's Quest for Autonomy* (Princeton: Princeton University Press, 1966), pp. 3–4. On the European tradition, see Raymond Aron, *Peace and War* (New York: Praeger, 1968), pp. 589–600; and Waltz, *Man, the State and War*, pp. 198–223.

sponse to the compulsions and dangers of a fluid, contingent world in which
the margin of choice for statesmen was limited. Although there was some latitude for choice regarding the goals and means of diplomacy, rivalry and strife
were seen as the normal conditions of relations among nations. Military power
was simply an element of statecraft that was used to establish a new but condi-
tional "balance of power." A strong military force was regarded as an essential
asset of the nation and, given the character of international relations, the
morality of war was never an issue.

This approach to international affairs constituted, during the modern era,
the response to world affairs of all "great powers" except the United States
and, to a lesser extent, Great Britain. Two world wars brought to an end the
"European Age" of power politics, but it did not, as many had hoped, rev-
olutionize the character of international relations by rendering obsolete both
the nation-state and interstate power politics. However, the U.S. Occupation,
in the heady idealism that immediately followed victory, embodied the idea
that power politics had been one of the root causes of the war and endeavored
to eradicate this force. Note these goals as expressed by General MacArthur:

A complete reformation of the Japanese people—reformation from human slavery
to human freedom, from immaturity that comes of mythical teachings and legendary ritualism to the maturity of enlightened knowledge and truth, from the blind
fatalism of war to the considered realism of peace.[6]

The moral platform from which this reformation took place was the American diplomatic tradition, a tradition born of the unique historical experience of
the United States and the political and moral principles of American democracy. Whereas the Japanese-European tradition stressed necessity in establishing foreign-policy goals, the American one assumed that there was wide
latitude for choice and that moral principles must be applied in such choices.
American values were seen as universal, and the purpose of war was a "just
and secure peace," not a new balance of power. MacArthur took the most mil-
lenarian aspects of this tradition and froze them in Article 9 of the new constitution.[7] Japan's security no longer rested on military force, but "on the good
faith and justice of mankind . . . on the evolution of mankind, under which
nations would develop, for mutual protection against war, a yet higher law of
international social and political morality."[8]

In the face of Cold War realities, the vision of *pacem in terris* gave way to Pax
Americana, but Japan had inherited an extreme principle of idealism from a

6. Douglas MacArthur, *A Soldier Speaks* (New York: Praeger, 1965), p. 182.

7. There is some dispute as to whether the Japanese (namely Shidehara Kijurō) or Mac-
Arthur first suggested Article 9. As there was no mention of prohibiting armed forces or re-
nouncing war in the Matsumoto committee draft of the constitution issued more than a week
after Shidehara reported this to MacArthur, it seems clear that the idea was American. See
John K. Emmerson, *Arms, Yen and Power* (Tokyo: Charles E. Tuttle, 1971), pp. 51–52.

8. MacArthur, *A Soldier Speaks*, pp. 182, 169.

unique diplomatic tradition. One legacy is the moral cast of the debate over Japanese security in the ensuing years (an orientation accepted by all parties); another is the sharp discontinuity with prewar diplomatic experience—a fractured diplomatic tradition. By defining the security issue in such completely moral terms, the Japanese have become, in one sense, more American than America, an ironic situation that has been allowed to develop because of the extraordinary security commitments of the United States to contain communism in Asia.

The new Japanese diplomatic tradition would have quickly withered without suitably favorable international conditions. The moral rejection of power politics in the United States in large part had grown out of its geographical isolation from the conflicts that constantly beset Europe. What geography did for the United States, the United States and the Cold War have done for Japan. East Asia, the main locus of Japan's security problem, has been convulsed by war and conflict almost continuously since World War II, but the virtually unqualified American commitment to the military containment of communism in the region has insulated Japan from the conflicts. As this anomalous isolation from East Asian politics dissolves in the multipolar order, however, the moralistic assumptions underlying Japanese security policy will be challenged. Any Japanese move away from an essentially apolitical, noninvolved position toward a posture of political engagement (with attendent pressures for positive military action) is likely to precipitate deep internal political cleavages comparable to those experienced in the United States—first in the 1940s, during its move from isolationism to internationalism, and more recently in the bitter turmoil touched off by the indecisive and "immoral" war in Vietnam.

Similarly, any challenge to the premises underlying Japanese security policy are likely to be generated first from changes in the international situation, not from a calculated choice initiated by government in Tokyo. Furthermore, because Japan has become so deeply enmeshed economically in the region and the world, only the highly improbable occurrence of a generation of peace would enable the Japanese to remain aloof from a broadened role in power politics. That the linkage between economics and political security matters in foreign policy has not, until very recently, been fully acknowledged in Japan is due in large part to the second dimension of the new Japanese diplomatic tradition and the Pax Americana that has sustained it.

Economics and political-security issues

Japan's approach to the issue of security has been that of an expanding international trading company, not that of a nation-state. The Japanese have become a major global economic force and the preeminent power in the East Asian region. They are more dependent on imports of critical raw materials than any major industrial nation and have highly vulnerable shipping lines to these resources, but they have steadfastly refused to acknowledge the need for an overseas security role. Not only has Japan refused to dispatch forces abroad, but up to now there has been no linkage between its overseas economic interests and national military capabilities. In this still-prevailing vision of global affairs, economics and politics are seen as separable, and armament and power politics are rejected as critical ingredients for a successful foreign policy. The assumptions on which this dimension of Japanese foreign policy rest are also derived from the American diplomatic tradition. They have been perpetuated by the singularly salutary international economic relations that prevailed under United States leadership from 1950 to 1970 among both Western industrial powers and underdeveloped nations.

The separability of economics and politics in foreign policy has been an implicit (and often explicit) premise in the policies of all postwar Japanese governments and a perspective widely shared by many left-wing critics as well.[9] In short, there has been a consensus that defined Japan's international role in narrowly economic terms within the framework of the nation-state system. This is not a novel concept. It was most fully developed in the thought of the nineteenth-century economic liberals, especially Jeremy Bentham and Thomas Cobden, but the American liberal ideal since the founding of the Republic has also stressed a repudiation of power politics and the substitution of commercial for political relations among states.[10]

In this liberal vision of the international system, free trade among nations promotes the "natural harmony of interests" among peoples, a harmony that was perverted by the ruling groups of mercantilist Europe in the eighteenth and nineteenth centuries. Similar distortions occur in the contemporary system through nation-centered economic and political policies (such as protectionist trade barriers) that distort the free operation of the economic marketplace. Thus, international trade is not only a vehicle for economic prosperity, but ultimately a guarantor of peace, superseding power politics.[11]

More recently, the development of increasing economic interdependence among the advanced industrial societies has led some to declare that "the state is an old-fashioned idea, badly adapted to serve the needs of our present complex world," and others to promote economic collaboration among these in-

9. Although the concept of "economic diplomacy" has been part of Japan's approach to the world since the end of the Occupation, the notion was first developed publicly by Foreign Minister Shigemitsu in setting forth the broad goals of the new foreign policy of the first Hatoyama cabinet. See *Yomiuri shimbun*, Dec. 10, 1954. For an example of the left-wing view, see Noguchi Yūichirō, "Keizai nashonarizumu," *Sēkai*, Jan. 1965, pp. 53–62.

10. See, for example, Felix Gilbert, *To the Farewell Address: Ideas of Early American Foreign Policy* (Princeton: Princeton University Press, 1961).

11. Edward L. Morse, "Crisis Diplomacy, Interdependence, and the Politics of International Economic Relations," *World Politics* 24 (spring 1972), supplemental issue: *Theory and Policy in International Relations*, pp. 129–130.

dustrialized nations as a solvent to international political problems.[12] This orientation is integral to the new Japanese diplomatic tradition. The deep-seated legitimacy that the rationale for the trading-company approach has within the Japanese political and business worlds will inhibit any shift to new security policies unless there are compelling external circumstances.

Until the enunciation of the Nixon Doctrine, American security policy made it possible and appropriate for the Japanese to conduct a one-sided economic foreign policy in keeping with the principles of their new liberal diplomatic tradition. Power politics, however, were not peripheral to the postwar international system; the international economic order in which Japan operated so well rested on the political-security arrangements that served to underwrite the Western bloc.[13] Pax Americana was the foundation on which an "American world economy" rested. Even in bilateral Japanese-American relations, the security tie was at least as important as mutual economic interests in establishing the special economic relationship marked most notably by easy access to the United States market.

The world in which Japanese liberalism flourished was shattered in the early 1970s by a series of events that has brought together the high politics of a changing politicomilitary era and international economic relations. Economically, the erosion and collapse of the postwar monetary system and the perpetration of a global resource crisis by the producing nations' political use of economic resources have seriously jeopardized the fragile arrangements fostering global interdependence during the period of the "American world economy." The specter of economic nationalism is made more real by a climate conducive to political nationalism, which features the proliferation of nuclear weapons and an explicit recognition by the superpowers (as well as other nations) that the commitments and capabilities of the United States and the Soviet Union are no longer global in the Cold War sense.

In these new circumstances, Japan has been forced to reconsider its international economic policy side-by-side with its political role in the world, especially with regard to the oil-producing states. This shift implicitly repudiates a basic premise of the foreign policy consensus of the past two decades, but its meaning for security policy has not been fully recognized, far less developed. Although the uncertainty and the nation-centered features of the contemporary international situation have emerged from a complex pattern of events beyond

12. George W. Ball, "The Promise of the Multinational Corporation," *Fortune*, vol. 75, no. 6 (June 1, 1967), p. 80. For a proposal explicitly aimed at Japan, see Zbigniew Brzezinski, *The Fragile Blossom: Crisis and Change in Japan* (New York: Harper and Row, 1972), pp. 140–142. The recently formed Trilateral Commission is designed to promote international harmony through nonpolitical patterns of interaction.

13. Robert Gilpin, "The Politics of Transnational Economic Relations," *International Organization*, vol. 25, no. 3 (summer 1971), pp. 401–402. For similar views from a moderate "revisionist" position, see David P. Calleo and Benjamin M. Rowland, *America and the World Political Economy* (Bloomington: Indiana University Press, 1973), especially chap. 3.

the control of any single state, the shift in the premises of American policy has been particularly important to Japan. Accordingly, it is both ironic and instructive that the Japanese should rightly despair that Henry Kissinger, as a latter-day practitioner of the European diplomatic tradition, should, in a fundamental sense, prove to be so un-American.

JAPANESE DOMESTIC POLICY
AND SECURITY POLICY

In considering the development of Japan's security policies, domestic political influences and the external environment must be scrupulously distinguished and separately evaluated. Normally, a nation's strategic policy reflects a dynamic balance between internal and international considerations, but in Japan this relationship has been disrupted. Prolonged withdrawal from all power politics and the peculiar features of the new diplomatic tradition have led to a perspective that is, to an extraordinary extent, derived from politics and ideals unique to conditions *within* the country. It is essential, therefore, to consider the evolution of the security policy with an eye to ascertaining (1) the substantive features of this policy; (2) the way in which this issue is caught up in the dynamics of domestic politics; and (3) the degree to which the nation has the capacity to formulate a pragmatic security policy appropriate to a fluid and uncertain multipolar world.

A fundamental assumption regarding most studies of Japanese security is that they have been calculated responses to the realities of world politics—a perspective that is seemingly supported by the remarkable success of Japan in gaining international status and wealth at minimal cost, while ostensibly adhering to humanitarian and pacifist principles. Virtually all commentaries by Japanese strategic specialists presuppose that their nation's policy-makers have selected and will continue to select the "appropriate" policy for the external realities and given set of values.[14] Western (primarily American) studies of Japanese defense have taken a similar perspective.[15] The premise is also implicit in the Nixon Doctrine, which presumes that various political and economic pressures will provoke an appropriate, calculated Japanese response.

14. See, for example, Kiichi Saeki, "Japan's Security in a Multipolar World," paper presented at a Brookings Institution Conference, "The United States and Japan in Asia," Racine, Wisconsin, Jan. 4–5, 1973.

15. Examples include those that have concentrated on the Japanese domestic scene, such as Martin E. Weinstein, *Japan's Postwar Defense Policy* (New York: Columbia University Press, 1971), and John Welfield, *Japan and Nuclear China*, Canberra Papers on Strategy and Defense no. 9 (Canberra: Australian National University Press, 1970); and others that have focused mainly on the imperatives of the external environment, such as Robert E. Osgood, *The Weary and the Wary: U.S. and Japanese Security Policies in Transition* (Baltimore: Johns Hopkins University Press, 1972).

A main thrust of my argument is to severely qualify the notion that security policy for Japan (or any nation) is fully, or even primarily, the result of calculated choice. Situational factors, both domestic and international, severely limit the options open to decision-makers and thus make any analysis of the policy dialogue based on assumptions of a full, equal range of alternatives an incomplete and misleading guide to the basic influences shaping a nation's role in the world. This is particularly true in postwar Japan, where Japanese decision-making institutions have inhibited and continue to inhibit rapid, flexible responses; they have produced reactive, not active, policies. The incapacity for bold leadership, the extremely politicized nature of the policy-making process, and the lack of a partisan consensus on security matters assure that Japanese policies will be largely a product of the tangled web of domestic political forces. Moreover, the indeterminacy and complexity of the multipolar world render it improbable that Japan (or any other nation) will long be able to manage international conflict merely through deft maneuvers by statesmen and professional diplomats. Consequently, in analyzing Japan's foreign policy in general, or security policy in particular, emphasis should not be on a priori scenarios postulating a reversal of history or the moral imperatives of the peace constitution, but rather on the complex and changing character of domestic (and international) politics, which will continue to determine the direction of this nation's role in the world.

Japan's approach to defense has been remarkably unvarying and subdued, being built around full and unqualified United States security guarantees. Beyond the American alliance, there has been virtually no strategic policy regarding external threats or regional conflict. Security has been defined in the narrow sense of preserving national territorial integrity. Government defense measures have been aimed first at maintaining internal order and, second, at supplementing American forces to cope with a conventional invasion—a contingency that has been singularly implausible since the early 1950s. Every Japanese government has supported this narrow definition of security as defense of the home islands,[16] within which there is unlikely to be a clear or present military danger from any country that could not be met by its own modest conventional forces.

The development of the Japanese Self-Defense Forces, despite the fact that they are structured around five-year plans, displays two general characteristics of Japanese foreign policy—a lack of clear, long-term goals involving more independent actions by the nation and an emphasis on domestic over external considerations. The very extensive dependence on the United States has allowed defense plans to develop in a kind of international vacuum, in which the

16. The vague extension of a "security interest" to South Korea and Taiwan in the Nixon-Satō communiqué of November 1969 is properly viewed as a response to American pressure related to the return of Okinawa, not as a carefully calculated strategic policy.

direction and tempo of expansion have been treated more as a budgetary issue than a strategic one—in essence, a kind of weapons procurement review. The extraordinarily modest level of military expenditures—a record completely out of line with comparable expenditures of other industrial powers—has many causes, including political opposition to rearmament and the demands of rapid economic growth. However, the basic causes lie in the dynamics of decision-making and in the low priority (indeed, almost inadvertent attention) that has been accorded the question of external defense. With no independent strategic goals beyond providing a holding operation for the United States, and with no immediate political incentives for establishing such goals, even the limited appropriations requests of the Defense Agency have been grist in the mill of the Finance Ministry and other powerful elements of the bureaucracy, which have reduced them to proportions in line with other ministries' demands.

Within the ruling conservative party, there has been a consensus on the need for the Mutual Security Treaty, the principle of collective defense, the gradual strengthening of the Self-Defense Forces, the education of the public on national defense requirements, and (with some dissent) the preservation of the constitution. Two aspects of the conservative politicians' posture on defense are notable: a reluctance to speak out on the security issue because of potential domestic political repercussions; and a willingness to keep a wide range of policy options open. Because the security issue is such a highly politicized and controversial question within the LDP (as with all the parties), it will inevitably be caught up in factional politics if and when a shift to a new strategic posture is undertaken.

The nature of the foreign-policy-making process in Japan has prevented bold leadership not only on security policy, but on all major questions involving political rather than economic matters. The fragmented structure of the LDP —a style of authority that requires at least tacit consensus among all the responsible participants involved in policy-making (in this case the party faction leaders)—and the extreme degree to which intraparty politics has been involved in all major foreign policy moves have produced a kind of immobilism in conservative decision-making.[17]

Furthermore, the vehement and unqualified opposition of the Japanese Left to a more activist position has discouraged government initiatives by increasing the domestic political risks that would be involved. More recently, the proliferation of opposition parties and the shrinking margin of the conservatives' control of the Diet has further limited the capacity of the government to act.[18] Barring an unexpected reversal of past trends, which would alter the relative strength

17. On this point, see my *Japanese Domestic Politics and Foreign Policy* (Berkeley and Los Angeles: University of California Press, 1969), chaps. 3 and 9; and *Japan and East Asia: The New International Order* (New York: Praeger, 1972), chap. 3.

18. For elaboration, see Masataka Kōsaka, "Options for Japan's Foreign Policy," *Adelphi Papers* no. 97 (London: International Institute for Strategic Studies, 1973), pp. 17–22.

and modes of operation of the parties, or the sudden emergence of a nationalist consensus, this style of policy formulation will continue to restrain leadership no matter what the personalities or issues of the moment. Further, it will prevent a Gaullist-type move in the direction of a more autonomous political and military role in the world. Rather, basic shifts in security policy, if they occur, will be closely tied to changes in the international milieu, not ones independently initiated by policy-makers in Tokyo.

Security has been a central concern to all of the opposition parties, and this has given broad definition to Japanese public opinion as well as structure to the debate in the mass media and intellectual journals regarding the defense question. Despite many differences regarding details, the two most significant effects of the opposition parties' actions have been to fuel anti-American feelings and to give political identity to pacifism. The Left has made Article 9 into the most dramatic symbol of the new constitution, so that, aside from the weak and abortive challenges offered by several conservative leaders in the 1950s, the issue of the peace clause has not been directly and effectively raised.[19] In consequence, the government has operated in a pacifist milieu and has been placed continuously on the defensive with respect to all efforts to develop a security policy. As the very legality of the military forces has been vehemently questioned by a portion of the Left, it is not surprising that it has proved difficult for the government to articulate clear and positive national strategic objectives. Above all, the idealism embodied in Article 9 has given all matters of defense a peculiarly moral cast; it has drawn the question of security deeply into the issue of constitutional revision and a consideration of the basic attitudes regarding the very foundations of the postwar political order—reaching even to the relationship between citizen and state. Thus, the emotional and political legacies of Article 9 stand as major imponderables affecting the future direction of Japanese defense policy.

Each of the opposition parties has different reasons for opposing the current military alliance with the United States, but the substantive differences among their respective positions are less important than the overall political effect: to feed protonationalist and anti-American sentiments. Much of the public partisan clamor against the security treaty has been provoked by periodic campaigns to exploit the issue. In a world featuring détente with Communist powers and intensified economic competition among all states, the conservatives will be increasingly vulnerable to attacks leveled against Cold War style dependence on the United States, with such attacks having an implicit nationalistic appeal.

Even a cursory examination of the nature of foreign-policy-making in Japan

19. On this point, see Haruhiro Fukui, "Twenty Years of Revisionism," in D.F. Henderson, ed., *The Constitution of Japan: Its First Twenty Years* (Seattle: University of Washington Press, 1968), pp. 45–58.

and the substance of the security debate raise profound doubts about the capacity of Japan to devise a security policy suitable for a world of fluidity, uncertainty, and conflict. The decision-making process is most appropriately described as immobilist, and even under optimal conditions it ensures that Japan proceeds incrementally from one issue to another without a strategic calculus. Beyond the American alliance, there has been no real consideration of strategic options, and the debate over defense policy takes on highly moral and emotional forms. Therefore, any attempt to devise a fresh policy will raise issues challenging the assumptions of the new diplomatic tradition and threatening the stability of the domestic political system. The main result of this situation is to assure a passive role for Japan in foreign affairs, at a time when change and uncertainty have come to characterize both the political and economic dimensions of the international order.

THE EXTERNAL ENVIRONMENT

The changing nature of threats likely to face the Japanese and the new directions in which their strategic policy is likely to move can be more fully understood by examining the major external forces impinging on Tokyo.

The American alliance

During the last quarter century, the single most important determinant of Japan's security role was American strategic policy toward East Asia. In the years immediately after World War II, Japan was still seen as the main threat to peace in Asia, but with the onset of the Cold War, the triumph of the Communists in China, and the outbreak of the Korean War, Japan became a major and essential ally. Japan thus returned to international politics in 1952 in a comprehensive political and economic alliance in which the United States was the dominant partner. Moreover, the attendant security arrangements were not cast simply in bilateral terms, but with regard "to the maintenance of international peace and security in the Far East," which brought them into accord with the broad Cold War aims of the United States in the region.

Changes in the international realities in Asia during the 1960s—China's development of nuclear weapons and the escalation of the Vietnam War—led to slight modifications in this policy as the United States tried to move Japan into a leadership role in Asia in economic and, to a lesser extent, political affairs. Still built around a one-sided military partnership featuring an American nuclear umbrella, the modified policy was founded on several assumptions: that the United States would remain deeply engaged militarily in the region, both on nuclear and conventional levels; that there was and would continue to be a basic identity of Japanese and American security interests; and that the economic and political dimensions of policy could be effectively separated from security matters. The war in Vietnam ultimately challenged all of these assumptions, demonstrated that the United States lacked the capacity to control conflict effectively in the region, and shattered the bipartisan, internationalist domestic consensus on which postwar American policy had been built. This led to the Nixon Doctrine, the first fundamental reordering of American foreign policy priorities since the start of the Cold War.

The new "doctrine" never achieved the status of a fully developed policy position; rather, it consisted of a set of responses to altered international conditions and reflected the shift in the mood within the United States away from internationalism and anticommunism. Despite the vagueness of the vision and the impact of the unique Nixon-Kissinger diplomatic style, the basic points of departure from previous policy are likely to endure as permanent features of future American policy toward Asia generally and Japan specifically.

First, in the multipolar global order, the United States will not intervene militarily to "contain communism," as in the past two decades. Despite the affirmation that existing alliances would be honored, President Nixon also made it clear that "we are not involved in the world because we have commitments; we have commitments because we are involved. Our interest must shape our commitments, rather than the other way around."[20] Thus, an atmosphere of "indeterminacy" has replaced the certitude of the containment era.[21] Second, there is a notable shift from the globalist ideals of earlier policy to an emphasis on more narrowly defined national security interests and a concomitant assumption that East Asian nations can and will assume fuller responsibility for their own defense. Finally, there is a clear expectation that a stable, new international order ("a generation of peace") can be created in the region through policies stressing diplomatic maneuvering with the other great powers (now including China as well as Japan) rather than the far-flung alliances and direct American military intervention that characterized the "era of confrontation" now ending.[22]

This fundamental shift in the aims of American policy cannot but test the basis of the Japanese-American alliance, especially as the change in priorities rests not simply on choice, but on the reduced capacities (or will) of the United States to maintain global peace and to manage conflict in Asia. Even if

20. President Richard M. Nixon, *U.S. Foreign Policy for the 1970s: A Report to the Congress* (Washington, D.C.: Government Printing Office, 1971), p. 13. This statement also appeared in the president's first annual report in 1970.

21. Robert J. Pranger, *Defense Implications of International Indeterminacy* (Washington, D.C.: American Enterprise Institute, 1972).

22. For a good discussion of the military implications of the Nixon Doctrine for Japan, see Osgood, *Weary and Wary*, pp. 14–17.

American statesmen are able to maintain a credible nuclear and strategic umbrella for the defense of Japanese territory, the existing security arrangements
are likely to prove inadequate because of Japan's place in the radically altered
international landscape. Two features of this landscape are particularly important: (1) the massive and growing involvement of Japan in regional and global
international affairs (especially with the politically volatile Third World); and
(2) the impact of the still unfolding world economic and resource crises on the
fundamental stability and *modus operandi* of the global international system.

It will thus become increasingly difficult to keep in proper balance the
economic and strategic aspects of Japanese-American relations. More importantly, the direction of Japan's security policy cannot but be shaped increasingly by factors other than American policy. Rather than conjecture about
whether or when Japan may move to a more autonomous and activist security
policy, it is more instructive to explore the general kinds of diplomatic challenges the Japanese will face and the implications they hold for the use of military power by Tokyo as an instrument of diplomacy.

Japan and conflict in a pluralistic world of scarcity

Are any future international conflicts involving war likely to impinge upon
Japan? An answer to this question is elusive, not only because of the peculiar
Japanese domestic political situation and the unusual and successful security
policies of the postwar era, but also because of the current uncertainties over
the place of war itself in international affairs. What is clear is the confluence of
destabilizing factors of staggering proportions on the contemporary international scene: an acute shortage of basic resources (most notably a Malthu-
sian situation in some poor countries); an incredibly massive and rapid shift of
wealth to oil-exporting countries; a general weakening of the international
economic and political institutions previously devised to mediate and moderate
conflict; a persistence of profound national and ideological differences; and
nuclear proliferation. As in most periods of extreme uncertainty in world affairs, views regarding the place of war tend to cluster around two poles: an
end to war as a calculated instrument of policy, except for the very strong (the
superpowers) or the very weak (the chronically poor on the periphery of world
society); or an inexorable drift toward war as part of a deeply rooted malaise
leading to Armageddon.[23]

23. The former view is implicitly and explicitly part of the huge literature treating
"supranationalism" and economic independence as the crucial variables in international
affairs (for example, Miriam Camps, *The Management of Interdependence* [New York: Council
on Foreign Relations, 1974]), whereas the latter runs through the equally profuse publications focused on the dire international consequences of the problems of population, ecology,
resource scarcity, and especially the politics of oil.

From either perspective, there is little need for Japan to maintain a security policy in the traditional sense of the word. Indeed, from the first viewpoint, more important because it moves beyond an almost wholly determinist position, the current nonmilitary posture of Japan can be seen not as a transient aberration, but "as a model of what all nations might become."[24] Three basic arguments, *inter alia*, are offered to support the obsolescence of a substantial security role for Japan: (1) the unlikelihood of military conflict in terms of the Communist/non-Communist lines of the Cold War (the détente syndrome); (2) a growing degree of economic "interdependence" among a wide range of countries, which makes conventional diplomacy involving national security policies obsolete and counterproductive; and (3) the obvious impracticality and irrationality of war itself in a nuclear and post-Vietnam era. However, a more careful look at each of these arguments in terms of Japan's specific international situation raises serious doubts that the Japanese can, in fact, proceed without major concern for an expanded security policy.

At first glance, détente seems to provide a formidable reason against change from the present strategic policy. The relaxation of tensions between the United States and the Communist world (most notably the Soviet Union and China), the concomitant efforts to expand diplomatic and economic contacts with these countries, and the modest progress in strategic arms limitation agreements with the Russians may have contributed to the short-term prospects for peace. Most certainly, these developments have altered the hegemonial Cold-War alliance systems and the global strategies of the superpowers. However, to alter the strategies related to the Cold War is not to suspend the use of force from a central place in international affairs. To assume that the Soviet Union and China will effectively renounce the use of force as a central component of their foreign policies as a result of détente is an untenable, utopian denial of the continuity of international politics. Moreover, as the Korean and Vietnamese wars illustrate, the situation in Asia is further complicated by the fact that several smaller Communist and non-Communist states have both the military and political capacities to initiate violent conflict under circumstances that the great powers can neither fully control nor totally ignore.

Regional conflicts will persist, détente notwithstanding, and in view of the preeminent economic and mounting political commitments of Japan in the region, complete aloofness for the indefinite future will prove increasingly difficult. The current relaxation of tensions will not banish military conflict to the periphery of international politics in Asia (in this generation at least) and thereby remove the need for a Japanese security policy. On the contrary, because of the implicit nationalist (as distinct from globalist) orientation of the current trend in international affairs, pressures will continue to mount on

24. William Bundy, "International Security Today," *Foreign Affairs*, vol. 53, no. 1 (Oct. 1974), p. 33.

Japan to look to itself more fully in defining national interests and adopting policies appropriate to those interests.

The immediate problems of the current international political situation, which may push Japan into an expanded security policy, center on the credibility of the United States as viewed from Tokyo, and the gap between the realities of the contemporary scene and the existing alliance arrangements. Even a cursory inspection of the Asian political landscape shows that the profound political and ideological differences generated during the last three decades between the Communist states and movements, on the one hand, and the non-Communist states and groups, on the other, remain as critical features and a potential cause of conflict in the region. Moreover, the web of political and economic ties binding Japan to the non-Communist states in the region are substantial.[25] At the same time, the indeterminacy of the contemporary pluralist world and the more nationalist orientation of American and Soviet policy have made the alliances between the superpowers and their primary Asian Cold War allies (the Japanese-American Mutual Security Treaty and especially the Sino-Soviet Treaty of Friendship and Alliance) fragile anachronisms.

In the immediate future, the credibility of the United States commitment to Tokyo will, in particular, be tested by two continuing problems: the disposition of Taiwan and the political division of Korea. The war in Indochina, a third test of recent times, has already ended in an American defeat of major proportions. Resolution of the Taiwan question—a controversial issue within Japan —remains basically in the hands of Washington and Peking, but the prospects for a major war in Korea can be substantially determined by local conditions. If large-scale military action takes place, particularly if it leads to an extension of Communist control, a limited American response would provide "final evidence" concerning the general security role of the United States in East Asia. Taiwan provides a similar test, should a resort to force in the near future occur.

In short, anything short of peace in the region will force Japan to reconsider its own policies and interests and, at the very least, to regard the bilateral security treaty in a new and more limited light. However, although realpolitik machinations could force Japan to reassess its security policy, the immediate cause for a move by Tokyo into power politics may well grow out of the nature of Japanese economic interests and how they are affected by power politics.

The future security policy of Japan will, of necessity, focus on access to vital raw materials and markets to assure the survival and health of the national economy. No matter how successful the government may be in the short run in solving the problems of cost and availability of resources and energy, Japan is likely to remain the most vulnerable of the advanced industrial societies to breakdowns in the international economic system and political machinations of Third-World countries involving critical raw materials.

25. On this point, see Hellmann, *Japan and East Asia*, especially chaps. 2 and 5.

There is little dispute over these assertions, but there are substantial differences over their implications for Japanese policy. Again, a polarization of views exists. Economists and political analysts, beguiled by the "interdependence" of the world economy, see the present highly restricted security policy of Japan as both appropriate and continuing. In their most extreme form, these arguments take on an extraordinary ahistorical cast: "multiple dependence on other countries" and "the effects of affluence" will keep Japan from "exerting traditional forms of power around the world";[26] the extension and permanent dependence by Japan on raw material, energy, and food imports has rendered obsolete power politics as a guideline to policy.[27] Others, starting from the same premise of interdependence, reach the sharply contrasting conclusion that the oil crisis and its attendant monetary problems have pushed the world to the brink of a situation "comparable in its potential for economic and political disaster to the Great Depression of the 1930s."[28] They seem to believe that only creative diplomacy and unprecedented cooperation could avert such a disaster. In a world of chaos, force would become the medium for the resolution of conflict.

If there is a total collapse of world order or, conversely, a withering away of international politics because of economic interdependence, the question of Japanese security will be wholly determined by factors beyond the reach of Tokyo. However, short of the millenium or an apocalyptic collapse, Japan is destined to live in a pluralist world of scarcity in which an expanded and more autonomous security policy is adopted in the course of establishing viable international economic relationships.

To a much greater extent than the United States, Japan is truly interdependent with the resource-exporting nations, which tend to be underdeveloped, chronically unstable, and increasingly prone to use their economic assets for political purposes. Extensive interdependence of this sort leads to either the creation of institutions for the regulation of mutual interests or a drive for dominance by one (or more) of the partners.[29] Efforts, such as those now under way to coordinate the energy policies of the industrialized, oil-importing nations, will have to be devised time and again to cope with recurring crises in a resource-scarce world; it is quixotic to postulate undeviating success. Under conditions of shortage, the possibility for international cooperation becomes more remote, the pressures for competition in terms of narrow national interests increase, and political power becomes deeply and inextricably linked

26. Bundy, "International Security Today," p. 32.

27. Saburo Okita, "Natural Resource Dependency and Japanese Foreign Policy," *Foreign Affairs*, vol. 52, no. 4 (July 1974), pp. 714–724.

28. Walter J. Levy, "World Oil Cooperation or International Chaos," *Foreign Affairs*, vol. 52, no. 4 (July 1972), p. 713.

29. For elaboration on this point, see Kenneth N. Waltz, "Conflict in World Politics" in S. Spiegel and K. Waltz, eds., *Conflict in World Politics* (Cambridge, Mass.: Winthrop Publishers, 1971), p. 46.

with economic policy. Under these conditions, interdependence does not lead away from security policy, but more likely provides the catalyst for Japanese participation in realpolitik.

There are, of course, limitless possible scenarios for when and under what circumstances Japan might be led to military intervention or a more active security policy, but the issues and problems are perhaps clearest in the East Asian region, where extensive economic interests are bolstered by special and longstanding political interests. Japan is not economically dependent on any country in Asia in the sense it is dependent on the Middle East for oil. Japan does, however, rely on countries such as Indonesia for imports of several critical materials (such as oil, bauxite, and timber). Moreover, a loss in the high level of trade and investment with a country such as South Korea would be costly in a precariously balanced economic situation, and would take a political and psychological toll as well. The cumulative commercial (trade and investment) and aid entanglements of Japan with these countries do not add up to a short-term economic *necessity* for Japanese military involvement. Incentives for any such drastic action would also be political—both external, in the form of pressures from nations fully participating in a world of realpolitik, and internal, in the form of political imperatives associated with maintaining a popularly accepted level of prosperity.

In a world of scarcity, the inherent propensity toward aggressive nationalistic actions can only intensify the pressure for drastic action. This is not to suggest that conflict (and Japan's military involvement in that conflict) will proceed from a kind of anarchy in Asia; there will certainly be a web of collective and cooperative endeavors in various fields, especially security. However, a basic and often forgotten condition of international politics is that in *all* international situations involving cooperative action (interdependence), one cannot always rely on the others, even when all agree on the goals and have an equal interest in the projects. Rousseau's parable of the stag suggests some of the difficulties inherent in cooperative endeavor; Kenneth Waltz has brilliantly and aptly applied the parable to international politics.

Assume that five men (nations) who have acquired a rudimentary ability to speak and to understand each other happen to come together at a time when all of them suffer from hunger. The hunger of each will be satisfied by the fifth part of a stag, so they agree to cooperate in a project to trap one. But also the hunger of any one of them will be satisfied by a hare, so as a hare comes within reach, one of them grabs it. The defector obtains the means of satisfying his hunger but in doing so permits the stag to escape. His immediate interest prevails over consideration of his fellows.[30]

It is important to recognize that the rabbit-snatcher was rational and predictable from *his* point of view and capricious only in regard to the others. The

30. Waltz, *Man, the State and War*, pp. 167–168.

United States seems to have learned the implied lesson and currently is taking the lead in a cooperative venture of sharing with the oil-importing nations (seeking the stag), while pressing hard on a project for energy self-sufficiency (approaching the hare).

For Japan, the implications of the parable are profound. Not only will domestic politics make it difficult for Tokyo to participate in cooperative ventures regarding security-economics, but the limited resources under Japanese political control make success in such cooperative ventures the only option open—other than a massive, autonomous expansion of security policy. As the mores regulating relations among states take on the more traditional political economy cast, the prospects for conflict and some sort of expanded security policy for Japan are very high indeed.

If war is to be a peripheral feature of internal politics, then the minimal security option currently followed by Japan is indeed the best.[31] American and Soviet development of nuclear arsenals in the 1950s and the doomsday character of the destructive force involved led many to conclude that the world had indeed crossed the technological threshold making war obsolete because of the costs involved for all parties. Furthermore, both the prolonged strategic stalemate between the superpowers and modest progress toward arms control seem to demonstrate that those with the capacity to act recognize the unacceptability of all-out war. However, efforts to prevent the spread of nuclear weapons have not worked. More important, the political conflicts that underlie the use of force in international affairs have persisted and led to widespread violence with conventional arms. As both Raymond Aron and Henry Kissinger early recognized, and as the history of the last quarter-century has shown, the issue was never total peace or complete annihilation, but really the role and implication of the nuclear dimension in the conduct of strategic policy by the major powers.[32] For Japan, as for other nations, the nuclear era does not mean an end to strategy, but simply a more complicated strategic calculus.

The Vietnam War and the other costly military excursions of the United States since the end of World War II have raised doubts about the utility (and even the legitimacy) of any large-scale military intervention abroad by any great power. But the notion that war is soon to be abandoned as an instrument of policy is highly questionable in a world of scarcity, economic interdependence, and polymorphous violence. To be sure, in certain areas of the world, most notably Western Europe, the possibility of war among the nations of the region in the manner of the past has been greatly reduced because of superpower strategic confrontation and prolonged, institutionalized economic coop-

---

31. See Louis J. Halle, "Does War Have a Future?" *Foreign Affairs*, vol. 52, no. 1 (Oct. 1973), pp. 20–34, for an illustrative example of the "no-war" argument.

32. See Raymond Aron, *On War* (Garden City, N.Y.: Doubleday, 1958); and Henry A. Kissinger, *Nuclear Weapons and Foreign Policy* (New York: Harper, 1957).

eration. In the Middle East, Asia, and other economically poor or politically precarious areas, however, there has been recurrent violent conflict. It is utterly quixotic to postulate the end of conventional or internationalized insurgency warfare in the Third World; it is only slightly less so to suggest that Japan (or other industrialized nations) can remain completely aloof from such conflicts indefinitely. Alteration in the nature of warfare has not destroyed the need for a security policy in Tokyo.

Security for Japan in a pluralist world of scarcity can no longer be conducted under the liberal diplomatic principles sustained by the bipolar Cold War era. Politics and economics are no longer separable, and Japan's extensive overseas economic involvement, especially in Asia, will force the development of a foreign policy in which strategic considerations have a greatly expanded role. The critical question is no longer whether Japan will accept realpolitik, but whether a broadened security policy can be devised without destabilizing the domestic political system.

Basic Trends in Japanese Security Policies

MAKATO MOMOI

> In the long run, however, rifles and swords can no longer prevail. . . . What grasps people's minds and functions as a gyrocompass for domestic and international politics will be . . . the power of moral justice and the spirit of rationalism.[1]

This was the first reference to a national security concept made by a Japanese premier after the surrender in August 1945. Addressing the Eighty-Ninth Imperial Parliament on January 28, 1946, Shidehara Kijurō reminded the public of a stern fact—that the government was too occupied with the administrative affairs related to postwar reconstruction to think about national security per se. His reference to the "power of moral justice" echoed Morito Tatsuo's thesis that the truly peaceful nation not only wants no war but possesses no war potential and that "a defeated Japan could now grasp the chance to live as a truly peaceful nation" and in this role "become a leader of the world."[2]

FROM "NO WAR" TO POLICE RESERVE FORCE

No one suspected at the time of Shidehara's address that he had met with General MacArthur four days earlier (January 24, 1946), and that they allegedly had discussed the now-famous no-war clause (Article 9) in the draft of the new constitution. One scholar has speculated that a renunciation of war was the "price" the government had to pay for the "generous act of the Allied nations

---

1. Naikaku Kanbō, ed., *Naikaku sōridaijin enzetsu shu* (Tokyo: Sōrifu Shuppon Kyoku, 1965), p. 410.
2. Morito Tatsuo, "Heiwa kokka no kensetsu," *Kaizō*, Jan. 1946, pp. 14-15.

in letting Japan keep its emperor system."[3] With many important postwar official documents still classified, it is difficult to determine who actually initiated Japan's no-war clause. It is clear, however, that Article 9 was not so much the product of a well-thought-out strategic decision as the result of current domestic and international political pressures. On December 1, 1945, the JCP had called for the "destruction of the emperor system," and when Nozaka Sanzō, later to be a key figure in the Communist Party, returned from China on January 14, 1946, he had pledged to "crush the emperor system." On January 16, Australia and New Zealand had submitted to the General Headquarters a list of war criminals which included the emperor's name, and two days before that, General MacArthur had met with Shidehara concerning the setting up of the Far Eastern Military Tribunal.

Regardless of who originally advocated Article 9, it was inserted in the constitution (promulgated on November 3, 1946) and has since remained a vital issue in all discussion of and planning for Japan's national defense. Short of an extremely unlikely constitutional revision or some political catastrophe, the article will remain the point at which all reviews and studies of Japanese defense policy must begin. The article has been both expedient and obstructive. Successive Japanese governments have found it expedient to point to this legal restriction in their efforts to resist U.S. pressures to rearm, and to put their resources into economic expansion instead. But the article has also been an obstacle to convincing the Japanese public that renouncement of war does not preclude a capacity for self-defense. Ironically, Nozaka Sanzō was the first to press the government for a distinction between "a just war, a war fought by an invaded country, and an unjust war, a war of aggression." Interestingly, Premier Yoshida replied, "The interpellator seems to argue that a war for the self-defense of a nation is just and right. . . . I consider it harmful to accept such an argument. [Applause] . . . Recognition of a right to self-defense can provoke a war [under the excuse] of a just war."[4]

Even the conservative premier, at least in 1945, received an ovation (apparently from conservatives) for denouncing "rights of belligerency" and even self-defense. It took four years, a series of international strategic developments, and instructions from MacArthur's headquarters before the Japanese government again considered its state of no armament. On July 12, 1950, seventeen days after the outbreak of the Korean War, General MacArthur "authorized" (meaning "instructed") the Japanese government to set up a 75,000-man Police Reserve Force to deal with internal disorders.[5] Although the character of

3. Ueyama Sumpei, *Daitōa sensō no isan* (Tokyo: Chūō Kōronsha, 1972), pp. 154–155.

4. Shimizu Shin, ed., *Chikujō Nihon koku kempō shingiroku* (Tokyo: Yunikaku, 1962), vol. 2, p. 81.

5. There were two methods for arriving at the magic number of 75,000 men: it was comparable to the number of men in the four U.S. divisions scheduled to leave Japan for Korea; and it was the balance of the 200,000 policemen authorized under the Potsdam Declaration minus the 125,000 already in force.

the Police Reserve Force has changed over the years, it has remained essentially a parapolice force. Organizationally, it was to report to the prime minister via a state minister in charge, and the contemporary Self-Defense Forces are also controlled directly by the prime minister.

FROM POLICE RESERVE
FORCE TO REARMAMENT

The establishment on August 10, 1950, of the Police Reserve Force triggered the first postwar debates over Japan's rearmament. Former Premier Ashida Hitoshi led a pro-rearmament group, whereas Prime Minister Yoshida opposed the idea of rearmament. Yoshida told the Tenth Diet Plenary Session (January 26, 1951) that "an argument for rearmament has already created unnecessary suspicions both overseas and in Japan. . . . In fact, large-scale armaments are something that a defeated Japan cannot afford to undertake." He then argued that the "safety and independence of a nation rests not exclusively on armament, but on a people's passion for independence and freedom."[6] For him, "just to think of rearmament is a stupid act of the foolish, and a wild dream of the ignorant; they know nothing about the situation in the world."[7] Yoshida advanced three reasons for his position: (1) rearmament was too expensive for the economy of a defeated Japan; (2) psychologically, the public did not support it; and (3) the scars of the defeat were still unhealed." With these arguments, he squarely opposed a suggestion for Japan's rearmament when he met with John Foster Dulles just three days before the outbreak of the Korean War.[8] Evidently unimpressed, Dulles told an American Club luncheon meeting on the same day that if Japan were to opt for a free world, it had to be capable of dealing with indirect aggression. Later, on September 15, Dulles told the State Department press corps that there should be no limits on the extent of Japan's rearmament or the size of the U.S. forces stationed in Japan.

Yoshida's views on national security, however, underwent a subtle change after his second meeting with Dulles in January 1951. Resorting to a concept of "historical inevitability"—that no nation could defend itself singlehandedly at a time when "common defense has become the dominant concept of defense" —he accepted the idea of a Japan-U.S. mutual security treaty system.[9] "Neither side imposed the system on the other," he insisted, "since both sides wanted to prepare against Communist aggressions."[10] In short, he still opposed

6. Naikaku Kanbō, ed., *Enzetsu shu*, p. 506.
7. Yoshida Shigeru, *Kaisō jūnen* (Tokyo: Shinchōsha, 1957), p. 160.
8. Ibid., p. 162.
9. Ibid., p. 161.
10. Ibid., p. 179.

Japan's full-scale rearmament, but recognized a need for a certain force to maintain internal order. As such an internal force would be insufficient to deal with an outside threat, he looked for an "appropriate external power" to fill the void. In his view, this was a job for the United Nations. In the absence of a clear-cut notion on how the U.N. could protect Japan from external aggression, however, Japan would have to rely on the U.S., the "central power . . . in terminating the [Pacific] war and managing the Occupation."[11]

Between September 1950 and January 1951, the Foreign Office produced its first three major papers on Japan's national security. Each of them called for the stationing of U.S. troops in Japan until the U.N. could become capable of guaranteeing Japan's security. A fourth paper—actually a revised version of the first—was completed on December 27 and stated explicitly that Japan "does not desire to rearm itself."[12] In the meantime, the rearmament advocate, Ashida, who had written his own memorandum and distributed it among the ranking officials at the General Headquarters, conferred with Yoshida on December 14, 1950. The Ashida memorandum reflected his fear of "an imminent outbreak of World War III" and his despair at Japan's "standing idly by . . . while the U.N. forces were engaged in a fierce battle so close to Japan." On January 1, 1951, MacArthur, in his New Year message, delivered his first public call for Japan's rearmament by asking Japan to repulse violence with force.

In October 1951, the Liberal party (Jiyūtō) published its "Basic Policy Outline in the Post-Peace Treaty Era" (Kōwa-go ni okeru kihon seisaku taikō), which is the first government party argument for (1) "establishment of a basic self-defense posture"; (2) gradual build-up of defense capability; and (3) reinforcement of the Police Reserve and Maritime Safety forces for the maintenance of internal order.[13] On January 31, 1952, Yoshida informed the lower-house Budget Committee that the Police Reserve Force would cease as such by the end of October, and that his government would like to consider "what one might call defense" (bōei to itta mono). This occasion was Yoshida's first public (reluctant, it would seem, judging from his peculiar phraseology) mention of the word defense (bōei). Three months later, the peace treaty, along with the U.S.-Japan security pact, went into effect. Under the terms of the pact, the U.S. forces stationed in Japan would deal with any direct aggression against Japan, and the Japanese paramilitaries—the ground (hoantai) and maritime (keibitai) forces—with indirect aggression (internal troubles, riots and natural disasters). On October 15, 1952, the Hoanchō (Security Agency) was established to control both the ground and maritime forces; it was to remain a "nonmilitary organization with sufficient capability to maintain internal order."[14]

11. Ibid., vol. 3, p. 116.
12. Frederick S. Dunn, *Peacemaking and the Settlement with Japan* (Princeton, N.J.: Princeton University Press, 1963), pp. 84–85.
13. Tsuji Seimei, ed., *Shiryō sengo nijūnen shi* (Tokyo: Nihon Hyōronsha, 1966), p. 94.
14. Bōeichō Rikujō Bakuryō Kambu, *Hoantai shi* (Tokyo: Sorifu Shuppon Kyoku, 1958), pp. 8–10.

During the negotiations for the Mutual Security Treaty concluded between Japan and the U.S. in 1953, the U.S. side allegedly suggested a 325,000-man land force for Japan. On October 11, 1953, Ikeda Hayato, the head of the Japanese delegation, elaborated the various legal, sociopolitical, economic, and physical factors that would prevent Japan from constructing such a force. These restrictive factors—Article 9, antimilitary sentiment, low national income, and a low recruitment rate, all of which are still more or less valid—somehow convinced the U.S. side to settle for a 180,000-man ground force, the size that remains in effect today.

THE DEFENSE AGENCY AND
THE FIRST POLICY PAPER

Following the passage of the defense bills in both houses of the Diet (in May and June 1954), the Defense Agency (Bōeichō) and the ground, maritime, and air Self-Defense Forces were formally set up on July 1, 1954. Although there was still no official basic defense policy, a euphemistically named Administrative System Study Committee (Seidochōsa Iinkai) had been created within the Security Agency on October 5, 1952, as a centralized office for studying the security issue. A vice-director (vice-minister) headed the committee, and its subcommittees on defense, economic affairs, and systems were chaired by high-ranking officials who, in practice, served as top-level advisers to the minister in charge of the agency and the prime minister, who was the legal supreme commander of the Self-Defense Forces.

Between May 1953 and April 1955, the then little-known committee studied a series of ten programs on the basis of three assumptions: (1) Japan must be able to prevent both direct and indirect aggression, secure sea-supply lanes, and protect its independence and safety (the inclusion of direct aggression is particularly noteworthy because the Security Agency was officially charged only with countering internal troubles); (2) Japan must remain within the collective security system of the free world; and (3) plans for Japan's defense must take into consideration the state of the Japanese economy and the state of mind of the people.

In April 1955, the committee completed its long-range "six-year defense plan" aimed primarily at "enabling the gradual withdrawal of U.S. forces as we build up forces in accordance with an increasing national potential."[15] Defense Agency Director Sugihara Arata reiterated this position on July 1, 1955, when he told the lowerhouse Cabinet Affairs Committee, "Our efforts are directed at establishing a proper and appropriate self-defense system necessary for an independent nation . . . and we hope that the U.S. forces, at least their ground troops, will withdraw [from Japan] in the course of this achievement."

15. Hatoyama Ichirō's address to the Twenty-Second Diet, April 25, 1955.

The Joint Chiefs of Staff of the Defense Agency had also circulated its first "strategic estimate," which pointed out that the U.S.-Soviet confrontation would not disappear in the coming ten years; the two powers would avoid an atomic war or an act of mutual annihilation; and a local conflict might break out in and around Japan if and when Japan's ties with the free world should be loosened.[16] The Joint Chiefs of Staff paper further speculated that "the Soviet Union might find no need for launching an amphibious operation [against Japan] if it could capture air and sea supremacy . . . and if Japan should lose the will to fight." Hence, the paper gave priority to the build-up of air and naval capabilities. Because of political rather than strategic considerations, however, the ground force actually received prime consideration. The ground force was more relevant for the early withdrawal of U.S. troops and the easiest of the three services to build up.[17]

On May 20, 1957, the Defense Council (Kokubō Kaigi, the Japanese counterpart of the U.S. National Security Council) announced the first—and, so far, only—Basic Policy of National Defense (BPND). The brief but precise paper (1) stressed the deterrent function of a defense capability; (2) pledged support for U.N. activities; (3) emphasized the need for a comprehensive national security policy; (4) called for a "gradual build-up of an efficient defense capability" exclusively for the purpose of self-defense, and finally, (5) argued that "the security system with the U.S. will be sufficient to deal with any external aggression."

FROM THE FIRST TO
THE FOURTH BUILD-UP PLANS

Between 1957 and 1972 the Japanese cabinets announced four defense build-up plans, each of which represented an increasingly autonomous position. The first plan, announced on June 14, 1957, one month after the publication of the BPND, was not based on any concrete strategic concept or goal. It merely served the political purpose of acquiring a minimum defense capability—a "quick build-up of the ground force to fill a possible vacuum that might be created by the withdrawal of U.S. troops." The plan was "not at all clear on what strategic situations the self-defense forces were designed to deal with," mainly due to a "lack of knowledge concerning nuclear arms and their future."[18]

The second plan, announced on July 18, 1961, for the five-year period 1962–1966, confronted a number of issues not dealt with in the first plan or other government defense papers. As Defense Minister Akagi Munenori

16. Asagumo Shimbunsha, ed., *Nihon no anzen hoshō* (Tokyo: Asagumo Shumbunsha, 1973), pp. 168–169.
17. Ibid., p. 169.   18. Ibid., p. 174.

earlier elaborated to reporters, it was drafted on the basis of a strategic concept calling for Japan to remain "strategically defensive," and for the U.S. to carry out offensive (retaliatory) operations.[19] Second, it specifically stated that the forces must be able to "deal effectively with an aggression lower in scale than a local conventional war," and recognized the need to deal with a fairly large-scale aggression, without U.S. help during the initial period. Finally, it emphasized the need to acquire missile capabilities and gave priority to air defense build-up.

A stress on an "autonomous posture" and a qualitative build-up emerged with the third plan announced on November 29, 1966. It specified defense capabilities that could "deal *most* effectively with an aggression lower in scale than a local conventional war" (italics added; "most" did not exist in the phraseology of the two earlier plans). The new plan also emphasized an "autonomous naval and air build-up," particularly naval, evidently reflecting Japan's concern over the expanding Soviet naval presence in the Far East.

The fourth plan of 1971–1972 and Japan's first Defense White Paper gave top priority to the "autonomy" of its defense posture in general. Partly in response to a shift in the overall U.S. strategic posture in Asia (suggested in the Guam Doctrine), Arita Kiichi was the first defense leader to openly mention the possibility of a "delay" in the arrival of U.S. help. In a draft White Paper, he reportedly argued that "if the arrival of U.S. help were delayed, Japan must be able to prevent any aggressor from achieving a *fait accompli*."[20] Japan no longer assumed that U.S. help would arrive in time. The Arita paper, however, was not formally approved by the cabinet before Arita was replaced by Nakasone Yasuhiro in a January 1970 cabinet reshuffle.

Japan's first Defense White Paper, which Nakasone finally published ten months later on October 20, 1970, did not emphasize, as Arita's draft had, a "rejection of nonaligned neutrality," but did stress the need to reverse the manner in which the Japanese viewed their security relations with the U.S. The paper proposed that the Mutual Defense Treaty should "supplement" (and not substitute for) Japan's own autonomous defense capability. Nakasone labeled his basic concept an "exclusively defensive posture" (*senshu bōei;* a euphemism designed to restrict Japan's military efforts to defensive actions). Other features of the first Defense White Paper were its consideration of the possibility of internal troubles that might invite intervention from an external power, and its strategic estimate that "it is most unlikely that a major nuclear war will break out and involve Japan." The paper further insisted that Japan ought to maintain an air and sea capacity sufficient to deal with any crisis (obviously for a limited, initial period before U.S. help arrived). The question Arita had raised—what would Japan do if U.S. help failed to arrive in time—remained unanswered.

19. Ibid., pp. 196–197.   20. *Asahi shimbun*, Sept. 17, 1969.

When Nakasone told the lower house Cabinet Affairs Committee on October 26, 1970, that he was planning a Fourth Defense Build-up Plan, which, he hinted, would cost about twice as much as the third plan, he set off a chain of controversies. The fourth plan draft was revised and scaled down before it was announced on December 1, 1971, following a series of events including Mishima Yukio's suicide (November 25, 1970) and a midair crash of an Air Self-Defense Force plane with a commercial airliner. The fourth plan had to wait until February 7, 1972, for its final Defense Council approval; eighteen days later, however, its budget was "frozen" by parliamentary decision because of its alleged "unauthorized weapons acquisition program." A month after the formation of the Tanaka cabinet (July 7, 1972), the agency revised the plan. The cabinet finally approved it on October 9, following Tanaka's return from Peking where he allegedly had ascertained that Japan's defense build-up plan was not necessarily provocative to Chinese leaders, as some Japanese had feared it would be. The ordeal for the ill-fated Fourth Build-up Plan was not over yet; late in December 1973, the final fatal blow came from an unrelated, nonmilitary source—the Arab oil embargo. The agency voluntarily scaled down its requirements for oil-consuming weapon systems (tanks, jets, and large ships). Rising weapon costs resulting from the higher oil prices further threatened planned procurement programs.

POLICY CHARACTERISTICS
AND PRINCIPLES

Some striking features of Japan's defense policies emerge from this brief review of the evolution of these policies over the past quarter-century.

Ambiguity. Both the official denial of the presence of potential enemies and the absence of any sense of threat among the general public—at least the threat of an immediate and large-scale attack—have inevitably led to ambiguous defense policies. Such ambiguity is often due to the way in which the policies are officially expressed, with the use (and abuse) of euphemism. The terminology not only defies exact translation into English (see, for example, the official English version of the Defense White Paper), but also precludes an easy, first-glance understanding to ordinary Japanese.

Coincidental good luck. Japan has simply been fortunate that it has not been involved in any armed conflict for over twenty-five years. So far (at least prior to the oil crisis), its build-up plans have happened to mesh with strategic trends and general developments in the international environment conducive to keeping Japan out of armed conflict. Consequently, as none of Japan's plans have ever been put to the test, the country has never felt a strong incentive to develop its own strategic concepts.

Internal restrictions. Numerous restrictive factors—geopolitical, demographic, sociopsychological, and legal—have kept Japan from intensive rearmament. Economic and industrial restrictions—in particular Japan's extreme dependency on overseas resources—have prevented Japan from developing its own comprehensive national security policy and have led to a certain fatalism, especially regarding protection of overseas assets.

Limited options. Japan's original rearmament was undertaken in the absence of a national consensus and accelerated in the context of bipolar confrontation. Now Japan faces diplomatic difficulties in adjusting to new external conditions such as the oil crisis, which has compounded Japan's difficulties mainly because of a lack of diplomatic experience in the Middle East, or the U.S.-Soviet nuclear détente, which is basically the type of political framework that Japan should welcome, but which confuses the hitherto Cold-War-oriented Japanese opinion leaders.

Basic vulnerability. "Autonomous defense" remains a euphemism, and a policy of continued reliance on the U.S. increasingly runs counter to recent neonationalist trends. Economic and geopolitical circumstances make Japan extremely vulnerable not only to an attack, but even to political or psychological bluff, such as the threat of an oil embargo or a Persian Gulf blockade.

Arrogance. Despite Japan's vulnerability and the many internal and external limitations on the country's defense policy, sentiment in Japan strongly favors "big powerism" and "independent diplomacy" (which no one can define) or "autonomous defense" (which in reality depends on U.S. help). Few Japanese realize how arrogant it must sound to most Asian nations when their government refers to its defense expenditure costing "less than 10 percent of Japan's GNP"; in real monetary terms, the amount is comparable to the total national budget in many other Asian countries.

Timidity. In contrast, however, to this unintended arrogance, the Japanese government is still timid about persuading the Japanese public of the need for national defense. The government has also failed to realize that its timidity can breed suspicion among other nations, such as the unfounded allegations that Japan might "go nuclear" or use military means to protect overseas assets and merchant ships.

WHERE WILL JAPAN GO FROM HERE?

The recent oil crisis has intensified Japan's sense of frustration over the security question and, in effect, overshadowed the defense issue itself. It is no longer national security, but "resource security" that must receive the major allocation of Japan's human and physical resources. Without oil, no destroyers or jets can move; nothing could more clearly show the layman where the real issue of national security lies. Such an understanding, however, could cause the Japanese to underestimate the importance of their self-defense capability at a time when it is imperative to balance allocations of national resources adequately among the several factors that will ensure Japan's national security and contribute to "international security as well."

The oil crisis undoubtedly accelerated a general trend toward "de-Americanization." Japanese leaders simply stopped talking about a wholesale reliance on the U.S. after witnessing how the U.S. behaved in recent years during the course of such events as the oil crisis, the Middle East War, and the Cyprus incident.[21] Some even voiced a fear that the next *shokku* (shock) might well be a U.S. ban on the export of agricultural products. These fears will disappear only if U.S.-Japan relations are maintained on a firmer, friendlier basis.

The changing conditions of the 1970s could provide Japan with a good opportunity for overhauling its strategic concepts, moving away from the carbon copy of past U.S. concepts. Even the United States has begun to move away from a concept based on mutual assured destruction toward a recognition that, in essence, the best way to win a war is to avoid it in the first place (see, for example, the Washington Agreement of June 1973). Such a shift would require a reversal in traditional strategic thinking, which has essentially forced planners to consider how a war might break out and, hence, how to fight in this or that contingency. Instead, they would concentrate on how a specific nation could terminate an armed conflict if one should break out despite all efforts to avoid it, and what preparations should or should not be made under such circumstances.

CONCEPTUAL CONVERGENCE: U.S. AND JAPANESE STRATEGIC THINKING

Throughout all the subtle, gradual shifts in Japan toward the build-up of a greater self-defense capability, the ties with the United States have been a permanent fixture in Japanese strategic thinking. Following the war, Japan had demilitarized so completely, both physically and psychologically, that it had no choice but to depend on Washington, its major occupier turned protector-in-residence. As Japan's successive defense build-up plans were essentially arms procurement and personnel organization programs—labeled "orderly preparedness plans" (*seibi-keikaku*)—it may sound as though Japan has wasted precious time and momentum in developing its own defense concepts. In timing, if not in substance, however, Japanese strategic thinking has not been far behind that of the U.S.

    21. Makoto Momoi, "Energy Problems and the Alliance System," paper submitted to the 1974 annual conference of the International Institute for Strategic Studies (Adelphi Paper series, 1975).

When Paul Nitze replaced George Kennan as the State Department's long-range planning chief on January 15, 1950, he began an intramural study of U.S. national security policy. The result was National Security Council Paper no. 68, which, among other things, called for a defense budget cut and preparation only for a large-scale war. National Security Council Paper no. 162, the first U.S. security paper in which the Department of Defense took the initiative, was not completed until October 1954. On December 9, 1954, the American Joint Chiefs of Staff completed a study in which they advised that various countries with which the U.S. had ties should assume the primary responsibility for their own defense, and that Japan and West Germany should rearm.

In Japan, Prime Minister Yoshida made his reference to "what one might call defense" two years after National Security Council Paper no. 68; and only six months after the completion of National Security Council Paper no. 162, the Japanese drafted their first long-range defense plan. The Japanese Defense Council announced its BPND about eighteen months after the U.S. formulation of its "new look" policy, and lessened emphasis on surface forces. As the U.S. held absolute strategic supremacy in both nuclear warheads and their delivery systems throughout the period prior to the announcement of the BPND, the Japanese assumed that the two superpowers would avoid an atomic war, even though the confrontation between them might last another decade. Nevertheless, Japanese analysts closely followed the developments in nuclear technology and strategic nuclear doctrines. For example, a Japanese air force colonel and a civilian analyst translated and published Henry A. Kissinger's *Nuclear Weapons and Foreign Policy* in May 1958, within a year after its publication in the U.S.

Official Japanese defense plans, however, did not reflect U.S. nuclear concepts or strategic thinking. Neither the BPND, the Japanese Joint Chiefs of Staff estimate, nor the First Build-up Plan made any reference to the prevailing U.S. strategic doctrines. Japanese defense planners lacked precise knowledge on nuclear arms and their future strategic implications, but perhaps more important, anything nuclear was taboo in official circles. Thus, the First Build-up Plan emphasized the Ground Self-Defense Force. In addition to filling a vacuum left by the withdrawal of U.S. troops, the build-up of the Ground Self-Defense Force was influenced by the "traditional concept of the former Imperial Army," which in turn barred a flexible accommodation to new strategic trends.[22]

Only three months after Japan's announcement of the BPND, however, the U.S. strategic supremacy was threatened; the Russians successfully tested their first ICBM (August 1957) and demonstrated their delivery capability with the launching of Sputnik I on October 4. If the U.S. had been confident in the pre-Sputnik period that there could be no direct, massive threat to its continent, the

22. *Nihon no anzen hoshō*, p. 174.

orbiting Sputnik revealed the potential for a direct attack on Washington, D.C., and completely shattered the already defunct massive retaliation theory. The era of a "delicate balance of terror" began, with the missile gap rapidly narrowing the U.S. margin of supremacy. In response, the U.S. undertook a crash missile and Polaris submarine program. Early in the 1960s, it looked as though the U.S. had regained supremacy, at least in second strike capability and later in assured destruction and damage limitation capabilities.

While this technological game was proceeding, the U.S.-Japan Mutual Security Treaty was revised in 1960. Moreover, with American assurances that the nuclear umbrella was still valid and effective, and with its encouragement that Japan should "firmly establish a defense posture capable of dealing effectively with aggression smaller in scale than a local war involving [only] conventional arms," Japan formally adopted its Second Defense Build-up Plan in July 1961. This was the first expression of a concept based on Japanese responsibility for "strategic defense," with the expectation that the U.S. would maintain a "strategic offense" capability in exchange for the base facilities and other privileges provided under the Status of Force Agreement. Interestingly enough, neither the Japanese public, officials, nor academics, have discussed the "hostage" value of having U.S. forces present on their soil in the way the Europeans, especially the Germans, have done. Rather, the Japanese have simply offered the base facilities to the U.S. as the political price the country must pay for being able to rely on U.S. deterrent capabilities and to maintain its free access to American markets.

This one-sided reliance on the United States has caused many Japanese to consider any event that might undermine the U.S. deterrent power as a destabilizing factor for Japan's overall national security. Hence, on October 25, 1962, Prime Minister Ikeda Hayato allegedly told President John F. Kennedy that the presence of Soviet missiles in Cuba would not only threaten the United States itself, but would also seriously damage the international equilibrium that had supported world peace in the postwar period. At the same time, Japan's opposition parties have consistently argued that an American military presence in Japan might function as a "magnet" to draw down a preemptive attack on Japan. Most recently, the opposition applied the magnet theory to the alleged existence of U.S. OTH radar sites in Japan, while the government continued to stress the need to accommodate Washington because Japan depended on its deterrent power. During the Vietnam War, the opposition repeatedly attacked the government for permitting the U.S. to use Okinawa as a B52 operational base. In response, the government carefully explained that the U.S. bombers were not given combat orders during their take-offs and emphasized that Japan was obligated to help the American effort to maintain peace and security in Asia.

'63 this issue came up

Even while Japan was consistently integrating its defense policy with American strategic concepts and, at times, closely cooperating with U.S. operations, the Japanese Defense Council quietly began its own strategic studies. Although it is difficult to determine precisely what motivated Japan to undertake its first conceptual study, the circumstantial evidence suggests that it was at least partially influenced by several threatening international events that had transpired since Japan adopted its Second Defense Build-up Plan. Following the Bay of Pigs fiasco, the Berlin Wall had been erected (August 13, 1961) and the Soviet Union had tested a fifty-eight megaton bomb in the atmosphere (August 30), which had caused the U.S. to resume its nuclear tests (April 25, 1962). On May 11, 1962, the U.S. Seventh Fleet had begun its patrol of the Taiwan Straits, and six days later the U.S. had sent a detachment to Thailand. The following October, the Cuban missile crisis erupted. During 1963, the Sino-Soviet dispute had intensified and France had withdrawn its Atlantic fleet from NATO. A partial nuclear test ban had been signed on July 25, 1963, while the conventional (and subconventional) war situation deteriorated in South Vietnam. The year 1963 also witnessed the tragic assassination of President Kennedy. Against such turmoil in international politics and the strategic situation, it was natural and timely that the Japanese Defense Council should produce, on July 8, 1964, its own basic strategy plan—the Japanese counterpart to National Security Council Paper no. 162.

The issues raised in the paper, the "Text of the Defense Council Basic Plan" (Kokubō-kaigi kihon-keikaku honbun),[23] reflected in part the Japanese reaction to a speech made by Senator Frank Church in the U.S. Senate on April 22, 1963, against continuing economic and military aid to Japan because the country had become economically independent. The Japanese interpreted Church's argument as a signal that Japan would have to go it alone, at least in weapon acquisitions and to some degree in its general defense posture. Thus, the Defense Council plan called for a study of the "trends of U.S. global strategy and Japan's defense posture" as well as a review of the existing alliance with the U.S. in terms of how to coordinate a common defense and an "autonomous defense"; whether the BPND was still valid; what threats would most likely emerge; how to integrate the self-defense capability with economic, social, and political policies; and how to deal with the gradual reduction of U.S. military aid and presence in Japan.

While the study was still in progress, China successfully detonated its first nuclear device (on October 16, 1964). Theoretically, this should have increased Japan's concern over the potential threat from such a nearby fifth member in the nuclear club. In reality, it did not provoke any Japanese demands for adjustments in its defense concepts. Japan's relatively complacent response was

23. *Asahi shimbun*, July 9, 1964.

based on Japanese estimates that China would require quite some time, perhaps a decade or longer, to acquire a full nuclear weapon system (MR/IRBMs with sophisticated command-control systems, long-range bombers, and submarine-based missiles) that could effectively threaten Japan's major urban-industrial centers. Moreover, as Japan's basic posture was purely defensive, it was generally considered unprovocative to Chinese leaders, who were also well aware of the U.S. commitment to Japan. Finally, Japan had been under the shadow of the Soviet nuclear threat long enough to make the country's leaders consider a nuclear China only a marginal additional threat. Although the Japanese displayed some sense of hopelessness over defending themselves against any nuclear attack, this feeling was partially alleviated by the Satō-Johnson joint communiqué of January 14, 1965, in which the U.S. president reconfirmed the security-treaty obligation to defend Japan "against any armed attack" from the outside. On April 16, 1966, the Foreign Office reiterated that "any armed attack" included nuclear attacks and therefore U.S. nuclear capabilities would remain the "major deterrent" to a nuclear attack against Japan.[24]

Although the Japanese Defense Council never published the results of its study, the Third Defense Build-up Plan—which was announced six months after China tested its first thermonuclear device—seems to have incorporated many of the study's objectives. The third plan placed priority on naval defense in Japan's peripheral waters and on air defense of vital territorial areas, and it emphasized the need to acquire the "most effective means" for dealing with aggression. One analyst argues that the new emphasis was a subtle expression on Japan's intent to "establish an autonomous defense posture as much as possible in place of a total reliance on U.S. military forces."[25] As complete autonomy was out of the question, Japan's new posture was more a psychological self-criticism of its past neglect of defense efforts and a practical decision to become increasingly self-reliant in arms production rather than de-Americanization of its total defense planning. Nevertheless, the third plan represents Japan's first effort to provide for its own defense—an attempt prompted by both Japan's desire to lessen its heavy dependency on the U.S. except in the area of nuclear deterrence, and increasing American pressure on Japan to provide more self-help. Although officially Japan made no specific references to either China's successive nuclear tests or Secretary McNamara's November 10 announcement (just nineteen days before the plan's publication) concerning Soviet ABM deployment, the plan also reflects Japan's response to the rapidly changing strategic situation.

Japan's policy makers had such a strong faith in the U.S. commitment to

24. *Nichi-Bei shiryō* (Tokyo: Nihon Hyōronsha, 1972), pp. 408–409.
25. *Nihon no anzen hoshō*, p. 212

Japan that they regarded the Mutual Security Treaty as an "absolute security in guaranteeing Japan's safety," and the presence of U.S. troops in Japan as "a direct deterrent against aggression."[26] Therefore, publicly, at least, Japanese policy makers remained unconcerned about their own anti-missile defense, even after September 18, 1967, when McNamara announced the U.S. decision to deploy the anti-Chinese Sentinel ABM system. Actually, any concern they might have had could not have been revealed publicly because, in the Japanese view, the ABM system constituted another politically taboo nuclear weapons system. In contrast to the situation in the 1950s, however, when Japan had been complacent out of ignorance about strategic realities, the attitude in 1966–1967 was based on Japan's careful assessment of several factors: that China might find that the Russians were its major "enemy" (thus reducing the probability of Japan becoming a primary target); that China would not become a real nuclear threat until the mid-1970s at the earliest; and that the U.S. had not applied pressure on Japan to deal with the new threats posed by China, for example, via such measures as new base facilities or deployment specifically oriented against China.

Preoccupation with internal political issues also helps explain Japanese policy-makers' complacency or the low-posture attitude taken toward security issues in the 1960s. First there were the after-effects of the so-called Three Arrow study, a hypothetical war-game covering the Korean peninsula, which had set off a series of controversies after its exposure in the Diet in March 1965. There was also the delicate issue of permitting (since 1964) U.S. nuclear-powered submarines and later the *Enterprise* (in 1967) to make port calls in Japan. The progress of the Vietnam War—and the U.S. use of Japanese bases as staging areas—further put the Japanese government on the defensive regarding security issues. The foremost issue in the policy-makers' minds however, was Okinawa—the first foreign policy question over which there had emerged a national consensus, at least on the issue of reversion itself. The manner and timing of reversion were still much debated. The question remained controversial until November 15, 1967, when Premier Satō and President Johnson issued a joint communiqué in Washington signaling a basic agreement on reversion "within a couple of years." The issue was settled on November 21, 1969, in a Satō-Nixon communiqué in which the Japanese premier said that the "security of Korea is essential to Japan's own security and peace" and "security in the Taiwan area is a very important matter," thus, for the first time associating, at least verbally, Japan's security with that of its two anti-Communist neighbors. For domestic consumption, however, this had to be played down, particularly in view of the imminent political issue of extending the security treaty in the following year (1970).

26. Jimintō Ampo chōsa kai, "Report," Aug. 28, 1967, *Seisaku geppō*, Oct. 1965, p. 42.

Although the so-called defense debate had been gaining momentum in Japan (and after China's first nuclear test in 1964, specialists had even begun to consider the previously taboo nuclear issue), the emphasis was primarily on the legal aspects of Japan's security relations with the U.S. Strangely, there was little discussion either in or out of the Diet on Chinese or Soviet strategic postures. The debates over nuclear matters were mainly limited to issues involving the United States and to such subsidiary issues as the environmental dangers of nuclear-powered submarines and carriers anchored in Japanese ports. Even on the reversion of Okinawa, the main thrust of popular arguments was over whether the islands could be returned to Japan "minus nuclear arms."[*]

On June 24, 1969, twenty-one days before Nixon announced his Guam Doctrine (July 15), Defense Minister Arita Kiichi informed the lower house Cabinet Affairs Committee of his plans to produce a defense white paper before the end of the year. When completed in September, the 452-page Arita paper defined, for the first time, the most likely contingencies for which Japan should prepare: a Cold-War type of covert operation; indirect aggression; and an armed attack by an external force. Situations that could lead to the third eventuality were identified as (1) a small-scale armed attack that could result either from an escalation of disputes over fishery rights or territorial (air and water) violations, or from the proliferation of a peripheral local war that eventually involved Japan as a collateral target (theater); (2) a limited war with Japan a primary target but with the conflict limited as to locus, targets, and duration; and (3) a conflict involving Japan as a result of a spill-over from a global war.

Arita argued that Japan's basic strategy consisted of "two pillars": Japan's own self-defense and reliance on the U.S. The first pillar required capabilities to (1) prevent any aggressor from achieving a military *fait accompli* such as occupation of a local area in Japan with an amphibious or paratroop landing, especially during an initial period when U.S. military help may not have yet arrived; (2) secure the minimum safety of sea transportation, a factor vital to national survival; and (3) maintain air supremacy for a considerable period.[27] Arita's implication that Japan must be able to take care of itself in the eventuality that U.S. aid did not arrive in time reflected a subtle Japanese reaction to the Guam Doctrine and its "new, more prudent policy toward Asia."

The Arita paper was never published. As Japan's policy-makers were preoccupied with the reversion of Okinawa and public attention was focused on Premier Satō's visit to Washington in November, the prevailing political climate was inappropriate. Arita's sweeping rebuttal of a "nonalliance-neutrality policy"—a pet posture maintained by the opposition parties—could have created Diet controversies at a time when the government badly needed a consensus on the Okinawa reversion question. The paper's emphasis on the primary importance of Japan's own defense efforts, with the security treaty to be

27. *Asahi shimbun*, Sept. 17, 1969.

merely complementary, might have encouraged some circles opposed to extending the treaty in the following year and created suspicion over the extent to which Japan was preparing to rearm. Finally, Arita's term in office ended before he could push through his version of Japan's strategic plans.

In January 1970, Nakasone Yasuhirō was appointed defense minister. Two months later (March 9), he told the National Security Study Committee of the LDP that Japan ought to have its own defense strategy and that it should "share security missions" with the U.S. "Sharing" would make the two nations "true partners," and with its own defense strategy, Japan could get rid of its "vague expectations [about what the United States could do for Japan] and its unilateral reliance, without principles of its own, on the U.S." He also pointed out that the Self-Defense Forces were already capable of repelling limited and localized aggressions, but that Japan would have to continue to depend on the U.S. for offensive operations.[28] To some, Nakasone's "sharing security missions" might have sounded like a partial de-Americanization of Japan's security arrangements.

Nakasone's plan set off a number of controversies. Within the government, it was considered too expensive. It would have meant an increase in the total defense budget 2.2 times greater than that which had been planned in the Third Build-up Plan. The opposition argued that Japan was heading toward full-scale rearmament, and that this would arouse criticism and suspicion among its Asian neighbors. Although Nakasone's thesis was mainly a response to American criticism of Japan's "free ride,"[29] the Japanese press interpreted it as an indication of emerging militarism, or at least a nationalistic attitude (which in Japan has been a synonym for ultramilitarism).

Nakasone nevertheless proceeded to inject his concepts into his version of the Defense White Paper, which was published in October 1970, following his trip to Washington and an extensive talk with Defense Secretary Laird. Although the paper sought, in part, to serve as "an answer to the criticism of militarism,"[30] its major emphasis was on Nakasone's "exclusively defensive posture," based on the strategic assessment that there would be no need for Japan to expand its defense perimeter beyond its immediate peripheral areas or to respond militarily, except in self-defense. For the latter purpose, he wanted Japan "to do what it can do best," as Laird suggested.[31] Later, in his fiscal year 1972

28. Yoshihara Kōichirō, *Nichi-Bei ampo joyaku taisei shi* (Tokyo: Sanshadō, 1970–1971), p. 314.

29. Melvin Laird, *Defense Posture Statement, Fiscal Year 1971* (Washington, D.C.: Government Printing Office, 1970), p. 57.

30. *Nihon no anzen hoshō*, p. 240.

31. "In many cases, our allies are able and willing to provide the forces if we can contribute some of the needed weapons, and in some circumstances, specialized military support. Under this approach, each partner would be doing what it can best do and both would benefit." Laird, *Defense Posture Statement, 1971*.

defense posture statement (published in March 1971), Laird acknowledged that "the Japanese have announced plans for continuing qualitative improvements in their self-defense forces, thereby enabling them to provide for substantially all of their conventional defense requirements."[32]

In the same statement, Laird submitted for the first time the concept of a total force under the heading of "Realistic Deterrence":

With regard to U.S. force capabilities in Asia, we do not plan for the long term to maintain separate large U.S. ground combat forces specifically oriented just to this theater, but we do intend to maintain strong air, naval and support capabilities. If a large land war involving the U.S. should occur in Asia, we would, of course, be prepared to mobilize, and would initially use our non-NATO-committed forces as well as portions of those forces based in the U.S. and earmarked for NATO, if required and feasible, and with emphasis on our air and naval capabilities. In the future, we expect the emphasis in Asia more and more to be placed on U.S. support to our allies who themselves will provide the required manpower.[33]

Laird's statement was the first official signal from the U.S. that its commitment in Asia might be limited to air and naval capabilities, and to support to allies who would provide their own manpower. Later, in his final report (January 8, 1973), Laird, referring to South Korean defense, stressed a "deterrence that does not rely on American ground combat power." His successor, Richardson, modified the statement by saying that "the military capabilities of our allies and the threat to their security will, in the near term, require that we maintain some well-equipped forces overseas for deterrence, or for an appropriate response if deterrence fails."[34]

One month after the publication of Laird's fiscal year 1972 posture statement, the Japanese Defense Agency completed a draft of the New Defense Build-up Plan (the fourth plan). The plan was labeled "new" instead of with the traditional number, partially to avoid giving a public impression that the build-up might continue indefinitely, but mainly to indicate the new need for Japan to deal with conventional contingencies in response to the Nixon Doctrine and recent U.S. official statements. The plan defined a basic defense concept in fairly logical sequence. First, Japan's defense capabilities should be able to deal with limited, direct aggression (by implication, without immediate U.S. involvement) by maintaining sea and air control in Japan's peripheries for the *limitation of damage* and an early elimination of the aggressor. Second, should Japan fail in the latter mission, it should be able to *deny and resist* any attempts by the aggressor to achieve a military *fait accompli* or to occupy a local area.

32. Melvin Laird, *Defense Posture Statement, Fiscal Year 1972* (Washington D.C.: Government Printing Office, 1971), p. 109.
33. Ibid., p. 77.
34. Elliot Richardson, *Defense Posture Statement, Fiscal Year 1974* (Washington, D.C.: Government Printing Office, 1973), p. 73.

Third, together with the necessary denial and resistance, Japan should be able to *terminate* the contingencies either with U.S. support under the security treaty or with a peace (truce) effort through the U.N. Finally, Japan must continue to depend on the U.S. for deterrence against nuclear threat.[35]

The new plan, with its comprehensive consideration of how Japan itself might resolve a conflict, demonstrated an unprecedented realism and rationality in Japan's defense thinking. By implication, the termination of a conflict (without prolonged occupation of even a local area, thereby avoiding a situation in which Japan would have to choose between an unconditional surrender or national suicide) needed both U.S. or, in the distant future, possibly U.N. help and above all Japan's own denial and resistance efforts until outside mediation or intervention could take place. As the draft paper was mainly for home, especially intragovernment, consumption, it avoided academic theorization. Nevertheless, any analyst can find in it a series of crisis management approaches under the overall concept of Japan's strategy for limited response. Japan could not expect to be able to do everything itself, but it did want to do what it could do best—the three major elements of crisis management italicized in the preceding summary of the draft.

Even this limited approach, however, would have required about ¥5,800 billion (then about U.S. $15 billion), a prospect that immediately provoked public controversy over the allocation of national resources. Moreover, before the plan could be formally adopted, Masuhara Keikichi succeeded Nakasone in an early-summer cabinet reshuffle. Then, the July 30 midair crash of an Air Self-Defense Force trainer plane with a commercial airliner created a "psychological effect that dampened the climate for autonomous defense efforts."[36] Nishimura Naomi, who pinch-hit for Masuhara, had no choice but to scale down the plan. He suggested a ¥500 billion cut. Before his budgetary revision was accepted, however, a Diet controversy over his alleged derogatory remarks about the U.N. forced his resignation.

Prior to leaving office, Nishimura explained his "philosophy on self-defense—on a strategy of limited response" to foreign correspondents in Tokyo (October 11, 1971). The basic strategy, which he admitted was still in the conceptual stage, was based on the belief that there is a "natural limit for any country, whatever its economic, technological, or spiritual potential, to counter military threat with military power." Moreover, "every country has its own list of priorities at a given time for the allocation of its resources." Therefore, the Japanese should (1) "objectively assess our own strategic and geopolitical vulnerability"; (2) "plan our comprehensive national security policy to maximize the effectiveness of our limited capabilities"; and (3) "make realistic options in terms of the most likely contingencies and our own limited capabilities for dealing with possible threats, both manmade and natural."

35. *Asahi shimbun*, April 29, 1971.
36. *Nihon no anzen hoshō*, p. 246.

Based on this line of thinking, Nishimura outlined his "three-point comprehensive national security policy":

(*a*) To maintain the minimum level of defense capability necessary to deter and resist an aggression against Japan whatever the changes in both threats and international environments;
(*b*) To secure air and sea safety in Japan's peripheral areas in a manner that will not threaten Japan's neighbors;
(*c*) To endeavor to stabilize Japan's diplomatic relations with others and to extend nonmilitary assistance to the rest, in particular to Asian nations.

Nishimura's thesis, although primarily philosophical, did define Japan's defense posture as one of limited response, which presumably ruled out the possibility of acquiring most "counterthreat" capabilities. Unfortunately, Nishimura left office before he had time to elaborate his concept further. The Fourth Build-up Plan, or the revised version of the New Defense Build-up Plan, was approved at the Defense Council meeting on February 27, 1972, twenty days before the announcement of the Sino-American Shanghai communiqué.

In essence, the new version was closer to the Third Build-up Plan than to the draft plan it replaced. As Ezaki Masumi, Nishimura's successor, explained to the upper house Cabinet Affairs Committee on June 6, 1972, it was designed primarily to "acquire arms that were in short supply and replace those that were obsolete." In the wake of Premier Tanaka's visit to Peking and the resulting climate of détente, however, the plan underwent a further scaling down. On October 9, the Defense Agency announced its own version—still an "extension of the third plan," but with a strong emphasis on Japan's defending itself without direct U.S. participation. Japan, it stressed, would have to "expel both indirect and small-scale aggression *by itself*" (italics added). As the Defense Affairs Bureau Director Kubo Takuya explained, "Aggressors might undertake armed aggression at a time and in a manner that would not allow full-scale U.S. support [for Japan], in an effort to establish a [military] *fait accompli.*"[37] Kubo also pointed out that the fourth plan was not drafted to comply with either the Nixon Doctrine or Laird's total force concept. Rather, he said, it was planned with an "emphasis on Japan's own defense build-up against the background of the [strategic] environment in which Japan is now placed." He did not, however, reject security ties with the U.S.; on the contrary, he insisted that Japan "can hardly scrap the Japan-U.S. security system until an alternative structure can replace it without undermining Japan's safety and advantage in existing environmental relations."[38]

In summary, the conceptual progress in Japanese defense thinking can be set forth in terms of four periods:

37. Takuya Kubo, "Yojibō no seikaku to tokuchō," *Kokubō*, Dec. 1972, pp. 22–23.
38. Ibid.

1950–1960: the period of "total reliance," both physically and conceptually on U.S. initiative. Initially, Japan had no defense concept at all. In these years, a premier could not even refer precisely to national security or defense, but to "what one might call defense." Toward the end of this period, which coincided with the first revision of the Mutual Security Treaty in 1960, the defense (ground force) build-up was used as a political instrument in bargaining for the early withdrawal of U.S. troops from Japan.

The Second Defense Build-up Plan through 1965: the period of "partial reliance." Total reliance on the U.S. had become impractical, and Japan began to pay for or produce arms itself. During this period, Japan slowly developed a concept of combining its own "strategic defense" with America's "strategic offense" under a conceptual barter arrangement that continued to provide for U.S. base facilities in Japan. Nevertheless, the exchange was far from equal; Japan still depended on U.S. protection or automatic U.S. military involvement. At the time, the U.S.-Japan joint communiqué of 1965, which stressed that the U.S. was committed to defending Japan "against any armed attack," was highly valued in Tokyo.

1966–1968: the period of "selective reliance." Although selective reliance was never actually mentioned in official language, the concept was evident in the Third Build-up Plan, which stressed Japan's own capabilities for dealing with air and sea aggression "most effectively." The idea of "autonomous defense" also began to appear in official statements, although there was still little concrete idea of how to achieve it. At the same time, references to U.S. military help in a Japanese land war virtually disappeared, and the expectation of immediate U.S. assistance in air and sea combat operations was, perhaps inadvertently, played down.

1969–1973: the period of "de-Americanization," which gradually emerged after the announcement of the Guam (Nixon) Doctrine. The Arita paper, Nakasone's "autonomous defense first" thesis, and Nishimura's "strategy of limited response" all represent the first serious Japanese efforts to develop their own defense concept. Most important, all avoided the previous Japanese tendency toward wishful thinking and proceeded to assess Japan's strategic environment more realistically. None of these plans survived in its original substance: Arita's was perhaps too provocative in the political climate then prevailing in Japan; Nakasone's was too ambitious budgetarily if not conceptually; and Nishimura's was too philosophical to gain public acceptance. Nevertheless, the changes in the international strategic environment that have developed since the October (1973) War in the Middle East have undeniably revealed the extent of Japan's strategic vulnerability. Japan's strategic options are indeed limited, but such limitation might impose a conceptual framework for the future development of Japan's strategic thinking.

JAPAN'S STRATEGIC OPTIONS

Any conceptual study of Japan's strategic considerations must attempt to assess realistically Japan's peculiar combination of vulnerabilities, some of which are permanent features of Japan's environment and others of which are imposed by contemporary conditions. Geopolitically, for instance, Japan lacks strategic depth. With a land mass of 142,726 square miles—a little smaller than the state of Montana—and a 16,470-mile-long coastline, no point in Japan is more than 75 miles from the coast. As of December 1970, the Japanese population was heavily concentrated around Tokyo (24 percent) and the Osaka-Kobe area (12 percent); by 1975, the Welfare Ministry expects that 52 percent of the population will be in these two metropolitan areas. Located close to the continent of Asia, the entire archipelago is within the range of TU-16s, not to mention MRBMs, and the northern part can even be reached with Mig 21s or IL-28s.

Politically and psychologically, the Japanese have had no experience with war on their own territory or with guerrilla warfare and, particularly in the urban areas, there is no popular support for a forward defense (a theoretical necessity for a country with virtually no strategic depth). Hence, Japan can expect little public understanding and psychological preparedness for a homeland resistance.

Socioeconomically, Japan is ill-prepared with emergency stockpilings of oil, food, medical supplies, and other strategic materials. Japan also has no plans for precrisis dispersal and shelter, or for arms production during a crisis. Ironically, however, Japan is well prepared, at least conceptually, to deal with a crisis overseas, whether or not the homeland is involved. The preparation, however, is entirely negative. As a former defense minister told foreign correspondents in Tokyo, "no self-defense force unit or personnel will be sent overseas to protect Japan's economic interests by force."[39] This presumably includes Japanese merchant ships. They are so widely dispersed in the world and so numerous (1,258 ships larger than 3,000 tons or a total of 25,879,000 metric tons as of January 1972) that an all-out escort would be impractical. Moreover, efforts to sustain their voyages to home port might be meaningless unless the conflict lasted a long time and, most important, unless the total transportation system (offshore safety, harbor facilities, unloading facilities, overland transportation, and plants) was functioning normally during the armed crisis.

Furthermore, Japan's current high-dependency on overseas sources for natural resources makes Japan extremely vulnerable, not only to military situations, but also to political instabilities in the resource-producing countries. As one policy-maker allegedly lamented, some resources, if used as a politicostrategic weapon, may prove (as oil did during the past crisis) "a far more powerful

39. Quotation by Nishimura Naomi.

threat to Japan than an ICBM." Even if such a commodity as oil is not used as a weapon, it may not flow into Japan if, for instance, the Gulf of Persia is involved in an armed conflict (whether or not the conflict involves Japan). Extended sea lanes, on which Japan depends for its survival, are also vulnerable to a wide spectrum of conflicts, such as harassment on the high seas or a blockade. Thus, Japan must consider its own security, not only in national or regional (East Asia) security terms, but also in the international context of global political affairs and nonmilitary issues.

In view of these basic vulnerabilities, Japan's strategic options are necessarily limited, with its priorities placed on war avoidance, conflict limitation, or quick termination. Japan has so far succeeded in the first through a combination of its alliance with the U.S. and its economic diplomacy. While maintaining the alliance with the U.S. as insurance, Japan may have to emphasize economic diplomacy even more strenuously and deliberately in the future. Essentially, this could mean offering bonuses in order to "buy friendship" with otherwise potentially unfriendly nations, maintaining existing harmonious ties even at a certain sacrifice to Japan in trade terms, and obtaining the cooperation of other Asian and coastal nations for the protection of Japan's overseas assets and sea lanes.

Such bonus-offering or bonus-deterrence might not invariably or perpetually work. A recipient could raise the ante or suddenly turn unfriendly even to the extent that Japan might be drawn into a conflict. If such a conflict should escalate into a direct armed attack on Japan, Japan's immediate response should be denial and resistance designed to limit the conflict and the damage to the Japanese people and their property. For Japan to be able to deny access to its territorial air and sea or a long occupation of its land, it must be able to achieve favorable terms for conflict termination through third-party mediation or intervention. Such a denial effort, moreover, would require an effective strategic intelligence system; an effective tactical data-processing mechanism; a limited forward interception capability; an ASW fleet to control a limited area (such as a "safety zone" set up during the crisis in Japan's periphery); and the "most effective means" to repel land aggression, including sophisticated air defense, antitank, antiship, and antitroop firepower with modern precision guidance munitions as their mainstays.

No matter how sophisticated the weapon system may be, however, there is obviously a limit to the homeland warfare. A nation cannot fight to the last man; there is a point, in any resistance, beyond which a national effort might prove to be merely counterproductive or even suicidal. The strategic planning for a country such as Japan must always consider security in terms of national survival or a termination of armed conflict under the best available conditions. In that sense, Japan's policy-makers may have to "give deeper thought to the fate of [their] devastated country and realize that what remains of the nation's future would largely depend on how the war, which had just begun, would come to an end.''[40]

For a favorable termination, however, Japan needs both its own resolute, determined resistance effort, without which no negotiation can succeed, and an effective, timely, diplomatic intervention by a third party, preferably the U.S. Japan has been trying to achieve the first condition in the context of making defense preparations that would prevent an aggressor from achieving a military *fait accompli*. The second condition has never been mentioned officially. It is important, nevertheless, at least theoretically, and especially in view of Japan's own historical experience—both the advantageous experience in 1905 and the bitter experience in 1945. This consideration will increase, not lessen, the importance of the existing security ties with the U.S. Although the U.S. might or might not be able to intervene with force and in time, it should feel the mutual benefit, if not the obligation of intervening diplomatically, provided the existing relations with Japan have not deteriorated too far from their present status.

40. Fred Iklé, *Every War Must End*.

V

A Summary

The Foundations of
Modern Japanese
Foreign Policy

SEIZABURO SATO

A nation's foreign policy may directly or indirectly be affected by a variety of factors.[1] Weather conditions, for example, can influence the bargaining power of a nation by increasing or decreasing its agricultural yield. Even a virus, by limiting the activity of an important diplomat—possibly claiming his life—can have an enormous impact on international politics. Yet neither weather conditions nor viruses can properly be considered elements of the "foundation" of foreign policy for the simple reason that their impact, no matter how great, remains all too accidental and ephemeral. To be included as a foundation for a nation's foreign policy, a given factor must not merely exert substantial influence, but also possess a high probability of exerting that influence continuously over time.

Factors with the potential for exercising such long-term influence on a nation's foreign policy may be divided into three groups: the realities of the international environment and national power; the attitudes within the society toward the international environment; and the special characteristics of a nation's foreign policy formulation process.

The international environment refers to the relatively durable patterns of mutual contact between a nation and the various countries with which it maintains relations. National power, which plays a particularly significant role in

1. I am deeply grateful to Glen W. Fukushima of Harvard University, who rendered valuable assistance in translating this article into English.

367

the shaping of these patterns, includes several components—for instance, military power, economic power, and political penetrative power—each possessing a complex base of its own.[2] These components however, have meaning only in comparison with their strength in other nations. Therefore, national power is both an element in the formation of the international environment and an element conditioned by it.

The widely shared attitudes (modal attitudes) held within a given society toward the international environment refer to the more or less durable and predictable responses that serve as the framework for perceptions and preferences on a particular issue. People do not respond directly to the objective environment but to the *perceived* environment. Thus the attitudes which define the perceptions and preferences toward the international environment function as intermediaries between the objective environment and any given foreign policy.

The special characteristics of the foreign policy formulation process include, among others, the degree of relative importance occupied by matters pertaining to foreign relations, the special features of the foreign policy decision-making structure, and the role of public opinion.

INTERNATIONAL ENVIRONMENT
AND NATIONAL POWER

A distinctive feature in the international environment surrounding modern Japan is its relative isolation from and peripheral position with reference to the world's major powers. During the premodern period, Japan was one of the eastern peripheral countries—*tōi* (Eastern barbarians)—of China, then the center of international order in East Asia. Moreover, the East China Sea and the Straits of Korea separating Japan from continental Asia were, by technical standards prior to the Industrial Revolution, sufficiently wide and rough to restrict large-scale movement across them. Thus, compared with such a country as Korea, Japan was indeed isolated from China. With the dramatic development of communication and transportation media since the Industrial Revolution, the rough seas could no longer isolate Japan from the international community. At the same time, however, the Industrial Revolution made international domination by the Western powers possible, a development that shifted the "center of the world" even farther away from Japan. Furthermore, the Western powers were both ethnically and culturally more removed from Japan than China had been. Thus, although Japan gradually but firmly became tied to the international community as modernization progressed, its relative isolation from the mainstream of that community, at least in comparison with other advanced powers, has continued until quite recently.

2. See Klaus E. Knorr, *Power and Wealth: The Political Economy of International Power* (New York: Basic Books, 1973).

This relative isolation and peripherality enabled Japan to insure its security rather easily, until the development of the airplane—and, subsequently, the rocket—eliminated distance as a meaningful guarantee of national security. Japan and Korea were the last Asian countries affected by the West. Moreover, Japan was much too remote for the Western powers in the nineteenth century—to mention nothing of the Iberians in the sixteenth—to subjugate effectively. Aside from the confrontation between Japan and the Western powers over opening the doors of the country in the late Tokugawa period, the only instance of a direct threat to Japan's security occurred when Russia advanced into Manchuria and further increased its influence over Korea early in the twentieth century. Japan's victory in the Russo-Japanese War and, later, the crippling effects of the Bolshevik Revolution on Russia temporarily removed this threat. By the 1930s, however, the Communist Party was in firm control in the USSR, and the Russian state had again begun to strengthen its military power in Northeast Asia. Particularly stunning to Japan was the Soviet army's decimation of Japanese ground forces during the Nomonhan Incident, which erupted in Mongolia in March 1939. Immediately thereafter, however, the Second World War broke out in Europe and caused a shift of Soviet military concerns away from Asia.

Until the First World War, Britain kept a sizable military force in East Asia. Britain, however, attempted to protect its territories and interests in Asia by forming an alliance with Japan. Therefore, the Japanese military never considered Britain a hypothetical enemy before 1936.[3] In contrast, with the adoption of the "Teikoku kokubō hōshin" (Imperial Japanese defense policy) in 1907, the Japanese ranked the United States second after Russia as a potential enemy, and following the Russian Revolution, the U.S. did become Japan's primary potential enemy. The U.S. presented no real military threat to Japan at the time, even though its navy had become one of the most powerful in the world. Actually until the Pacific War, it was practically impossible for the American navy to engage in large-scale military maneuvers in the western Pacific over an extended period; the Pacific Ocean was too vast an expanse to permit such activity at the time.[4]

The advances in military technology since the beginning of the Second World War have completely eliminated distance as a guarantee of security and caused the two superpowers to become the only nations capable of maintaining their security single-handedly. Thus, following the Second World War, Japan's security has been dependent on the American nuclear deterrent and on the stabilization of relations among the United States, the Soviet Union, and China—presently the three nuclear powers in East Asia.

3. See Bōeichō Boeikenshūjo Senshi-Shitsu, ed., *Daihonei rikugun bu*, vol. 1 (Tokyo: Asa-gumo Shimbunsha, 1967).
4. Satō Seizaburō, "Kyōchō to jiritsu to no aida," in Nihon Seiji Gakkai, ed., *Kokusai kin-chō kanwa no seiji katei* (Tokyo: Iwamani Shoten, 1970), p. 116.

During the early part of the twentieth century, the relative isolation of East
Asia from the major powers and their primary military concerns also contributed to the ease with which Japan was able to establish a predominant position in the area despite its limited national power. The fact that China, Korea,
and the other neighboring Asian countries were incapable of modernizing as
efficiently as Japan further facilitated Japan's expansion. In the thirty years
from 1880—when Japan's possession of the Ryukyu Islands was recognized
and the area of Japan proper thereby definitely established—until 1910 and the
annexation of Korea, Japanese territory nearly doubled from 383,000 square
kilometers to 675,000 square kilometers (or 679,000 square kilometers, including the leased territory on the Liaotung peninsula). Although Japan was
barely able to maintain its independence in 1880, by 1910 it had become an
"empire" in East Asia with a land force ranking alongside that of Russia and
the most powerful navy in the area. The First World War and the Great
Depression further decreased the Western powers' concern with East Asia,
thereby producing a power vacuum in the region favorable to Japanese expansion. Japan took advantage of this situation to reinforce its commanding position through such means as the Twenty-One Demands and the Manchurian
Incident in East Asia.

Although Japan was able to secure both national security and predominance
in East Asia without undue difficulty, its national power was still clearly inferior to that of other major countries—signaling a second characteristic of
Japan's relationship to the international environment. National power comprises various components and dimensions (Lasswell and Kaplan offer weight,
domain, and scope as dimensions of power; Deutsch adds a fourth, range[5]),
which are exceedingly difficult to measure accurately. Nevertheless, in terms of
economic strength—the most important base for national power in the modern
age—Japan's weakness and fragility were indeed obvious.

Japan acquired international competitive power comparatively early in light
industries—particularly textiles—at least in Asia.[6] In heavy industries, however, which are more important as a foundation for military power, Japan's
prewar production scale was Lilliputian compared to that of the major powers
(see Table 1). Japan's level of technology was also low. As late as the 1930s,
Japan was at least partially dependent on imports for armaments, especially
sophisticated weapons.

In the prewar era, Japan concentrated on building up armaments (begin-

5. Harold D. Lasswell and Abraham Kaplan, *Power and Society: A Framework for Political
Inquiry* (New Haven: Yale University Press, 1950), p. 77; Karl W. Deutsch, *The Analysis of
International Relations* (New Jersey: Prentice Hall, 1968), pp. 24–39.

6. See H.G. Moulton, *Japan, an Economic and Financial Appraisal* (Washington, D.C.: The
Brookings Institution, 1931).

Table 1
Industrial Production of the Major Powers

		Japan	U.K.	U.S.A.	Germany	France
1913	Pig iron	56	10,260	30,653	19,000	5,126
	(thousand metric tons)	(1)	(183)	(545)	(340)	(92)
	Steel	13	7,664	31,301	18,631	4,614
	(thousand metric tons)	(1)	(590)	(2,405)	(1,435)	(355)
	Coal	21,650	321,920	590,646	305,700	--
	(thousand long tons)	(1)	(15)	(27)	(14)	
	Number of spindles*	3,320	57,000	19,600	--	--
	(in thousands)	(1)	(5.8)	(3.4)		
1930	Pig iron	1,628	6,167	31,441	11,423	9,874
	(thousand long tons)	(1.0)	(3.8)	(19.4)	(7.1)	(6.1)
	Steel	2,203	7,299	40,278	13,259	9,296
	(thousand long tons)	(1.0)	(3.3)	(18.3)	(6.0)	(4.2)
	Coal	31	246	484	154	--
	(million metric tons)	(1.0)	(7.9)	(15.6)	(5.0)	
	Number of spindles	7,072	55,207	24,025	--	--
	(in thousands)	(1.0)	(7.8)	(3.4)		
	Rayon	35,100	49,700	119,000	50,300	41,600
	(thousand pounds)	(1.0)	(1.4)	(3.4)	(1.4)	(1.2)
	Shipbuilding	130	1,211	45	47	--
	(thousand tons)	(1.0)	(9.3)	(0.3)	(0.4)	

SOURCE: Ouchi Tsutomu, *Nihon keizai ron*, vol. 1 (Tokyo, 1962), p. 155.
NOTE: Figures in parentheses indicate ratio to Japanese production.
*Figures for number of spindles for the year 1919.

ning in 1890, excluding the 1920s, military expenditures normally accounted for about 40 percent of the national budget).[7] Although this enabled Japan to maintain a substantial peacetime military force, its overall combat capacity, including weaponry, was still exceedingly low. A comparison of certain statistics before and during the Pacific War reveals Japan's weak military capacity. One scholar estimates that, in 1938, Japan's total combat munitions output was less than one-fifth that of Germany, although it was one and a half times that of the United States, for the latter country was currently pursuing isolationist policies. By 1942, however, although such production had grown to slightly more than

7. Emi Kōichi and Shionoya Yūichi, *Zaisei shishutsu* (Tokyo: Tōyō Keizai Shimpōsha, 1966), pp. 18–22.

one-fifth that of Germany, it had plunged to one-fifth the comparable figure for the United States.[8]

Today, the situation is considerably different in certain respects. Japan's heavy and chemical industries have drawn abreast of those of the other major powers since the late 1950s, and its overall economic power has developed far beyond the prewar level. Thus, it would be possible for Japan's military potential to grow to considerable proportions. In contrast to the prewar years, however, as is well known, Japan has allocated only a small proportion of its wealth to defense expenditures even since the end of the Occupation period. Domestic criticism against any military build-up, moreover, particularly one involving nuclear weapons, remains substantial. Japan, therefore, still lags behind in terms of military technology. It does not possess its own guided missile system, nor does it have the technical know-how necessary to condense uranium. Even if Japan should decide to become a military power—a highly unlikely prospect in the near future—it would be next to impossible for it to develop and maintain sufficient military strength to match that of the United States or the Soviet Union in the foreseeable future. Furthermore, Japan is highly vulnerable economically due to her extensive dependence on other nations for important raw materials and foodstuffs. And, because there exist no indispensable commodities produced solely by Japan, its ability to blackmail other countries economically is relatively limited.

Distance from the international economic and political centers together with deep ethnic and cultural dissimilarities from the other major powers have also made it difficult for Japan to wield significant influence in areas outside East Asia. Japan first participated with Western powers in an international conference at the Peking Conference of 1901, convened to deal with the aftermath of the Boxer Rebellion. Since then, Japan has sent representatives to a large number of important international conferences, but they have seldom, if ever, assumed active positions of leadership. Instead, the Japanese delegates have either conformed to the general trend or confined themselves to pressing for Japan's interests.

Prewar Japan (or, more accurately, Japan after the Russo-Japanese War) was the poorest and weakest of the major powers, as well as the only "yellow" power. The economically rejuvenated postwar Japan is a militarily weak economic power and remains, as before, the only nonwhite industrially advanced nation. The ambiguity stemming from this unique position constitutes the third characteristic of modern Japan's international environment.

Even in premodern times, Japan's international position was unclear. Since antiquity Japan had striven to import Chinese culture; the shared *kanji* (Chinese ideographs), Confucianism, and Mahayana Buddhism clearly demon-

8. Klaus E. Knorr, *The War Potentials of Nations* (Princeton: Princeton University Press, 1956), p. 34.

strate Japan's inclusion in the Chinese cultural area. Yet, except for two periods (between the third and the beginning of the sixth centuries, and again between the early fifteenth and mid-sixteenth centuries), Japan did not consider China a suzerain state. The emperors of China never appointed Japan's rulers or gave them the initial seal. Japan's diplomatic documents did not employ the Chinese calendar or reign titles. Moreover, no formal diplomatic relations existed between the two countries from the end of the ninth century to the end of the fourteenth century and from the mid-sixteenth century until the Treaty of Peace and Amity between Japan and the Ch'ing dynasty in 1871. During these periods, Sino-Japanese relations rested almost entirely on Japanese reception of Chinese culture and the trade that took place between the two countries.

The Chinese themselves corroborate the view that premodern Japan was not completely incorporated into the Chinese empire. The *Wan-li hui-tien* (the Collected Statutes printed in 1587 during the reign of the Wan-li emperor in the Ming dynasty) identified Japan as a tributary. The *Chia-ch'ing hui-tien* of 1818, however, although it listed the "Western Ocean" (Portugal, the Papacy, and England) as tributaries, classified Japan, along with such countries as France, Sweden, and Norway, as among "countries having commercial relations with China."[9]

At the same time, it was impossible for the rulers of premodern Japan either to conquer China and seize the throne of the Chinese empire or to establish a separate empire with Japan as its center. Toyotomi Hideyoshi (1536–1598), who entertained the grand dream of conquering China and India and thereafter moving Japan's capital to Peking, failed in the first step of his plan—the subjugation of Korea—and thereby hastened the collapse of his reign. Ever since Japan's two-century-long domination of the southern Korean peninsula was overturned by Silla around the middle of the sixth century, premodern Japan held no territories outside of Japan proper nor, with the exception of the Ryūkyū kingdom which was attached to Satsuma, did it possess any tributaries. Thus, premodern Japan, although greatly influenced by Chinese culture, was only briefly a tributary of the Chinese empire, and remained outside the inner network of the international relations of an empire it could neither successfully challenge nor wholly ignore.

The Sinocentric East Asian world order crumbled following the Opium War, as the countries of the area—excluding Japan—underwent colonization. The international law that regulated relations among the "civilized" (that is, Western) countries was not applied to the relations between these powers and

9. Banno Masataka, *Kindai Chūgoku seiji gaikō shi* (Tokyo: Tokyo University Press, 1973), pp. 83–91; John K. Fairbank, ed., *The Chinese World Order: Traditional China's Foreign Relations* (Cambridge, Mass.: Harvard University Press, 1968), pp. 11–14.

the "uncivilized" countries of Asia. Thus, an unstable balance of power resulting from Western competition for colonies, interests, and concessions was
the only international order that emerged to replace the old Chinese world
order. As all the countries of Asia, except Japan, became fully or semi-colo-
nized, they could not participate in the formation of a new Asian world order.
The balance of power among the Western nations was, of course, extremely
fluid, and the rapid rise of Chinese nationalism in the aftermath of the First
World War further heightened the instability of international relations in Asia.

These trends reached a climax in post-World War II East Asia as the region
became a principal stage of mutual confrontation between the United States
and the Soviet Union, the United States and China, and the Soviet Union and
China. In addition, three of the four divided countries produced by the Cold
War were situated in East Asia: mainland China and Taiwan, North and
South Korea, and North and South Vietnam. The majority of Asian countries
that attained independence following the Second World War, including China, have yet to achieve full political and economic stability, and even with the
recent Sino-U.S. rapprochement, East Asia still remains one of the most unstable areas of the world.

Japan's position and role in this new international environment has been
even more troubled and uncertain than in the premodern period. Although
Japan had earlier secured a predominant position in East Asia with relative
ease, it was never able to exercise the type of long-term, far-reaching stability in
the region that the United States achieved over the Western hemisphere.

Classified according to the criterion of "East" or "West," Japan clearly
belongs to the former. When, however, one applies the criteria of strong or
weak, advanced or underdeveloped, "civilized" or "uncivilized," Japan has,
since the early twentieth century, been recognized as a member of the exclusive
club of strong, advanced, "civilized" nations comprising the Western powers.
Yet Japan was the most recent member to join this club, and thus represents a
weak country among the strong, an underdeveloped country among the advanced, and an "uncivilized" country among the "civilized." Thus, Japan's
small East Asian empire was consequently unable to belong in any stable fashion to either the East or the West, and was, until its collapse at the end of
World War II, never capable of overcoming its anomalous position.

Japan's defeat in the Second World War and the Cold War which followed
temporarily clarified Japan's international position: defeat turned Japan into a
weak nation even in comparison with the other countries of Asia. As a result of
the Cold War, the term "East" came to denote not Asia but the Communist
camp, and Japan was therefore firmly attached to the West. In essence, Japan's
position definitely became that of a weak nation in the Western camp. But
Japan's subsequent economic development, the easing of Cold War tensions,
and the multipolarization of international society have once again made its po-

sition and role ambiguous. Possessing a weak military force and heavily dependent on imports for most essential raw materials, therefore having limited influence and bargaining power, Japan is still in the process of searching for its role in this new era, an era that has seen state-to-state cooperation and confrontation take on exceedingly complex, multidimensional qualities.

ATTITUDES TOWARD THE INTERNATIONAL ENVIRONMENT

Not all Japanese, of course, have shared the same kind of attitude or the same level of concern toward the international environment. Diverse factors such as the historical period involved and social position or educational background have naturally affected individual perceptions, preferences, and degrees of concern regarding foreign affairs. At the same time, however, it would be difficult to deny that both the elite and the masses in modern Japan have shared certain common attitudes in this respect. The principal attitudes characterizing the perceptions and preferences of both the elite and the attentive public toward the international environment over the past one hundred years include (1) a strong sense of belonging to Japan and the Japanese race, coupled with deep-rooted feelings of inferiority; (2) an intense concern with improving the country's international status; (3) a deep anxiety over being isolated internationally; (4) a desire to conform to world trends (*sekai no taisei*); and (5) an emotional commitment to Asia, which has resulted in a focusing of attention on that area.

Since antiquity, Japan has not only been in continuous contact with cultures more advanced than its own but it has also endeavored to adopt them. Yet, except for the American Occupation in the postwar period, Japan has not experienced actual subjugation by another culture; thus the country's acceptance of foreign cultures has not destroyed the indigenous culture or culturally dismembered Japan proper. On the contrary, advanced cultures, imported in small quantities, have coexisted harmoniously with the native culture and gradually have been diffused throughout the country. As a result, Japan has remained highly homogeneous and unique, both culturally and ethnically. From ancient times, practically all the inhabitants of the Japanese archipelago have been ethnically Japanese; conversely, almost all those ethnically classifiable as Japanese have resided within the confines of the islands. The Japanese language, moreover, could be used anywhere within the country, but could rarely be understood elsewhere.

This consciousness among Japanese, both of the existence of more advanced cultures and of their own homogeneity and uniqueness, has developed in them a sense of belonging to Japan and, simultaneously, a feeling of inferiority. That the Japanese were the first people within the Chinese cultural area to create, around the end of the eighth century, an original syllabary different from the Chinese ideographs demonstrates the early development of ethnic self-consciousness in Japan. The Korean alphabet (han'gul) did not come into being until the middle of the fifteenth century, and Vietnam did not develop her own written language until it was colonized by France. Nevertheless, the Japanese named their syllabary kana (kari no moji; that is, the provisional or unauthorized characters), which reveals their sense of inferiority to China and its written language and culture.

It should be noted that Japanese intellectuals have played a major role in perpetuating the view that Japan was a culturally backward, small country compared with China and India—and, later, compared with the Western powers. Moreover, the resolution of the conflict between their sense of inferiority, on the one hand, and their feelings of belonging to a special group which cultivated a strong national pride, on the other hand, has posed enormously difficult problems. With the coming of the modern period, the Japanese sense of crisis toward the outside world has intensified. As one result, domestic, political, social, and economic integration was strengthened. Challenge and response, moreover, both produced an increase in nationalistic sentiments. Yet at the same time, the huge inflow of advanced Western culture heightened the Japanese sense of inferiority.

Attempts to compensate for this feeling of inferiority and to overcome the ambivalence toward Japan assumed many forms.[10] At one extreme were those xenophiles who sought psychological refuge from Japan and tried to identify with the advanced nations and their culture. Among the Edo Confucian scholars who ardently admired Chinese culture and the Meiji Western scholars who devoted themselves to the study of Western culture, not a few chose this path. At the other extreme were the aggressive nationalists who argued that Japan was the supreme nation of the world. Representative of this group were those Kokugaku scholars—and the fanatic nationalists of the 1930s who echoed them—who insisted that because the country had been ruled uninterruptedly by the emperor, a descendant of the Sun Goddess, Japan was not only the Divine Land (shinkoku), but the Father Country (oyaguni) of all the nations on earth.

Psychological refuge in the advanced countries, however, was difficult to reconcile with a strong sense of belonging to Japan. And those who narcissistically glorified Japan found it hard to account fully for such questions as why had Japan depended so heavily on foreign cultures or why was Japan—supposedly the Father Country—so small in territorial size. The most effective way to resolve the ambivalence toward Japan was to separate an advanced culture

10. See Satō Seizaburō, "Bakumatsu Meiji shoki ni okeru taigai ishiki no shoruikei," in Satō Seizaburō and Roger Dingman, eds., Nihonjin no taigai ishiki, (Tokyo: University of Tokyo Press, 1974).

from the society that had produced it—and to elevate culture to a universal principle transcending both time and place, and to use that principle as a standard by which to relativize existing conditions in the advanced nations; or, alternatively, to pay attention only to specific parts of the advanced cultures and to catch up with them in that particular area.

For example, Ogyū Sorai (1666–1728) made an absolute standard out of the ruling techniques of the legendary sage-kings of ancient China and the doctrines of Confucius, in whose name had been recorded a comprehensive compilation of these methods. He then criticized post-Confucius China and prided himself on being a "barbarous Japanese" who understood the teachings of the sage-kings of old China better than the Chinese themselves.[11] Fukuzawa Yukichi (1834–1901) universalized civilization by asserting that it was nothing other than the progress of the intellect and morality (chitoku) of all mankind. He thereby made a logical distinction between Westernization and the process of civilization and relativized Western culture.[12]

Only a few exceptional intellectuals, however, could assume such a universalistic position. A much more prominent tendency was the attempt to catch up with the advanced countries by adopting the syncretic attitude of utilizing their merits to compensate for Japan's shortcomings. By the end of the tenth century, the term Yamato damashii (Japanese spirit) was used to denote resourcefulness in managing daily life (seikatsu no chie) in contrast to kara zae (Chinese learning), which signified scholarly knowledge. By the Muromachi period (1392–1573), the phrase wakon kansai (Japanese spirit, Chinese learning) expressed the ideal for combining human abilities. After the Meiji Restoration the phrase was transformed into wakon yōsai (Japanese spirit, Western learning).

The meaning of the terms kansai and yōsai in these syncretic slogans was relatively clear-cut and concrete. Wakon, on the other hand, was undefined and synthesized with the other two terms in an ambiguous way. Yet, precisely because of this vagueness these slogans permitted the Japanese to camouflage the conflict between their sense of belonging and their feelings of inferiority. Thus, the slogans were effective in that they promoted the attempt to compensate for inferiority by focusing on catching up with one specific area of the advanced countries. Moreover, this syncretism suited the Japanese experience of importing foreign cultures without destroying their indigenous culture.

The importance of hierarchy in interpersonal as well as intergroup relations is a well-known characteristic in Japanese society. As the Japanese feel a strong bond with the group to which they belong, they tend to focus keen concern on

11. See Yoshikawa Kōjirō, "Sorai gakuan," in Yoshikawa Kōjirō et al., eds., Ogyū Sorai (Tokyo: Iwanami Shoten, 1973); and Yoshikawa Kojiro, "Minzokushugi sha to shite no Sorai," Sekai, Jan. 1974, pp. 246–271.

12. Fukuzawa Yukichi, "Bunmeiron no gairyaku," in Fukuzawa yukichi zenshū (Tokyo: Iwanami Shoten, 1959), vol. 4, 1–212.

the social rank of their group. When these attitudes are directed toward international society, interstate relations similarly come to be viewed hierarchically, and the Japanese sense of belonging to the Japanese state makes them extremely sensitive to the international status of their country. The will to compensate for their sense of inferiority has historically been an important source of energy for elevating Japan's international position.

A precondition for raising a country's international status lies in its recognition as a full-fledged member of the community of nations. Wishing to be acknowledged internationally as a "civilized" country, Japan in the early Meiji period strove to import and adopt the legal system of the "civilized" (Western) powers. A prime reason Japan promulgated a written constitution relatively early was that the possession of such a constitution was regarded as an important prerequisite of a "civilized" nation. Moreover, the revision of the unequal treaties, concluded during the Tokugawa period with the Western powers, became as urgent task because they symbolized that Japan had not yet achieved the status of a legitimate member of the community of nations. The imperial rescript declaring war against Ch'ing China instructed the government to fight the enemy, "exhausting every means, insofar as international laws are not violated."[13] The aim of this, of course, was for Japan to be recognized by the world as a "civilized" nation by strictly observing the international laws which served as a form of agreement among "civilized" nations.

The tentative realization of treaty revision in 1894, the victory in the Sino-Japanese War in 1895, and the inauguration of the Anglo-Japanese Alliance in 1902 were all welcomed enthusiastically as proof that Japan had at last attained equal status with the Western powers. A leading article in one influential newspaper of the time expressed Japan's elation over the establishment of the Anglo-Japanese Alliance:

Within some four decades since the opening of our doors, and but a few years since demonstrating our true strength in the Sino-Japanese War, our country has elevated itself to such an advanced position. When we consider that Japan has now practically leaped into the ranks of the international powers, it seems as if it were all merely an ecstatic dream. But no, it is not a utopian fantasy: it is in fact reality.[14]

Ranking naturally requires criteria for comparison. Since the Meiji Restoration, the most popular criteria were military power and economic strength —epitomized in the well-known slogan *fukoku kyōhei* (rich country, strong military). After achieving a semblance of parity with the Western powers, many Japanese focused their urgent attention on the question, Where precisely

13. Gaimushō, ed., *Nihon gaikō nenpyō narabini shuyō bunsho* (Tokyo: Hara Shobo, 1965), vol. 1, p. 1.
14. "Nichi ei dōmei no kōka," *Jiji shimpō*, Feb. 14, 1902.

does Japan stand internationally in terms of strength? Since the early Meiji period, a wide readership has intently followed the frequently published tables and charts of comparative statistics on subjects such as population, territory, military power, and economic strength.

The outcome of the Russo-Japanese War drew Japan into the ranks of the "eight great powers" (as number eight); and the First World War elevated the country to the number five position. Even the Washington Naval Treaty of 1922—the terms of which were not necessarily satisfactory to the Japanese naval authorities—was accepted quite consciously because it clearly showed that Japan possessed the world's third most powerful navy.

Although defeat in war often fortifies nationalism, most Japanese experienced a deep sense of impotence for a period immediately following the holocaust of World War II; they felt that Japan had plummeted militarily and economically to the status of a fourth-rate power and would not be able, at least in the near future, to raise its international position. There were even those who believed that Japan had "reverted . . . to the Eskimo stage of development."[15] Under these conditions, their first concern was to "return to the community of nations." The cooperation with the United States Occupation forces, the effort to democratize Japan, and the active adoption of Article 9 of the Constitution were all motivated by the desire to recover the world's trust and confidence in Japan.

With Japan's rapid economic development since the 1950s and the consequent uplifting of Japan's international economic status, the Japanese have again focused attention on economic power as a criterion for grading nations. Until the 1970s—when the intensification of environmental pollution and the resource crisis began to raise doubts concerning the wisdom of unlimited economic growth—a majority of the Japanese people felt immense pride in the rapid rise, measured in terms of gross national product, of Japan's international position.

The existence of a deep concern with world recognition and elevation of status also implies an intense fear of being isolated internationally. The historical peripherality and ambiguity of Japan's international status have heightened this anxiety and at times have elicited responses verging on delusions of persecution. A widespread apprehension among Japanese high government officials at the time of the First World War illustrates this Japanese fear of persecution.[16] Many Western observers at the time thought that World War I would be the last war among the "civilized nations," and that all efforts should be directed toward that end. Some Japanese, however, viewed the war merely as the final conflict among countries of the white race and believed that a future

15. Rōyama Masamichi, *Yomigaeru Nihon* (Tokyo: Chūō Koronsha, 1967), pp. 125–126.

16. For example, Yamagata Aritomo, "Taishi seisaku ikensho" (1914), in Oyama Azusa, ed., *Yamagata Aritomo ikensho* (Tokyo: Hara Shobō, 1966), pp. 339–345.

racial war would pit a coalition of the white races against the weaker yellow peoples.

In the 1930s a widespread fear developed that Japan was being isolated by the United States *(A)*, Britain *(B)*, China *(C)*, and Holland *(D)*—the "ABCD encirclement against Japan." An overwhelming desire to redress this condition led Japan to form its alliance with Germany and Italy, an alliance of the "have-nots."

Japanese fears of isolation abated somewhat as Japan became firmly bound to the Western camp during the Cold War confrontation. With the easing of world tensions and the multipolarization of international relations, however, the specter has reappeared. President Nixon's announcements in the summer of 1971 of his plans to visit China and to adopt a new protective economic policy were especially shocking to the Japanese because they aggravated this reviving fear of international isolation. One nightmarish scenario warned that the United States and China, wary of Japan's economic strength and military potential, might link together in an anti-Japanese alliance reminiscent of the prewar ABCD encirclement. Another masochistic self-image suggested that an economically strong Japan would incur worldwide antipathy and become a victim of a *fukuro dataki* (violent drubbing).[17] "Don't become an orphan of the world" and "cooperate with the powers" have been repeatedly emphasized maxims of Japanese diplomacy in both the pre- and postwar periods.

To avoid becoming isolated internationally, it is necessary to understand properly the trend of the world and not to deviate from it. When the Western powers demanded that Japan open its doors to the outside, the country submitted to an abandonment of its sacred tradition of seclusion (*sakoku*) rather than to plunge Japan into a reckless war. Since that time Japanese diplomacy has coped with the fluctuating international environment by being both practical and opportunistic. Thus, "don't miss the boat" has been another important maxim of Japanese diplomacy.

The army officers who planned and executed the Manchurian Incident believed that the powers would do little more than issue moral denunciations against the act because the United States and Britain were busily absorbed in reconstructing their domestic economies and the Soviet army in Siberia was not yet sufficiently strong. Their judgment proved to be correct, and the remarkable success of this venture provided a solid fillip to Japan's overseas advance. If, however, Nazi Germany had not been so overwhelmingly victorious in the early stages of World War II; if Holland and France had not capitulated to Germany and thereby left the vast power vacuum in Southeast Asia; and if the initiation of hostilities between Germany and the Soviet Union had not freed

17. Takeyama Yasuo, *Fukuro dataki no Nihon: Amaku nai heiwa kokka no michi* (Tokyo: Saimuru Shuppan, 1972).

Japan from the threat of the Soviet military, Japan probably would not have advanced militarily into Southeast Asia in such an open manner. Furthermore, if the United States had not imposed such retaliatory measures as the total commercial embargo—including oil—and demanded the total withdrawal of all Japanese military forces from China, the war between the United States and Japan would probably not have erupted, at least in 1941. Of course, the fanatic nationalists and aggressive expansionists of the period had their influence, but the leaders of Japan—including the military command—were eminently practical. They were both opportunistic and reactive in their response to the new trend of the world; in this regard they did not differ greatly from their Meiji predecessors.

The desire to conform with the trend of the times leads to the practical diplomacy of betting on the "winning horse." Already in 1858, Hashimoto Sanai (1834–1859) observed that the world's most powerful nations were Russia and Britain, and that because the former was more likely to gain international popularity in the future, Japan should ally itself with Russia.[18] Yet later, other leaders perceived England to be the more promising power. Excluding the post-World War II Occupation period, during which Japan had lost its independence, the only period since the beginning of the twentieth century in which the country did not maintain an alliance with at least one powerful nation was from 1923, when the Anglo-Japanese Alliance expired, until 1940, when Japan joined the Tripartite Pact with Germany and Italy. Even then from 1923 until the Manchurian Incident in 1931, Japan joined with the United States, Britain, and France in a loose collective security arrangement for East Asia under the Four-Power Treaty.

With the advance of the Western powers into East Asia, the term *tōyō* (Eastern Ocean) came to have a special meaning for Japan. In contrast to the West, the Eastern Ocean represented the area with which Japanese felt cultural familiarity. Furthermore, Japan and the rest of East Asia had shared a common experience in being confronted by the threat of the Western powers. Even as the Japanese strove to adopt Western culture with a practical, syncretic attitude, the prodigious inflow of highly heterogeneous Western cultures inevitably resulted in an "identity crisis," which created a strong and persistent feeling of nostalgia for the East.

The arrogant racial discrimination of the West toward the Japanese and other yellow peoples—as represented by the "yellow peril" theme—deeply injured the pride of the already vulnerable Japanese and further intensified their emotional commitment to Asia. Thus Tokutomi Sohō (1863–1957) wrote indignantly in 1894, "Westerners who think highly of the Japanese think we are

18. Keigaku Kai, ed., *Hashimoto Keigaku zenshū* (Tokyo: Iwanami Shoten, 1939), vol. 1, pp. 552–554.

some kind of human being next to the monkey; those who think ill of us think we are some kind of monkey next to human beings."[19] At a time when the Western powers justified their domination of Asia as a result of the superiority of the white over the yellow race, it was only natural for Japan to argue that its expansion was in the cause of justice to "liberate the East."

Japanese territorial expansion was possible, moreover, only in Asia. Japan's overseas investments before the war and its greatest commercial partners in both exports and imports were almost entirely in East Asia, particularly China. In 1914, when Japan maintained seventeen consulate generals around the world, seven were in China; of twenty-nine consulates, seventeen were in China.[20]

A Japanese expansion that tried to draw East Asia into its own sphere of influence could not be fully reconciled with the concept of "liberating the East." As long as the nationalistic feelings of other Asians had not yet awakened, this anomaly could be smoothed over temporarily. Once the flames of national liberation movements began to spread throughout the region, however, the contradiction inevitably surfaced. Yet the more difficult it becomes to justify one's actions, the more fervently one tends to grope for an ideology to rationalize those actions. Japan is indeed symbolic of this paradigm: when the Chinese national liberation movement reached the point of demanding that the imperialist powers—including Japan—return the territories and concessions previously seized, Japan, waving the banner of "liberation of the East," sparked the Manchurian Incident and thereby embarked on a full collision course with China. From the late 1930s, Asianism peaked in Japan precisely as Japan's domination of Asia became most unrestrained.

Asianism declined significantly after the Second World War. First, Japan's conduct during the war had so tainted the flag of Asianism that it had utterly lost its attraction as an ideology. Second, the Cold War had divided East Asia into the Communist and Western camps, and stripped the confrontation between East and West of its former meaning. Third, Japan's economic activity has grown to global proportions, and as the share of Japan's investment in and commerce with Asia has decreased, interested concern was not focused so exclusively on Asia. Asia's share in Japan's economy has declined as a natural result of the overall growth of Japanese economic power. But seen from the other side, it is clear that Japan's role in trade and other economic activities in the rest of Asia has in fact increased significantly compared to the prewar era. Fourth, the three great military powers—the United States, the Soviet Union, and China—are competing for influence in Asia. At the same time, the tremendous upsurge of nationalism throughout the region has made it impossible for

19. Tokutomi Sohō, "Seishin no shin igi," quoted in Kawahara Hiroshi, *Ajia eno shisō* (Tokyo: Kawashima Shoten, 1968), p. 119.

20. Banno Masataka, *Gendai gaikō no bunseki* (Tokyo: University of Tokyo Press, 1971), p. 50.

Japan, with such a tarnished record, to assume a position of dominance in East Asia, despite the magnitude of its economic role therein.

Even now, Japan's attitude toward Communist China is quite different from its attitude toward Communist Russia, a difference that undeniably arises from Japan's sense of guilt and emotional commitment to Asia. Moreover, the easing of Cold War tensions and the worsening of the Sino-Soviet rift are eliminating one factor that would restrain the development of Asianism. If the competition among the advanced nations over markets and resources should intensify significantly, the possibility that Asianism will emerge again cannot be totally discounted.

THE FOREIGN POLICY
FORMULATION PROCESS

From the oligarchic government of Meiji times to the present-day parliamentary democracy the framework of modern Japan's political system and its foreign policy formulation process have undergone great changes. At the same time, certain distinctive features have persisted, such as the strong tendency toward centralization and the institutionalization of factionalism (or the factionalization of institutions) in the modern Japanese political process.

Among the enduring characteristics of Japan's foreign policy formulation process is the remarkable degree of professionalism in the Foreign Ministry. As much of the work in a foreign ministry is secret and highly technical, foreign ministries of all countries require a certain degree of professionalism. Nevertheless professionalism appeared especially early in Japan, as the government found it necessary to rely on diplomatic specialists to deal with the modern diplomatic rules and customs that had originated in the very heterogeneous societies, cultures, and languages of the West. Table 2 shows the number of full-time holders of a ministry portfolio as a ratio of the total number of cabinets. The ratio is lowest for the navy and war ministers in the prewar period and for the prime minister since the war, but in overall comparison with the other ministries, a relatively small number of persons has held the Foreign Ministry portfolio.

From the time of Shidehara Kijūrō's (1872–1951) appointment as foreign minister in 1924, there were only three prewar exceptions to the practice of naming career diplomats who had passed the HFSE (Higher Foreign Service Examination) as full-time foreign ministers. (All three exceptions—one army general and two navy admirals—assumed the portfolio in the latter half of the 1930s when the influence of the military had become strong.) In addition almost all of the ambassadors and ministers sent abroad had also passed the HFSE. After the war, the tendency to name experienced Foreign Ministry peo-

Table 2
Ratio of Number of Full-Time Cabinet Ministry
Portfolio-Holders to Number of Cabinets

	Prewar period (1885–1945)			Postwar period (1945–1973)		
	A	B	$\frac{A}{B}$	A	B	$\frac{A}{B}$
	Number of full-time portfolio-holders	Number of cabinets		Number of full-time portfolio-holders	Number of cabinets	
Prime minister	29	42	0.69	11	23	0.48
Foreign minister	28	42	0.67	12	23	0.52
Home minister	42	42	1.00	6	4	1.50
Finance minister	29	42	0.69	17	23	0.74
War minister	26	42	0.62	--	--	--
Navy minister	18	42	0.43	--	--	--
Defense minister	--	--	--	22	16	1.38
Justice minister	35	42	0.83	26	23	1.13
Education minister	48	42	1.14	25	23	1.09
Agriculture and Commerce minister	28	24	1.17	--	--	--
Agriculture minister	14	17	0.82	30	22	1.36
Commerce and Industry minister	22	17	1.29	6	6	1.00
International Trade and Industry minister	--	--	--	21	18	1.17
Communication minister	38	40	0.95	31	21	1.48
Welfare minister	8	9	0.89	28	23	1.22
Labor minister	--	--	--	25	20	1.25
Construction minister	--	--	--	24	19	1.26
Economic Planning minister	--	--	--	22	21	1.05
Administrative Management minister	--	--	--	20	19	1.05
Local Autonomy minister	--	--	--	27	18	1.50

ple as foreign ministers continued for a time. From the Higashikuni cabinet (established immediately after the defeat) through the third Hatoyama cabinet (resigned December 1956), only four foreign ministers served in the twelve cabinets, and all had been career diplomats.

With the Ishibashi cabinet, which followed the Hatoyama cabinet, the trend changed toward choosing cabinet members on the basis of their seniority and influence in the various factions within the LDP. Thus the important post of foreign minister usually went to an influential member of a major faction, and from the time of Kishi Nobusuke (1896– , foreign minister in the Ishibashi cabinet) to the present, not one of the eight foreign ministers has had a background as a career diplomat. Three were formerly with Finance Ministry, two with Ministry of Commerce and Industry (the predecessor to MITI), two were business leaders, and one who was purely a party politician. Six, however, were either factional bosses (*jitsuryokusha*) at the time they assumed the portfolio, or later became bosses. Due to their long service in foreign countries, Foreign Ministry officials lack the patronage necessary to cultivate the electorate. Naturally they find it difficult to become factional bosses or even to win an election. At present only three former career diplomats are members of the lower house of the Diet (more than twenty members of the same body are Finance Ministry alumni), and not one is a factional boss.

Despite the great change in the background of foreign ministers, diplomats still predominate within the ministry. For a time after the Occupation a number of businessmen were appointed as ambassadors and ministers, but nearly all resigned soon afterward. Now, as in prewar times, career diplomats hold almost all of the principal diplomatic posts.[21] This is one mark of privileged status which clearly sets those who have passed the examination apart from all others.

Diplomacy, however, is not the monopoly of the Foreign Ministry. The scope of international relations has become more extensive even as its concerns have become more intensive. Moreover, as the boundary between domestic and diplomatic problems has become increasingly vague, other branches of the government have become concerned with diplomatic issues. These other ministries have also emphasized professionalism, which has led to rivalries with the Foreign Ministry.

Under the Meiji constitution a complicated system of checks and balances was maintained among the central organizations—the cabinet, Diet, military authorities, and Privy Council—each of which derived its authority from its direct link to the emperor. Even within the cabinet, the prime minister's authority over members of his cabinet was legally limited. Therefore, it was extremely difficult to regulate discord among the various branches of the government, especially the army and navy. The prerogative of supreme command, the requirement that war and navy ministers be active service officers, and the right of war and navy ministers to appeal directly to the throne, all combined to make them an *imperium in imperio* with enormous independence from the rest of the cabinet.

In the Meiji period, frequent exchange of personnel among the branches of government and the existence of the *genrō* (senior political leaders) helped to

21. See Haruhiro Fukui, "Policy-Making in the Japanese Foreign Ministry," in this volume.

regulate the discord among the various branches. Gradually, however, each of the branches became increasingly professional and closed off from the others, and the ability of the *genrō* to control discord declined as its members grew old and died. As a result Japanese diplomacy often fell into a state of confusion. For example, the army's strategic concern with China led to remarkable paradoxes in Japan's policy toward that country—frequently the Foreign Ministry and the army pursued separate and quite contradictory China policies. This kind of disintegration into what has been called a "double government" of foreign policies and policy-makers is a second distinctive feature of prewar Japan's foreign policy formulation process.[22]

Under this prewar "double government," the army was gradually able to centralize its control as it administered the areas it had occupied through the succession of *faits accomplis* presented by its military actions. After the Manchurian Incident, the army established the Taiman Jimukyoku (Executive Offices for Manchurian Affairs) in 1934. It was followed by the Kōa-in (Asian Development Agency), established in 1938 to take charge of policy toward China after the outbreak of the Sino-Japanese War, and by the Dai Tōa-shō (Ministry of Greater East Asian Affairs), organized in 1942 to take charge of policy toward all occupied territories including China. All were designed to unify diplomacy by reducing the influence of the Foreign Ministry bureaus responsible for Asian relations.

After the Second World War, the abolition of privileged structures not subject to public election, such as the House of Peers and the Privy Council, and establishment of parliamentary government strengthened the authority of the prime minister over members of his cabinet. The military authorities were also entirely dissolved, then re-established as the Self-Defense Forces under civilian control and without their former independence. But the LDP (and its predecessor, the Democratic Liberal Party), which has continually controlled the government since the end of the Occupation, is essentially a coalition of the factions. Competition among these factions imposes checks and balances on the LDP leadership and produces much compromising in the decision-making process. Moreover, the LDP must depend on the government bureaucracy for talented policy-makers. Thus, although the LDP administration is highly stable and the likelihood of its losing its rein over the government in the near future is slight, the regulation of sectionalism among branches of the government still poses a great challenge.

As the scope of international relations has rapidly expanded since World War II, almost all branches of government have begun to participate in diplomatic affairs. For example, the present-day Japanese embassy in Washington is staffed not only by Foreign Ministry personnel, but also by people sent there from most other ministries in the government. As a result, the opportunities for

22. See Yoshino Sakuzō, *Nijū seifu to iaku jōsō* (Tokyo, 1922).

discord between the Foreign Ministry and other ministries over foreign policy and diplomatic negotiations have increased. This is especially true since the so-called economic diplomacy concerning such matters as international finance and economic aid has become so important. In the postwar period, the antagonism between the Foreign Ministry and economic authorities, notably the Finance Ministry and MITI, is particularly conspicuous.

Although discord between the Foreign Ministry and other ministries is apt to cause confusion or even paralysis in Japanese dipomacy, the Diet has not played a large role in foreign policy formulation in either prewar or postwar times. Under the Meiji constitution, diplomacy was a prerogative of the emperor. The Privy Council, not the Diet, ratified treaties signed by the government. This is not to say, however, that the Imperial Diet had no influence whatsoever on the formulation of foreign policy. From the Twenty-Fifth Imperial Diet of 1909 onward, the foreign minister addressed both the upper and lower houses of the Diet concerning foreign policy. Even before that time the prime minister devoted a significant part of his administrative address to an explanation of foreign policy. Questions and answers concerning these speeches constituted an important part of debates in the Diet. Although the Imperial Diet lacked the power of ratification, its power to criticize the government's foreign policy, if skillfully handled, could arouse public opinion and, by causing divisions within the government, aggravating existing cleavages, or exerting influence on the deliberations of the Privy Council, could force the government into a difficult situation. For example, at the time of 1930 London Naval Disarmament Treaty, the opposition Seiyūkai joined with the naval general staff and the members of the Privy Council strongly opposed to the treaty, and harassed the Hamaguchi cabinet with repeated sharp criticism of the government in the Diet. Under the Meiji constitution the various organs of government were separated in pluralist fashion, and it was possible for an opposition party to attain some influence with respect to foreign policy if it utilized that separation with skill. Nevertheless, if the government firmly adhered to its decision, it could defy the opposition of the Diet. The London Disarmament Treaty, in the end, was ratified by the Privy Council.

After World War II the Diet acquired the power to ratify treaties. Except for the confused periods immediately following the defeat and Occupation, the LDP has managed (up to 1976) to have a comfortable majority in both houses of the Diet, and despite the factionalism within the party, its discipline in Diet votes has been strict. Furthermore, the opposition parties' disagreements with the LDP, which have been greatest in the area of foreign policy, have tended to focus on abstract principles. The result has limited the opposition parties' ability to use discord within the LDP and among the government ministries in the deliberations over diplomatic questions. Blocked in the Diet, the opposition parties have sought to inflame public opinion by organizing mass agitation

outside the Diet and "blocking with their bodies" any decision on treaty ratification or related measures inside the Diet. These tactics, however, expose the
opposition parties to criticism of their frequent use of violence. Although the
movement to oppose the 1960 U.S.-Japan Security Treaty was the most successful example of these tactics, it was not able to block the treaty.

A fourth characteristic of Japan's foreign policy formulation process is the
continual diplomatic anxiety and frustration caused by the ambiguity and
relative weakness of Japan's international position. Moreover, the government's
policies of opportunism and its efforts to follow general world trends have tended to create dissatisfaction among the intellectuals, most of whom prefer a foreign policy with an idealistic basis. The combination of these two elements has
led to criticism of the government's practical foreign policy as *tsuizui gaikō*
(copy-cat diplomacy) or *nanyyaku gaiko* (weak-kneed diplomacy) and demands
for international firmness. Ever since the *jōi* (expel the barbarians) exponents of
late Tokugawa days, advocacy of international firmness has been the most
characteristic form of antigovernment criticism. The major specific demands,
however, have varied according to the time and the foreign policy issue at hand:
during the Meiji Restoration the issue centered on *jōi;* from the 1880s to the
1890s, on the revision of the unequal treaties; during the first decade of the
1900s, on measures to deal with the Russians; from the 1910s to the 1920s, on a
resolute counteroffensive against Chinese nationalism; during the 1930s, on a
strong stand against the United States; and in the postwar years, on criticism of
the security arrangements with the United States.

As, in practice, following the world trend in the prewar era meant pursuing
those trends discerned among the Western powers, supporters of a firm stand
viewed the government's foreign policies as paying heed only to the Western
powers and ignoring the rest of Asia. This also goes far toward explaining why,
in the prewar years, Asianism became the most powerful ideology among the
antigovernment theorists pressing for hard-line policies. By comparison, pacifism has been the most influential theme in the postwar period. The lack of
harmony between the widespread pacifist sentiment among the people and the
ideology of Article 9 of the constitution, on the one hand, and the commitment
of the Japanese government to American Cold War diplomacy, on the other,
has made the government very vulnerable to criticism on this point.

Parties with slight possibilities of gaining political power are able to advocate
a hard line internationally. From the 1890s through the first decades of the
twentieth century, the minority Kaishintō, Kenseihontō, and Kokumintō usually favored a firmer foreign policy than that which the Jiyūtō and Seiyūkai—
in power during that period—actually pursued. Similarly, the opposition parties since World War II have found it easy to advocate idealistic pacifism, for
there has been almost no possibility of their gaining political power. They have
also found it effective at election time to appeal to the people's pacifist sen-

timents by insisting on "beautiful" idealism, rather than accepting "dirty" realism. In the 1950s, the leftist wing of the Socialist Party greatly increased its strength with the slogan, "Young people! Don't take up arms! Mothers! Don't send your sons off to the battlelines again!"

In addition, in an international environment controlled by Cold War confrontation, the opposition parties' position of idealistic neutralism has enabled them to perform the role of go-between in negotiations, trade, and cultural exchanges between Japan and the Soviet Union, China, North Korea, and other nations in the Communist sphere. The significance of such accomplishments has been one of the few pleasures afforded the politically powerless opposition parties. With the recent reduction of tension, however, the Japanese government has renewed direct negotiations with the governments of the Communist countries, thus sharply reducing the initiatives possible for the opposition parties in the diplomatic sphere. The alleviation of tension has also reduced the appeal of idealistic pacifism. This fact, together with the increasing importance of international questions such as those related to the environment and natural resources, will doubtless produce further changes in the approach of the opposition parties to foreign policy.

These characteristics of the foreign policy formulation process, together with Japan's strong desire to avoid international isolation and to conform to world trends, have made Japanese foreign policy ad hoc, reactive, and equivocating. Thus, at best, Japan's foreign policy is characterized by a shrewd pragmatism and, at worst, by an irresponsible immobilism.

Hata: J. as 'normal power'

Perspectives on Modern
Japanese Foreign Policy

ROBERT A. SCALAPINO

The foreign policy of modern Japan has been decisively affected by two sweeping developments of the past 150 years. The first relates to geography and geopolitics. In the early nineteenth century, the Japanese islands were in a remote, nearly inaccessible part of the world, totally removed from a larger economic or political context. In the late twentieth century, Japan is at the center of a highly strategic region, which involves other major societies, including the two current superpowers, in the most direct manner. Indeed, Northeast Asia is as important from the standpoint of international relations as any region of the contemporary world.

The traditional notion that a nation's geographic position—hence, certain geopolitical factors that establish the perimeters for its foreign policy—remains fixed is true only in the most formal sense. Today, revolutionary changes in transport and communication, together with equally dramatic changes in weaponry, resource needs, and political ties, serve to alter geography and, more particularly, the character of geographic strictures on politics, domestic and foreign. Japan's movement from remoteness to centrality in the global arena is striking evidence of this fact.

Second, Japan has moved from a position of total self-reliance to one of heavy dependence on the external world.[1] In general, this movement was closely connected with the particular form that the Japanese modernization process took, namely, the ever-increasing need for technology, raw materials, and, eventually, manpower. Once again, this kind of massive trend bears greatly on both options and attitudes in foreign policy.

1. See Tada Minoru, "Nihon gaikō wo dō kaweru ka?" *Ushio*, vol. 97 (June 1969), pp. 168–175.

- all this just happened "

Changes in these aspects will not necessarily cease, nor is their broad direction irreversible. The time may come when the relative importance of Northeast Asia declines. Even more possibly, Japan's current high level of international dependency may be reduced. For example, new sources of energy, including solar energy, and new methods of obtaining raw materials (the greater utilization of the ocean) may alter the picture. A shift of significant proportions, however, does not lie on the immediate horizon.[2] Meanwhile, the basic thrust of these developments has made Japanese involvement in the world ever more essential. Total defeat in World War II, to be sure, resulted in a hiatus and, even now, contributes to certain unique conditions. On the whole, however, Japanese involvement in the world has been progressive in the modern era, and it has also taken on new and varied dimensions.

Yet a major problem has long existed. The rapidly advancing necessity for internationalism has not been uniformly matched by corresponding adjustments within Japanese society. Thus, the gap between the demands of a successful international policy and the proclivities of Japan's political culture have generally grown wider. This is not to assert that Japanese society has remained in a static, traditional mold. Changes of truly major proportions have taken place and, since 1945, they have accelerated. In part, moreover, the gap noted here exists because, in comparison with other states, Japan's need to be internationalist is so great. No society could easily adjust its internal structure, values, and relations to the requirements imposed on Japan in its external relations. But this is not the entire story. That particular admixture of tradition and modernity applied so successfully to internal goals has served less well when brought to the international arena.

The behavioral patterns and attitudes of Japanese society clash with the requirements for an optimally successful foreign policy in several respects. First, Japan came to a sense of cultural identity at a relatively early date, which correspondingly created a strong feeling of separateness from other cultures, particularly those outside the traditional Confucian orbit. Qualities of xenophobia and exclusiveness followed. The counterforces accompanying modernization have not removed these elements from Japanese culture.[3]

passive tense

The nature of Japanese social organization, moreover, has placed certain limits or restraints on the outward projection of relationships. It has long been

2. Among many sources, see Tsuchiya Kiyoshi, "Nihon wa enerugi de tsubureru?" *Shakai shisō kenkyū,* vol. 22 (Dec. 1970), pp. 2–10; Umezu Kazuro, "Sōgō enerugī seisaku no ronri," *Sekai keizai hyōron,* vol. 15 (Dec. 1971), pp. 22–30, 40; "Nihon no enerugī mondai: zōdai suru jukyū to seisaku no hōkō," *Tsūsho sangyō kenkyu,* vol. 160 (March 1971); "Kaiyōkoku Nihon no shigen mondai," *Keizaijin,* vol. 25 (April 1971), pp. 6–15; "Nihon no shigen mondai no shikaku," *Keizai hyōron,* vol. 20 (May 1971), pp. 6–26; "Enerugī yosoku no mondai ten," *Keizai hyōron,* vol. 19 (Dec. 1970).

3. See Uchiyama Masateru, "Nihon gaikō no dentō to kakushin," *Hōgaku kenkyū,* vol. 26 (Aug. 1963), pp. 1–17; Nagai Yonosuke, "Nihon gaikō ni okeru kōsoku to sentaku," *Chūō kōron,* no. 81 (March 1966), pp. 46–85.

noted that the political genius of Japan has lain in oligarchy. Expressed in broader social terms, Japanese culture has revolved heavily around the small group, a discrete cluster of individuals, kinship or nonkinship, tightly connected via a complex set of reciprocal obligations. The creation of larger units capable of taking action or wielding power involves the aggregation of these small groups, necessitating an intricate system of liaison and consensus. The further the projection of intergroup relations, the more diluted the actual relationship, and the less compelling, particularly at the individual level.[4]

Like Great Britain, a society with which Japan shares certain social and geopolitical features, Japan has retained a strongly hierarchical social structure in the course of its modern development. Superior-inferior and inferior-superior patterns have created the key reference points for all relations and have also provided the basis on which each individual has established his own identity. The Japanese appear to have established their national identity in similar fashion, with the concept of equality in international relations difficult for them both to perceive and to execute.

These features of Japan's political culture have deeply affected its foreign relations in policies and in style. Two caveats, however, are in order. One must guard against the temptations to treat the problem of meshing indigenous behavioral patterns with foreign relations as one unique to Japan. No nation comes easily to extensive relations beyond its immediate cultural orbit, and irrespective of its particular cultural attributes, every society faces complex problems in adjusting its political values and style to the requirements of its external relations. If the Japanese problem seems special, it is only because the kind of development characterizing modern Japan has placed a high premium on internationalism, while Japan's particular set of cultural attributes has run sharply counter to this need in certain respects, especially in the postcolonial, mass-communications era.

My second caveat concerns the relations between foreign policy and the citizen. Political culture as a concept, being an effort to capture the full range of political attitudes and relations, applies to the whole of a society. The conceptualization and execution of foreign policy, on the other hand, is essentially an elitist operation, the task of the power holder and the specialist. Any given foreign policy must reflect the special concerns and the broader consciousness of the political elite, which may diverge—sometimes widely—from mass perceptions and values. This does occur, in Japan as elsewhere. Too much, however, should not be made of this fact. Generally, the Japanese political elite have shared fully in the cultural attributes of the society as a whole, which has served to make them a part of mass as well as elitist culture. Thus, divergence in policy has been tactical, not strategic. Whether the citizen of Japan in recent

4. For a recent stimulating—and controversial—analysis, see Nakane Chie, *Japanese Society* (Berkeley and Los Angeles: University of California Press, 1970).

times has played an increasing role in establishing the permissible perimeters of foreign policy, if not in the formulation of such policy, is a separate but related question.

Within the preceding framework is contained the underlying raison d'être for modern Japanese foreign policy and, at the same time, those aspects of the indigenous culture that at once challenge and shape that policy. When applied to several critical issues of foreign policy confronting Japan over time, it can help provide greater insight into Japan's real options of today. It is appropriate to commence with the question of Japan's relations with the Asian continent, because this has been an issue of continuous importance from earliest times.[5]

Prior to the Meiji Restoration, the continental policies of Japan had oscillated from those of significant involvement to those of near-total isolation. Interaction took various forms: cultural and economic exchange, marked by extensive Japanese borrowing from China, often via Korea; and military confrontation in which Japan played both offensive and defensive roles. When the role was offensive, the target was Korea, a society so geographically and culturally positioned as to cause concern on the one hand, and provide an access to the continent on the other.

A balance sheet on continental involvement in the traditional period would include, on the plus side, the opportunities for a vigorous yet relatively underdeveloped society to borrow from one of the great civilizations of all times. The impact of China on Japanese thought, religion, literature, and art can scarcely be exaggerated. Further, dominance of at least a portion of Korea afforded control over neighboring seas as well as over the chief invasion route, a route used by the ancestors of the Japanese themselves.[6]

Yet the negative aspects of continental involvement were substantial. Not until the Satsuma Rebellion was quelled in 1877 could Japan be considered truly unified despite the major accomplishments of earlier times. Always the areas of primary concern to central leaders had been precisely those fiefdoms closest to the continent. Foreign involvement, indeed, had invariably complicated the problem of internal unification by giving additional strength to the powerful "outer" lords.

Moreover, as the later involvement with the West was to illustrate anew, the impact of a foreign religion, a foreign literature, and foreign political ideas could also be traumatic. Intensive interaction with the continent exacted a psychological price. Japanese were required to accept a lower position in the hierarchical Confucian world, acknowledging the supremacy of China in those respects that mattered most. Indeed, Japanese nationalism first emerged in

5. For a variety of positions, see Ichiko Chūzō, *Kindai Nihon no tairiku hatten* (Tokyo, 1941); Ueda Toshio, *Nihon no tairiku hatten to sono hōkai katei* (Tokyo, 1948); Etō Shinkichi, *Higashi Ajia seiji shi kenkyū* (Tokyo, 1968); Ho Takushu, *Meiji shoki Ni-Kan shin kankei no kenkyū* (Tokyo, 1969).

6. Two works with different positions are Hatada Takashi, *Nihon to Chōsen* (Tokyo, 1965); and Nakamura Hidetaka, *Ni-Sen kankei shi no kenkyū* (Tokyo, 1969).

protest against a lower status. Finally, there were certain military costs and risks, such as the barely averted Mongol invasion and Japanese defeat at the hands of the Koreans.

The West, however, tilted the scales decisively against all foreign involvement at the beginning of the Tokugawa era. At this point, Japan had obtained what the Asian continent had to offer and could afford a period of consolidation and further refinement. Viewed from Edo, the risks posed by Western intrusion far outranked the benefits.

Japanese historians have discussed extensively the costs and benefits of Tokugawa isolation.[7] It enabled Japan to concentrate on internal unification, which, in turn, made possible new forms of economic growth. It also provided impetus for the deeper, more uniform spread of a common culture throughout the islands. It may even have been the decisive factor that enabled Japan to avoid the kinds of subordination to the West that affected much of Asia. At the same time, isolation no doubt reinforced that exclusiveness and privatism which are prominent aspects of modern Japan.

With the Meiji era, the issue of continental involvement reemerged, juxtaposed against the awesome problem of how to deal with the West. Given Perry and others, isolation was no longer a viable route. At an early point, however, priorities were established, the initial goal being the kind of internal development that would propitiate (and ward off) the West. Thus, when continental involvement began anew, first via Korea and subsequently throughout Asia, Japan was in the ascendency, whether the reference point was military, economic, or political.

Korea, it should be emphasized, was not merely the crucial first step, but the most important subsequent element in Japan's continental policies. To the Meiji leaders, a Korea dominated by either China or Russia represented an unacceptable threat to Japan's own security, and a self-reliant, independent Korea was regarded as an impossibility. Strategic more than economic considerations operated at this point, but once Korea was incorporated into Greater Japan, with an effort to make it an integral part of the homeland, the security issues loomed even larger. Japan had become an immediate part of the Asian continent at a time when much of that continent was characterized by weakness, political instability, and the intrusion of external forces, Western and Russian. Under these circumstances, it is scarcely surprising that Japan would seek to shape the indigenous forces of continental Asia into political units favorable to it. Henceforth, the Japanese debate over continental policy was not "whether" but "how"—how best to influence events so that Japanese interests would be protected.

One prominent school favored reliance on economic and political measures. Had conditions on the continent been different, this school might well have

7. In particular, see Watsuji Tetsurō, *Sakoku: Nihon no higeki* (Tokyo, 1951); and Kobayashi Ryōsei, *Tokugawa sakoku: baku-han hōken* (Tokyo, 1957).

396

prevailed. Given the existing vacuum of power, however, and developments on the global level, those advocating a more forceful set of policies involving military measures triumphed, with consequences too well known to need repetition here. It is important, however, to assert that despite the significant economic factors present, Japan's pre-1941 Northeast Asian policies were at root based on security considerations. They stemmed from the deep Japanese concern over the growing power of the USSR, including its capacity to exert political influence via the Communist movement, and the constant fear of a close linkage between China and leading Western powers. These dual concerns gave Japan its mission: rid Asia of both communism and Western imperialism.[8]

The issues underlying Japan's policies in Southeast Asia were different and basically economic. As Japan moved toward major power status, its dependence on external energy and raw material sources had steadily grown, and in this era Southeast Asia was a leading supplier. As the West controlled this region, it could deny Japan access to those materials, an intolerable situation if Japan's broader policies were to be maintained.[9]

Although the so-called military solution was ultimately adopted, there was no abandonment of economic and political approaches. Even now, there has been insufficient study of Japan's major effort in the decade immediately before World War II to align its policies with the cause of Asian nationalism and to work toward a regional economic community under Japanese leadership. The Japanese challenge to Western imperialism in Asia *and* to Soviet influence via the Communist movement was a massive one with substantial success initially.

The final failure, however, was not merely a military one. As a number of Asian nationalists have testified, certain factors springing from Japanese political culture ultimately inhibited or made more difficult the kind of genuine cooperation that might have rendered Japanese economic and political policies effective. In the final analysis, Japanese nationalism seemed the dominant force in the new order, and thus to many Asians—and not merely Chinese—another imperialism now confronted them. The relationships, moreover, were largely superior-inferior ones, with the traits of exclusiveness and commandism often in evidence. At the individual level, there were striking contrasts in this general picture, but they were not sufficient to change the total image. When the era of Japanese military power in Asia ended, therefore, Japan's political standing was correspondingly low.[10]

8. For an extreme view, see Akao Bin, *Genkyō han-So ka, han-Ei, Bei ka?* (Tokyo, 1940); see also Maruyama Kunio, *Harris-Perry shinryaku gaikō tenmatsu* (Tokyo, 1944).

9. See Takada Hōma, *Minzoku to keizai* (Tokyo, 1940).

10. Among the many works, for diverse perspectives, see Kajima Institute of International Peace, ed., *Daitō-A sensō gaishi*, 24 vols. (Tokyo, 1971); *Nihon gaikō shi*, 25 vols.; *Daitō-A sensō: shūsen gaikō* (Tokyo, 1972); Tamura Kōsaku, *Taiheiyō sensō gaikō shi* (Tokyo, 1966); Shigemitsu Mamoru, *Gaikō kaisō roku* (Tokyo, 1953); Tōgō Shigenori, *Jidai no ichimen: Taisen gaikō no shūkō* (Tokyo, 1965).

Defeat produced a total Japanese withdrawal from the continent, and once again a period of (enforced) isolation ensued. But within less than three decades, Japan had reemerged on the Asian mainland. In Northeast Asia, reemergence took the form of a commanding economic presence in South Korea, with promising, if limited, probes of a similar nature toward both the People's Republic of China and the Soviet Union. In Southeast Asia, the nature of the presence was similar. By 1970, Japan had achieved an economic position throughout the region unequaled by any other foreign power. These developments had occurred in conjunction with an economic explosion that had projected Japan into the foremost ranks of the world's industrial nations, resulting in Japan's greatly expanded requirements from external sources, on the one hand, and its strongly magnified capacity to render economic services to a wide range of societies, on the other hand. To some, the Greater East Asia Co-Prosperity Sphere was in the process of being realized without its earlier political and military connotations.

Rather than probing this inexact historical parallel, I shall note both the continuing and the new issues tied to Japan's continental involvement. The strategic situation, in its most basic dimensions, is new.[11] Southeast Asia remains troubled by a variety of weaknesses, legacy in part of the still-recent colonial era. In Northeast Asia, however, a vacuum of power no longer exists. Although China continues to manifest many of the uncertainties marking a developing society, it is also in the course of creating a formidable military establishment, nuclear and nonnuclear. As one result of the Sino-Soviet quarrel, moreover, the Soviet Union has moved substantial military forces into Northeast Asia. And even if the present tension is significantly reduced at some future date, there is every reason to expect that Russia will expand its military facilities in Siberia in accompaniment with the economic development of this area. The Soviet Union intends to be a major Asian as well as Western nation. As the United States also has vital interests in Northeast Asia, it too maintains military as well as political commitments in the area. Thus, all of the Pacific-Asian societies of key importance are highly visible and show every indication of regarding the region

11. See Etō Shinkichi et al., *Taikoku Nihon no shinro* (Tokyo, 1971); "Shichi jūnen Ampo to kyokutō jōsei," *Ajia kuotarī*, vol. 2, no. 3 (July 1970), pp. 2–161; "Ni-Chū kankei no mondai ten", *Ajia kuotarī*, vol. 3, no. 2 (April 1971), pp. 2–178; "Ajia gaikō no shiten," *Ekonomisto*, vol. 49, no. 35 (Aug. 24, 1971), pp. 28–42; "Bei-Chū sekkin to Ajia," *Sekai*, vol. 310 Sept. 1971), pp. 10-37; Hanai Hitoshi, "Shichijūninen Ajia to Nihon: Ajia no yon kyoku kōzō to Nihon," *Jiyū*, vol. 14 (Jan. 1972), pp. 72–78.

For approaches by American scholars, See Edwin O. Reischauer, *Beyond Vietnam: The United States and Asia* (New York: Knopf, 1967); Donald C. Hellmann, *Japan and East Asia: The New International Order* (New York: Praeger, 1972); Zbigniew Brzezinski, *The Fragile Blossom: Crisis and Change in Japan* (New York: Harper and Row, 1972); Herman Kahn, *The Emerging Japanese Superstate: Challenge and Response* (Englewood Cliffs, N.J.: Prentice-Hall, 1970); Frank Langdon, *Japanese Foreign Policy;* and Robert A. Scalapino, *Asia and the Major Powers: Implications for the International Order* (Washington, D.C.: American Enterprise Institute for Public Policy Research, and the Hoover Institution, 1972).

as one relating strongly to their national interests. Moreover, given the fact that certain unresolved issues of considerable importance are therein contained, for example, Korea and Taiwan, this is a region of global significance, possessing the ingredients for peace or war, international cooperation or confrontation.[12]

These conditions—the strategic importance of Northeast Asia today as a fulcrum of major power interaction, and the unprecedented reliance of Japan on external resources and markets—set the broad perimeters within which Japanese foreign policy must operate. The dilemma is clear. Given the trends toward multipolarism and economic interdependency, isolation from any major part of the world, and particularly from the Asian continent, is unthinkable; gradually, an accommodation to this fact is taking place via concrete policies. Yet what will the nature of this involvement be? Today the states of continental Asia are predominately operating under Communist systems, Southeast Asia being the only partial exception. Even there the future is far from clear. Can Japan interact with Communist states in such a fashion as to safeguard and advance both its economic and its political-strategic interests? Another question is of equal importance: can Japanese interaction with Asia's open and quasi-open societies be conducted in such a manner as to avoid sharp nationalist reactions against abuses and the threat of dominance?

After a lengthy period of minimal economic interaction across non-Communist and Communist barriers, the major nations of the world are now exploring the possibilities of much more extensive relations in this sphere. It is too early to be certain of the results. How will the various Communist ruling elites draw up the balance sheet between the significant economic advantages and the "subversion of the system" potential in such exchanges? Notwithstanding the existing problems and uncertainties, we appear to stand on the threshold of an intriguing new era of interaction between so-called capitalist and socialist economic systems, and certainly no country has more at stake than Japan.

Such interaction may have broad political and strategic implications for all parties concerned. How far will various states or blocs go in using trade and other forms of economic intercourse as political weapons? How will heightened economic relations affect the relative military capacities of various nations, and the overall strategic balance of power? Specifically, will Japan find that, in sharing its technology and goods with the People's Republic of China and the Soviet Union, it has made both the economic competition and the military-strategic position of one or both of these major societies more formidable? Or, will an old economic principle obtain: namely, that despite elements of competition, economic interaction among more advanced states is of the greatest all-around benefit, and that increased economic intercourse with the Communist states can strengthen the hands of the "moderates" within the system

12. For further amplification, see my *Asia and the Road Ahead* (Berkeley and Los Angeles: University of California Press, 1975).

and raise the priorities on internal development, including higher living standards? In contemplating its growing involvement with the Communist societies of continental Asia, these are issues that will ultimately present themselves to Japanese policy-makers.

What of economic interaction with the non-Communist states of continental Asia (and the off-shore states)? Here dramatic increases have already occurred, as is well known, and the character of issues is substantially different. If Japan's stance vis-à-vis the two major Communist states is innately defensive (that of the "inferior"), its stance toward South Korea, Taiwan, and various Southeast Asian countries is essentially offensive (that of the "superior"). A threat from these sources measured in traditional terms is inconceivable, and before them Japan's strengths as an "advanced" society capable of meshing effectively with their economic systems have stood out. Indeed, this is precisely the problem, and the source of a new threat. Already in such diverse settings as Seoul, Bangkok, and Jakarta, sharp nationalistic reactions to an excessive Japanese presence and a growing catalogue of abuses have burst forth.[13] It is perhaps ironic that, in the presence of minimal political commitments and a small military establishment oriented toward defensive purposes only, Japan should face charges of "neocolonialism" and find its image tarnished in those very societies where logic would seem to dictate a substantial range of mutual interests— proof that even "purely economic policies" have serious political repercussions.

Clearly, continental involvement, in whatever form, presents difficulties for Japan. In part, the difficulties relate to a major paradox: intensive economic penetration in most cases has not been accompanied by forms of cultural interaction perceived to be beneficial. Hence, the economic input—whatever its utility to the economy of the host country—is viewed as a manifestation of selfishness. The combination of intensive economic penetration and cultural exclusiveness leads to swift political deterioration, especially at the critical secondary elite levels, namely, at that level just below the top political-military elite of the nation involved.

For these and other reasons, Pan-Asianism, still a dream for some Japanese, is highly unrealistic. Diversity, and strong elements of competition and conflict will characterize inter-Asian relations for the foreseeable future. Even without the conditions previously noted, Japan would not be in a position to make regionalism the primary focus of its foreign policies, economic or political. The nature of its development has made Japan one of the few societies of the contemporary world with truly global interests. Its future hinges partly on the emergence of a new economic internationalism among the world's advanced nations and partly on maximal access to global resources. Exclusively or primarily regional policies would not serve either of these requirements, although

13. For a different viewpoint, see Kawai Hidekazu, "Tōnan Ajia to Chūgoku to Nihon: Ajia no tabi kara," *Sekai*, vol. 310 (Sept. 1971), pp. 183–190.

this does not negate the importance of certain regional concerns and institutions.[14]

Although Pan-Asianism is not the route of the future, it would be equally
mistaken to assume that Japan can in some manner be transformed into an
Asian appendage of the West, with its policies wholly focused on interaction
with the advanced industrial world. The recent ventures in trilateralism—
the efforts to bring into closer coordination the views and policies of Japan,
the United States, and West Europe—are very important. Constructive approaches to a number of vital international issues, including monetary, trade,
and investment policies, depend heavily on cooperation among these nations.
But some intensely Europocentric elements seek to extend this process too far.
They show resentment over the fact that Japan is in Asia and almost literally
seek to move it into the Atlantic, treating it as a nation that should have its exclusive concerns there. This too will fail, and if pushed too strongly, it will exacerbate the age-old conflict within Japan between those who are drawn to
Asia as an expression of identity and purpose and those who look to the West
as a means of development and change.

For modern Japan it cannot be either/or. Japan's complex task is to accord
importance simultaneously to different regions and levels in its foreign policies.
For some purposes, bilateral relations remain supremely important, as recent
developments pertaining to the United States, the People's Republic of China,
and the USSR so clearly indicate. Indeed, we have not yet reached the stage
where such relations have been surpassed in importance by those of a broader,
more complex character. At the same time, Japan is now one of the few global
powers, albeit of a special character. Its concerns with regional relations,
therefore, both of a geographic and of a developmental nature, have correspondingly increased. Thus, East Asia represents a geographic region involving
Japan's security as well as its most elemental political and economic relations.
The "Third World," particularly—though not exclusively—the Middle East,
comprises Japan's resource lifeline. The advanced industrial West, meanwhile,
also provides indispensable resources as well as technology and markets.

Like other major states, moreover, Japan faces the necessity of rapidly restructuring both its thought processes and its institutional capacities to deal
with truly global issues that cut across regions of whatever type. This is an era
in which there is the need to work toward an entirely new set of international
rules, procedures, and institutions pertaining to food, population, maritime and
space jurisdiction, resource procurement and management, arms control,
peaceful coexistence, and a host of other issues. Increasingly, the Japanese are
speaking of the North-South problem in an effort to encompass these problems,
but some of them, being variously West-East and regional problems as well, do
not fit into this rubric neatly.

14. See "Shōwa yonjūshichinen no uchi to soto," *Ushio*, vol. 17 (April 1972), pp. 26–37.

Meanwhile, Japan's complex task is to accord importance *simultaneously* to various levels of international relations. Its bilateral relations, especially with the United States, remain essential, particularly as they are closely connected with potentialities at other levels. Pacific-Asian regional programs and institutions offer the possibility of developing a sense of community without which Japanese economic policies will continue to pose threats to others. At the same time, Japan's stake in the broader international issues is clear. Thus, although the question of continental involvement versus isolation has, in the most fundamental sense, been resolved, involvement has not yet produced any real sense of community, nor can it serve as an exclusive, or even primary, reliance in the quest for a comprehensive foreign policy serving Japan's interests.

I shall now turn to a second basic policy dilemma long present in the Japanese scene. What are the advantages and disadvantages of alliance versus various forms of "independent" or "neutralist" foreign policy? In the pre-1945 era, Japan's leaders periodically decided that alliances out of Asia would benefit policies being pursued in Asia. Indeed, such alliances on occasion helped to determine those policies. For the first two decades of the twentieth century, the Anglo-Japanese Alliance was the cornerstone of Japanese foreign policy.[15] Having made the fateful decision to align Japan with Great Britain rather than with Russia, Japanese leaders were free to pursue expansionist policies in Northeast Asia in exchange for certain restraints with respect to Southern Asia. China remained an uncertain, troublesome testing ground for rival ambitions.

Shortly after World War I, the Anglo-Japanese alliance was abandoned in favor of a vague multipolarism in the form of the Washington Treaties of 1921. Now, reciprocal advantages, hence restraints, were less clear. The dependence was on moral suasion. As tensions mounted and the international order of this era progressively disintegrated, Japan returned to an alliance out of Asia, this time with the so-called Axis powers, Germany and Italy. Although this alliance was of a limited, realpolitik character, it also provided Japan with additional flexibility with respect to policies within Asia. Indecision remained as to whether to settle accounts with Russia or challenge the more formidable Western alliance spearheaded by the United States. There can be no doubt that the final decision was greatly influenced by the course of American policies in the critical period after 1939.[16]

15. For a recent English language study, see Ian H. Nish, *Alliance in Decline: A Study in Anglo-Japanese Relations, 1908–1923* (London: Athlone Press, 1973).

16. In addition to the works cited, see Tsunoda Jun and the Japanese International Politics Association, eds., *Taiheiyō sensō e no michi*, 7 vols. (Tokyo, 1962–1963); Tagaki Sōkichi, *Shikan Taiheiyō sensō* (Tokyo, 1969); Kojima Noboru, *Taiheiyō sensō* (Tokyo: Chūō Kōronsha, 1965); Ienaga Saburō, *Taiheiyō sensō* (Tokyo, 1968); Hattori Takushirō, *Daitō-A sensō zenshi* (Tokyo, 1965): Nihon Gaikō Gakkai, ed., *Taiheiyō sensō gen'in ron* (Tokyo, 1953); and Okumura Fusao, *Nichi-Bei kōshō to Taiheiyō sensō* (Tokyo, 1970). For official American accounts, see U.S. Department of State, *Foreign Relations of the United States: Japan, 1931–1941*, 2 vols. (Washington: Government Printing Office, 1943), and *Foreign Relations of the U.S.: The*

Thus, in the post-1945 period, Japan has not come to the concept of alliance without experience. Yet the alliance with the United States, which represents Japan's third alliance in modern times and which has endured for nearly a quarter of a century, is different from the others. Comparatively, it has been a far more pervasive alliance, affecting the cultures as well as the politics and economics of both societies, and involving a wide network of people-to-people relations as well as governmental ties. Within the strictures of their culture, Japanese, particularly those from the higher educational brackets, have sought a meaningful relationship with Americans. Indeed, since Japan's advent as a modern nation, this quest has been more serious with respect to Americans than with any other foreigners (with the possible exception of the Chinese).

In recent times, however, the American-Japanese alliance has been in trouble.[17] Perhaps it is symbolic, moreover, that as doubts concerning the relationship with Americans emerged, the Japanese public showed a proclivity for restoration of closer ties with China, another nation that has profoundly affected Japanese culture at various points in the history of the Japanese people.[18] It is as if the common man of Japan, irrespective of certain economic and political realities of the late twentieth century, is weary and apprehensive concerning the "turn toward the West," and now seeks the comfort of more intimate ties with a people within his historical cultural orbit. Great swings of the pendulum, first outward to the intensely foreign West, and then back to an emphasis on the indigenous and the culturally familiar, have been one pronounced characteristic of Japan's modernization process. With the swing back, moreover, has come a reassertion of Japanese nationalism, together with intensified manifestations of the "privatism" that is so deeply implanted in the Japanese way of life.

Should one then take the recent strains in the American-Japanese alliance as an illustration of the paradox between Japan's growing international requirements and its still constrained psychological and cultural capacities? Before reaching any such conclusion, a hard look at the pressures put on that alliance in recent years is necessary. It should be remembered that the

---

Far East, 1941 (Washington: Government Printing Office, 1956), vol. 4. For American works of continuing value, see Herbert Feis, *The Road to Pearl Harbor* (Princeton: Princeton University Press, 1950); Roberta Wohlstetter, *Pearl Harbor: Warning and Decision* (Stanford: Stanford University Press, 1961); and Nobutake Ike, trans. and ed., *Japan's Decision for War* (Stanford: Stanford University Press, 1967).

17. For recent accounts of American-Japanese relations other than those previously cited, see Gerald L. Curtis, *Japanese-American Relations in the 1970s* (Washington, D.C.: The American Assembly, Columbia Books, 1970); and Robert A. Scalapino, *American-Japanese Relations in a Changing Era* (New York: The Washington Papers, The Library Press, 1972).

18. For early data on Japanese public opinion as it relates to foreign policy, see Douglas H. Mendel, Jr., *The Japanese People and Foreign Policy* (Berkeley and Los Angeles, University of California Press, 1961); for recent data, showing the shift toward China, see Hugh L. Burleson, *The Nixon Doctrine in Northeast Asia: Strategic Implications of Japanese Reactions* (Carlisle Barracks, Penna.: U.S. Army War College, 1973).

American-Japanese alliance was inaugurated under nearly optimal conditions. Both parties had strongly perceived interests in maintaining close ties, interests that encompassed every major field—economic, political, and strategic. The alliance, moreover, was well attuned to the current psychological proclivities of each side. Japan, totally defeated in a massive war and deeply disillusioned with the old order, was prepared to accept the subordinate role. The United States, having achieved a new self-confidence and power, was prepared to lead, playing the role of tutor and protector.[19] Given these conditions, the fact that alliances were relatively all-encompassing and exclusive in character during the so-called Cold War era merely reinforced the security to be derived from such a Japanese-American relationship and enabled the Japanese to fit it more easily into a pattern with which they were completely familiar. A new "small group" had been formed, with clear-cut, reciprocal obligations of loyalty and protection.

Gradually changes running counter to the central premises initially underwriting the American-Japanese alliance occurred, both with respect to the two nations centrally concerned and the international environment. Economic and political trends blurred the basis on which the old superior-inferior relationship had rested. The sense of need also declined—on the political-security front for Japan and in economic matters for America. Meanwhile, global trends operated against exclusive alliances, favoring elements of flexibility, ambiguity, and irregularity that could be profoundly disturbing psychologically to those involved in close bilateral ties.

In this setting, the roles played by key political actors became a significant variable not predetermined by events. With respect to economic problems between the two nations, the Satō administration badly misjudged the American mood and, admittedly under strenuous domestic pressures to hold the line, unwisely procrastinated in taking actions that would have provided greater equity in bilateral economic relations. In turn, President Nixon followed the thesis that Japan would respond readily only to harsh measures and applied a series of shocks in both the economic and political arenas. He and Henry Kissinger, while paying homage rhetorically to the supreme importance of the alliance, in their personal approaches and private statements raised substantial doubts about their true attitudes toward Japan. In Japan the ranks of the anti-American forces swelled.

Thus, in addition to the underlying, impersonal factors adversely affecting the alliance, the actions and nonactions of prominent individuals and groups caused the emotional atmosphere surrounding the alliance to deteriorate. Now

19. For some excellent recent Japanese works, see Kamiya Fuji, ed., *Nihon to Amerika: kyōchō to tairitsu no kōzō* (Tokyo, 1973); Nagai Yōnosuke and Kamiya Fuji, eds., *Nichi-Bei keizai kankei no seijiteki kōzō* (Tokyo, 1972); and Etō Jun, "Nihon to Amerika: hitotsu no shōsatsu," *Chūō kōron*, vol. 86 (Dec. 1971), pp. 54–67.

relations were troubled by issues of credibility, respect, and even civility. Echoing these issues, trends in public opinion, notably in Japan, showed a declining support for the alliance. The latest trends have been mixed. On the one hand, the Lockheed scandal had profound and adverse repercussions, contributing to the crisis within the LDP and its meager showing in the December 1976 elections—thus seeming to accelerate the trend toward less political stability and an ultimate end to traditional conservative dominance. On the other hand, 1976 public opinion polls paradoxically indicated some upswing in the popularity of the United States.

This is the recent background. What are the broad alternatives for Japan in the coming decade and beyond? Is an alliance with some other society a possibility? Or is a "balanced" relationship with all major powers a more logical accommodation to the so-called multipolar era? Can Japan in this fashion find a more suitable degree of independence?

If the quest is for a substitute alliance, only two states, China or Russia, represent even remote possibilities. An alliance with China—de jure or de facto—would be an alliance between two highly dissimilar societies.[20] Notwithstanding the historic cultural legacy that the two peoples share and some lingering elements of commonality that stem from that legacy, Japan and China have moved in radically different directions in recent times. As a result, the political systems and economic structures of the two societies are widely at variance, which controls and inhibits their cultural relations. Thus a Sino-Japanese alliance would have to be based primarily on the mutual benefits to be derived from the economic interaction between an advanced and a developing society. Not even in the security realm could such an alliance be meaningful at this point. Here a negative advantage might exist: neither party would pose a threat to the other. The capacity of a Sino-Japanese alliance to deter the Soviet Union, however, would be minimal, and such an alliance would certainly create Russian apprehensions. Moreover, whatever economic gains are to be achieved in Japanese-Chinese relations can be obtained without an alliance. Five years after normalization of Sino-Japanese relations, economic interaction is expanding rather rapidly, but it remains heavily dependent on certain basic economic decisions made in Peking, as well as on the general state of political and economic health of both societies, and it still represents only about 3 percent of total Japanese trade.

From a strictly logical standpoint, an alliance with the Soviet Union has greater potential benefit to Japan than an alliance with China. The Soviet Union could provide the same security guarantees as the United States, and theoretically at least, the benefits from close economic interaction, although

20. See *Ni-Chū kankei no naka no "Taiwan mondai"* (Tokyo, 1970); and *Nihon kokusai bōeki sokushin kyōkai* (Tokyo, 1970); Ishikawa Tadao, "Ni-Chū mondai no kangaekata," *Dōmei*, Oct. 1971, pp. 58–70.

similar to those involved in Sino-Japanese relations, could have more immediate importance. The full extent of Siberian resources has yet to be measured, but indications are that they exceed anything available in China. Nor are the Russians reticent in indicating their desire for development of this area.

A Soviet-Japanese alliance, however, is most improbable. Here the full weight of historical and emotional restraints makes itself felt. Soviet generosity and credibility are both in short supply for Japan, and there is a deep resentment among most Japanese toward the Russians for actions past and present. Even with new policies, such as a Soviet agreement to return the Southern Kurile islands to Japan (a move still improbable), it would take time—and repeated evidence—to alter the emotional-political foundations necessary for any intimate relationship.[21] Moreover, the same basic gap between the political and economic institutions of the two nations exists as in the case of China, and as the Soviet Union is far more foreign culturally, it is difficult to imagine the kind of interchange that would underwrite an alliance.[22]

At root Sino-Japanese and Soviet-Japanese relations are two excellent illustrations of a crucial variable, namely, the relationship between emotional-political predispositions—hence, pressures—on the one hand, and realistic economic and political considerations (realpolitik), on the other. For Japan, the importance of this variable has unquestionably increased in recent decades as public opinion, and more particularly middle-level elitist opinion, is having an impact on policy-making. At least in the recent past, grass-roots sentiment favorable to Sino-Japanese relations has run considerably ahead of the political realities. The recognition and exploitation of the sentiment testifies to the shrewdness of Chinese foreign policy makers, although they constantly confront the risk of overplaying their hand. The reverse is true for Soviet-Japanese relations; both Japanese and Soviet leaders are seemingly at a loss (or restrained by other factors) in formulating new approaches.

Thus, to move toward another bilateral alliance in place of the American-Japanese alliance would not fit Japanese interests, either now or in the foreseeable future, even though the struggle between "Pan-Asianists" and "pro-Westerners" can be expected to continue. Has some variant of "neutralism" become more realistic as a result of the trends toward multipolarism? There can be no doubt that the character of all alliances has undergone a profound change in recent years. From the exclusiveness, breadth, and centrality characteristic of the Cold War era the movement has been toward porousness,

21. For a careful study of the complexities involved in earlier Japanese-Soviet negotiations, see Donald C. Hellmann, *Japanese Domestic Politics and Foreign Policy: The Peace Agreement with the Soviet Union* (Berkeley and Los Angeles: University of California Press, 1969). For an account of recent developments, see Elizabeth Pond, "Japan and Russia: The View from Tokyo," *Foreign Affairs*, Oct. 1973, pp. 141–152.

22. See Matsumoto Shun'ichi, *Mosukuwa ni kakeru niji: Nisso kokkō kaifuku hiroku* (Tokyo: Asahi Shimbunsha, 1966).

partiality, and flexibility in those bilateral alliances that have endured. Is the age of alliance over? If so, there is no clearly discernible trend toward more highly integrated political units at the supranational level. Rather, the resurgent force everywhere seems to be nationalism, bolstered perhaps by the receding threat of global conflict and the trend within economic development toward strenuous competition. Even in cases where economic integration has steadily progressed, as within the European Economic Community, unity in the political and strategic realms seems remote.

Thus, trends with respect to the American-Japanese alliance are a part of, not apart from, broader international trends. Strengthened elements of reciprocity and independence within the relationship were to be expected. But the question remains: is a truly neutral or equidistant foreign policy for Japan desirable or possible? This may not be merely a matter of theoretical concern. The future governance of Japan is in some doubt. The so-called progressives have made significant gains in recent years, particularly in metropolitan areas. Their mainstream has long been committed to a neutralist foreign policy with a considerable element of anti-Americanism.[23] Even if Japan were to move into LDP-dominated coalition politics, foreign policy might become a major issue, particularly if the balance of power within the LDP shifts toward more nationalistic elements.

A policy of equidistance (and perhaps this is a better designation than neutralism) could take several forms. One possibility would be to move to the staunchly pacifist position long advocated by the Socialist Party, hinging Japan's security to major power guarantees and such moral suasion as might be exercised by others, including the United Nations. Not even the major Communist states, however, favor this policy currently, because they do not have sufficient trust in each other, nor do they believe that the ultimate domestic repercussion from such a policy would be healthy. There is no sign, moreover, that such a policy would garner majority support within Japan today, from either the people or the political elite.

Another variant would be to keep Japan substantially within the orbit of "the advanced world," but progressively shift emphasis and attention from bilateral to trilateral relations, seeking to interact more fully with Western Europe as well as with the United States and, on occasion, when it seemed in the Japanese interest, standing with Europe against American policies. In its own way, Peking has been cultivating such a policy by designating both Japan and Western Europe in the Second Intermediate Zone—nations that must struggle to avoid domination by the superpowers. Whatever the merits of this policy from a Japanese standpoint, however, it has several serious defects.

---

23. Among the voluminous materials on the JSP and its current position, the official party newspaper, *Shakai shimbun*, offers the most comprehensive, ongoing data.

Western Europe is neither capable of nor interested in underwriting Japan's security. Moreover, the European Economic Community is presently deeply concerned over Japanese economic inroads. Hence, protectionism remains popular, and there is scant interest in close cooperation with Tokyo. Indeed, at this point, Japan has considerably more in common economically with the United States than with the European Economic Community. A Japan-EEC coalition within a trilateral grouping is feasible neither from a political nor an economic standpoint. Trilateralism has a place in Japanese foreign policy, but not as the dominant element.

The most strident form of independence for Japan would be a Gaullist-type policy.[24] It would involve the cultivation of an independent military capacity, including nuclear weapons, together with a sharp increase in international political activity with a conscious effort to manipulate the major powers to serve Japanese interests, and special attention to a new Pan-Asianism in which Japan would play a key role. The obstacles besetting any such policy are presently so great, however, as to make it hopelessly unrealistic.[25] The Japanese people themselves, including current economic, political, and military elites, show no signs of being prepared to support such a policy. None of the major powers could be expected to cooperate or look favorably on such a development. The small Asian states, moreover, would consider Japan a threat rather than an ally, exacerbating already growing problems. And in the final analysis, it should be remembered, Gaullism has not been successful as a foreign policy in the nation of its origin.

If Japan should abandon its reliance on the American-Japanese alliance, the most rational alternative would probably be a fairly complex set of policies involving the following steps: (1) augmenting current military forces while keeping them nonnuclear and for defense purposes only; (2) seeking a three-power guarantee (the U.S., the USSR, and the PRC) as a substitute for the Mutual Security Treaty; and (3) requesting the dissolution of all other defense treaties in the Northeast Asian area directed against Japan. Japan would exchange reliance on a broad political-military Asian equilibrium to which it is a party for the acceptance of a strategic disequilibrium, with military superiority inside

24. See Ōmori Minoru, "Nihon no kihon gensoku o tou," *Chūō kōron*, vol. 78 (Jan. 1963), pp. 148–159.
25. For additional discussions of rearmament and the nuclear weapons issue in English, see James Morley, ed., *Forecast for Japan: Security in the 1970s* (Princeton: Princeton University Press, 1972); John K. Emmerson, *Arms, Yen and Power: The Japanese Dilemma* (New York: Dunellen Press, 1971); Martin E. Weinstein, *Japan's Postwar Defense Policy, 1947–1968* (New York: Columbia University Press, 1971); Kamiya Fuji, "Japan-U.S. Relations and the Security Treaty: A Japanese Perspective," *Asian Survey*, Sept. 1972, pp. 717–724; Paul F. Langer, *Japanese National Security Policy: Domestic Determinents* (Santa Monica, Calif.: The Rand Corporation, 1972); Robert E. Osgood, *The Weary and the Wary: U.S. and Japanese Security Policies in Transition* (Baltimore: Johns Hopkins University Press, 1972); and George A. Quester, "Japan and Nuclear Non-Proliferation," *Asian Survey*, Sept. 1970, pp. 765–777.

the immediate region resting with China and Russia. The United States, removed from any primary responsibility for Japanese security, would not be likely to find it in its own interests to maintain its current commitments to other states in the region, namely, South Korea and Taiwan. With respect to the Republic of Korea at least, the U.S. might seek arrangements similar to those involving Japan. In any case, a deliberate Japanese move toward independence would probably accelerate an American military retrenchment, essentially falling back to the mid-Pacific.

Under such conditions, Japan would have to exercise its leverage on both the major states of the region (Russia and China) and the minor states (North Korea, South Korea, and Taiwan) without counting on external assistance and from a position of military inferiority. Thus, in the final analysis, both Japan's security and the most likely prospects for satisfying its interests would rest on several conditions: the avoidance of serious disputes with any of the states in the region; the continuance of the Sino-Soviet cleavage, thereby preventing any greater aggregation of potentially hostile power and enabling Japan to use Communist divisions to its own ends; and finally, the restraint of all major states, not merely in their adjustment of disputes with Japan, but also on minor states still affiliated with them in some degree.

In its essence, such a policy would have its greatest chance of success in a status-quo situation with minimal crises. It would take a brave observer to envisage the immediate future of Asia in these terms, particularly if balance-of-power politics are abandoned in favor of an international order for which the basic requisites do not yet exist. The risks in such a Japanese policy would be substantial—for both Japan and the rest of the Pacific-Asian area. It could trigger a sharp reversion to militancy in Japan and the dangers associated with miscalculations elsewhere—the kind that have led to two wars since 1945, in Korea and Vietnam.

Japan may find, therefore, that there are no sweeping alternatives to the present policies that would offer better opportunities. Sometimes, undramatic as it may be, adjustment rather than massive change is the sounder, more meaningful route. This is not to assert that current policies could not be revitalized and in some respects amended to advantage. At root, Japanese foreign policy rests on continued close relations with the United States, with the effort simultaneously to raise the level of relations with both the People's Republic of China and the USSR in more or less balanced fashion. Needless to say, such a policy depends not merely on Japan, and recent events have clearly indicated that it will not be easy to effectuate. Relations with the United States became frayed in part because the two most prominent elements in fixing those relations—the governmental and business communities of both parties—had not established the proper rapport. Methods of handling grievances, signaling systems, and communications in general remain unsatisfactory. Outside these two communities, relations are tenuous and exert little independent leverage. The implacable hostility to America and the strong partisanship of a portion of the Japanese press, including such influential newspapers as *Asahi*, further exacerbate the problem.

Meanwhile, Tokyo is discovering that China and Russia each have different assets and liabilities for Japan, which makes the balancing of Sino-Japanese and Soviet-Japanese relations extremely difficult. China has the advantages of cultural access, significant political allies within Japan, and the absence of any immediate threat. The Soviet Union offers greater overall economic opportunities but also presents the greater immediate challenge, both in terms of unresolved issues and broader security matters. The Chinese advantages appear to outweigh those of the Soviet Union by a considerable measure, but the longer range developments are less easy to predict.

A third major and interrelated issue facing contemporary Japanese policymakers concerns Japan's near-exclusive reliance on economic policies to protect its basic interests, an unprecedented experiment on the part of a major society. Indeed, some have argued that Japan has no foreign policy, only entrepreneurial policies; hence, the label "economic animal" is appropriate. In any case, the issue is whether reliance on economic policies alone is feasible and, if not, what alternatives or modifications are available.

Clearly, Japan can use its economic power to political effect in certain instances, such as in the case of the South Korean Kim Tai-jung affair. Moreover, even with major societies like the People's Republic of China and the USSR, Japan's economic capacities are a desideratum of no small importance, hence, a bargaining instrument of value. Nevertheless, Japan's basic economic position makes it extremely vulnerable to economic countermeasures in any vital dispute. The Middle East crisis of 1973–1974 highlighted the vulnerability of Japan to external developments affecting its markets or resource and energy sources.

There are no simple answers to this problem. Obviously, Japan, even more than other major industrial nations, must concentrate on diversifying its sources of supply and seeking substitutes, such as solar energy, that will reduce its vulnerability to the international arena. Yet for Japan the basic answers do not lie in this direction. Its greatest hope lies in the emergence of a new international economic order encompassing monetary, trade, investment, pricing, and developmental policies. We are at a particularly crucial juncture in the world's future in this respect. On every front nationalist tides are mounting, yet the future welfare of the overwhelming majority of the globe's population can best be advanced through more sophisticated and coordinated economic policies than have thus far been devised. Indeed, for the so-called advanced states, the alternatives may be crisis and mounting hostility.

To date, internationalization in the economic realm, with the notable exception of Western Europe, has proceeded largely via the multilateral corporation, with its attendant benefits and abuses. The recurrent troubles of recent years, however, make it clear that the constant threat of economic chaos hanging over the key democratic states poses not merely a welfare problem but also issues extending to the broadest reaches of politics and security. Democracy as we know it is threatened. And as Japan has a major stake in the outcome, would it not be appropriate for it to assume greater initiatives in this field? Such initiatives could take a variety of forms from convening public and private international conferences to underwriting the studies of Japanese experts so as to encourage concrete proposals for international consideration. Thus far, Japan's timid ventures into the realm of international initiatives have come mainly via proposals for regional conferences with an emphasis on security matters. It is in the economic arena, however, especially on an interregional basis, that Japan has the most to offer, and the most to lose or gain. Here Japanese leadership, proceeding from real strengths, could be credible.

The other side of the international economic coin relates to the so-called emerging states. In this arena Japan is in serious trouble, especially in Asia. The Japanese government, not without reason, has treated its private industrial sector as "a national treasure," and in many ways has facilitated its expansion abroad. At the same time, the government has paid only minimal attention to the overseas behavior of Japanese enterprises, with the result that various unethical practices have become sufficiently commonplace to tarnish the entire Japanese image. The most elemental dictates of self-interest require new Japanese initiatives. Some governmental sanctions against unscrupulous Japanese business practices abroad should be undertaken and widely publicized. On the positive side, Japan is a logical site for an International Study Center on Economic Growth. By pooling expertise, providing research funds for continuing studies, and interpreting the issues of growth in such a fashion as to encompass social and political as well as economic issues, Japan could make a major contribution to what will surely be one central problem of the late twentieth century.

Such economically oriented activities do not negate the possibility of more purely political efforts. Undoubtedly Japan will continue its drive for greater political recognition. Regional initiatives, particularly to states in Northeast Asia, are within Japanese capabilities and directly connected with its national interests. Any such initiatives, however, must be kept at a relatively low level of risk. One possibility with long-range consequences would be to expand greatly Japan's cultural exchange program, bringing larger numbers of foreigners to Japan for study, specialized training, and interaction with their counterpart interest groups. Ultimately this could promote greater "internationalization" of Japanese culture itself, one of the critical variables. Via such organizations as the Japan Foundation, this trend is underway.

Even under optimal conditions, however, the Japanese government and people are likely to experience many frustrations with respect to foreign relations in the years immediately ahead. Today Japan finds its relations with nearly all of the states in its immediate environs either minimal or troubled. Meanwhile, the pressures will continue to mount for any government in power to concentrate heavily on domestic issues, because these will constitute the primary concerns and chief annoyances for the average citizen. There are no "solutions" in sight to such difficulties as inflation, pollution, congestion, housing, and the myriad of other problems related to rapid growth. Yet most, if not all, of these problems are also closely related to the international environment with which Japan must cope and from which it cannot conceivably withdraw.

In a general analysis of perspectives on Japanese foreign policy the primary lessons would appear to be twofold. First, a minimal foreign policy can no longer produce the benefits that accrued during the first two decades following World War II. It is therefore essential to educate the Japanese public to this vital fact, a task that government and opinion-makers alike have scarcely acknowledged. Simultaneously, Japan must find methods of expanding its foreign policy beyond the narrow confines of the past in such a fashion as to serve Japanese needs and interests without falling into those excesses that would set in motion a new or exacerbated cluster of problems. The second lesson follows. The composite range of factors, domestic and foreign, bearing on Japanese foreign policy in this era strongly supports the case for modification or revision of current policies, notably those of continuing special ties with the United States, while seeking increased interaction with both China and Russia, but not an overturn of such policies. Once the alternatives are carefully surveyed, it becomes clear that any "revolution" in Japanese foreign policy would be destabilizing, hence unconducive to the goals of peace and development in Asia and adverse to Japan's own interests.

The primary risk today is not of a Japan militant, aggressive, and politically or militarily expansionist. It is rather of a Japan uncertain, indecisive, and clinging to those minimal policies of the past which are no longer applicable. Perhaps another threat is now rising on the horizon—that of a Japan under a new kind of leadership, which, in an effort to avoid all risks and keep in tune with the current priorities and the prevailing psychology of its constituency, elects to experiment with "neutralism" or rely on "multilaterism" before the conditions appropriate for such experimentation exist. Such an experimentation *may* be valid at some later point in time. But timing is the essence of success in politics, domestic or foreign. And the time for such a risk is clearly not the present.

For the scholar, unlike the policy-maker, the advocacy of ideas—or policies—that are dramatic, bold, and new, is always the preferred route. It signifies creativity, innovation, the kind of breakthrough for which he continuously strives. Yet on frequent occasions, the course of action, hence advocacy, dictated by the available evidence is not dramatic but incremental, not revolution but revision, and such is the case when the alternatives confronting Japan are examined.

Index

413